# The Annotated Two Years Before the Mast

# The Annotated Two Years Before the Mast

Richard Henry Dana

Annotated by Rod Scher

Essex, Connecticut

An imprint of Globe Pequot, the trade division of
The Rowman & Littlefield Publishing Group, Inc.
4501 Forbes Blvd., Ste. 200
Lanham, MD 20706
www.rowman.com

Distributed by NATIONAL BOOK NETWORK


First edition published 2013
First paperback edition published 2023



British Library Cataloguing in Publication Information available

**Library of Congress Cataloging-in-Publication Data**

Dana, Richard Henry, 1815–1882.
[Two years before the mast]
The annotated Two years before the mast / Richard Henry Dana ; annotated by Rod Scher.
pages cm
1. Dana, Richard Henry, 1815–1882—Travel. 2. Voyages and travels. 3. Pilgrim (Brig) 4. Alert (Brig : 1843-1862) 5. Seafaring life. 6. Horn, Cape (Chile) I. Scher, Rod. II. Title.
G540.D2 2013
910.4'5—dc23
2013024020

ISBN 9781574093100 (cloth) | ISBN 9781493075980 (paperback) | ISBN 9781574093193 (electronic)

™ The paper used in this publication meets the minimum requirements of American National Standard for Information Sciences—Permanence of Paper for Printed Library Materials, ANSI/NISO Z39.48-1992.

# Contents

## A Note for Educators

Richard Henry Dana's *Two Years Before the Mast* is taught in both secondary schools and colleges: mostly in English courses, but occasionally in sociology, history, or other disciplines. If you are using this annotated edition with your class, you can find a free online study guide at the author's website, www.rodscher.com.

The study guide includes discussion questions—some suitable for high school and others more appropriate for post-secondary study—to help unpack themes, characters and motivations, events and plot mechanisms, and terms and expressions. A sample response is supplied for each question to help prompt students as needed. The study guide also contains a list of suggested resources (articles, websites, videos, etc.) for those who wish to learn more about the legacy of tall ships and Dana's life.

# INTRODUCTION

## Two Years Before the Mast

*Two Years Before the Mast* is a classic twice over. First, it set the stage for generations of nautical (and non-nautical) travel narratives and novels to come; without *Two Years Before the Mast*, there would be no *Moby Dick*, possibly no *Sailing Alone Around the World*, and perhaps even no *Caine Mutiny*. It was Richard Henry Dana who, in writing the story of his journey to California and back aboard the *Pilgrim* and the *Alert*, set out to tell his tale in as straightforward a manner as possible. In Dana's tale, there is little of the then-prevalent seagoing romanticism to which 19th-century readers were accustomed: Instead of the clash of sabers and the glitter of officers' medal-bedecked tunics, in Dana's book we hear the gripes and groans of those who live "before the mast," that is, in the cramped quarters forward of the foremost mast—this as opposed to the more leisurely, privileged domain of officers and paying passengers who lived in relative luxury after the mast. These were battered men who alternately sweated and froze as they strained at tarred hemp ropes and clambered precipitously upward to tend to sails and rigging in good weather and in bad. It is a grim and grisly world of hard work, little leisure, and unrelenting danger—all overseen by an absolute and sometimes tyrannical master who is well within his rights to imprison or flog a sailor whom he has determined to be lazy, dishonest, or mutinous. There was knowledge to be gained by shipping aboard as a common seaman, and hard work enough to toughen weak muscles, and there were adventures to be had, enough to provide stories for one's pub-mates well into old age. But there was nothing pretty about life before the mast. And one must, after all, contrive to *live* through the journey if one intends to spend his old age telling those stories in that pub.

Of course, the book is a fine adventure yarn, even (or perhaps especially) absent the cloying romanticism of then-contemporary nautical writers such as James Fenimore Cooper and Nathaniel Ames. (The latter of whom is now almost unknown, though Cooper of course had a long, respectable career. But even Cooper was influenced by Dana, say many critics, and his later books were much grittier and less romanticized than his early efforts.) But *Two Years Before the Mast* is more than merely an adventure and much more than simply a travelogue. It is a book that set the stage for Dana's later involvement in a lifelong fight for what he saw as social justice as it applied to the sailors of the merchant marine: Within the limits of his time and class, Dana would devote much of his career as an attorney to helping sailors fight for their rights, as Dana saw them. (There were limits, certainly, to Dana's open-minded benevolence. He never sought, for example, to curtail the captain's absolute power over ship and crew, feeling that on the high seas that power was necessary to keep order.) Out of this concern would come a second book, *The Seaman's Friend* (in Britain, *The Seaman's Manual*), a nautical treatise that aimed to explain to its readers both the basics of seamanship and the rights of sailors. While Dana was something of a rebel (he was once "rusticated"—temporarily expelled from school—for supporting a student rebellion) and surely something of a compassionate liberal (he became an abolitionist in all but name), he is nonetheless a member of the upper class and constrained by both his times and his station. He therefore aims not at the abolition of the captain's unfettered power, but at its wise and compassionate use. Thus, he says of the typical ship's master, "If he is profane, passionate, tyrannical, indecent, or intemperate . . . the same qualities will. . . break out among officers and men. He may make his ship almost anything he chooses, and may render the lives and duties of his officers and men pleasant and profitable to them, or may introduce disagreements, discontent, tyranny, resistance . . . ." On the other hand, he notes, a wise and compassionate captain, though omnipotent on the high seas, may "be a benefactor to the numbers . . . under his command," and "do much to raise the character of the calling."

So there is in *Two Years Before the Mast* an embryonic sense of Dana's blossoming compassion, a gentle sensibility that grows out of his honest experience (and blunt portrayal) of the petty—and sometimes vicious—actions of *Pilgrim*'s savagely tyrannical master, Captain Thompson. (As Dana himself notes in the book, he is honor-bound, if and when it becomes possible, to "redress the grievances and relieve the sufferings" of those with whom he sailed.)

In the end, the book—surely planned from the moment he hauled his duffel up the *Pilgrim*'s gangplank at Boston Harbor—led Dana to a fruitful career as an attorney, and allowed him to dedicate a not insignificant portion of that career to righting what he saw as the wrongs impressed upon a largely defenseless population of often uneducated laborers who toiled mostly for the gain of others.

**Richard Henry Dana**

Richard Henry Dana was the scion of a once-wealthy, still impressively well-to-do and connected Boston family that counted among its ancestors poets, jurists, politicians, professors, and more. Though in somewhat reduced circumstances due to recent financial reverses, Dana's family was nonetheless privileged and powerful.

As the eldest son of a relatively well-known poet and literary critic, among other of his father's many accomplishments, Dana was destined for a good education and a lucrative, respectable career at the bar, the counting house, or the Church.

He entered Harvard in 1831, but an attack of measles during his sophomore year weakened his eyes to the point that he was forced to take time off from school. A young man (Dana was just 19 years old) from a wealthier family might have taken the opportunity to travel to Europe, but that was beyond Dana's means. Knowing that he would be bored without meaningful work to do, he determined on a sea voyage, but rather than travel as a paying passenger (or as a companion to a paying passenger), Dana decided to ship out as a seaman "before the mast." He reasoned (correctly) that the hard work and strict diet would be good for his health, and that the chance to live with others not of his class would broaden his mind.

Dana may not have known quite what he was getting into. Shipping out before the mast was more than simply taking on hard work and a strict diet. It was a rigorously demanding, often dangerous undertaking during which Dana would be far from his home, his friends, and his upper-class environment. It would be a bit like one of our 21st-century teenagers signing up for a two-year stint of boot camp, with—as Dr. Johnson once said when comparing living aboard a boat to the seemingly identical experience of living in a prison—the added possibility of drowning.

But there was more. Dana had signed on not realizing that the voyage was essentially open-ended. Given the vagaries of sea travel and of the hide trade, the *Pilgrim* could be gone for two years, as was ostensibly the intent of the ship's owners, or it could be plying the coast for three or four years, or longer. (The realization that he could be stuck on board ship and away from civilization for more than two years finally drove Dana to take advantage of his powerful family ties, and he pulled strings to arrange passage back on the *Alert*. This caused some friction with the crew, some of whom resented Dana using his money and connections to find for himself what was literally an easier berth.To his credit, though, this is as far as we know the *only* time Dana took advantage of his position.)

**Dana's "Failure"**

*Two Years Before the Mast* was a tremendous success. It forever cemented Dana's literary reputation and it energized his fledgling legal practice, much of which was in fact devoted to maritime law and specifically to defending the rights of the common sailor.

Although Dana would go on to write another well-received volume, *The Seaman's Friend,* none of his subsequent writings would match either the impact or the passion of his first effort. Sadly, Dana would forever think of himself as a minor author.

In truth, this would have been acceptable to him, because his real goal was a career in politics: Dana saw himself as a potential statesman of the first order. The fact that he never achieved that goal left him feeling forever a failure, worried that the only thing of importance he'd accomplished was this early book.

But what an accomplishment it was. The book launched a genre, helped secure the rights of sailors the world over, and told a great yarn to boot. (In the absence of reliable travel advice, it even came to serve as something of a guidebook for those headed to California during the first heady days of the 1849 Gold Rush.) This is a book that has been in print ever since the first edition was published in 1840; over 180 years later, it is still as entertaining, as informative, and as important as it was when it was new. *Two Years Before the Mast* has been read by millions, and is still taught to students ranging from middle school to college. It has found an audience with readers interested in the sea, in the law, in history, and in literature—and there is no reason to suppose that its appeal will be any less 180 years from now. It is at once a history, a sailing primer, a polemic, and a damned good story.

Because of his failure to achieve high political office and the fact that he never managed to repeat the success of *Two Years Before the Mast*, Dana may have considered himself something of a failure, but we know better. He wrote a powerful (and powerfully moving) book that impacted the world and may have saved some lives; certainly it improved many. It has entertained and enlightened millions. It helped provide for his family and, after he died, his children and theirs. It is an accomplishment that few of us could ever hope to match.

— Rod Scher

## PREFACE

I am unwilling to present this narrative to the public without a few words in explanation of my reasons for publishing it. Since Mr. Cooper's Pilot and Red Rover, there have been so many stories of sea-life written, that I should really think it unjustifiable in me to add one to the number without being able to give reasons in some measure warranting me in so doing.

With the single exception, as I am quite confident, of Mr. Ames's entertaining, but hasty and desultory work, called "Mariner's Sketches," all the books professing to give life at sea have been written by persons who have gained their experience as naval officers, or passengers, and of these, there are very few which are intended to be taken as narratives of facts.

Now, in the first place, the whole course of life, and daily duties, the discipline, habits and customs of a man-of-war are very different from those of the merchant service; and in the next place, however entertaining and well written these books may be, and however accurately they may give sea-life as it appears to their authors, it must still be plain to every one that a naval officer, who goes to sea as a gentleman, "with his gloves on," (as the phrase is,) and who associated only with his fellow-officers, and hardly speaks to a sailor except through a boatswain's mate, must take a very different view of the whole matter from that which would be taken by a common sailor.

Besides the interest which every one must feel in exhibitions of life in those forms in which he himself has never experienced it; there has been, of late years, a great deal of attention directed toward common seamen, and a strong sympathy awakened in their behalf. Yet I believe that, with the single exception which I have mentioned, there has not been a book written, professing to give their life and experiences, by one who has been of them, and can know what their life really is. A voice from the forecastle has hardly yet been heard.

**Mr. Cooper's Pilot and Red Rover...** James Fenimore Cooper (1789-1851), the first volume of whose *Leatherstocking Tales* was published in 1823, wrote romanticized tales of the frontier and of the sea. *The Red Rover* (1828) and *The Pilot* (1823) were unrealistic nautical tales told mainly from the privileged perspective of officers.

**...Mr. Ames's entertaining, but hasty and desultory work...** Nathaniel Ames' *A Mariner's Sketches*, published in 1830, was a lighthearted collection of nautically themed essays. (Desultory is used here to mean "superficial," in which sense it's been used since the 16th century.)

In the news
**1840**

The city fathers of Boston and nearby cities are finishing a granite monument in Charlestown, MA, to commemorate the Battle of Bunker Hill.

**... goes to sea as a gentleman...** Dana, who in fact *is* a gentleman, nonetheless goes to sea as a common sailor.

**...from that which would be taken by a common sailor.** Dana's goal here is to live as the common sailor lives. He wishes to experience (for a while) the rough and hardy life of a "tar" (see later note).

**...a strong sympathy awakened in their behalf.** One of Dana's goals is to help redress the grievances of powerless sailors wronged by powerful captains and officers.

**A voice from the forecastle...** The forecastle is that portion of the ship forward of the foremost mast, under the decks of which live the common sailor. The forecastle is cramped, dark, dank, and uncomfortable, and life there is not for the weak or the soft. Until Dana's book was published, the sailors living "before the mast" had no real voice.

In the following pages I design to give an accurate and authentic narrative of a little more than two years spent as a common sailor, before the mast, in the American merchant service. It is written out from a journal which I kept at the time, and from notes which I made of most of the events as they happened; and in it I have adhered closely to fact in every particular, and endeavored to give each thing its true character. In so doing, I have been obliged occasionally to use strong and coarse expressions, and in some instances to give scenes which may be painful to nice feelings; but I have very carefully avoided doing so, whenever I have not felt them essential to giving the true character of a scene. My design is, and it is this which has induced me to publish the book, to present the life of a common sailor at sea as it really is,–the light and the dark together.

**...a journal which I kept at the time...** Actually, Dana's journal was lost when he arrived back in Boston, and most of the book was written from (occasionally flawed) memory and from about 16 pages' worth of notes that remained.

In the news

**February, 1840**

Queen Victoria marries her cousin, the German Prince Albert. They would have nine children, and his death in 1861 would plunge Victoria into deep mourning. Victoria would reign until her death in 1901, a total of almost 64 years. Hers was the longest reign of a British monarch until Queen Elizabeth II's recently ended reign.

**...the light and the dark together.** Dana's goal was to present a realistic, unvarnished look at life in the merchant marine, and he succeeded. The book is a straightforward, unromantic, sometimes brutal look at life aboard.

There may be in some parts a good deal that is unintelligible to the general reader; but I have found from my own experience, and from what I have heard from others, that plain matters of fact in relation to customs and habits of life new to us, and descriptions of life under new aspects, act upon the inexperienced through the imagination, so that we are hardly aware of our want of technical knowledge. Thousands read the escape of the American frigate through the British channel, and the chase and wreck of the Bristol trader in the Red Rover, and follow the minute nautical manoeuvres with breathless interest, who do not know the name of a rope in the ship; and perhaps with none the less admiration and enthusiasm for their want of acquaintance with the professional detail.

**There may be in some parts a good deal that is unintelligible to the general reader...** Many critics have commented on the flood of nautical jargon in the book, and some have recommended skipping it—just as some have recommended skipping the "cetology chapters" in Melville's *Moby Dick*. It's not necessary to know all about whales, lines, sails, or shrouds to enjoy either book, of course. But as a neophyte sailor who is literally "learning the ropes" (a phrase that comes to us in exactly the fashion you're now thinking), Dana is justifiably proud of his new-found nautical expertise, and he's determined to show it off.

In preparing this narrative I have carefully avoided incorporating into it any impressions but those made upon me by the events as they occurred, leaving to my concluding chapter, to which I shall respectfully call the reader's attention, those views which have been suggested to me by subsequent reflection.

These reasons, and the advice of a few friends, have led me to give this narrative to the press. If it shall interest the general reader, and call more attention to the welfare

**...have led me to give this narrative to the press.** It's possible that Dana is being disingenuous here. Some critics have commented that the author may have intended to write this book from the moment he began thinking about shipping out, believing (correctly, as it happens) that it would generate interest in his future law practice.

of seamen, or give any information as to their real condition, which may serve to raise them in the rank of beings, and to promote in any measure their religious and moral improvement, and diminish the hardships of their daily life, the end of its publication will be answered.

R.H.D., Jr.
Boston, July, 1840.

**...the end of its publication will be answered.** That is, its purpose will have been served. In fact, *Two Years Before the Mast* will serve to garner some sympathy, in both England and the United States, for the common sailors of the merchant marine. However, Dana's subsequent book, *The Seaman's Friend*, will do even more to redress the plight of the sailor living "before the mast."

In the news
**July, 1840**

As Dana prepares to publish *Two Years Before the Mast*, the first Hawaiian constitution is proclaimed. The people the *Pilgrim's* crew had called the Sandwich Islanders were now ruled by a constitutional monarchy. Hawaii would become a republic on July 4, 1894, and a U.S. territory in 1898—although that annexation was disputed and is sometimed characterized as illegal and imperialistic. Hawaii became a U.S. state in August of 1959.

# CHAPTER I

## DEPARTURE

The fourteenth of August was the day fixed upon for the sailing of the brig Pilgrim on her voyage from Boston round Cape Horn to the western coast of North America. As she was to get under weigh early in the afternoon, I made my appearance on board at twelve o'clock, in full sea-rig, and with my chest, containing an outfit for a two or three years' voyage, which I had undertaken from a determination to cure, if possible, by an entire change of life, and by a long absence from books and study, a weakness of the eyes, which had obliged me to give up my pursuits, and which no medical aid seemed likely to cure.

The change from the tight dress coat, silk cap and kid gloves of an undergraduate at Cambridge, to the loose duck trowsers, checked shirt and tarpaulin hat of a sailor, though somewhat of a transformation, was soon made, and I supposed that I should pass very well for a jack tar. But it is impossible to deceive the practised eye in these matters; and while I supposed myself to be looking as salt as Neptune himself, I was, no doubt, known for a landsman by every one on board as soon as I hove in sight. A sailor has a peculiar cut to his clothes, and a way of wearing them which a green hand can never get. The trowsers, tight round the hips, and thence hanging long and loose round the feet, a superabundance of checked shirt, a low-crowned, well varnished black hat, worn on the back of the head, with half a fathom of black ribbon hanging over the left eye, and a peculiar tie to the black silk neckerchief, with sundry other minutiae, are signs, the want of which betray the beginner, at once.

Besides the points in my dress which were out of the way, doubtless my complexion and hands were enough to distinguish me from the regular salt, who, with a sunburnt cheek, wide step, and rolling gait, swings his bronzed and toughened hands athwartships, half open, as though just ready to grasp a

**The fourteenth of August...** This would have been in the year 1834.

**...get under weigh early...** Most editions have, more correctly, "under way" or "underway." The error is common, though, perhaps reflecting an erroneous link with the idea of *weighing* (raising) anchor. Thus, the persistent error is in effect a nautical form of folk etymology.

**...a weakness of the eyes...** Dana had been stricken with measles, an affliction which—especially when combined with a lack of vitamin A—can weaken the eyes, occasionally causing blindness.That said, measles may or may not have been the real issue: It would not be at all unusual (then or now) for a 19-year-old college student to make almost any excuse for dropping out of school for a time to see the world.

**...I should pass very well for a jack tar.** An experienced seaman, perhaps so-called because tar was commonly used aboard ship to seal clothes and to protect hemp ropes.

**In the news**
**August, 1834**

Ony a few months prior to Dana's departure, Boston city fathers had moved a chunk of the putative Plymouth Rock (the huge chunk of granite had split years before) to a place of honor in front of Pilgrim Hall.

**...want of which betray the beginner...** Merely looking like an "old salt" was not enough; besides, it was not a look an inexperienced landman could carry off. At this point, Dana is a scrawny college student with pale skin and soft scholar's hands that have never handled a rope.

**...swings his bronzed and toughened hands athwartships...** From one side (of a ship) to the other; thus, walking with a swaying, rolling gait.

rope.

"With all my imperfections on my head," I joined the crew, and we hauled out into the stream, and came to anchor for the night. The next day we were employed in preparations for sea, reeving studding-sail gear, crossing royal yards, putting on chafing gear, and taking on board our powder. On the following night, I stood my first watch. I remained awake nearly all the first part of the night from fear that I might not hear when I was called; and when I went on deck, so great were my ideas of the importance of my trust, that I walked regularly fore and aft the whole length of the vessel, looking out over the bows and taffrail at each turn, and was not a little surprised at the coolness of the old salt whom I called to take my place, in stowing himself snugly away under the long boat, for a nap. That was a sufficient look-out, he thought, for a fine night, at anchor in a safe harbor.

The next morning was Saturday, and a breeze having sprung up from the southward, we took a pilot on board, hove up our anchor, and began beating down the bay. I took leave of those of my friends who came to see me off, and had barely opportunity to take a last look at the city, and well-known objects, as no time is allowed on board ship for sentiment. As we drew down into the lower harbor, we found the wind ahead in the bay, and were obliged to come to anchor in the roads. We remained there through the day and a part of the night. My watch began at eleven o'clock at night, and I received orders to call the captain if the wind came out from the westward. About midnight the wind became fair, and having called the captain, I was ordered to call all hands. How I accomplished this I do not know, but I am quite sure that I did not give the true hoarse, boatswain call of "A-a-ll ha-a-a-nds! up anchor, a-ho-oy!" In a short time every one was in motion, the sails loosed, the yards braced, and we began to heave up the anchor, which was our last hold upon Yankee land. I could take but little part in all these preparations. My little knowledge of a vessel was all at fault. Unintelligible orders were so rapidly given and so

**With all my imperfections on my head...** From *Hamlet* (Act I, Scene V), in which the ghost of Hamlet's father laments having died before atoning for his sins. Although signed on as a common seaman, Dana is a well-to-do and well-educated young man, occasionally given to quoting Shakespeare.

**...taffrail...** A rail around the stern (rear; aft portion) of a ship.

**That was a sufficient look-out, he thought...** Dana is being self-deprecatingly ironic. The old salt, though derilect in his duties, is probably correct in assuming that little harm could befall a ship safe in its harbor on a calm night.

In the news
**August, 1834**

Days before Dana ships out, the British Emancipation Act abolishes slavery throughout the Empire, some 29 years before Lincoln issues the Emancipation Proclamation.

**...we took a pilot on board...** A pilot is a captain familiar with the local waters whose job it is to help guide a ship out to sea or, if returning to port, into the harbor. Note that, as was recently reaffirmed (2003) in a case involving a ship being steered by a harbor pilot, the captain remains responsible for his ship, regardless of who is at the helm. To "beat" is to sail against the wind, or as close to it as possible in a square-sailed ship. (A brig is a two-masted vessel with square sails; such a ship is fast and fairly maneuverable, but cannot sail very effectively into the wind.)

**...the true hoarse, boatswain call...** The boatswain (pronounced—and often spelled—*bo'sun* or *bos'n*) is a ship's officer charged with caring for rigging and with calling the crew to duty.

**...so helpless and pitiable an object...** To his credit, Dana is not too proud to admit that he knows little of the sea and lacks the standing of even the rawest of neophytes. He is determined to work hard and learn quickly—and in fact he does so, amassing a considerable bit of nautical know-how in a brief period of time, while at the same time transforming himself into a "rough and ready" tar.

**...the windlass...** A machine featuring a pulley (hand-cranked in those days) with which a rope or chain is wound around a cylinder and by which an anchor is raised or other heavy weight lifted.

**...we were under weigh.** Another example of this edition's misuse of the term, as earlier noted. The misspelling may have been added by an overzealous (and landlubberly) editor at Harpers', since that firm held the copyright (and issued several editions of the book) until the copyright reverted to Dana in 1868. Between the various Harpers' editions and later revisions made by Dana himself, there are several versions of the text in circulation.

In the news
**August, 1834**

As Dana sets out on a journey that will eventually take him to the coast of California, the Mexican government representative in the little pueblo (village) of San Francisco (which Dana would soon visit; see Ch. 26) has been ordered to secularize the California missions. Yankee traders, including William H. Davis, have been trading with the Mexicans, establishing outposts and, in some cases, huge fortunes. California-born Spanish subject Mariano Guadalupe Vallejo is made captain of the San Francisco Company, and is eventually given Rancho Petaluma as a reward for his efforts at establishing a secular Mexican government.

immediately executed; there was such ahurrying about, and such an intermingling of strange cries and stranger actions, that I was completely bewildered. There is not so helpless and pitiable an object in the world as a landsman beginning a sailor's life. At length those peculiar, longdrawn sounds, which denote that the crew are heaving at the windlass, began, and in a few moments we were under weigh. The noise of the water thrown from the bows began to be heard, the vessel leaned over from the damp night breeze, and rolled with the heavy ground swell, and we had actually begun our long, long journey. This was literally bidding "good night" to my native land.

## CHAPTER II

## FIRST IMPRESSIONS—"SAIL HO!"

The first day we passed at sea was Sunday. As we were just from port, and there was a great deal to be done on board, we were kept at work all day, and at night the watches were set, and everything was put into sea order. When we were called aft to be divided into watches, I had a good specimen of the manner of a sea-captain. After the division had been made, he gave a short characteristic speech, walking the quarter-deck with a cigar in his mouth, and dropping the words out between the puffs.

"Now, my men, we have begun a long voyage. If we get along well together, we shall have a comfortable time; if we don't, we shall have hell afloat. All you have got to do is to obey your orders, and do your duty like men,— then you will fare well enough; if you don't, you will fare hard enough,— I can tell you. If we pull together, you will find me a clever fellow; if we don't, you will find me a bloody rescal. That's all I've got to say. Go below, the larboard watch!"

I, being in the starboard or second mate's watch, had the opportunity of keeping the first watch at sea. Stimson, a young man making, like myself, his first voyage, was in the same watch, and as he was the son of a professional man, and had been in a merchant's counting-room in Boston, we found that we had some acquaintances and topics in common. We talked these matters over— Boston, what our friends were probably doing, our voyage, &c.— until he went to take his turn at the lookout, and left me to myself. I had now a good opportunity for reflection. I felt for the first time the perfect silence of the sea. The officer was walking the quarter-deck, where I had no right to go, one or two men were talking on the forecastle, whom I had little inclination to join, so that I was left open to the full impression of everything about me. However much I was affected by the

**...we were kept at work all day...** While it's understandable that there is much work to be done, the fact that the men are kept at work during what is normally a day of rest foreshadows a problem that will shortly become apparent: The captain of the *Pilgrim* is something of a tyrant, caring little for the welfare (or the morale) of his men.

**...divided into watches...** Onboard ship, watches are normally of four hours' duration.

**...a bloody rascal.** Keep in mind that, for the time, this is pretty frank language. It's also, as it turns out, quite accurate.

**...the larboard watch!** Most editions include here Dana's subsequent note that the British and American merchant marine had recently adopted the now-familiar term "port" to replace "larboard." Larboard, meaning the lefthand side of a vessel (assuming one is looking toward the bow, that is, the front) goes back to at least the 14th century. Possibly derived from *ladde-borde*, the "boarding (or loading) side" of a ship, the term was dropped in order to avoid confusion with "starboard," used to signify the right-hand side of a vessel.

**...we found that we had some acquaintances and topics in common.** Although he has shipped out as a common seaman living "before the mast" (that is, in the forecastle—the space in front of the foremost mast—with the common sailors), Dana never forgets that he's a member of a patrician class. He spends much of the book noting how much he misses civilized Boston and living amongst others of his station. While he truly feels for and empathizes with the sailors (and will eventually prove it), he is not *of* them. His upbringing and his education set him apart, and he is well aware of (and occasionally pained by) that fact.

**...to prevent my becoming insensible to the value of what I was losing.** This is a central theme of the book, and a prime motivator for Dana. It's not that he wishes to leave civilization behind, abandoning it for a more rustic life; rather, he wishes to experience a more rustic life precisely so that he can better appreciate and enjoy (what he sees as) true civilization. He wishes to learn not to take that civilization for granted.

**...trim the yards...** To brace the sails such that the wind will strike them at the correct angle. A yard is a spar suspended across a mast to support a sail.

**...eight bells were struck...** Indicating the end of a watch. Metaphorically, "eight bells" has come to mean the end or finish of *anything*.

**...steerage...** The deck below the main deck of a ship, often used for cargo or for carrying passengers of little means. In the 17th century, this was the level of the ship through which ran control lines for the rudder—thus, steerage.

**..."hurrah's nest"...** In complete disorder; a confused or disorderly mass. Found in 1829 (in Longfellow) and earlier, and derived from the shout of "hurrah!" (or more commonly today, "hooray!"), meaning a great hubbub or fanfare. ("Hurrah" itself may be derived from "huzzah," a soldier's battlecry.)

**...ahoy!...** From the German, a call or greeting used to hail a ship. In this context, a call to the crew.

In the news
**1834**

Dana's not-yet-famous neighbor, Oliver Wendell Holmes, will soon become a practicing physician, having attended Phillips Academy, Andover, and Harvard. Holmes' reputation as a writer of prose and poetry will eventually overshadow his accomplishments as a physican and anatomy professor.

beauty of the sea, the bright stars, and the clouds driven swiftly over them, I could not but remember that I was separating myself from all the social and intellectual enjoyments of life. Yet, strange as it may seem, I did then and afterwards take pleasure in these reflections, hoping by them to prevent my becoming insensible to the value of what I was losing.

But all my dreams were soon put to flight by an order from the officer to trim the yards, as the wind was getting ahead; and I could plainly see by the looks the sailors occasionally cast to windward, and by the dark clouds that were fast coming up, that we had bad weather to prepare for, and I had heard the captain say that he expected to be in the Gulf Stream by twelve o'clock. In a few minutes eight bells were struck, the watch called, and we went below. I now began to feel the first discomforts of a sailor's life. The steerage, in which I lived, was filled with coils of rigging, spare sails, old junk, and ship stores, which had not been stowed away. Moreover, there had been no berths put up for us to sleep in, and we were not allowed to drive nails to hang our clothes upon. The sea, too, had risen, the vessel was rolling heavily, and everything was pitched about in grand confusion. There was a complete "hurrah's nest," as the sailors say, "everything on top and nothing at hand." A large hawser had been coiled away on my chest; my hats, boots, mattress, and blankets had all fetched away and gone over to leeward, and were jammed and broken under the boxes and coils of rigging. To crown all, we were allowed no light to find anything with, and I was just beginning to feel strong symptoms of sea-sickness, and that listlessness and inactivity which accompany it. Giving up all attempts to collect my things together, I lay down on the sails, expecting every moment to hear the cry, "All hands ahoy!" which the approaching storm would make necessary. I shortly heard the raindrops falling on deck thick and fast, and the watch evidently had their hands full of work, for I could hear the loud and repeated orders of the mate, trampling of feet, creaking of the blocks, and all the accompaniments of a coming storm. In a few minutes the slide of the hatch was thrown back, which let down the noise and tumult of the deck still louder, the cry of "All hands ahoy! tumble up here and take in sail," saluted our ears, and the hatch was quickly shut again. When I got upon deck, a new scene and a new experience was before me.

The little brig was close-hauled upon the wind, and lying over, as it then seemed to me, nearly upon her beam ends. The heavy head sea was beating against her bows with the noise and force almost of a sledgehammer, and flying over the deck, drenching us completely through. The topsail halyards had been let go, and the great sails were filling out and backing against the masts with a noise like thunder; the wind was whistling through the rigging; loose ropes were flying about; loud and, to me, unintelligible orders constantly given, and rapidly executed; and the sailors "singing out" at the ropes in their hoarse and peculiar strains.

In addition to all this, I had not got my "sea legs on," was dreadfully sea-sick, with hardly strength enough to hold on to anything, and it was "pitch dark." This was my condition when I was ordered aloft, for the first time, to reef topsails.

How I got along, I cannot now remember. I "laid out" on the yards and held on with all my strength. I could not have been of much service, for I remember having been sick several times before I left the topsail yard, making wild vomits into the black night, to leeward. Soon all was snug aloft, and we were again allowed to go below. This I did not consider much of a favor, for the confusion of everything below, and that inexpressible sickening smell, caused by the shaking up of bilge water in the hold, made the steerage but an indifferent refuge from the cold, wet decks. I had often read of the nautical experiences of others, but I felt as though there could be none worse than mine; for, in addition to every other evil, I could not but remember that this was only the first night of a two years' voyage. When we were on deck, we were not much better off, for we were continually ordered about by the officer, who said that it was good for us to be in motion. Yet anything was better

**The little brig was close-hauled...** A brig is a sailboat with two masts and square sails. To sail close-hauled is to "beat," attempting to sail as near to upwind as possible. This is a rough point of sail, and often results in an uncomfortable passage.

In the news
**August, 1834**

A female living in Boston in 1834 would likely not be included in the Boston Directory. Women were listed only if they were in business (offering rooms, for example) or if they were widows—in which case, the word "widow" was actually appended to their names.

**...and it was "pitch dark."** The phrase was used as far back as 1704, in Defoe. "Pitchy," meaning "dark as pitch," is found in Douglas' 1522 translation of the *Aeneid*. Pitch itself is a dark resin (often distilled from petroleum) used for waterproofing or caulking.

**...to leeward.** Always to leeward—that is, to the side opposite that from which the wind comes. As any sailor, modern or otherwise, would tell you, it's always best to "puke on the down side." Another way of saying that one does not vomit *into* the wind.

**This I did not consider much of a favor...** In spite of the understandable urge to hide away below, a seasick person usually feels better on deck, where he can see the horizon.

**...an effectual emetic.** An emetic is any medicine used to induce vomiting (i.e., emesis). Like Dana, most people become immune to seasickness over time, but it's pure misery for the few days it lasts. And of course, some never do become immune.

than the horrible state of things below. I remember very well going to the hatchway and putting my head down, when I was oppressed by nausea, and always being relieved immediately. It was an effectual emetic.

**This state of things continued for two days.** Dana has a penchant for wry understatement.

This state of things continued for two days.

**I stood in the waist on the weather side...** The waist is the middle portion of a ship's deck. As the "fulcrum" in the "lever" formed by the decks, the middle section is the one that moves the least. Staying in the waist would be like straddling the middle portion of a child's "teeter-totter": Both ends would rise and fall a fair amount, but the middle section would move only a little. The waist would therefore be most comfortable for one who is feeling ill.

**"Old Ocean's gray and melancholy waste."** A quote from William Cullen Bryant's poem, "Thanatopsis." Dana is an educated young man, and often quotes famous authors or alludes to their works. As it happens, the poem was published by Dana's father in the magazine the senior Dana helped edit, the *North American Review*. The poem, much of which was written when Bryant was a teenager, is a meditation on death. (So, no, there's nothing new about young people's current brooding fixation with death, as evidenced by the goth and emo movements and by our ongoing fascination with zombies and with vampiric legend.)

Wednesday, August 20th. We had the watch on deck from four till eight, this morning. When we came on deck at four o'clock, we found things much changed for the better. The sea and wind had gone down, and the stars were out bright. I experienced a corresponding change in my feelings, yet continued extremely weak from my sickness. I stood in the waist on the weather side, watching the gradual breaking of the day, and the first streaks of the early light. Much has been said of the sunrise at sea; but it will not compare with the sunrise on shore. It lacks the accompaniments of the songs of birds, the awakening hum of humanity, and the glancing of the first beams upon trees, hills, spires, and house-tops, to give it life and spirit. There is no scenery. But, although the actual rise of the sun at sea is not so beautiful, yet nothing will compare for melancholy and dreariness with the early breaking of day upon "Old Ocean's gray and melancholy waste."

**...melancholy foreboding...** Note that, for someone who loves the sea and wishes to get away from "civilization," Dana is often depressed by and regularly expresses his distaste for rustic living, and bemoans the lack of civilized company, books, etc.

There is something in the first gray streaks stretching along the eastern horizon and throwing an indistinct light upon the face of the deep, which combines with the boundlessness and unknown depth of the sea around, and gives one a feeling of loneliness, of dread, and of melancholy foreboding, which nothing else in nature can. This gradually passes away as the light grows brighter, and when the sun comes up, the ordinary monotonous sea day begins.

**...rig the headpump!** The headpump (or head-pump) is a small pump at the bow that pumps seawater up to the vessel, often for cleaning the deck.

**..."turn to" at the first light.** Often rendered as "turn *up*," this is the oppsite of the command to "turn in" or "turn out," i.e., go below to rest in one's bunk.

From such reflections as these, I was aroused by the order from the officer, "Forward there! rig the head-pump!" I found that no time was allowed for daydreaming, but that we must "turn to" at the first light. Having called up the "idlers," namely, carpenter, cook, and steward, and rigged the pump, we began washing down the decks. This operation, which is performed every morning at sea, takes nearly two hours; and I had hardly strength enough to get through it. After we had finished, swabbed down decks, and coiled up the rigging, I sat on the spars, waiting for seven bells, which was the signal for breakfast. The officer, seeing my lazy posture, ordered me to slush the mainmast, from the royal-mast-head down. The vessel was then rolling a little, and I had taken no food for three days, so that I felt tempted to tell him that I had rather wait till after breakfast; but I knew that I must "take the bull by the horns," and that if I showed any sign of want of spirit or backwardness, I should be ruined at once. So I took my bucket of grease and climbed up to the royal-mast-head. Here the rocking of the vessel, which increases the higher you go from the foot of the mast, which is the fulcrum of the lever, and the smell of the grease, which offended my fastidious senses, upset my stomach again, and I was not a little rejoiced when I had finished my job and got upon the comparative terra firma of the deck. In a few minutes seven bells were struck, the log hove, the watch called, and we went to breakfast. Here I cannot but remember the advice of the cook, a simple-hearted African. "Now," says he, "my lad, you are well cleaned out; you haven't got a drop of your 'long-shore swash aboard of you. You must begin on a new tack,— pitch all your sweetmeats overboard, and turn to upon good hearty salt beef and ship bread, and I'll promise you, you'll have your ribs well sheathed, and be as hearty as any of 'em, afore you are up to the Horn." This would be good advice to give to passengers, when they set their hearts on the little niceties which they have laid in, in case of sea-sickness.

I cannot describe the change which half a pound of cold salt beef and a biscuit or two produced in me. I was a new being. Having a watch below until noon, so that I had some time to myself, I got a huge piece of strong, cold salt beef from the cook, and kept gnawing upon it until twelve o'clock. When we went on deck, I felt somewhat like a man, and could begin to learn my sea duty with considerable spirit. At about two o'clock, we heard the loud cry of "Sail ho!" from aloft, and soon saw two sails to windward, going directly athwart our

**...if I showed any sign of want of spirit or backwardness, I should be ruined at once.** This is Dana's first real chance to make an impression on the officers and on his fellow-sailors, and he desperately wishes to make a good one.

**...the smell of the grease...** The grease, or slush, often came from boiled barrel-scrapings or skimming from the top of a pan of boiling beef. Slush was sometimes sold by the cooks, the money thereby collected becoming known as a "slush fund." (See Chapter XXXI for more about slush funds.)

**...turn to upon good hearty salt beef and ship bread...** The cook advises Dana that a simple diet will serve him well onboard ship.

**...cold salt beef...** Salt beef is exactly what it sounds like: beef that has been salted (pickled) and stored in barrels. Similar to what we would now call "corned beef," it was a staple of sailors of the time. Salt pork was also common fare onboard.

**...going directly athwart our hawse.** A ship at anchor has cables stretched from the bow (and possibly the stem); since the anchor is called a "hawse," the term "athwart our hawse" therefore refers to a vessel crossing those cables. (Crossing *within* the triangle formed by the cable, the ship, and the sea could, of course, be disastrous.)

**They passed to leeward...** To the side opposite the side from which the wind originates.

hawse. This was the first time that I had seen a sail at sea. I thought then, and have always since, that no sight exceeds it in interest, and few in beauty. They passed to leeward of us, and out of hailing distance; but the captain could read the names on their sterns with the glass. They were the ship Helen Mar, of New York, and the brig Mermaid, of Boston. They were both steering westward, and were bound in for our "dear native land."

Thursday, August 21st. This day the sun rose clear; we had a fine wind, and everything was bright and cheerful. I had now got my sea legs on, and was beginning to enter upon the regular duties of a sea life. About six bells, that is, three o'clock P.M., we saw a sail on our larboard bow. I was very desirous, like every new sailor, to speak her. She came down to us, backed her main-top-sail, and the two vessels stood "head on," bowing and curveting at each other like a couple of war-horses reined in by their riders. It was the first vessel that I had seen near, and I was surprised to find how much she rolled and pitched in so quiet a sea. She plunged her head into the sea, and then, her stern settling gradually down, her huge bows rose up, showing the bright copper, and her stem and breasthooks dripping, like old Neptune's locks, with the brine. Her decks were filled with passengers, who had come up at the cry of "Sail ho!" and who, by their dress and features, appeared to be Swiss and French emigrants. She hailed us at first in French, but receiving no answer, she tried us in English. She was the ship La Carolina, from Havre, for New York. We desired her to report the brig Pilgrim, from Boston, for the northwest coast of America, five days out. She then filled away and left us to plough on through our waste of waters.

There is a settled routine for hailing ships at sea: "Ship a-hoy!" Answer, "Hulloa!" "What ship is that, pray?" "The ship Carolina, from Havre, bound to New York. Where are you from?" "The brig Pilgrim, from Boston, bound to the coast of California, five days out." Unless there is leisure, or something special to say, this form is not much varied from.

**...the brig Mermaid...** A brig has two masts; a ship had, in those days, three. Today the distinction has more to do with size and capacity: In most cases, a vessel that can carry another vessel is called a ship. There are exceptions, including the submarine, which is always called a boat, regardless of size.

**...to speak her.** To maneuver close enough to exchange greetings.

**In the news**
**August, 1834**

On August 18, Mt. Vesuvius erupts. The volcano, about 5 1/2 miles from Naples, Italy, had destroyed the Roman city of Pompeii in A.D. 79. Vesuvius was active more or less continuously from 1660 to 1944. The last serious eruption, in March of 1944, destroyed several villages and damaged aircraft belonging to the U.S. Army Air Force's 340th Bombardment Group.

**...like old Neptune's locks.** Neptune was the Roman god of the sea. The image is of seawater streaming from his hair as he arises from the ocean.

**...the ship La Carolina, from Havre...** This is apparently a reference to a passenger ship from Le Havre, a city in northwestern France.

**In the news**
**August, 1834**

On almost this exact date, naturalist Charles Darwin is in Valparaiso, Chile, very near where Dana will be in a few months. Somewhat weary of his sea journey in the *Beagle*, Darwin will take in the Chilean vista and write, "There was equally little doubt, how much more beautiful a foreground a plain makes, where distances can be measured, than an expanse of water."

This day ended pleasantly; we had got into regular and comfortable weather, and into that routine of sea life which is only broken by a storm, a sail, or the sight of land.

[1] Of late years, the British and American marine, naval and mercantile, have adopted the word "port" instead of larboard, in all cases on board ship, to avoid mistake from similarity of sound. At this time "port" was used only at the helm.

**Of late years...** See previous note relating to the recent (at that time) adoption of the term "port."

### In the news
### August, 1834

On the 11th and 12th of August, anti-Catholic mobs near Boston burn down a Roman Catholic convent. The riots were sparked by rumors of a woman being "kept against her will" in the convent. The *Boston Evening Transcript* noted, somewhat breathlessly, "The subject of universal interest in the city today has been the work of destruction accomplished by a mob, last night and this morning, at and about the Ursuline Convent, on Mount Benedict, in Charlestown—resulting in the complete sacking of the principal building itself—a four-story handsome brick edifice, with wings, and front about eighty feet—together with the farm house, cottage, and every other building upon the premises, and also with the demolition or consumption by fire of all the furniture and chattels of every description, appurtant to the whole."

# CHAPTER III

## SHIP'S DUTIES—TROPICS

As we had now a long "spell" of fine weather, without any incident to break the monotony of our lives, there can be no better place to describe the duties, regulations, and customs of an American merchantman, of which ours was a fair specimen.

The captain, in the first place, is lord paramount. He stands no watch, comes and goes when he pleases, and is accountable to no one, and must be obeyed in everything, without a question, even from his chief officer. He has the power to turn his officers off duty, and even to break them and make them do duty as sailors in the forecastle. When there are no passengers and no supercargo, as in our vessel, he has no companion but his own dignity, and no pleasures, unless he differs from most of his kind, but the consciousness of possessing supreme power, and, occasionally, the exercise of it.

The prime minister, the official organ, and the active and superintending officer, is the chief mate. He is first lieutenant, boatswain, sailing-master, and quarter-master. The captain tells him what he wishes to have done, and leaves to him the care of overseeing, of allotting the work, and also the responsibility of its being well done. The mate (as he is always called, par excellence) also keeps the log-book, for which he is responsible to the owners and insurers, and has the charge of the stowage, safe keeping, and delivery of the cargo. He is also, ex-officio, the wit of the crew; for the captain does not condescend to joke with the men, and the second mate no one cares for; so that when "the mate" thinks fit to entertain "the people" with a coarse joke or a little practical wit, every one feels bound to laugh.

The second mate's is proverbially a dog's berth. He is neither officer nor man. The men do not respect him as an officer, and he is obliged to go aloft to reef and furl the topsails, and to put his hands into the tar and slush, with the rest. The crew call him the "sailor's waiter," as

**... accountable to no one...** This was at the time quite true: The captain of a ship was its lord and master. To some extent this is still true, but in those days a captain could mistreat his crew, punishing crew members by withholding food or drink, by confinement, or by flogging. In extreme cases, he could execute a violent or mutinous crew member. Many captains wore this responsibility well and wielded power honorably, but that, we will come to see, is not the case with the captain of the *Pilgrim*.

**...supercargo...** The owner's agent.

**...no pleasures, unless he differs from most of his kind, but the consciousness of possessing supreme power, and, occasionally, the exercise of it.** Consider Lord Acton's comment: "Power tends to corrupt, and absolute power corrupts absolutely. Great men are almost always bad men." It is perhaps dangerous to confer great power upon one who fervently desires it.

**...par excellence...** By virtue of one's superiority. In general, the first mate is the most experienced sailor on board, and is—or ought to be—highly respected by the men.

**In the news**
**1834**

As Dana sails for the West Coast, Francisco de Haro is elected San Francisco's first alcalde, or mayor. California has been a part of Mexico since the 1820s, but the state is sparsely settled. In 1834, San Francisco is still known as Yerba Buena ("good herb" or "good grass"), after the aromatic shrubs surrounding the pueblo.

**...a dog's berth.** As is sometimes the case with very junior officers, the second mate is uncomfortable with (and looked down upon by) both common sailors and officers.

he has to furnish them with spun-yarn, marline, and all other stuffs that they need in their work, and has charge of the boatswain's locker, which includes serving-boards, marline-spikes, etc. He is expected by the captain to maintain his dignity and to enforce obedience, and still is kept at a great distance from the mate, and obliged to work with the crew. He is one to whom little is given and of whom much is required. His wages are usually double those of a common sailor, and he eats and sleeps in the cabin; but he is obliged to be on deck nearly all the time, and eats at the second table, that is, makes a meal out of what the captain and chief mate leave.

The steward is the captain's servant, and has charge of the pantry, from which every one, even the mate himself, is excluded. These distinctions usually find him an enemy in the mate, who does not like to have any one on board who is not entirely under his control; the crew do not consider him as one of their number, so he is left to the mercy of the captain.

The cook is the patron of the crew, and those who are in his favor can get their wet mittens and stockings dried, or light their pipes at the galley on the night watch. These two worthies, together with the carpenter and sailmaker, if there be one, stand no watch, but, being employed all day, are allowed to "sleep in" at night, unless all hands are called.

The crew are divided into two divisions, as equally as may be, called the watches. Of these the chief mate commands the larboard, and the second mate the starboard. They divide the time between them, being on and off duty, or, as it is called, on deck and below, every other four hours. If, for instance, the chief mate with the larboard watch have the first night-watch from eight to twelve; at the end of the four hours, the starboard watch is called, and the second mate takes the deck, while the larboard watch and the first mate go below until four in the morning, when they come on deck again and remain until eight; having what is called the morning watch. As they will have been on deck eight hours out of the

**...which includes serving-boards, marline-spikes, etc.** A serving-board is a thin board with gouges on the edges; onboard ship it's used for holding and helping one unravel (i.e., "serve") small ropes. A marlingspike is a pointed wooden or iron pin used to lift strands of rope when splicing.

In the news
**August, 1834**

Philadelphia, the "city of brotherly love," is torn apart by proslavery race riots, which destroy some 45 homes in the city's African-American community.

**...the crew do not consider him as one of their number...** Like the second mate, the steward is neither seaman nor officer. He is somewhat privileged, though, answering directly (and only) to the captain; this privilege can rankle other members of the crew, though, including (and perhaps especially) the mate.

**...those who are in his favor...** He who controls the stove (for heat) and the food wields power beyond his station. Ask any school custodian or cafeteria manager.

**...together with the carpenter and sailmaker...** Even today, sailing the open sea is very rough on one's gear, the sails, the rigging, and on the vessel itself. Out of sight of land, the ability to fashion and repair equipment and sails may be all that stands between a vessel and disaster. Thus, the sailmaker and carpenter were highly valued (and highly skilled) members of the crew, and often received special privileges.

**...the chief mate commands the larboard, and the second mate the starboard.** As earlier noted, the larboard is the port (or left) side of a vessel, while starboard is the right, when facing the bow. Traditional watches are divided into two—and then normally into two again, giving a total of four rotating watches of four hours each.

twelve, while those who had the middle watch—from twelve to four, will only have been up four hours, they have what is called a "forenoon watch below," that is, from eight, A.M., till twelve, M. In a man-of-war, and in some merchantmen, this alteration of watches is kept up throughout the twenty-four hours; but our ship, like most merchantmen, had "all hands" from twelve o'clock till dark, except in bad weather, when we had "watch and watch."

**...except in bad weather, when we had "watch and watch."** During bad weather, both halves of the watch alternate duty every four hours—but with both watch's subsets of sailors included, so that twice as many people are on watch at any given time.

In the news
**1834**

A few months before Dana's departure, another New Englander, Isaac Fischer, patents a process for making sandpaper. Around the same time, Cyrus Hall McCormick patents the reaping machine.

An explanation of the "dog watches" may, perhaps, be of use to one who has never been at sea. They are to shift the watches each night, so that the same watch need not be on deck at the same hours. In order to effect this, the watch from four to eight, P.M., is divided into two half, or dog watches, one from four to six, and the other from six to eight. By this means they divide the twenty-four hours into seven watches instead of six, and thus shift the hours every night. As the dog watches come during twilight, after the day's work is done, and before the night watch is set, they are the watches in which everybody is on deck. The captain is up, walking on the weather side of the quarter-deck, the chief mate is on the lee side, and the second mate about the weather gangway. The steward has finished his work in the cabin, and has come up to smoke his pipe with the cook in the galley. The crew are sitting on the windlass or lying on the forecastle, smoking, singing, or telling long yarns. At eight o'clock, eight bells are struck, the log is hove, the watch set, the wheel relieved, the galley shut up, and the other watch goes below.

**...the chief mate is on the lee side, and the second mate about the weather gangway.** The lee side is the side opposite that from which the wind is coming, while the weather gangway is the passageway on the side toward the wind.

**...log is hove...** Hove is the (archaic) past tense of *heave*. A log (as used here) is a device for calculating the speed of a vessel. It is attached to a knotted line and thrown (hove) overboard; speed is measured by counting the knots as another sailor measures the time. (This is why nautical speed is to this day expressed in knots. A vessel may be said to be traveling at seven knots, for example—not "seven-knots per hour," just "seven knots.")

The morning commences with the watch on deck's "turning-to" at day-break and washing down, scrubbing, and swabbing the decks. This, together with filling the "scuttled butt" with fresh water, and coiling up the rigging, usually occupies the time until seven bells, (half after seven,) when all hands get breakfast. At eight, the day's work begins, and lasts until sun-down, with the exception of an hour for dinner.

**...filling the "scuttled butt" with fresh water...** A scuttlebutt is a cask used to store water. (A butt being a cask or barrel. Since a scuttle is an opening, this is a cask with an opening for a tin or dipper.) It's also the origin of the term "scuttlebutt," meaning gossip or rumor—derived from the talk of men gathered around the cask.

Before I end my explanations, it may be well to define a day's work, and to correct a mistake prevalent among landsmen about a sailor's life. Nothing is more common than to hear people say—"Are not sailors very idle at sea?—what can they find to do?" This is a very natural mistake, and being very frequently made, it is one which every sailor feels interested in having corrected. In the first place, then, the discipline of the ship requires every man to be at work upon something when he is on deck, except at night and on Sundays. Except at these times, you will never see a man, on board a well-ordered vessel, standing idle on deck, sitting down, or leaning over the side. It is the officers' duty to keep every one at work, even if there is nothing to be done but to scrape the rust from the chain cables. In no state prison are the convicts more regularly set to work, and more closely watched. No conversation is allowed among the crew at their duty, and though they frequently do talk when aloft, or when near one another, yet they always stop when an officer is nigh.

With regard to the work upon which the men are put, it is a matter which probably would not be understood by one who has not been at sea. When I first left port, and found that we were kept regularly employed for a week or two, I supposed that we were getting the vessel into sea trim, and that it would soon be over, and we should have nothing to do but sail the ship; but I found that it continued so for two years, and at the end of the two years there was as much to be done as ever. As has often been said, a ship is like a lady's watch, always out of repair. When first leaving port, studding-sail gear is to be rove, all the running rigging to be examined, that which is unfit for use to be got down, and new rigging rove in its place: then the standing rigging is to be overhauled, replaced, and repaired, in a thousand different ways; and wherever any of the numberless ropes or the yards are chafing or wearing upon it, there "chafing gear," as it is called, must be put on. This chafing gear consists of worming, parcelling, roundings, battens, and service of all kinds—both rope-yarns, spun-yarn, marline and seizing-stuffs. Taking off, putting on, and mending the chafing gear alone, upon a vessel, would find constant employment for two or three men, during working hours, for a whole voyage.

**...the discipline of the ship requires every man to be at work...** In spite of his empathy for the downtrodden sailor, Dana is a product of his times and a believer in discipline and order. And given that the lives of all aboard depend on the vessel being in good repair, one can understand why the men are kept busy ensuring that everything is...well, *shipshape*. The practice also keeps the men out of trouble and instills in them the (normally admirable) habit of following officers' orders.

**...at the end of the two years there was as much to be done as ever.** The sea is a rugged and destructive environment, and on a vessel there is always something needing either repair or maintenance designed to avoid the necessity of repair. This is as true now as it was then, although our equipment and tools are generally better and longer-lasting, these days.

**...the standing rigging...** A boat or ship has two kinds of rigging: Cables, stays, guylines and similar contrivances are usually called "standing rigging." They're meant to be installed, adjusted, and then largely left alone, except when further adjustment or repair are needed. "Running rigging" are the ropes and other gear that are contantly being pulled and hauled upon to adjust and position the sails.

### In the news
### August, 1834

In nearby New York City, Cornelius Lawrence becomes the first mayor to be elected by popular vote in a city election. Lawrence will die in 1861, after a long career in banking and as a Congressman representing New York.

**...manufactured into spun-yarn.** Small rope made by twisting together multiple strands.

In the news
**August, 1834**

As Dana is heading for the Cape, astronomer and aviation pioneer Samuel Pierpont Langley is born in Aiken, South Carolina. Langley became chair of mathematics at the U.S. Naval Academy, and then a professor of astronomy at the Western University of Pennsylvania.

**...such a connection between different parts of a vessel, that one rope can seldom be touched without altering another.** This is still true today: If one adjusts one portion of the standing rigging—say, the stay or cable in front of a mast—it generally means that any other rigging attached to that mast—e.g., the stay at the rear—must now be readjusted.

**...reefing, furling, bracing...** Reefing is reducing the exposed area of a sail, often by rolling the sail around a spar or boom and tying it down, furling is rolling the sail up completely, and bracing is to prop the sail and spar in a support or to immobilize it with rope.

**Wherein the cub-drawn bear would couch...** Another allusion to Shakespeare, this one from King Lear (III, i). A cub-drawn bear is one that suckles her young. College-educated Dana is appropriating Shakespeare's description of a wild and dangerous storm, during which even wild animals—hungry though they might be—dare not venture abroad. Sailors, though, must tend their vessel regardless of the weather.

The next point to be considered is, that all the "small stuffs" which are used on board a ship—such as spun-yarn, marline, seizing-stuff, etc.—are made on board. The owners of a vessel buy up incredible quantities of "old junk," which the sailors unlay, after drawing out the yarns, knot them together, and roll them up in balls. These "rope-yarns" are constantly used for various purposes, but the greater part is manufactured into spun-yarn. For this purpose every vessel is furnished with a "spun-yarn winch;" which is very simple, consisting of a wheel and spindle. This may be heard constantly going on deck in pleasant weather; and we had employment, during a great part of the time, for three hands in drawing and knotting yarns, and making them spun-yarn.

Another method of employing the crew is, "setting up" rigging. Whenever any of the standing rigging becomes slack, (which is continually happening), the seizings and coverings must be taken off, tackles got up, and after the rigging is bowsed well taut, the seizings and coverings replaced; which is a very nice piece of work. There is also such a connection between different parts of a vessel, that one rope can seldom be touched without altering another. You cannot stay a mast aft by the back stays, without slacking up the head stays, etc. If we add to this all the tarring, greasing, oiling, varnishing, painting, scraping, and scrubbing which is required in the course of a long voyage, and also remember this is all to be done in addition to watching at night, steering, reefing, furling, bracing, making and setting sail, and pulling, hauling, and climbing in every direction, one will hardly ask, "What can a sailor find to do at sea?"

If, after all this labor—after exposing their lives and limbs in storms, wet and cold,

"Wherein the cub-drawn bear would couch;
The lion and the belly-pinched wolf
Keep their fur dry;—"

the merchants and captain think that they have not

earned their twelve dollars a month, (out of which they clothe themselves,) and their salt beef and hard bread, they keep them picking oakum—ad infinitum. This is the usual resource upon a rainy day, for then it will not do to work upon rigging; and when it is pouring down in floods, instead of letting the sailors stand about in sheltered places, and talk, and keep themselves comfortable, they are separated to different parts of the ship and kept at work picking oakum. I have seen oakum stuff placed about in different parts of the ship, so that the sailors might not be idle in the snatches between the frequent squalls upon crossing the equator. Some officers have been so driven to find work for the crew in a ship ready for sea, that they have set them to pounding the anchors (often done) and scraping the chain cables. The "Philadelphia Catechism" is,

"Six days shalt thou labor and do all thou art able,
And on the seventh—holystone the decks and scrape the cable."

This kind of work, of course, is not kept up off Cape Horn, Cape of Good Hope, and in extreme north and south latitudes; but I have seen the decks washed down and scrubbed, when the water would have frozen if it had been fresh; and all hands kept at work upon the rigging, when we had on our pea-jackets, and our hands so numb that we could hardly hold our marline-spikes.

I have here gone out of my narrative course in order that any who read this may form as correct an idea of a sailor's life and duty as possible. I have done it in this place because, for some time, our life was nothing but the unvarying repetition of these duties, which can be better described together. Before leaving this description, however, I would state, in order to show landsmen how little they know of the nature of a ship, that a ship-carpenter is kept in constant employ during good weather on board vessels which are in, what is called, perfect sea order.

**... picking oakum...** That is, picking bits of rope and yarn apart to be used as caulking.

In the news
**August, 1834**

Joseph Marie Jacquard, French weaver and inventor, dies in Oullins, France. Jacquard invented a mechanical loom that utilized punch cards to weave certain patterns automatically. The Jacquard loom, therefore, is a direct forerunner of programmable machines such as computers.

**Six days shalt thou labor...** Used by several denominations (but often associated with Catholicism), a catechism is a book of basic instruction in a church's religious tenets. The *Philadelphia Baptist Catechism* currently consists of 31 chapters and a brief introduction. Naturally, it says nothing about sailors keeping their ships clean; Dana jokes that ensuring that sailors have plenty of work to do and very little leisure time is as common and as inviolate as any religious precept found in such a book.

**...the water would have frozen...** Adding salt (or any other solute) to water tends to lower its freezing point—a phneomenon known as "freezing point depression." This is why salt sprinkled on roadways helps prevent the formation of ice. Saltwater *will* freeze, of course, but the water temperature has to be quite low: A temperature of about -6 degrees Fahrenheit will freeze even fully saturated water—i.e., water with a salt content of about 23%.

**... our life was nothing but the unvarying repetition of these duties...** Dana rightfully assumes that a linear narrative in which he describes the same events occurring day after day would be quite boring. Therefore, he lumps them all together and describes them in detail in one place.

## Chapter IV

### A Rogue–Trouble On Board– "Land Ho!"–Pompero–Cape Horn

After speaking the Carolina, on the 21st August, nothing occurred to break the monotony of our life until Friday, September 5th, when we saw a sail on our weather (starboard) beam. She proved to be a brig under English colors, and passing under our stern, reported herself as forty-nine days from Buenos Ayres, bound to Liverpool. Before she had passed us, "sail ho!" was cried again, and we made another sail, far on our weather bow, and steering athwart our hawse. She passed out of hail, but we made her out to be an hermaphrodite brig, with Brazilian colors in her main rigging. By her course, she must have been bound from Brazil to the south of Europe, probably Portugal.

Sunday, Sept. 7th. Fell in with the north-east trade winds. This morning we caught our first dolphin, which I was very eager to see. I was disappointed in the colors of this fish when dying. They were certainly very beautiful, but not equal to what has been said of them. They are too indistinct. To do the fish justice, there is nothing more beautiful than the dolphin when swimming a few feet below the surface, on a bright day. It is the most elegantly formed, and also the quickest fish, in salt water; and the rays of the sun striking upon it, in its rapid and changing motions, reflected from the water, make it look like a stray beam from a rainbow.

This day was spent like all pleasant Sabbaths at sea. The decks are washed down, the rigging coiled up, and everything put in order; and throughout the day, only one watch is kept on deck at a time. The men are all dressed in their best white duck trowsers, and red or checked shirts, and have nothing to do but to make the necessary changes in the sails. They employ themselves in reading, talking, smoking, and mending their clothes. If the weather is pleasant, they bring their work and their books upon deck, and sit down upon the forecastle and windlass. This is the only day on which these privi-

**...after speaking the Carolina...** That is, after drawing close enough to exchange greetings and news (and occasionally, provisions).

**...forty-nine days from Buenos Ayres...** That is, Buenos Aires, the capital of Argentina. She is bound for Liverpool, England.

**...an hermaphrodite brig...** A brig is, as was earlier noted, a square-rigged vessel with two masts. A hermaprodite brig also has two masts, but only the forward mast is rigged with square sails; the aft mast has triangular sails running fore-and-aft.

**...disappointed in the colors of this fish...** Dana is correct here in calling the "dolphin" a fish. Unlike the marine mammal to which most of us are referring when we use the term, the fish he's describing here is probably the mahi-mahi or dorado. It's a true fish, and its colors are indeed striking, but fade quickly as the fish dies.

**In the news**
**September, 1834**

According to a notice in the September issue of the *Boston Medical and Surgical Journal*, doctors are still arguing about and attempting to understand William Harvey's theory of blood circulation, first published in 1628.

**...dressed in their best white duck trowsers...** Duck is a linen or cotton fabric that's strong enough to be made into light sails or tents, but light enough to be made into pants and jackets.

**This is the only day on which these privileges are allowed them.** Historically, the Sabbath is a day of rest onboard as it is elsewhere. Of course, the captain has the right (some might say the duty) to call the men to work if the vessel is threatened or in need of repair.

leges are allowed them. When Monday comes, they put on their tarry trowsers again, and prepare for six days of labor.

To enhance the value of the Sabbath to the crew, they are allowed on that day a pudding, or, as it is called, a "duff." This is nothing more than flour boiled with water, and eaten with molasses. It is very heavy, dark, and clammy, yet it is looked upon as a luxury, and really forms an agreeable variety with salt beef and pork. Many a rascally captain has made friends of his crew by allowing them duff twice a week on the passage home.

On board some vessels this is made a day of instruction and of religious exercises; but we had a crew of swearers, from the captain to the smallest boy; and a day of rest, and of something like quiet, social enjoyment, was all that we could expect.

We continued running large before the north-east trade winds for several days, until Monday–

September 22d; when, upon coming on deck at seven bells in the morning, we found the other watch aloft throwing water upon the sails; and looking astern, we saw a small clipper-built brig with a black hull heading directly after us. We went to work immediately, and put all the canvas upon the brig which we could get upon her, rigging out oars for studding-sail yards; and continued wetting down the sails by buckets of water whipped up to the mast-head, until about nine o'clock, when there came on a drizzling rain. The vessel continued in pursuit, changing her course as we changed ours, to keep before the wind. The captain, who watched her with his glass, said that she was armed, and full of men, and showed no colors. We continued running dead before the wind, knowing that we sailed better so, and that clippers are fastest on the wind. We had also another advantage. The wind was light, and we spread more canvas than she did, having royals and sky-sails fore and aft, and ten studding-sails; while she, being an hermaphrodite brig, had only a gaff topsail, aft. Early in the morning she was overhauling us a little, but after the

**... their tarry trowsers...** That is, their work trousers, stained with grime, tar, and slush.

**...they are allowed on that day a pudding...** Something like what we might call a dumpling. It may not sound too appetizing, but it was no doubt a pleasant change from the typical diet of salted beef and pork.

**...we had a crew of swearers, from the captain to the smallest boy...** Dana is a man of faith—and he may have become even more religious by the time he returned from his journey to write this book. (And more religious still by the time of his later [1868] amendments to the book.) A recurring theme in *Two Years Before the Mast* is the idea that religious instruction would serve the sailors well, and that without it they tend to lead dissolute lives filled with strong drink and women of questionable virtue. Dana, however, does not always practice what he preaches.

**...the north-east trade winds...** The tradewinds are so-called because they can be relied upon to blow steadily, and are thus utilized by sailing ships following the trade routes to buy, sell, and transport goods.

**... small clipper-built brig with a black hull...** Clippers are very fast vessels with three or more masts and a raked bow that allowed the ship to rake (or "clip") through the waves. In this case, the captain of the *Pilgrim* surmises that the clipper pursuing them might be crewed by pirates, since she was armed but was not flying a flag—that is, she "showed no colors."

**...We continued running dead before the wind...** Dana is saying that the *Pilgrim's* fastest point of sail is with the wind directly behind her—that is, sailing "on a run." It may seem counterintuitive, but this is not generally true of modern sailboats; most can actually travel faster when sailing just *off* the wind.

rain came on and the wind grew lighter, we began to leave her astern. All hands remained on deck throughout the day, and we got our arms in order; but we were too few to have done anything with her, if she had proved to be what we feared. Fortunately there was no moon, and the night which followed was exceedingly dark, so that by putting out all the lights and altering our course four points, we hoped to get out of her reach. We had no light in the binnacle, but steered by the stars, and kept perfect silence through the night. At daybreak there was no sign of anything in the horizon, and we kept the vessel off to her course.

Wednesday, October 1st. Crossed the equator in long. 24° 24' W. I now, for the first time, felt at liberty, according to the old usage, to call myself a son of Neptune, and was very glad to be able to claim the title without the disagreeable initiation which so many have to go through. After once crossing the line you can never be subjected to the process, but are considered as a son of Neptune, with full powers to play tricks upon others. This ancient custom is now seldom allowed, unless there are passengers on board, in which case there is always a good deal of sport.

It had been obvious to all hands for some time that the second mate, whose name was F—-, was an idle, careless fellow, and not much of a sailor, and that the captain was exceedingly dissatisfied with him. The power of the captain in these cases was well known, and we all anticipated a difficulty. F—- (called Mr. by virtue of his office) was but half a sailor, having always been short voyages and remained at home a long time between them. His father was a man of some property, and intended to have given his son a liberal education; but he, being idle and worthless, was sent off to sea, and succeeded no better there; for, unlike many scamps, he had none of the qualities of a sailor– he was "not of the stuff that they make sailor of." He was one of that class of officers who are disliked by their captain and despised by the crew. He used to hold long yarns with the crew, and talk about the captain, and play with the boys, and relax discipline in every way. This kind of

**...and we got our arms in order...** The *Pilgrim*'s crew was ready to fight, armed as they were with muskets, sabers, and the like. (Rifled muskets—and true rifles—would soon become popular, but were not yet widely available when Dana sailed.) The vessel also carried four small cannon.

**...the binnacle...** A box or pedestal in which the compass is kept.

**...altering our course four points...** The mariner's compass of that era was divided into 16 cardinal points, and subdivided again into a total of 32. (Today's compasses are much more accurate, with bearings noted in degrees from 1 to 360.) Altering course by four points is roughly equivalent to saying that the vessel changed course by 45 degrees.

**Crossed the equator in long. 24° 24' W.** Most navies and merchant fleets commemorate one's first crossing of the equator with a ceremony, skits, mild hazing, etc. (The hazing was not always mild, though, and in the past it occasionally resulted in serious injury.) Dana's note about the *Pilgrim*'s longitude and latitude puts the brig in the South Atlantic ocean, about 1,000 nautical miles west of what would eventually be Gabon, in west-central Africa, and about 1,400 nautical miles east of Belém, in northern Brazil. The Pilgrim is some 3,400 miles from Boston, although she's sailed much farther than that, having tacked back and forth along the way.

**...whose name was F—-, was an idle, careless fellow...** In other editions and in his notes, Dana calls the mate *Forster*, but the man's name is actually George Foster.

**...talk about the captain, and play with the boys, and relax discipline in every way.** It is unwise of the second mate to attempt to "pal around" with the crew and gossip about the captain. It's an attempt to be "one of the boys" and to be accepted, but the attempt fails, as all such attempts eventually do.

conduct always makes the captain suspicious, and is never pleasant, in the end, to the men; they preferring to have an officer active, vigilant, and distant as may be, with kindness. Among other bad practices, he frequently slept on his watch, and having been discovered asleep by the captain, he was told that he would be turned off duty if he did it again. To prevent it in every way possible, the hen-coops were ordered to be knocked up, for the captain never sat down on deck himself, and never permitted an officer to do so.

The second night after crossing the equator, we had the watch from eight till twelve, and it was "my helm" for the last two hours. There had been light squalls through the night, and the captain told Mr. F—-, who commanded our watch, to keep a bright look-out. Soon after I came to the helm, I found that he was quite drowsy, and at last he stretched himself on the companion and went fast asleep. Soon afterwards, the captain came very quietly on deck, and stood by me for some time looking at the compass. The officer at length became aware of the captain's presence, but pretending not to know it, began humming and whistling to himself, to show that he was not asleep, and went forward, without looking behind him, and ordered the main royal to be loosed. On turning round to come aft, he pretended surprise at seeing the master on deck. This would not do. The captain was too "wide awake" for him, and beginning upon him at once, gave him a grand blow-up, in true nautical style– "You're a lazy, good-for-nothing rascal; you're neither man, boy, soger, nor sailor! you're no more than a thing aboard a vessel! you don't earn your salt! you're worse than a Mahon soger!" and other still more choice extracts from the sailor's vocabulary. After the poor fellow had taken the harangue, he was sent into his stateroom, and the captain stood the rest of the watch himself.

At seven bells in the morning, all hands were called aft and told that F—- was no longer an officer on board, and that we might choose one of our own number for second mate. It is usual for the captain to make this offer, and it is very good policy, for the crew think

**...he frequently slept on his watch...** Obviously, the second mate is lazy and undisciplined. The captain orders the chicken coops broken down so that they can't be used as convenient seats on deck.

**...it was "my helm" for the last two hours.** That is, Dana was steering the vessel. The helm is the place where the vessel's steering device (wheel, tiller, etc.) is located. A modern vessel may have more than one helm.

In the news

**October, 1834**

Henry Blair is granted a patent for a corn planting machine. Blair appears to have been the second African-American to receive a United States patent. The first is said to be Thomas Jennings, a New York City tailor who patented a drycleaning process in 1820. Both were free men; slaves, of course, could not be granted patents.

**...the companion...** A wooden cover over a staircase leading to a cabin.

**...the main royal...** A royal is a small, light sail just above a top-gallant; the top-gallant is the third sail above the deck—that is, there are two sails below the top-gallant.

**The captain was too "wide awake" for him...** Too sharp, too clever, too experienced for the mate to fool.

**... neither man, boy, soger, nor sailor!** To call a sailor a "soger" (i.e., a soldier) was an insult of the worst kind. "Mahon" was a reference to a fort taken from the British by the French in 1756 during the early days of the Seven Years' War; so, a "Mahon soger," having been defeated in battle and had his fort seized, wasn't even a good soldier, let alone a competent sailor. Thus, this is meant to be doubly insulting.

**...born near the Kennebee...** Dana's memory is imperfect; the man's name is actually Hill. An experienced sailor, Hall/Hill was actually from Pittston, in central Maine. While Dana recalls him being born and bred to the sea, Pittston is actually on the Pennobscot River, about 15 nautical miles northeast of Merrymeeting Bay and some 25 nautical miles from the sea itself.

**...knives and forks and tea-cups.** Dana is being somewhat snide, but accurate. Seamen used few utensils, other than a good knife, and usually ate from a common tin or trencher. Officers, on the other hand, used knives and forks and ate at a table.

**This was done to determine our longitude...** If a ship sails in an east/west direction (i.e., a direction of constant latitude), readings of coastal landmarks (unavailable at sea, of course) can help determine the vessel's longitude. The captain has many years' experience, and is beginning to doubt that his clock is keeping time correctly. For accurate readings with a sextant, a precise measurement of time is essential. He eventually determines that the timepiece is in error.

**... the port of Pernambuco.** The town—in northeast Brazil— was actually called Recife. Pernambuco was the name of the state. Now at sea for about 51 days, the *Pilgrim* is some 3,500 nautical miles from Boston.

**...catamarans.** A catamaran consists of two hulls with a cabin (or, in smaller boats, a net or other platform) in between. Within limits, a catamaran is quite stable, heeling (tipping to leeward) only slightly, and is thus a comfortable vessel to sail. However, if a catamaran is forced to heel at an extreme angle (in a storm, for example), the heeled vessel may exceed its *righting moment*, and thus be unable to recover; at that point, the vessel will capsize. Many single-hulled, keeled vessels are self-righting, and a capsized sailboat can often right itself. But once a catamaran is capsized, it must be manually righted.

themselves the choosers and are flattered by it, but have to obey, nevertheless. Our crew, as is usual, refused to take the responsibility of choosing a man of whom we would never be able to complain, and left it to the captain. He picked out an active and intelligent young sailor, born near the Kennebee, who had been several Canton voyages, and proclaimed him in the following manner: "I choose Jim Hall–he's your second mate. All you've got to do is, to obey him as you would me; and remember that he is Mr. Hall." F— went forward into the forecastle as a common sailor, and lost the handle to his name, while young fore-mast Jim became Mr. Hall, and took up his quarters in the land of knives and forks and tea-cups.

Sunday, October 5th. It was our morning watch; when, soon after the day began to break, a man on the forecastle called out, "Land ho!" I had never heard the cry before, and did not know what it meant, (and few would suspect what the words were, when hearing the strange sound for the first time,) but I soon found, by the direction of all eyes, that there was land stretching along our weather beam. We immediately took in studding-sails and hauled our wind, running in for the land. This was done to determine our longitude; for by the captain's chronometer we were in 25° W., but by his observations we were much farther, and he had been for some time in doubt whether it was his chronometer or his sextant which was out of order. This land-fall settled the matter, and the former instrument was condemned, and becoming still worse, was never afterwards used.

As we ran in towards the coast, we found that we were directly off the port of Pernambuco, and could see with the telescope the roofs of the houses, and one large church, and the town of Olinda. We ran along by the mouth of the harbor, and saw a full-rigged brig going in. At two, P.M., we again kept off before the wind, leaving the land on our quarter, and at sun-down, it was out of sight. It was here that I first saw one of those singular things called catamarans. They are composed of logs lashed together upon the water; have one large sail, are quite fast, and, strange as it may seem, are trusted as good sea boats. We saw several, with from one to three men in each, boldly putting out to sea, after it had become almost dark. The Indians go out in them after fish, and as the weather is regular in certain seasons, they have no fear. After taking a new departure from Olinda, we kept off on our way to Cape Horn.

We met with nothing remarkable until we were in the latitude of the river La Plata. Here there are violent gales from the south-west, called Pomperos, which are very destructive to the shipping in the river, and are felt for many leagues at sea. They are usually preceded by lightning. The captain told the mates to keep a bright look-out, and if they saw lightning at the south-west, to take in sail at once. We got the first touch of one during my watch on deck. I was walking in the lee gangway, and thought that I saw lightning on the lee bow. I told the second mate, who came over and looked out for some time. It was very black in the south-west, and in about ten minutes we saw a distinct flash. The wind, which had been south-east, had now left us, and it was dead calm. We sprang aloft immediately and furled the royals and top-gallant-sails, and took in the flying jib, hauled up the mainsail and trysail, squared the after yards, and awaited the attack. A huge mist capped with black clouds came driving towards us, extending over that quarter of the horizon, and covering the stars, which shone brightly in the other part of the heavens. It came upon us at once with a blast, and a shower of hail and rain, which almost took our breath from us. The hardiest was obliged to turn his back. We let the halyards run, and fortunately were not taken aback. The little vessel "paid off" from the wind, and ran on for some time directly before it, tearing through the water with everything flying. Having called all hands, we close-reefed the topsails and trysail, furled the courses and job, set the fore-top-mast staysail, and brought her up nearly to her course, with the weather braces hauled in a little, to ease her.

This was the first blow, that I had seen, which could really be called a gale. We had reefed our topsails in the Gulf Stream, and I thought it something serious, but an

**...the river La Plata.** The rio de la Plata (the Plate [meaning silver plate] River) is a 180-mile long river on the border between what is now Argentina and Uruguay.

**...on the lee bow.** Toward the front of the ship, on the side opposite the side from which the wind is coming.

**We sprang aloft...** The crew is hurrying to minimize the amount of sail exposed before the storm hits.

## In the news
## October, 1834

As the *Pilgrim* approaches the Rio Plata, botanist Thomas Nuttall is on the Oregon Trail as part of the Wyeth expedition, collecting samples as he accompanies a party of explorers, missionaries, and settlers on an overland trip. Oddly, Dana and Nuttall know each other from Harvard, where Dana is a student and Nuttall a botany professor. They will soon be aboard ship together, Dana as a common seaman, and Nuttall as a passenger. It's a small world, in spite of its immensity.

**...not taken aback.** That is, the sails were not blown backward against the mast. (This is the origin of the phrase *taken aback*, which we now use to mean *startled*, *suprised*, or *shocked*.)

**...furled the courses...** A course is the lowest square sail on a mast—essentially the same thing as the mainsail. If there is more than one mast, then there are multiple courses.

**...a gale.** A gale is a storm in which the wind moves at speeds of 45 to 55 knots or so, although definitions vary widely. A wind of 55 knots is blowing at over 60 mph, so it is quite strong. Such a wind is strong enough to break or uproot trees and damage buildings. At sea, a 55 knot wind would cause heavy rolling and 20 to 30 ft. waves.

**...which is in such general use...** In this edition, Dana takes the time to explain the use of the word "lay" in a nautical context. An educated young man, he is well aware that the verb "lay" takes a direct object, which he points out is understood here. Thus, "lay [go] forward" is to be understood as "lay *yourselves* forward," so that the word, in his estimation, is being used correctly.

In the news
**October, 1834**

By now, some 30,000 anglos live in Coahuila y Tejas, vastly outnumbering the Mexican-born citizens of the country that had only 14 years before won its independence from Spain. The influx of U.S. settlers (called Texians) would raise tensions and, exacerbated by economic issues, eventually (1835) result in the Texas War of Independence.

**...have the weather earing passed...** The "weather" side of anything is the side from which the wind blows; the weather earing is a rope attached to (in this case, the weather side of) a sail and used to furl or bend (fasten) it.

**...no "sogering,"...** That is, no acting like a soldier. As noted earlier, an insult to any real sailor.

**...to make up the bunt.** The bunt is the middle of the sail.

older sailor would have thought nothing of it. As I had now become used to the vessel and to my duty, I was of some service on a yard, and could knot my reef-point as well as anybody. I obeyed the order to lay(1) aloft with the rest,

---

1. This word "lay," which is in such general use on board ship, being used in giving orders instead of "go"; as "Lay forward!" "Lay aft!" "Lay aloft!" etc., I do not understand to be the neuter verb, lie, mispronounced, but to be the active verb lay, with the objective case understood; as "Lay yourselves forwards!" "Lay yourselves aft!" etc.

---

and found the reefing a very exciting scene; for one watch reefed the fore-topsail, and the other the main, and every one did his utmost to get his topsail hoisted first. We had a great advantage over the larboard watch, because the chief mate never goes aloft, while our new second mate used to jump into the rigging as soon as we began to haul out the reef-tackle, and have the weather earing passed before there was a man upon the yard. In this way we were almost always able to raise the cry of "Haul out to leeward" before them, and having knotted our points, would slide down the shrouds and back-stays, and sing out at the topsail halyards to let it be known that we were ahead of them. Reefing is the most exciting part of a sailor's duty. All hands are engaged upon it, and after the halyards are let go, there is no time to be lost–no "sogering," or hanging back, then. If one is not quick enough, another runs over him. The first on the yard goes to the weather earing, the second to the lee, and the next two to the "dog's ears;" while the others lay along into the bunt, just giving each other elbow-room. In reefing, the yard-arms (the extremes of the yards) are the posts of honor; but in furling, the strongest and most experienced stand in the slings, (or, middle of the yard,) to make up the bunt. If the second mate is a smart fellow, he will never let any one take either of these posts from him; but if he is wanting either in seamanship, strength, or activity, some better man will get the bunt and earings from him; which immediately brings him into disrepute.

We remained for the rest of the night, and throughout the next day, under the same close sail, for it continued to blow very fresh; and though we had no more hail, yet there was a soaking rain, and it was quite cold and uncomfortable; the more so, because we were not prepared for cold weather, but had on our thin clothes. We were glad to get a watch below, and put on our thick clothing, boots, and south-westers. Towards sun-down the gale moderated a little, and it began to clear off in the south-west. We shook our reefs out, one by one, and before midnight had top-gallant sails upon her.

We had now made up our minds for Cape Horn and cold weather, and entered upon every necessary preparation.

Tuesday, Nov. 4th. At day-break, saw land upon our larboard quarter. There were two islands, of different size but of the same shape; rather high, beginning low at the water's edge, and running with a curved ascent to the middle. They were so far off as to be of a deep blue color, and in a few hours we sank them in the north-east. These were the Falkland Islands. We had run between them and the main land of Patagonia. At sunset the second mate, who was at the masthead, said that he saw land on the starboard bow. This must have been the island of Staten Land; and we were now in the region of Cape Horn, with a fine breeze from the northward, top-mast and top-gallant studding-sails set, and every prospect of a speedy and pleasant passage round.

**...to blow very fresh...** A fresh breeze is a moderate one, say, 15 to 20 knots.

**...south-westers.** Oiled canvas or cloth hats with a long back brim used to prevent water from running down the back of a sailor's neck.

**We shook our reefs out...** Just as one reefs (shortens) sail during bad weather, one takes reefs out, adding sail, as the weather improves.

**...made up our minds for Cape Horn...** The *Pilgrim* is now nearing a difficult and dangerous part of the journey: rounding Cape Horn, a region where ice, bad weather, and tumultuous seas are common.

**These were the Falkland Islands.** Located in the South Atlantic, these islands have long been the subject of dispute. In Dana's day, they had just been reclaimed by the British. The *Pilgrim* is now about 6,900 nautical miles from Boston and about 300 nautical miles from Cape Horn, the southernmost tip of South America. According to tradition, sailors who made the perilous passage around "The Horn" were entitled to wear an earring in their left ears, a custom that is still sometimes followed. (And which may be why we so often picture pirates wearing earrings: They were worn to signify various voyages taken.) In any event, there is nothing new about the idea of men wearing earrings: The King James Bible (Judges viii. 24) has "For they had golden earrings, because they were Ishmaelites."

**In the news**

**November, 1834**

Franklin Pierce, the future 14th President of the United States, marries Jane Appleton. Pierce will become a colonel during the Mexican-American War, and will command the troops that eventually capture Mexico City.

## Chapter V

## Cape Horn–A Visit

Wednesday, Nov. 5th. The weather was fine during the previous night, and we had a clear view of the Magellan Clouds, and of the Southern Cross. The Magellan Clouds consist of three small nebulae in the southern part of the heavens,–two bright, like the milky-way, and one dark. These are first seen, just above the horizon, soon after crossing the southern tropic. When off Cape Horn, they are nearly overhead. The cross is composed of four stars in that form, and is said to be the brightest constellation in the heavens.

**...a clear view of the Magellan Clouds...** The Magellanic Clouds are galaxies visible, in good weather, from our southern hemisphere. The Southern Cross (or Crux) is a constellation visible in the southern hemisphere. The flag of New Zealand features the four stars that make up the cross.

In the news
**November, 1834**

Father Vicente Pascual Oliva has recently (August) become the officiating father at the San Diego Mission, which Dana will visit shortly. The mission, founded in 1769 by Father Junipero Serra, was the first of 21 Spanish missions that would eventually stretch to Sonoma, California. The missions served not only as places of worship, but also as farms run by the Spanish with the (often involuntary) help of Native Americans that the Spanish fathers hoped to convert to Christianity.

During the first part of this day (Wednesday) the wind was light, but after noon it came on fresh, and we furled the royals. We still kept the studding-sails out, and the captain said he should go round with them, if he could. Just before eight o'clock, (then about sun-down, in that latitude,) the cry of "All hands ahoy!" was sounded down the fore scuttle and the after hatchway, and hurrying upon deck, we found a large black cloud rolling on toward us from the south-west, and blackening the whole heavens. "Here comes the Cape Horn!" said the chief mate; and we had hardly time to haul down and clew up, before it was upon us. In a few moments, a heavier sea was raised than I had ever seen before, and as it was directly ahead, the little brig, which was no better than a bathing machine, plunged into it, and all the forward part of her was under water; the sea pouring in through the bow-ports and hawse-hole and over the knight-heads, threatening to wash everything overboard. In the lee scuppers it was up to a man's waist. We sprang aloft and double reefed the topsails, and furled all the other sails, and made all snug. But this would not do; the brig was laboring and straining against the head sea, and the gale was growing worse and worse. At the same time the sleet and hail were driving with all fury against us. We clewed down, and hauled out the reef-tackles again, and close-reefed the fore-topsail, and furled the main, and hove her to on the starboard tack. Here was an end to our fine prospects. We made up our

**...we had hardly time to haul down and clew up...** That is, to furl the sails by gathering the clews, or lower corners of the sails. A way to hurriedly furl the sails in an emergency.

**...the little brig...** The *Pilgrim* truly is a small vessel, especially to be sailing in these latitudes. Built in 1825 at a cost of $50,000, the 180-ton vessel is 85' in length, with a 21' beam, and is crewed by a dozen or so men.

**...the bow-ports and hawse-hole...** Holes in the bow through which run cables for anchors and other gear.

**...hove her to on the starboard tack.** That is, "came about" so that the wind is coming over her starboard (right, when viewed facing the bow) side.

minds to head winds and cold weather; sent down the royal yards, and unrove the gear, but all the rest of the top hamper remained aloft, even to the sky-sail masts and studding-sail booms.

Throughout the night it stormed violently–rain, hail, snow, and sleet beating down upon the vessel–the wind continuing to break ahead, and the sea running high. At daybreak (about three, A.M.) the deck was covered with snow. The captain sent up the steward with a glass of grog to each of the watch; and all the time that we were off the Cape, grog was given to the morning watch, and to all hands whenever we reefed topsails. The clouds cleared away at sun-rise, and the wind becoming more fair, we again made sail and stood nearly up to our course.

Thursday, Nov. 6th. It continued more pleasant through the first part of the day, but at night we had the same scene over again. This time, we did not heave to, as on the night before, but endeavored to beat to windward under close-reefed top-sails, balance-reefed trysail, and fore top-mast stay-sail. This night it was my turn to steer, or, as the sailors say, my trick at the helm, for two hours. Inexperienced as I was, I made out to steer to the satisfaction of the officer, and neither S— nor myself gave up our tricks, all the time that we were off the Cape. This was something to boast of, for it requires a good deal of skill and watchfulness to steer a vessel close hauled, in a gale of wind, against a heavy head sea. "Ease her when she pitches," is the word; and a little carelessness in letting her ship a heavy sea, might sweep the decks, or knock masts out of her.

Friday, Nov. 7th. Towards morning the wind went down, and during the whole forenoon we lay tossing about in a dead calm, and in the midst of a thick fog. The calms here are unlike those in most parts of the world, for there is always such a high sea running, and the periods of calm are so short, that it has no time to go down; and vessels, being under no command of sails or rudder, lie like logs upon the water. We were obliged to steady the booms and yards by guys and braces, and

**...the top hamper...** The uppermost sails and rigging.

**...a glass of grog...** In this context, a drink often made with one part rum and one or two parts water.

**In the news**
**November, 1834**

John C. Stewart leaves Boston on the *Alert*, destined for California. Stewart, a common seaman at the time, will sail with Dana when they both return to Boston on the *Alert*. By that time, Stewart will have been promoted to second mate. In 1845, Stewart will marry Rosa Machado, daughter of Jose Manuel Machado, who served in the old Spanish army in California; the marriage was typical of the manner in which the old Spanish, newer Mexican, and newer still "yankee" Californians intermarried until distinctions among the three began to fall away.

**...the wind becoming more fair...** A fair wind is one that blows in the direction you need it to blow in order to stay on course.

**...my trick at the helm...** A "trick" is a tour or watch; the time allotted to a task or station.

**...neither S— nor myself...** In some editions, Dana notes (incorrectly) that the other sailor's name is "Stimpson," but it's actually *Stimson*. Benjamin Stimson, only 18 at the time of the Dana's 1834 voyage, lived in Dedham, MA.

**...lash everything well below.** In rough weather, gear that is not tied down securely can be tossed about with great force, injuring men or damaging the vessel.

**...and the sea as smooth as though oil had been poured upon it...** Oil poured on "troubled" water does in fact have a calming effect.

**...and grampuses...** The term "grampus" can refer to either a killer whale (an orca) or a type of dolphin called Risso's dolphin. The dolphin, however, is normally found only in tropical and temperate waters, so Dana is probably referring to killer whales.

In the news
**November, 1834**

The governor of Alta California, Jose Figueroa, reports that there are only three primary schools in all of California—and none in San Diego, where Dana will eventually disembark. Partly this is due to the influence of the Franciscan missionaries, who felt that a secular education was unnecessary, especially for a populace of "savage" natives whose main role had been to toil on the mission farms.

to lash everything well below. We now found our top hamper of some use, for though it is liable to be carried away or sprung by the sudden "bringing up" of a vessel when pitching in a chopping sea, yet it is a great help in steadying a vessel when rolling in a long swell; giving it more slowness, ease, and regularity to the motion.

The calm of the morning reminds me of a scene which I forgot to describe at the time of its occurrence, but which I remember from its being the first time that I had heard the near breathing of whales. It was on the night that we passed between the Falkland Islands and Staten Land. We had the watch from twelve to four, and coming upon deck, found the little brig lying perfectly still, surrounded by a thick fog, and the sea as smooth as though oil had been poured upon it; yet now and then a long, low swell rolling over its surface, slightly lifting the vessel, but without breaking the glassy smoothness of the water. We were surrounded far and near by shoals of sluggish whales and grampuses; which the fog prevented our seeing, rising slowly to the surface, or perhaps lying out at length, heaving out those peculiar lazy, deep, and long-drawn breathings which give such an impression of supineness and strength. Some of the watch were asleep, and the others were perfectly still, so that there was nothing to break the illusion, and I stood leaning over the bulwarks, listening to the slow breathing of the mighty creatures–now one breaking the water just alongside, whose black body I almost fancied that I could see through the fog; and again another, which I could just hear in the distance–until the low and regular swell seemed like the heaving of the ocean's mighty bosom to the sound of its heavy and long-drawn respirations.

In the news
**November, 1834**

The *Beagle*, with Charles Darwin aboard, leaves Valparaiso, headed for Tres Montes, Chile.

Towards the evening of this day, (Friday 7th,) the fog cleared off, and we had every appearance of a cold blow; and soon after sun-down it came on. Again it was clew up and haul down, reef and furl, until we had got her down to close-reefed topsails, double-reefed trysail, and reefed forespenser. Snow, hail, and sleet were driving upon us most of the night, and the sea was breaking over the bows and covering the forward part of the little vessel; but as she would lay her course the captain refused to heave her to.

Saturday, Nov. 8th. This day commenced with calm and thick fog, and ended with hail, snow, a violent wind, and close-reefed topsails.

Sunday, Nov. 9th. To-day the sun rose clear and continued so until twelve o'clock, when the captain got an observation. This was very well for Cape Horn, and we thought it a little remarkable that, as we had not had one unpleasant Sunday during the whole voyage, the only tolerable day here should be a Sunday. We got time to clear up the steerage and forecastle, and set things to rights, and to overhaul our wet clothes a little. But this did not last very long. Between five and six–the sun was then nearly three hours high–the cry of "All starbowlines ahoy!" summoned our watch on deck; and immediately all hands were called. A true specimen of Cape Horn was coming upon us. A great cloud of a dark slate-color was driving on us from the south-west; and we did our best to take in sail, (for the light sails had been set during the first part of the day,) before we were in the midst of it. We had got the light sails furled, the courses hauled up, and the topsail reef-tackles hauled out, and were just mounting the fore-rigging, when the storm struck us. In an instant the sea, which had been comparatively quiet, was running higher and higher; and it became almost as dark as night. The hail and sleet were harder than I had yet felt them; seeming to almost pin us down to the rigging. We were longer taking in sail than ever before; for the sails were stiff and wet, the ropes and rigging covered with snow and sleet, and we ourselves cold and nearly blinded with the violence of the storm. By the time we had got down upon deck again, the little brig was plunging madly into a tremendous head sea, which at every drive rushed in through the bow-ports and over the bows, and buried all the forward part of the vessel. At this instant the chief mate, who was standing on the top of the windlass, at the foot of the spenser mast, called out, "Lay out there and furl the jib!" This was no agreeable or safe duty, yet it must be done. An old Swede, (the best sailor on

**...as she would lay her course the captain refused to heave her to.** Although the weather was extremely rough, the vessel was under control and on course. The captain therefore opted not to heave to, or adjust *Pilgrim*'s sails such that she made as little headway as possible, and could thus wait out the storm in relative comfort.

**...the captain got an observation.** That is, was able to get a position reading using his sextant, something possible only in good weather.

**"All starbowlines ahoy!"** That is, all men of the starboard watch.

In the news
**November, 1834**

Back in Dana's New England, travelers could purchase $3 tickets on the stagecoach leaving Newport, MA at 7:30 a.m. and arriving in Boston almost 12 hours later—at 7:00 p.m. Today, this journey is a leisurely 90-minute drive.

**... and we ourselves cold and nearly blinded with the violence of the storm.** This is when the Cape is at its most dangerous: It's dark and very cold, the seas are high, and the wind is blowing hard. The men are tired, and the ropes and sails with which they're attempting to work are frozen stiff.

**...who belonged on the forecastle...** That is, by virtue of his skill and hard work, the Swede really should have been an officer.

board,) who belonged on the forecastle, sprang out upon the bowsprit. Another one must go: I was near the mate, and sprang forward, threw the down-haul over the windlass, and jumped between the knight-heads out upon the bowsprit. The crew stood abaft the windlass and hauled the jib down, while we got out upon the weather side of the jib-boom, our feet on the foot ropes, holding on by the spar, the great jib flying off to leeward and slatting so as almost to throw us off of the boom. For some time we could do nothing but hold on, and the vessel diving into two huge seas, one after the other, plunged us twice into the water up to our chins. We hardly knew whether we were on or off; when coming up, dripping from the water, we were raised high into the air. John (that was the sailor's name) thought the boom would go, every moment, and called out to the mate to keep the vessel off, and haul down the staysail; but the fury of the wind and the breaking of the seas against the bows defied every attempt to make ourselves heard, and we were obliged to do the best we could in our situation. Fortunately, no other seas so heavy struck her, and we succeeded in furling the jib "after a fashion"; and, coming in over the staysail nettings, were not a little pleased to find that all was snug, and the watch gone below; for we were soaked through, and it was very cold. The weather continued nearly the same through the night.

**...jumped between the knight-heads...** The knight-heads are two pieces of timber used to support the windlass, a hand-operated machine used to raise the anchor or to lift buckets and other heavy items.

**The crew stood abaft the windlass...** Because Dana was eager to show off his newly aquired nautical expertise, the book is awash (if you'll pardon the expression) in nautical terminology, much of it now obsolete. Some critics have recommended that confused readers simply skip over the sailing terms and concentrate on the story itself, much as other critics have recommended skipping the so-called cetology chapters of *Moby Dick*. (A novel written, as it happens, by an author who would come to know—and be much indebted to—Dana.)

**..."after a fashion"...** This slightly deprecatory phrase (meaning *tolerably*, or *more or less*) sounds modern, but used in this sense it actually goes back to the early 1600s.

Monday, Nov. 10th. During a part of this day we were hove to, but the rest of the time were driving on, under close-reefed sails, with a heavy sea, a strong gale, and frequent squalls of hail and snow.

Tuesday, Nov. 11th. The same.

Wednesday, Nov. 12th. The same.

Thursday, Nov. 13th. The same.

**The same.** This sort of understated repetition, called *syntactic parallelism*, is a very effective rhetorical device. The men are living in a nightmare—and that nightmare is repeated day after day, with seemingly no end to the misery.

We had now got hardened to Cape weather, the vessel was under reduced sail, and everything secured on deck and below, so that we had little to do but steer and to stand our watch. Our clothes were all wet through, and

In the news
**November, 1834**

This quarter's issue of the *North American Review*, edited by none other than Dana's father (Richard Henry Dana Sr.), contains a somewhat worshipful analysis of the poems of Samuel Taylor Coleridge (including "The Rime of The Ancient Mariner," mentioned below) and a spirited defense of the poet.

the only change was from wet to more wet. It was in vain to think of reading or working below, for we were too tired, the hatchways were closed down, and everything was wet and uncomfortable, black and dirty, heaving and pitching. We had only to come below when the watch was out, wring out our wet clothes, hang them up, and turn in and sleep as soundly as we could, until the watch was called again. A sailor can sleep anywhere–no sound of wind, water, wood or iron can keep him awake–and we were always fast asleep when three blows on the hatchway, and the unwelcome cry of "All starbowlines ahoy! eight bells there below! do you hear the news?" (the usual formula of calling the watch), roused us up from our berths upon the cold, wet decks. The only time when we could be said to take any pleasure was at night and morning, when we were allowed a tin pot full of hot tea, (or, as the sailors significantly call it, "water bewitched,") sweetened with molasses. This, bad as it was, was still warm and comforting, and, together with our sea biscuit and cold salt beef, made quite a meal. Yet even this meal was attended with some uncertainty. We had to go ourselves to the galley and take our kid of beef and tin pots of tea, and run the risk of losing them before we could get below. Many a kid of beef have I seen rolling in the scuppers, and the bearer lying at his length on the decks. I remember an English lad who was always the life of the crew, but whom we afterwards lost overboard, standing for nearly ten minutes at the galley, with this pot of tea in his hand, waiting for a chance to get down into the forecastle; and seeing what he thought was a "smooth spell," started to go forward. He had just got to the end of the windlass, when a great sea broke over the bows, and for a moment I saw nothing of him but his head and shoulders; and at the next instant, being taken off of his legs, he was carried aft with the sea, until her stern lifting up and sending the water forward, he was left high and dry at the side of the long-boat, still holding on to his tin pot, which had now nothing in it but salt water. But nothing could ever daunt him, or overcome, for a moment, his habitual good humor. Regaining his legs, and shaking his fist at the man at the wheel, he rolled below, saying, as he passed, "A man's no sailor, if he

**A sailor can sleep anywhere...** Like firefighters, emergency room physicians, and others who work long hours and must be ready at any time, sailors learn to sleep whenever and wherever sleep is possible.

**...as the sailors significantly call it, "water bewitched,"...** A sarcastic term signifying any weak tea, punch, beer, or watered-down alcoholic drink.

**Many a kid of beef...** A kid was a sailor's mess tub—a small wooden tub containing food or drink.

**...whom we afterwards lost overboard...** George Ballmer (or Bellamer). See Chapter VI.

**In the news**
**November, 1834**

At this point, of all the California ports at which Dana and other hide traders will call, the dingy and desolate-looking port of San Pedro—some 30 miles from El Pueblo de Los Angeles—has earned a reputation as the richest source of hides on the coast.

can't take a joke." The ducking was not the worst of such an affair, for, as there was an allowance of tea, you could get no more from the galley; and though sailors would never suffer a man to go without, but would always turn in a little from their own pots to fill up his, yet this was at best but dividing the loss among all hands.

**The cook had just made for us a mess of hot "scouse"...** A variant of "lobscouse," meat stewed with vegetables, biscuit, etc.

Something of the same kind befell me a few days after. The cook had just made for us a mess of hot "scouse"– that is, biscuit pounded fine, salt beef cut into small pieces, and a few potatoes, boiled up together and seasoned with pepper. This was a rare treat, and I, being the last at the galley, had it put in my charge to carry down for the mess. I got along very well as far as the hatchway, and was just getting down the steps, when a heavy sea, lifting the stern out of water, and passing forward, dropping it down again, threw the steps from their place, and I came down into the steerage a little faster than I meant to, with the kid on top of me, and the whole precious mess scattered over the floor. Whatever your feelings may be, you must make a joke of everything at sea; and if you were to fall from aloft and be caught in the belly of a sail, and thus saved from instant death, it would not do to look at all disturbed, or to make a serious matter of it.

**I came down into the steerage a little faster than I meant to...** Dana is using *meiosis*, ironic understatement or minimization, to point out the humor in the fact the he essentially fell down the ladder into steerage, the food ending up on top of him. Many euphemisms are good examples of such understatement, including such phrases "the recent unpleasantness" to refer to the Civil War. In *Monty Python and the Holy Grail*, meiosis is used (or perhaps overused) to comic effect: the Black Knight (John Cleese)—having had various limbs hacked off by King Arthur (Graham Chapman)—refuses to concede defeat, insisting, "It's just a flesh wound!"

**Whatever your feelings may be, you must make a joke of everything at sea...** Not too different than the way that soldiers, police officers, etc., normally avoid admitting to being afraid.

Friday, Nov. 14th. We were now well to the westward of the Cape and were changing our course to the northward as much as we dared, since the strong south-west winds, which prevailed then, carried us in toward Patagonia. At two, P.M., we saw a sail on our larboard beam, and at four we made it out to be a large ship, steering our course, under single-reefed topsails. We at that time had shaken the reefs out of our topsails, as the wind was lighter, and set the main top-gallant sail. As soon as our captain saw what sail she was under, he set the fore top-gallant sail and flying jib; and the old whaler– for such, his boats and short sail showed him to be–felt a little ashamed, and shook the reefs out of his topsails, but could do no more, for he had sent down his top-gallant masts off the Cape. He ran down for us, and answered our hail as the whale-ship, New England, of

**...in toward Patagonia.** A region (not a specific city or state) in the southernmost portions of South America, Patagonia is located in Chile and Argentina.

**...shook the reefs out of his topsails, but could do no more...** The two are engaged in a bit of one-upmanship designed to show who is the "saltier" captain.

**the whale-ship, New England, of Poughkeepsie...** The ship hails from Poughkeepsie, a New York town on the Hudson River.

Poughkeepsie, one hundred and twenty days from New York. Our captain gave our name, and added, ninety-two days from Boston. They then had a little conversation about longitude, in which they found that they could not agree. The ship fell astern, and continued in sight during the night. Toward morning, the wind having become light, we crossed our royal and skysail yards, and at daylight we were seen under a cloud of sail, having royal and skysails fore and aft. The "spouter," as the sailors call a whaleman, had sent up his main top-gallant mast and set the sail, and made signal for us to heave to. About half-past seven their whale-boat came alongside, and Captain Job Terry sprang on board, a man known in every port and by every vessel in the Pacific ocean. "Don't you know Job Terry? I thought everybody knew Job Terry," said a green-hand, who came in the boat, to me, when I asked him about his captain. He was indeed a singular man. He was six feet high, wore thick, cowhide boots, and brown coat and trowsers, and, except a sun-burnt complexion, had not the slightest appearance of a sailor; yet he had been forty years in the whale trade, and, as he said himself, had owned ships, built ships, and sailed ships. His boat's crew were a pretty raw set, just out of the bush, and as the sailor's phrase is, "hadn't got the hayseed out of their hair." Captain Terry convinced our captain that our reckoning was a little out, and, having spent the day on board, put off in his boat at sunset for his ship, which was now six or eight miles astern. He began a "yarn" when he came on board, which lasted, with but little intermission, for four hours. It was all about himself, and the Peruvian government, and the Dublin frigate, and Lord James Townshend, and President Jackson, and the ship Ann M'Kim of Baltimore. It would probably never have come to an end, had not a good breeze sprung up, which sent him off to his own vessel. One of the lads who came in his boat, a thoroughly countrified-looking fellow, seemed to care very little about the vessel, rigging, or anything else, but went round looking at the live stock, and leaned over the pig-sty, and said he wished he was back again tending his father's pigs.

**...royal and skysails fore and aft.** As previously noted, a royal is a light sail above the topgallant; a skysail is a light sail above the royal.

**I thought everybody knew Job Terry...** There is now a small cemetery in Freetown, MA named after Terry's father, also named Job Terry. Captain Terry died in 1861, aged 78, and is interred there. (Terry's father, wife, and two daughters are also buried there.) The *New England*—owned by former captain and now owner of a whaling fleet, David S. Shearman—was a vessel of 375 tons, significantly larger than the *Pilgrim*. Her voyage would be quite successful, with the ship bringing home some 800 barrels of sperm oil and 2000 barrels of other whale oil.

**Captain Terry convinced our captain that our reckoning was a little out...** That is, that our captain was mistaken in his estimate of our position.

**...the Dublin frigate, and Lord James Townshend...** The *Dublin* was a fast, 50-gun British warship built during the War of 1812 to fight American privateers. Townshend was a British statesman and naval commander.

**...bound for Juan Fernandez.** An island about 400 miles off the coast of Chile. In 1704, Scotsman Alexander Selkirk was marooned on the island and was rescued four years later. His story became the basis of Daniel Defoe's *Robinson Crusoe*. (In 1966, the Chilean government would officially rename the island Robinson Crusoe Island.)

**...we saw the fellow, all white, directly ahead of us, asleep upon the waves...** The albatross is among the largest of flying birds, and feeds on fish, shrimp, and other sealife. In Coleridge's 1798 poem, "Rime of the Ancient Mariner," a mariner is punished for killing an albatross by being forced to wear the dead bird around his neck. (Dana had almost certainly read the poem.) Although the bird was considered a good omen and was a majestic animal, sailors of Dana's day often killed and ate albatrosses.

In the news
**November, 1834**

As Dana is contemplating the majesty and beauty of the albatross, Marcus Albert Reno is born in Carrollton, IL. Reno will become a career military officer and serve in the Civil War. Promoted to major, Reno is assigned to the 7th Cavalry, becoming the highest-ranking officer to serve under General George Armstrong Custer. Holding a position to the southwest of Custer, Reno manages to avoid the 1876 slaughter at the Battle of Little Bighorn. He will go on to command Fort Abercrombie in North Dakota, but his drinking will cause him problems, as will accusations that he acted in a cowardly fashion at Little Bighorn.

At eight o'clock we altered our course to the northward, bound for Juan Fernandez.

This day we saw the last of the albatrosses, which had been our companions a great part of the time off the Cape. I had been interested in the bird from descriptions which I had read of it, and was not at all disappointed. We caught one or two with a baited hook which we floated astern upon a shingle. Their long, flapping wings, long legs, and large, staring eyes, give them a very peculiar appearance. They look well on the wing; but one of the finest sights that I have ever seen, was an albatross asleep upon the water, during a calm, off Cape Horn, when a heavy sea was running. There being no breeze, the surface of the water was unbroken, but a long, heavy swell was rolling, and we saw the fellow, all white, directly ahead of us, asleep upon the waves, with his head under his wing; now rising on the top of a huge billow, and then falling slowly until he was lost in the hollow between. He was undisturbed for some time, until the noise of our bows, gradually approaching, roused him, when, lifting his head, he stared upon us for a moment, and then spread his wide wings and took his flight.

## Chapter VI

### Loss of a Man–Superstition

Monday, Nov. 19th. This was a black day in our calendar. At seven o'clock in the morning, it being our watch below, we were aroused from a sound sleep by the cry of "All hands ahoy! a man overboard!" This unwonted cry sent a thrill through the heart of every one, and hurrying on deck we found the vessel hove flat aback, with all her studding-sails set; for the boy who was at the helm left it to throw something overboard, and the carpenter, who was an old sailor, knowing that the wind was light, put the helm down and hove her aback. The watch on deck were lowering away the quarter-boat, and I got on deck just in time to heave myself into her as she was leaving the side; but it was not until out upon the wide Pacific, in our little boat, that I knew whom we had lost. It was George Ballmer, a young English sailor, who was prized by the officers as an active lad and willing seaman, and by the crew as a lively, hearty fellow, and a good shipmate. He was going aloft to fit a strap round the main top-mast-head, for ringtail halyards, and had the strap and block, a coil of halyards and a marline-spike about his neck. He fell from the starboard futtock shrouds, and not knowing how to swim, and being heavily dressed, with all those things round his neck, he probably sank immediately. We pulled astern, in the direction in which he fell, and though we knew that there was no hope of saving him, yet no one wished to speak of returning, and we rowed about for nearly an hour, without the hope of doing anything, but unwilling to acknowledge to ourselves that we must give him up. At length we turned the boat's head and made towards the vessel.

Death is at all times solemn, but never so much so as at sea. A man dies on shore; his body remains with his friends, and "the mourners go about the streets;" but when a man falls overboard at sea and is lost, there is a suddenness in the event, and a difficulty in realizing it, which give to it an air of awful mystery. A man dies on shore–you follow his body to the grave, and a stone

**This unwonted cry...** "Unwonted" is different than "unwanted." The former means "unfamiliar" or not commonly heard or seen.

**...we found the vessel hove flat aback...** That is, with her sails set such that she was making no headway, so that the vessel was still—or as still as possible, given the motion of the water.

In the news
**November, 1834**

This week the *HMS Beagle*, with Charles Darwin aboard, anchors at the Bay of San Carlos, Chile. Darwin describes Chiloe Island (the second largest island in South America) as being heavily forested, "partly cultivated & pleasant-looking," and the Indians there as living a sparse but peaceful life.

**...and not knowing how to swim...** Generally speaking, few sailors of that day knew how to swim. George, weighted down with gear, stood little chance of surviving such a fall.

**Death is at all times solemn...** Dana is taken aback (a term which is itself of nautical origin) by the speed with which death can strike at sea and by how difficult it is to deal with in the small, closed world of a ship. At least on land, he notes, one normally has a chance to mourn, to say one's good-byes. Dana's remark may be an echo of an article in the September 1833 *Monthly Review*, in which the author, Charles Wall, writing about capital punishment in Great Britain, comments, "Death is at all times terrible, but must be more so when it is violent and disgraceful: most who suffer are frightened...but fear is not penitence, nor is it repentance for their sins." Dana may well have read the article, since the capital punishment debate was—then as now—in full swing, and since his family was deeply involved in the social, legal, and literary issues of the day.

marks the spot. You are often prepared for the event. There is always something which helps you to realize it when it happens, and to recall it when it has passed. A man is shot down by your side in battle, and the mangled body remains an object, and a real evidence; but at sea, the man is near you–at your side–you hear his voice, and in an instant he is gone, and nothing but a vacancy shows his loss. Then, too, at sea–to use a homely but expressive phrase–you miss a man so much. A dozen men are shut up together in a little bark, upon the wide, wide sea, and for months and months see no forms and hear no voices but their own, and one is taken suddenly from among them, and they miss him at every turn. It is like losing a limb. There are no new faces or new scenes to fill up the gap. There is always an empty berth in the forecastle, and one man wanting when the small night watch is mustered. There is one less to take the wheel, and one less to lay out with you upon the yard. You miss his form, and the sound of his voice, for habit had made them almost necessary to you, and each of your senses feels the loss.

All these things make such a death peculiarly solemn, and the effect of it remains upon the crew for some time. There is more kindness shown by the officers to the crew, and by the crew to one another. There is more quietness and seriousness. The oath and the loud laugh are gone. The officers are more watchful, and the crew go more carefully aloft. The lost man is seldom mentioned, or is dismissed with a sailor's rude eulogy– "Well, poor George is gone! His cruise is up soon! He knew his work, and did his duty, and was a good shipmate." Then usually follows some allusion to another world, for sailors are almost all believers; but their notions and opinions are unfixed and at loose ends. They say,–"God won't be hard upon the poor fellow," and seldom get beyond the common phrase which seems to imply that their sufferings and hard treatment here will excuse them hereafter,–"To work hard, live hard, die hard, and go to hell after all, would be hard indeed!" Our cook, a simple-hearted old African, who had been through a good deal in his day, and was rather seriously inclined, always going to church twice a day

In the news
**November, 1834**

While Dana comes to grips with a hard life at sea and subsists on boiled beef, salt pork, and hardtack, Delmonico's (a fine restaurant in New York City) provides a full dinner, including soup, steak, coffee, and pie, for 12 cents.

**It is like losing a limb.** A German proverb notes, "The death of a friend is equivalent to the loss of a limb."

**All these things make such a death peculiarly solemn...** Meditating upon death is typical of this age, as much contemporary art and poetry shows, including the previously mentioned *Thanatopsis*. Even absent any literary considerations, though, keep in mind that Dana is 19 years old and serving in the rough-and-tumble man's world of the 19th century merchant marine. In a way, he is coming to grips with his own mortality. He is struck by the reality of death and by the realization that he too could die—suddenly, painfully, and futilely. That's a stunning and humbling (and perhaps frightening) realization that ultimately comes to every young person, and Dana—in spite of his ambitions and elevated station—is thus typical of his age.

**Well, poor George is gone!** This seems a common expression of resignation in the face of loss, and perhaps a faint echo of Shakespeare: "Alas, poor Yorick! I knew him, Horatio...."

**Our cook, a simple-hearted old African...** We might use either the phrase "simple-minded" or "kind-hearted," but "simple-hearted" has actually been used in this sense since the 15th century. Here, it means "unsophisticated and sincere."

when on shore, and reading his Bible on a Sunday in the galley, talked to the crew about spending their Sabbaths badly, and told them that they might go as suddenly as George had, and be as little prepared.

Yet a sailor's life is at best, but a mixture of a little good with much evil, and a little pleasure with much pain. The beautiful is linked with the revolting, the sublime with the commonplace, and the solemn with the ludicrous.

We had hardly returned on board with our sad report, before an auction was held of the poor man's clothes. The captain had first, however, called all hands aft and asked them if they were satisfied that everything had been done to save the man, and if they thought there was any use in remaining there longer. The crew all said that it was in vain, for the man did not know how to swim, and was very heavily dressed. So we then filled away and kept her off to her course.

The laws regulating navigation make the captain answerable for the effects of a sailor who dies during the voyage, and it is either a law or a universal custom, established for convenience, that the captain should immediately hold an auction of his things, in which they are bid off by the sailors, and the sums which they give are deducted from their wages at the end of the voyage. In this way the trouble and risk of keeping his things through the voyage are avoided, and the clothes are usually sold for more than they would be worth on shore. Accordingly, we had no sooner got the ship before the wind, than his chest was brought up upon the forecastle, and the sale began. The jackets and trowsers in which we had seen him dressed but a few days before, were exposed and bid off while the life was hardly out of his body, and his chest was taken aft and used as a store-chest, so that there was nothing left which could be called his. Sailors have an unwillingness to wear a dead man's clothes during the same voyage, and they seldom do so unless they are in absolute want.

As is usual after a death, many stories were told about

**...a sailor's life is at best, but a mixture of a little good with much evil, and a little pleasure with much pain.** Compare to: "...even so may the life of man be well compared to the Ocean Seas, that for every calm hath a thousand storms; for a little pleasure, much pain; and for high desire, much discontent..." *The Declaration of Captain James Hind* (London, 1651).

**...filled away...** After being "hove to," the sails are let out and fill with air as the vessel gets underway.

**...that the captain should immediately hold an auction of his things...** It may seem heartless, but such an auction ensures that the dead sailor's effects will be put to good use on a future voyage, and it offers crew members the chance to secure a memento of the deceased. The proceeds from such sales normally go to the sailor's family or to a charity. (The tradition does indeed seem to be custom, rather than law.)

**In the news**
**November, 1834**

A few years after Dana's visit, the Archeological Institute of America points out that at the time Dana came to California, some 200,000 Native Americans lived there. A few years later, disease and (mostly dishonored) treaties will have reduced that number to 17,000. While the Southern California Indians were moved and given practically uninhabitable desert land from which to attempt to scratch a living, the Northern California tribes were given nothing.

George. Some had heard him say that he repented never having learned to swim, and that he knew that he should meet his death by drowning. Another said that he never knew any good to come of a voyage made against the will, and the deceased man shipped and spent his advance and was afterwards very unwilling to go, but not being able to refund, was obliged to sail with us. A boy, too, who had become quite attached to him, said that George talked to him during most of the watch on the night before, about his mother and family at home, and this was the first time that he had mentioned the subject during the voyage.

In the news
**November, 1834**

The Leonid meteor shower of November, 1834 (though not mentioned by Dana) is seen and commented on by ship captains off the coast of California. Associated with the comet Tempel-Tuttle, the Leonids are in fact most visible in November.

The night after this event, when I went to the galley to get a light, I found the cook inclined to be talkative, so I sat down on the spars, and gave him an opportunity to hold a yarn. I was the more inclined to do so, as I found that he was full of the superstitions once more common among seamen, and which the recent death had waked up in his mind. He talked about George's having spoken of his friends, and said he believed few men died without having a warning of it, which he supported by a great many stories of dreams, and the unusual behavior of men before death. From this he went on to other superstitions, the Flying Dutchman, etc., and talked rather mysteriously, having something evidently on his mind.

**...the Flying Dutchman...** A legendary "ghost ship" doomed to forever sail the seas. The first popular literary reference to the legend appears to have been in Sir Walter Scott's 1813 poem, *Rokeby*, but the legend was also mentioned in earlier works, including George Barrington's 1795 *A Voyage to Botany Bay*. The spectral ship was the subject of Richard Wagner's 1843 opera, *The Flying Dutchman*.

At length he put his head out of the galley and looked carefully about to see if any one was within hearing, and being satisfied on that point, asked me in a low tone–

In the news
**November, 1834**

This month, back in Dana's hometown of Boston, theologian Abner Kneeland becomes the last man in America to be charged with (and, four years later, tried for) blasphemy. Kneeland campaigned for equal rights for women, supported the idea of married women being able to keep their own property, and refused to condemn interracial marriage. Such beliefs brought him into conflict with more conservative churchmen.

"I say! you know what countryman 'e carpenter be?"

"Yes," said I; "he's a German."

"What kind of a German?" said the cook.

"He belongs to Bremen," said I.

"Are you sure o' dat?" said he.

I satisfied him on that point by saying that he could speak no language but the German and English.

"I'm plaguy glad o' dat," said the cook. "I was mighty 'fraid he was a Fin. I tell you what, I been plaguy civil to that man all the voyage."

I asked him the reason of this, and found that he was fully possessed with the notion that Fins are wizards, and especially have power over winds and storms. I tried to reason with him about it, but he had the best of all arguments, that from experience, at hand, and was not to be moved. He had been in a vessel at the Sandwich Islands, in which the sail-maker was a Fin, and could do anything he was of a mind to. This sail-maker kept a junk bottle in his berth, which was always just half full of rum, though he got drunk upon it nearly every day. He had seen him sit for hours together, talking to this bottle, which he stood up before him on the table. The same man cut his throat in his berth, and everybody said he was possessed.

He had heard of ships, too, beating up the gulf of Finland against a head wind, and having a ship heave in sight astern, overhaul and pass them, with as fair a wind as could blow, and all studding-sails out, and find she was from Finland.

"Oh ho!" said he; "I've seen too much of them men to want to see 'em 'board a ship. If they can't have their own way, they'll play the d—l with you."

As I still doubted, he said he would leave it to John, who was the oldest seaman aboard, and would know, if anybody did. John, to be sure, was the oldest, and at the same time the most ignorant, man in the ship; but I consented to have him called. The cook stated the matter to him, and John, as I anticipated, sided with the cook, and said that he himself had been in a ship where they had a head wind for a fortnight, and the captain found out at last that one of the men, whom he had had some hard words with a short time before, was a Fin, and immediately told him if he didn't stop the head wind he would

**...plaguy glad o' dat...** *Plaguy* is an archaic word going back to the 16th century; not surprisingly, it means "having to do with the plague," and by extension, anything that's distressful or troublesome, especially if it can be viewed as a punishment.

**...the notion that Fins are wizards...** The cook is not alone in his belief. In years past, Scandinavian natives believed that the land to the east was in fact inhabited by wizards.

**...a vessel at the Sandwich Islands...** What we now call the Hawaiian Islands. They were named after John Montagu, the 4th Earl of Sandwich in the 1770s by Captain James Cook; the earl was a supporter of Cook's voyages. (The earl probably did not invent the sandwich, by the way, but may well have served to popularize it.)

In the news

**November, 1834**

As Dana makes his way to the coast of California, the population of the little pueblo of Los Angeles stands at about 1500 people, many of them Native Americans brought in to work the farms, dig ditches, and serve as domestic help. Unlike the Native American mission workers, the Native Los Angeles workers were at least paid—in goods, clothing, cash, and liquor. They nonetheless remained at the bottom of the pecking order and were often mistreated, sometimes grievously.

**...the oldest, and at the same time the most ignorant.** The rhetorical technique called *antithesis*, in which opposites are paired, is quite effective. It's even more dramatic in this case, because of the additional irony: We normally expect the eldest to also be the wisest.

**...a fortnight...** Two weeks. A contraction "fourteen nights," the term goes all the way back to the 11th century.

shut him down in the fore peak, and would not give him anything to eat. The Fin held out for a day and a half, when he could not stand it any longer, and did something or other which brought the wind round again, and they let him up.

**You think, 'cause you been to college, you know better than anybody.** Dana worries (quite naturally) that the other sailors will view him as a "college boy" who thinks he's better than them, and who uses his position to curry favor. Most of the time, he goes to great lengths to ensure that he works just as hard (or harder) than they, and asks for no special treatment. Throughout the voyage, he also works hard at being a "regular guy," one who gets along with the sailors and avoids "putting on airs."

"There," said the cook, "what do you think o' dat?"

I told him I had no doubt it was true, and that it would have been odd if the wind had not changed in fifteen days, Fin or no Fin.

"Oh," says he, "go 'way! You think, 'cause you been to college, you know better than anybody. You know better than them as 'as seen it with their own eyes. You wait till you've been to sea as long as I have, and you'll know."

In the news

**November, 1834**

At this point, the first regular transatlantic steamship service, which would be inaugurated by the sidewheeler *Sirius*, was still four years away. *Sirius* traveled from London to New York, arriving in the latter city in April of 1838.

## Chapter VII

## Juan Fernandez–The Pacific

We continued sailing along with a fair wind and fine weather until Tuesday, Nov. 25th, when at daylight we saw the island of Juan Fernandez, directly ahead, rising like a deep blue cloud out of the sea. We were then probably nearly seventy miles from it; and so high and so blue did it appear, that I mistook it for a cloud, resting over the island, and looked for the island under it, until it gradually turned to a deader and greener color, and I could mark the inequalities upon its surface. At length we could distinguish trees and rocks; and by the afternoon, this beautiful island lay fairly before us, and we directed our course to the only harbor. Arriving at the entrance soon after sun-down, we found a Chilian man-of-war brig, the only vessel, coming out. She hailed us, and an officer on board, whom we supposed to be an American, advised us to run in before night, and said that they were bound to Valparaiso. We ran immediately for the anchorage, but, owing to the winds which drew about the mountains and came to us in flaws from every point of the compass, we did not come to an anchor until nearly midnight. We had a boat ahead all the time that we were working in, and those aboard were continually bracing the yards about for every puff that struck us, until about 12 o'clock, when we came-to in 40 fathoms water, and our anchor struck bottom for the first time since we left Boston–one hundred and three days. We were then divided into three watches, and thus stood out the remainder of the night.

I was called on deck to stand my watch at about three in the morning, and I shall never forget the peculiar sensation which I experienced on finding myself once more surrounded by land, feeling the night breeze coming from off shore, and hearing the frogs and crickets. The mountains seemed almost to hang over us, and apparently from the very heart there came out, at regular intervals, a loud echoing sound, which affected me as hardly human. We saw no lights, and could hardly account for the sound, until the mate, who had been

**...the island of Juan Fernandez...** As noted, Juan Fernandez, about 360 nautical miles off the coast of Chile, is where Alexander Selkirk was marooned for nearly four years. Selkirk's story is said to have been the inspiration for Daniel Defoe's *Robinson Crusoe*.

In the news
**November, 1834**

This is the birthday of Grace Darling, who was born in 1815 in Northumberland, England, not far from the Scottish coast. She and her father, William, in charge of a lighthouse off the Northumberland coast, will save nine people from drowning when the steamship *Forfarshire* breaks up on the rocks near the lighthouse in September, 1838. Grace, who lived until October of 1842, became an instant heroine.

**a Chilian man-of-war brig...** A brig, as already noted, is a square-rigged, two-masted vessel. But the definition of "man of war" (or "man o' war") is imprecise and often debated. It may be best to stick with the oldest definition, going back to the 15th century, as provided by the *OED*: A man of war is "any vessel equipped for warfare; a commissioned warship belonging to the recognized navy of a country." That original definition is probably generic enough to satisfy everyone. Or possibly no one. The more interesting question is: Why was an American officer aboard a Chilean warship? The answer is that many American officers joined the Chilean Navy to help that nation fight for its independence from Spain, and stayed to fight in later Chilean conflicts with Bolivia and Peru.

**...40 fathoms water...** A fathom is six feet, so *Pilgrim* is anchored in some 240 feet of water.

**...the "Alerta"...** Spanish for "alarm."

**...this romantic, I may almost say, classic island.** The island is certainly beautiful, with translucent, greenish-blue water leading to white, sandy beaches surrounded by craggy mountains and dense forests. Defoe's book, published in 1719, had indeed become a classic, and one with which Dana was no doubt familiar.

**This, of course, was dignified by the title of Presidio.** Although Dana recognizes the rugged beauty of the places he vists, he tends to look down on the various inhabitants and to belittle their accomplishments and their culture. In this case, he can't resist sarcastic comments about the fact that the governor's house is "only" one story, and about the title of "Presidio" (in Spanish, a reinforced position, barricade, fort, or outpost) "dignifying" the "low brown-looking" building. A product of his times, Dana occasionally strikes us now as something of a chauvinist.

In the news
**November, 1834**

As Dana sails into the harbor in Chile, back home in the U.S. the widespread movement of settlers to the West begins. As one barely literate emigrant notes in a letter back to his kin in Tennessee, "Thare is good land on the Missura for a poar mans home." Literate or not (and he was probably more educated than most such travelers), the man who wrote this was tough as nails to have survived the trek in the first place and perfectly correct about the opportunities in the emerging West.

**...my friend S—- and myself ...** Benjamin Stimson. Other editions have it as "my friend Ben."

**...the quarter-boat...** A boat hung at a vessel's quarter, that is, at the side just aft of the middle of the vessel.

there before, told us that it was the "Alerta" of the Spanish soldiers, who were stationed over some convicts confined in caves nearly halfway up the mountain. At the expiration of my watch I went below, feeling not a little anxious for the day, that I might see more nearly, and perhaps tread upon, this romantic, I may almost say, classic island.

When all hands were called it was nearly sunrise, and between that time and breakfast, although quite busy on board in getting up water-casks, etc., I had a good view of the objects about me. The harbor was nearly landlocked, and at the head of it was a landing-place, protected by a small breakwater of stones, upon which two large boats were hauled up, with a sentry standing over them. Near this was a variety of huts or cottages, nearly an hundred in number, the best of them built of mud and white washed, but the greater part only Robinson Crusoe like– of posts and branches of trees. The governor's house, as it is called, was the most conspicuous, being large, with grated windows, plastered walls, and roof of red tiles; yet, like all the rest, only of one story. Near it was a small chapel, distinguished by a cross; and a long, low brown-looking building, surrounded by something like a palisade, from which an old and dingy-looking Chilian flag was flying. This, of course, was dignified by the title of Presidio. A sentinel was stationed at the chapel, another at the governor's house, and a few soldiers armed with bayonets, looking rather ragged, with shoes out at the toes, were strolling about among the houses, or waiting at the landing-place for our boat to come ashore.

The mountains were high, but not so overhanging as they appeared to be by starlight. They seemed to bear off towards the centre of the island, and were green and well wooded, with some large, and, I am told, exceedingly fertile valleys, with mule-tracks leading to different parts of the island.

I cannot forget how my friend S—- and myself got the laugh of the crew upon us for our eagerness to get on shore. The captain having ordered the quarter-boat to be lowered, we both sprang down into the forecastle, filled our jacket pockets with tobacco to barter with the people ashore, and when the officer called for "four hands in the boat," nearly broke our necks in our haste to be first over the side, and had the pleasure of pulling ahead of the brig with a tow-line for a half an hour, and coming on board again to be laughed at by the crew, who had seen our manoeuvre.

After breakfast the second mate was ordered ashore with five hands to fill the water-casks, and to my joy I was among the number. We pulled ashore with the empty casks; and here again fortune favored me, for the water was too thick and muddy to be put into the casks, and the governor had sent men up to the head of the stream to clear it out for us, which gave us nearly two hours of leisure. This leisure we employed in wandering about among the houses, and eating a little fruit which was offered to us. Ground apples, melons, grapes, strawberries of an enormous size, and cherries, abounded here. The latter are said to have been planted by Lord Anson. The soldiers were miserably clad, and asked with some interest whether we had any shoes to sell on board. I doubt very much if they had the means of buying them. They were very eager to get tobacco, for which they gave shells, fruits, etc. Knives also were in demand, but we were forbidden by the governor to let any one have them, as he told us that all the people there, except the soldiers and a few officers, were convicts sent from Valparaiso, and that it was necessary to keep all weapons from their hands. The island, it seems, belongs to Chili, and had been used by the government as a sort of Botany Bay for nearly two years; and the governor–an Englishman who had entered the Chilian navy– with a priest, half a dozen task-masters, and a body of soldiers, were stationed there to keep them in order. This was no easy task; and only a few months before our arrival, a few of them had stolen a boat at night, boarded a brig lying in the harbor, sent the captain and crew ashore in their boat, and gone off to sea. We were informed of this, and loaded our arms and kept strict watch on board through the night, and were careful not to let the convicts get our knives from us when

**...the pleasure of pulling ahead of the brig with a tow-line...** Dana and his friend think they're going to be first ashore; instead they end up working, and then end up back on the *Pilgrim*, becoming the butt of the other crewmembers' jokes.

In the news

**November, 1834**

In San Pedro, Calif., which Dana will shortly visit, Alta California governor Jose Figueroa grants 31,600 acres, including the town of San Pedro, to the two sons of Don Jose Sepulveda in the hope of settling a dispute between the Sepulvedas and another prominent Mexican family.

**... eating a little fruit...** At sea for more than three months, it has been some time since Dana and his crewmates have eaten fresh fruit. Although we now know that fruit (especially citrus) and vegetables can cure (or help one avoid) scurvy, and although James Lind had offered proof of that back in the 1750s, it wasn't until the 1860s that the British navy instituted a daily lime ration. (From whence came "limeys" as a nickname for British sailors.) In Dana's day, scurvy was still a problem, although Dana himself notes the rapid recovery of a sailor who was given raw potatoes and onions to eat. (See Ch. 35.)

**...as a sort of Botany Bay...** That is, as a place to which the government would ship criminals and other undesirables. Botany Bay, in what is now Sydney, NSW, Australia, was a penal colony used by the British government. (Notwithstanding the fact that the country was in fact populated at the time by some 350,000 aboriginal natives who'd been living there for many thousands of years.) The colony at Botany Bay actually failed and was re-established at Port Jackson, farther north, but the original name continued to be used to refer to the colony. Between 1788 and 1853, some 165,000 British convicts, male and female, were sent to Australia.

**...a paseo...** A walk.

**...too lazy to speak fast...** As earlier noted, Dana is a product of his chauvinistic times. He will feel much the same about the natives of California, when he arrives there shortly. In general, Dana—although willing to traffic with man of all classes and origins—cannot help but look down upon those who do not share his privileged (he might say, "civilized") background. This makes him neither a bad person nor an unfeeling ogre; he is in fact quite sympathetic to the aims (if not always the means) of, say, abolitionists, to take one example. He is certainly more than merely empathetic when it comes to ensuring the rights of the common seaman; in fact, this book is partly a protest against the denial of those rights.

**...dirty regimentals...** That is, in military dress, but looking unkempt. (The word "unkempt," by the way, originally meant having untrimmed, neglected hair, but we now use it to mean disheveled and slovenly of dress, in addition to possibly unshaven or shaggy.)

**...whaleman, of New Bedford...** New Bedford, in southeastern Massachusetts, was at that time a very important whaling port.

**...to see if there were any vessels from round the Horn...** Cape Horn (from the Dutch *Kaap Hoorn*) is at the southernmost tip of Chile and near (but not quite at) the southernmost portion of Argentina. Before the opening of the Panama Canal (in 1914), one route from the U.S. East Coast to the West Coast, was to head south and "round the Cape" (as *Pilgrim* has done) and then sail north off the western shore of the coast of South America. (When the Canal opened, the journey from one coast to the other was shortened by thousands of miles.)

on shore. The worst part of the convicts, I found, were locked up under sentry in caves dug into the side of the mountain, nearly halfway up, with mule-tracks leading to them, whence they were taken by day and set to work under task-masters upon building an aqueduct, a wharf, and other public works; while the rest lived in the houses which they put up for themselves, had their families with them, and seemed to me to be the laziest people on the face of the earth. They did nothing but take a paseo into the woods, a paseo among the houses, a paseo at the landing-place, looking at us and our vessel, and too lazy to speak fast; while the others were driving–or rather, driven–about, at a rapid trot, in single file, with burdens on their shoulders, and followed up by their task-masters, with long rods in their hands, and broadbrimmed straw hats upon their heads. Upon what precise grounds this great distinction was made, I do not know, and I could not very well know, for the governor was the only man who spoke English upon the island, and he was out of my walk.

Having filled our casks, we returned on board, and soon after, the governor, dressed in a uniform like that of an American militia officer, the Padre, in the dress of the grey friars, with hood and all complete, and the Capitan, with big whiskers and dirty regimentals, came on board to dine. While at dinner, a large ship appeared in the offing, and soon afterwards we saw a light whale-boat pulling into the harbor. The ship lay off and on, and a boat came alongside of us, and put on board the captain, a plain young Quaker, dressed all in brown. The ship was the Cortes, whaleman, of New Bedford, and had put in to see if there were any vessels from round the Horn, and to hear the latest news from America. They remained aboard a short time and had a little talk with the crew, when they left us and pulled off to their ship, which, having filled away, was soon out of sight.

A small boat which came from the shore to take away the governor and suite–as they styled themselves–brought, as a present to the crew, a large pail of milk, a few shells, and a block of sandal wood. The milk, which was the first we had tasted since leaving Boston, we soon despatched; a piece of the sandal wood I obtained, and learned that it grew on the hills in the centre of the island. I have always regretted that I did not bring away other specimens of the products of the island, having afterwards lost all that I had with me–the piece of sandal wood, and a small flower which I plucked and brought on board in the crown of my tarpaulin, and carefully pressed between the leaves of a book.

About an hour before sun-down, having stowed our water casks, we commenced getting under weigh, and were not a little while about it; for we were in thirty fathoms water, and in one of the gusts which came off shore had let go our other bow anchor; and as the southerly wind draws round the mountains and comes off in uncertain flaws, we were continually swinging round, and had thus got a very foul hawse. We hove in upon our chain, and after stoppering and unshackling it again and again, and hoisting and hauling down sail, we at length tipped our anchor and stood out to sea. It was bright starlight when we were clear of the bay, and the lofty island lay behind us, in its still beauty, and I gave a parting look, and bid farewell, to the most romantic spot of earth that my eyes had ever seen. I did then, and have ever since, felt an attachment for that island, altogether peculiar. It was partly, no doubt, from its having been the first land that I had seen since leaving home, and still more from the associations which every one has connected with it in their childhood from reading Robinson Crusoe. To this I may add the height and romantic outline of its mountains, the beauty and freshness of its verdure, and the extreme fertility of its soil, and its solitary position in the midst of the wide expanse of the South Pacific, as all concurring to give it its peculiar charm.

When thoughts of this place have occurred to me at different times, I have endeavored to recall more particulars with regard to it. It is situated in about 33° 30' S., and is distant a little more than three hundred miles from Valparaiso, on the coast of Chili, which is in the same latitude. It is about fifteen miles in length and five in breadth. The harbor in which we anchored (called by

**...a piece of the sandal wood...** An aromatic wood grown in South America and the West Indies, sandalwood is often used in carving and in perfumes. The sandalwood tree was overexploited on the island (as elsewhere), and is now extinct there.

**In the news**
**November, 1834**

The San Juan Capistrano, San Gabrial, and other California missions are scenes of revolt as many of the Native American workers either disobey the orders of the friars or simply refuse to work altogether until granted both their freedom and fair treatment. "The Indians want the freedom of vagabonds.... No Padre is able to get anything out of them," says Padre Narciso Duran. "I must suffer the pain of being obliged to suspend work for want of hands," complains Pablo de la Portilla, a Mexican officer.

**...had let go our other bow anchor...** *Pilgrim* is (or was) anchored bow and stem in deep water, but had lost her bow anchor. The ship thus swung wildly in the wind, twisting the remaining anchor rope and fouling the cutaway areas (the hawse-holes) through which the anchor ropes and chains pass.

**...felt an attachment for that island, altogether peculiar.** The island, which today has a population of some 500 or so, really is beautiful. Hundreds of tourists visit each year, many of whom wish to see the cave in which "Robinson Crusoe" (really, Alexander Selkirk) lived while marooned there.

Lord Anson, Cumberland bay) is the only one in the island; two small bights of land on each side of the main bay (sometimes dignified by the name of bays) being little more than landing-places for boats. The best anchorage is at the western side of the bay, where we lay at about three cables' lengths from the shore, in a little more than thirty fathoms water. This harbor is open to the N.N.E., and in fact nearly from N. to E., but the only dangerous winds being the south-west, on which side are the highest mountains, it is considered very safe. The most remarkable thing perhaps about it is the fish with which it abounds. Two of our crew, who remained on board, caught in a few minutes enough to last us for several days, and one of the men, who was a Marblehead man, said that he never saw or heard of such an abundance. There were cod, breams, silver-fish, and other kinds whose names they did not know, or which I have forgotten.

**...Lord Anson...** Anson was Admiral of the Fleet and saw service service during the Seven Years' War between Britain and France (and their respective allies.) Anson entered the bay in 1741 to refit his ships.

**...about three cables' lengths from the shore...** A cable was generally 120 fathoms in length; since a fathom is six feet, the vessel lay some 2,160 feet (not quite half a mile) offshore.

In the news

**November, 1834**

Sir Robert Peel becomes Prime Minister of of the U.K. Something of a progressive, Peel reduced the number of crimes punishable by death, established the Metropolitan Police Force (whose members were known ever after as "Bobbies" or "Peelers" in his honor), and introduced the idea of educating prisoners while they were confined.

There is an abundance of the best of water upon the island, small streams running through every valley, and leaping down from the sides of the hills. One stream of considerable size flows through the centre of the lawn upon which the houses are built, and furnishes an easy and abundant supply to the inhabitants. This, by means of a short wooden aqueduct, was brought quite down to our boats. The convicts had also built something in the way of a breakwater, and were to build a landing-place for boats and goods, after which the Chilian government intended to lay port charges.

**...the Chilian government intended to lay port charges.** That is, charges levied on ships that moor in the harbor. The charges are supposed to pay for building and maintaining the harbor and for any required personnel. In some cases, such fees might also help pay for wood, water, or other of the vessel's necessities.

Of the wood I can only say, that it appeared to be abundant; the island in the month of November, when we were there, being in all the freshness and beauty of spring, appeared covered with trees. These were chiefly aromatic, and the largest was the myrtle. The soil is very loose and rich, and wherever it is broken up, there spring up immediately radishes, turnips, ground apples, and other garden fruits. Goats, we were told, were not abundant, and we saw none, though it was said we might, if we had gone into the interior. We saw a few bullocks winding about in the narrow tracks upon the sides of the mountains, and the settlement was com-

In the news

**November, 1834**

In Boston, the fourth section of the Boston & Albany Railroad opens, providing a rail route from Boston to Westborough. About seven months later, the line will be complete, terminating in Worcester.

**...bullocks...** Castrated bulls or oxen.

pletely overrun with dogs of every nation, kindred, and degree. Hens and chickens were also abundant, and seemed to be taken good care of by the women. The men appeared to be the laziest people upon the face of the earth; and indeed, as far as my observation goes, there are no people to whom the newly-invented Yankee word of "loafer" is more applicable than to the Spanish Americans. These men stood about doing nothing, with their cloaks, little better in texture than an Indian's blanket, but of rich colors, thrown over their shoulders with an air which it is said that a Spanish beggar can always give to his rags; and with great politeness and courtesy in their address, though with holes in their shoes and without a sou in their pockets. The only interruption to the monotony of their day seemed to be when a gust of wind drew round between the mountains and blew off the boughs which they had placed for roofs to their houses, and gave them a few minutes' occupation in running about after them. One of these gusts occurred while we were ashore, and afforded us no little amusement at seeing the men look round, and if they found that their roofs had stood, conclude that they might stand too, while those who saw theirs blown off, after uttering a few Spanish oaths, gathered their cloaks over their shoulders, and started off after them. However, they were not gone long, but soon returned to their habitual occupation of doing nothing.

It is perhaps needless to say that we saw nothing of the interior; but all who have seen it, give very glowing accounts of it. Our captain went with the governor and a few servants upon mules over the mountains, and upon their return, I heard the governor request him to stop at the island on his passage home, and offer him a handsome sum to bring a few deer with him from California, for he said that there were none upon the island, and he was very desirous of having it stocked.

A steady, though light south-westerly wind carried us well off from the island, and when I came on deck for the middle watch I could just distinguish it from its hiding a few low stars in the southern horizon, though my

**The men appeared to be the laziest people upon the face of the earth...** Once again, we see Dana's cultural bias. What appears to him to be laziness may simply be the cultural norm; it's not how many of us are comfortable living, but it's a mistake—and an overbroad generalization—simply to dismiss it as laziness.

**...the newly-invented Yankee word of "loafer"...** Dana is correct about the etymology of this word. It first appears in print in the July 10th, 1830 issue of *Mechanic's Press*, and then shortly afterward in *Knickerbocker*. It meant then exactly what it means now: an idle person. (In 1939, the word was first applied to a type of shoe—one meant to be comfortable enough to wear while lounging [idly?] about.)

**... afforded us no little amusement...** Dana thinks little of these people, and enjoys poking fun at them.

In the news

**November, 1834**

This month, teacher and transcendentalist philosopher Amos Bronson Alcott writes in his journal about his young daughter: "Louisa manifests uncommon activity and force of mind at present...by force of will and practical talent, [she] realizes all that she conceives...." Louisa May Alcott will grow up to be a successful writer, author of *Little Women*.

**...there were none upon the island...** Actually, while it's home to many species of plants, fish, and seabirds, there are no native land mammals (or reptiles) on the island at all. (One true native seagoing mammal on the island is the South American fur seal.) Except for the village and a small airfield, the entire island is now a national park.

**...saw no more land until we arrived upon the western coast of the great continent of America.** At this point, Dana has been at sea for almost four months, has traveled about 8,000 nautical miles, and is about one fourth of the way through his voyage, in terms of distance traveled. (But not in terms of time, since he spends several months in various ports on the coast of California.)

unpracticed eyes would hardly have known it for land. At the close of the watch a few trade-wind clouds which had arisen, though we were hardly yet in their latitude, shut it out from our view, and the next day,

Thursday, Nov. 27th, upon coming on deck in the morning, we were again upon the wide Pacific, and saw no more land until we arrived upon the western coast of the great continent of America.

## Chapter VIII

## "Tarring Down"–Daily Life– "Going Aft"–California

As we saw neither land nor sail from the time of leaving Juan Fernandez until our arrival in California, nothing of interest occurred except our own doing on board. We caught the south-east trades, and run before them for nearly three weeks, without so much as altering a sail or bracing a yard. The captain took advantage of this fine weather to get the vessel in order for coming upon the coast. The carpenter was employed in fitting up a part of the steerage into a trade-room; for our cargo, we now learned, was not to be landed, but to be sold by retail from on board; and this trade-room was built for the samples and the lighter goods to be kept in, and as a place for the general business. In the mean time we were employed in working upon the rigging. Everything was set up taught, the lower rigging rattled down, or rather rattled up, (according to the modern fashion,) an abundance of spun-yarn and seizing-stuff made, and finally, the whole standing-rigging, fore and aft, was tarred down. This was my first essay at this latter business, and I had enough of it; for nearly all of it came upon my friend S— and myself. The men were needed at the other work, and M—, the other young man who came out with us, was laid up with the rheumatism in his feet, and the boy was rather too young and small for the business; and as the winds were light and regular, he was kept during most of the daytime at the helm; so that nearly all the tarring came upon us. We put on short duck frocks, and taking a small bucket of tar and a bunch of oakum in our hands we went aloft, one at the main royal-mast-head and the other at the fore, and began tarring down. This is an important operation, and is usually done about once in six months in vessels upon a long voyage. It was done in our vessel several times afterwards, but by the whole crew at once, and finished off in a day; but at this time, as most of it came upon two of us, and we were new at the business, it took us several days. In this operation they always begin at the mast-head and work down, tarring the shrouds, back-stays, standing parts of the lifts, the ties,

**...altering a sail or bracing a yard.** One of the advantages of the tradewinds is that they are very predictable, always blowing at roughly the same rate and in essentially the same direction. (That's why they were used by trading vessels.) If the men do not need to constantly be adjusting the sails, they can attend to other duties.

**...this trade-room was built for the samples...** In effect, they are building an onboard store, from which they will sell to the coastal Californians such goods and trinkets as they brought with them from Boston.

**...Everything was set up taught...** We would write "taut."

**...or rather rattled up...** This has nothing to do with rats, but refers to the practice of securing ratlines (pronounced "ratlins")—lines strung horizontally across shrouds to form rope ladders for the sailors to use when going aloft or when descending. "Rattled up" means that the lines were strung beginning at the bottom.

**...laid up with the rheumatism...** "M" is Henry Mellus, an 18-year-old seaman. When the *Pilgrim* departs California, Mellus will stay behind, eventually settling in Los Angeles. Doctors today do not ordinarily use the word "rheumatism" to refer to a specific disease, since it's a very vague term that can refer to any disorder of the joints and connective tissues. However, a physician may, for example, refer to arthritis in which the joints and connective tissues are affected as "rheumatoid arthritis."

**In the news**
**December, 1834**

After the death of his wife Ellen, Ralph Waldo Emerson moves from Boston to Concord, where he will live for most of the rest of his life. In 1835 he marries Lydia Jackson, with whom he has four children.

runners, etc., and go out to the yard-arms, and come in, tarring, as they come, the lifts and foot-ropes. Tarring the stays is more difficult, and is done by an operation which the sailors call "riding down." A long piece of rope– top-gallant-studding-sail halyards, or something of the kind– is taken up to the mast-head from which the stay leads, and rove through a block for a girt-line, or, as the sailors usually call it, a gant-line; with the end of this a bowline is taken round the stay, into which the man gets with his bucket of tar and a bunch of oakum, and the other end being fast on deck, with some one to tend it, he is lowered down gradually, and tars the stay carefully as he goes. There he "sings aloft 'twixt heaven and earth," and if the rope slips, breaks, or is let go, or if the bowline slips, he falls overboard or breaks his neck. This, however, is a thing which never enters into a sailor's calculation. He thinks only of leaving no holy-days, (places not tarred,) for in case he should, he would have to go over the whole again; or of dropping no tar upon deck, for then there would be a soft word in his ear from the mate. In this manner I tarred down all the head-stays, but found the rigging about the jib-booms, martingale, and spritsail yard, upon which I was afterwards put, the hardest. Here you have to hang on with your eye-lids and tar with your hands.

This dirty work could not last forever, and on Saturday night we finished it, scraped all the spots from the deck and rails, and, what was of more importance to us, cleaned ourselves thoroughly, rolled up our tarry frocks and trowsers and laid them away for the next occasion, and put on our clean duck clothes, and had a good comfortable sailor's Saturday night. The next day was pleasant, and indeed we had but one unpleasant Sunday during the whole voyage, and that was off Cape Horn, where we could expect nothing better. On Monday we commenced painting, and getting the vessel ready for port. This work, too, is done by the crew, and every sailor who has been long voyages is a little of a painter, in addition to his other accomplishments. We painted her, both inside and out, from the truck to the water's edge. The outside is painted by lowering stages over the side by ropes, and on those we sat, with our brushes and

**...sailors call "riding down."** Generally, "riding down" is a process whereby the men climb aloft and hang from the halyards, using their weight to help hoist the sails. In this case, the men are hanging with tar buckets, tarring the rigging as they descend.

**...taken round the stay...** A bowline is a knot that forms a temporary loop; the loop can be used to form a larger bight to lift or carry anything from a bucket to a man. The bowline is among the most important knots a sailor learns how to tie. (It's also useful in climbing and in lifesaving and rescue.)

**...He thinks only of leaving no holy-days...** We're used to thinking of "holy days" as days of religious observance, but the word "holiday" to mean "a spot that has been missed" has a long nautical history that goes back to the 18th century. It was defined as such in Grose's 1785 *Dictionary of the Vulgar Tongue*. (In which publication "vulgar" meant "everyday" or "common.")

**...then there would be a soft word in his ear from the mate.** Dana is once again employing the rhetorical technique known as meiosis—a purposeful understatement. The mate would normally yell at the sailor.

**...hang on with your eye-lids and tar with your hands.** An echo of the seaman's adage, "one hand for yourself, and one for the boat," or variations thereof.

In the news

**December, 1834**

In *The New England Magazine*, a writer decries the growth of atheism, declaring that the press publishes mainly "the works of atheistical writers." There is some truth to this, made even more impactful by the fact that during this same year (see previous note) a man can be charged in court with the "crime" of blasphemy.

paint-pots by us, and our feet half the time in the water. This must be done, of course, on a smooth day, when the vessel does not roll much. I remember very well being over the side painting in this way, one fine afternoon, our vessel going quietly along at the rate of four or five knots, and a pilot-fish, the sure precursor of the shark, swimming alongside of us. The captain was leaning over the rail watching him, and we quietly went on with our work. In the midst of our painting, on

Friday, Dec. 19th, we crossed the equator for the second time. I had the feeling which all have when, for the first time, they find themselves living under an entire change of seasons; as, crossing the line under a burning sun in the midst of December, and, as I afterwards was, beating about among ice and snow on the fourth of July.

Thursday, Dec. 25th. This day was Christmas, but it brought us no holiday. The only change was that we had a "plum duff" for dinner, and the crew quarrelled with the steward because he did not give us our usual allowance of molasses to eat with it. He thought the plums would be a substitute for the molasses, but we were not to be cheated out of our rights in this way.

Such are the trifles which produce quarrels on shipboard. In fact, we had been too long from port. We were getting tired of one another, and were in an irritable state, both forward and aft. Our fresh provisions were, of course, gone, and the captain had stopped our rice, so that we had nothing but salt beef and salt pork throughout the week, with the exception of a very small duff on Sunday. This added to the discontent; and a thousand little things, daily and almost hourly occurring, which no one who has not himself been on a long and tedious voyage can conceive of or properly appreciate,–little wars and rumors of wars,–reports of things said in the cabin,–misunderstanding of words and looks,–apparent abuses,–brought us into a state in which everything seemed to go wrong. Every encroachment upon the time allowed for rest, appeared unnecessary. Every shifting of the studding-sails was only to "haze"(1) the crew.

**...a pilot-fish, the sure precursor of the shark...** Pilot fish are fish that swim with sharks and other fish, eating the parasites that live on the larger fish. The relationship between the two is symbiotic: the shark is rid of harmful parasites, while the pilot fish gain food and protection. (Some pilot fish will actually swim into a shark's mouth to clean food fragments from the shark's teeth. A risky—or at least, nerve-wracking—way to make a living, one assumes.)

**...living under an entire change of seasons...** That is, living in the Southern Hemisphere (the portion of the planet south of the equator), where the seasons are reversed.

**...a "plum duff" for dinner...** A plum duff is a rich pudding made with raisins, spices, and fruits. Quite a treat for men who've been living mostly on boiled meat and biscuits.

**...we had been too long from port.** The men have been mostly at sea for about five months now, with only occasional—and brief—landfall. Tempers are beginning to fray.

## In the news
### December, 1834

This month the first U.S. dental society is organized in New York City. Known as The Society of Dental Surgeons of the City and State of New York, the group was formed by Solyman Brown, variously known as the father of professional dentistry and the "Poet Laureate of Dentistry." Prior to this time, the practice of dentistry was in chaos: There were no legal requirements for treating patients and no schools of dentistry, and charlatans and quacks were common.

**Every shifting of the studding-sails was only to "haze"(1) the crew.** That is, it was simply "make-work" invented to harass the crew and keep them busy.

**You will be "worked up," if you are not a better man...** Dana's explanatory note cautions that once an officer decided to haze a sailor, the sailor has no alternative but to take it for longer than the officer can dish it out. Used in the sense of *stir up* or *agitate*, "worked up" goes back to the 17th century.

**...petitioned the captain for leave to shift our berths from the steerage...** As dark and dim and uncomfortable as the forecastle is, the steerage (see previous note) is usually worse, so Dana and Stimson are delighted that they can move into the forecastle.

In the news

**December, 1834**

The inventor of the Hansom Cab, London's Joseph Hansom, receives a patent on his invention, which combines speed with a low center of gravity, allowing it to carry passengers around town quickly and safely.

**...as independent as a wood-sawyer's clerk...** A wood-sawyer is one who saws wood. A supply of wood was critical to the shipping industry (and would become even more so in the age of steam), and wood suppliers were very important people. Thus a wood-sawyer could afford to be somewhat independent; perhaps his clerk—who kept and settled his accounts—could afford to be even more independent than the sawyer himself. (That, by the way, explains the origins of the surname Sawyer: It was applied to a man—or a family—who made a living sawing wood.)

---

1. Haze is a word of frequent use on board ship, and never,

I believe, used elsewhere. It is very expressive to a sailor, and means to punish by hard work. Let an officer once say, "I'll haze you," and your fate is fixed. You will be "worked up," if you are not a better man than he is.

---

In this midst of this state of things, my messmate S— and myself petitioned the captain for leave to shift our berths from the steerage, where we had previously lived, into the forecastle. This, to our delight, was granted, and we turned in to bunk and mess with the crew forward. We now began to feel like sailors, which we never fully did when we were in the steerage. While there, however useful and active you may be, you are but a mongrel,–and sort of afterguard and "ship's cousin." You are immediately under the eye of the officers, cannot dance, sing, play, smoke, make a noise, or growl, (i.e. complain,) or take any other sailor's pleasure; and you live with the steward, who is usually a go-between; and the crew never feel as though you were one of them. But if you live in the forecastle, you are "as independent as a wood-sawyer's clerk," (nautice',) and are a sailor. You hear sailor's talk, learn their ways, their peculiarities of feeling as well as speaking and acting; and moreover pick up a great deal of curious and useful information in seamanship, ship's customs, foreign countries, etc., from their long yarns and equally long disputes. No man can be a sailor, or know what sailors are, unless he has lived in the forecastle with them–turned in and out with them, eaten of their dish and drank of their cup. After I had been a week there, nothing would have tempted me to go back to my old berth, and never afterwards, even in the worst of weather, when in a close and leaking forecastle off Cape Horn, did I for a moment wish myself in the steerage. Another thing which you learn better in the forecastle than you can anywhere else, is, to make and mend clothes, and this is indispensable to sailors. A large part of their watches below they spend at this work, and here I learned that art which stood me in so good stead afterwards.

But to return to the state of the crew. Upon our coming into the forecastle, there was some difficulty about the uniting of the allowances of bread, by which we thought we were to lose a few pounds. This set us into a ferment. The captain would not condescend to explain, and we went aft in a body, with a Swede, the oldest and best sailor of the crew, for spokesman. The recollection of the scene that followed always brings up a smile, especially the quarter-deck dignity and eloquence of the captain. He was walking the weather side of the quarter-deck, and seeing us coming aft, stopped short in his walk, and, with a voice and look intended to annihilate us, called out, "Well, what do you want now?" Whereupon we stated our grievances as respectfully as we could, but he broke in upon us, saying that we were getting fat and lazy, didn't have enough to do, and that made us find fault. This provoked us, and we began to give word for word. This would never answer. He clenched his fist, stamped and swore, and sent us all forward, saying, with oaths enough interspersed to send the words home,–"Away with you! go forward every one of you! I'll haze you! I'll work you up! You don't have enough to do! You've mistaken your man. I'm F—- T—-, all the way from 'down east.' I've been through the mill, ground, and bolted, and come out a regular-built down-east johnny-cake, good when it's hot, but when it's cold, sour and indigestible;–and you'll find me so!" The latter part of the harangue I remember well, for it made a strong impression, and the "down-east johnny-cake" became a by-word for the rest of the voyage. So much for our petition for the redress of grievances. The matter was however set right, for the mate, after allowing the captain due time to cool off, explained it to him, and at night we were all called aft to hear another harangue, in which, of course, the whole blame of the misunderstanding was thrown upon us. We ventured to hint that he would not give us time to explain; but it wouldn't do. We were driven back discomforted. Thus the affair blew over, but the irritation caused by it remained; and we never had peace or a good understanding again so long as the captain and

## In the news
## December, 1834

English economist Thomas Malthus dies. Malthus, author of *An Essay on the Principle of Population*, theorized that the population would continue to increase until, if left unchecked, it would eventually surpass the ability of the planet to support it. His theory was a forerunner of the idea of natural selection, and other researchers, including Charles Darwin, used some of his ideas to form their own theories. Malthus did not actually foresee a looming global disaster, believing that hunger, war, disease—as well as prostitution, birth control, and postponement of marriage—would hold the population down to manageable levels.

**...I'm F— T—...** The captain is Frank Thompson. He is something of a martinet, and we'll soon see that he can be a cruel, heartless, petty man.

**...down-east johnny-cake, good when it's hot, but when it's cold, sour and indigestible...** A Johnny-cake (or Jonny-cake, or any of several other variants—and sometimes called a hoecake) is a fried flatbread made mainly of cornmeal. The Captain is saying that if the men treat him well and fairly, he will do the same, but if they give him trouble, they'll regret it.

**...we never had peace or a good understanding again so long as the captain and crew remained together.** This is true; the disagreement set the tone for the crew's relationship with the captain for a long time to come.

crew remained together.

We continued sailing along in the beautiful temperate climate of the Pacific. The Pacific well deserves its name, for except in the southern part, at Cape Horn, and in the western parts, near the China and Indian oceans, it has few storms, and is never either extremely hot or cold. Between the tropics there is a slight haziness, like a thin gauze, drawn over the sun, which, without obstructing or obscuring the light, tempers the heat which comes down with perpendicular fierceness in the Atlantic and Indian tropics. We sailed well to the westward to have the full advantage of the north-east trades, and when we had reached the latitude of Point Conception, where it is usual to make the land, we were several hundred miles to the westward of it. We immediately changed our course due east, and sailed in that direction for a number of days. At length we began to heave-to after dark, for fear of making the land at night on a coast where there are no light-houses and but indifferent charts, and at daybreak on the morning of

Tuesday, Jan 13th, 1835, we made the land at Point Conception, lat 34º 32' N., long 120º 06' W. The port of Santa Barbara, to which we were bound, lying about sixty miles to the southward of this point, we continued sailing down the coast during the day and following night, and on the next morning,

Jan. 14th, 1835, we came to anchor in the spacious bay of Santa Barbara, after a voyage of one hundred and fifty days from Boston.

**...well deserves its name...** The word, meaning "peaceful and free from disturbance," comes to us from the French. Pacific Ocean (named by Ferdinand Magellan in 1521) is indeed calm and peaceful much of the time.

In the news
**January, 1835**

In Washington, D.C., Richard Lawrence, a deranged painter who believes that he is king of England, attempts (unsuccessfully) to assassinate President Andrew Jackson.

**...we began to heave-to after dark...** In an era when sailors could not be exactly sure of their location, it made (and still makes) sense to avoid a possible nighttime landfall—especially during a time well before the aids to navigation we now take for granted.

**...lat 34º 32' N., long 120º 06' W.** Lines of latitude are imaginary horizontal circles around the surface of the Earth. The band at the equator is 0º. Latitudes north of the equator are designated N (as in 34º N), while latitudes south of the equator are designated S. The bands are numbered in degrees, and—in those days—the degrees were subdivided into minutes and then into seconds. (A decimal system is more common now.) Vertical bands stretching from pole to pole represent degrees of longitude. The two sets of points along both lines thus constitute a coordinate system that allows one to pinpoint a fairly precise location on the globe.

**...bay of Santa Barbara...** Modern-day Santa Barbara is a thriving city of slightly less than 100,000 people. When Dana landed there, however, the area was sparsely populated, with much of the land held in the form of huge "ranchos" granted by the government to prominent Mexican cattle ranchers. Dana is now on the California coast, ready to engage in commerce and in the acquisition of tanned hides; this is the real purpose of the voyage.

## Chapter IX

## California–A South-Easter

California extends along nearly the whole of the western coast of Mexico, between the gulf of California in the south and the bay of Sir Francis Drake on the north, or between the 22d and 38th degrees of north latitude. It is subdivided into two provinces–Lower or Old California, lying between the gulf and the 32d degree of latitude, or near it; (the division line running, I believe, between the bay of Todos Santos and the port of San Diego;) and New or Upper California, the southernmost port of which is San Diego, in lat. 32° 39', and the northernmost, San Francisco, situated in the large bay discovered by Sir Francis Drake, in lat. 37° 58', and called after him by the English, though the Mexicans call it Yerba Buena. Upper California has the seat of its government at Monterey, where is also the custom-house, the only one on the coast, and at which every vessel intending to trade on the coast must enter its cargo before it can commence its traffic. We were to trade upon this coast exclusively, and therefore expected to go to Monterey at first; but the captain's orders from home were to put in at Santa Barbara, which is the central port of the coast, and wait there for the agent who lives there, and transacts all the business for the firm to which our vessel belonged.

The bay, or, as it was commonly called, the canal of Santa Barbara, is very large, being formed by the main land on one side, (between Point Conception on the north and Point St. Buena Ventura on the south,) which here bends in like a crescent, and three large islands opposite to it and at the distance of twenty miles. This is just sufficient to give it the name of a bay, while at the same time it is so large and so much exposed to the south-east and north-west winds, that it is little better than an open roadstead; and the whole swell of the Pacific ocean rolls in here before a southeaster, and breaks with so heavy a surf in the shallow waters, that it is highly dangerous to lie near to the shore during the south-easter season; that is, between the months of

**...the bay of Sir Francis Drake on the north...** Dana is likely speaking of Drakes Bay, north and west of San Francisco Bay and bordered on the northwest by Pt. Reyes.

**...the bay of Todos Santos...** All Saints' Bay. A bay near Ensenada in what is now Baja, California, Mexico. The area is now a popular tourist and fishing destination.

**... situated in the large bay discovered by Sir Francis Drake...** This is a mistake on Dana's part. Drake did not discover San Francisco Bay, and it was not named for him.

**...though the Mexicans call it Yerba Buena.** Or "good herb," after the many aromatic plants that surround the area.

**Upper California has the seat of its government at Monterey...** Keep in mind that at this time the entire area is part of Mexico. So, when Dana says "seat of its government," he means the *Mexican* government of Upper California.

**...wait there for the agent who lives there, and transacts all the business for the firm to which our vessel belonged.** The agent is Alfred Robinson. He is contracted to the firm that owns the *Pilgrim* (Bryant, Sturgis & Co.) and he conducts business in California on behalf of the firm. In 1846, Robinson will write *Life in California*, an influential, well-received, and sympathetic portrait of California as it existed when it was part of Mexico.

**... three large islands opposite to it...** These would be the Channel Islands: San Miguel, Santa Rosa, and Santa Cruz, actually about 12 nautical miles off of the coast of Santa Barbara. A fourth (much smaller) island, Anacapa, is also nearby. To the south lie Santa Catalina, San Nicolas, Santa Barbara, and San Clemente islands.

November and April.

This wind (the south-easter) is the bane of the coast of California. Between the months of November and April, (including a part of each,) which is the rainy season in this latitude, you are never safe from it, and accordingly, in the ports which are open to it, vessels are obliged, during these months, to lie at anchor at a distance of three miles from the shore, with slip-ropes on their cables, ready to slip and go to sea at a moment's warning. The only ports which are safe from this wind are San Francisco and Monterey in the north, and San Diego in the south.

As it was January when we arrived, and the middle of the south-easter season, we accordingly came to anchor at the distance of three miles from the shore, in eleven fathoms water, and bent a slip-rope and buoys to our cables, cast off the yard-arm gaskets from the sails, and stopped them all with rope-yarns. After we had done this, the boat went ashore with the captain, and returned with orders to the mate to send a boat ashore for him at sundown. I did not go in the first boat, and was glad to find that there was another going before night; for after so long a voyage as ours had been, a few hours is long to pass in sight and out of reach of land. We spent the day on board in the usual avocations; but as this was the first time we had been without the captain, we felt a little more freedom, and looked about us to see what sort of a country we had got into, and were to spend a year or two of our lives in.

In the first place, it was a beautiful day, and so warm that we had on straw hats, duck trowsers, and all the summer gear; and as this was mid-winter, it spoke well for the climate; and we afterwards found that the thermometer never fell to the freezing-point throughout the winter, and that there was very little difference between the seasons, except that during a long period of rainy and south-easterly weather, thick clothes were not uncomfortable.

The large bay lay about us, nearly smooth, as there was

**...the bane of the coast of California.** Technically, a "bane" is a murderer, one who causes the death of another, and the word has been used in that sense since the 9th century. (It appears in the epic poem, *Beowulf*.) Around the 16th century it came to mean *anything* that negatively affects one's well-being.

**...ready to slip and go to sea at a moment's warning.** Although the idea makes non-sailors nervous, in a violent storm, a ship is much safer far out at sea than near the shore. Close to land, wind and waves can drive a vessel onto the rocks, with devastating results. During bad weather, a ship captain prefers to have "sea room" for the same reason that a pilot prefers to have altitude: They act as buffers, giving the crew time to react to problems.

**...three miles from the shore, in eleven fathoms water...** The *Pilgrim* is, for reasons explained above, anchored quite a ways from land in about 66 ft. of water. Using "slip ropes" allows the crew to depart quickly if the weather turns bad.

In the news

**January, 1835**

Los Angeles officially becomes a city, and the Mexican government declares it the capital of California, replacing Monterey.

**...we afterwards found that the thermometer never fell to the freezing-point throughout the winter, and that there was very little difference between the seasons...** Mostly true, especially along the coast. The standing joke is that Southern California doesn't have weather, it has *climate*.

hardly a breath of wind stirring, though the boat's crew who went ashore told us that the long ground swell broke into a heavy surf upon the beach. There was only one vessel in the port–a long, sharp brig of about 300 tons, with raking masts and very square yards, and English colors at her peak. We afterwards learned that she was built at Guayaquil, and named the Ayacucho, after the place where the battle was fought that gave Peru her independence, and was now owned by a Scotchman named Wilson, who commanded her, and was engaged in the trade between Callao, the Sandwich Islands, and California. She was a fast sailer, as we frequently afterwards perceived, and had a crew of Sandwich Islanders on board. Beside this vessel there was no object to break the surface of the bay. Two points ran out as the horns of the crescent, one of which–the one to the westward–was low and sandy, and is that to which vessels are obliged to give a wide berth when running out for a south-easter; the other is high, bold, and well wooded, and, we were told, has a mission upon it, called St. Buenaventura, from which the point is named. In the middle of this crescent, directly opposite the anchoring ground, lie the mission and town of Santa Barbara, on a low, flat plain, but little above the level of the sea, covered with grass, though entirely without trees, and surrounded on three sides by an amphitheatre of mountains, which slant off to the distance of fifteen or twenty miles. The mission stands a little back of the town, and is a large building, or rather a collection of buildings, in the centre of which is a high tower, with a belfry of five bells; and the whole, being plastered, makes quite a show at a distance, and is the mark by which vessels come to anchor. The town lies a little nearer to the beach–about half a mile from it–and is composed of one-story houses built of brown clay–some of them plastered–with red tiles on the roofs. I should judge that there were about an hundred of them; and in the midst of them stands the Presidio, or fort, built of the same materials, and apparently but little stronger. The town is certainly finely situated, with a bay in front, and an amphitheatre of hills behind. The only thing which diminishes its beauty is, that the hills have no large trees upon them, they having been all

**...now owned by a Scotchman named Wilson, who commanded her, and was engaged in the trade...** John Wilson acquired *Ayacucho* in about 1831. At one time, the brig had a reputation as being the fastest vessel on the coast. Dana may be wrong about the vessel's size, since contemporary records indicate that she was actually either 204 or 130 tons. Captain Wilson eventually became a cattle rancher and landowner, marrying into a prominent Mexican family. When California became a U.S. state (1850), Wilson became the first treasurer of San Luis Obispo. He died in 1861.

**...called St. Buenaventura, from which the point is named.** Dana is most likely mistaken, and his geography (here and elsewhere in the book) is suspect: Mission Buenaventura (founded in 1782 and still an active Catholic parish) does not stand on a point, and Mission Santa Barbara has *two* towers. (Keep in mind, though, that Dana is working from memory, with only a few tattered pages of notes—his original journal having been lost—to guide him.)

**The mission stands a little back of the town...** This is no longer true, the town having grown, mostly to the west and north of the mission.

**In the news**

**January, 1835**

In London, preparations are underway for the celebration of the birthday of William IV's wife, Adelaide. With William unable to produce an heir, his niece, Victoria, would in 1837 succeed him as ruler of England, and she would remain queen until her death in 1901.

**...burnt by a great fire...** Santa Barbara's summers are hot and dry, and the city is surrounded by chaparral. Fires in the area are common, and many have threatened to destroy the town, even in modern times.

In the news
**January, 1835**

During this year, some 40,000 slaves will travel (unwillingly, of course) on 117 separate voyages from their homes in Africa to Brazil, Cuba, the Caribbean, and Central America, from which ports a large number will be sold once more, many ending up in the U.S.

**...breaking in loud and high "combers" upon the beach.** A comber is a long wave that curls and slopes.

**...talking and halooing in their outlandish tongue.** The Hawaiian language would indeed have sounded outlandish to Dana and his compatriots. A Polynesian variant, the language had no written form until missionaries created an alphabet for it. The language almost died out, but the 20th century saw a determined effort to revitalize it, and in a 1978 election, Hawaiians voted to reestablish it as the official language of the state.

**...We saw, at once, how it was to be done...** These waves are good for surfing, but not so good for landing a small boat on the beach. (And, as Dana will later discover, they also make it very difficult to carry hides out to a waiting boat.) The *Pilgrim*'s second mate wisely waits to see how the vastly more experienced Sandwich Islanders (Hawaiians) handle the task.

burnt by a great fire which swept them off about a dozen years before, and they had not yet grown up again. The fire was described to me by an inhabitant, as having been a very terrible and magnificent sight. The air of the whole valley was so heated that the people were obliged to leave the town and take up their quarters for several days upon the beach.

Just before sun-down the mate ordered a boat's crew ashore, and I went as one of the number. We passed under the stern of the English brig, and had a long pull ashore. I shall never forget the impression which our first landing on the beach of California made upon me. The sun had just gone down; it was getting dusky; the damp night wind was beginning to blow, and the heavy swell of the Pacific was setting in, and breaking in loud and high "combers" upon the beach. We lay on our oars in the swell, just outside of the surf, waiting for a good chance to run in, when a boat, which had put off from the Ayacucho just after us, came alongside of us, with a crew of dusky Sandwich Islanders, talking and halooing in their outlandish tongue. They knew that we were novices in this kind of boating, and waited to see us go in. The second mate, however, who steered our boat, determined to have the advantage of their experience, and would not go in first. Finding, at length, how matters stood, they gave a shout, and taking advantage of a great comber which came swelling in, rearing its head, and lifting up the stern of our boat nearly perpendicular, and again dropping it in the trough, they gave three or four long and strong pulls, and went in on top of the great wave, throwing their oars overboard, and as far from the boat as they could throw them, and jumping out the instant that the boat touched the beach, and then seizing hold of her and running her up high and dry upon the sand. We saw, at once, how it was to be done, and also the necessity of keeping the boat "stern on" to the sea; for the instant the sea should strike upon her broad-side or quarter, she would be driven up broad-side-on, and capsized. We pulled strongly in, and as soon as we felt that the sea had got hold of us and was carrying us in with the speed of a race-horse, we threw the oars as far from the boat as we could, and took hold of the gunwale, ready to spring out and seize her when she struck, the officer using his utmost strength to keep her stern on. We were shot up upon the beach like an arrow from a bow, and seizing the boat, ran her up high and dry, and soon picked up our oars, and stood by her, ready for the captain to come down.

Finding that the captain did not come immediately, we put our oars in the boat, and leaving one to watch it, walked about the beach to see what we could, of the place. The beach is nearly a mile in length between the two points, and of smooth sand. We had taken the only good landing-place, which is in the middle; it being more stony toward the ends. It is about twenty yards in width from high-water mark to a slight bank at which the soil begins, and so hard that it is a favorite place for running horses. It was growing dark, so that we could just distinguish the dim outlines of the two vessels in the offing; and the great seas were rolling in, in regular lines, growing larger and larger as they approached the shore, and hanging over the beach upon which they were to break, when their tops would curl over and turn white with foam, and, beginning at one extreme of the line, break rapidly to the other, as a long card-house falls when the children knock down the cards at one end. The Sandwich Islanders, in the mean time, had turned their boat round, and ran her down into the water, and were loading her with hides and tallow. As this was the work in which we were soon to be engaged, we looked on with some curiosity. They ran the boat into the water so far that every large sea might float her, and two of them, with their trowsers rolled up, stood by the bows, one on each side, keeping her in her right position. This was hard work; for beside the force they had to use upon the boat, the large seas nearly took them off their legs. The others were running from the boat to the bank, upon which, out of the reach of the water, was a pile of dry bullocks' hides, doubled lengthwise in the middle, and nearly as stiff as boards. These they took upon their heads, one or two at a time, and carried down to the boat, where one of their number stowed them away. They were obliged to carry them on their heads, to keep them out of the water, and we

In the news
**January, 1835**

In Boston, the Revolutionary War and the Boston Tea Party are far from ancient history; alive at the time are several men who were teenagers at the time of the Tea Party (1773). In January of 1835, Benjamin B. Thatcher publishes a book that lists—apparently for the first time—the names of those who took part.

**...loading her with hides and tallow.** Hides, of course, were used for making clothing and other leather goods. Throughout history, tallow—the processed, purified fat from animals—has been used to make soap, candles, and other goods, and also as a dressing for leather. Its use is less common now, but in Dana's day, tallow was quite valuable. (During Joshua Slocum's incredible 1893-1895 solo sail around the world, he came across an unclaimed cargo of tallow and profited handsomely from its sale.)

In the news
**January, 1835**

The *Neva*, a convict transport carrying some 150 female convicts and several children to Australia, sets sail from Cork, Ireland. A few months later, she will break up on the rocks near King Island, Tasmania, and quickly sink. Most of the women—many of them drunk on rum carried in the ship's hold—drown. In the end, there are only 15 survivors.

**...These they took upon their heads, one or two at a time...** Dana and his colleagues watched the Sandwich Islanders very carefully; in the end, the crew of the *Pilgrim* would adopt a similar technique when carrying hides out to the boat for transfer to the ship.

**...it did not look very encouraging.** Naturally not; it looked like very hard work, which it was. Nothing like a college boy might be used to, as the other sailors said teasingly.

**...a common meal bag...** That is, a large bag in which meal (such as cornmeal) is typically shipped and stored.

In the news
**January, 1835**

Andrew Jackson pays off the national debt. (A lifelong hater of debt, he had previously called it "a national curse.") He is the only U.S. president to pay off the national debt, and he did so in part by refusing to spend a penny on any infrastructure projects: roads, railways, etc. In fact, as of January 1st, 1835, the U.S. treasury showed a balance of $440,000. By the following year, though, prosperity had ended, the economy contracted, and the national debt was back for good.

**...it was high time for "the old man," as the captain is generally called, to come down.** The phrase "old man" as applied to someone in authority goes back to the 17th century or earlier, appearing in Dryden's *Sir Martin Marall*. It was applied specifically to a ship's captain as early as 1821 and has since become common usage, even today.

**...blanket cloak or surreppa...** What we would now call a "serape." (Which, in fact, is how some editions spell it.)

observed that they had on thick woolen caps. "Look here, Bill, and see what you're coming to!" said one of our men to another who stood by the boat. "Well, D—," said the second mate to me, "this does not look much like Cambridge college, does it? This is what I call 'head work.'" To tell the truth, it did not look very encouraging.

After they had got through with the hides, they laid hold of the bags of tallow, (the bags are made of hide, and are about the size of a common meal bag,) and lifting each upon the shoulders of two men, one at each end, walked off with them to the boat, and prepared to go aboard. Here, too, was something for us to learn. The man who steered, shipped his oar and stood up in the stern, and those that pulled the after oars sat upon their benches, with their oars shipped, ready to strike out as soon as she was afloat. The two men at the bows kept their places; and when, at length, a large sea came in and floated her, seized hold of the gunwale, and ran out with her till they were up to their armpits, and then tumbled over the gunwale into the bows, dripping with water. The men at the oars struck out, but it wouldn't do; the sea swept back and left them nearly high and dry. The two fellows jumped out again; and the next time they succeeded better, and, with the help of a deal of outlandish hallooing and bawling, got her well off. We watched them till they were out of the breakers, and saw them steering for their vessel, which was now hidden in the darkness.

The sand of the beach began to be cold to our bare feet; the frogs set up their croaking in the marshes, and one solitary owl, from the end of the distant point, gave out his melancholy note, mellowed by the distance, and we began to think that it was high time for "the old man," as the captain is generally called, to come down. In a few minutes we heard something coming towards us. It was a man on horseback. He came up on the full gallop, reined up near us, addressed a few words to us, and receiving no answer, wheeled around and galloped off again. He was nearly as dark as an Indian, with a large Spanish hat, blanket cloak or surreppa, and leather leggins, with a long knife stuck in them. "This is the seventh city that ever I was in, and no Christian one neither," said Bill Brown. "Stand by!" said Tom, "you haven't seen the worst of it yet." In the midst of this conversation the captain appeared; and we winded the boat round, shoved her down, and prepared to go off. The captain, who had been on the coast before and "knew the ropes," took the steering oar, and we went off in the same way as the other boat. I, being the youngest, had the pleasure of standing at the bow, and getting wet through. We went off well, though the seas were high. Some of them lifted us up, and sliding from under us, seemed to let us drop through the air like a flat plank upon the body of the water. In a few minutes we were in the low, regular swell, and pulled for a light, which, as we came up, we found had been run up to our trysail gaff.

Coming aboard, we hoisted up all the boats, and diving down into the forecastle, changed our wet clothes, and got our supper. After supper the sailors lighted their pipes, (cigars, those of us who had them,) and we had to tell all we had seen ashore. Then followed conjectures about the people ashore, the length of the voyage, carrying hides, etc., until eight bells, when all hands were called aft, and the "anchor watch" set. We were to stand two in a watch, and as the nights were pretty long, two hours were to make a watch. The second mate was to keep the deck until eight o'clock, and all hands were to be called at daybreak, and the word was passed to keep a bright look-out, and to call the mate if it should come on to blow from the south-east. We had also orders to strike the bells every half-hour through the night, as at sea. My watchmate was John, the Swedish sailor, and we stood from twelve to two, he walking the larboard side, and I the starboard. At daylight all hands were called, and we went through the usual process of washing down, swabbing, etc., and got breakfast at eight o'clock. In the course of the forenoon, a boat went aboard of the Ayacucho and brought off a quarter of beef, which made us a fresh bite for dinner. This we were glad enough to have, and the mate told us that we should live upon fresh beef while we were on the coast,

**...and no Christian one neither," said Bill Brown. "Stand by!" said Tom...** William Brown, an able seaman, hailed from Baltimore. Tom may be Thomas Curtis, the *Pilgrim*'s cook. Note that an able seaman, being more experienced, ranks above an ordinary seaman.

**The captain, who had been on the coast before and "knew the ropes," took the steering oar...** As captain of the ship, he certainly *should* "know the ropes"—that is, he should understand the purpose of the various lines and rigging on board a vessel, which is where this phrase comes from. (In spite of the fact that sailors normally called them "sheets" or "lines," not "ropes.") Although the term was already familiar by 1840, when Dana was writing this book, *Two Years Before the Mast* is in fact one of the first places the phrase had appeared in print.

**In the news**
**January, 1835**

Back in Boston, Ralph Waldo Emerson delivers his first public lectures, a series of biographies, at the Boston Masonic Temple. The lectures will prove popular, but will remain unpublished until 1959.

**...and the "anchor watch" set.** The anchor watch is a small detachment of sailors left on board to see to the vessel while at anchor.

**My watchmate was John, the Swedish sailor...** John Linden was the eldest seaman on board, and perhaps the most experienced sailor.

**...a quarter of beef...** This is a substantial amount of beef. Then again, it's meant to feed 12 to 15 hungry men.

**The ship's colors had puzzled us, and we found that she was from Genoa...** Genoa is now an Italian port city, but in 1834 it was a protectorate of Sardinia. Italy did not become a fully unified, sovereign state until several years later.

**...stood out...** That is, the vessel headed without tacking toward some destination.

**...what the sailors call a butter-box.** So-called because of her unappealing—and perhaps unseaworthy—lines. A box for butter being somewhat squared-off and ungainly and certainly not fit for sailing. The term, originally used in a broader pejorative sense, may have derived from the Anglo-Dutch wars of the mid-1600s. The British referred to the Dutch as "butter boxes." Note that Dutch is in fact the name of a language, not a people. Dutch is spoken by the people of The Netherlands, Denmark, and Flanders.

**...has little to do...** That is, unless he is also acting in some clerical, legal, or commercial capacity as a representative of the owner.

In the news
**January, 1835**

The Society for the Diffusion of Useful knowledge reports that Dana's home town of Boston now boasts 80 public schools, with 7,430 "scholars in attendance." Sponsored in America by such luminaries as Emerson and Thoreau, the Society is part of the Lyceum Movement, groups that sponsored lectures, concerts, and other programs for the edification of the public.

**...we were worse off in the end...** A mate who wants to be everyone's friend is not a good mate. A crew needs discipline, and the men need someone to be in charge. This mate is weak, and his inability to be a leader is already causing trouble.

as it was cheaper here than the salt. While at dinner, the cook called, "Sail ho!" and coming on deck, we saw two sails coming round the point. One was a large ship under top-gallant sails, and the other a small hermaphrodite brig. They both backed their topsails and sent boats aboard of us. The ship's colors had puzzled us, and we found that she was from Genoa, with an assorted cargo, and was trading on the coast. She filled away again, and stood out; being bound up the coast to San Francisco. The crew of the brig's boat were Sandwich Islanders, but one of them, who spoke a little English, told us that she was the Loriotte, Captain Nye, from Oahu, and was engaged in this trade. She was a lump of a thing –what the sailors call a butter-box. This vessel, as well as the Ayacucho, and others which we afterwards saw engaged in the same trade, have English or Americans for officers, and two or three before the mast to do the work upon the rigging, and to rely upon for seamanship, while the rest of the crew are Sandwich Islanders, who are active, and very useful in boating.

The three captains went ashore after dinner, and came off again at night. When in port, everything is attended to by the chief mate; the captain, unless he is also supercargo, has little to do, and is usually ashore much of his time. This we thought would be pleasanter for us, as the mate was a good-natured man and not very strict. So it was for a time, but we were worse off in the end; for wherever the captain is a severe, energetic man, and the mate is wanting in both these qualities, there will always be trouble. And trouble we had already begun to anticipate. The captain had several times found fault with the mate, in presence of the crew; and hints had been dropped that all was not right between them. When this is the case, and the captain suspects that his officer is too easy and familiar with the crew, then he begins to interfere in all the duties, and to draw the reins taughter, and the crew have to suffer.

In the news

**January, 1835**

In Chile, Charles Darwin witnesses the eruption of Mount Osorno in the Los Lagos region of Chile. The eruption had actually begun in November of 1834 and would continue until the end of February, 1835. Although active since the Middle Ages, Osorno has not had any major eruptions since 1869.

## Chapter X

### A South-Easter–Passage Up the Coast

This night, after sundown, it looked black at the southward and eastward, and we were told to keep a bright look-out. Expecting to be called up, we turned in early. Waking up about midnight, I found a man who had just come down from his watch, striking a light. He said that it was beginning to puff up from the south-east, and that the sea was rolling in, and he had called the captain; and as he threw himself down on his chest with all his clothes on, I knew that he expected to be called. I felt the vessel pitching at her anchor, and the chain surging and snapping, and lay awake, expecting an instant summons. In a few minutes it came–three knocks on the scuttle, and "All hands ahoy! bear-a-hand up and make sail." We sprang up for our clothes, and were about halfway dressed, when the mate called out, down the scuttle, "Tumble up here, men! tumble up! before she drags her anchor." We were on deck in an instant. "Lay aloft and loose the topsails!" shouted the captain, as soon as the first man showed himself. Springing into the rigging, I saw that the Ayacucho's topsails were loosed, and heard her crew singing-out at the sheets as they were hauling them home. This had probably started our captain; as "old Wilson" (the captain of the Ayacucho) had been many years on the coast, and knew the signs of the weather. We soon had the topsails loosed; and one hand remaining, as usual, in each top, to overhaul the rigging and light the sail out, the rest of us laid down to man the sheets. While sheeting home, we saw the Ayacucho standing athwart our bows, sharp upon the wind, cutting through the head sea like a knife, with her raking masts and sharp bows running up like the head

**...bear-a-hand up and make sail.** According to a note added by Dana to other editions, to "bear-a-hand" means to make haste. The phrase may have legal origins, having meant "to maintain or assert, to charge or accuse."

**Tumble up here, men!** Another phrase meaning "to make haste." A ship dragging its anchor is not under control, and the anchor may foul or be lost.

**This had probably started our captain...** That is, since (the more experienced) Wilson's crew was hurriedly preparing to set sail, the *Pilgrim*'s captain decided to do likewise.

**While sheeting home...** That is, while pulling on the rope that hauls the sail up and out to its full extent. Aboard a ship, ropes (not sails) are called "sheets."

**...with a turn round the timber-heads.** The ends of timber that protrude up through the decks are used for belaying (wrapping, but not tying) large ropes.

In the news
**January, 1835**

As a tactic for achieving statehood, the territorial legislature of Michigan calls for a constitutional convention. Congress agrees, but only if the territory can resolve the boundary dispute (known as the "Toledo War") that pitted Michigan against Ohio, each of which claimed the mouth of the Maumee River as its own.

**It now began to blow fresh...** That is, briskly.

**...well clear of the point.** Whatever his other failings, Captain Thompson is an experienced seaman. Even though having that much sail up makes for a rough, perhaps even somewhat dangerous sail in the storm, he does not wish to risk the loss of control that might result from reducing sail until the vessel is clear of the point, lest she be driven onto the rocks before she has a chance to clear.

In the news
**January, 1835**

This month marks Robert E. Lee's 28th birthday. A first lieutenant, Lee is assigned to help civil engineer Andrew Talcott, a U.S. Army captain at the time, survey the southern Michigan border. Talcott and Lee would become friends for life.

**When the watch came up, we wore ship...** To wear (or ware) ship is to change direction by bringing the stern around. ("Tacking," on the other hand, is to change direction by bringing the *bow* around.)

of a greyhound. It was a beautiful sight. She was like a bird which had been frightened and had spread her wings in flight. After the topsails had been sheeted home, the head yards braced aback, the fore-top-mast staysail hoisted, and the buoys streamed, and all ready forward, for slipping, we went aft and manned the slip-rope which came through the stern port with a turn round the timber-heads. "All ready forward?" asked the captain. "Aye, aye, sir; all ready," answered the mate. "Let go!" "All gone, sir;" and the iron cable grated over the windlass and through the hawse-hole, and the little vessel's head swinging off from the wind under the force of her backed head sails, brought the strain upon the slip-rope. "Let go aft!" Instantly all was gone, and we were under weigh. As soon as she was well off from the wind, we filled away the head yards, braced all up sharp, set the foresail and trysail, and left our anchorage well astern, giving the point a good berth. "Nye's off too," said the captain to the mate; and looking astern, we could just see the little hermaphrodite brig under sail standing after us.

It now began to blow fresh; the rain fell fast, and it grew very black; but the captain would not take in sail until we were well clear of the point. As soon as we left this on our quarter, and were standing out to sea, the order was given, and we sprang aloft, double reefed each topsail, furled the foresail, and double reefed the trysail, and were soon under easy sail. In those cases of slipping for south-easters, there is nothing to be done, after you have got clear of the coast, but to lie-to under easy sail, and wait for the gale to be over, which seldom lasts more than two days, and is often over in twelve hours; but the wind never comes back to the southward until there has been a good deal of rain fallen. "Go below the watch," said the mate; but here was a dispute which watch it should be, which the mate soon however settled by sending his watch below, saying that we should have our turn the next time we got under weigh. We remained on deck till the expiration of the watch, the wind blowing very fresh and the rain coming down in torrents. When the watch came up, we wore ship, and stood on the other tack, in towards land. When we came up again, which was at four in the morning, it was very dark, and there was not much wind, but it was raining as I thought I had never seen it rain before. We had on oil-cloth suits and south-wester caps, and had nothing to do but to stand bolt upright and let it pour down upon us. There are no umbrellas, and no sheds to go under, at sea.

While we were standing about on deck, we saw the little brig drifting by us, hove to under her fore topsail double reefed; and she glided by like a phantom. Not a word was spoken, and we saw no one on deck but the man at the wheel. Toward morning the captain put his head out of the companion-way and told the second mate, who commanded our watch, to look out for a change of wind, which usually followed a calm and heavy rain; and it was well that he did; for in a few minutes it fell dead calm, the vessel lost her steerage-way, and the rain ceased. We hauled up the trysail and courses, squared the after yards, and waited for the change, which came in a few minutes, with a vengeance, from the north-west, the opposite point of the compass. Owing to our precautions, we were not taken aback, but ran before the wind with square yards. The captain coming on deck, we braced up a little and stood back for our anchorage. With the change of wind came a change of weather, and in two hours the wind moderated into the light steady breeze, which blows down the coast the greater part of the year, and, from its regularity, might be called a trade-wind. The sun came up bright, and we set royals, skysails, and studding-sails, and were under fair way for Santa Barbara. The little Loriotte was astern of us, nearly out of sight; but we saw nothing of the Ayacucho. In a short time she appeared, standing out from Santa Rosa Island, under the lee of which she had been hove to, all night. Our captain was anxious to get in before her, for it would be a great credit to us, on the coast, to beat the Ayacucho, which had been called the best sailer in the North Pacific, in which she had been known as a trader for six years or more. We had an advantage over her in light winds, from our royals and skysails which we carried both at the fore and main, and also in our studding-sails;

**...it was well that he did...** Again, Captain Thompson is an experienced mariner, and his knowledge of the sea is once again made evident.

**...it fell dead calm, the vessel lost her steerage-way, and the rain ceased.** Steerageway is the forward movement a vessel requires in order to maintain control of her direction. If she does not make steerageway, she simply drifts and wallows. (Close to shore, she could drift onto the rocks, in fact.)

**In the news**
**January, 1835**

Allen B. Light, an African-American man said to have accompanied Dana on the *Pilgrim* (though Dana never mentions him), arrives at Santa Barbara. Light carries a document identifying him as a free man; he apparently hid that document for safekeeping in a building wall in San Diego, where it was finally discovered in 1948.

**... under the lee of which she had been hove to, all night.** The *Ayacucho* hove to on the lee side of the island, protected from the wind. If she had been on the windward side, the storm might have driven her ashore; on the lee side, even if her anchors dragged, she would be driven *away* from the land, which would have been better than the alternative.

**We had an advantage over her in light winds...** In light winds, *Pilgrim* usually fares better than the *Ayacucho* because she carries more sail—the better to take advantage of the little wind that is available.

**...come upon a taught bowline...** Once clear of the point, there was more wind (figuratively speaking, enough to stretch a bowline taut), at which point *Ayacucho* once more has the advantage.

**...a very nice piece of work.** Indeed it is. Imagine a vessel of many tons under sail, with no motor to control her speed or direction. Wilson, and Thompson, too, were seamen enough to bring a ship right up to where her mooring cables lie, such that the crew could grab her mooring ropes and tie off. Even now, a sailor in a small day boat can earn a quick round of applause—or an appreciative smile—by bringing his vessel under sail smoothly up to a dock or mooring line and nonchalantly tying her off. Imagine the skill it took to accomplish this in ships of this size.

**In the news**

**January, 1835**

San Diego officially becomes a pueblo, with a mayor and aldermen. However, over the next few years, its population would decline until, unable to remain a municipality on its own, it becomes part of Los Angeles, administered by judges appointed by the governor.

**...touch of California...** That is, they'd best get used to dealing with constant wind, strong tides, and bad harbors.

**...our agent, Mr. R...** Alfred Robinson. Captain Thompson is accompanied by his brother, Alpheus B. Thompson, and his brother's wife, the former Francisca Carrillo. At this time, Alpheus had recently settled in Santa Barbara. In 1846, Alpheus Thompson would receive from the governor of Mexico a grant for a rancho of over 35,000 acres in what are today Stainslaus and San Joaquin counties. (Of course, Thompson has married the daughter of the governor—a move that is almost guaranteed to benefit him socially and financially.)

for Captain Wilson carried nothing above top-gallant-sails, and always unbent his studding-sails when on the coast. As the wind was light and fair, we held our own, for some time, when we were both obliged to brace up and come upon a taught bowline, after rounding the point; and here he had us on fair ground, and walked away from us, as you would haul in a line. He afterwards said that we sailed well enough with the wind free, but that give him a taught bowline, and he would beat us, if we had all the canvas of the Royal George.

The Ayacucho got to the anchoring ground about half an hour before us, and was furling her sails when we came up to it. This picking up your cables is a very nice piece of work. It requires some seamanship to do it, and come to at your former moorings, without letting go another anchor. Captain Wilson was remarkable, among the sailors on the coast, for his skill in doing this; and our captain never let go a second anchor during all the time that I was with him. Coming a little to windward of our buoy, we clewed up the light sails, backed our main topsail, and lowered a boat, which pulled off, and made fast a spare hawser to the buoy on the end of the slip-rope. We brought the other end to the captain, and hove in upon it until we came to the slip-rope, which we took to the windlass, and walked her up to her chain, the captain helping her by backing and filling the sails. The chain is then passed through the hawse-hole and round the windlass, and bitted, the slip-rope taken round outside and brought into the stern port, and she is safe in her old berth. After we had got through, the mate told us that this was a small touch of California, the like of which we must expect to have through the winter.

After we had furled the sails and got dinner, we saw the Loriotte nearing, and she had her anchor before night. At sun-down we went ashore again, and found the Loriotte's boat waiting on the beach. The Sandwich Islander who could speak English, told us that he had been up to the town; that our agent, Mr. R—-, and some other passengers, were going to Monterey with us, and that we were to sail the same night. In a few minutes Captain T—-, with two gentlemen and one female, came down, and we got ready to go off. They had a good deal of baggage, which we put into the bows of the boat, and then two of us took the señora in our arms, and waded with her through the water, and put her down safely in the stern. She appeared much amused with the transaction, and her husband was perfectly satisfied, thinking any arrangement good which saved his wetting his feet. I pulled the after oar, so that I heard the conversation, and learned that one of the men, who, as well as I could see in the darkness, was a young-looking man, in the European dress, and covered up in a large cloak, was the agent of the firm to which our vessel belonged; and the other, who was dressed in the Spanish dress of the country, was a brother of our captain, who had been many years a trader on the coast, and had married the lady who was in the boat. She was a delicate, dark-complexioned young woman, and of one of the best families in California. I also found that we were to sail the same night. As soon as we got on board, the boats were hoisted up, the sails loosed, the windlass manned, the slip-ropes and gear cast off; and after about twenty minutes of heaving at the windlass, making sail, and bracing yards, we were well under weigh, and going with a fair wind up the coast to Monterey. The Loriotte got under weigh at the same time, and was also bound up to Monterey, but as she took a different course from us, keeping the land aboard, while we kept well out to sea, we soon lost sight of her. We had a fair wind, which is something unusual when going up, as the prevailing wind is the north, which blows directly down the coast; whence the northern are called the windward, and the southern the leeward ports.

**...one of the best families in California.** The Carrillos were in fact a powerful family of some standing. The branch into which Alpheus Thompson married was descended from José Raimundo Carrillo, a member of the 1769 Portolà expedition, and included José Antonio Carrillo, the mayor of Los Angeles and Juan José Carrillo, who was to become the mayor of both Santa Monica and Santa Barbara, California. Thompson's wife, Francisca, was the daughter of Carlos Antonio de Jesus Carrillo, the governor of Alta California.

**In the news**
**January, 1835**

In accordance with the edicts of the Mexican government, the San Diego mission is secularized: turned over to "secular clergy"—ministers who did not belong to a religious order. The priests of the Catholic church thus lose control of the property and of the natives who run the farms, gardens, and orchards attached to the mission.

**We had a fair wind...** A fair wind is any wind that blows in a direction that will drive a vessel in the direction one wishes to travel.

**...off Point Conception...** Point Conception, near present-day Santa Barbara, is sometimes considered the dividing line between Southern and Central California. Popular with tourists and surfers, the Point gets its name from the nearby Mission of the Immaculate Conception of the Most Holy Virgin Mary, which was established in 1787.

**...we doused the sky-sails...** That is, lowered them suddenly.

**His brother and Mr. R——...** Alfred Robinson, the owners' agent.

**...letting them know how he could carry sail.** Captain Thompson certainly does know his ship and how much sail she can safely carry—and he knows the sea in general quite well. But the fact that he feels obliged to prove it is worrisome, and does not bode well for the fate of the voyage.

In the news

**January, 1835**

As Dana lands at Monterey, the capital of California at this time, the region is in some turmoil because Indians have been stealing horses from ranches in the area. The governor of Mexico steps in to warn ranchers not to chase down the local Indians, because in their efforts to catch and punish the thieves, the Mexicans have several times captured and killed members of the Tulare Indian tribe—a tribe that was friendly to the Mexicans and whose members were in fact *not* the ones stealing horses. The thefts would continue, and a year or two later, one visitor would note that the Indians "plunder the farms of the colonists of horses, which they eat in preference to beef."

# CHAPTER XI

## PASSAGE UP THE COAST—MONTEREY

We got clear of the islands before sunrise the next morning, and by twelve o'clock were out of the canal, and off Point Conception, the place where we first made the land upon our arrival. This is the largest point on the coast, and is uninhabited headland, stretching out into the Pacific, and has the reputation of being very windy. Any vessel does well which gets by it without a gale, especially in the winter season. We were going along with studding-sails set on both sides, when, as we came round the point, we had to haul our wind, and take in the lee studding-sails. As the brig came more upon the wind, she felt it more, and we doused the sky-sails, but kept the weather studding-sails on her, bracing the yards forward so that the swinging-boom nearly touched the sprit-sail yard. She now lay over to it, the wind was freshening, and the captain was evidently "dragging on to her." His brother and Mr. R——, looking a little squally, said something to him, but he only answered that he knew the vessel and what she would carry. He was evidently showing off his vessel, and letting them know how he could carry sail. He stood up to windward, holding on by the backstays, and looking up at the sticks, to see how much they would bear; when a puff came which settled the matter. Then it was "haul down," and "clew up," royals, flying-jib, and studding-sails, all at once. There was what the sailors call a "mess"—everything let go, nothing hauled in, and everything flying. The poor Spanish woman came to the companion-way, looking as pale as a ghost, and nearly frightened to death. The mate and some men forward were trying to haul in the lower studding-sail, which had blown over the sprit-sail yard-arm and round the guys; while the topmast-studding-sail boom, after buckling up and springing out again like a piece of whalebone, broke off at the boom-iron. I sprang aloft to take in the main top-gallant studding-sail, but before I got into the top, the tack parted, and away went the sail, swinging forward of the top-gallant-sail, and tearing and slatting itself to pieces. The halyards were at this moment let go by the run; and such a piece of work I never had before, in taking in a sail. After great exertions I got it, or the remains of it, into the top, and was making it fast, when the captain, looking up, called out to me, "Lay aloft there, D——, and furl that main royal." Leaving the studding-sail, I went up to the cross trees; and here it looked rather squally. The foot of the top-gallant-mast was working between the cross and trussel trees, and the royal-mast lay over at a fearful angle with the mast below, while everything was working, and cracking, strained to the utmost.

There's nothing for Jack to do but to obey orders, and I went up upon the yard; and there was a worse "mess," if possible, than I had left below. The braces had been let go, and the yard was swinging about like a turnpike-gate, and the whole sail having blown over to leeward, the lee leach was over the yard-arm, and the sky-sail was all adrift and flying over my head. I looked down, but it was in vain to attempt to make myself heard, for every one was busy below, and the wind roared, and sails were flapping in every direction. Fortunately, it was noon and broad daylight, and the man at the wheel, who had his eyes aloft, soon saw my difficulty, and after numberless signs and gestures, got some one to haul the necessary ropes taut. During this interval I took a look below. Everything was in confusion on deck; the little vessel was tearing through the water as if she were mad, the seas flying over her, and the masts leaning over at an angle of forty-five degrees from the vertical. At the other royal-mast-head was S——, working away at the sail, which was blowing from him as fast as he could gather it in. The top-gallant-sail below me was soon clewed up, which relieved the mast, and in a short time I got my sail furled, and went below; but I lost overboard a new tarpaulin hat, which troubled me more than anything else. We worked for about half an hour with might and main; and in an hour from the time the squall struck us, from having all our flying kites abroad, we came down to double-reefed top-sails and the storm-sails.

The wind had hauled ahead during the squall, and we

**Lay aloft there, D——...** Dana. Possibly reflecting an intent to be discreet or circumspect, 18th and early 19th-century authors often referred to non-fictional characters by an initial, rather than by surname. This device fell out of favor by the mid-19th century, and Dana himself included the full names of characters in his own 1869 edition of *Two Years Before the Mast.*

**...between the cross and trussel trees...** In later editions, Dana changed this to the more modern (and commonly accepted) "trestle trees," meaning two fore-and-aft pieces of timber set on opposite sides of a masthead whose purpose is to support portions of the mast and rigging above.

**There's nothing for Jack to do but to obey orders...** The helplessness of the common seaman (Jack, from "Jack Tar," possibly from the tar used to waterproof tarpaulins or used in sailors' hair to keep it dry) in the face of unfair (and sometimes savagely violent) captains is a recurring theme in Dana's work. Dana eventually came to lead what was, to some extent, a life of advocacy: In his legal practice, political aspirations, and in other published works, Dana worked to represent and defend these oft-mistreated men.

**...forty-five degrees from the vertical.** *Pilgrim* is heeling quite a bit and moving fast. Though not normally dangerous, a 45 degree tilt can make for an uncomfortable sail, and working conditions would be less than optimal.

**At the other royal-mast-head was S——...** Ordinary seaman Benjamin Stimson.

**...with might and main...** Vigorously; with the greatest of possible power or strength. The phrase goes back at least to the 12th century. See Spenser: "Those great warriors, which did ouercomme The world with conquest of their might and maine."

**...the pleasant prospect of beating up to Monterey...** Dana is being sarcastic. Beating (sailing against the wind) is an uncomfortable, tiresome point of sail, and to do it in rough weather for 100 miles (i.e., several days' worth of sailing) is not something to which one would look forward.

**...our fore topmast was sprung...** That is, had been jarred loose or possibly cracked.

**...taking the sun every day at noon.** That is, using a sextant to take readings of the sun in order to determine the vessel's latitude. (Determining longitude with a sextant is also possible, but that would require either an accurate timepiece or lunar sights, which can then be used to determine Greenwich Mean Time; an accurate determination of GMT is necessary in order to find longitude.)

**...what a miserable and forlorn creature a sea-sick passenger is.** Seasickness appears to derive from disturbances in the inner ear. Most people who are prone to it recover within a few days—but it's a very miserable few days.

**...we made the land at Point Pinos...** "Point of the Pines," near what would be present-day Pacific Grove, CA. When Dana was there, the forest grew almost to the water's edge. At the time, these were fairly dangerous waters: Many ships mistook an inlet near the Point for the entrance to Monterey Bay and sailed onto the rocks. Some 20 years after Dana's visit, the town of Pacific Grove would erect what would eventually become the West Coast's oldest continually operating lighthouse there.(Alcatraz Island actually had a lighthouse several months before the Point Pinos lighthouse, but the one at Alcatraz was torn down to make room for expansion of the soon-to-be-famous prison.) At the time of Dana's visit, the land around the point was part of a then-recent 2,667-acre grant from the Mexican government to Jose Maria Armenta.

were standing directly in for the point. So, as soon as we had got all snug, we wore round and stood off again, and had the pleasant prospect of beating up to Monterey, a distance of an hundred miles, against a violent head wind. Before night it began to rain; and we had five days of rainy, stormy weather, under close sail all the time, and were blown several hundred miles off the coast. In the midst of this, we discovered that our fore topmast was sprung, (which no doubt happened in the squall,) and were obliged to send down the fore topgallant-mast and carry as little sail as possible forward. Our four passengers were dreadfully sick, so that we saw little or nothing of them during the five days. On the sixth day it cleared off, and the sun came out bright, but the wind and sea were still very high. It was quite like being at sea again: no land for hundreds of miles, and the captain taking the sun every day at noon. Our passengers now made their appearance, and I had for the first time the opportunity of seeing what a miserable and forlorn creature a sea-sick passenger is. Since I had got over my own sickness, the third day from Boston, I had seen nothing but hale, hearty men, with their sea legs on, and able to go anywhere, (for we had no passengers;) and I will own there was a pleasant feeling of superiority in being able to walk the deck, and eat, and go about, and comparing one's self with two poor, miserable, pale creatures, staggering and shuffling about decks, or holding on and looking up with giddy heads, to see us climbing to the mast-heads, or sitting quietly at work on the ends of the lofty yards. A well man at sea has little sympathy with one who is seasick; he is too apt to be conscious of a comparison favorable to his own manhood. After a few days we made the land at Point Pinos, (pines,) which is the headland at the entrance of the bay of Monterey. As we drew in, and ran down the shore, we could distinguish well the face of the country, and found it better wooded than that to the southward of Point Conception. In fact, as I afterwards discovered, Point Conception may be made the dividing line between two different faces of the country. As you go to the northward of the point, the country becomes more wooded, has a richer appearance, and is better supplied with water. This is the case with Monterey, and still more so with San Francisco; while to the southward of the point, as at Santa Barbara, San Pedro, and particularly San Diego, there is very little wood, and the country has a naked, level appearance, though it is still very fertile.

The bay of Monterey is very wide at the entrance, being about twenty-four miles between the two points, Año Nuevo at the north, and Pinos at the south, but narrows gradually as you approach the town, which is situated in a bend, or large cove, at the south-eastern extremity, and about eighteen miles from the points, which makes the whole depth of the bay. The shores are extremely well wooded, (the pine abounding upon them,) and as it was now the rainy season, everything was as green as nature could make it,—the grass, the leaves, and all; the birds were singing in the woods, and great numbers of wild-fowl were flying over our heads. Here we could lie safe from the south-easters. We came to anchor within two cable lengths of the shore, and the town lay directly before us, making a very pretty appearance; its houses being plastered, which gives a much better effect than those of Santa Barbara, which are of a mud-color. The red tiles, too, on the roofs, contrasted well with the white plastered sides and with the extreme greenness of the lawn upon which the houses—about an hundred in number—were dotted about, here and there, irregularly. There are in this place, and in every other town which I saw in California, no streets, or fences, (except here and there a small patch was fenced in for a garden,) so that the houses are placed at random upon the green, which, as they are of one story and of the cottage form, gives them a pretty effect when seen from a little distance.

It was a fine Saturday afternoon when we came to anchor, the sun about an hour high, and everything looking pleasantly. The Mexican flag was flying from the little square Presidio, and the drums and trumpets of the soldiers, who were out on parade, sounded over the water, and gave great life to the scene. Every one was delighted with the appearance of things. We felt as though we had got into a Christian (which in the sailor's vocabulary means civilized) country. The first impres-

**...a naked, level appearance...** This is largely true: The land around San Diego is mostly desert-like, especially a few miles inland, and has never been heavily forested.

### In the news
### January, 1835

In Springfield, Illinois, the state senate meets to vote for officers. A young lawyer and former militiaman named Abraham Lincoln casts votes for his choices, all of whom are elected. Lincoln had only been elected and confirmed as the representative from Sangamon County the previous August.

**...safe from the south-easters.** A south-easter (or sou'easter) is a large storm typical of the region, which approaches from the southeast. Monterey Bay is broad and well-protected from storms from either north or south, with its only real exposure being to the west.

**...the houses—about an hundred in number...** Today, Monterey is a picturesque community of about 30,000 year-round residents. Although small, Monterey was at the time a bustling port of call, the main port in California, and a town very important to the burgeoning trade in hides and tallow. About 10 years after Dana's visit, the town would become the site of the Battle of Monterey, in which the United States Navy attacked the town during the Mexican American War (1846 to 1848) and claimed Monterey—and all of California—for the U.S.

**...we had got into a Christian (which in the sailor's vocabulary means civilized) country.** Dana's sarcastic remark indicates that he's well aware that, although the typical uneducated sailor might equate Christianity with civilization, such a belief is narrow-minded and . . . well, parochial.

sion which California had made upon us was very disagreeable:—the open roadstead of Santa Barbara; anchoring three miles from the shore; running out to sea before every south-easter; landing in a high surf; with a little dark-looking town, a mile from the beach; and not a sound to be heard, or anything to be seen, but Sandwich Islanders, hides, and tallow-bags. Add to this the gale off Point Conception, and no one can be at a loss to account for our agreeable disappointment in Monterey. Beside all this, we soon learned, which was of no small importance to us, that there was little or no surf here, and this afternoon the beach was as smooth as a duck-pond.

**...our agreeable disappointment in Monterey.** Dana is being witty. "Agreeable disappointment" is both an oxymoron and paradox: He is not at all disappointed to discover that the *Pilgrim* can anchor relatively close to shore and that the crew need not endure the pounding of the surf that they encountered when working off Point Conception.

We landed the agent and passengers, and found several persons waiting for them on the beach, among whom were some, who, though dressed in the costume of the country, spoke English; and who, we afterwards learned, were English and Americans who had married and settled in the country.

**...viz...** Latin for *as follows*.

**...seamanship—sending down a royal-yard.** The royal yard is the sail fourth from the deck of the vessel, so it is a long way up the mast. This is a complicated and difficult task, and Dana acquits himself well.

I also connected with our arrival here another circumstance which more nearly concerns myself; viz, my first act of what the sailors will allow to be seamanship—sending down a royal-yard. I had seen it done once or twice at sea, and an old sailor, whose favor I had taken some pains to gain, had taught me carefully everything which was necessary to be done, and in its proper order, and advised me to take the first opportunity when we were in port, and try it. I told the second mate, with whom I had been pretty thick when he was before the mast, that I would do it, and got him to ask the mate to send me up the first time they were struck. Accordingly I was called upon, and went up, repeating the operations over in my mind, taking care to get everything in its order, for the slightest mistake spoils the whole. Fortunately, I got through without any word from the officer, and heard the "well done" of the mate, when the yard reached the deck, with as much satisfaction as I ever felt at Cambridge on seeing a "bene" at the foot of a Latin exercise.

In the news
**January, 1835**

Iwasaki Yataro is born in Aki, Japan to a family that had once been samurai, but which had now been reduced to relative poverty, with the head of the family forced to work as a clerk. Yataro works his way up in business, and in 1870 he forms a company that specializes in mining and, of all things, shoe repair. The company is called, then and now, Mitsubishi.

**...as much satisfaction as I ever felt at Cambridge on seeing a "bene" at the foot of a Latin exercise.** "Bene" (Latin for good), is what a Latin professor might write at the bottom of a student's test or essay if it were particularly well-done.

## CHAPTER XII

## LIFE AT MONTEREY

The next day being Sunday, which is the liberty-day among merchantmen, when it is usual to let a part of the crew go ashore, the sailors had depended upon a day on land, and were already disputing who should ask to go, when, upon being called in the morning, we were turned-to upon the rigging, and found that the topmast, which had been sprung, was to come down, and a new one to go up, and top-gallant and royal-masts, and the rigging to be set up. This was too bad. If there is anything that irritates sailors and makes them feel hardly used, it is being deprived of their Sabbath. Not that they would always, or indeed generally, spend it religiously, but it is their only day of rest. Then, too, they are often necessarily deprived of it by storms, and unavoidable duties of all kinds, that to take it from them when lying quietly and safely in port, without any urgent reason, bears the more hardly. The only reason in this case was, that the captain had determined to have the custom-house officers on board on Monday, and wished to have his brig in order. Jack is a slave aboard ship; but still he has many opportunities of thwarting and balking his master. When there is danger, or necessity, or when he is well used, no one can work faster than he; but the instant he feels that he is kept at work for nothing, no sloth could make less headway. He must not refuse his duty, or be in any way disobedient, but all the work that an officer gets out of him, he may be welcome to. Every man who has been three months at sea knows how to "work Tom Cox's traverse"—"three turns round the long-boat, and a pull at the scuttled-butt." This morning everything went in this way. "Sogering" was the order of the day. Send a man below to get a block, and he would capsize everything before finding it, then not bring it up till an officer had called him twice, and take as much time to put things in order again. Marline-spikes were not to be found; knives wanted a prodigious deal of sharpening, and, generally, three or four were waiting round the grindstone at a time. When a man got to the mast-head, he would come slowly down again to

**In the news**
**January, 1835**

Juan Maria Osuna is elected the first alcalde (mayor) of tiny San Diego, which village Dana is now visiting. After fighting in the Mexican revolution (in which Mexico won its independence from Spain), Osuna retired as a corporal and served as a minor city official. Prior to Osuna's election as alcalde, the town had been under military rule.

**Not that they would always, or indeed generally, spend it religiously...** Dana is complaining, but also poking fun, noting that although sailors consider this their "Sabbath," most generally spend their day off (as we will see) in decidedly secular pursuits.

**Jack is a slave aboard ship...** This is almost literally true, and it's a recurring theme of Dana's. As he notes, though, even a slave can thwart his master, if he does so cleverly.

**Every man who has been three months at sea knows how to "work Tom Cox's traverse"...** That is, to bustle about wildly, attempting to look busy while accomplishing nothing. (A stratagem still employed today in many offices and at worksites around the world.) That is, to behave as what Dickens called an "artful dodger."

**"Sogering" was the order of the day.** As noted previously, a "soger" (i.e., a soldier) was a lazy good-for-nothing who knew nothing about seamanship. The men are doing their best to pay Captain Thompson back for making them work on a Sunday.

get something which he had forgotten; and after the tackles were got up, six men would pull less than three who pulled "with a will." When the mate was out of sight, nothing was done. It was all uphill work; and at eight o'clock, when we went to breakfast, things were nearly where they were when we began.

**...but that was mutiny...** Any refusal of a direct order was mutiny, punishable by extreme means, up to and including hanging, if the captain felt it was justified. (More typically, the mutineers would instead be thrown in the brig and taken home to stand trial.)

**...the men quoted "Father Taylor"...** The Reverend Edward T. Taylor was the pastor of the seaman's church in Boston.

During our short meal, the matter was discussed. One proposed refusing to work; but that was mutiny, and of course was rejected at once. I remember, too, that one of the men quoted "Father Taylor," (as they call the seamen's preacher at Boston,) who told them that if they were ordered to work on Sunday, they must not refuse their duty, and the blame would not come upon them. After breakfast, it leaked out, through the officers, that if we would get through our work soon, we might have a boat in the afternoon and go fishing. This bait was well thrown, and took with several who were fond of fishing; and all began to find that as we had one thing to do, and were not to be kept at work for the day, the sooner we did it, the better.

In the news
**January, 1835**

Runaway slaves being subject to capture and return to their owners, slaveowners typically posted flyers or ran ads promising rewards for the return of runaway slaves, much as we might post a flyer or run an ad seeking the return of a lost dog or misplaced bracelet. One such notice appeared in a Henrico, Virginia newspaper of the day. It describes a 6-foot tall 20-year-old runaway named Billy, and offers a reward of $20 for his return. That's a fair amount of money, perhaps $500 or so in today's dollars.

Accordingly, things took a new aspect; and before two o'clock this work, which was in a fair way to last two days, was done; and five of us went a fishing in the jolly-boat, in the direction of Point Pinos; but leave to go ashore was refused. Here we saw the Loriotte, which sailed with us from Santa Barbara, coming slowly in with a light sea-breeze, which sets in towards afternoon, having been becalmed off the point all the first part of the day. We took several fish of various kinds, among which cod and perch abounded, and F——, (the ci-devant second mate,) who was of our number, brought up with his hook a large and beautiful pearl-oyster shell. We afterwards learned that this place was celebrated for shells, and that a small schooner had made a good voyage, by carrying a cargo of them to the United States.

**...and F——, (the ci-devant second mate,)...** "F" is George Foster (though Dana consistently spells it "Forster" in other editions), the recently demoted second mate. "Ci-devant" is a French term meaning *former*.

**...found the Loriotte at anchor, within a cable's length of the Pilgrim.** As noted previously, a cable is normally 120 fathoms, or about 720 feet, in length. The *Loriot*, which Dana misspells, was a hermaphrodite brig built in Massachusetts in 1828. Her exact displacement is unknown, but is documented variously as 70, 90, and 96 tons.

We returned by sun-down, and found the Loriotte at anchor, within a cable's length of the Pilgrim. The next day we were "turned-to" early, and began taking off the hatches, overhauling the cargo, and getting everything ready for inspection. At eight, the officers of the customs, five in number, came on board, and began overhauling the cargo, manifest, etc.

The Mexican revenue laws are very strict, and require the whole cargo to be landed, examined, and taken on board again; but our agent, Mr. R——, had succeeded in compounding with them for the two last vessels, and saving the trouble of taking the cargo ashore. The officers were dressed in the costume which we found prevailed through the country. A broad-brimmed hat, usually of a black or dark-brown color, with a gilt or figured band round the crown, and lined inside with silk; a short jacket of silk or figured calico, (the European skirted body-coat is never worn;) the shirt open in the neck; rich waistcoat, if any; pantaloons wide, straight, and long, usually of velvet, velveteen, or broadcloth; or else short breeches and white stockings. They wear the deer-skin shoe, which is of a dark-brown color, and, (being made by Indians,) usually a good deal ornamented. They have no suspenders, but always wear a sash round the waist, which is generally red, and varying in quality with the means of the wearer. Add to this the never-failing cloak, and you have the dress of the Californian. This last garment, the cloak, is always a mark of the rank and wealth of the owner. The "gente de razón," or aristocracy, wear cloaks of black or dark blue broadcloth, with as much velvet and trimmings as may be; and from this they go down to the blanket of the Indian; the middle classes wearing something like a large table-cloth, with a hole in the middle for the head to go through. This is often as coarse as a blanket, but being beautifully woven with various colors, is quite showy at a distance. Among the Mexicans there is no working class; (the Indians being slaves and doing all the hard work;) and every rich man looks like a grandee, and every poor scamp like a broken-down gentleman. I have often seen a man with a fine figure, and courteous manners, dressed in broadcloth and velvet, with a noble horse completely covered with trappings; without a real in his pocket, and absolutely suffering for something to eat.

**...our agent, Mr. R——...** Robinson.

**In the news**
**January, 1835**

Naturalist Charles Darwin, aboard the *Beagle*, anchors off the Chonos Archipelago, near the coast of Chile. He encounters huge numbers of seals, and notes the presence of turkey vultures, which he calls (somewhat oddly for an objective, dispassionate scientist), "this disgusting bird."

**...pantaloons wide, straight, and long...** This is the source of the word *pants*, which was only beginning to come into common usage at the time of Dana's voyage. However, long before the mid-19th century, pantaloons was used to refer to long, close-fitting trousers. The word comes from the style of garment worn by Pantaloon, a character in 14th-century Italian comedy who represented the older generation and who was depicted as a hypocritical, foolish old man.

**The "gente de razón"...** This is a phrase with a somewhat racist history: Literally, it means "people of reason" or "intelligent people." It was applied by the Mexicans to those who spoke Spanish, rather than an Indian language.

**...the Indians being slaves...** Strictly speaking, this is not true, although their freedom was certainly limited by the missionaries for whom they worked. In his 1869 edition of the book, Dana wrote "practically serfs."

**...absolutely suffering for something to eat.** Compare this to someone today spending a small fortune on a fancy car or a cool smart phone so that he can impress his peers, even though he has no money for decent food or living quarters. A real was a small silver coin worth about one-eighth of a dollar—or about 12 cents or so. Keep in mind, though, that $1 in 1835 would be equivalent to over $30 now in terms of consumer prices.

**...fitted up in the steerage...** One of the goals of this voyage was to carry cargo to California, and sell it to the coastal residents. The cargo of pins, cloth, tea, and other goods thus served both as ballast and as a way to help recoup costs. The crew sets up a "store" in steerage, and the locals come aboard to make purchases.

**...M——, a young man who came out from Boston with us...** "M" is Henry Mellus. Having proved his clerking talents, he will remain in California, become a clerk for other ship owners, and ultimately settle in Los Angeles.

In the news
**January, 1835**

Up the coast in San Luis Obispo, Domingo Amador (in his 50s, as near as we can tell from confirmation records) signs on to teach at the local school, which he does from January 1835 to August 1835 for $15 per month. The first primary school had opened in December of 1794 at San Jose. School was held during the early morning and late afternoon, "in order that in the interval the children might aid their parents in the necessary labor of the household or the field."

**The Californians are an idle, thriftless people...** An educated, privileged American, Dana looks down his nose at cultures he believes are inferior and points out examples of what he considers to be the locals' laziness and stupidity. While he seeks to share the lot of the common man, Dana wishes to share only so much and only for so long; he is in fact dismissive of the fate of the common man when those "common men" are natives of other, "lesser" countries. In this, Dana reflects his age's prevailing world-view, one in which white Europeans are presumed to occupy a place at the apex of humanity.

# CHAPTER XIII

## TRADING—A BRITISH SAILOR

The next day, the cargo having been entered in due form, we began trading. The trade-room was fitted up in the steerage, and furnished out with the lighter goods, and with specimens of the rest of the cargo; and M——, a young man who came out from Boston with us, before the mast, was taken out of the forecastle, and made supercargo's clerk. He was well qualified for the business, having been clerk in a counting-house in Boston. He had been troubled for some time with the rheumatism, which unfitted him for the wet and exposed duty of a sailor on the coast. For a week or ten days all was life on board. The people came off to look and to buy—men, women, and children; and we were continually going in the boats, carrying goods and passengers,—for they have no boats of their own. Everything must dress itself and come aboard and see the new vessel, if it were only to buy a paper of pins. The agent and his clerk managed the sales, while we were busy in the hold or in the boats. Our cargo was an assorted one; that is, it consisted of everything under the sun. We had spirits of all kinds, (sold by the cask,) teas, coffee, sugars, spices, raisins, molasses, hardware, crockery-ware, tinware, cutlery, clothing of all kinds, boots and shoes from Lynn, calicoes and cottons from Lowell, crepes, silks; also shawls, scarfs, necklaces, jewelry, and combs for the ladies; furniture; and in fact, everything that can be imagined, from Chinese fire-works to English cart-wheels—of which we had a dozen pairs with their iron rims on.

The Californians are an idle, thriftless people, and can make nothing for themselves. The country abounds in grapes, yet they buy bad wines made in Boston and brought round by us, at an immense price, and retail it among themselves at a real (12½ cents) by the small wine-glass. Their hides, too, which they value at two dollars in money, they give for something which costs seventy-five cents in Boston; and buy shoes (like as not, made of their own hides, and which have been carried twice around Cape Horn) at three or four dollars, and "chicken-skin" boots at fifteen dollars apiece. Things sell, on an average, at an advance of nearly three hundred per cent upon the Boston prices. This is partly owing to the heavy duties which the government, in their wisdom, with the intent, no doubt, of keeping the silver in the country, has laid upon imports. These duties, and the enormous expenses of so long a voyage, keep all merchants, but those of heavy capital, from engaging in the trade. Nearly two-thirds of all the articles imported into the country from round Cape Horn, for the last six years, have been by the single house of Bryant, Sturgis & Co., to whom our vessel belonged, and who have a permanent agent on the coast.

This kind of business was new to us, and we liked it very well for a few days, though we were hard at work every minute from daylight to dark; and sometimes even later.

By being thus continually engaged in transporting passengers with their goods, to and fro, we gained considerable knowledge of the character, dress, and language of the people. The dress of the men was as I have before described it. The women wore gowns of various texture—silks, crape, calicoes, etc.,—made after the European style, except that the sleeves were short, leaving the arm bare, and that they were loose about the waist, having no corsets. They wore shoes of kid, or satin; sashes or belts of bright colors; and almost always a necklace and ear-rings. Bonnets they had none. I only saw one on the coast, and that belonged to the wife of an American sea-captain who had settled in San Diego, and had imported the chaotic mass of straw and ribbon, as a choice present to his new wife. They wear their hair (which is almost invariably black, or a very dark brown) long in their necks, sometimes loose, and sometimes in long braids; though the married women often do it up on a high comb. Their only protection against the sun and weather is a large mantle which they put over their heads, drawing it close round their faces, when they go out of doors, which is generally only in pleasant weather. When in the house, or sitting out in

**...and "chicken-skin" boots...** Oddly, chicken skin really can be used for boots, belts, wallets, and such gear.

**...expenses of so long a voyage, keep all merchants, but those of heavy capital, from engaging in the trade.** Dana bemoans the barriers to entry that keep all but the wealthiest of entrepreneurs from taking part in this sort of trade.

In the news

**January, 1835**

This month's *Baptist Magazine* recounts the receipt of a letter from Baptist ministers in England, requesting that the American church join the British in declaring themselves against slavery. The American Baptists refuse to do so, on the grounds that "we are precluded by our constitution from taking any part in the discussion of the subject...." Instead, they offer a resolution proclaiming that they respect the British members, and that they "earnestly desire a closer intimacy with their Baptist brethren in England." Later, Dana will become a virulent anti-slavery advocate and a tireless campaigner for abolition.

**...gowns of various texture—silks, crape...** Not a misspelling so much as the use of an anglicized version of the perhaps more common *crêpe*. (Itself originally spelled *crespe*.) The word has been in use (and spelled with an "a") since at least the 15th century.

**...the amount of Spanish blood they can lay claim to.** Given that the Spanish conquerors had claimed the country, the more Spanish blood one had, the higher one's station in life.

In the news
**January, 1835**

Now that San Diego is growing and has officially become a pueblo, a new representative, José Antonio Carrillo, is sent to the Mexican Congress. One of the prime issues to be considered by Carrillo and his colleagues is the Mexican government's order that the inhabitants of Alta California be disarmed. This did not sit well with many, especially not the Tejanos (or Texians) who had settled in what would eventually be the U.S. state of Texas; Texans—then and now—were unlikely to have willingly submitted to such an order. The ensuing unrest eventually became a full-fledged rebellion that led to Mexico's war with Texas and the eventual establishment of the Republic of Texas.

**...until you come to the pure Indian, who runs about with nothing upon him but a small piece of cloth...** The Indians—that is, the original inhabitants of the land claimed first by the Spanish and then by Mexico—were at the bottom of the social ladder.

**Yet the least drop of Spanish blood, if it be only of quadroon or octoroon...** A quadroon would be a person with one-fourth (in this case, Spanish) blood; an octoroon is one with one-eighth Spanish blood. At one time, this language was also applied to African-Americans who were partially white. The usage is archaic, and these days the distinction is so meaningless as to be ignored. In years past, though, it was an important determinant of one's social class.

front of it, which they often do in fine weather, they usually wear a small scarf or neckerchief of a rich pattern. A band, also, about the top of the head, with a cross, star, or other ornament in front, is common. Their complexions are various, depending—as well as their dress and manner—upon their rank; or, in other words, upon the amount of Spanish blood they can lay claim to. Those who are of pure Spanish blood, having never intermarried with the aborigines, have clear brunette complexions, and sometimes, even as fair as those of English women. There are but few of these families in California; being mostly those in official stations, or who, on the expiration of their offices, have settled here upon property which they have acquired; and others who have been banished for state offences. These form the aristocracy; inter-marrying, and keeping up an exclusive system in every respect. They can be told by their complexions, dress, manner, and also by their speech; for, calling themselves Castilians, they are very ambitious of speaking the pure Castilian language, which is spoken in a somewhat corrupted dialect by the lower classes. From this upper class, they go down by regular shades, growing more and more dark and muddy, until you come to the pure Indian, who runs about with nothing upon him but a small piece of cloth, kept up by a wide leather strap drawn round his waist. Generally speaking, each person's caste is decided by the quality of the blood, which shows itself, too plainly to be concealed, at first sight. Yet the least drop of Spanish blood, if it be only of quadroon or octoroon, is sufficient to raise them from the rank of slaves, and entitle them to a suit of clothes—boots, hat, cloak, spurs, long knife, and all complete, though coarse and dirty as may be,—and to call themselves Españolos, and to hold property, if they can get any.

The fondness for dress among the women is excessive, and is often the ruin of many of them. A present of a fine mantle, or of a necklace or pair of ear-rings, gains the favor of the greater part of them. Nothing is more common than to see a woman living in a house of only two rooms, and the ground for a floor, dressed in spangled satin shoes, silk gown, high comb, and gilt, if not gold, ear-rings and necklace. If their husbands do not dress them well enough, they will soon receive presents from others. They used to spend whole days on board our vessels, examining the fine clothes and ornaments, and frequently made purchases at a rate which would have made a seamstress or waiting-maid in Boston open her eyes.

**...made purchases at a rate which would have made a seamstress or waiting-maid in Boston open her eyes.** A seamstress, of course, would make volume purchases as required by her business. A waiting-maid would make many purchases (often of costly goods) for the fine lady whom she served.

Next to the love of dress, I was most struck with the fineness of the voices and beauty of the intonations of both sexes. Every common ruffian-looking fellow, with a slouched hat, blanket cloak, dirty under-dress, and soiled leather leggins, appeared to me to be speaking elegant Spanish. It was a pleasure, simply to listen to the sound of the language, before I could attach any meaning to it. They have a good deal of the Creole drawl, but it is varied with an occasional extreme rapidity of utterance, in which they seem to skip from consonant to consonant, until, lighting upon a broad, open vowel, they rest upon that to restore the balance of sound. The women carry this peculiarity of speaking to a much greater extreme than the men, who have more evenness and stateliness of utterance. A common bullock-driver, on horseback, delivering a message, seemed to speak like an ambassador at an audience. In fact, they sometimes appeared to me to be a people on whom a curse had fallen, and stripped them of everything but their pride, their manners, and their voices.

**It was a pleasure, simply to listen to the sound of the language...** In spite of the disdain with which Dana views the inhabitants of California, he is enamored—as many have been—of the romantic, lilting sound of the Spanish language. Of course, then he has to note that they seem "a people on whom a curse had fallen," implying that a beautiful language is about *all* they had.

## In the news
### January, 1835

In San Francisco, which has just been granted status as a pueblo, José Cornelio Bernal requests a grant of "one square league" of land. (Originally, a league was the distance a man could walk in one hour. These days, that's taken to mean about three miles, although the designation is no longer in use.) Since San Francisco has just officially become a city, Governor Fegueroa denies Bernal's petition, ruling that, "...the petition is not granted, as it cannot be given in ownership (en propiedad), but the party interested may keep his cattle there, the same as other citizens do."

Another thing that surprised me was the quantity of silver that was in circulation. I certainly never saw so much silver at one time in my life, as during the week that we were at Monterey. The truth is, they have no credit system, no banks, and no way of investing money but in cattle. They have no circulating medium but silver and hides—which the sailors call "California bank notes." Everything that they buy they must pay for in one or the other of these things. The hides they bring down dried and doubled, in clumsy ox-carts, or upon mules' backs, and the money they carry tied up in a handkerchief;—fifty, eighty, or an hundred dollars and half dollars.

**...they have no credit system, no banks, and no way of investing money...** Another sly and somewhat demeaning reference to the country's lack of culture—in this case, culture in a commercial sense. Dana is saying, in so many words, that these people lack sophistication.

**...I got the name of a great linguist...** Dana is intelligent, educated, and motivated, and has the advantage of understanding English, French, and Latin grammar (and of course, all of these share many cognates with Spanish). When it comes to learning a language, he is a quick study, and this facility for language serves him well aboard ship.

In the news
**January, 1835**

In England, the Whigs—known as social reformers, and thus a party that might have been supported by Dana and his liberal-leaning family—win the general election. Tory Robert Peel remains in office temporarily, at the request of King William IV. (In April, Lord Melbourne, a Whig, takes over as Prime Minister. Melbourne will remain Prime Minister until 1841.)

**...decidedly the pleasantest and most civilized-looking place in California.** In spite of shipping out to escape the cultured confines of Boston, Dana repeatedly makes a big deal out of the lack of sophistication on board and ashore, and also a big deal out of any examples of sophistication he does happen to encounter.

**This is the "Presidio," or fort.** The presidio at Monterey was established in June of 1770, by Captain Don Gaspar de Portola, who commanded the military contingent of Father Junipero Serra's Spanish missionary expedition. The fort was specifically built to defend against attacks by Russians, whom the missionaries felt might attack at any time. (Altogether, the Spanish established 21 missions and four forts.) By the time that Dana visited, the fort was actually looking somewhat dilapidated, since the Mexican government had taken over for the Spaniards in 1822.

I had never studied Spanish while at college, and could not speak a word, when at Juan Fernandez; but during the latter part of the passage out, I borrowed a grammar and dictionary from the cabin, and by a continual use of these, and a careful attention to every word that I heard spoken, I soon got a vocabulary together, and began talking for myself. As I soon knew more Spanish than any of the crew, (who indeed knew none at all,) and had been at college and knew Latin, I got the name of a great linguist, and was always sent for by the captain and officers to get provisions, or to carry letters and messages to different parts of the town. I was often sent to get something which I could not tell the name of to save my life; but I liked the business, and accordingly never pleaded ignorance. Sometimes I managed to jump below and take a look at my dictionary before going ashore; or else I overhauled some English resident on my way, and got the word from him; and then, by signs, and the help of my Latin and French, contrived to get along. This was a good exercise for me, and no doubt taught me more than I should have learned by months of study and reading; it also gave me opportunities of seeing the customs, characters, and domestic arrangements of the people; beside being a great relief from the monotony of a day spent on board ship.

Monterey, as far as my observation goes, is decidedly the pleasantest and most civilized-looking place in California. In the centre of it is an open square, surrounded by four lines of one-story plastered buildings, with half a dozen cannon in the centre; some mounted, and others not. This is the "Presidio," or fort. Every town has a presidio in its centre; or rather, every presidio has a town built around it; for the forts were first built by the Mexican government, and then the people built near them for protection. The presidio here was entirely open and unfortified. There were several officers with long titles, and about eighty soldiers, but they were poorly paid, fed, clothed, and disciplined. The governor-general, or, as he is commonly called, the "general," lives here; which makes it the seat of government. He is appointed by the central government at Mexico, and is the chief civil and military officer. In addition to him, each town has a commandant, who is the chief military officer, and has charge of the fort, and of all transactions with foreigners and foreign vessels; and two or three alcaldes and corregidores, elected by the inhabitants, who are the civil officers. Courts and jurisprudence they have no knowledge of. Small municipal matters are regulated by the alcaldes and corregidores; and everything relating to the general government, to the military, and to foreigners, by the commandants, acting under the governor-general. Capital cases are decided by him, upon personal inspection, if he is near; or upon minutes sent by the proper officers, if the offender is at a distant place. No Protestant has any civil rights, nor can he hold any property, or, indeed, remain more than a few weeks on shore, unless he belong to some vessel. Consequently, the Americans and English who intend to remain here become Catholics, to a man; the current phrase among them being,—"A man must leave his conscience at Cape Horn."

**...alcaldes and corregidores...** Mayors and municipal administrators or judges.

**"A man must leave his conscience at Cape Horn."** That is, in California, one must become Catholic for the sake of convenience, whatever one's actual beliefs. One critic has noted that Dana somewhat overstates the religious/political situation in California, commenting that it was quite possible for Protestants to remain in the region, so long as they did not intend to become naturalized citizens.

But to return to Monterey. The houses here, as everywhere else in California, are of one story, built of clay made into large bricks, about a foot and a half square and three or four inches thick, and hardened in the sun. These are cemented together by mortar of the same material, and the whole are of a common dirt-color. The floors are generally of earth, the windows grated and without glass; and the doors, which are seldom shut, open directly into the common room; there being no entries. Some of the more wealthy inhabitants have glass to their windows and board floors; and in Monterey nearly all the houses are plastered on the outside. The better houses, too, have red tiles upon the roofs. The common ones have two or three rooms which open into each other, and are furnished with a bed or two, a few chairs and tables, a looking-glass, a crucifix of some material or other, and small daubs of paintings enclosed in glass, and representing some miracle or martyrdom. They have no chimneys or fire-places in the houses, the climate being such as to make a fire unnecessary; and all their cooking is done in a small cook-house, separated from the house. The Indians, as I have said before, do all the hard work, two or three

**...large bricks, about a foot and a half square and three or four inches thick, and hardened in the sun.** Probably not simply clay, but what we would call—and what the Mexicans called—*adobe*. Adobe is a mixture of mud and clay, sand, water, and some kind of fibrous material (hay, straw, etc.) used as a binder. Adobe is quite durable, and some of the oldest buildings in the world are made of it.

**...windows grated and without glass...** Windows without glass were not uncommon at the time, especially in mild climates. Glass panes existed, of course, but were fragile and expensive; purchasing glass windows and having them shipped around the Horn was very expensive, and only the wealthiest could afford to do so.

**...two or three rooms which open into each other...** Dana makes this arrangement sound a bit unsophisticated—as if having a larger number of enclosed rooms (as had many homes in New England) would be better. In fact, though, having larger, airy rooms that opened onto one another is an advantage in temperate climates, the better to provide adequate light and good ventilation.

being attached to each house; and the poorest persons are able to keep one, at least, for they have only to feed them and give them a small piece of coarse cloth and a belt, for the males; and a coarse gown, without shoes or stockings, for the females.

In Monterey there are a number of English and Americans (English or "Ingles" all are called who speak the English language) who have married Californians, become united to the Catholic church, and acquired considerable property. Having more industry, frugality, and enterprise than the natives, they soon get nearly all the trade into their hands. They usually keep shops, in which they retail the goods purchased in larger quantities from our vessels, and also send a good deal into the interior, taking hides in pay, which they again barter with our vessels. In every town on the coast there are foreigners engaged in this kind of trade, while I recollect but two shops kept by natives. The people are generally suspicious of foreigners, and they would not be allowed to remain, were it not that they become good Catholics, and by marrying natives, and bringing up their children as Catholics and Mexicans, and not teaching them the English language, they quiet suspicion, and even become popular and leading men. The chief alcaldes in Monterey and Santa Barbara were both Yankees by birth.

The men in Monterey appeared to me to be always on horseback. Horses are as abundant here as dogs and chickens were in Juan Fernandez. There are no stables to keep them in, but they are allowed to run wild and graze wherever they please, being branded, and having long leather ropes, called "lassos," attached to their necks and dragging along behind them, by which they can be easily taken. The men usually catch one in the morning, throw a saddle and bridle upon him, and use him for the day, and let him go at night, catching another the next day. When they go on long journeys, they ride one horse down, and catch another, throw the saddle and bridle upon him, and after riding him down, take a third, and so on to the end of the journey. There are probably no better riders in the world. They get

In the news
**January, 1835**

As Dana is visiting the West Coast, Prof. Thomas Nuttall, having completed his journey along the Oregon Trail, arrives at the Sandwich Islands (i.e., Hawaii). Nuttall and Dana are acquainted, and will eventually return to Boston together.

**Having more industry, frugality, and enterprise than the natives...** One doubts that *all* "Ingles" were truly more industrious and frugal than the natives, but Dana rarely misses a chance to portray the local populace as lazy bumpkins, inferior in every way to the white European stock from which Dana himself springs. In spite of his very genuine sympathies for the underdog, Dana is after all a product of his times.

**The chief alcaldes in Monterey and Santa Barbara were both Yankees by birth.** As mentioned, an alcalde was equivalent to a mayor. In Monterey, Scotsman David Spence was Monterey's alcalde at the time. In Santa Barbara, oddly enough, the alcalde in 1836 was Dana's cousin, William Goodwin Dana. Odder still, Dana never mentions him in the book.

**Horses are as abundant here as dogs and chickens...** Certainly true, and quite interesting, given that domesticated horses were completely unknown in North America until the Spanish conquest; it is generally accepted that the vast herds of horses that wandered the Great Plains originated from animals that had escaped from the Spanish. (One reason that the Spaniards were able to conquer the native Aztecs and Incas only about 300 years prior to Dana's voyage was that many of the natives were terrified of the huge animals ridden by the Spaniards. Of course, the fact that the Spanish also possessed armor and firearms also helped the invaders' cause.)

upon a horse when only four or five years old, their little legs not long enough to come half way over his sides; and may almost be said to keep on him until they have grown to him. The stirrups are covered or boxed up in front, to prevent their catching when riding through the woods; and the saddles are large and heavy, strapped very tight upon the horse, and have large pommels, or loggerheads, in front, round which the "lasso" is coiled when not in use. They can hardly go from one house to another without getting on a horse, there being generally several standing tied to the door-posts of the little cottages. When they wish to show their activity, they make no use of their stirrups in mounting, but striking the horse, spring into the saddle as he starts, and sticking their long spurs into him, go off on the full run. Their spurs are cruel things, having four or five rowels, each an inch in length, dull and rusty. The flanks of the horses are often sore from them, and I have seen men come in from chasing bullocks with their horses' hind legs and quarters covered with blood. They frequently give exhibitions of their horsemanship, in races, bull-baitings, etc.; but as we were not ashore during any holyday, we saw nothing of it. Monterey is also a great place for cock-fighting, gambling of all sorts, fandangos, and every kind of amusement and knavery. Trappers and hunters, who occasionally arrive here from over the Rocky mountains, with their valuable skins and furs, are often entertained with every sort of amusement and dissipation, until they have wasted their time and their money, and go back, stripped of everything.

Nothing but the character of the people prevents Monterey from becoming a great town. The soil is as rich as man could wish; climate as good as any in the world; water abundant, and situation extremely beautiful. The harbor, too, is a good one, being subject only to one bad wind, the north; and though the holding-ground is not the best, yet I heard of but one vessel's being driven ashore here. That was a Mexican brig, which went ashore a few months before our arrival, and was a total wreck, all the crew but one being drowned. Yet this was from the carelessness or ignorance of the cap-

**and have large pommels...** A pommel is a knob at the front of a saddle that provides the rider with a handgrip.

**They can hardly go from one house to another without getting on a horse...** There is a wonderful but completely unintended irony here, given that 150 years later people would say the same thing about Californians and their cars.

**Their spurs are cruel things, having four or five rowels...** A rowel is a small spiked wheel on a spur. Neither a native word nor an English one, *spur* comes from Anglo-Saxon via Medieval High German. The word is quite old, appearing in recognizable form as far back as AD 725.

**Monterey is also a great place for cock-fighting, gambling of all sorts, fandangos...** Not surprisingly, no mention is made of cock-fighting and "knavery" in the official history of this very old city. (Monterey was founded in 1770). "Knavery" is lying, cheating, or stealing—that is, something a knave (a deceitful scoundrel) might do. A fandango is a lively dance.

**...every sort of amusement and dissipation...** Dissipation is an indulgence in sensual pleasure. In other words, says Dana, the trappers threw away their money on liquor, women, and gambling, and often went home penniless. Later in the book, Dana will make similar observations about his sailor colleagues, but will remain silent about any of his own indulgences.

**...was a total wreck...** The brig *Natalia*, with a crew of 13 men, went down at Monterey in December of 1834. Some records contradict Dana's version of the story, indicating that only three people were killed when *Natalia* beached about two miles north of the town. While some sources say that this is the same vessel on which Napoleon Bonaparte escaped confinement at Elba in 1815, more reliable records say that the ship Napoleon used to return to France was the *Inconstant*.

tain, who paid out all his small cable before he let go his other anchor. The ship Lagoda, of Boston, was there at the time, and rode out the gale in safety, without dragging at all, or finding it necessary to strike her top-gallant masts.

**In the news**
**January, 1835**

Some things never change. This month at Ft. Nisqually (in what is now Tacoma, WA), the diary kept by the commander notes, somewhat petulantly, that it rained 21 out of 31 days. He also notes that their hunters killed during the year 46 bears, 1038 beavers, and 700 rats.

The only vessel in port with us was the little Loriotte. I frequently went on board her, and became very well acquainted with her Sandwich Island crew. One of them could speak a little English, and from him I learned a good deal about them. They were well formed and active, with black eyes, intelligent countenances, dark-olive, or, I should rather say, copper complexions and coarse black hair, but not woolly like the negroes. They appeared to be talking continually. In the forecastle there was a complete Babel. Their language is extremely guttural, and not pleasant at first, but improves as you hear it more, and is said to have great capacity. They use a good deal of gesticulation, and are exceedingly animated, saying with their might what their tongues find to say. They are complete water-dogs, therefore very good in boating. It is for this reason that there are so many of them on the coast of California; they being very good hands in the surf. They are also quick and active in the rigging, and good hands in warm weather; but those who have been with them round Cape Horn, and in high latitudes, say that they are useless in cold weather. In their dress they are precisely like our sailors. In addition to these Islanders, the vessel had two English sailors, who acted as boatswains over the Islanders, and took care of the rigging. One of them I shall always remember as the best specimen of the thoroughbred English sailor that I ever saw. He had been to sea from a boy, having served a regular apprenticeship of seven years, as all English sailors are obliged to do, and was then about four or five and twenty. He was tall; but you only perceived it when he was standing by the side of others, for the great breadth of his shoulders and chest made him appear but little above the middle height. His chest was as deep as it was wide; his arm like that of Hercules; and his hand "the fist of a tar—every hair a rope-yarn." With all this he had one of the pleasantest smiles I ever saw. His cheeks were of a

**It is for this reason that there are so many of them on the coast of California; they being very good hands in the surf.** It is by watching the Sandwich Islanders (i.e., Hawaiians) that *Pilgrim*'s crew learns how to safely and efficiently carry hides through the surf to their waiting boat, and then to transfer the hides from the boat to their ship.

**...the best specimen of the thoroughbred English sailor...** Several critics have remarked upon the fact that Dana singles out this sailor and describes him almost as one would describe a Greek god. (Hercules himself being a mythical Greek figure.) One writer notes, "One might think that after months at sea, the sight of Spanish senoritas would rouse in Dana some dream of feminine beauty," but he (and later, Melville) instead spend much more time on descriptions of manly beauty. In fact, it's very possible that Dana's description of sailor Bill Jackson influenced Herman Melville, who would some 50 years later write (but not yet publish) *Billy Budd*, a novella about a (perhaps Christ-like?) sailor who is the epitome of manly beauty, maritime skill, and dignified goodness.

handsome brown; his teeth brilliantly white; and his hair, of a raven black, waved in loose curls all over his head, and fine, open forehead; and his eyes he might have sold to a duchess at the price of diamonds, for their brilliancy. As for their color, they were like the Irishman's pig, which would not stay to be counted, every change of position and light seemed to give them a new hue; but their prevailing color was black, or nearly so. Take him with his well-varnished black tarpaulin stuck upon the back of his head; his long locks coming down almost into his eyes; his white duck trowsers and shirt; blue jacket; and black kerchief, tied loosely round his neck; and he was a fine specimen of manly beauty. On his broad chest he had stamped with India ink "Parting moments;"—a ship ready to sail; a boat on the beach; and a girl and her sailor lover taking their farewell. Underneath were printed the initials of his own name, and two other letters, standing for some name which he knew better than I did. This was very well done, having been executed by a man who made it his business to print with India ink, for sailors, at Havre. On one of his broad arms, he had the crucifixion, and on the other the sign of the "foul anchor."

**...he had stamped with India ink...** That is, he was tattooed. "India ink," however, was probably invented not in India, but in China. Some components, however, may indeed have come from India, and the ink itself has been in use in India since about the 4th century BC, thus giving rise to the term.

In the news

**January, 1835**

In Salem, only a few miles from Dana's home town of Boston, the trinitarian (and teetotalling) Rev. George Cheever publishes the satirical "Inquire at Deacon Giles' Distillery," aimed at Unitarian deacon (and distillery owner) John Stone. The publication causes a furor, and Cheever is beaten by one of Stone's foremen, then found guilty of libel and jailed.

He was very fond of reading, and we lent him most of the books which we had in the forecastle, which he read and returned to us the next time we fell in with him. He had a good deal of information, and his captain said he was a perfect seaman, and worth his weight in gold on board a vessel, in fair weather and in foul. His strength must have been great, and he had the sight of a vulture. It is strange that one should be so minute in the description of an unknown, outcast sailor, whom one may never see again, and whom no one may care to hear about; but so it is. Some people we see under no remarkable circumstances, but whom, for some reason or other, we never forget. He called himself Bill Jackson; and I know no one of all my accidental acquaintances to whom I would more gladly give a shake of the hand than to him. Whoever falls in with him will find a handsome, hearty fellow, and a good shipmate.

**...the "foul anchor."** A popular naval insignia depicting an anchor with a chain wrapped around it—that is, an anchor that has been fouled.

**...he had the sight of a vulture.** Dana continues his catalog of Jackson's manly and endearing attributes.

**...It is strange that one should be so minute in the description of an unknown, outcast sailor...** Dana is correct: It is strange that an author should, out of nowhere, devote this much space (over 540 words) to describing a sailor from another ship, and one whom Dana will in all likelihood never see again.

**....it brought us no holyday.** Dana is complaining (again) about the lack of liberty on a Sunday. Note the spelling: The word "holiday" does indeed mean a "holy day"—originally a day of religious observance, marked by a festival. Yet, it was not spelled "holyday" until the 16th century, though it was in use long before that time.

**Our cidevant second mate...** George Foster, the former second mate, now demoted. A rash, ill-tempered young man lacking in common sense. Dressing for liberty before it is granted is imprudent, presumptuous, rude, and not at all customary. (Cidevant means "from before.")

**...if there was a wrong way of doing a thing, was sure to hit upon it.** We've all known people like this—perhaps this even describes us, at one time or another. With Foster, this seems to be his normal mode of operation.

**The captain took two or three turns...** That is, two or three walks around the deck.

**What the captain said to him, we never could get him to tell...** Considering that the captain—and this captain was notoriously short-tempered and tyrannical—held something very close to the power of life and death over Foster, it's not surprising that he could have quite an effect on the man.

Sunday came again while we were at Monterey, but as before, it brought us no holyday. The people on shore dressed themselves and came off in greater numbers than ever, and we were employed all day in boating and breaking out cargo, so that we had hardly time to eat. Our cidevant second mate, who was determined to get liberty if it was to be had, dressed himself in a long coat and black hat, and polished his shoes, and went aft and asked to go ashore. He could not have done a more imprudent thing; for he knew that no liberty would be given; and besides, sailors, however sure they may be of having liberty granted them always go aft in their working clothes, to appear as though they had no reason to expect anything, and then wash, dress, and shave, after they get their liberty. But this poor fellow was always getting into hot water, and if there was a wrong way of doing a thing, was sure to hit upon it. We looked to see him go aft, knowing pretty well what his reception would be. The captain was walking the quarter-deck, smoking his morning cigar, and F—— went as far as the break of the deck, and there waited for him to notice him. The captain took two or three turns, and then walking directly up to him, surveyed him from head to foot, and lifting up his forefinger, said a word or two, in a tone too low for us to hear, but which had a magical effect upon poor F——. He walked forward, sprang into the forecastle, and in a moment more made his appearance in his common clothes, and went quietly to work again. What the captain said to him, we never could get him to tell, but it certainly changed him outwardly and inwardly in a most surprising manner.

## CHAPTER XIV

## SANTA BARBARA—HIDE-DROGHING—HARBOR DUTIES—DISCONTENT—SAN PEDRO

After a few days, finding the trade beginning to slacken, we hove our anchor up, set our topsails, ran the stars and stripes up to the peak, fired a gun, which was returned from the Presidio, and left the little town astern, running out of the bay, and bearing down the coast again, for Santa Barbara. As we were now going to leeward, we had a fair wind and a plenty of it. After doubling Point Pinos, we bore up, set studding-sails alow and aloft, and were walking off at the rate of eight or nine knots, promising to traverse in twenty-four hours the distance which we were nearly three weeks in traversing on the passage up. We passed Point Conception at a flying rate, the wind blowing so that it would have seemed half a gale to us, if we had been going the other way and close hauled. As we drew near the islands off Santa Barbara, it died away a little but we came-to at our old anchoring-ground in less than thirty hours from the time of leaving Monterey.

**...finding the trade beginning to slacken...** Recall that the *Pilgrim* carried with her from Boston many items to be sold to the coastal Californians. After selling what they could at Point Conception, the ship now heads for Santa Barbara.

**...fired a gun, which was returned from the Presidio...** The ship fires a gun in salute, and the fort at Monterey answers with its own salute.

**As we were now going to leeward...** Heading south from Monterey toward Santa Barbara (a total distance of about 240 nautical miles), *Pilgrim* was heading more or less in the direction the wind was blowing. For a brig rigged mainly with square sails, this is a fairly efficient point of sail. For some other rigs (a sloop, for instance), sailing straight downwind is (somewhat counter-intuitively) not its fastest point of sail.

**...it would have seemed half a gale to us, if we had been going the other way and close hauled.** Beating, or sailing close-hauled so as to sail as nearly as possible into the wind, is a very rough point of sail.

Here everything was pretty much as we left it—the large bay without a vessel in it; the surf roaring and rolling in upon the beach; the white mission; the dark town and the high, treeless mountains. Here, too, we had our south-easter tacks aboard again,—slip-ropes, buoy-ropes, sails furled with reefs in them, and rope-yarns for gaskets. We lay here about a fortnight, employed in landing goods and taking off hides, occasionally, when the surf was not high; but there did not appear to be one-half the business doing here that there was in Monterey. In fact, so far as we were concerned, the town might almost as well have been in the middle of the Cordilleras. We lay at a distance of three miles from the beach, and the town was nearly a mile farther; so that we saw little or nothing of it. Occasionally we landed a few goods, which were taken away by Indians in large, clumsy ox-carts, with the yoke on the ox's neck instead of under it, and with small solid wheels. A few hides were brought down, which we carried off in

**We lay here about a fortnight, employed in landing goods and taking off hides...** The ship spends about two weeks at Santa Barbara, selling goods and purchasing hides.

**...the town might almost as well have been in the middle of the Cordilleras.** That is, there was so little business that the town felt as if it were in another country. (A cordillera is a mountain range near a coastline; Dana could be referring specifically to the Southern Pacific Cordilleras, a mountain range in the Philippines, or to the ranges that run through North America and into Central and South America.)

the California style. This we had now got pretty well accustomed to; and hardened to also; for it does require a little hardening even to the toughest.

**...then we rake them upon our heads, one at a time, or two, if they are small, and wade out with them and throw them into the boat...** This is dangerous, backbreaking work, and there are several months of it ahead. Dana and his shipmates discover that there is no easy way to accomplish the task of hauling hides out to the boat, and from there to the ship. The hides must be kept dry, so placing them on one's head is the only way to get them to the boat, even though the hides are heavy and unwieldy.

The hides are always brought down dry, or they would not be received. When they are taken from the animal, they have holes cut in the ends, and are staked out, and thus dried in the sun without shrinking. They are then doubled once, lengthwise, with the hair side usually in, and sent down, upon mules or in carts, and piled above highwater mark; and then we rake them upon our heads, one at a time, or two, if they are small, and wade out with them and throw them into the boat, which as there are no wharves, we are usually kept anchored by a small kedge, or keelek, just outside of the surf. We all provided ourselves with thick Scotch caps, which would be soft to the head, and at the same time protect it; for we soon found that however it might look or feel at first the "head-work" was the only system for California. For besides that the seas, breaking high, often obliged us to carry the hides so, in order to keep them dry, we found that, as they were very large and heavy, and nearly as stiff as boards, it was the only way that we could carry them with any convenience to ourselves. Some of the crew tried other expedients, saying that they looked too much like West India negroes; but they all came to it at last. The great art is in getting them on the head. We had to take them from the ground, and as they were often very heavy, and as wide as the arms could stretch and easily taken by the wind, we used to have some trouble with them. I have often been laughed at myself, and joined in laughing at others, pitching themselves down in the sand, trying to swing a large hide upon their heads, or nearly blown over with one in a little gust of wind. The captain made it harder for us, by telling us that it was "California fashion" to carry two on the head at a time; and as he insisted upon it, and we did not wish to be outdone by other vessels, we carried two for the first few months; but after falling in with a few other "hide-droghers," and finding that they carried only one at a time we "knocked off" the extra one, and thus made our duty somewhat easier.

In the news
**January, 1835**

Near Cape Town, South Africa, an uprising of Xhosa natives results in retaliatory attacks and then in an outright war that lasts until the following September. The treaty signed in that month stipulates that the Xhosa are British citizens. The Xhosa are forced to relinquish some 60,000 head of cattle as partial payment for the cattle and sheep stolen by the tribe during the hostilities.

**falling in with a few other "hide-droghers,"...** A hide-drogher is a coastal vessel engaged in the hide trade—or those who practiced such a trade. A drogher is a coastal trading vessel of whatever sort.

**...finding that they carried only one at a time we "knocked off" the extra one...** The captain may have misled the men in an attempt to get more work out of them. Given Thompson's temperament, this sort of deception would not be at all surprising.

After we had got our heads used to the weight, and had learned the true California style of tossing a hide, we could carry off two or three hundred in a short time, without much trouble; but it was always wet work, and, if the beach was stony, bad for our feet; for we, of course, always went barefooted on this duty, as no shoes could stand such constant wetting with salt water. Then, too, we had a long pull of three miles, with a loaded boat, which often took a couple of hours.

We had now got well settled down into our harbor duties, which, as they are a good deal different from those at sea, it may be well enough to describe. In the first place, all hands are called at daylight, or rather—especially if the days are short—before daylight, as soon as the first grey of the morning. The cook makes his fire in the galley; the steward goes about his work in the cabin; and the crew rig the head pump, and wash down the decks. The chief mate is always on deck, but takes no active part, all the duty coming upon the second mate, who has to roll up his trowsers and paddle about decks barefooted, like the rest of the crew. The washing, swabbing, squilgeeing, etc., lasts, or is made to last, until eight o'clock, when breakfast is ordered, fore and aft. After breakfast, for which half an hour is allowed, the boats are lowered down, and made fast astern, or out to the swinging booms, by ges-warps, and the crew are turned-to upon their day's work. This is various, and its character depends upon circumstances. There is always more or less of boating, in small boats; and if heavy goods are to be taken ashore, or hides are brought down to the beach for us, then all hands are sent ashore with an officer in the long boat. Then there is always a good deal to be done in the hold: goods to be broken out; and cargo to be shifted, to make room for hides, or to keep the trim of the vessel. In addition to this, the usual work upon the rigging must be done. There is a good deal of the latter kind of work which can only be done when the vessel is in port;—and then everything must be kept taut and in good order; spun-yarn made; chafing gear repaired; and all the other ordinary work. The great difference between sea and harbor duty is in the division of time. Instead of having a

In the news

**January, 1835**

In Germany, at the time still just a loosely joined confederation of states, steelmaker Alfred Krupp returns from a tour to show off his first marketable product: a strong, weldable steel that can be formed into precision tools almost impervious to wear and breakage. The product will enable his company to become perhaps the 20th century's best-known arms manufacturer and the chief supplier of weaponry to Hitler's Third Reich.

**The washing, swabbing, squilgeeing...** Using what we would now call a squeegee.

**...out to the swinging booms, by ges-warps...** Today these would be called "guess-warps"—ropes used to tie up the end of a boat to a wharf. In some cases, any rope used to attach a boat to the stern of a vessel. Like most nautical terms, this one is very old, going back at least to the 15th century. Also known as a "guest-rope": a rope thrown from one vessel to another for towing or to enable the second vessel to tie up alongside the first.

**...cargo to be shifted, to make room for hides, or to keep the trim of the vessel.** Keep in mind the commercial nature of *Pilgrim*'s voyage: Part of her original ballast was in the form of goods to be sold in California. As those are sold, they're replaced in the holds with hides that are literally squeezed in. The constant exchange and movement of cargo must be accounted for and the ship kept correctly trimmed, because at any moment (say, if a storm should arise) she may have to head to sea for safety.

**...an "anchor-watch" is kept...** A detachment of the crew kept on deck and charged with the safety of the ship as she lies at anchor.

**...except in the binnacle...** The box (often on a pedestal, and generally near the helm) in which the compass is placed.

**Some religious captains give their crews Saturday afternoons to do their washing and mending in, so that they may have their Sundays free. This is a good arrangement, and does much toward creating the preference sailors usually show for religious vessels.** An important point that Dana takes care to note. Allowing the men to attend to personal duties on Saturday not only makes for a more contented crew, but one that is more godly and perhaps more likely to attend worship on the following Sunday. (Or at least we can assume that is the claim to be made by sailors seeking a berth with such a captain. Regardless, Captain Thompson, of course, is not about to allow his crew two full days off.)

**...uncertainty, which hung over the nature and length of our voyage.** The voyage—and Dana did not realize this at the time he signed on—was essentially open-ended. It might last one year, or two, or three, or more. It would end when *Pilgrim* had collected enough hides, and Captain Thompson (not a man Dana trusted) would be the one to decide when that would be.

watch on deck and a watch below, as at sea, all hands are at work together, except at meal times, from daylight till dark; and at night an "anchor-watch" is kept, which consists of only two at a time; the whole crew taking turns. An hour is allowed for dinner, and at dark, the decks are cleared up; the boats hoisted; supper ordered; and at eight, the lights put out, except in the binnacle, where the glass stands; and the anchor-watch is set. Thus, when at anchor, the crew have more time at night, (standing watch only about two hours,) but have no time to themselves in the day; so that reading, mending clothes, etc., has to be put off until Sunday, which is usually given. Some religious captains give their crews Saturday afternoons to do their washing and mending in, so that they may have their Sundays free. This is a good arrangement, and does much toward creating the preference sailors usually show for religious vessels. We were well satisfied if we got Sunday to ourselves, for, if any hides came down on that day, as was often the case when they were brought from a distance, we were obliged to bring them off, which usually took half a day; and as we now lived on fresh beef, and ate one bullock a week, the animal was almost always brought down on Sunday, and we had to go ashore, kill it, dress it, and bring it aboard, which was another interruption. Then, too, our common day's work was protracted and made more fatiguing by hides coming down late in the afternoon, which sometimes kept us at work in the surf by star-light, with the prospect of pulling on board, and stowing them all away, before supper.

But all these little vexations and labors would have been nothing,—they would have been passed by as the common evils of a sea-life, which every sailor, who is a man, will go through without complaint,—were it not for the uncertainty, or worse than uncertainty, which hung over the nature and length of our voyage. Here we were, in a little vessel, with a small crew, on a half-civilized coast, at the ends of the earth, and with a prospect of remaining an indefinite period, two or three years at the least. When we left Boston we supposed that it was to be a voyage of eighteen months, or two years, at most; but upon arriving on the coast, we learned something more of the trade, and found that in the scarcity of hides, which was yearly greater and greater, it would take us a year, at least, to collect our own cargo, beside the passage out and home; and that we were also to collect a cargo for a large ship belonging to the same firm, which was soon to come on the coast, and to which we were to act as tender. We had heard rumors of such a ship to follow us, which had leaked out from the captain and mate, but we passed them by as mere "yarns," till our arrival, when they were confirmed by the letters which we brought from the owners to their agent. The ship California, belonging to the same firm, had been nearly two years on the coast; had collected a full cargo, and was now at San Diego, from which port she was expected to sail in a few weeks for Boston; and we were to collect all the hides we could, and deposit them at San Diego, when the new ship, which would carry forty thousand, was to be filled and sent home; and then we were to begin anew, and collect our own cargo. Here was a gloomy prospect before us, indeed. The California had been twenty months on the coast, and the Lagoda, a smaller ship, carrying only thirty-one or thirty-two thousand, had been two years getting her cargo; and we were to collect a cargo of forty thousand beside our own, which would be twelve or fifteen thousand; and hides were said to be growing scarcer. Then, too, this ship, which had been to us a worse phantom than any flying Dutchman, was no phantom, or ideal thing, but had been reduced to a certainty; so much so that a name was given her, and it was said that she was to be the Alert, a well-known India-man, which was expected in Boston in a few months, when we sailed. There could be no doubt, and all looked black enough. Hints were thrown out about three years and four years;—the older sailors said they never should see Boston again, but should lay their bones in California; and a cloud seemed to hang over the whole voyage. Besides, we were not provided for so long a voyage, and clothes, and all sailors' necessaries, were excessively dear—three or four hundred per cent. advance upon the Boston prices. This was bad enough for them; but still worse was it for me, who did not mean to be a sailor for life; having intended only to be gone eighteen

**...the scarcity of hides, which was yearly greater and greater...** Note that even as early as 1835, hides are getting more difficult to come by. As time passes, hide droghers will have to range farther and farther afield in order to collect enough hides to make their voyages worthwhile.

**...a cargo for a large ship belonging to the same firm...** The larger ship will turn out to be the *Alert*—the ship on which Dana will return to Boston.

**...we passed them by as mere "yarns,"...** We're used to thinking of "stories" (especially "tall tales") as yarns, no matter the tale's source. But used in this sense, the word is nautical in origin, going back to the early 1800s. It may have to do with an earlier usage in which, in some dialects, a "yarn" was a fisherman's net. (Which in turn may have derived from an Old English term meaning "strong.")

**Here was a gloomy prospect before us, indeed.** Dana is bemoaning the fact that, if *Pilgrim* suddenly becomes a mere tender (that is, a supply and provisioning vessel) for the much larger *Alert*, the voyage could be extended by years.

**... a worse phantom than any flying Dutchman...** As noted earlier, the *Flying Dutchman* is a legendary ghost ship, condemned to forever sail the sea.

**...a well-known India-man...** That is, a merchant ship used in trade (for spices and other goods) with India.

**...we were not provided for so long a voyage...** This is not idle whining: Consider how long your clothes might last under normal circumstances. A year for a pair of jeans? Two years for a jacket, maybe? Now think about how long they'd last if you were constantly engaged in hard physical labor aboard a ship. Clothes and gear will wear out quickly aboard ship, and there are no nearby stores.

**Three or four years would make me a sailor in every respect, mind and habits, as well as body—nolens volens...** This is a constant worry of Dana's: that he will become so accustomed to a sailor's life that any other sort of life, including the privileged and intellectually stimulating life he led in Boston, would be lost to him. He wants to be a sailor—"one of the guys"—but not forever. (*Nolens volens* is Latin for "willy-nilly," or, in this context, "willingly or unwillingly.")

**...to be master of a vessel, must be the height of my ambition.** If he does end up a sailor for life, he could perhaps become a ship's captain, but that would be the extent of his life's accomplishments. (Of course, one could do much worse than to be the captain of a ship, although Dana doesn't seem to see it that way.)

**We lost all interest in the voyage...** The morale of the men is suffering terribly under Captain Thompson's tyrannical rule.

In the news

**January, 1835**

We are accustomed to living amidst complaints that cities and states (and indeed the federal government) have spent unwisely and are therefore now saddled with burdensome debt. However, this has long been the case, and a January 1835 address by Boston's mayor (Theodore Lyman, Jr.) complains that the city is now spending more than it earns, partly due to expenditures on improvements to streets, a new city wharf, and for costs related to fighting a city-wide cholera epidemic. He notes, "We bequeath to our children a debt created for purposes concerning which they cannot . . . be consulted."

months or two years. Three or four years would make me a sailor in every respect, mind and habits, as well as body—nolens volens; and would put all my companions so far ahead of me that college and a profession would be in vain to think of; and I made up my mind that, feel as I might, a sailor I must be, and to be master of a vessel, must be the height of my ambition.

Beside the length of the voyage, and the hard and exposed life, we were at the ends of the earth; on a coast almost solitary; in a country where there is neither law nor gospel, and where sailors are at their captain's mercy, there being no American consul, or any one to whom a complaint could be made. We lost all interest in the voyage; cared nothing about the cargo, which we were only collecting for others; began to patch our clothes; and felt as though we were fixed beyond all hope of change.

In addition to, and perhaps partly as a consequence of, this state of things, there was trouble brewing on board the vessel. Our mate (as the first mate is always called, par excellence) was a worthy man;—a more honest, upright, and kind-hearted man I never saw; but he was too good for the mate of a merchantman. He was not the man to call a sailor a "son of a b—-h," and knock him down with a handspike. He wanted the energy and spirit for such a voyage as ours, and for such a captain. Captain T—— was a vigorous, energetic fellow. As sailors say, "he hadn't a lazy bone in him." He was made of steel and whalebone. He was a man to "toe the mark," and to make every one else step up to it. During all the time that I was with him, I never saw him sit down on deck. He was always active and driving; severe in his discipline, and expected the same of his officers. The mate not being enough of a driver for him, and being perhaps too easy with the crew, he was dissatisfied with him, became suspicious that discipline was getting relaxed, and began to interfere in everything. He drew the reins tauter; and as, in all quarrels between officers, the sailors side with the one who treats them best, he became suspicious of the crew. He saw that everything went wrong—that nothing was done "with a will;" and in his attempt to remedy the difficulty by severity, he made everything worse. We were in every respect unfortunately situated. Captain, officers, and crew, entirely unfitted for one another; and every circumstance and event was like a two-edged sword, and cut both ways. The length of the voyage, which made us dissatisfied, made the captain, at the same time, feel the necessity of order and strict discipline; and the nature of the country, which caused us to feel that we had nowhere to go for redress, but were entirely at the mercy of a hard master, made the captain feel, on the other hand, that he must depend entirely upon his own resources. Severity created discontent, and signs of discontent provoked severity. Then, too, ill-treatment and dissatisfaction are no "linimenta laborum;" and many a time have I heard the sailors say that they should not mind the length of the voyage, and the hardships, if they were only kindly treated, and if they could feel that something was done to make things lighter and easier. We felt as though our situation was a call upon our superiors to give us occasional relaxations, and to make our yoke easier. But the contrary policy was pursued. We were kept at work all day when in port; which, together with a watch at night, made us glad to turn-in as soon as we got below. Thus we got no time for reading, or—which was of more importance to us—for washing and mending our clothes. And then, when we were at sea, sailing from port to port, instead of giving us "watch and watch," as was the custom on board every other vessel on the coast, we were all kept on deck and at work, rain or shine, making spun-yarn and rope, and at other work in good weather, and picking oakum, when it was too wet for anything else. All hands were called to "come up and see it rain," and kept on deck hour after hour in a drenching rain, standing round the deck so far apart as to prevent our talking with one another, with our tarpaulins and oil-cloth jackets on, picking old rope to pieces, or laying up gaskets and robands. This was often done, too, when we were lying in port with two anchors down, and no necessity for more than one man on deck as a look-out. This is what is called "hazing" a crew, and "working their old iron up."

**...nothing was done "with a will;"...** That is, the captain begins to believe that the crew is shirking.

**...entirely unfitted for one another; and every circumstance and event was like a two-edged sword, and cut both ways.** By this time, everyone is at everyone else's throats, the captain is suspicious of both officers and crew, and the situation is becoming untenable. Spending the next year (or two or three) on this ship with this crew begins to seem like a horror.

**...Severity created discontent, and signs of discontent provoked severity.** This is a vicious cycle, and one that Thompson does not know how (or perhaps feel the need) to break: The men do not respond well to severe treatment, so they are unhappy and troublesome, which causes the captain to react even more harshly.

**..."linimenta laborum;"...** Latin for "liniments for labor"—that is, something to make the work more enjoyable.

**...if they were only kindly treated...** *Two Years Before the Mast* is a quest and a sea-yarn, and also a coming-of-age story. But it is also an explication of the merchantman's lot and a call to improve the situation of the men who labor "before the mast." That is a recurring theme of the book, and something to which Dana will (much to his credit) devote himself for the rest of his life.

**...instead of giving us "watch and watch," as was the custom...** That is, four hours on and four off.

**...kept on deck hour after hour in a drenching rain...** Thompson is hazing the crew: harassing them by forcing them to stand on deck and do make-work and other distasteful (and perhaps unnecessary) tasks.

**...covering the mountain, and hanging down over the town, appearing almost to rest upon the roofs of the houses.** On occasion, Dana reminds us that he can be a fine writer, with a touch of the poet in him.

**...we found ourselves drifted nearly ten leagues from the anchorage...** A league is roughly three miles—or in this case, three nautical miles. *Pilgrim* has drifted nearly 30 miles.

**...our orders were to stop at an intermediate port called San Pedro...** Because of its location, its accessibility, and its fine weather, San Pedro quickly became the most important port on the coast. In 1909, the Port of San Pedro will become part of Los Angeles, but keep in mind that at the time of Dana's visit, the port—and in fact, all of California—is part of Mexico.

**...instead of shipping some hands to make our work easier...** Adding another officer when *Pilgrim* is so shorthanded is probably not a good management move, at least, not from the perspective of those who are working so hard to make up for the lack of manpower. The men feel that they have plenty of officers; they would much prefer an additional sailor or two.

**...appearing level or moderately uneven...** Critic and editor John Haskell Kemble has noted that Dana's description of the coast between San Pedro and Santa Barbara is somewhat inaccurate. With a few exceptions, the coast in that area consists of steep cliffs that drop down almost to the water's edge. Then again, Dana is (as mentioned earlier) working mostly from memory, having lost most of his notes.

While lying at Santa Barbara, we encountered another south-easter; and, like the first, it came on in the night; the great black clouds coming round from the southward, covering the mountain, and hanging down over the town, appearing almost to rest upon the roofs of the houses. We made sail, slipped our cable, cleared the point, and beat about, for four days, in the offing, under close sail, with continual rain and high seas and winds. No wonder, thought we, they have no rain in the other seasons, for enough seemed to have fallen in those four days to last through a common summer. On the fifth day it cleared up, after a few hours, as is usual, of rain coming down like a four hours' shower-bath, and we found ourselves drifted nearly ten leagues from the anchorage; and having light head winds, we did not return until the sixth day. Having recovered our anchor, we made preparations for getting under weigh to go down to leeward. We had hoped to go directly to San Diego, and thus fall in with the California before she sailed for Boston; but our orders were to stop at an intermediate port called San Pedro, and as we were to lie there a week or two, and the California was to sail in a few days, we lost the opportunity. Just before sailing, the captain took on board a short, red-haired, round-shouldered, vulgar-looking fellow, who had lost one eye, and squinted with the other, and introducing him as Mr. Russell, told us that he was an officer on board. This was too bad. We had lost overboard, on the passage, one of the best of our number, another had been taken from us and appointed clerk, and thus weakened and reduced, instead of shipping some hands to make our work easier, he had put another officer over us, to watch and drive us. We had now four officers, and only six in the forecastle. This was bringing her too much down by the stern for our comfort.

Leaving Santa Barbara, we coasted along down, the country appearing level or moderately uneven, and, for the most part, sandy and treeless; until, doubling a high, sandy point, we let go our anchor at a distance of three or three and a half miles from shore. It was like a vessel, bound to Halifax, coming to anchor on the Grand Banks; for the shore being low, appeared to be at a greater distance than it actually was, and we thought we might as well have staid at Santa Barbara, and sent our boat down for the hides. The land was of a clayey consistency, and, as far as the eye could reach, entirely bare of trees and even shrubs; and there was no sign of a town,—not even a house to be seen. What brought us into such a place, we could not conceive. No sooner had we come to anchor, than the slip-rope, and the other preparations for south-easters, were got ready; and there was reason enough for it, for we lay exposed to every wind that could blow, except the north-west, and that came over a flat country with a range of more than a league of water. As soon as everything was snug on board, the boat was lowered, and we pulled ashore, our new officer, who had been several times in the port before, taking the place of steersman. As we drew in, we found the tide low, and the rocks and stones, covered with kelp and sea-weed, lying bare for the distance of nearly an eighth of a mile. Picking our way barefooted over these, we came to what is called the landing-place, at high-water mark. The soil was as it appeared at first, loose and clayey, and except the stalks of the mustard plant, there was no vegetation. Just in front of the landing, and immediately over it, was a small hill, which, from its being not more than thirty or forty feet high, we had not perceived from our anchorage. Over this hill we saw three men coming down, dressed partly like sailors and partly like Californians; one of them having on a pair of untanned leather trowsers and a red baize shirt. When they came down to us, we found that they were Englishmen, and they told us that they had belonged to a small Mexican brig which had been driven ashore here in a south-easter, and now lived in a small house just over the hill. Going up this hill with them, we saw, just behind it, a small, low building, with one room, containing a fire-place, cooking apparatus, etc., and the rest of it unfinished, and used as a place to store hides and goods. This, they told us, was built by some traders in the Pueblo, (a town about thirty miles in the interior, to which this was the port,) and used by them as a storehouse, and also as a lodging place when they came down to trade with the vessels. These three men were employed by them to keep the house in order,

In the news

**January, 1835**

John Ablewhite, a Boston harness maker and wheelwright finds himself in court in London, England, having been arrested for insolvency. In 1835, debtors' prisons were still common in Europe, in spite of the fact that someone imprisoned for failure to pay a debt was obviously unable to make enough money while in prison to pay the debt. In the U.S. (where Ablewhite probably should have stayed), debtors' prisons had been outlawed in 1833.

**...a red baize shirt.** Baize is a soft fabric made of wool. It looks like (and is often called) felt, but it's neither as fine nor as soft as true felt.

**...a small Mexican brig which had been driven ashore...** The brig *Fazio*, with a crew of 11 men, went ashore at San Pedro shortly before Dana's arrival. (Bancroft's *History of California* notes that *Pilgrim* "rescued" *Fazio*. It's difficult to credit this meeting as any sort of rescue, but see a later note.)

**...the Pueblo, (a town about thirty miles in the interior, to which this was the port,) and used by them as a storehouse...** The "Pueblo" (village) to which Dana refers is El Pueblo de Nuestra Señora la Reina de los Ángeles del Río de Porciúncula (The Town of Our Lady the Queen of the Angels of the Porciúncula River): That is, the sleepy Mexican village that would eventually become Los Angeles, California. At the time, though, the population of Los Angeles was only about 1000.

**...peculiar kind of bean...** At the time, "peculiar" was commonly used to mean special or particular. Only more recently did the word take on the sense of *odd*.

In the news

**January, 1835**

A small British publisher prints a 500-copy edition of Alexis de Tocqueville's *Democracy in America*. An aristocratic Frenchman, de Tocqueville traveled America in 1831, taking notes and writing commentary about the new country's political institutions. Many historians believe that the book is still one of the most insightful examinations of the American systems of justice and politics ever written.

**...having a large house there...** A so-called "hide house." Dana would spend many months stationed at his agent's hide house.

**...smoking ship...** A form of fumigation in which fires are built on board to create smoke that kills or drives out vermin such as rats, cockroaches, scorpions, etc.

In the news

**January, 1835**

The first of some 50 "Crockett Almanacs" appears, purportedly written or authorized by Crockett or "his heirs," and recounting the life of the famous frontiersman. The pamphlets contain many tall tales about Crockett, Kit Carson, and other such figures. Crockett will die at The Alamo in 1836.

**...Pueblo de los Angelos...** The short name for the "City of Angels"—Los Angeles. (Note that, even with only 1000 inhabitants, it was said to be the largest town in California.)

and to look out for the things stored in it. They said that they had been there nearly a year; had nothing to do most of the time, living upon beef, hard bread, and frijoles (a peculiar kind of bean very abundant in California). The nearest house, they told us, was a Rancho, or cattle-farm, about three miles off; and one of them went up, at the request of our officer, to order a horse to be sent down, with which the agent, who was on board, might go up to the Pueblo. From one of them, who was an intelligent English sailor, I learned a good deal, in a few minutes' conversation, about the place, its trade, and the news from the southern ports. San Diego, he said, was about eighty miles to the leeward of San Pedro; that they had heard from there, by a Mexican who came up on horseback, that the California had sailed for Boston, and that the Lagoda, which had been in San Pedro only a few weeks before, was taking in her cargo for Boston. The Ayacucho was also there, loading for Callao, and the little Loriotte, which had run directly down from Monterey, where we left her. San Diego, he told me, was a small, snug place, having very little trade, but decidedly the best harbor on the coast, being completely land-locked, and the water as smooth as a duck-pond. This was the depot for all the vessels engaged in the trade; each one having a large house there, built of rough boards, in which they stowed their hides, as fast as they collected them in their trips up and down the coast, and when they had procured a full cargo, spent a few weeks there, taking it in, smoking ship, supplying wood and water, and making other preparations for the voyage home. The Lagoda was now about this business. When we should be about it, was more than I could tell; two years, at least, I thought to myself.

I also learned, to my surprise, that the desolate-looking place we were in was the best place on the whole coast for hides. It was the only port for a distance of eighty miles, and about thirty miles in the interior was a fine plane country, filled with herds of cattle, in the centre of which was the Pueblo de los Angelos—the largest town in California—and several of the wealthiest missions; to all of which San Pedro was the sea-port.

Having made our arrangements for a horse to take the agent to the Pueblo the next day, we picked our way again over the green, slippery rocks, and pulled aboard. By the time we reached the vessel, which was so far off that we could hardly see her, in the increasing darkness, the boats were hoisted up, and the crew at supper. Going down into the forecastle, eating our supper, and lighting our cigars and pipes, we had, as usual, to tell all we had seen or heard ashore. We all agreed that it was the worst place we had seen yet, especially for getting off hides, and our lying off at so great a distance looked as though it was bad for south-easters. After a few disputes as to whether we should have to carry our goods up the hill, or not, we talked of San Diego, the probability of seeing the Lagoda before she sailed, etc., etc.

The next day we pulled the agent ashore, and he went up to visit the Pueblo and the neighboring missions; and in a few days, as the result of his labors, large ox-carts, and droves of mules, loaded with hides, were seen coming over the flat country. We loaded our long-boat with goods of all kinds, light and heavy, and pulled ashore. After landing and rolling them over the stones upon the beach, we stopped, waiting for the carts to come down the hill and take them; but the captain soon settled the matter by ordering us to carry them all up to the top, saying that, that was "California fashion." So what the oxen would not do, we were obliged to do. The hill was low, but steep, and the earth, being clayey and wet with the recent rains, was but bad holding-ground for our feet. The heavy barrels and casks we rolled up with some difficulty, getting behind and putting our shoulders to them; now and then our feet slipping, added to the danger of the casks rolling back upon us. But the greatest trouble was with the large boxes of sugar. These, we had to place upon oars, and lifting them up rest the oars upon our shoulders, and creep slowly up the hill with the gait of a funeral procession. After an hour or two of hard work, we got them all up, and found the carts standing full of hides, which we had to unload, and also to load again with our own goods; the lazy Indians, who came down with them, squatting down on their hams, looking on, doing nothing, and

**...so far off that we could hardly see her...** In those days, the harbor at San Pedro was quite shallow, with mud flats; ships were obliged to anchor several miles out.

In the news
**January, 1835**

Chicago's "fire-bucket ordinance" requires every occupant of a store or dwelling "to have one good painted leather fire-bucket, with the initials of the owner's name painted thereon" for each fireplace or stove in the building. About 20 years later, the city's first real fire department is formed. None of this does any good at all when the city erupts in flames on October 8th,1871. The fire, which was *not* started by a cow belonging to a Mrs. O'Leary, kills hundreds and destroys several square miles of the city.

**...as the result of his labors...** Making all the business arrangements is one of the jobs of an owner's agent. In this case, the agent (Alfred Robinson) purchases the raw hides and has them readied for treatment and transport.

In the news
**January, 1835**

Olympia Brown is born in Prairie Ronde, Michigan. Her mother, to encourage her daughters' education, decrees that they need not do housework if they were studying. Soon after her graduation in 1863, Brown was ordained by the Northern Universalist Association, the first ordination of a woman by any regularly constituted American denomination. In 1866 Brown was invited to the founding convention of the Equal Rights Association.

**...shaking their heads, or drawling out "no quiero."** That is, "I don't want [to]."

**...covered with dust, and our clothes torn**. This is very difficult, dangerous work, and the crew can look forward to much more of the same.

In the news
**January, 1835**

The *Texas Republican* is published at Brazoria, Texas, just west of Galveston and south of Houston. A subscription costs $5 per year. One ad in a Nov. issue notes an auction at which visitors could bid on the estate of a recently deceased citizen. The estate included, "5 likely young Negro Men, 1 boy about 17 years of age, 200 cows, 3 horses, 1 likely gentle male, 180 heads of hogs, 1 silver watch, 1 box of silver smith's tools, 1 rifle, 1 shot gun...."

**...a violent blow...** That is, a storm. Since the wind was coming from the shore, *Pilgrim* was not in danger of being driven ashore.

**...ship-shape and Bristol fashion...** That is, clean, organized, and in order. Ship-shape means "stowed neatly as required, and ready for sea or for homecoming." The term "Bristol fashion" may have derived from the fact that ships at Bristol (an ancient seaport in England) were at one time careened (beached and left lying on their sides) whenever the tide went out. Thus, the ships—and everything on and in them—had to be well-designed and strongly made. Ships were often careened in order to clean the hull or make repairs.

**...everything above the cross-trees was left to us...** Stimson and Dana, two of the youngest of the crew, have proven themselves able sailors and are now entrusted with tasks requiring skill and experience.

when we asked them to help us, only shaking their heads, or drawling out "no quiero."

Having loaded the carts, we started up the Indians, who went off, one on each side of the oxen, with long sticks, sharpened at the end, to punch them with. This is one of the means of saving labor in California;—two Indians to two oxen. Now, the hides were to be got down; and for this purpose, we brought the boat round to a place where the hill was steeper, and threw them down, letting them slide over the slope. Many of them lodged, and we had to let ourselves down and set them agoing again; and in this way got covered with dust, and our clothes torn. After we had got them all down, we were obliged to take them on our heads, and walk over the stones, and through the water, to the boat. The water and the stones together would wear out a pair of shoes a day, and as shoes were very scarce and very dear, we were compelled to go barefooted. At night, we went on board, having had the hardest and most disagreeable day's work that we had yet experienced. For several days, we were employed in this manner, until we had landed forty or fifty tons of goods, and brought on board about two thousand hides; when the trade began to slacken, and we were kept at work, on board, during the latter part of the week, either in the hold or upon the rigging. On Thursday night, there was a violent blow from the northward, but as this was off-shore, we had only to let go our other anchor and hold on. We were called up at night to send down the royal-yards. It was as dark as a pocket, and the vessel pitching at her anchors, I went up to the fore, and my friend S——, to the main, and we soon had them down "ship-shape and Bristol fashion," for, as we had now got used to our duty aloft, everything above the cross-trees was left to us, who were the youngest of the crew, except one boy.

CHAPTER XV

## A FLOGGING—A NIGHT ON SHORE—THE STATE OF THINGS ON BOARD—SAN DIEGO

For several days the captain seemed very much out of humor. Nothing went right, or fast enough for him. He quarrelled with the cook, and threatened to flog him for throwing wood on deck; and had a dispute with the mate about reeving a Spanish burton; the mate saying that he was right, and had been taught how to do it by a man who was a sailor! This, the captain took in dudgeon, and they were at sword's points at once. But his displeasure was chiefly turned against a large, heavy-moulded fellow from the Middle States, who was called Sam. This man hesitated in his speech, and was rather slow in his motions, but was a pretty good sailor, and always seemed to do his best; but the captain took a dislike to him, thought he was surly, and lazy; and "if you once give a dog a bad name"—as the sailor-phrase is—"he may as well jump overboard." The captain found fault with everything this man did, and hazed him for dropping a marline-spike from the main-yard, where he was at work. This, of course, was an accident, but it was set down against him. The captain was on board all day Friday, and everything went on hard and disagreeably. "The more you drive a man, the less he will do," was as true with us as with any other people. We worked late Friday night, and were turned-to early Saturday morning. About ten o'clock the captain ordered our new officer, Russell, who by this time had become thoroughly disliked by all the crew, to get the gig ready to take him ashore. John, the Swede, was sitting in the boat alongside, and Russell and myself were standing by the main hatchway, waiting for the captain, who was down in the hold, where the crew were at work, when we heard his voice raised in violent dispute with somebody, whether it was with the mate, or one of the crew, I could not tell; and then came blows and scuffling. I ran to the side and beckoned to John, who came up, and we leaned down the hatchway; and though we could see no one, yet we knew that the captain had the advantage, for his voice was loud and clear—

**...reeving a Spanish burton...** To reeve is to pass the end of a line through something, such as a block-and-tackle. Not surprisingly, a Spanish burton is a particular arrangement of block-and-tackle.

**This, the captain took in dudgeon...** That is, with anger or resentment. (Then again, the mate saying that he'd been taught "by a sailor"—implying that the captain was not a true sailor—was quite offensive.)

**... large, heavy-moulded fellow from the Middle States...** Samuel Sparks was a 25-year-old seaman from Virginia. The implication here is that Sam was a bit slow, but the captain took that as a sign of laziness.

In the news
**January, 1835**

After most of the Seminole Indian chiefs renounce the terms of the proposed Treaty of Payne's Landing (which would have forced them to move west and to live with or near their much unloved Creek cousins), the Second Seminole War begins with the murder by Seminole Chief Osceola of Indian Agent Wiley Thompson and the ambush of American soldiers near Fort King. The natives retreat into the Everglades and spend the next seven years waging a guerrilla campaign. The war is a bitter one (as most are), and in this case, even some of the soldiers feel that it is unjustified. Says one officer: "The government is in the wrong, and this is the chief cause of the persevering opposition of the Indians, who have nobly defended their country against our attempt to enforce a fraudulent treaty. The natives used every means to avoid a war, but were forced into it by the tyranny of our government."

### In the news
### January, 1835

Patterned after a Haitian slave revolt, the (failed) Malê Revolt is perhaps the most significant slave rebellion in Brazil. On a Sunday during Ramadan in January 1835, in the city of Salvador da Bahia, a group of black slaves and freedmen, mostly African Muslims, rebel against the government. Many consider this rebellion to be the turning point of slavery in Brazil. Although slavery itself existed for more than fifty years after the revolt, the slave trade was abolished in 1851.

**"I never have been, sir," said Sam.** Sam simply cannot make himself promise to stop doing something he feels he has never done in the first place, so he stubbornly refuses to submit to the captain.

**Seize that man up, Mr. A——! Seize him up!** Mr. A is Andrew B. Amazeen, the first mate. To "seize him up" is to bind him with rope.

### In the news
### January, 1835

Writer William Seton is born in New York City. While in Europe around 1886 he becomes interested in science and begins making yearly trips to Paris, where he comes to know scientists Albert Gaudry and Albert de Lapparent. His first published work is a novel, *Nat Gregory*, followed by other novels and a book of poems, but he is most famous for popularizing of the theory of evolution currently being formulated by Charles Darwin as he sails on the *Beagle*.

"You see your condition! You see your condition! Will you ever give me any more of your jaw?" No answer; and then came wrestling and heaving, as though the man was trying to turn him. "You may as well keep still, for I have got you," said the captain. Then came the question, "Will you ever give me any more of your jaw?"

"I never gave you any, sir," said Sam; for it was his voice that we heard, though low and half choked.

"That's not what I ask you. Will you ever be impudent to me again?"

"I never have been, sir," said Sam.

"Answer my question, or I'll make a spread eagle of you! I'll flog you, by G—d."

"I'm no negro slave," said Sam.

"Then I'll make you one," said the captain; and he came to the hatchway, and sprang on deck, threw off his coat, and rolling up his sleeves, called out to the mate—"Seize that man up, Mr. A——! Seize him up! Make a spread eagle of him! I'll teach you all who is master aboard!"

The crew and officers followed the captain up the hatchway, and after repeated orders the mate laid hold of Sam, who made no resistance, and carried him to the gangway.

"What are you going to flog that man for, sir?" said John, the Swede, to the captain.

Upon hearing this, the captain turned upon him, but knowing him to be quick and resolute, he ordered the steward to bring the irons, and calling upon Russell to help him, went up to John.

"Let me alone," said John. "I'm willing to be put in

irons. You need not use any force;" and putting out his hands, the captain slipped the irons on, and sent him aft to the quarter-deck. Sam by this time was seized up, as it is called, that is, placed against the shrouds, with his wrists made fast to the shrouds, his jacket off, and his back exposed. The captain stood on the break of the deck, a few feet from him, and a little raised, so as to have a good swing at him, and held in his hand the bight of a thick, strong rope. The officers stood round, and the crew grouped together in the waist. All these preparations made me feel sick and almost faint, angry and excited as I was. A man—a human being, made in God's likeness—fastened up and flogged like a beast! A man, too, whom I had lived with and eaten with for months, and knew almost as well as a brother. The first and almost uncontrollable impulse was resistance. But what was to be done? The time for it had gone by. The two best men were fast, and there were only two beside myself, and a small boy of ten or twelve years of age. And then there were (beside the captain) three officers, steward, agent and clerk. But beside the numbers, what is there for sailors to do? If they resist, it is mutiny; and if they succeed, and take the vessel, it is piracy. If they ever yield again, their punishment must come; and if they do not yield, they are pirates for life. If a sailor resist his commander, he resists the law, and piracy or submission are his only alternatives. Bad as it was, it must be borne. It is what a sailor ships for. Swinging the rope over his head, and bending his body so as to give it full force, the captain brought it down upon the poor fellow's back. Once, twice—six times. "Will you ever give me any more of your jaw?" The man writhed with pain, but said not a word. Three times more. This was too much, and he muttered something which I could not hear; this brought as many more as the man could stand; when the captain ordered him to be cut down, and to go forward.

"Now for you," said the captain, making up to John and taking his irons off. As soon as he was loose, he ran forward to the forecastle. "Bring that man aft," shouted the captain. The second mate, who had been a shipmate of John's, stood still in the waist, and the mate walked

**...the captain slipped the irons on...** The captain now has both John and Sam in custody.

**...the bight of a thick, strong rope.** A bight is a bend or a loop.

**...fastened up and flogged like a beast!** Dana abhors cruelty in any form. Not surprisingly, in later years he became something of an abolitionist, representing many fugitive slaves as they fought their return to slavery under the (1850) Fugitive Slave Act, which required the return of runaway slaves. Under the law, slaves had no right to a jury trial, nor were they allowed to testify on their own behalf. Some sources say that Dana refused all fees for his antislavery work.

**...what is there for sailors to do? If they resist, it is mutiny; and if they succeed, and take the vessel, it is piracy.** A key point in Dana's treatise: The law is on the side of the captain and officers. When Dana graduates from law school, he will set up a law practice largely devoted to defending men such as this.

In the news

**February, 1835**

An ad for the period touts a $1.50 medicinal preparation made "solely from vegetable matter" which purports to cure "Dyspepsia, Loss of Appetite, Indigestion, Inflamation of the Stomach, Heart Burn, Diarrhea, Dysentary or Flux, Piles, Fistula, Obstructed Menstruation, Ague," and other conditions, including "excessive gas."

**...The second mate, who had been a shipmate of John's, stood still in the waist...** Neither the first nor the second mates want any part of this, but they're bound to obey orders. The other officer, however, is eager to endear himself to the captain. The waist is the part of the vessel's upper deck between the fore- and main-masts.

slowly forward; but our third officer, anxious to show his zeal, sprang forward over the windlass, and laid hold of John; but he soon threw him from him. At this moment I would have given worlds for the power to help the poor fellow; but it was all in vain. The captain stood on the quarter-deck, bare-headed, his eyes flashing with rage, and his face as red as blood, swinging the rope, and calling out to his officers, "Drag him aft!—Lay hold of him! I'll sweeten him!" etc., etc. The mate now went forward and told John quietly to go aft; and he, seeing resistance in vain, threw the blackguard third mate from him; said he would go aft of himself; that they should not drag him; and went up to the gangway and held out his hands; but as soon as the captain began to make him fast, the indignity was too much, and he began to resist; but the mate and Russell holding him, he was soon seized up. When he was made fast, he turned to the captain, who stood turning up his sleeves and getting ready for the blow, and asked him what he was to be flogged for. "Have I ever refused my duty, sir? Have you ever known me to hang back, or to be insolent, or not to know my work?"

"No," said the captain, "it is not that that I flog you for; I flog you for your interference—for asking questions."

"Can't a man ask a question here without being flogged?"

"No," shouted the captain; "nobody shall open his mouth aboard this vessel, but myself;" and began laying the blows upon his back, swinging half round between each blow, to give it full effect. As he went on, his passion increased, and he danced about the deck, calling out as he swung the rope,—"If you want to know what I flog you for, I'll tell you. It's because I like to do it!—because I like to do it!—It suits me! That's what I do it for!"

The man writhed under the pain, until he could endure it no longer, when he called out, with an exclamation more common among foreigners than with us—"Oh, Jesus Christ! Oh, Jesus Christ!"

**In the news**
**February, 1835**

A museum in Baltimore, Maryland advertises that it offers for patrons' viewing a "cameleopard" (i.e., a giraffe), which it says is "the only one in this country." Admission is usually 25 cents, except during "extraordinary exhibitions," when it is raised to 50 cents.

**I'll sweeten him!** That is, make him more agreeable.

**...nobody shall open his mouth aboard this vessel...** The captain is now clearly enraged and irrational.

**In the news**
**January, 1835**

Joseph Smith, founder of the Mormon church, calls a meeting of church leaders, telling them that he had spoken to God and was told that Jesus would return within the next 56 years. This is the latest in a long line of doomsday scenarios announced seemingly every year, not just by members of Christian religions, but also by practitioners of other religions and philosophies.

**It's because I like to do it!** The captain admits that he enjoys flogging his crew, that he does it because he can, and because it gives him pleasure.

"Don't call on Jesus Christ," shouted the captain; "he can't help you. Call on Captain T——, he's the man! He can help you! Jesus Christ can't help you now!"

At these words, which I never shall forget, my blood ran cold. I could look on no longer. Disgusted, sick, and horror-struck, I turned away and leaned over the rail, and looked down into the water. A few rapid thoughts of my own situation, and of the prospect of future revenge, crossed my mind; but the falling of the blows and the cries of the man called me back at once. At length they ceased, and turning round, I found that the mate, at a signal from the captain had cut him down. Almost doubled up with pain, the man walked slowly forward, and went down into the forecastle. Every one else stood still at his post, while the captain, swelling with rage and with the importance of his achievement, walked the quarter-deck, and at each turn, as he came forward, calling out to us,—"You see your condition! You see where I've got you all, and you know what to expect!"—"You've been mistaken in me—you didn't know what I was! Now you know what I am!"—"I'll make you toe the mark, every soul of you, or I'll flog you all, fore and aft, from the boy, up!"—"You've got a driver over you! Yes, a slave-driver—a negro-driver! I'll see who'll tell me he isn't a negro slave!" With this and the like matter, equally calculated to quiet us, and to allay any apprehensions of future trouble, he entertained us for about ten minutes, when he went below. Soon after, John came aft, with his bare back covered with stripes and wales in every direction, and dreadfully swollen, and asked the steward to ask the captain to let him have some salve, or balsam, to put upon it. "No," said the captain, who heard him from below; "tell him to put his shirt on; that's the best thing for him; and pull me ashore in the boat. Nobody is going to lay-up on board this vessel." He then called to Mr. Russell to take those men and two others in the boat, and pull him ashore. I went for one. The two men could hardly bend their backs, and the captain called to them to "give way," "give way!" but finding they did their best, he let them alone. The agent was in the stern sheets, but during the

**Call on Captain T——, he's the man!** Captain Thompson has gone over the edge, reveling in his power and in his ability to make the men suffer. This whole exchange is a bit reminiscent of Herman Wouk's *The Caine Mutiny*. At one point, Queeg, the crazed captain in that novel, says, "Some misguided sailors on this ship still think they can pull a fast one on me. Well, they're very much mistaken. Since you've taken this course, the innocent will be punished with the guilty. There will be no liberty for any member of this crew for three months. I will not be made a fool of! Do you hear me?" At another point, the *Caine*'s captain says: "Aboard my ship, excellent performance is standard, standard performance is substandard, and sub-standard performance is not permitted to exist—that, I warn you."

**...swelling with rage and with the importance of his achievement...** Dana is being sarcastic; the captain has achieved little, other than making the men hate him even more. Fear does motivate, but it is not an effective long-term management technique.

**Nobody is going to lay-up on board this vessel.** Captain Thompson refuses to allow John to dress his wounds. To "lay up" a ship is to take it out of service. Thompson is saying that no one on board (including the wounded John Linden) will be allowed to slack off.

**The agent was in the stern sheets...** The owner's agent, Alfred Robinson, watched the whole episode from the stern sheets—an area near the stern of the open boat—without trying to stop the captain. (Keep in mind, though, that on board a ship, the captain's word truly was law; there was little that Robinson could have done, even if he had wanted to.)

whole pull—a league or more—not a word was spoken. We landed; the captain, agent, and officer went up to the house, and left us with the boat. I, and the man with me, staid near the boat, while John and Sam walked slowly away, and sat down on the rocks. They talked some time together, but at length separated, each sitting alone. I had some fears of John. He was a foreigner, and violently tempered, and under suffering; and he had his knife with him, and the captain was to come down alone to the boat. But nothing happened; and we went quietly on board. The captain was probably armed, and if either of them had lifted a hand against him, they would have had nothing before them but flight, and starvation in the woods of California, or capture by the soldiers and Indian blood-hounds, whom the offer of twenty dollars would have set upon them.

After the day's work was done, we went down into the forecastle, and ate our plain supper; but not a word was spoken. It was Saturday night; but there was no song—no "sweethearts and wives." A gloom was over everything. The two men lay in their berths, groaning with pain, and we all turned in, but for myself, not to sleep. A sound coming now and then from the berths of the two men showed that they were awake, as awake they must have been, for they could hardly lie in one posture a moment; the dim, swinging lamp of the forecastle shed its light over the dark hole in which we lived; and many and various reflections and purposes coursed through my mind. I thought of our situation, living under a tyranny; of the character of the country we were in; of the length of the voyage, and of the uncertainty attending our return to America; and then, if we should return, of the prospect of obtaining justice and satisfaction for these poor men; and vowed that if God should ever give me the means, I would do something to redress the grievances and relieve the sufferings of that poor class of beings, of whom I then was one.

The next day was Sunday. We worked as usual, washing decks, etc., until breakfast-time. After breakfast, we pulled the captain ashore, and finding some hides there which had been brought down the night before, he

**In the news**

**February, 1835**

In a move calculated to exacerbate feelings about the so-called "Toledo War," (see earlier note) the state of Ohio sets up county governments along and within a disputed strip of land that the territory of Michigan also claims as its own. Michigan's (somewhat hot-headed) 24-year-old territorial governor, Stevens T. Mason, responds by passing a law making it a crime to carry out "governmental actions" in the strip, and instructs the state militia to prepare to act with force against any trespassers. Ohio responds by sending its own forces to the area, and tensions run high. President Jackson sends representatives to arbitrate the dispute.

**..."sweethearts and wives."** This could be a reference to a then-popular song, or it could simply refer to a toast popular among sailors (and perhaps other travelers) at the time: "To [absent] sweethearts and wives."

**...swinging lamp of the forecastle shed its light over the dark hole in which we lived...** The tone here has become, like the atmosphere on board the Pilgrim, quite gloomy.

**...vowed that if God should ever give me the means, I would do something to redress the grievances and relieve the sufferings of that poor class of beings...** True to his word, Dana spends much of the rest of his life fighting for the rights of merchant sailors.

**We worked as usual...** Note that once again the men are forced to work through at least part of a Sunday, even though they're not at sea.

ordered me to stay ashore and watch them, saying that the boat would come again before night. They left me, and I spent a quiet day on the hill, eating dinner with the three men at the little house. Unfortunately, they had no books, and after talking with them and walking about, I began to grow tired of doing nothing. The little brig, the home of so much hardship and suffering, lay in the offing, almost as far as one could see; and the only other thing which broke the surface of the great bay was a small, desolate-looking island, steep and conical, of a clayey soil, and without the sign of vegetable life upon it; yet which had a peculiar and melancholy interest to me, for on the top of it were buried the remains of an Englishman, the commander of a small merchant brig, who died while lying in this port. It was always a solemn and interesting spot to me. There it stood, desolate, and in the midst of desolation; and there were the remains of one who died and was buried alone and friendless. Had it been a common burying-place, it would have been nothing. The single body corresponded well with the solitary character of everything around. It was the only thing in California from which I could ever extract anything like poetry. Then, too, the man died far from home; without a friend near him; by poison, it was suspected, and no one to inquire into it; and without proper funeral rites; the mate, (as I was told,) glad to have him out of the way, hurrying him up the hill and into the ground, without a word or a prayer.

I looked anxiously for a boat, during the latter part of the afternoon, but none came; until toward sundown, when I saw a speck on the water, and as it drew near, I found it was the gig, with the captain. The hides, then, were not to go off. The captain came up the hill, with a man, bringing my monkey jacket and a blanket. He looked pretty black, but inquired whether I had enough to eat; told me to make a house out of the hides, and keep myself warm, as I should have to sleep there among them, and to keep good watch over them. I got a moment to speak to the man who brought my jacket.

"How do things go aboard?" said I.

**Unfortunately, they had no books...** Dana is a cultured gentleman and a scholar. He craves books and rejoices when he encounters someone who has one to share, trade, or sell.

**...a small, desolate-looking island...** The small, rocky island came to be called Dead Man's Island (or Deadman's Island). It was demolished in 1928 when the harbor at Los Angeles was enlarged. During that demolition, work crews discovered on the island the almost complete skeleton of a man. (But the skeleton may not have been that of the brig captain to whom Dana refers, because the island was also used as a burial ground during the Mexican-American war, which occurred 10 years after Dana's visit.)

<u>In the news</u>

**February, 1835**

Philadelphia businessman Stephen Girard dies, leaving some $30,000 (almost $800,000 in today's dollars) to the Pennsylvania Hospital, to be used to provide nurses. Girard's trust also pays his slave, Hannah, $200 per year for the rest of her life, and the will also stipulates that Hannah is now a free woman. Girard also gives a total of $80,000 to other public and philanthropic entities, several thousand more to various family members, and $6,000 to be used to build a school "for poor [male and female] white children."

**I found it was the gig, with the captain.** The hides, then, were not to go off. A gig is a small boat used to ferry people and supplies to and from the shore. It's not large enough to carry hides, so Dana realizes that he is to stay on shore and guard the hides until the next day.

“Bad enough,” said he; “hard work and not a kind word spoken.”

**...from stem to stern, and from the waterways to the keelson.** That is, from front to back and from deck level to the bilge. A keelson is a long piece of wood bolted above the keel to provide additional strength. It sounds as if the crew is being given “make-work,” arduous chores used to keep them busy and to punish them for their presumed insolence.

**....“treinta uno,” a sort of Spanish “everlasting.”** “Thirty-one.” Like “War,” a card game that goes on for a very long time, because no one wins until he has won all of the cards. (These days—and possibly also during Dana's time—also used as a drinking game.)

**...take up my bivouack...** A bivouac (to use the correct spelling) is a military camp with tents used for shelter. Dana is referring to his “camping out” among the hides.

**The coati...** A relative of the racoon, there is a South American mammal called a coati, but Dana almost certainly means “coyote” here. Later editions have it as “coyata.”

In the news
**February, 1835**

The city of Baltimore, Maryland expands its police department to 12 men, paying them $220 per year, plus an additional $20 per man per year "for night duty."

**...succeeded in finding a part of a volume of Scott's Pirate...** Published in 1821, Sir Walter Scott's *The Pirate* is a romantic (some might say overly so) swashbuckling tale based on the life of true-life pirate John Gow.

“What,” said I, “have you been at work all day?”

“Yes! no more Sunday for us. Everything has been moved in the hold, from stem to stern, and from the waterways to the keelson.”

I went up to the house to supper. We had frijoles, (the perpetual food of the Californians, but which, when well cooked, are the best bean in the world,) coffee made of burnt wheat, and hard bread. After our meal, the three men sat down by the light of a tallow candle, with a pack of greasy Spanish cards, to the favorite game of “treinta uno,” a sort of Spanish “everlasting.” I left them and went out to take up my bivouack among the hides. It was now dark; the vessel was hidden from sight, and except the three men in the house, there was not a living soul within a league. The coati (a wild animal of a nature and appearance between that of the fox and the wolf) set up their sharp, quick bark, and two owls, at the end of two distant points running out into the bay, on different sides of the hills where I lay, kept up their alternate, dismal notes. I had heard the sound before at night, but did not know what it was, until one of the men, who came down to look at my quarters, told me it was the owl. Mellowed by the distance, and heard alone, at night, I thought it was the most melancholy, boding sound I had ever heard. Through nearly all the night they kept it up, answering one another slowly, at regular intervals. This was relieved by the noisy coati, some of which came quite near to my quarters, and were not very pleasant neighbors. The next morning, before sunrise, the long-boat came ashore, and the hides were taken off.

We lay at San Pedro about a week, engaged in taking off hides and in other labors, which had now become our regular duties. I spent one more day on the hill, watching a quantity of hides and goods, and this time succeeded in finding a part of a volume of Scott's Pirate, in a corner of the house; but it failed me at a most interesting moment, and I betook myself to my acquaintances on shore, and from them learned a good deal about the customs of the country, the harbors, etc. This, they told me, was a worse harbor than Santa Barbara, for south-easters; the bearing of the headland being a point and a half more to windward, and it being so shallow that the sea broke often as far out as where we lay at anchor. The gale from which we slipped at Santa Barbara, had been so bad a one here, that the whole bay, for a league out, was filled with the foam of the breakers, and seas actually broke over the Dead Man's island. The Lagoda was lying there, and slipped at the first alarm, and in such haste that she was obliged to leave her launch behind her at anchor. The little boat rode it out for several hours, pitching at her anchor, and standing with her stern up almost perpendicularly. The men told me that they watched her till towards night, when she snapped her cable and drove up over the breakers, high and dry upon the beach.

**...so shallow that the sea broke often as far out as where we lay at anchor.** Shallow waters are not necessarily safer than deep waters: Often they can be whipped up by the winds and tides. This is one reason waters in the Great Lakes can be so treacherous.

**The Lagoda...** *Lagoda* was a 300-ton, three-masted ship that was eventually converted into a whaler. She was ultimately wrecked near Yokahama, Japan, and then sold and used to transport coal. In 1899, she was sold to the Japanese and burned.

On board the Pilgrim, everything went on regularly, each one trying to get along as smoothly as possible; but the comfort of the voyage was evidently at an end. "That is a long lane which has no turning"—-"Every dog must have his day, and mine will come by-and-by"—and the like proverbs, were occasionally quoted; but no one spoke of any probable end to the voyage, or of Boston, or anything of the kind; or if he did, it was only to draw out the perpetual, surly reply from his shipmate—"Boston, is it? You may thank your stars if you ever see that place. You had better have your back sheathed, and your head coppered, and your feet shod, and make out your log for California for life!" or else something of this kind—"Before you get to Boston the hides will wear the hair off your head, and you'll take up all your wages in clothes, and won't have enough left to buy a wig with!"

**That is a long lane which has no turning...** The men are very unhappy and morale aboard ship is low. They console themselves with proverbs that speak of a better day to come.

In the news

**February, 1835**

The town of Newark, New Jersey announces (in capital letters) that Newark's exports for the year "will exceed the immense amount of EIGHT MILLIONS OF DOLLARS." Exports manufactured in Newark include such goods as harnesses, carriages, cutlery, window blinds, jewelry, and trunks.

The flogging was seldom if ever alluded to by us, in the forecastle. If any one was inclined to talk about it, the others, with a delicacy which I hardly expected to find among them, always stopped him, or turned the subject. But the behavior of the two men who were flogged

**...and John never, by word or deed, let anything escape him to remind the other that it was by interfering to save his shipmate, that he had suffered.** The two men, at least in Dana's telling, are much more noble—more human, even—than the captain who flogged them.

**...disposition of a crew be discovered better than in getting under weigh.** Getting underway is a complex and sometimes dangerous undertaking; as Dana points out, it is during this operation that one can see the skill of the crew, as well as their pride and motivation. In this case, though, the men's morale is low. Work goes slowly, and the men are disagreeable and loath to exert themselves on behalf of such a tyrannical master.

In the news
**February, 1835**

Darwin is present when an earthquake strikes Valdivia, Chile. He writes, "the world, the very emblem of all that is solid, moves beneath our feet like a crust over a fluid; one second of time conveys to the mind a strange idea of insecurity."

**...before a light fair wind...** As noted earlier, a "fair" wind is not one that blows gently, but one that blows in a direction favorable to your intended route.

toward one another showed a delicacy and a sense of honor, which would have been worthy of admiration in the highest walks of life. Sam knew that the other had suffered solely on his account, and in all his complaints, he said that if he alone had been flogged, it would have been nothing; but that he never could see that man without thinking what had been the means of bringing that disgrace upon him; and John never, by word or deed, let anything escape him to remind the other that it was by interfering to save his shipmate, that he had suffered.

Having got all our spare room filled with hides, we hove up our anchor and made sail for San Diego. In no operation can the disposition of a crew be discovered better than in getting under weigh.

Where things are "done with a will," every one is like a cat aloft: sails are loosed in an instant; each one lays out his strength on his handspike, and the windlass goes briskly round with the loud cry of "Yo heave ho! Heave and pawl! Heave hearty ho!" But with us, at this time, it was all dragging work. No one went aloft beyond his ordinary gait, and the chain came slowly in over the windlass. The mate, between the knight-heads, exhausted all his official rhetoric, in calls of "Heave with a will!—Heave hearty, men!—heave hearty!"—"Heave and raise the dead!"—"Heave, and away!" etc., etc.; but it would not do. Nobody broke his back or his handspike by his efforts. And when the cat-tackle-fall was strung along, and all hands—cook, steward, and all—laid hold, to cat the anchor, instead of the lively song of "Cheerily, men!" in which all hands join in the chorus, we pulled a long, heavy, silent pull, and—as sailors say a song is as good as ten men—the anchor came to the cat-head pretty slowly. "Give us 'Cheerily!'" said the mate; but there was no "cheerily" for us, and we did without it. The captain walked the quarterdeck, and said not a word. He must have seen the change, but there was nothing which he could notice officially.

We sailed leisurely down the coast before a light fair wind, keeping the land well aboard, and saw two other missions, looking like blocks of white plaster, shining in the distance; one of which, situated on the top of a high hill, was San Juan Campestrano, under which vessels sometimes come to anchor, in the summer season, and take off hides. The most distant one was St. Louis Rey, which the third mate said was only fifteen miles from San Diego. At sunset on the second day, we had a large and well wooded headland directly before us, behind which lay the little harbor of San Diego. We were becalmed off this point all night, but the next morning, which was Saturday, the 14th of March, having a good breeze, we stood round the point, and hauling our wind, brought the little harbor, which is rather the outlet of a small river, right before us. Every one was anxious to get a view of the new place. A chain of high hills, beginning at the point, (which was on our larboard hand, coming in,) protected the harbor on the north and west, and ran off into the interior as far as the eye could reach. On the other sides, the land was low, and green, but without trees. The entrance is so narrow as to admit but one vessel at a time, the current swift, and the channel runs so near to a low stony point that the ship's sides appeared almost to touch it. There was no town in sight, but on the smooth sand beach, abreast, and within a cable's length of which three vessels lay moored, were four large houses, built of rough boards, and looking like the great barns in which ice is stored on the borders of the large ponds near Boston; with piles of hides standing round them, and men in red shirts and large straw hats, walking in and out of the doors. These were the hide-houses. Of the vessels: one, a short, clumsy, little hermaphrodite brig, we recognized as our old acquaintance, the Loriotte; another, with sharp bows and raking masts, newly painted and tarred, and glittering in the morning sun, with the blood-red banner and cross of St. George at her peak, was the handsome Ayacucho. The third was a large ship, with top-gallant-masts housed, and sails unbent, and looking as rusty and worn as two years' "hide-droghing" could make her. This was the Lagoda. As we drew near, carried rapidly along by the current, we overhauled our chain, and clewed up the topsails. "Let go the anchor!" said the captain but either there was not chain enough forward of the windlass, or the anchor went down foul, or we

**...San Juan Campestrano...** Mission San Juan Capistrano was founded in 1775; it then burned and was re-founded in 1776. In any case, the mission is not visible from the sea.

**... the little harbor of San Diego.** San Diego, which had a population of barely 600 when Dana was there, is now the eighth-largest city in the United States. The "little harbor" is now home to the Port of San Diego, which boasts two cargo terminals, a cruise ship terminal, over a dozen public parks, and several wildlife reserves.

**...outlet of a small river...** Either the Agua Dulce (i.e., "Sweetwater River") or the San Diego River, both of which now empty into San Diego Bay. (Although the latter river originally emptied into what is now Mission Bay, prior to changing course sometime during the 1820s.)

**...larboard hand...** That is, the port or left side of a vessel, if facing the bow.

In the news

**February, 1835**

Johnson Patrick builds Kalamazoo, Michigan's second hotel, The Exchange. Looking back 34 years, the 1869 City Directory notes that the establishment "speedily became famous for its excellent table and appointments, and was a favorite inn for the citizen, stranger and speculator." The hotel came to be called the Sheridan House, and it still exists, though it is now a bed-and-breakfast.

**...blood-red banner and cross of St. George...** The cross of St. George (a blood-red cross on a white background) is used on the flags of many countries, cities, and provinces. The cross figures heavily in the design of the flags of England and Australia, for example. The hermaphrodite brig Loriotte (or Loriot) was of American registry.

**...and we gave it to her; but it would not do.** In spite of the efforts of the men, the ship is out of control in the strong current and drifts into the Lagoda.

**She lost her martingale.** A martingale is a piece of rigging (a stay) that's used to hold down the jib-boom—that is, the extension of the bowsprit that's used to extend the foot of the jib. (See what can happen when you try to define nautical terms by using other nautical terms?)

In the news
**February, 1835**

President Andrew Jackson appoints Meriwether Lewis Randolph as Secretary of the Arkansas Territory. Randolph, who was named after—but was not related to—explorer Meriwether Lewis, remains territorial secretary until Arkansas becomes a state in June of 1836.

**We drifted fairly into the Loriotte...** In this context, "fairly" means "gently." Pilgrim has now managed to drift into two ships.

**...breaking off her larboard bumpkin, and one or two stanchions above the deck.** On a ship, a bumpkin is a spar that extends over the stem of a vessel. A stanchion is a support along the deck for the ship's guardrail.

**We now began to drift down toward the Ayacucho...** *Ayacucho* is an English brig under the command of Captain John Wilson, a well-respected seaman of vast experience.

had too much headway on, for it did not bring us up. "Pay out chain!" shouted the captain; and we gave it to her; but it would not do. Before the other anchor could be let go, we drifted down, broadside on, and went smash into the Lagoda. Her crew were at breakfast in the forecastle, and the cook, seeing us coming, rushed out of his galley, and called up the officers and men.

Fortunately no great harm was done. Her jib-boom ran between our fore and main masts, carrying away some of our rigging, and breaking down the rail. She lost her martingale. This brought us up, and as they paid out chain, we swung clear of them, and let go the other anchor; but this had as bad luck as the first, for, before any one perceived it, we were drifting on to the Loriotte. The captain now gave out his orders rapidly and fiercely, sheeting home the topsails, and backing and filling the sails, in hope of starting or clearing the anchors; but it was all in vain, and he sat down on the rail, taking it very leisurely, and calling out to Captain Nye, that he was coming to pay him a visit. We drifted fairly into the Loriotte, her larboard bow into our starboard quarter, carrying away a part of our starboard quarter railing, and breaking off her larboard bumpkin, and one or two stanchions above the deck. We saw our handsome sailor, Jackson, on the forecastle, with the Sandwich Islanders, working away to get us clear. After paying out chain, we swung clear, but our anchors were no doubt afoul of hers. We manned the windlass, and hove, and hove away, but to no purpose. Sometimes we got a little upon the cable, but a good surge would take it all back again. We now began to drift down toward the Ayacucho, when her boat put off and brought her commander, Captain Wilson, on board. He was a short, active, well-built man, between fifty and sixty years of age; and being nearly twenty years older than our captain, and a thorough seaman, he did not hesitate to give his advice, and from giving advice, he gradually came to taking the command; ordering us when to heave and when to pawl, and backing and filling the topsails, setting and taking in jib and trysail, whenever he thought best. Our captain gave a few orders, but as Wilson generally countermanded them, saying, in an easy, fatherly kind of way, "Oh no! Captain T——, you don't want the jib on her," or "it isn't time yet to heave!" he soon gave it up. We had no objections to this state of things, for Wilson was a kind old man, and had an encouraging and pleasant way of speaking to us, which made everything go easily. After two or three hours of constant labor at the windlass, heaving and "Yo ho!"-ing with all our might, we brought up an anchor, with the Loriotte's small bower fast to it, Having cleared this and let it go, and cleared our hawse, we soon got our other anchor, which had dragged half over the harbor. "Now," said Wilson, "I'll find you a good berth;" and setting both the topsails, he carried us down, and brought us to anchor, in handsome style, directly abreast of the hide-house which we were to use. Having done this, he took his leave, while we furled the sails, and got our breakfast, which was welcome to us, for we had worked hard, and it was nearly twelve o'clock. After breakfast, and until night, we were employed in getting out the boats and mooring ship.

**Wilson was a kind old man, and had an encouraging and pleasant way of speaking to us, which made everything go easily.** This, Dana wants us to understand, is how a captain should act. Wilson is kind, and he encourages the men gently and with good humor, even as he gives orders.

**...we brought up an anchor, with the Loriotte's small bower fast to it...** A bower is one of a pair of bow anchors that, in spite of being called "small" and "large" bowers, are actually the same size; the "small bower" is the one that hangs on the port side. *Pilgrim*'s anchor chain has fouled *Loriotte*'s small bower.

After supper, two of us took the captain on board the Lagoda. As he came alongside, he gave his name, and the mate, in the gangway, called out to the captain down the companion-way—"Captain T—— has come aboard, sir!" "Has he brought his brig with him?" said the rough old fellow, in a tone which made itself heard fore and aft. This mortified our captain a little, and it became a standing joke among us for the rest of the voyage. The captain went down into the cabin, and we walked forward and put our heads down the forecastle, where we found the men at supper, "Come down, shipmates! Come down!" said they, as soon as they saw us; and we went down, and found a large, high forecastle, well lighted; and a crew of twelve or fourteen men, eating out of their kids and pans, and drinking their tea, and talking and laughing, all as independent and easy as so many "wood-sawyer's clerks." This looked like comfort and enjoyment, compared with the dark little forecastle, and scanty, discontented crew of the brig. It was Saturday night; they had got through with their work for the week; and being snugly moored, had nothing to do until Monday, again. After two years' hard service, they

**Has he brought his brig with him?** Captain Wilson jests at Captain Thompson's expense. Note that Thompson is probably not the kind of man who laughs at himself easily.

**...we went down, and found a large, high forecastle, well lighted; and a crew of twelve or fourteen men, eating out of their kids and pans, and drinking their tea, and talking and laughing...** This is the sort of crew with which (and the sort of ship on which) Dana would like to serve. Morale is good, and the men are content. Not only are they not forced to work on Sundays, at least when they're at anchor, they don't even work on Saturdays.

had seen the worst, and all, of California;—had got their cargo nearly stowed, and expected to sail in a week or two, for Boston. We spent an hour or more with them, talking over California matters, until the word was passed—"Pilgrims, away!" and we went back with our captain. They were a hardy, but intelligent crew; a little roughened, and their clothes patched and old, from California wear; all able seamen, and between the ages of twenty and thirty-five. They inquired about our vessel, the usage, etc., and were not a little surprised at the story of the flogging. They said there were often difficulties in vessels on the coast, and sometimes knock-downs and fightings, but they had never heard before of a regular seizing-up and flogging. "Spread-eagles" were a new kind of bird in California.

Sunday, they said, was always given in San Diego, both at the hide-houses and on board the vessels, a large number usually going up to the town, on liberty. We learned a good deal from them about curing and stowing of hides, etc. and they were anxious to have the latest news (seven months old) from Boston. One of their first inquiries was for Father Taylor, the seamen's preacher in Boston. Then followed the usual strain of conversation, inquiries, stories, and jokes, which, one must always hear in a ship's forecastle, but which are perhaps, after all, no worse, nor, indeed, more gross, than that of many well-dressed gentlemen at their clubs.

In the news
**February, 1835**

Thomas Babington Macaulay, who had lived in India for several years, speaks out against the India Bill of 1833. He notes that natives in India (at the time a colony of Britain's) must be allowed to hold high office and that to deny them that would be "a despicable policy." He is a product of his age, however, and further comments that "for the good of India itself, the admission of natives to high office must be effected by slow degrees."

**"Spread-eagles" were a new kind of bird in California.** Dana employs here a metaphor meant to convey the image of a man roped (spread-eagle) to a mast, ready to be whipped. The men of the *Lagoda* are taken aback to learn that this sort of thing occurs; they've not seen any floggings on their voyages.

**One of their first inquiries was for Father Taylor...** As noted earlier, Reverend Edward Thomson Taylor was a popular figure amongst Massachusetts sailors.

**...jokes, which, one must always hear in a ship's forecastle...** Men are men, Dana seems to be saying, and no matter where they are gathered, or of what social class they are members, they tend to be crude. (And women might well be the same, of course, but Dana has no way of knowing this.)

## Chapter XVI

## Liberty-Day On Shore

The next day being Sunday, after washing and clearing decks, and getting breakfast, the mate came forward with leave for one watch to go ashore, on liberty. We drew lots, and it fell to the larboard, which I was in. Instantly all was preparation. Buckets of fresh water, (which we were allowed in port,) and soap, were put in use; go-ashore jackets and trowsers got out and brushed; pumps, neckerchiefs, and hats overhauled; one lending to another; so that among the whole each one got a good fit-out. A boat was called to pull the "liberty men" ashore, and we sat down in the stern sheets, "as big as pay passengers," and jumping ashore, set out on our walk for the town, which was nearly three miles off.

It is a pity that some other arrangement is not made in merchant vessels, with regard to the liberty-day. When in port, the crews are kept at work all the week, and the only day they are allowed for rest or pleasure is the Sabbath; and unless they go ashore on that day, they cannot go at all. I have heard of a religious captain who gave his crew liberty on Saturdays, after twelve o'clock. This would be a good plan, if shipmasters would bring themselves to give their crews so much time. For young sailors especially, many of whom have been brought up with a regard for the sacredness of the day, this strong temptation to break it, is exceedingly injurious. As it is, it can hardly be expected that a crew, on a long and hard voyage, will refuse a few hours of freedom from toil and the restraints of a vessel, and an opportunity to tread the ground and see the sights of society and humanity, because it is on a Sunday. It is too much like escaping from prison, or being drawn out of a pit, on the Sabbath day.

I shall never forget the delightful sensation of being in the open air, with the birds singing around me, and escaped from the confinement, labor, and strict rule of a vessel–of being once more in my life, though only for a day, my own master. A sailor's liberty is but for a day;

**...it fell to the larboard, which I was in.** That is, the larboard watch (of which Dana was a member) was selected for liberty on shore. Larboard, you may recall, is the soon-to-be-obsolete term for the left-hand side of a vessel (when facing forward). Even after "port" came to be used for "larboard" in most cases, it held on for a time in usages such as this.

**...fresh water, (which we were allowed in port,)...** At sea, fresh water is precious and used very sparingly. Most sailors bathed (when they bathed) with salt water. Even today, sailors and yachtsmen utilize saltwater as much as possible for bathing, dishwashing, etc., often with special soaps made for use with seawater.

**....pumps...** Formal shoes with low heels. Not a recent coinage at all, but one that, used in this sense, goes back to the 16th century.

**..."as big as pay passengers,"...** That is, as if they were high-class passengers living in luxury and used to being waited upon, rather than simple sailors who lived in steerage or in the forecastle.

**...this strong temptation to break it, is exceedingly injurious.** Dana's argument seems to be that if the men were allowed Saturday off, they would spend Sunday in worship. The argument is a bit weak; there's every likelihood that the men would simply spend *both* days drinking, playing cards, and chasing women. But Dana is 19 years old, after all, and still a bit naive. Either that, or he's simply being disingenuous.

**A sailor's liberty...** Dana revels in the now unfamiliar feeling of freedom, which he gave up when he signed on for this voyage. A privileged child of a powerful (though not particularly wealthy) family, Dana has traded his relatively carefree life as a student for that of a hardworking merchant sailor. He's (rightfully) proud of what he's learned and what he's accomplished, but he also misses his former life.

yet while it lasts it is perfect. He is under no one's eye, and can do whatever, and go wherever, he pleases. This day, for the first time, I may truly say, in my whole life, I felt the meaning of a term which I had often heard–the sweets of liberty. My friend S— was with me, and turning our backs upon the vessels, we walked slowly along, talking of the pleasure of being our own masters, of the times past, and when we were free in the midst of friends, in America, and of the prospect of our return; and planning where we would go, and what we would do, when we reached home. It was wonderful how the prospect brightened, and how short and tolerable the voyage appeared, when viewed in this new light. Things looked differently from what they did when we talked them over in the little dark forecastle, the night after the flogging at San Pedro. It is not the least of the advantages of allowing sailors occasionally a day of liberty, that it gives them a spring, and makes them feel cheerful and independent, and leads them insensibly to look on the bright side of everything for some time after.

S— and myself determined to keep as much together as possible, though we knew that it would not do to cut our shipmates; for, knowing our birth and education, they were a little suspicious that we would try to put on the gentleman when we got ashore, and would be ashamed of their company; and this won't do with Jack. When the voyage is at an end, you may do as you please, but so long as you belong to the same vessel, you must be a shipmate to him on shore, or he will not be a shipmate to you on board. Being forewarned of this before I went to sea, I took no "long togs" with me, and being dressed like the rest, in white duck trowsers, blue jacket and straw hat, which would prevent my going in better company, and showing no disposition to avoid them, I set all suspicion at rest. Our crew fell in with some who belonged to the other vessels, and, sailor-like, steered for the first grog-shop. This was a small mud building, of only one room, in which were liquors, dry and West India goods, shoes, bread, fruits, and everything which is vendible in California. It was kept by a yankee, a one-eyed man, who belonged formerly to Fall River, came out to the Pacific in a whale-ship, left

**My friend S—...** Stimson, Dana's young friend.

**It was wonderful how the prospect brightened, and how short and tolerable the voyage appeared, when viewed in this new light.** It's especially wonderful for Dana. A key to understanding Dana's outlook is this: He has an out. That is, no matter how bleak things are, he will—at some point relatively soon—be returning to a "civilized" life among sophisticated, cultured people. One can stand almost any misery or punishment, if one knows that it will soon end, and in the back of his mind—and no matter how much he tries to be "one of the guys"—Dana knows that this is not his lot forever. Few of the other crew members can say that.

**...knowing our birth and education, they were a little suspicious...** Dana and Stimson, both educated and coming from relative wealth, realize that they stand out from the rest of the group. They therefore try to avoid "putting on airs."

**...I took no "long togs" with me...** That is, clothes more befitting a landsman than a sailor.

**...sailor-like, steered for the first grog-shop.** A grog shop is a bar or pub, so-called after the traditional seaman's onboard ration of rum (usually mixed with water). Used in this general sense, of course, a grog-shop might sell *any* type of liquor, not just rum. Note that Dana is well aware of sailors' tendency to misbehave while on leave—doing so is, after all, a time-honored tradition. Note also that he avoids any mention of his *own* such misbehaviors, though some critics and researchers contend that he was no different than his colleagues in that respect.

her at the Sandwich Islands, and came to California and set up a "Pulperia." S—- and I followed in our shipmates' wake, knowing that to refuse to drink with them would be the highest affront, but determining to slip away at the first opportunity. It is the universal custom with sailors for each one, in his turn, to treat the whole, calling for a glass all round, and obliging every one who is present, even the keeper of the shop, to take a glass with him. When we first came in, there was some dispute between our crew and the others, whether the new comers or the old California rangers should treat first; but it being settled in favor of the latter, each of the crews of the other vessels treated all round in their turn, and as there were a good many present, (including some "loafers" who had dropped in, knowing what was going on, to take advantage of Jack's hospitality,) and the liquor was a real (12½ cents) a glass, it made somewhat of a hole in their lockers. It was now our ship's turn, and S—- and I, anxious to get away, stepped up to call for glasses; but we soon found that we must go in order–the oldest first, for the old sailors did not choose to be preceded by a couple of youngsters; and bon gré mal gré, we had to wait our turn, with the twofold apprehension of being too late for our horses, and of getting corned; for drink you must, every time; and if you drink with one and not with another, it is always taken as an insult.

Having at length gone through our turns and acquitted ourselves of all obligations, we slipped out, and went about among the houses, endeavoring to get horses for the day, so that we might ride round and see the country. At first we had but little success, all that we could get out of the lazy fellows, in reply to our questions, being the eternal drawling "Quien sabe?" ("who knows?") which is an answer to all questions. After several efforts, we at length fell in with a little Sandwich Island boy, who belonged to Captain Wilson of the Ayacucho, and was well acquainted in the place; and he, knowing where to go, soon procured us two horses, ready saddled and bridled, each with a lasso coiled over the pommel. These we were to have all day, with the privilege of riding them down to the beach at night, for

**... Pulperia.** That is, a grocery store, but one that sells liquor in addition to its other goods.

**...obliging every one who is present...** This custom helps explain the drunkenness that was common in such settings—and not so uncommon today in other settings: If a party of five or six or eight enter, and if every person is obliged to buy a round of drinks, that means that every person will consume ("for drink you must, every time," Dana says a few sentences later) five or six or eight drinks at a minimum.

In the news

**March, 1835**

A medical student and diarist describes making rounds at a large hospital in France. He examines the dead body of a woman who had succumbed to what was then called puerperal fever—sometimes called childbed fever, since it often affected newly delivered mothers. Given that one of the primary treatments was to "bleed" patients, it's not surprising that death was a fairly common outcome.

**...bon gré mal gré..** With good grace or bad; that is, willingly or not.

**...all that we could get out of the lazy fellows...** Dana is culturally tone-deaf, as was common at the time (and not completely unheard of now). He is always ready to ascribe to laziness the fact that the natives are not in any particular hurry to help him entertain himself.

**...a little Sandwich Island boy...** That is a Hawaiian. Probably not a slave, but very possibly a servant—so, "belonged" in the sense of "being a part of," in much the way one "belongs" to a political party.

**...Horses are the cheapest thing in California...** As noted earlier, horses, though quite common by this time, were unknown in the area prior to the arrival of the Spanish conquistadores.

**...the old ruinous presidio...** The presidio (fort) at San Diego was established (along with Father Junipero Serra's first mission) in 1769, making it the earliest permanent European settlement on the coast. When the Mexicans won their independence from Spain in 1821, they took over the forts and the missions, secularizing the latter. However, the Mexicans did not invest much in maintaining the presidios or the missions, and they rapidly fell into disuse. Today, nothing is left of the San Diego presidio itself, although there is a park (Presidio Park) where the fort once stood.

**...one of which was spiked...** That is, rendered inoperable, normally by driving a large nail into the hole used to ignite the gunpowder. The gun may have been spiked by the departing Spanish, or it may have been disabled more recently because it had become unsafe to fire.

**...gente de razón...** We encountered this term earlier in the book. Literally, it means "people of reason." Meaning Hispanic people, its use implied that the original Indian inhabitants of the area were *not* capable of reason—that is, that they were, quite literally, "dumb brutes." It's difficult to conceive of a more racist term.

a dollar, which we had to pay in advance. Horses are the cheapest thing in California; the very best not being worth more than ten dollars apiece, and very good ones being often sold for three, and four. In taking a day's ride, you pay for the use of the saddle, and for the labor and trouble of catching the horses. If you bring the saddle back safe, they care but little what becomes of the horse. Mounted on our horses, which were spirited beasts, and which, by the way, in this country, are always steered by pressing the contrary rein against the neck, and not by pulling on the bit,–we started off on a fine run over the country. The first place we went to was the old ruinous presidio, which stands on a rising ground near the village, which it overlooks. It is built in the form of an open square, like all the other presidios, and was in a most ruinous state, with the exception of one side, in which the commandant lived, with his family. There were only two guns, one of which was spiked, and the other had no carriage. Twelve, half clothed, and half starved looking fellows, composed the garrison; and they, it was said, had not a musket apiece. The small settlement lay directly below the fort, composed of about forty dark brown looking huts, or houses, and two larger ones, plastered, which belonged to two of the "gente de razón." This town is not more than half as large as Monterey, or Santa Barbara, and has little or no business. From the presidio, we rode off in the direction of the mission, which we were told was three miles distant. The country was rather sandy, and there was nothing for miles which could be called a tree, but the grass grew green and rank, and there were many bushes and thickets, and the soil is said to be good. After a pleasant ride of a couple of miles, we saw the white walls of the mission, and fording a small river, we came directly before it. The mission is built of mud, or rather of the unburnt bricks of the country, and plastered. There was something decidedly striking in its appearance: a number of irregular buildings, connected with one another, and disposed in the form of a hollow square, with a church at one end, rising above the rest, with a tower containing five belfries, in each of which hung a large bell, and with immense rusty iron crosses at the tops. Just outside of the buildings, and under the walls, stood twenty or thirty small huts, built of straw and of the branches of trees, grouped together, in which a few Indians lived, under the protection and in the service of the mission.

Entering a gate-way, we drove into the open square, in which the stillness of death reigned. On one side was the church; on another, a range of high buildings with grated windows; a third was a range of smaller buildings, or offices; and the fourth seemed to be little more than a high connecting wall. Not a living creature could we see. We rode twice round the square, in the hope of waking up some one; and in one circuit, saw a tall monk, with shaven head, sandals, and the dress of the Grey Friars, pass rapidly through a gallery, but he disappeared without noticing us. After two circuits, we stopped our horses, and saw, at last, a man show himself in front of one of the small buildings. We rode up to him, and found him dressed in the common dress of the country, with a silver chain round his neck, supporting a large bunch of keys. From this, we took him to be the steward of the mission, and addressing him as "Mayordomo," received a low bow and an invitation to walk into his room. Making our horses fast, we went in. It was a plain room, containing a table, three or four chairs, a small picture or two of some saint, or miracle, or martyrdom, and a few dishes and glasses. "Hay algunas cosa de comer?" said I. "Si Señor!" said he. "Que gusta usted?" Mentioning frijoles, which I knew they must have if they had nothing else, and beef and bread, and a hint for wine, if they had any, he went off to another building, across the court, and returned in a few moments, with a couple of Indian boys, bearing dishes and a decanter of wine. The dishes contained baked meats, frijoles stewed with peppers and onions, boiled eggs, and California flour baked into a kind of macaroni. These, together with the wine, made the most sumptuous meal we had eaten since we left Boston; and, compared with the fare we had lived upon for seven months, it was a regal banquet. After despatching our meal, we took out some money and asked him how much we were to pay. He shook his head, and crossed himself, saying that it was charity: –that the Lord gave

**...under the protection and in the service of the mission.** The original intent of the missions was to convert the natives to Catholicism. The fathers thought of their Indian charges as "children," and did indeed feel they were protecting them. In turn, the Indians worked on the mission farms and as laborers or domestics. They were not slaves, however, and (at least, theoretically) were free to leave the missions.

**...we drove into the open square, in which the stillness of death reigned.** One reason for this may be the fact that it's the middle of the afternoon, when most Californians rested out of the heat of the sun. (The "siesta" is a tradition in many cultures, especially those in warm or temperate climates.) Another possibility is that everyone is in fact awake but out working the fields, engaged in prayer, or attending services.

**...the dress of the Grey Friars...** That is, Franciscan friars. The Franciscans, an order founded by St. Francis of Assisi, founded the missions along the California coast.

**...a small picture or two of some saint, or miracle, or martyrdom...** Dana has the 19th century Protestant's disdain for what he sees as the "superstitions" of this mostly Catholic country, and it comes across in comments in which he lumps together insignificant items such as "a few dishes and glasses" with saints and miracles.

**"Hay algunas cosa de comer?"** Are there (that is, "do you have") things to eat?

**After despatching our meal...** This is the British spelling of what Americans these days spell "dispatch." Dana uses many British spellings (such as "grey" for "gray"), which was not uncommon at the time, since American spellings had not yet completely differentiated themselves from their British origins. In other cases (using "color" instead of "colour," for example), Dana uses the Americanized spellings of words.

**...willing to receive a present...** The father will not charge for the meal, but he is willing to accept a "donation" to the mission. *Dios se lo pague* translates as *God bless* [or, somewhat more accurately, *reward*] *you.*

**The language of these people, which is spoken by all the Indians of California, is the most brutish and inhuman language...** Dana thinks even less of the Indians than he does of the Mexicans, and characterizes their language as "a slabber"—the noise one might make when drooling or slobbering. An educated man, he knows of the glories of the Aztec empire and cannot believe that such accomplished people could have spoken like this. The language of the California Indians was actually quite diverse, consisting of dozens of language groups and hundreds of dialects.

**...taking hold of his lids with his fingers, lifted them up to look at us...** The old man may be suffering from blepharospasm, a form of focal dystonia or movement disorder in which the eyelids remain closed and the patient is unable to open them, even though his eyesight is actually normal. Even today, the cause is sometimes unknown, although a blow to the back of the head has been known to cause it. Unconfirmed recent research indicates that it may also be a complication of syphilis. Another possibility is that the old man has myasthenia gravis, a disease in which the muscles that control eye and eyelid movement, facial expressions, chewing, talking, and swallowing are weakened. While symptoms are often intermittent, the first noticeable indication is often a weakness of the eye muscles.

**... they have no need of the genteel trot...** It's clever of Dana to notice first of all that the horses tend to lack the ability to trot (genteel means "in a refined manner"), and then to ascribe that fact to a perfectly understandable cause: There are no streets, and there is therefore no *need* to trot; these horses have three speeds: a headlong gallop, a walk, and a full stop.

it to us. Knowing the amount of this to be that he did not sell it, but was willing to receive a present, we gave him ten or twelve reals, which he pocketed with admirable nonchalance, saying, "Dios se lo pague." Taking leave of him, we rode out to the Indians' huts. The little children were running about among the huts, stark naked, and the men were not much better; but the women had generally coarse gowns, of a sort of tow cloth. The men are employed, most of the time, in tending the cattle of the mission, and in working in the garden, which is a very large one, including several acres, and filled, it is said, with the best fruits of the climate. The language of these people, which is spoken by all the Indians of California, is the most brutish and inhuman language, without any exception, that I ever heard, or that could well be conceived of. It is a complete slabber. The words fall off of the ends of their tongues, and a continual slabbering sound is made in the cheeks, outside of the teeth. It cannot have been the language of Montezuma and the independent Mexicans.

Here, among the huts, we saw the oldest man that I had ever seen; and, indeed, I never supposed that a person could retain life and exhibit such marks of age. He was sitting out in the sun, leaning against the side of a hut; and his legs and arms, which were bare, were of a dark red color, the skin withered and shrunk up like burnt leather, and the limbs not larger round than those of a boy of five years. He had a few grey hairs, which were tied together at the back of his head; and he was so feeble that, when we came up to him, he raised his hands slowly to his face, and taking hold of his lids with his fingers, lifted them up to look at us; and being satisfied, let them drop again. All command over the lid seemed to have gone. I asked his age, but could get no answer but "Quien sabe?" and they probably did not know the age.

Leaving the mission, we returned to village, going nearly all the way on a full run. The California horses have no medium gait, which is pleasant, between walking and running; for as there are no streets and parades, they have no need of the genteel trot, and their riders usually keep them at the top of their speed until they are fired, and then let them rest themselves by walking. The fine air of the afternoon; the rapid rate of the animals, who seemed almost to fly over the ground; and the excitement and novelty of the motion to us, who had been so long confined on shipboard, were exhilarating beyond expression, and we felt willing to ride all day long. Coming into the village, we found things looking very lively. The Indians, who always have a holyday on Sunday, were engaged at playing a kind of running game of ball, on a level piece of ground, near the houses. The old ones sat down in a ring, looking on, while the young ones–men, boys and girls–were chasing the ball, and throwing it with all their might. Some of the girls ran like greyhounds. At every accident, or remarkable feat, the old people set up a deafening screaming and clapping of hands. Several blue jackets were reeling about among the houses, which showed that the pulperias had been well patronized. One or two of the sailors had got on horseback, but being rather indifferent horsemen, and the Spaniards having given them vicious horses, they were soon thrown, much to the amusement of the people. A half dozen Sandwich Islanders, from the hide-houses and the two brigs, who are bold riders, were dashing about on the full gallop, hallooing and laughing like so many wild men.

**....engaged at playing a kind of running game of ball...** This could have been any of several games, many of which go back to the Azetcs. The Chumash of California played a game called *tikauwich*, the object of which was to use sticks to drive a small wooden ball through the opponent's goal posts.

In the news
**March, 1835**

Congress authorizes the establishment of a U.S. mint at New Orleans, Louisiana. Purposely established far from Washington in order to encourage the development of the nation's western frontier, the mint served for a time as the Confederate Mint when it was seized during the Civil War by state authorities. Minting operations were halted in 1909, and the building is now a museum.

It was now nearly sundown, and S—- and myself went into a house and sat quietly down to rest ourselves before going down to the beach. Several people were soon collected to see "los Ingles marineros," and one of them–a young woman–took a great fancy to my pocket handkerchief, which was a large silk one that I had before going to sea, and a handsomer one than they had been in the habit of seeing. Of course, I gave it to her; which brought us into high favor; and we had a present of some pears and other fruits, which we took down to the beach with us. When we came to leave the house, we found that our horses, which we left tied at the door, were both gone. We had paid for them to ride down to the beach, but they were not to be found. We went to the man of whom we hired them, but he only shrugged his shoulders, and to our question, "Where are the hors-

**...los Ingles marineros...** The English mariners, or sailors.

**...pears and other fruits...** Sailors value fresh fruits highly, since they're in short supply at sea.

**...as he was very easy...** That is, since he was not angry or upset.

**...in "high snuff."** That is, in high spirits; very cheerful.

**...steering pretty wild...** That is, staggering drunk and not likely to make any real headway.

In the news
**March, 1835**

Charles Darwin, in the *Beagle,* leaves Santiago, Chile, heading for Portillo Pass and from there to Mendoza, Argentina. In his diary he describes crossing the pass with the aid of a small mare, the Madrina, which wore a bell, the sound of which the expedition's numerous mules seem to follow willingly: "It is quite curious to see how steadily the mules follow the sound of the Bell, — if four large troops are grazing together during the night, the Muleteers in the morning have only to draw a little apart each Madrina & tinkle the Bell, & immediately the mules although 2–300 together, will all go to their proper troop. — The affection of the mules for the Madrina saves an infinity of trouble...."

es?" only answered–"Quien sabe?" but as he was very easy, and made no inquiries for the saddles, we saw that he knew very well where they were. After a little trouble, determined not to walk down,–a distance of three miles–we procured two, at four reals apiece, with an Indian boy to run on behind and bring them back. Determined to have "the go" out of the horses, for our trouble, we went down at full speed, and were on the beach in fifteen minutes. Wishing to make our liberty last as long as possible, we rode up and down among the hide-houses, amusing ourselves with seeing the men, as they came down, (it was now dusk,) some on horseback and others on foot. The Sandwich Islanders rode down, and were in "high snuff." We inquired for our shipmates, and were told that two of them had started on horseback and had been thrown or had fallen off, and were seen heading for the beach, but steering pretty wild, and by the looks of things, would not be down much before midnight.

The Indian boys having arrived, we gave them our horses, and having seen them safely off, hailed for a boat and went aboard. Thus ended our first liberty-day on shore. We were well tired, but had had a good time, and were more willing to go back to our old duties. About midnight, we were waked up by our two watchmates, who had come aboard in high dispute. It seems they had started to come down on the same horse, double-backed; and each was accusing the other of being the cause of his fall. They soon, however, turned-in and fell asleep, and probably forgot all about it, for the next morning the dispute was not renewed.

## Chapter XVII

### San Diego–A Desertion–San Pedro Again–Beating the Coast

The next sound we heard was "All hands ahoy!" and looking up the scuttle, saw that it was just daylight. Our liberty had now truly taken flight, and with it we laid away our pumps, stockings, blue jackets, neckerchiefs, and other go-ashore paraphernalia, and putting on old duck trowsers, red shirts, and Scotch caps, began taking out and landing our hides. For three days we were hard at work, from the grey of the morning until starlight, with the exception of a short time allowed for meals, in this duty. For landing and taking on board hides, San Diego is decidedly the best place in California. The harbor is small and land-locked; there is no surf; the vessels lie within a cable's length of the beach; and the beach itself is smooth, hard sand, without rocks or stones. For these reasons, it is used by all the vessels in the trade, as a depot; and, indeed, it would be impossible, when loading with the cured hides for the passage home, to take them on board at any of the open ports, without getting them wet in the surf, which would spoil them. We took possession of one of the hide-houses, which belonged to our firm, and had been used by the California. It was built to hold forty thousand hides, and we had the pleasing prospect of filling it before we could leave the coast; and toward this, our thirty-five hundred, which we brought down with us, would do but little. There was not a man on board who did not go a dozen times into the house, and look round, and make some calculation of the time it would require.

**For landing and taking on board hides, San Diego is decidedly the best place in California.** This is why the companies locate their hide-houses here.

<u>In the news</u>
**March, 1835**

In an effort to enhance their presence in North America, the British goverment begins offering cheap land in Canada to citizens who are willing to settle there. The government advertises "One Million Acres of Land, in Farms of 100 Acres and upwards, situated in the healthy and fertile Eastern Townships of Lower Canada, distant from 50 to 100 miles from Montreal, Three Rivers and Quebec. Prices from Four Shillings to Ten Shillings currency per Acre."

**It was built to hold forty thousand hides...** Dana (correctly) sees many months of work ahead, if the crew is to fill this huge hide house; the 3,500 hides they currently have amount to only about 8% of what they'll need.

The hides, as they come rough and uncured from the vessels, are piled up outside of the houses, whence they are taken and carried through a regular process of pickling, drying, cleaning, etc., and stowed away in the house, ready to be put on board. This process is necessary in order that they may keep, during a long voyage, and in warm latitudes. For the purpose of curing and taking care of these hides, an officer and a part of the crew of each vessel are usually left ashore and it was

**...as they come rough and uncured from the vessels...** The hides must be cured and dried before being packed away in the hide houses. Otherwise, they would spoil on the journey home.

**...the report of the flogging had got among them...** Captain Thompson's reputation is causing him trouble. The Hawaiians, though willing to work for him on shore, are unwilling to serve on his vessel.

for this business, we found, that our new officer had joined us. As soon as the hides were landed, he took charge of the house, and the captain intended to leave two or three of us with him, hiring Sandwich Islanders to take our places on board; but he could not get any Sandwich Islanders to go, though he offered them fifteen dollars a month; for the report of the flogging had got among them, and he was called "aole maikai," (no good,) and that was an end of the business. They were, however, willing to work on shore, and four of them were hired and put with Mr. Russell to cure the hides.

**She had been the pet of the cook during the whole passage...** Pigs actually can make good pets. They're normally well-behaved and (contrary to what most think), left to their own devices, they're quite clean. Of course, most breeds get quite large, so having a pig as a pet can be something like having a rowdy, 100 lb. 3-year old running around the house. It's not for the faint of heart.

**Tom Cringle says...** The "Tom Cringle" books were early nautical adventures in which a young English boy recounts his adventurous sea voyages. Published in magazines as early as 1829, the series would be published in book form beginning in 1834.

**...it almost broke our poor darky's heart...** There is a tendency, even amongst sympathetic anti-slavery activists such as Dana, to condescend to African-Americans, treating them as "simple" and in need of counsel from "better," smarter (read: white) people. Keep in mind that this isn't really Dana talking as much as it's an era speaking. It's difficult to think outside of your own culture's world-view; that's what makes it a world-view, after all.

**"'Vast there! 'vast!" said the mate...** That is, "avast." An order to cease or stop. The word goes back to the 17th century. It may have derived from the Italian *basta*—or *enough*.

After landing our hides, we next sent ashore all our spare spars and rigging; all the stores which we did not want to use in the course of one trip to windward; and, in fact, everything which we could spare, so as to make room for hides: among other things, the pig-sty, and with it "old Bess." This was an old sow that we had brought from Boston, and which lived to get around Cape Horn, where all the other pigs died from cold and wet. Report said that she had been a Canton voyage before. She had been the pet of the cook during the whole passage, and he had fed her with the best of everything, and taught her to know his voice, and to do a number of strange tricks for his amusement. Tom Cringle says that no one can fathom a negro's affection for a pig; and I believe he is right, for it almost broke our poor darky's heart when he heard that Bess was to be taken ashore, and that he was to have the care of her no more during the whole voyage. He had depended upon her as a solace, during the long trips up and down the coast. "Obey orders, if you break owners!" said he. "Break hearts," he meant to have said; and lent a hand to get her over the side, trying to make it as easy for her as possible. We got a whip up on the main-yard, and hooking it to a strap around her body, swayed away; and giving a wink to one another, ran her chock up to the yard. "'Vast there! 'vast!" said the mate; "none of your skylarking! Lower away!" But he evidently enjoyed the joke. The pig squealed like the "crack of doom," and tears stood in the poor darky's eyes; and he muttered something about having no pity on a dumb beast. "Dumb beast!" said Jack; "if she's what you call a dumb beast, then my eyes a'n't mates." This produced a laugh from all but the cook. He was too intent upon seeing her safe in the boat. He watched her all the way ashore, where, upon her landing, she was received by a whole troop of her kind, who had been sent ashore from the other vessels, and had multiplied and formed a large commonwealth. From the door of his galley, the cook used to watch them in their manoeuvres, setting up a shout and clapping his hands whenever Bess came off victorious in the struggles for pieces of raw hide and half-picked bones which were lying about the beach. During the day, he saved all the nice things, and made a bucket of swill, and asked us to take it ashore in the gig, and looked quite disconcerted when the mate told him that he would pitch the swill overboard, and him after it, if he saw any of it go into the boats. We told him that he thought more about the pig than he did about his wife, who lived down in Robinson's Alley; and, indeed, he could hardly have been more attentive, for he actually, on several nights, after dark, when he thought he would not he seen, sculled himself ashore in a boat with a bucket of nice swill, and returned like Leander from crossing the Hellespont.

The next Sunday the other half of our crew went ashore on liberty, and left us on board, to enjoy the first quiet Sunday which we had had upon the coast. Here were no hides to come off, and no south-easters to fear. We washed and mended our clothes in the morning, and spent the rest of the day in reading and writing. Several of us wrote letters to send home by the Lagoda. At twelve o'clock the Ayacucho dropped her fore topsail, which was a signal for her sailing. She unmoored and warped down into the bight, from which she got under way. During this operation, her crew were a long time heaving at the windlass, and I listened for nearly an hour to the musical notes of a Sandwich Islander, called Mahannah, who "sang out" for them. Sailors, when heaving at a windlass, in order that they may heave together, always have one to sing out; which is done in a peculiar, high and long-drawn note, varying with the motion of the windlass. This requires a high voice, strong lungs, and much practice, to be done well. This

**...had multiplied and formed a large commonwealth.** Dana is making a joke, comparing the herd of feral pigs to a commonwealth (an organized group of people under a single government). He thus humorously describes the pigs in human terms, and at the same time pokes a bit of gentle fun at the people themselves.

**...made a bucket of swill...** Wet feed, generally made up of garbage, kitchen waste, sour milk, etc. (Honest, if you were a pig, it would sound heavenly.)

**...returned like Leander from crossing the Hellespont.** Dana's education is showing. This is a reference to the Greek myth of Hero and Leander who, separated by a strait called the Hellespont, carry on a love affair during which the intrepid (but not very smart) Leander swims across the strait every night to be with her. The affair ends tragically, as these things tend to; the wind blows out the light that Hero has used to guide Leander to shore, Leander drowns, and Hero in her grief throws herself from a tower. The myth is mentioned in Shakespeare's *Two Gentlemen of Verona,* when Valentine speaks to Proteus: "That's on some shallow story of deep love: How young Leander cross'd the Hellespont."

**Here were no hides to come off, and no south-easters to fear.** Dana's initial stay at San Diego (he will leave shortly and then return) is relatively pleasant. The hides they have are already in the hide-house, the ship is in good shape, the weather is good, and the harbor is a safe one.

**...not enough of the boatswain hoarseness...** The boatswain (pronounced "bosun" and sometimes spelled "bos'n" or "bo'sun") is an officer in charge of cables, sails, rigging, and the like, and whose duty it is to "call out" to control the work of the sailors.

**She was bound to Callao, and thence to the Sandwich Islands...** As noted earlier, the brig *Ayacucho*, under the command of Captain John Wilson, was known at the time as the fastest vessel on the coast. Records indicate that the ship sank off the coast of what is now Pt. Reyes, CA in 1860. (However, by that time Captain Wilson had retired, because we know that Dana visits him in 1859 and finds him "an elderly gentleman, thin . . . [with] one shriveled hand." Callao is a port on the west coast of Peru.

**...delayed a day or two by the running away of F—.** Foster, who had previously been second mate, jumps ship. He is widely derided (by men and officers alike) as a "soger," about which term see Dana's note.The captain was determined to break Foster's spirit ("ride him down"), and he succeeded.

**"Marine" is the term applied more particularly to a man who is ignorant and clumsy...** Note that the sailors' jargon differentiates between a man who is lazy (a shirker) and one who is merely clumsy. The former is a "soger," while the latter is a "marine."

fellow had a very peculiar, wild sort of note, breaking occasionally into a falsetto. The sailors thought it was too high, and not enough of the boatswain hoarseness about it; but to me it had a great charm. The harbor was perfectly still, and his voice rang among the hills, as though it could have been heard for miles. Toward sundown, a good breeze having sprung up, she got under weigh, and with her long, sharp head cutting elegantly through the water, on a taught bowline, she stood directly out of the harbor, and bore away to the southward. She was bound to Callao, and thence to the Sandwich Islands, and expected to be on the coast again in eight or ten months.

At the close of the week we were ready to sail, but were delayed a day or two by the running away of F—-, the man who had been our second mate, and was turned forward. From the time that he was "broken," he had had a dog's berth on board the vessel, and determined to run away at the first opportunity. Having shipped for an officer when he was not half a seaman, he found little pity with the crew, and was not man enough to hold his ground among them. The captain called him a "soger,"(1)

---

1. Soger (soldier) is the worst term of reproach that can be applied to a sailor. It signifies a skulk, a sherk,–one who is always trying to get clear of work, and is out of the way, or hanging back, when duty is to be done. "Marine" is the term applied more particularly to a man who is ignorant and clumsy about seaman's work–a green-horn–a land-lubber. To make a sailor shoulder a handspike, and walk fore and aft the deck, like a sentry, is the most ignominious punishment that could be put upon him. Such a punishment inflicted upon an able seaman in a vessel of war, would break his spirit down more than a flogging.

---

and promised to "ride him down as he would the main tack;" and when officers are once determined to "ride a man down," it is a gone case with him. He had had several difficulties with the captain, and asked leave to go home in the Lagoda; but this was refused him. One night he was insolent to an officer on the beach, and refused to come aboard in the boat. He was reported to the captain; and as he came aboard,–it being past the proper hour,–he was called aft, and told that he was to have a flogging. Immediately, he fell down on the deck, calling out–"Don't flog me, Captain T—; don't flog me!" and the captain, angry with him, and disgusted with his cowardice, gave him a few blows over the back with a rope's end and sent him forward. He was not much hurt, but a good deal frightened, and made up his mind to run away that very night. This was managed better than anything he ever did in his life, and seemed really to show some spirit and forethought. He gave his bedding and mattress to one of the Lagoda's crew, who took it aboard his vessel as something which he had bought, and promised to keep it for him. He then unpacked his chest, putting all his valuable clothes into a large canvas bag, and told one of us, who had the watch, to call him at midnight. Coming on deck, at midnight, and finding no officer on deck, and all still aft, he lowered his bag into a boat, got softly down into it, cast off the painter, and let it drop silently with the tide until he was out of hearing, when he sculled ashore.

The next morning, when all hands were mustered, there was a great stir to find F—. Of course, we would tell nothing, and all they could discover was, that he had left an empty chest behind him, and that he went off in a boat; for they saw it lying up high and dry on the beach. After breakfast, the captain went up to the town, and offered a reward of twenty dollars for him; and for a couple of days, the soldiers, Indians, and all others who had nothing to do, were scouring the country for him, on horseback, but without effect; for he was safely concealed, all the time, within fifty rods of the hide-houses. As soon as he had landed, he went directly to the Lagoda's hide-house, and a part of her crew, who were living there on shore, promised to conceal him and his traps until the Pilgrim should sail, and then to intercede with Captain Bradshaw to take him on board the ship. Just behind the hide-houses, among the thickets and underwood, was a small cave, the entrance to

**...managed better than anything he ever did in his life, and seemed really to show some spirit and forethought.** Dana delights in the irony: Here's a stupid, lazy man who has never succeeded at anything, finally succeeding—at running away.

**In the news**
**March, 1835**

For years, people thought that Mars was (or had once been) inhabited, because astronomers had supposedly found evidence of canals having been dug on the planet. This mistake was caused by Italian astronomer Giovanni Schiaparelli, born on the 14th of this month. He meant to describe the planet's surface features as "channels," but mistakenly used the Italian word for "canals," instead.

**...a reward of twenty dollars...** A fair amount of money, really, worth more than $500 today.

**...within fifty rods of the hide-houses.** A rod is a measure of length, equal to 5.5 yards, or 16.5 feet.

**...promised to conceal him and his traps...** In this context and at this time, "traps" refers to personal effects or belongings. The word may come from a shortening of "trappings" and in this form goes back to the very early 1800s.

**...intercede with Captain Bradshaw to take him on board the ship.** This is the first time Bradshaw is mentioned and, except for the comment a few sentences later, he never again appears in the book. There is record of a Captain John Bradshaw, at one time master of a vessel called the *Franklin*. If it's the same man, then Bradshaw has a bit of a checkered past, having several times been held by the Mexican authorities on (possibly trumped-up) charges, including smuggling. In an appendix written 24 years later, Dana does mention him, but only briefly.

which was known only to two men on the beach, and which was so well concealed that, though, when I afterwards came to live on shore, it was shown to me two or three times, I was never able to find it alone. To this cave he was carried before daybreak in the morning, and supplied with bread and water, and there remained until he saw us under weigh and well round the point.

**...we made sail, dropping slowly down with the tide and light wind.** *Pilgrim* is heading back to San Pedro to retrieve more hides. Due to light winds and contrary tides, her passage is slow. (Remember that San Pedro, which Dana calls "a desolate-looking place," is nonetheless a popular spot for acquiring hides.)

In the news
**March, 1835**

The Treaty of Washington is signed by Cherokee and U.S. representatives and directs the Cherokee Nation to assemble in New Echota, Georgia, and to "cede, relinquish, and convey to the United States, all their right and title to all the lands owned, claimed, and possessed by them, including the lands reserved by them for a school fund, east of the Mississippi river." Later, General John E. Wool informs the Cherokees that they have until May 25,1837 to move to a territory west of the Mississippi, or "else be forced to remove by U.S. soldiers."

Friday, March 27th. The captain, having given up all hope of finding F—-, and being unwilling to delay any longer, gave orders for unmooring the ship, and we made sail, dropping slowly down with the tide and light wind. We left letters with Captain Bradshaw to take to Boston, and had the satisfaction of hearing him say that he should be back again before we left the coast. The wind, which was very light, died away soon after we doubled the point, and we lay becalmed for two days, not moving three miles the whole time, and a part of the second day were almost within sight of the vessels. On the third day, about noon, a cool sea-breeze came rippling and darkening the surface of the water, and by sundown we were off San Juan's, which is about forty miles from San Diego, and is called half way to San Pedro, where we were now bound. Our crew was now considerably weakened. One man we had lost overboard; another had been taken aft as clerk; and a third had run away; so that, beside S—- and myself, there were only three able seamen and one boy of twelve years of age. With this diminished and discontented crew, and in a small vessel, we were now to battle the watch through a couple of years of hard service; yet there was not one who was not glad that F—- had escaped; for, shiftless and good for nothing as he was, no one could wish to see him dragging on a miserable life, cowed down and disheartened; and we were all rejoiced to hear, upon our return to San Diego, about two months afterwards, that he had been immediately taken aboard the Lagoda, and went home in her, on regular seaman's wages.

**With this diminished and discontented crew, and in a small vessel, we were now to battle the watch through a couple of years of hard service.** It's interesting to note that, although the men dislike Foster, they're rooting for him, because they hate to see someone treated the way that Captain Thompson is treating him. *Pilgrim* really is "a small vessel," with a length of only about 90 feet. Seaworthy, certainly, but not the safest or most comfortable vessel on which to make a voyage of this length and distance.

After a slow passage of five days, we arrived, on Wednesday, the first of April, at our old anchoring ground at San Pedro. The bay was as deserted, and

**...at our old anchoring ground at San Pedro.** It's now April 1st, 1835, so Dana has been away from Boston for about eight months.

looked as dreary, as before, and formed no pleasing contrast with the security and snugness of San Diego, and the activity and interest which the loading and unloading of four vessels gave to that scene. In a few days the hides began to come slowly down, and we got into the old business of rolling goods up the hill, pitching hides down, and pulling our long league off and on. Nothing of note occurred while we were lying here, except that an attempt was made to repair the small Mexican brig which had been cast away in a south-easter, and which now lay up, high and dry, over one reef of rocks and two sand-banks. Our carpenter surveyed her, and pronounced her capable of refitting, and in a few days the owners came down from the Pueblo, and, waiting for the high spring tides, with the help of our cables, kedges, and crew, got her off and afloat, after several trials. The three men at the house on shore, who had formerly been a part of her crew, now joined her, and seemed glad enough at the prospect of getting off the coast.

On board our own vessel, things went on in the common monotonous way. The excitement which immediately followed the flogging scene had passed off, but the effect of it upon the crew, and especially upon the two men themselves, remained. The different manner in which these men were affected, corresponding to their different characters, was not a little remarkable. John was a foreigner and high-tempered, and, though mortified, as any one would be at having had the worst of an encounter, yet his chief feeling seemed to be anger; and he talked much of satisfaction and revenge, if he ever got back to Boston. But with the other, it was very different. He was an American, and had had some education; and this thing coming upon him, seemed completely to break him down. He had a feeling of the degradation that had been inflicted upon him, which the other man was incapable of. Before that, he had a good deal of fun, and mused us often with queer negro stories,–(he was from a slave state); but afterwards he seldom smiled; seemed to lose all life and elasticity; and appeared to have but one wish, and that was for the voyage to be at an end. I have often known him to draw

**...pulling our long league off and on...** As noted earlier, a league was a measurement (no longer in use) about equal to three miles.

**...an attempt was made to repair the small Mexican brig...** This, rather than the earlier mention (see Ch. 14), is the point at which *Pilgrim* "rescues" the brig *Fazio*, which had gone aground at San Pedro.

In the news
**April, 1835**

On the way from Mendoza to Santiago, Chile, Darwin discovers that "...some thief had stolen one of our mules & the bell from the Madrina; we only rode a short distance to the remains of the old Guard House." (See previous note regarding la Madrina.)

**...the effect of it upon the crew, and especially upon the two men themselves, remained.** The entire crew is feeling the effects of the flogging, but especially the two men who had received the punishment. Being an American, Dana seems to be saying, Samuel Sparks is more sensitive to the degradation or feelings of abasement; perhaps because, as an American, Sparks is used to enjoying his right to a certain amount of liberty and freedom. Yet, when another man has every right to "sieze you up" and flog you, then the freedom you thought was your birthright is something of a delusion. Interestingly, Sparks comes from a slave state (Virginia) and often tells "queer negro stories." One wonders if he now has a better understanding of what it means to be a slave.

a long sigh when he was alone, and he took but little part or interest in John's plans of satisfaction and retaliation.

**...slipped...** That is, slipped anchor and headed to sea. As noted earlier, being at sea during a storm is safer than being near land, because near land your vessel could be driven ashore and possibly broken up on the rocks. Better to have some "sea room" between you and the land.

**...under weigh for Santa Barbara.** Having finished their business at San Pedro, *Pilgrim* now heads for Santa Barbara, some 90 or so (nautical) miles up the coast.

After a stay of about a fortnight, during which we slipped for one south-easter, and were at sea two days, we got under weigh for Santa Barbara. It was now the middle of April, and the south-easter season was nearly over; and the light, regular trade-winds, which blow down the coast, began to set steadily in, during the latter part of each day. Against these, we beat slowly up to Santa Barbara–a distance of about ninety miles–in three days. There we found, lying at anchor, the large Genoese ship which we saw in the same place, on the first day of our coming upon the coast. She had been up to San Francisco, or, as it is called, "chock up to windward," had stopped at Monterey on her way down, and was shortly to proceed to San Pedro and San Diego, and thence, taking in her cargo, to sail for Valparaiso and Cadiz. She was a large, clumsy ship, and with her topmasts stayed forward, and high poop-deck, looked like an old woman with a crippled back. It was now the close of Lent, and on Good Friday she had all her yards a'cock-bill, which is customary among Catholic vessels. Some also have an effigy of Judas, which the crew amuse themselves with keel-hauling and hanging by the neck from the yard-arms.

**...Valparaiso and Cadiz.** Busy ports in Chile and Spain.

**...which is customary among Catholic vessels.** Tipping the yards (a horizontal spar used to support a square sail) at an angle (i.e., a'cock-bill) is a sign of mourning, usually due to the death of a crew member. In this case, it is to commemorate Good Friday.

**... amuse themselves with keel-hauling...** Keelhauling was a punishment (now illegal) in which a crew member (almost never an officer, unless he was mutinous) was dragged beneath the ship from one side to another. The result was often death by drowning, but even if the victim escaped death, he was badly lacerated by being dragged against the barnacles that grew on the ship's hull. In this case, the crew of the Genoese ship is symbolically keelhauling a representation of Judas Iscariot, the Apostle who betrayed Christ.

## Chapter XVIII

### Easter Sunday–"Sail Ho!"–Whales–San Juan–Romance of Hide-Droghing–San Diego Again

The next Sunday was Easter Sunday, and as there had been no liberty at San Pedro, it was our turn to go ashore and misspend another Sabbath. Soon after breakfast, a large boat, filled with men in blue jackets, scarlet caps, and various colored under-clothes, bound ashore on liberty, left the Italian ship, and passed under our stern; the men singing beautiful Italian boat-songs, all the way, in fine, full chorus. Among the songs I recognized the favorite "O Pescator dell' onda." It brought back to my mind pianofortes, drawing-rooms, young ladies singing, and a thousand other things which as little befitted me, in my situation, to be thinking upon. Supposing that the whole day would be too long a time to spend ashore, as there was no place to which we could take a ride, we remained quietly on board until after dinner. We were then pulled ashore in the stern of the boat, and, with orders to be on the beach at sundown, we took our way for the town. There, everything wore the appearance of a holyday. The people were all dressed in their best; the men riding about on horseback among the houses, and the women sitting on carpets before the doors. Under the piazza of a "pulperia," two men were seated, decked out with knots of ribbons and bouquets, and playing the violin and the Spanish guitar. These are the only instruments, with the exception of the drums and trumpets at Monterey that I ever heard in California; and I suspect they play upon no others, for at a great fandango at which I was afterwards present, and where they mustered all the music they could find, there were three violins and two guitars, and no other instrument. As it was now too near the middle of the day to see any dancing and hearing that a bull was expected down from the country, to be baited in the presidio square, in the course of an hour or two we took a stroll among the houses. Inquiring for an American who, we had been told, had married in the place, and

**...and misspend another Sabbath.** Dana is only half jesting; the men do indeed "misspend" the Sabbath, spending their time drinking and dancing, rather than in worship.

**In the news**
**April, 1835**

At the time, one "solution" to the problem of slavery (and of former slaves who were now landless and jobless) was thought to be repatriating all who wished to move to Liberia, a West African colony begun expressly for the purpose of relocating former slaves. In April of 1835, the brig *Rover* reported transporting 71 former slaves, many of them family members, to the colony. Some 23 of them died en route.

**Among the songs I recognized the favorite "O Pescator dell' onda."** A light-hearted Venetian duet composed about 1819. The title means "the fisherman of the waves." The song is also mentioned in James Fenimore Cooper's *The Bravo* (1831).

**It brought back to my mind pianofortes, drawing-rooms, young ladies singing...** Having shipped out on his adventure as a common sailor, Dana, eager to return to his former life, again laments the lack of culture and sophistication. One critic notes that Dana's tale is, among other things, the story of a "cultural dislocation."

**...a bull was expected down from the country, to be baited in the presidio square...** Not at all the same thing as a bullfight. In bull-baiting, specially trained dogs are set loose on the bull, with the object of attacking and ultimately killing the bull. (The bulldog was bred for a variant of this sport—its powerful jaws were meant to latch onto the bull's snout and not let go until the bull was dead.) Even in "civilized" Britain, the sport was legal until the passage of the 1835 Cruelty to Animals Act.

kept a shop, we were directed to a long, low building, at the end of which was a door, with a sign over it, in Spanish. Entering the shop, we found no one in it, and the whole had an empty, deserted appearance. In a few minutes the man made his appearance, and apologized for having nothing to entertain us with, saying that he had had a fandango at his house the night before, and the people had eaten and drunk up everything.

"Oh yes!" said I, "Easter holydays?"

"No!" said he, with a singular expression to his face; "I had a little daughter die the other day, and that's the custom of the country."

Here I felt a little strangely, not knowing what to say, or whether to offer consolation or no, and was beginning to retire, when he opened a side door and told us to walk in. Here I was no less astonished; for I found a large room, filled with young girls, from three or four years of age up to fifteen and sixteen, dressed all in white, with wreaths of flowers on their heads, and bouquets in their hands. Following our conductor through all these girls, who were playing about in high spirits, we came to a table, at the end of the room, covered with a white cloth, on which lay a coffin, about three feet long, with the body of his child. The coffin was lined on the outside with white cloth, and on the inside with white satin, and was strewed with flowers. Through an open door we saw, in another room, a few elderly people in common dresses; while the benches and tables thrown up in a corner, and the stained walls, gave evident signs of the last night's "high go." Feeling, like Garrick, between tragedy and comedy, an uncertainty of purpose and a little awkwardness, I asked the man when the funeral would take place, and being told that it would move toward the mission in about an hour, took my leave.

To pass away the time, we took horses and rode down to the beach, and there found three or four Italian sailors, mounted, and riding up and down, on the hard sand, at a furious rate. We joined them, and found it fine

In the news

**April, 1835**

In this month's issue of *The New England Magazine*, the editors contend that Edward Everett exhibits a "peculiar fitness" for the office of governor of the state of Massachusetts, which office Everett now seeks. The magazine notes that Everett, a renowned orator and an experienced legislator, "...has been obliged to encounter a common prejudice, that eminence in one department of intellectual labor can only be obtained at the price of mediocrity in all others." Everett wins the election, taking office in January of 1836.

**Here I felt a little strangely...** Dana is truly in a foreign country. He does not understand the customs of this strange land.

**...signs of the last night's "high go."** A "high go" is a frolic or a bout of merriment. Dana sees the signs of last night's party, and he finds it incongruous that the occasion of the party is the small girl whose dead body lies in a coffin at one end of the room.

**Feeling, like Garrick, between tragedy and comedy...** David Garrick was a famous 18th-century British actor. Artist Joshua Reynolds painted a famous portrait of Garrick in which the actor is pictured between two feminine figures, one representing tragedy and the other comedy. (The treatment may have been based on the myth of Hercules being forced to choose between pleasure and virtue. Not surprisingly—he is Hercules, after all—he chooses virtue, although this is not made clear in all versions of the myth.)

sport. The beach gave us a stretch of a mile or more, and the horses flew over the smooth, hard sand, apparently invigorated and excited by the salt sea-breeze, and by the continual roar and dashing of the breakers. From the beach we returned to the town, and finding that the funeral procession had moved, rode on and overtook it, about half-way to the mission. Here was as peculiar a sight as we had seen before in the house; the one looking as much like a funeral procession as the other did like a house of mourning. The little coffin was borne by eight girls, who were continually relieved by others, running forward from the procession and taking their places. Behind it came a straggling company of girls, dressed as before, in white and flowers, and including, I should suppose by their numbers, nearly all the girls between five and fifteen in the place. They played along on the way, frequently stopping and running all together to talk to some one, or to pick up a flower, and then running on again to overtake the coffin. There were a few elderly women in common colors; and a herd of young men and boys, some on foot and others mounted, followed them, or walked or rode by their side, frequently interrupting them by jokes and questions. But the most singular thing of all was, that two men walked, one on each side of the coffin, carrying muskets in their hands, which they continually loaded, and fired into the air. Whether this was to keep off the evil spirits or not, I do not know. It was the only interpretation that I could put upon it.

As we drew near the mission, we saw the great gate thrown open, and the pádre standing on the steps, with a crucifix in hand. The mission is a large and deserted-looking place, the out-buildings going to ruin, and everything giving one the impression of decayed grandeur. A large stone fountain threw out pure water, from four mouths, into a basin, before the church door; and we were on the point of riding up to let our horses drink, when it occurred to us that it might be consecrated, and we forbore. Just at this moment, the bells set up their harsh, discordant clang; and the procession moved into the court. I was anxious to follow, and see the ceremony, but the horse of one of my companions had

### In the news
### April, 1835

*The North American Review* prints articles on poet Samuel Taylor Coleridge (author of "The Rime of The Ancient Mariner" noted earlier), European politics, and a favorable review of E.L. Bulwer's *The Last Days of Pompeii*, a novel detailing the destruction of the city in A.D. 79 by the eruption of Mt. Vesuvius. Of special interest to us is the fact that Dana's father, Richard Henry Dana Sr., is the editor of (and a frequent contributor to) the magazine.

**Whether this was to keep off the evil spirits or not, I do not know.** Dana is most likely correct. Many old funereal customs do indeed have their origins in attempts to frighten away evil spirits or to comfort the recently departed spirit. A "dead bell," for example, was used during British funerals, originally to frighten away spirits. Even today, the famed New Orleans jazz funeral is known for loud music and clashing symbols, the original purpose of which were to frighten away such spirits.

**...it occurred to us that it might be consecrated, and we forbore.** A wise decision on Dana's part. The fountain may indeed have been consecrated (or declared holy) during a religious ceremony. Given Dana's disdain of Catholicism, it's nice to see this sign of respect.

become frightened, and was tearing off toward the town; and having thrown his rider, and got one of his feet caught in the saddle, which had slipped, was fast dragging and ripping it to pieces. Knowing that my shipmate could not speak a word of Spanish, and fearing that he would get into difficulty, I was obliged to leave the ceremony and ride after him. I soon overtook him, trudging along, swearing at the horse, and carrying the remains of the saddle, which he had picked up on the road. Going to the owner of the horse, we made a settlement with him, and found him surprisingly liberal. All parts of the saddle were brought back, and, being capable of repair, he was satisfied with six reáls. We thought it would have been a few dollars. We pointed to the horse, which was now half way up one of the mountains; but he shook his head, saying, "No importe!" and giving us to understand that he had plenty more.

**... dragging and ripping it to pieces.** Keep in mind that, while horses are cheap and plentiful in California (after all, they happily reproduce themselves without any effort or expense on our part), saddles are very dear, and take many, many hours and a good deal of skill to create. It's one thing to lose a horse, but losing or destroying a saddle is a serious issue.

**"No importe!"** That is, "It's not important."

Having returned to the town, we saw a great crowd collected in the square before the principal pulperia, and riding up, found that all these people–men, women, and children–had been drawn together by a couple of bantam cocks. The cocks were in full tilt, springing into one another, and the people were as eager, laughing and shouting, as though the combatants had been men. There had been a disappointment about the bull; he had broken his bail, and taken himself off, and it was too late to get another; so the people were obliged to put up with a cock-fight. One of the bantams having been knocked in the head, and had an eye put out, he gave in, and two monstrous prize-cocks were brought on. These were the object of the whole affair; the two bantams having been merely served up as a first course, to collect the people together. Two fellows came into the ring holding the cocks in their arms, and stroking them, and running about on all fours, encouraging and setting them on. Bets ran high, and, like most other contests, it remained for some time undecided. They both showed great pluck, and fought probably better and longer than their masters would have done. Whether, in the end, it was the white or the red that beat, I do not recollect; but, whichever it was, he strutted off with the true veni-vidi-vici look, leaving the other lying panting on his

**The cocks were in full tilt, springing into one another...** Much like the bull baiting noted earlier, cockfighting is a "blood sport" of ancient origins. In this case, two cocks (roosters) are placed in a ring (the cockpit) and the birds fight until one of them is injured or dead. In some regions, sharp spurs are attached to the birds' legs to help them injure one another. (They are so sharp and so dangerous, in fact, that—somewhat ironically—birds have been known to injure or even kill their handlers.) Like bull (and bear) baiting, cockfighting is now illegal in most countries.

**...the two bantams having been merely served up as a first course...** Dana puns here; obviously, such birds often really *are* one course in a meal.

**...fought probably better and longer than their masters would have done.** Dana affects to appear unconcerned by and nonchalant about this brutality. And yet, note the snide remark implying that the birds may be better (and are certainly tougher) than their owners.

beam-ends.

This matter having been settled, we heard some talk about "caballos" and "carrera" and seeing the people all streaming off in one direction, we followed, and came upon a level piece of ground, just out of the town, which was used as a race-course. Here the crowd soon became thick again; the ground was marked off; the judges stationed; and the horses led up to one end. Two fine-looking old gentlemen –Don Carlos and Don Domingo, so called–held the stakes, and all was now ready. We waited some time, during which we could just see the horses twisting round and turning, until, at length, there was a shout along the lines, and on they came–heads stretched out and eyes starting;–working all over, both man and beast. The steeds came by us like a couple of chain-shot–neck and neck; and now we could see nothing but their backs, and their hind hoofs flying in the air. As fast as the horses passed, the crowd broke up behind them, and ran to the goal. When we got there, we found the horses returning on a slow walk, having run far beyond the mark, and heard that the long, bony one had come in head and shoulders before the other. The riders were light-built men; had handkerchiefs tied round their heads; and were bare-armed and bare-legged. The horses were noble-looking beasts, not so sleek and combed as our Boston stable-horses, but with fine limbs, and spirited eyes. After this had been settled, and fully talked over, the crowd scattered again and flocked back to the town.

Returning to the large pulperia, we found the violin and guitar screaming and twanging away under the piazza, where they had been all day. As it was now sundown, there began to be some dancing. The Italian sailors danced, and one of our crew exhibited himself in a sort of West India shuffle, much to the amusement of the bystanders, who cried out, "Bravo!" "Otra vez!" and "Vivan los marineros!" but the dancing did not become general, as the women and the "gente de razón" had not yet made their appearance. We wished very much to stay and see the style of dancing; but, although we had had our own way during the day, yet we were, after all,

**...veni-vidi-vici...** "I came-I saw-I conquered." From Julius Caesar's message to the Roman Senate after his victory, in 47 B.C., at Zela, in north-central Turkey.

**...talk about "caballos" and "carrera"...** The crowd is yelling about horses and a horse race.

**Two fine-looking old gentlemen – Don Carlos and Don Domingo...** In Italian, Spanish, and some other Latinate languages, "Don" is a title of respect. It is used with a given name (i.e., a first name) rather than with a surname.

**The steeds came by us like a couple of chain-shot...** Chain-shot is a form of ammunition used by warships in the days of sail. It consisted of two small iron balls chained together (an iron bar was sometimes used instead of a chain), and was quite destructive, often used to bring down masts, shrouds, and other rigging.

**In the news**

**April, 1835**

We know Edgar Allan Poe as a writer of gothic horror and mystery—and possibly as the inventor of the detective/mystery story in the form in which we've come to know it. But he first came to prominence as a literary critic, and this month's issue of the *Southern Literary Messenger* includes both a Poe story ("Morella") and a critical review of Laughton Osborn's *Confessions of a Poet.*

**...screaming and twanging...** One gets the impression that Dana doesn't think much of the Californians' music.

**..."Otra vez!" and "Vivan los marineros!"...** "Again!" And "Hooray for [actually, "long live"] the sailors!"

**...we were, after all, but 'foremast Jacks...** That is, we are but simple sailors and subject to our masters' orders. Note that Dana says "fore-mast," not "foremost." He means that they sail "before the mast"; in other words, they are low-ranking seamen whose quarters are in the forecastle.

**...which, from some cause or other, always brings on, or precedes a heavy sea.** There are certainly many documented instances of rough seas accompanying (or being preceded by) fog, but most authorities note that fog is usually accompanied by *calm* seas. The calm seas that normally accompany fog are in fact fortuitious, since the fact that the sailors cannot see is bad enough without also having to deal with rough seas.

**....set to work "tarring down" the rigging.** Tarring the rigging (coating the sheets [i.e., ropes] in tar so as to protect them from the elements) is a difficult, smelly, dangerous job. It requires that the sailors be hauled up and down the masts and shrouds by the use of ropes and pulleys, all while carrying heavy buckets of hot tar.

**...we had the satisfaction of seeing the Italian ship's boat go ashore...** Dana is being sarcastically snide. While his crew is confined to the boat doing various dirty jobs, the Genoese crew is off to shore. A baracolla (or baracolle) is a boating song.

**There's no danger of Catholicism's spreading in New England; Yankees can't afford the time to be Catholics.** A bit more of Dana's snide commentary. This time he manages to insult both Catholicism *and* ship captains.

but 'foremast Jacks; and having been ordered to be on the beach by sundown, did not venture to be more than an hour behind the time; so we took our way down. We found the boat just pulling ashore through the breakers, which were running high, there having been a heavy fog outside, which, from some cause or other, always brings on, or precedes a heavy sea. Liberty-men are privileged from the time they leave the vessel until they step on board again; so we took our places in the stern sheets, and were congratulating ourselves upon getting off dry, when a great comber broke fore and aft the boat, and wet us through and through, filling the boat half full of water. Having lost her buoyancy by the weight of the water, she dropped heavily into every sea that struck her, and by the time we had pulled out of the surf into deep water, she was but just afloat, and we were up to our knees. By the help of a small bucket and our hats, we bailed her out, got on board, hoisted the boats, eat our supper, changed our clothes, gave (as is usual) the whole history of our day's adventures to those who had staid on board, and having taken a night-smoke, turned-in. Thus ended our second day's liberty on shore.

On Monday morning, as an offset to our day's sport, we were all set to work "tarring down" the rigging. Some got girt-lines up for riding down the stays and back-stays, and others tarred the shrouds, lifts, etc., laying out on the yards, and coming down the rigging. We over-hauled our bags and took out our old tarry trowsers and frocks, which we had used when we tarred down before, and were all at work in the rigging by sunrise. After breakfast, we had the satisfaction of seeing the Italian ship's boat go ashore, filled with men, gaily dressed, as on the day before, and singing their bar-carollas. The Easter holydays are kept up on shore during three days; and being a Catholic vessel, the Crew had the advantage of them. For two successive days, while perched up in the rigging, covered with tar and engaged in our disagreeable work, we saw these fellows going ashore in the morning, and coming off again at night, in high spirits. So much for being Protestants. There's no danger of Catholicism's spreading in New England; Yankees can't afford the time to be Catholics.

American shipmasters get nearly three weeks more labor out of their crews, in the course of a year, than the masters of vessels from Catholic countries. Yankees don't keep Christmas, and ship-masters at sea never know when Thanksgiving comes, so Jack has no festival at all.

About noon, a man aloft called out "Sail ho!" and looking round, we saw the head sails of a vessel coming round the point. As she drew round, she showed the broadside of a full-rigged brig, with the Yankee ensign at her peak. We ran up our stars and stripes, and, knowing that there was no American brig on the coast but ourselves, expected to have news from home. She rounded-to and let go her anchor, but the dark faces on her yards, when they furled the sails, and the Babel on deck, soon made known that she was from the Islands. Immediately afterwards, a boat's crew came aboard, bringing her skipper, and from them we learned that she was from Oahu, and was engaged in the same trade with the Ayacucho, Loriotte, etc., between the coast, the Sandwich Islands, and the leeward coast of Peru and Chili. Her captain and officers were Americans, and also a part of her crew; the rest were Islanders. She was called the Catalina, and, like all the other vessels in that trade, except the Ayacucho, her papers and colors were from Uncle Sam. They, of course, brought us no news, and we were doubly disappointed, for we had thought, at first, it might be the ship which we were expecting from Boston.

After lying here about a fortnight, and collecting all the hides the place afforded, we set sail again for San Pedro. There we found the brig which we had assisted in getting off lying at anchor, with a mixed crew of Americans, English, Sandwich Islanders, Spaniards, and Spanish Indians; and, though much smaller than we, yet she had three times the number of men; and she needed them, for her officers were Californians. No vessels in the world go so poorly manned as American and English; and none do so well. A Yankee brig of that size would have had a crew of four men, and would have worked round and round her. The Italian ship had a

**...we saw the head sails of a vessel coming round the point.** The head-sails are the sails forward of the foremast.

**...the Babel on deck...** The Hawaiians' (i.e., the Sandwich Islanders') language sounds completely. . .well, *foreign*, given that it is not related to any language with which any of the *Pilgrim*'s sailors would have been familiar. In other words, it sounded like senseless *babble*, a word that comes to us courtesy of the Biblical story of the Babylonians who built the famous (or infamous) Tower of Babel in an ill-advised attempt to reach the heavens. Since the people at this point all speak the same language, God determines to "confound their speech" in order to punish them and to prevent completion of the tower. This, according to some interpretations of the Bible, is why different peoples speak different languages today.

**... her papers and colors were from Uncle Sam.** Yes, the use of this term to personify the U.S. government goes back this far—and a bit further, really: It was first used during the War of 1812.

**... she had three times the number of men; and she needed them, for her officers were Californians.** Dana is at pains throughout the book to show how little he thinks of most of the Californians. In this case he points out that a comparable vessel crewed by American or British sailors and officers would have required a fraction of the manpower and would have performed much better.

**... like a parcel of "Yahoos," and running about decks...** The Yahoos (a name invented by Jonathan Swift in the satirical novel *Gulliver's Travels*) were an imaginary race of brutes in the form of men.

**..."turned to account."** That is, put to good use; to result in profit. The phrase sounds Victorian, but goes back to the 17th century. Swift (see the previous note about "Yahoos") used it in *A Modest Proposal* in 1729. Dana is saying that singing looks and sounds like leisure, but can result in improved performance.

**... And mitigates the harshest clime.** Dana's education is showing again. This is from William Wordsworth's "On the Power of Sound," among the last of Wordsworth's poems, and only recently published (1828) when Dana heads to sea. Dana quotes the poem because it expresses, in more poetic form, what he's been saying: Music helps lighten even a slave's burden.

**...San Pedro, as well as all the other open ports upon the coast, was filled with whales...** These are most likely gray whales, which (then and now) make a yearly 6000-mile migratory trip stretching from Alaska to Baja California, Mexico to bear their young. These whales were not as sought-after as sperm whale and some other species, but they were (and are) hunted for their oil nonetheless. About 100 years after Dana notes that the area was "filled with whales," the California gray whale would be driven nearly to extinction. Thanks to bans on hunting (not always honored by all nations), there are now estimated to be some 16,000 or so California gray whales in existence—not as many as there once were, but no longer at risk of extinction.

crew of thirty men; nearly three times as many as the Alert, which was afterwards on the coast, and was of the same size; yet the Alert would get under weigh and come-to in half the time, and get two anchors, while they were all talking at once–jabbering like a parcel of "Yahoos," and running about decks to find their cat-block.

There was only one point in which they had the advantage over us, and that was in lightening their labors in the boats by their songs. The Americans are a time and money saving people, but have not yet, as a nation, learned that music may be "turned to account." We pulled the long distances to and from the shore, with our loaded boats, without a word spoken, and with discontented looks, while they not only lightened the labor of rowing, but actually made it pleasant and cheerful, by their music. So true is it, that–

"For the tired slave, song lifts the languid oar,
  And bids it aptly fall, with chime
That beautifies the fairest shore,
  And mitigates the harshest clime."

We lay about a week in San Pedro, and got under weigh for San Diego, intending to stop at San Juan, as the south-easter season was nearly over, and there was little or no danger.

This being the spring season, San Pedro, as well as all the other open ports upon the coast, was filled with whales, that had come in to make their annual visit upon soundings. For the first few days that we were here and at Santa Barbara, we watched them with great interest–calling out "there she blows!" every time we saw the spout of one breaking the surface of the water; but they soon became so common that we took little notice of them. They often "broke" very near us; and one thick, foggy night, during a dead calm, while I was standing anchor-watch, one of them rose so near, that he struck our cable, and made all surge again. He did not seem to like the encounter much himself, for he sheered off, and spouted at a good distance. We once came very near running one down in the gig, and should probably have been knocked to pieces and blown sky-high. We had been on board the little Spanish brig, and were returning, stretching out well at our oars, the little boat going like a swallow; our backs were forward, (as is always the case in pulling,) and the captain, who was steering, was not looking ahead, when, all at once, we heard the spout of a whale directly ahead. "Back water! back water, for your lives!" shouted the captain; and we backed our blades in the water and brought the boat to in a smother of foam. Turning our heads, we saw a great, rough, hump-backed whale, slowly crossing our fore foot, within three or four yards of the boat's stem. Had we not backed water just as we did, we should inevitably have gone smash upon him, striking him with our stem just about amidships. He took no notice of us, but passed slowly on, and dived a few yards beyond us, throwing his tail high in the air. He was so near that we had a perfect view of him and as may be supposed, had no desire to see him nearer. He was a disgusting creature; with a skin rough, hairy, and of an iron-grey color. This kind differs much from the sperm, in color and skin, and is said to be fiercer. We saw a few sperm whales; but most of the whales that come upon the coast are fin-backs, hump-backs, and right-whales, which are more difficult to take, and are said not to give oil enough to pay for the trouble. For this reason whale-ships do not come upon the coast after them. Our captain, together with Captain Nye of the Loriotte, who had been in a whale-ship, thought of making an attempt upon one of them with two boats' crews, but as we had only two harpoons and no proper lines, they gave it up.

During the months of March, April, and May, these whales appear in great numbers in the open ports of Santa Barbara, San Pedro, etc., and hover off the coast, while a few find their way into the close harbors of San Diego and Monterey. They are all off again before midsummer, and make their appearance on the "off-shore ground." We saw some fine "schools" of sperm whales, which are easily distinguished by their spout, blowing away, a few miles to windward, on our passage to San Juan.

**...we saw a great, rough, hump-backed whale...** There is a species of whale known as the humpback whale. It's roughly the size and shape of a gray whale, though often a bit larger than the latter. Humpbacks are sometimes spotted near the California coast, so Dana could mean a true humpback, or possibly just a somewhat misshapen (or misidentified) gray whale. Either one, if aroused, could certainly make short work of a small boat.

In the news

**April, 1835**

Financier "Diamond Jim" James Fisk is born this month. At a young age Fisk ran away and joined a circus, became a waiter, and then a peddler. He became a stockbroker in 1864, and ended up controlling (with Jay Gould) the Erie Railroad. A man of unbridled (and unprincipled) financial and sexual appetites, Fisk was eventually shot by a former partner who had fallen in love with one of Fisk's mistresses.

**...as we had only two harpoons and no proper lines, they gave it up.** And a wise decision that was, too. To take out after full-grown whale (of whatever species) with only a couple of harpoons, no decent lines, and—perhaps most importantly—an inexperienced crew, would be incredibly risky, verging on suicidal. (Keep in mind that most sailors of the 1830s did not know how to swim. If a whale destroyed a boat, any sailor who could not grab onto a piece of floating timber would likely drown.)

**... whales appear in great numbers in the open ports of Santa Barbara, San Pedro, etc., and hover off the coast...** This is still the case, and whale-watching along the California and Oregon coats has become quite popular.

**...we came to anchor, in twenty fathoms' water...** Since 20 fathoms is 120 feet, *Pilgrim* truly is "almost out at sea."

**We pulled the agent ashore, and were ordered to wait for him...** The agent, Robinson, has business to conduct: As the owner's representative, the agent has to arrange for the acquisition and transport of hides.

**San Juan is the only romantic spot in California.** San Juan Capistrano may indeed be romantic, but this paragraph has befuddled critics for over 170 years. Dana's description of the coast at San Juan is completely at odds with the actual geography: The mission itself is not even visible, either from the sea or from the tops of what few cliffs are present. Then again, as noted earlier, most of Dana's journals have disappeared by the time he sits down to write this book. He is back in Boston working (four years after the fact) from memory and from a few pages of scrawled notes.

**...a small cove, or "bight," which gave us, at high tide, a few square feet of sand-beach...** A bight is usually a curve or loop in a rope; hence a curving piece of land.

In the news

**May, 1835**

Charles Darwin travels to Illapel, Chile. He notes, "I determined to strike in the country to the [copper] mining town of Illapel. — It was a long days journey & we had to cross a Cuesta I should think at least 2000 ft high....Illapel is a very regular & pretty little town, its flourishing condition depends on the numerous mines, chiefly Copper, in the vicinity."

Coasting along on the quiet shore of the Pacific, we came to anchor, in twenty fathoms' water, almost out at sea, as it were, and directly abreast of a steep hill which overhung the water, and was twice as high as our royal-mast-head. We had heard much of this place, from the Lagoda's crew, who said it was the worst place in California. The shore is rocky, and directly exposed to the south-east, so that vessels are obliged to slip and run for their lives on the first sign of a gale; and late as it was in the season, we got up our slip-rope and gear, though we meant to stay only twenty-four hours. We pulled the agent ashore, and were ordered to wait for him, while he took a circuitous way round the hill to the mission, which was hidden behind it. We were glad of the opportunity to examine this singular place, and hauling the boat up and making her well fast, took different directions up and down the beach, to explore it.

San Juan is the only romantic spot in California. The country here for several miles is high table-land, running boldly to the shore, and breaking off in a steep hill, at the foot of which the waters of the Pacific are constantly dashing. For several miles the water washes the very base of the hill, or breaks upon ledges and fragments of rocks which run out into the sea. Just where we landed was a small cove, or "bight," which gave us, at high tide, a few square feet of sand-beach between the sea and the bottom of the hill. This was the only landing-place. Directly before us, rose the perpendicular height of four or five hundred feet. How we were to get hides down, or goods up, upon the table-land on which the mission was situated, was more than we could tell. The agent had taken a long circuit, and yet had frequently to jump over breaks, and climb up steep places, in the ascent. No animal but a man or monkey could get up it. However, that was not our look-out; and knowing that the agent would be gone an hour or more, we strolled about, picking up shells, and following the sea where it tumbled in, roaring and spouting, among the crevices of the great rocks. What a sight, thought I, must this be in a south-easter! The rocks were as large as those of Nahant or Newport, but, to my eye, more grand and broken. Beside, there was a grandeur in everything around, which gave almost a solemnity to the scene: a silence and solitariness which affected everything! Not a human being but ourselves for miles; and no sound heard but the pulsations of the great Pacific! and the great steep hill rising like a wall, and cutting us off from all the world, but the "world of waters!" I separated myself from the rest and sat down on a rock, just where the sea ran in and formed a fine spouting horn. Compared with the plain, dull sand-beach of the rest of the coast, this grandeur was as refreshing as a great rock in a weary land. It was almost the first time that I had been positively alone–free from the sense that human beings were at my elbow, if not talking with me–since I had left home. My better nature returned strong upon me. Everything was in accordance with my state of feeling, and I experienced a glow of pleasure at finding that what of poetry and romance I ever had in me, had not been entirely deadened by the laborious and frittering life I had led. Nearly an hour did I sit, almost lost in the luxury of this entire new scene of the play in which I had been so long acting, when I was aroused by the distant shouts of my companions, and saw that they were collecting together, as the agent had made his appearance, on his way back to our boat.

**...the great steep hill rising like a wall, and cutting us off from all the world, but the "world of waters!"** The phrase is from James Thomson's 1729 poem, "Britannia."

**It was almost the first time that I had been positively alone–free from the sense that human beings were at my elbow...** Dana is quite literally correct: On board a fairly small vessel, a crew of 12 to 15 men live and work in very close proximity, and there is little chance for any privacy. In fact, the term "close quarters," originally a nautical phrase dating back to the mid-18th century, is an apt description of living arrangements on board a merchant vessel or warship, then and now.

**...finding that what of poetry and romance I ever had in me, had not been entirely deadened by the laborious and frittering life I had led.** It may seem odd, but Dana truly is worried about this. He is afraid that, after many months or years before the mast, he will no longer be intellectually fit for sophisticated company. A seaman's life, he frets, may be all he can aspire to.

We pulled aboard, and found the long-boat hoisted out, and nearly laden with goods; and after dinner, we all went on shore in the quarter-boat, with the long-boat in tow. As we drew in, we found an ox-cart and a couple of men standing directly on the brow of the hill; and having landed, the captain took his way round the hill, ordering me and one other to follow him. We followed, picking our way out, and jumping and scrambling up, walking over briers and prickly pears, until we came to the top. Here the country stretched out for miles as far as the eye could reach, on a level, table surface; and the only habitation in sight was the small white mission of San Juan Capistrano, with a few Indian huts about it, standing in a small hollow, about a mile from where we were. Reaching the brow of the hill where the cart stood, we found several piles of hides, and Indians sit-

**...found the long-boat hoisted out....we all went on shore in the quarter-boat...** Technically, a long-boat is simply the largest boat that happens to belong to a sailing vessel. In practice, the term generally refers to an open boat that can accomodate two rows of oarsmen. A quarter-boat is a somewhat smaller boat hung at a vessel's quarter—that is, at the side of a ship near the stem.

ting round them. One or two other carts were coming slowly on from the mission, and the captain told us to begin and throw the hides down. This, then, was the way they were to be got down: thrown down, one at a time, a distance of four hundred feet! This was doing the business on a great scale. Standing on the edge of the hill and looking down the perpendicular height, the sailors,

–"That walk upon the beach, Appeared like mice; and our tall anchoring bark Diminished to her cock; her cock a buoy Almost too small for sight."

Down this height we pitched the hides, throwing them as far out into the air as we could; and as they were all large, stiff, and doubled, like the cover of a book, the wind took them, and they swayed and eddied about, plunging and rising in the air, like a kite when it has broken its string. As it was now low tide, there was no danger of their falling into the water, and as fast as they came to ground, the men below picked them up, and taking them on their heads, walked off with them to the boat. It was really a picturesque sight: the great height; the scaling of the hides; and the continual walking to and fro of the men, who looked like mites, on the beach! This was the romance of hide-droghing!

Some of the hides lodged in cavities which were under the bank and out of our sight, being directly under us; but by sending others down in the same direction, we succeeded in dislodging them. Had they remained there, the captain said he should have sent on board for a couple of pairs of long halyards, and got some one to have gone down for them. It was said that one of the crew of an English brig went down in the same way, a few years before. We looked over, and thought it would not be a welcome task, especially for a few paltry hides; but no one knows what he can do until he is called upon; for, six months afterwards, I went down the same place by a pair of top-gallant studding-sail halyards, to save a half a dozen hides which had lodged there.

Having thrown them all down, we took our way back

**This, then, was the way they were to be got down: thrown down, one at a time...** The sailors are told to throw the hides down the cliff to the beach below, a time-consuming and potentially dangerous operation.

**That walk upon the beach, Appeared like mice...** Almost an exact quote from Shakespeare's *King Lear*. The lines are actually:

*The fishermen, that walk upon the beach, Appear like mice; and yond tall anchoring bark, Diminish'd to her cock; her cock, a buoy Almost too small for sight: the murmuring surge, That on the unnumber'd idle pebbles chafes, Cannot be heard so high.*

In both tellings, the point being made is that the men are so far up the mountain that the fairly good-sized ship looks very, very small, and the skiffs look even smaller.

In the news
**May, 1835**

The first railway in continental Europe opens between Brussels and Mechelen, Antwerp. Prodded along by engineers Pierre Simons and Gustave De Ridder, the country imports three engines from Britain.

**...until he is called upon...** This is certainly true of men and women called upon, perhaps in an emergency, to accomplish some feat previously thought beyond them. But it's also true in a larger sense, and Dana's entire voyage, like any quest or coming-of-age novel, is partly his attempt to answer that question: Of what feats is he capable? Can he learn to become a sailor? Can he leave his peers and his pampered, cultured environment and plunge into a whole different life? These are questions of the sort that young people have always asked themselves and always will; finding the answers to those sorts of questions is part of finding out who you are.

again, and found the boat loaded and ready to start. We pulled off; took the hides all aboard; hoisted in the boats; hove up our anchor; made sail; and before sundown, were on our way to San Diego.

Friday, May 8th, 1835. Arrived at San Diego. Here we found the little harbor deserted. The Lagoda, Ayacucho, Loriotte, and all, had left the coast, and we were nearly alone. All the hide-houses on the beach, but ours, were shut up, and the Sandwich Islanders, a dozen or twenty in number, who had worked for the other vessels and been paid off when they sailed, were living on the beach, keeping up a grand carnival. A Russian discovery-ship which had been in this port a few years before, had built a large oven for baking bread, and went away, leaving it standing. This, the Sandwich Islanders took possession of, and had kept, ever since, undisturbed. It was big enough to hold six or eight men–that is, it was as large as a ship's forecastle; had a door at the side, and a vent-hole at top. They covered it with Oahu mats, for a carpet; stopped up the vent-hole in bad weather, and made it their head-quarters. It was now inhabited by as many as a dozen or twenty men, who lived there in complete idleness–drinking, playing cards, and carousing in every way. They bought a bullock once a week, which kept them in meat, and one of them went up to the town every day to get fruit, liquor, and provisions. Besides this, they had bought a cask of ship-bread, and a barrel of flour from the Lagoda, before she sailed. There they lived, having a grand time, and caring for nobody. Captain T—- was anxious to get three or four of them to come on board the Pilgrim, as we were so much diminished in numbers; and went up to the oven and spent an hour or two trying to negotiate with them. One of them,–a finely built, active, strong and intelligent fellow,– who was a sort of king among them, acted as spokesman. He was called Mannini,–or rather, out of compliment to his known importance and influence, Mr. Mannini–and was known all over California. Through him, the captain offered them fifteen dollars a month, and one month's pay in advance; but it was like throwing pearls before swine, or rather, carrying coals to Newcastle. So long as they had money, they would not

**...a large oven for baking bread...** This would have been patterned after the typical brick ovens used in Russia both to heat homes and to bake bread and other goods. Constructed to retain heat for long periods of time, Russian ovens have been around since at least the 15th century. This one, meant to supply bread for a large company of sailors, was built large enough to serve as a shelter for several men after its abandonment by the Russians.

**...Oahu mats...** Woven mats such as the islanders had been used to making back home. Oahu is the third-largest of what are now called the Hawaiian Islands. With a permanent population of about 1 million, the island is home to the Pearl Harbor National Monument and the USS Arizona Memorial.

**...a cask of ship-bread...** Ship-bread is another name for biscuit or hardtack, an unleavened cracker made of flour, water, and salt. Not very tasty, but fairly nutritious and long-lasting.

**...it was like throwing pearls before swine, or rather, carrying coals to Newcastle.** Both sayings, the former often used as an insult, mean to waste one's time and resources on a fool's errand. The former because the effort is unappreciated and the latter because the effort is unnecessary. (Pigs don't care about pearls, and people in Newcastle don't need imported coal, having plenty of their own, since Newcastle is a coal-mining center.) In this case, the Islanders have no need for paid work; they're enjoying themselves too much at the moment.

**By-'em-by money pau–all gone; then Kanaka work plenty.** *Kanaka* means a Pacific Islander from any of a number of the islands. Over the years, the term has in some regions picked up negative connotations and can be interpreted as mildly insulting. The islanders have no need of work; they intend to play until they run out of money, and *then* they will work. This strikes both Dana and the captain as foolish, so they resolve to simply wait until the islanders need money and come looking for work, at which point they can hire them for less than they had been willing to pay earlier.

In the news
**May, 1835**

James Gordon Bennett, Sr. publishes the first issue of the *New York Herald*. The *Herald*, which would eventually sell some 15,000 copies daily, specializes in crime stories, with an emphasis on lurid murders. Within a few years of the sensational 1836 Jewett murder case, a coalition of clergymen, financiers, and rival editors wage a "Moral War" against Bennett and his sensationalizing newspaper. (Helen Jewett was a New York City prostitute whose alleged murderer, Richard Robinson, was ultimately acquitted.)

**...mollia tempora fandi...** Latin for, "times favorable for speaking." That is, he caught them at a more propitious time, and this time Mr. Mannini was interested in hiring on.

**...went up to the hide-house to take up my quarters for a few months.** Dana is being left ashore at San Diego to take care of the hide-house while *Pilgrim* continues plying the coast and picking up more hides.

work for fifty dollars a month, and when their money was gone, they would work for ten.

"What do you do here, Mr. Mannini?" said the captain.

"Oh, we play cards, get drunk, smoke–do anything we're a mind to."

"Don't you want to come aboard and work?"

"Aole! aole make make makou i ka hana. Now, got plenty money; no good, work. Mamule, money pau–all gone. Ah! very good, work!– maikai, hana hana nui!"

"But you'll spend all your money in this way," said the captain.

"Aye! me know that. By-'em-by money pau–all gone; then Kanaka work plenty."

This was a hopeless case, and the captain left them, to wait patiently until their money was gone.

We discharged our hides and tallow, and in about a week were ready to set sail again for the windward. We unmoored, and got everything ready, when the captain made another attempt upon the oven. This time he had more regard to the "mollia tempora fandi," and succeeded very well. He got Mr. Mannini in his interest, and as the shot was getting low in the locker, prevailed upon him and three others to come on board with their chests and baggage, and sent a hasty summons to me and the boy to come ashore with our things, and join the gang at the hide-house. This was unexpected to me; but anything in the way of variety I liked; so we got ready, and were pulled ashore. I stood on the beach while the brig got under weigh, and watched her until she rounded the point, and then went up to the hide-house to take up my quarters for a few months.

## Chapter XIX

### The Sandwich Islanders–Hide-Curing–Wood-Cutting–Rattle-Snakes–New-Comers

Here was a change in my life as complete as it had been sudden. In the twinkling of an eye, I was transformed from a sailor into a "beach-comber" and a hide-curer; yet the novelty and the comparative independence of the life were not unpleasant. Our hide-house was a large building, made of rough boards, and intended to hold forty thousand hides. In one corner of it, a small room was parted off, in which four berths were made, where we were to live, with mother earth for our floor. It contained a table, a small locker for pots, spoons, plates, etc., and a small hole cut to let in the light. Here we put our chests, threw our bedding into the berths, and took up our quarters. Over our head was another small room, in which Mr. Russell lived, who had charge of the hide-house; the same man who was for a time an officer of the Pilgrim. There he lived in solitary grandeur; eating and sleeping alone, (and these were his principal occupations,) and communing with his own dignity. The boy was to act as cook; while myself, a giant of a Frenchman named Nicholas, and four Sandwich Islanders, were to cure the hides. Sam, the Frenchman, and myself, lived together in the room, and the four Sandwich Islanders worked and ate with us, but generally slept at the oven. My new messmate, Nicholas, was the most immense man that I had ever seen in my life. He came on the coast in a vessel which was afterwards wrecked, and now let himself out to the different houses to cure hides. He was considerably over six feet, and of a frame so large that he might have been shown for a curiosity. But the most remarkable thing about him was his feet. They were so large that he could not find a pair of shoes in California to fit him, and was obliged to send to Oahu for a pair; and when he got them, he was compelled to wear them down at the heel. He told me once, himself, that he was wrecked in an American brig on the Goodwin Sands, and was sent up to London, to the charge of the American consul, without clothing to his back or shoes to his feet, and was obliged to go

**...the novelty and the comparative independence of the life were not unpleasant.** For Dana, life on the beach at San Diego is actually quite pleasant. His accomodations are decent enough—certainly no worse than on board ship, and probably better, since it's not as crowded in the hide-house. The work is not difficult, and the company is generally enjoyable. After months of chafing under the tyrannical rule of Captain Thompson, the months spent at the hide-house must have seemed a bit like a vacation.

**In the news**
**May, 1835**

The city of Chicago is growing rapidly. On May 16, the following article appears in the *Niles' Register*. "...[As] Chicago in Illinois, [is] a place destined to take rank very soon among the first commercial cities of the west, a few remarks relating to the prospects of this place may not be uninteresting to the public: Chicago contains at present between three and four thousand inhabitants. Three years since it was only a military station. The state is rapidly settling with emigrants of industry and character...."

**...communing with his own dignity.** Dana is being sarcastic. Russell, who was simply a sailor chosen to watch over the hide-house, has delusions of grandeur. He seems at pains to ensure that the others respect what he seems to think of as his lofty station.

**He was considerably over six feet...** Keep in mind that in Dana's time, men were somewhat smaller than today, mainly due to poor diet. These days, it's not at all uncommon for men to be over six feet tall, but in 1834 it was unusual.

about London streets in his stocking feet three or four days, in the month of January, until the consul could have a pair of shoes made for him. His strength was in proportion to his size, and his ignorance to his strength–"strong as an ox, and ignorant as strong." He neither knew how to read nor write. He had been to sea from a boy, and had seen all kinds of service, and been in every kind of vessel: merchantmen, men-of-war, privateers, and slavers; and from what I could gather from his accounts of himself, and from what he once told me, in confidence, after we had become better acquainted, he had even been in worse business than slave-trading. He was once tried for his life in Charleston, South Carolina, and though acquitted, yet he was so frightened that he never would show himself in the United States again; and I could not persuade him that he could never be tried a second time for the same offence. He said he had got safe off from the breakers, and was too good a sailor to risk his timbers again.

**...strong as an ox, and ignorant as strong...** From *Tales*, a collection of poems by George Crabbe (1754-1832). Once again, Dana can't resist a literary allusion.

**I could not persuade him that he could never be tried a second time for the same offence.** Dana, who intends to study law and who in fact does become a lawyer, is speaking of the concept of "double jeopardy," a defense that forbids a defendant from being tried more than once on the same charge. The Fifth Amendment of the U.S. Constitution (the same amendment that prohibits a defendant being forced to bear witness against himself) explicitly notes that no person shall "be subject for the same offense to be twice put in jeopardy of life or limb...."

Though I knew what his life had been, yet I never had the slightest fear of him. We always got along very well together, and, though so much stronger and larger than I, he showed a respect for my education, and for what he had heard of my situation before coming to sea. "I'll be good friends with you," he used to say, "for by-and-by you'll come out here captain, and then you'll haze me well!" By holding well together, we kept the officer in good order, for he was evidently afraid of Nicholas, and never ordered us, except when employed upon the hides. My other companions, the Sandwich Islanders, deserve particular notice.

**...by-and-by you'll come out here captain, and then you'll haze me well!** Nicholas forsees Dana rising to a lofty station in life (which indeed he does), perhaps even becoming a ship's captain and some day returning to San Diego. If that happens, Nicholas would benefit if Dana were in his debt.

In the news
**May, 1835**

Nine fairy tales written by Hans Christian Andersen are published in a series of three installments in Copenhagen, Denmark. This is Andersen's first attempt at writing fairy tales. Some of the tales are based on folktales Andersen had heard in his childhood; others are his own invention. Andersen is paid $36 for the manuscript.

A considerable trade has been carried on for several years between California and the Sandwich Islands, and most of the vessels are manned with Islanders; who, as they, for the most part, sign no articles, leave whenever they choose, and let themselves out to cure hides at San Diego, and to supply the places of the men of the American vessels while on the coast. In this way, quite a colony of them had become settled at San Diego, as their headquarters. Some of these had recently gone off in the Ayacucho and Loriotte, and the Pilgrim had taken

Mr. Mannini and three others, so that there were not more than twenty left. Of these, four were on pay at the Ayacucho's house, four more working with us, and the rest were living at the oven in a quiet way; for their money was nearly gone, and they must make it last until some other vessel came down to employ them.

**...at the Ayacucho's house...** That is, at the hide-house belonging to the *Ayacucho*.

During the four months that I lived here, I got well acquainted with all of them, and took the greatest pains to become familiar with their language, habits, and characters. Their language, I could only learn, orally, for they had not any books among them, though many of them had been taught to read and write by the missionaries at home. They spoke a little English, and by a sort of compromise, a mixed language was used on the beach, which could be understood by all. The long name of Sandwich Islanders is dropped, and they are called by the whites, all over the Pacific ocean, "Kanákas," from a word in their own language which they apply to themselves, and to all South Sea Islanders, in distinction from whites, whom they call "Haole." This name, "Kanaka," they answer to, both collectively and individually. Their proper names, in their own language, being difficult to pronounce and remember, they are called by any names which the captains or crews may choose to give them. Some are called after the vessel they are in; others by common names, as Jack, Tom, Bill; and some have fancy names, as Ban-yan, Fore-top, Rope-yarn, Pelican, etc., etc. Of the four who worked at our house one was named "Mr. Bingham," after the missionary at Oahu; another, Hope, after a vessel that he had been in; a third, Tom Davis, the name of his first captain; and the fourth, Pelican, from his fancied resemblance to that bird. Then there was Lagoda-Jack, California-Bill, etc., etc. But by whatever names they might be called, they were the most interesting, intelligent, and kind-hearted people that I ever fell in with. I felt a positive attachment for almost all of them; and many of them I have, to this time, a feeling for, which would lead me to go a great way for the mere pleasure of seeing them, and which will always make me feel a strong interest in the mere name of a Sandwich Islander.

**...a mixed language was used on the beach, which could be understood by all.** In other words, the two groups communicate via a pidgin language. Although the terms "pidgin" and "creole" are sometimes used interchangeably, a pidgin is a simplified "contact" language used between groups that do not have a language in common. It's the result of two different groups attempting to imitate each other's language—the result is a hybrid of sorts. A creole is an actual, stable language, with a grammar; it has, in effect, become the language of a group of people. A creole may have evolved from a pidgin, but they are not the same thing.

**...they were the most interesting, intelligent, and kind-hearted people that I ever fell in with.** It's a little difficult to understand Dana's affection for the kanakas, given his usual contempt for what he views as simple, unsophisticated cultures. After all, he sees the Californians (i.e., the Mexicans) as lazy and shiftless (although he thinks their language quite beautiful). He's said as much about the kanakas, pointing out that they will work only when they run out of money; when they have money, they're content to lie around the beach, drinking and eating. Perhaps the difference is simply that he's had a chance to live and work with the kanakas (he's writing this four years after the fact, remember), and he is familiar with their work onboard a variety of ships. One hopes that if he were given the chance to work alongside the Mexicans for months or years at a time, he would also come to appreciate *their* better qualities.

**...quick of apprehension...** He learned quickly.

**He must have been over fifty years of age...** This doesn't sound very old to us now, but life expectancy in the 1830s was much less than it is today. A man in the 1830s could expect to live into his fifties, but few would live much beyond that. (By comparison, a male's life expectancy in the U.S. today is close to 80 years.) Keep in mind that in 1835 there were no vaccines, no antibiotics, and no health insurance.

**Me pikinini–small–so high–no more!** That is, "I was a very small child at the time!" The word "pikinini" is actually a variant spelling of "picaninny" (itself of Portugese origin), meaning a small (usually black) child. The word, which goes back to the 17th century, was often applied not only to African-American children, but also to any non-white child. The term is now considered offensive.

**None of them liked to have anything said about Captain Cook, for the sailors all believe that he was eaten...** British explorer Captain James Cook was killed in a skirmish with Sandwich Islanders in 1779. He probably was *not* eaten, although the funeral preparations by the islanders (who held him in great respect and therefore gave him a chief's funeral) might have led some to believe that he was to be devoured by the Hawaiians: His body was baked to remove the flesh, and the cleaned bones were put on display.

**...Kamehameha, the Charlemagne of the Sandwich Islands...** King Kamehameha (1758-1819) unified the Hawaiian Islands under his rule.

**...Captain Lord Byron...** Not the poet, but his lesser-known cousin, George Anson Byron. Captain (later admiral) Byron was a career naval officer who sailed to the islands on *HMS Blonde* in 1824.

Tom Davis knew how to read, write, and cipher in common arithmetic; had been to the United States, and spoke English quite well. His education was as good as that of three-quarters of the Yankees in California, and his manners and principles a good deal better, and he was so quick of apprehension that he might have been taught navigation, and the elements of many of the sciences, with the most perfect ease. Old "Mr. Bingham" spoke very little English–almost none, and neither knew how to read nor write; but he was the best-hearted old fellow in the world. He must have been over fifty years of age, and had two of his front teeth knocked out, which was done by his parents as a sign of grief at the death of Kamehameha, the great king of the Sandwich Islands. We used to tell him that he ate Captain Cook, and lost his teeth in that way. That was the only thing that ever made him angry. He would always be quite excited at that; and say–"Aole!" (no.) "Me no eat Captain Cook! Me pikinini–small–so high–no more! My father see Captain Cook! Me–no!" None of them liked to have anything said about Captain Cook, for the sailors all believe that he was eaten, and that, they cannot endure to be taunted with.–"New Zealand Kanaka eat white man;–Sandwich Island Kanaka–no. Sandwich Island Kanaka ua like pu na haole–all 'e same a' you!"

Mr. Bingham was a sort of patriarch among them, and was always treated with great respect, though he had not the education and energy which gave Mr. Mannini his power over them. I have spent hours in talking with this old fellow about Kamehameha, the Charlemagne of the Sandwich Islands; his son and successor Riho Riho, who died in England, and was brought to Oahu in the frigate Blonde, Captain Lord Byron, and whose funeral he remembered perfectly; and also about the customs of his country in his boyhood, and the changes which had been made by the missionaries. He never would allow that human beings had been eaten there; and, indeed, it always seemed like an insult to tell so affectionate, intelligent, and civilized a class of men, that such barbarities had been practised in their own country within the recollection of many of them. Certainly, the history of no people on the globe can show anything like so rapid an advance. I would have trusted my life and my fortune in the hands of any one of these people; and certainly had I wished for a favor or act of sacrifice, I would have gone to them all, in turn, before I should have applied to one of my own countrymen on the coast, and should have expected to have seen it done, before my own countrymen had got half through counting the cost. Their costumes, and manner of treating one another, show a simple, primitive generosity, which is truly delightful; and which is often a reproach to our own people. Whatever one has, they all have. Money, food, clothes, they share with one another; even to the last piece of tobacco to put in their pipes. I once heard old Mr. Bingham say, with the highest indignation, to a Yankee trader who was trying to persuade him to keep his money to himself–"No! We no all 'e same a' you!–Suppose one got money, all got money. You;–suppose one got money–lock him up in chest.–No good!"–"Kanaka all 'e same a' one!" This principle they carry so far, that none of them will eat anything in the sight of others without offering it all round. I have seen one of them break a biscuit, which had been given him, into five parts, at a time when I knew he was on a very short allowance, as there was but little to eat on the beach.

My favorite among all of them, and one who was liked by both officers and men, and by whomever he had anything to do with, was Hope. He was an intelligent, kind-hearted little fellow, and I never saw him angry, though I knew him for more than a year, and have seen him imposed upon by white people, and abused by insolent officers of vessels. He was always civil, and always ready, and never forgot a benefit. I once took care of him when he was ill, getting medicines from the ship's chests, when no captain or officer would do anything for him, and he never forgot it. Every Kanaka has one particular friend, whom he considers himself bound to do everything for, and with whom he has a sort of contract,–an alliance offensive and defensive,–and for whom he will often make the greatest sacrifices. This friend they call aikane; and for such did Hope adopt me. I do not believe I could have wanted anything which he had, that he would not have given me. In return for this,

**In the news**
**June, 1835**

In early June, William A. Richardson is appointed Captain of the Port of San Francisco. On June 25, 1835, he chooses a site and sets up a temporary dwelling made from a sail and some redwood posts. This was the first residence at Yerba Buena Cove, site of the future city of San Francisco.

**Whatever one has, they all have.** This is not uncommon in so-called primitive societies. Some have argued that members of such tribes have no concept of ownership, but that is far from clear. It is clear, though, that their concept of ownership may *differ* from ours. In any case, in small isolated groups that face danger from without, it may be advantageous to share resources in order to allay attack or to prevent some members from starving.

**I once took care of him when he was ill, getting medicines from the ship's chests, when no captain or officer would do anything for him, and he never forgot it.** The fact that Dana cared for Hope when the latter was ill is revealing. At some risk to himself, Dana nurses Hope, takes care of him, and intercedes with others (including the captain of a ship—unfortunately, to no avail) on the islander's behalf. Dana may sometimes come across as jingoistic and also as condescending toward those he has been taught to think of as "lesser" peoples, but his dedication to and affection for Hope (indeed, for all of the islanders) speaks well of him.

**They were all astonishingly quick...** With our modern sensibilities, we may find this passage (and Dana's thought process) a bit grating: "Gee! Imagine that! Who would have thought that people of color could be so smart?!" he seems to be saying. But Dana is doing the best that he can given the times in which he lives and considering his upbringing. He even understands (and notes, a sentence or two later) that when the islanders *do* fail to understand a concept, the fault may lie not with the islanders but with Dana himself.

In the news
**June, 1835**

José Castro becomes governor of Alta California. Castro, born in Monterey, California in 1808, will become Commandante General of the Mexican army during the Mexican-American War, which begins in 1846. In 1860, Castro is assassinated by a bandit. Castro's legacy lives on in San Francisco, where both a street and a district of the city are named for him.

I was always his friend among the Americans, and used to teach him letters and numbers; for he left home before he had learned how to read. He was very curious about Boston (as they call the United States); asking many questions about the houses, the people, etc., and always wished to have the pictures in books explained to him. They were all astonishingly quick in catching at explanations, and many things which I had thought it utterly impossible to make them understand, they often seized in an instant, and asked questions which showed that they knew enough to make them wish to go farther. The pictures of steamboats and railroad cars, in the columns of some newspapers which I had, gave me great difficulty to explain. The grading of the road, the rails, the construction of the carriages, they could easily understand, but the motion produced by steam was a little too refined for them. I attempted to show it to them once by an experiment upon the cook's coppers, but failed; probably as much from my own ignorance as from their want of apprehension; and, I have no doubt, left them with about as clear an idea of the principle as I had myself. This difficulty, of course, existed in the same force with the steamboats and all I could do was to give them some account of the results, in the shape of speed; for, failing in the reason, I had to fall back upon the fact. In my account of the speed I was supported by Tom, who had been to Nantucket, and seen a little steamboat which ran over to New Bedford.

A map of the world, which I once showed them, kept their attention for hours; those who knew how to read pointing out the places and referring to me for the distances. I remember being much amused with a question which Hope asked me. Pointing to the large irregular place which is always left blank round the poles, to denote that it is undiscovered, he looked up and asked.– "Pau?" (Done? ended?)

**...afraid of doubling Cape Horn, for they suffer much in cold weather...** Even now, anyone with half a brain would fear doubling (sailing around) Cape Horn. The weather is terrible, the seas are violent, and many ships have been lost there. Doubling the cape is a sailor's rite of passage, but it's not something that any sailor anticipates without trepidation.

The system of naming the streets and numbering the houses, they easily understood, and the utility of it. They had a great desire to see America, but were afraid of doubling Cape Horn, for they suffer much in cold weather, and had heard dreadful accounts of the Cape, from those of their number who had been round it.

They smoke a great deal, though not much at a time; using pipes with large bowls, and very short stems, or no stems at all. These, they light, and putting them to their mouths, take a long draught, getting their mouths as full as they can hold, and their cheeks distended, and then let it slowly out through their mouths and nostrils. The pipe is then passed to others, who draw, in the same manner, one pipe-full serving for half a dozen. They never take short, continuous draughts, like Europeans, but one of these "Oahu puffs," as the sailors call them, serves for an hour or two, until some one else lights his pipe, and it is passed round in the same manner. Each Kanaka on the beach had a pipe, flint, steel, tinder, a hand of tobacco, and a jack-knife, which he always carried about with him.

That which strikes a stranger most peculiarly is their style of singing. They run on, in a low, guttural, monotonous sort of chant, their lips and tongues seeming hardly to move, and the sounds modulated solely in the throat. There is very little tune to it, and the words, so far as I could learn, are extempore. They sing about persons and things which are around them, and adopt this method when they do not wish to be understood by any but themselves; and it is very effectual, for with the most careful attention I never could detect a word that I knew. I have often heard Mr. Mannini, who was the most noted improvisatore among them, sing for an hour together, when at work in the midst of Americans and Englishmen; and, by the occasional shouts and laughter of the Kanakas, who were at a distance, it was evident that he was singing about the different men that he was at work with. They have great powers of ridicule, and are excellent mimics; many of them discovering and imitating the peculiarities of our own people, before we had seen them ourselves.

These were the people with whom I was to spend a few months; and who, with the exception of the officer, Nicholas the Frenchman, and the boy, made the whole population of the beach. I ought, perhaps, to except the

**...a hand of tobacco, and a jack-knife...** A hand of tobacco is a bundle of leaves tied together. (The individual leaves being compared to fingers.) A jackknife is a large clasp knife that one keeps in a pocket (rather than in a sheath on a belt). The term may have been of nautical origin, sailors being known as "Jack" back to the mid-17th century. Another possibility is that the word derived from a meaning common in the 16th century: The word "Jack" was applied at the time to anyone who was deemed low-bred, common, or ill-mannered; the assumption there is that such a person would have kept a knife handy, but hidden.

**...the words, so far as I could learn, are extempore.** That is, the words are made up on the spur of the moment. ("Spur of the moment," meanwhile, probably derives from the fact that one uses a spur to hurry a horse along; thus, things done quickly and without much time for thought are said to have been done "on the spur of the moment.")

**In the news**
**June, 1835**

Former Chargé d'Affaires Anthony Butler (whom one source calls "a man eminently unqualified for any position of trust") travels to New York in an attempt to talk officials into annexing California to the United States, even if doing so requires bribing Mexican officials. In a letter, Butler notes that the area is ripe for takeover, commenting on the "rich and beautiful country which excited the cupidity of the American pioneer; [and] the indolence and effeminacy of the inhabitants which inspired the backwoodsman's contempt...."

dogs, for they were an important part of our settlement. Some of the first vessels brought dogs out with them, who, for convenience, were left ashore, and there multiplied, until they came to be a great people. While I was on the beach, the average number was about forty, and probably an equal, or greater number are drowned, or killed in some other way, every year. They are very useful in guarding the beach, the Indians being afraid to come down at night; for it was impossible for any one to get within half a mile of the hide-houses without a general alarm. The father of the colony, old Sachem, so called from the ship in which he was brought out, died while I was there, full of years, and was honorably buried. Hogs, and a few chickens, were the rest of the animal tribe, and formed, like the dogs, a common company, though they were all known and marked, and usually fed at the houses to which they belonged.

**The father of the colony, old Sachem...** *Sachem* is a name for an Indian chief of the Algonquian tribe. There have been U.S. Navy ships with that name, but it's unlikely that one of those brought the dog to San Diego. Instead, the most likely candidate is the merchant ship with which the hide trade essentially began in 1822. That *Sachem* carried guns, spices, shoes, and other goods to California, where she traded those goods for hides. If this is the ship on which the dog was transported to San Diego, then the animal was indeed fairly old, perhaps 13 to 15 years of age.

I had been but a few hours on the beach, and the Pilgrim was hardly out of sight, when the cry of "Sail ho!" was raised, and a small hermaphrodite brig rounded the point, bore up into the harbor, and came to anchor. It was the Mexican brig Fazio, which we had left at San Pedro, and which had come down to land her tallow, try it all over, and make new bags, and then take it in, and leave the coast. They moored ship, erected their try-works on shore, put up a small tent, in which they all lived, and commenced operations. They made an addition to our society, and we spent many evenings in their tent, where, amid the Babel of English, Spanish, French, Indian, and Kanaka, we found some words that we could understand in common.

**...which had come down to land her tallow, try it all over...** Tallow is animal fat used for candle-making, waterproofing, and lubrication. Once it has been processed (tried), it can be kept at room temperature for long periods of time without spoiling. Tallow (or any other fat, including whale blubber) is tried by boiling it and skimming off the impurities.

The morning after my landing, I began the duties of hide-curing. In order to understand these, it will be necessary to give the whole history of a hide, from the time it is taken from a bullock until it is put on board the vessel to be carried to Boston. When the hide is taken from the bullock, holes are cut round it, near the edge, by which it is staked out to dry. In this manner it dries without shrinking. After they are thus dried in the sun, they are received by the vessels, and brought down to the depot at San Diego. The vessels land them, and

**...it will be necessary to give the whole history of a hide...** And he does. Like Melville explaining everything one could possibly want to know about whales in the so-called cetology chapters in *Moby Dick*, Dana goes on (and on) at length here about the job of hide-curing. But it's actually an interesting process, and it does let us know how Dana will spend his time on the beach when he's not eating or drinking with his kanaka buddies. (As it happens, Melville read *Two Years Before the Mast*, and thought highly of it and of its author. The author of *Moby Dick* said on more than one occasion that without Dana's book, there would have been no *Moby Dick*.)

leave them in large piles near the houses.

Then begins the hide-curer's duty. The first thing is to put them in soak. This is done by carrying them down at low tide, and making them fast, in small piles, by ropes, and letting the tide come up and cover them. Every day we put in soak twenty-five for each man, which, with us, made an hundred and fifty. There they lie forty-eight hours, when they are taken out, and rolled up, in wheelbarrows, and thrown into the vats. These vats contain brine, made very strong; being sea-water, with great quantities of salt thrown in. This pickles the hides, and in this they lie forty-eight hours; the use of the sea-water, into which they are first put, being merely to soften and clean them. From these vats, they are taken, and lie on a platform twenty-four hours, and then are spread upon the ground, and carefully stretched and staked out, so that they may dry smooth. After they were staked, and while yet wet and soft, we used to go upon them with our knives, and carefully cut off all the bad parts:– the pieces of meat and fat, which would corrupt and infect the whole if stowed away in a vessel for many months, the large flippers, the ears, and all other parts which would prevent close stowage. This was the most difficult part of our duty: as it required much skill to take everything necessary off and not to cut or injure the hide. It was also a long process, as six of us had to clean an hundred and fifty, most of which required a great deal to be done to them, as the Spaniards are very careless in skinning their cattle. Then, too, as we cleaned them while they were staked out, we were obliged to kneel down upon them, which always gives beginners the back-ache. The first day, I was so slow and awkward that I cleaned only eight; at the end of a few days I doubled my number; and in a fortnight or three weeks, could keep up with the others, and clean my proportion –twenty-five.

This cleaning must be got through with before noon; for by that time they get too dry. After the sun has been upon them a few hours, they are carefully gone over with scrapers, to get off all the grease which the sun brings out. This being done, the stakes are pulled up,

**In the news**
**June, 1835**

Alta California Governor José Figueroa commissions Lieutenant Antonio del Valle to secularize the mission at San Fernando Rey de Espana, paying del Valle a salary of $800 per year. These days, San Fernando is an incorporated city (pop. around 24,000) in Los Angeles County. The mission, originally founded in 1797 and now in a mixed residential-commercial area, is still open to visitors.

**This pickles the hides...** Pickling a hide preserves it and prepares it for exposure to tannins.

**In the news**
**June, 1835**

Back in Dana's hometown of Boston, on a cool June morning, Nathaniel Hawthorne (recently relocated from Salem, Massachusetts) takes a Sunday stroll around the city. He notes scenes of fashionable pretension as foppishly dressed men and fashionable women lounge about doing nothing productive—and certainly not participating in any form of worship. The scene will be recounted and analyzed in Hawthorne's "Sunday at Home," published in 1837.

**...the Spaniards are very careless in skinning their cattle.** Another dig at the native populace.

**...many of them, very probably, in the end, brought back again to California in the shape of shoes, and worn out in pursuit of other bullocks. . .** Dana takes some pleasure in the irony here: Many of the hides will end up being sold right back to the Californians in the form of shoes and other leather goods. Like his earlier comment about the Californians paying a premium for mediocre wine shipped from Boston when they could have grown and processed their own grapes, this is something of a subtle dig, implying that if the Californians were only a bit more industrious, they could save themselves a great deal of time, trouble, and money by doing their own leather working. (Which in fact they eventually do.)

and the hides carefully doubled, with the hair side out, and left to dry. About the middle of the afternoon they are turned upon the other side, and at sundown piled up and covered over. The next day they are spread out and opened again, and at night, if fully dry, are thrown upon a long, horizontal pole, five at a time, and beat with flails. This takes all the dust from them. Then, being salted, scraped, cleaned, dried, and beaten, they are stowed away in the house. Here ends their history, except that they are taken out again when the vessel is ready to go home, beaten, stowed away on board, carried to Boston, tanned, made into shoes and other articles for which leather is used; and many of them, very probably, in the end, brought back again to California in the shape of shoes, and worn out in pursuit of other bullocks, or in the curing of other hides.

### In the news
### June, 1835

On the road to eventual war with Texas (and then with the U.S.), during the summer of 1835, Mexican officials led by Captain Antonio Tenorio attempt to collect taxes from Texans shipping goods. In June, Tenorio arrests two merchants for refusal to pay the tariff. William B. Travis and a group of volunteers march from Harrisburg to the Brazos to free the merchants, and Tenorio surrenders in order to avoid bloodshed.

By putting an hundred and fifty in soak every day, we had the same number at each stage of curing, on each day; so that we had, every day, the same work to do upon the same number: an hundred and fifty to put in soak; an hundred and fifty to wash out and put in the vat; the same number to haul from the vat and put on the platform to drain; the same number to spread and stake out and clean; and the same number to beat and stow away in the home. I ought to except Sunday; for, by a prescription which no captain or agent has yet ventured to break in upon, Sunday has been a day of leisure on the beach for years. On Saturday night, the hides, in every stage of progress, are carefully covered up, and not uncovered until Monday morning. On Sundays we had absolutely no work to do, unless it was to kill a bullock, which was sent down for our use about once a week, and sometimes came on Sunday. Another good arrangement was, that we had just so much work to do, and when that was through, the time was our own. Knowing this, we worked hard, and needed no driving. We "turned out" every morning at the first signs of daylight, and allowing a short time, about eight o'clock, for breakfast, generally got through our labor between one and two o'clock, when we dined, and had the rest of the time to ourselves; until just before sundown, when we beat the dry hides and put them in the house, and cov-

**Knowing this, we worked hard, and needed no driving.** Dana's book is partly a polemic on the rights of sailors. In a more general sense, though, it's a treatise on how a good captain (or any other leader) should manage men to get the most out of them. As Dana points out here, when dedicated, skilled men know their jobs, are left to do them without interference or petty hazing, and are rewarded promptly and appropriately for having completed their work, that work tends to be done quickly and well.

ered over all the others. By this means we had about three hours to ourselves every afternoon; and at sundown we had our supper, and our work was done for the day. There was no watch to stand, and no topsails to reef. The evenings we generally spent at one another's houses, and I often went up and spent an hour or so at the oven; which was called the "Kanaka Hotel," and the "Oahu Coffee-house." Immediately after dinner we usually took a short siésta to make up for our early rising, and spent the rest of the afternoon according to our own fancies. I generally read, wrote, and made or mended clothes; for necessity, the mother of invention, had taught me these two latter arts. The Kanakas went up to the oven, and spent the time in sleeping, talking, and smoking; and my messmate, Nicholas, who neither knew how to read or write, passed away the time by a long siésta, two or three smokes with his pipe, and a paséo to the other houses. This leisure time is never interfered with, for the captains know that the men earn it by working hard and fast, and that if they interfered with it, the men could easily make their twenty-five hides apiece last through the day. We were pretty independent, too, for the master of the house–"capitan de la casa"– had nothing to say to us, except when we were at work on the hides, and although we could not go up to the town without his permission, this was seldom or never refused.

The great weight of the wet hides, which we were obliged to roll about in wheelbarrows; the continual stooping upon those which were pegged out to be cleaned; and the smell of the vats, into which we were often obliged to get, knee-deep, to press down the hides; all made the work disagreeable and fatiguing;– but we soon got hardened to it, and the comparative independence of our life reconciled us to it; for there was nobody to haze us and find fault; and when we got through, we had only to wash and change our clothes, and our time was our own. There was, however, one exception to the time's being our own; which was, that on two afternoons of every week we were obliged to go off and get wood, for the cook to use in the galley. Wood is very scarce in the vicinity of San Diego; there

**... necessity, the mother of invention...** From a phrase usually ascribed to Plato. While some sources assert that it does not appear in Plato's works, it can in fact be found in *The Republic*, "Book II," in the section entitled "Socrates - ADEIMANTUS."

*...let us begin and create in idea a State; and yet the true creator is necessity, who is the mother of our invention.*

**...a paséo...** A walk or a stroll. From the Spanish verb *pasar*, to pass or go.

**In the news**
**June, 1835**

A bill of sale dated 13 June, 1835, documents the sale of two slave children, Linus and Sue, to a South Carolina planter named Lewis O'Bryan. O'Bryan pays $550 (about $14,000 today) for the two children. The terms guarantee O'Bryan "...said two Negro slaves together with the future issue & increase of the female." Notice that O'Bryan purchased not just two slaves, but also any children ("future issue") to which one of those slaves might give birth. Sue has no right to her own children, should she have any; O'Bryan owns them even before they're born.

being no trees of any size, for miles. In the town, the inhabitants burn the small wood which grows in thickets, and for which they send out Indians, in large numbers, every few days. Fortunately, the climate is so fine that they had no need of a fire in their houses, and only use it for cooking. With us the getting of wood was a great trouble; for all that in the vicinity of the houses had been cut down, and we were obliged to go off a mile or two, and to carry it some distance on our backs, as we could not get the hand-cart up the hills and over the uneven places. Two afternoons in the week, generally Monday and Thursday, as soon as we had got through dinner, we started off for the bush, each of us furnished with a hatchet and a long piece of rope, and dragging the hand-cart behind us, and followed by the whole colony of dogs, who were always ready for the bush, and were half mad whenever they saw our preparations. We went with the hand-cart as far as we could conveniently drag it, and leaving it in an open, conspicuous place, separated ourselves; each taking his own course, and looking about for some good place to begin upon. Frequently, we had to go nearly a mile from the hand-cart before we could find any fit place. Having lighted upon a good thicket, the next thing was to clear away the under-brush, and have fair play at the trees. These trees are seldom more than five or six feet high, and the highest that I ever saw in these expeditions could not have been more than twelve; so that, with lopping off the branches and clearing away the underwood, we had a good deal of cutting to do for a very little wood. Having cut enough for a "back-load," the next thing was to make it well fast with the rope, and heaving the bundle upon our backs, and taking the hatchet in hand, to walk off, up hill and down dale, to the hand-cart. Two good back-loads apiece filled the hand-cart; and that was each one's proportion. When each had brought down his second load, we filled the hand-cart, and took our way again slowly back, and unloading, covering the hides for the night, and getting our supper, finished the day's work.

**...followed by the whole colony of dogs, who were always ready for the bush...** For the dogs, this is something of an adventure—possibly one in which the exertions of the men stir up game such as grouse or rabbits.

**...we had a good deal of cutting to do for a very little wood.** In other words, not a very efficient operation. Luckily, the climate is such that wood is not needed for heat, just for cooking.

**...followed by a troop of dogs...** Troop or troupe? A perennial debate. Both are from the French—and both evolved from the same root. The latter means a company or a band, especially a band of actors, singers, or musicians. A troop, meanwhile, is a body of soldiers (or a quasi-military group such as a complement of state troopers—that is, police officers whose jurisdiction extends throughout a specific state). Dana could have used either form here and been correct: He was being metaphorical, and the metaphor could have been one in which the dogs were being compared *either* to a group of actors (or a similar such band) or to a group of soldiers.

These wooding excursions had always a mixture of something rather pleasant in them. Roaming about in the woods with hatchet in hand, like a backwoodsman, followed by a troop of dogs; starting up of birds, snakes, hares and foxes, and examining the various kinds of trees, flowers, and birds' nests, was at least, a change from the monotonous drag and pull on shipboard. Frequently, too, we had some amusement and adventure. The coati, of which I have before spoken,–a sort of mixture of the fox and wolf breeds,–fierce little animals, with bushy tails and large heads, and a quick, sharp bark, abound here, as in all other parts of California. These, the dogs were very watchful for, and whenever they saw them, started off in full run after them. We had many fine chases; yet, although our dogs ran finely, the rascals generally escaped. They are a match for the dog,—one to one,–but as the dogs generally went in squads, there was seldom a fair fight. A smaller dog, belonging to us, once attacked a coati, single, and got a good deal worsted, and might perhaps have been killed had we not come to his assistance. We had, however, one dog which gave them a good deal of trouble, and many hard runs. He was a fine, tall fellow, and united strength and agility better than any dog that I have ever seen. He was born at the Islands, his father being an English mastiff, and his mother a greyhound. He had the high head, long legs, narrow body, and springing gait of the latter, and the heavy jaw, thick jowls, and strong fore-quarters of the mastiff. When he was brought to San Diego, an English sailor said that he looked, about the face, precisely like the Duke of Wellington, whom he had once seen at the Tower; and, indeed, there was something about him which resembled the portraits of the Duke. From this time he was christened "Welly," and became the favorite and bully of the beach. He always led the dogs by several yards in the chase, and had killed two coati at different times in single combats. We often had fine sport with these fellows. A quick, sharp bark from a coati, and in an instant every dog was at the height of his speed. A few moments made up for an unfair start, and gave each dog his relative place. Welly, at the head, seemed almost to skim over the bushes; and after him came Fanny, Feliciana, Childers, and the other fleet ones,– the spaniels and terriers; and then behind, followed the

**The coati, of which I have before spoken...** Dana means "coyote," of course, which is in fact *not* a "mixture of the fox and wolf breeds." Foxes are vulpines, while wolves are canine; despite persistent anecdotal reports of fox-wolf hybrids, they are too distantly related to breed successfully. However, a coyote is a species of canine, and therefore it *can* breed with a wolf. (And recent DNA studies indicate that the two have bred and produced hybrid offspring many times.)

**...his father being an English mastiff, and his mother a greyhound.** This would be a formidable animal. An English mastiff is quite large, with adult males routinely weighing about 160 pounds. (In fact, an English mastiff holds the record for the greatest weight recorded for a dog: 343 pounds.) They are normally gentle, but can be very protective, having been bred to accompany soldiers into battle. The greyhound is also fairly large, but tall and slender, weighing 60 pounds or more. Bred for speed, the greyhound is said to be the fastest dog in the world, capable of reaching speeds in excess of 40 miles per hour. "Welly" would be more than a match for any coyote—or almost anything else the men and dogs might encounter.

**In the news**
**June, 1835**

The city of New Orleans gives the U.S. government Jackson Square, to be used as the site of a new U.S. mint. Other branches included the original mint in Philadelphia and facilities in Charlotte, North Carolina and Dahlonega, Georgia.

heavy corps–bulldogs, etc., for we had every breed. Pursuit by us was in vain, and in about half an hour a few of them would come panting and straggling back.

Beside the coati, the dogs sometimes made prizes of rabbits and hares, which are very plentiful here, and great numbers of which we often shot for our dinners. There was another animal that I was not so much disposed to find amusement from, and that was the rattlesnake. These are very abundant here, especially during the spring of the year. The latter part of the time that I was on shore, I did not meet with so many, but for the first two months we seldom went into "the bush" without one of our number starting some of them. The first that I ever saw, I remember perfectly well. I had left my companions, and was beginning to clear away a fine clump of trees, when just in the midst of the thicket, not more than eight yards from me, one of these fellows set up his hiss. It is a sharp, continuous sound, and resembles very much the letting off of the steam from the small pipe of a steamboat, except that it is on a smaller scale. I knew, by the sound of an axe, that one of my companions was near, and called out to him, to let him know what I had fallen upon. He took it very lightly, and as he seemed inclined to laugh at me for being afraid, I determined to keep my place. I knew that so long as I could hear the rattle, I was safe, for these snakes never make a noise when they are in motion. Accordingly, I kept at my work, and the noise which I made with cutting and breaking the trees kept him in alarm; so that I had the rattle to show me his whereabouts. Once or twice the noise stopped for a short time, which gave me a little uneasiness, and retreating a few steps, I threw something into the bush, at which he would set his rattle agoing; and finding that he had not moved from his first place, I was easy again. In this way I continued at my work until I had cut a full load, never suffering him to be quiet for a moment. Having cut my load, I strapped it together, and got everything ready for starting. I felt that I could now call the others without the imputation of being afraid; and went in search of them. In a few minutes we were all collected, and began an attack upon the bush. The big Frenchman,

In the news
**June, 1835**

Attorney and storekeeper John Clemens and his family arrive in Florida, Missouri. A few months later, Mrs. Clemens will give birth to a son, Samuel Longhorne Clemens—better known as Mark Twain. In November of 1839, the family will move to Hannibal, Missouri, where Twain will spend his formative years.

**These are very abundant here, especially during the spring of the year.** Rattlesnakes are still common in and around San Diego. In many parks in the area, signs go up every summer to warn of the danger: "Watch for rattlesnakes." Four different species of rattlesnake can be found in the area.

**...these snakes never make a noise when they are in motion.** A myth, and one that Dana was lucky not to have attempted to test. If the snake is eight yards (or 24 feet) from him, Dana is relatively safe; the snake is not going to chase him. (Except for one or two species, and the rattlesnake is not one of them, snakes do not chase people.)

In the news
**June, 1835**

The ship *Hector,* a 325-ton vessel built in 1819, departs London with a load of 134 convicts (all of them female) bound for the penal colony at Tasmania. The average sentence for the women is nine years, although 13 of them are to serve life sentences. The voyage takes 129 days.

who was the one that I had called to at first, I found as little inclined to approach the snake as I had been. The dogs, too, seemed afraid of the rattle, and kept up a barking at a safe distance; but the Kanakas showed no fear, and getting long sticks, went into the bush, and keeping a bright look-out, stood within a few feet of him. One or two blows struck near him, and a few stones thrown, started him, and we lost his track, and had the pleasant consciousness that he might be directly under our feet. By throwing stones and chips in different directions, we made him spring his rattle again, and began another attack. This time we drove him into the clear ground, and saw him gliding off, with head and tail erect, when a stone, well aimed, knocked him over the bank, down a declivity of fifteen or twenty feet, and stretched him at his length. Having made sure of him, by a few more stones, we went down, and one of the Kanakas cut off his rattle. These rattles vary in number it is said, according to the age of the snake; though the Indians think they indicate the number of creatures they have killed. We always preserved them as trophies, and at the end of the summer had quite a number. None of our people were ever bitten by them, but one of our dogs died of a bite, and another was supposed to have been bitten, but recovered. We had no remedy for the bite, though it was said that the Indians of the country had, and the Kanakas professed to have an herb which would cure it, but it was fortunately never brought to the test.

**The dogs, too, seemed afraid of the rattle...** The dogs are not stupid. It makes good sense to fear a hidden snake of unknown size.

**These rattles vary in number it is said, according to the age of the snake...** This is more or less the case, but it is *not* true that the number of rattles is equal to the number of years the snake has been alive. A new rattle is added when the snake sheds its skin, and a rattlesnake can shed its skin once or several times per year, depending on many things, including the local food supply. Rattlesnakes can also *lose* rattles, because they can be broken off.

**...the Kanakas professed to have an herb which would cure it...** Certain herbs, such as Echinacea, are said by some to be useful in treating rattlesnake bite, although their efficacy has never been proven.

Hares and rabbits, as I said before, were abundant, and, during the winter months, the waters are covered with wild ducks and geese. Crows, too, were very numerous, and frequently alighted in great numbers upon our hides, picking at the pieces of dried meat and fat. Bears and wolves are numerous in the upper parts, and in the interior, (and, indeed, a man was killed by a bear within a few miles of San Pedro, while we were there,) but there were none in our immediate neighborhood. The only other animals were horses. Over a dozen of these were owned by different people on the beach, and were allowed to run loose among the hills, with a long lasso attached to them, and pick up feed wherever they could

**In the news**
**June, 1835**

Chicago is still growing. On June 6 there appears the following article: "Three years ago the number of inhabitants in Chicago was fifty-four,—now it is four thousand, including about forty merchants. Five churches have been erected, of various sizes, and for various denominations. A steamboat communication, twice a week, is established with Buffalo, and by sloops and schooners, flour is transported from one place to the other at a freight of 25 cents per barrel."

find it. We were sure of seeing them once a day, for there was no water among the hills, and they were obliged to come down to the well which had been dug upon the beach. These horses were bought at, from two, to six and eight dollars apiece, and were held very much as common property. We generally kept one fast to one of the houses every day, so that we could mount him and catch any of the others. Some of them were really fine animals, and gave us many good runs up to the Presidio and over the country.

## Chapter XX

### Leisure–News From Home–"Burning the Water"

After we had been a few weeks on shore, and had begun to feel broken into the regularity of our life, its monotony was interrupted by the arrival of two vessels from the windward. We were sitting at dinner in our little room, when we heard the cry of "Sail ho!" This, we had learned, did not always signify a vessel, but was raised whenever a woman was seen coming down from the town; or a squaw, or an ox-cart, or anything unusual, hove in sight upon the road; so we took no notice of it. But it soon became so loud and general from all parts of the beach, that we were led to go to the door; and there, sure enough, were two sails coming round the point, and leaning over from the strong north-west wind, which blows down the coast every afternoon. The headmost was a ship, and the other, a brig. Everybody was alive on the beach, and all manner of conjectures were abroad. Some said it was the Pilgrim, with the Boston ship, which we were expecting; but we soon saw that the brig was not the Pilgrim, and the ship with her stump top-gallant masts and rusty sides, could not be a dandy Boston Indiaman. As they drew nearer, we soon discovered the high poop and top-gallant forecastle, and other marks of the Italian ship Rosa, and the brig proved to be the Catalina, which we saw at Santa Barbara, just arrived from Valparaiso. They came to anchor, moored ship, and commenced discharging hides and tallow. The Rosa had purchased the house occupied by the Lagoda, and the Catalina took the other spare one between ours and the Ayacucho's, so that, now, each one was occupied, and the beach, for several days, was all alive. The Catalina had several Kanakas on board, who were immediately besieged by the others, and carried up to the oven, where they had a long pow-wow, and a smoke. Two Frenchmen, who belonged to the Rosa's crew, came in, every evening, to see Nicholas; and from them we learned that the Pilgrim was at San Pedro, and was the only other vessel now on the coast. Several of the Italians slept on shore at their hide-house; and there, and at the tent in which the

In the news
**June, 1835**

Australian businessman John Batman signs a treaty with the Aborigines, entitling him to the land that would eventually become the village (then city) of Melbourne. Among the first to recognize that the Aborigines (rather than Britain) owned the land, Batman arranges for annual rents to be paid to the natives. (The government later declares the treaty invalid, but the city flourishes in spite of that.)

**...the ship with her stump top-gallant masts and rusty sides, could not be a dandy Boston Indiaman.** An Indiaman was any large merchant ship that followed the trade routes to and from India. A "Boston Indiaman," as part of a large and regularly profitable enterprise, was sure to be in better repair than the stumpy *Rosa.* (Actually, the ship's name was *La Rosa.*)

**...hides and tallow...** Keep in mind that in the days before gaslights and electric lanterns, tallow (rendered animal fat often used in the making of candles) was quite a valuable commodity. It provided the only reliable and convenient form of light available after sundown.

**...the beach, for several days, was all alive.** That is, the beach was busy.

**...they had a long pow-wow...** *Powwow* is of course not a term of Hawaiian origin, but a North American Narragansett Indian word that has been used in English going back to the early 17th century. It may have originated as *Powah,* a name for a Native American priest or shaman. It eventually came to mean a religious or magical ceremony, and thus *any* important conversation or council.

**...barcarollas, provincial airs...** Boatmen's songs and unsophisticated folksongs of a specific country—in this case, Italy.

**...as clear as a clarionet.** That is, a clarinet. "Clarionet" was a common (mis)spelling well into the 1800s. There is some etymological basis for the spelling, though; after all, a clarionet is a sort of "small clarion," that is, a medieval brass instrument used to call or signal.

**...representatives from almost every nation under the sun...** On the beach at San Diego is a veritable United Nations of sailors and hide-droghers, all of whom seem to get along well.

**...three Frenchmen (two of whom were Normans, and the third from Gascony...** Normandy and Gascony are regions in France.

**...one Otaheitan...** That is, a Tahitian. At one time, the southern Pacific island we now call Tahiti was known as Otaheite.

**...Och! mein lieber Augustin!** Actually called "Oh du lieber Augustin," this is a 1679 Viennese song that tells the story of a beloved drunken balladeer who passes out and, mistaken for a plague victim, is thrown into a pit with the victims' bodies. He awakes, and the townspeople rescue him.

**...we three Yankees made an attempt at the "Star-spangled Banner."** At the time, this song (written by Francis Scott Key to commemorate the shelling of Fort McHenry by the British during the War of 1812) was only 20 years old. The words are Key's but, somewhat ironically, the melody is that of a popular British song of the day. If you've ever attempted to sing it and had trouble, there's no need to be ashamed: With a range of one and a half octaves, it's notoriously difficult to sing. It officially became the U.S. national anthem in 1931.

Fazio's crew lived, we had some very good singing almost every evening. The Italians sang a variety of songs–barcarollas, provincial airs, etc.; in several of which I recognized parts of our favorite operas and sentimental songs. They often joined in a song, taking all the different parts; which produced a fine effect, as many of them had good voices, and all seemed to sing with spirit and feeling. One young man, in particular, had a falsetto as clear as a clarionet.

The greater part of the crews of the vessels came ashore every evening, and we passed the time in going about from one house to another, and listening to all manner of languages. The Spanish was the common ground upon which we all met; for every one knew more or less of that. We had now, out of forty or fifty, representatives from almost every nation under the sun: two Englishmen, three Yankees, two Scotchmen, two Welshmen, one Irishman, three Frenchmen (two of whom were Normans, and the third from Gascony,) one Dutchman, one Austrian, two or three Spaniards, (from old Spain,) half a dozen Spanish-Americans and half-breeds, two native Indians from Chili and the Island of Chiloe, one Negro, one Mulatto, about twenty Italians, from all parts of Italy, as many more Sandwich Islanders, one Otaheitan, and one Kanaka from the Marquesas Islands.

The night before the vessels were ready to sail, all the Europeans united and had an entertainment at the Rosa's hide-house, and we had songs of every nation and tongue. A German gave us "Och! mein lieber Augustin!" the three Frenchmen roared through the Marseilles Hymn; the English and Scotchmen gave us "Rule Britannia," and "Wha'll be King but Charlie?" the Italians and Spaniards screamed through some national affairs, for which I was none the wiser; and we three Yankees made an attempt at the "Star-spangled Banner." After these national tributes had been paid, the Austrian gave us a very pretty little love-song, and the Frenchmen sang a spirited thing called "Sentinelle! O prenez garde a vous!" and then followed the melange which might have been expected. When I left them, the aguardiente and annisou was pretty well in their heads, and they were all singing and talking at once, and their peculiar national oaths were getting as plenty as pronouns.

The next day, the two vessels got under weigh for the windward, and left us in quiet possession of the beach. Our numbers were somewhat enlarged by the opening of the new houses, and the society of the beach a little changed. In charge of the Catalina's house, was an old Scotchman, who, like most of his countrymen, had a pretty good education, and, like many of them, was rather pragmatical, and had a ludicrously solemn conceit. He employed his time in taking care of his pigs, chickens, turkeys, dogs, etc., and in smoking his long pipe. Everything was as neat as a pin in the house, and he was as regular in his hours as a chronometer, but as he kept very much by himself, was not a great addition to our society. He hardly spent a cent all the time he was on the beach, and the others said he was no shipmate. He had been a petty officer on board the British frigate Dublin, Capt. Lord James Townshend, and had great ideas of his own importance. The man in charge of the Rosa's house was an Austrian by birth, but spoke, read, and wrote four languages with ease and correctness. German was his native tongue, but being born near the borders of Italy, and having sailed out of Genoa, the Italian was almost as familiar to him as his own language. He was six years on board of an English man-of-war, where he learned to speak our language with ease, and also to read and write it. He had been several years in Spanish vessels, and had acquired that language so well, that he could read any books in it. He was between forty and fifty years of age, and was a singular mixture of the man-of-war's-man and Puritan. He talked a great deal about propriety and steadiness, and gave good advice to the youngsters and Kanakas, but seldom went up to the town, without coming down "three sheets in the wind." One holyday, he and old Robert (the Scotchman from the Catalina) went up to the town, and got so cozy, talking over old stories and giving one another good advice, that they came down double-backed, on a horse, and both rolled off into the

**... aguardiente and annisou...** That should probably be "aguardiente and anisado," that is, "brandy and anisette." Things are getting a little rowdy on the beach, what with dozens of people of all nationalities drinking and carrying on. Anisette is a licorice-flavored, colorless liqueur made from aniseed. Anisette is very potent, with an alcohol content of around 29%. (Compare that to typical beers, the alcoholic content of which ranges from 5% or 6%, 10% at the most.)

**He hardly spent a cent all the time he was on the beach, and the others said he was no shipmate.** Here Dana buys into the stereotype of the Scotsman-as-skinflint. And a self-important skinflint, at that. The stereotype (like similar ideas about Jews) was very common at one time: Until recently, the store (value) brand of one California grocery chain was "Scotch Buy." One mid-50s car company (Studebaker) even offered a bare-bones station wagon called The Scotsman. The stereotype is less prevalent today. (Then again, we can still buy Scotch Tape, right?)

In the news
**June, 1835**

The pueblo of Sonoma is established, partly to control the Indians, but mainly as a bulwark against presumed Russian expansion. Mission San Francisco Solano de Sonoma itself was the last of the 21 California missions, having been founded in 1823.

**...a singular mixture of the man-of-war's-man and Puritan.** That is, he was a true sailor—and as wild a carouser as any of them. But he was also experienced enough to give good advice to the younger men about staying away from liquor. However, it doesn't seem as if he ever took his own advice.

**...double-backed, on a horse...** That is, riding double.

**...had a chest-full of books, which he willingly lent me to read.** Schmidt, for all his drunkenness, is well-read, articulate, and intelligent. He is someone whom Dana must have been overjoyed to encounter, especially since he lent the younger man books to read.

**He made it a point to get drunk once a fortnight...** That is, every two weeks.

**...had nothing more to do until she should come down again...** Dana and the kanakas have completed their jobs. The hides are all prepared and ready for stowage, and all the equipment has been cleaned. Now they wait for *Pilgrim* to return.

In the news
**July, 1835**

According to some (disputed) sources, the Liberty Bell, in Philadelphia, Pennsylvania, cracks as it tolls the death of Chief Justice John Marshall.

**...there was not a watch on the beach...** In 1835, Dana would have meant a pocket-watch, not a wristwatch. The former has been around since about the 17th century, while the latter was not invented until the early 1900s.

**...we had collected several cords...** A cord of wood is a stack that occupies a volume of 128 cubic feet. Generally speaking, that means a stack that's about four feet wide by four feet tall by eight feet long, or the equivalent.

sand as soon as the horse stopped. This put an end to their pretensions, and they never heard the last of it from the rest of the men. On the night of the entertainment at the Rosa's house, I saw old Schmidt, (that was the Austrian's name) standing up by a hogshead, holding on by both hands, and calling out to himself–"Hold on, Schmidt! hold on, my good fellow, or you'll be on your back!" Still, he was an intelligent, good-natured old fellow, and had a chest-full of books, which he willingly lent me to read. In the same house with him was a Frenchman and an Englishman; the latter a regular-built "man-of-war Jack;" a thorough seaman; a hearty, generous fellow; and, at the same time, a drunken, dissolute dog. He made it a point to get drunk once a fortnight, (when he always managed to sleep on the road, and have his money stolen from him,) and to battle the Frenchman once a week. These, with a Chilian, and a half a dozen Kanakas, formed the addition to our company.

In about six weeks from the time when the Pilgrim sailed, we had got all the hides which she left us cured and stowed away; and having cleared up the ground, and emptied the vats, and set everything in order, had nothing more to do until she should come down again, but to supply ourselves with wood. Instead of going twice a week for this purpose, we determined to give one whole week to getting wood, and then we should have enough to last us half through the summer. Accordingly, we started off every morning, after an early breakfast, with our hatchets in hand, and cut wood until the sun was over the point,–which was our only mark of time, as there was not a watch on the beach–and then came back to dinner, and after dinner, started off again with our hand-cart and ropes, and carted and "backed" it down, until sunset. This, we kept up for a week, until we had collected several cords, –enough to last us for six or eight weeks–when we "knocked off" altogether, much to my joy; for, though I liked straying in the woods, and cutting, very well, yet the backing the wood for so great a distance, over an uneven country, was, without exception, the hardest work I had ever done. I usually had to kneel down and contrive to heave the load, which was well strapped together, upon my back, and then rise up and start off with it up the hills and down the vales, sometimes through thickets,–the rough points sticking into the skin, and tearing the clothes, so that, at the end of the week, I had hardly a whole shirt to my back.

We were now through all our work, and had nothing more to do until the Pilgrim should come down again. We had nearly got through our provisions too, as well as our work; for our officer had been very wasteful of them, and the tea, flour, sugar, and molasses, were all gone. We suspected him of sending them up to the town; and he always treated the squaws with molasses, when they came down to the beach. Finding wheat-coffee and dry bread rather poor living, we dubbed together, and I went up to the town on horseback with a great salt-bag behind the saddle, and a few reáls in my pocket, and brought back the bag full of onions, pears, beans, water-melons, and other fruits; for the young woman who tended the garden, finding that I belonged to the American ship, and that we were short of provisions, put in a double portion. With these we lived like fighting-cocks for a week or two, and had, besides, what the sailors call "a blow-out on sleep;" not turning out in the morning until breakfast was ready. I employed several days in overhauling my chest, and mending up all my old clothes, until I had got everything in order–patch upon patch, like a sand-barge's mainsail. Then I took hold of Bowditch's Navigator, which I had always with me. I had been through the greater part of it, and now went carefully through it, from beginning to end working out most of the examples. That done, and there being no signs of the Pilgrim, I made a descent upon old Schmidt, and borrowed and read all the books there were upon the beach. Such a dearth was there of these latter articles, that anything, even a little child's story-book, or the half of a shipping calendar, appeared like a treasure. I actually read a jest-book through, from beginning to end, in one day, as I should a novel, and enjoyed it very much. At last, when I thought that there were no more to be got, I found, at the bottom of old Schmidt's chest, "Mandeville, a

**We suspected him of sending them up to the town; and he always treated the squaws with molasses...** The officer, Russell, may have made "arrangements" with some of the women in town, trading favors for food, or he may simply be *attempting* to win those favors by plying the women with food.

**...what the sailors call "a blow-out on sleep;"...** Sailors' watches are so arranged that few of the men get enough sleep. (And even that sleep is often interrupted by shipboard emergencies.) When they get a chance to do nothing *but* sleep, they take advantage of it in order to make up for lost sleep. (However, recent studies indeicate that serious sleep deficits in fact cannot be made up.)

**...I took hold of Bowditch's Navigator, which I had always with me.** Usually referred to simply as *Bowditch's*, the full title of the book was *The American Practical Navigator*, and it was for many decades a valuable handbook and the standard navigation text for sailors and officers. It is still important today, both as a source of nautical information and as an enduring nautical tradition. (In recent decades, though, it has been largely replaced by *Chapman Piloting: Seamanship & Small Boat Handling*—now in its 65th edition, and usually known simply as *Chapman's*.)

Romance, by Godwin, in five volumes." This I had never read, but Godwin's name was enough, and after the wretched trash I had devoured, anything bearing the name of a distinguished intellectual man, was a prize indeed. I bore it off, and for two days I was up early and late, reading with all my might, and actually drinking in delight. It is no extravagance to say that it was like a spring in a desert land.

**...a Romance, by Godwin, in five volumes.** A novel by William Godwin, originally published in 1817. Godwin was well known as a liberal crusader, and his books often attacked aristocratic privilege. He married pioneering feminist Mary Wollstonecraft. Their daughter, Mary Shelley, would go on to write, at the age of 19, *Frankenstein*.

**...it was like a spring in a desert land.** Dana's book is full of references such as this—comments that make it obvious how much he misses the sophisticated culture he left behind in Boston. He misses the culture, the books, the newspapers and journals, the long conversations with family and friends and professors. Although he has undertaken a voyage during which he labors as a lowly sailor (and does a fine job of it, in fact), he longs to return to his former life.

From the sublime to the ridiculous–so with me, from Mandeville to hide-curing, was but a step; for

Wednesday, July 18th, brought us the brig Pilgrim from the windward. As she came in, we found that she was a good deal altered in her appearance. Her short top-gallant masts were up; her bowlines all unrove (except to the courses); the quarter boom-irons off her lower yards; her jack-cross-trees sent down; several blocks got rid of; running-rigging rove in new places; and numberless other changes of the same character. Then, too, there was a new voice giving orders, and a new face on the quarter-deck,–a short, dark-complexioned man, in a green jacket and a high leather cap. These changes, of course, set the whole beach on the qui-vive, and we were all waiting for the boat to come ashore, that we might have things explained. At length, after the sails were furled and the anchor carried out, the boat pulled ashore, and the news soon flew that the expected ship had arrived at Santa Barbara, and that Captain T—- had taken command of her, and her captain, Faucon, had taken the Pilgrim, and was the green-jacketed man on the quarter-deck. The boat put directly off again, without giving us time to ask any more questions, and we were obliged to wait till night, when we took a little skiff, that lay on the beach, and paddled off. When I stepped aboard, the second mate called me aft, and gave me a large bundle, directed to me, and marked "Ship Alert." This was what I had longed for, yet I refrained from opening it until I went ashore. Diving down into the forecastle, I found the same old crew, and was really glad to see them again. Numerous inquiries passed as to the new ship, the latest news from Boston, etc., etc. S—- had received letters from home, and nothing remark-

**... there was a new voice giving orders...** We need not concern ourselves overly much with the physical changes aboard *Pilgrim*, except to say that she has been cleaned up and trimmed, and is looking a bit more "shipshape" than when we last saw her. What is important to note, though, is the fact that the vessel has a new captain. Hailing from Boston, Edward H. Faucon takes over *Pilgrim*, as Thompson takes over Faucon's vessel, the *Alert*, which is still plying the coast. We will shortly learn much more of both Faucon and the *Alert*.

**...set the whole beach on the qui-vive...** Dana is showing off a bit. "Qui-vive" is French for "on the alert."

**This was what I had longed for...** Dana is exercising considerable self-restraint. The bundle seems to indicate that he is being transferred to the *Alert*, a finer ship, and due back in Boston long before *Pilgrim*.

able had happened. The Alert was agreed on all hands to be a fine ship, and a large one: "Larger than the Rosa"–"Big enough to carry off all the hides in California"–"Rail as high as a man's head"–"A crack ship"–"A regular dandy," etc., etc. Captain T—- took command of her, and she went directly up to Monterey; from thence she was to go to San Francisco, and probably would not be in San Diego under two or three months. Some of the Pilgrim's crew found old shipmates aboard of her, and spent an hour or two in her forecastle, the evening before she sailed. They said her decks were as white as snow–holystoned every morning, like a man-of-war's; everything on board "shipshape and Bristol fashion;" a fine crew, three mates, a sailmaker and carpenter, and all complete. "They've got a man for mate of that ship, and not a bloody sheep about decks!"–"A mate that knows his duty, and makes everybody do theirs, and won't be imposed upon either by captain or crew." After collecting all the information we could get on this point, we asked something about their new captain. He had hardly been on board long enough for them to know much about him, but he had taken hold strong, as soon as he took comand;–sending down the top-gallant masts, and unreeving half the rigging, the very first day.

**...A crack ship–A regular dandy...** In this context and at that time, "crack" meant "first class," or "excellent." Used in that sense, the word goes back to the late 1700s. "Dandy," meanwhile, meant (and still means) anything fine, neat, or correct. Calling a man a dandy is a bit of an insult, though, implying that he might be *excessively* well-dressed and perhaps a bit "dainty."

**...her decks were as white as snow–holystoned every morning, like a man-of-war's...** *Pilgrim* is definitely looking better under Faucon's command than she did under Thompson's. Of course, much of the crew is also different, so we must not assume that Thompson was the only problem.

**"They've got a man for mate of that ship, and not a bloody sheep about decks!"** This mate is a real seaman: He's not worried about currying favor with the men, nor is he concerned about toadying to the captain. Unlike the previous mate, he is knowledgeable, hard-working, and intent on getting the job done correctly. This will have a definite (and positive) effect on how the ship is run.

Having got all the news we could, we pulled ashore; and as soon as we reached the house, I, as might be supposed, proceeded directly to opening my bundle, and found a reasonable supply of duck, flannel shirts, shoes, etc., and, what was still more valuable, a packet of eleven letters. These I sat up nearly all the night to read, and put them carefully away, to be read and re-read again and again at my leisure. Then came a half a dozen newspapers, the last of which gave notice of Thanksgiving, and of the clearance of "ship Alert, Edward H. Faucon, master, for Callao and California, by Bryant, Sturgis & Co." No one has ever been on distant voyages, and after a long absence received a newspaper from home, who cannot understand the delight that they give one. I read every part of them –the houses to let; things lost or stolen; auction sales, and all. Nothing carries you so entirely to a place, and makes

**...I read every part of them...** Dana is desperate for both reading material and news from home. He's so desperate that he reads *everything*: the want-ads, the house rental lists, even the results of auctions.

**"Tityre, tu patulae recubans sub tegmine fagi."** Latin for "Tityrus, you who lie under cover of the spreading beech-tree." This is a line from Virgil's *Eclogues*, which presented a vision of peaceful rural, pastoral life—but with a tinge of both erotica and political intrigue. (Not surprisingly, the *Eclogues* were a great success.) Captain Faucon's comment serves two purposes: First, he establishes himself as an educated man, Dana's intellectual equal. Second, the fact that he stops to comment at all (see below) points out (to Dana and to us) that Faucon is a much different person than Captain Thompson.

**...a kind word from a captain is a thing not to be slighted...** It's difficult to imagine the effect something like this might have on a sailor, especially a sensitive intellectual such as Dana. For almost a full year, he has been either ignored or bullied by his captain. A simple kind word from the ship's commander means a great deal to the one on whom it is bestowed. Faucon is capable of such a gesture; Thompson is not.

**All the duck I received from home...** Duck is a strong cloth made from linen or cotton.

**...displayed, every Sunday, a complete suit of my own make...** Dana is rightfully proud of the skills he's gained during the voyage. He has grown not merely stronger, but also much more self-sufficient.

**...craw-fish.** To us, crawfish (or crayfish) are freshwater crustaceans much like small lobsters. In the 1830s, however, the term was used to describe *all* edible crustacea, whether fresh- or saltwater. Dana and his colleagues are fishing for lobster. (Imagine a time when lobster were so common on the West Coast that they could be captured in this fashion and in these numbers, and within a few feet of shore.)

you feel so perfectly at home, as a newspaper. The very name of "Boston Daily Advertiser" "sounded hospitably upon the ear."

The Pilgrim discharged her hides, which set us at work again, and in a few days we were in the old routine of dry hides–wet hides–cleaning–beating, etc. Captain Faucon came quietly up to me, as I was at work, with my knife, cutting the meat from a dirty hide, asked me how I liked California, and repeated–"Tityre, tu patulae recubans sub tegmine fagi." Very apropos, thought I, and, at the same time, serves to show that you understand Latin. However, a kind word from a captain is a thing not to be slighted; so I answered him civilly, and made the most of it.

Saturday, July 11th. The Pilgrim set sail for the windward, and left us to go on in our old way. Having laid in such a supply of wood, and the days being now long, and invariably pleasant, we had a good deal of time to ourselves. All the duck I received from home, I soon made up into trowsers and frocks, and displayed, every Sunday, a complete suit of my own make, from head to foot, having formed the remnants of the duck into a cap. Reading, mending, sleeping, with occasional excursions into the bush, with the dogs, in search of coati, hares, and rabbits, or to encounter a rattlesnake, and now and then a visit to the Presidio, filled up our spare time after hide-curing was over for the day. Another amusement, which we sometimes indulged in, was "burning the water" for craw-fish. For this purpose, we procured a pair of grains, with a long staff like a harpoon, and making torches with tarred rope twisted round a long pine stick, took the only boat on the beach, a small skiff, and with a torch-bearer in the bow, a steersman in the stern, and one man on each side with the grains, went off, on dark nights, to burn the water. This is fine sport. Keeping within a few rods of the shore, where the water is not more than three or four feet deep, with a clear sandy bottom, the torches light everything up so that one could almost have seen a pin among the grains of sand. The craw-fish are an easy prey, and we used soon to get a load of them. The other fish were more difficult to catch, yet we frequently speared a number of them, of various kinds and sizes. The Pilgrim brought us down a supply of fish-hooks, which we had never had before, on the beach, and for several days we went down to the Point, and caught a quantity of cod and mackerel. On one of these expeditions, we saw a battle between two Sandwich Islanders and a shark. "Johnny" had been playing about our boat for some time, driving away the fish, and showing his teeth at our bait, when we missed him, and in a few moments heard a great shouting between two Kanakas who were fishing on the rock opposite to us: "E hana hana make i ka ia nui!" "E pii mai Aikane!" etc., etc.; and saw them pulling away on a stout line, and "Johnny Shark" floundering at the other end. The line soon broke; but the Kanakas would not let him off so easily, and sprang directly into the water after him. Now came the tug of war. Before we could get into deep water, one of them seized him by the tail, and ran up with him upon the beach; but Johnny twisted round, turning his head under his body, and, showing his teeth in the vicinity of the Kanaka's hand, made him let go and spring out of the way. The shark now turned tail and made the best of his way, by flapping and floundering, toward deep water; but here again, before he was fairly off, the other Kanaka seized him by the tail, and made a spring towards the beach, his companion at the same time paying away upon him with stones and a large stick. As soon, however, as the shark could turn, he was obliged to let go his hold; but the instant he made toward deep water, they were both behind him, watching their chance to seize him. In this way the battle went on for some time, the shark, in a rage, splashing and twisting about, and the Kanakas, in high excitement, yelling at the top of their voices; but the shark at last got off, carrying away a hook and liner and not a few severe bruises.

**...the Kanakas would not let him off so easily, and sprang directly into the water after him.** A number of species of sharks can be found around the San Diego area.The shark being toyed with by the kanakas was almost certainly not a great white, which even as an adolescent can reach 7 to 10 feet in length; adults can weight 2,000 pounds or more. But numerous other species abound in the area and sometimes venture close to shore, including leopard sharks, tiger sharks, thresher sharks, and gray smoothhound sharks. (The latter of which is a bottom-feeder and is not considered dangerous to humans.) Catching sharks by hand is apparently a time-honored custom in the islands. There is documentation that in the 1870s in Oahu, tourists would gather to watch islanders riding on the backs of tiger sharks and catching sharks by hand. And Dutch explorers in the area wrote of seeing natives catching sharks by hand as far back as 1643.

**...carrying away a hook and liner...** Subsequent editions have "...hook and line...."

# CHAPTER XXI

## CALIFORNIA AND ITS INHABITANTS

**...I had added much to my vocabulary...** Dana is a quick study, and he doesn't really have all that much else to do but study the people, language, and institutions of the Californians.

We kept up a constant connection with the Presidio, and by the close of the summer I had added much to my vocabulary, beside having made the acquaintance of nearly everybody in the place, and acquired some knowledge of the character and habits of the people, as well as of the institutions under which they live.

**California was first discovered in 1536...** In the following passages, Dana's history and geography are questionable at best. In the first place, although Cortes (a Spanish conquistador) did discover the Baja California peninsula, he'd been beaten to it by survivors of Fortún Jimenez's (also spelled Ximénez) mutinous expedition to New Spain. That group was searching for the mythical California—a beautiful, peaceful land populated only by women. After the mutiny (during which Captain Diego de Becerra was killed), Jimenez's band landed in 1532 near what is today the city of La Paz.

**No sooner was the importance of the country known, than the Jesuits obtained leave to establish themselves in it...** Actually, the Jesuits did not "establish themselves" there until about 1696. The presidios were established in this order: San Diego (1769), Monterey (1770), San Francisco (1776), and Santa Barbara (1782). (Note that some of these errors were corrected in later editions of the book.)

California was first discovered in 1536, by Cortes, and was subsequently visited by numerous other adventurers as well as commissioned voyagers of the Spanish crown. It was found to be inhabited by numerous tribes of Indians, and to be in many parts extremely fertile; to which, of course, was added rumors of gold mines, pearl fishery, etc. No sooner was the importance of the country known, than the Jesuits obtained leave to establish themselves in it, to Christianize and enlighten the Indians. They established missions in various parts of the country toward the close of the seventeenth century, and collected the natives about them, baptizing them into the church, and teaching them the arts of civilized life. To protect the Jesuits in their missions, and at the same time tc support the power of the crown over the civilized Indians, two forts were erected and garrisoned, one at San Diego, and the other at Monterey. These were called Presidios, and divided the command of the whole country between them. Presidios have since been established at Santa Barbara and San Francisco; thus dividing the country into four large districts, each with its presidio, and governed by the commandant. The soldiers, for the most part, married civilized Indians; and thus, in the vicinity of each presidio, sprung up, gradually, small towns. In the course of time, vessels began to come into the ports to trade with the missions, and received hides in return; and thus began the great trade of California. Nearly all the cattle in the country belonged to the missions, and they employed their Indians, who became, in fact, their slaves, in tending their vast herds. In the year 1793, when Vancouver visited San Diego, the mission had obtained great wealth

**...when Vancouver visited San Diego...** George Vancouver was a British explorer and naval officer. Between 1791 and 1795 he charted much of the Pacific Northwest, and several cities and landmarks in the area are named after him.

and power, and are accused of having depreciated the country with the sovereign, that they might be allowed to retain their possessions. On the expulsion of the Jesuits from the Spanish dominions, the missions passed into the hands of the Franciscans, though without any essential change in their management. Ever since the independence of Mexico, the missions have been going down; until, at last, a law was passed, stripping them of all their possessions, and confining the priests to their spiritual duties; and at the same time declaring all the Indians free and independent Rancheros. The change in the condition of the Indians was, as may be supposed, only nominal: they are virtually slaves, as much as they ever were. But in the missions, the change was complete. The priests have now no power, except in their religious character, and the great possessions of the missions are given over to be preyed upon by the harpies of the civil power, who are sent there in the capacity of administradores, to settle up the concerns; and who usually end, in a few years, by making themselves fortunes, and leaving their stewardships worse than they found them. The dynasty of the priests was much more acceptable to the people of the country, and indeed, to every one concerned with the country, by trade or otherwise, than that of the administradores. The priests were attached perpetually to one mission, and felt the necessity of keeping up its credit. Accordingly, their debts were regularly paid, and the people were, in the main, well treated, and attached to those who had spent their whole lives among them. But the administradores are strangers sent from Mexico, having no interest in the country; not identified in any way with their charge, and, for the most part, men of desperate fortunes—broken down politicians and soldiers—whose only object is to retrieve their condition in as short a time as possible. The change had been made but a few years before our arrival upon the coast, yet, in that short time, the trade was much diminished, credit impaired, and the venerable missions going rapidly to decay. The external arrangements remain the same. There are four presidios, having under their protection the various missions, and pueblos, which are towns formed by the civil power, and containing no mission or presidio. The most

**...a law was passed, stripping them of all their possessions, and confining the priests to their spiritual duties...** This reflects the Mexican government's decision to secularize the missions.

**The priests have now no power, except in their religious character...** Of course, some would say (and many did say) this is as it should be. And today, that's pretty much what we expect: The members of the priesthood, as respected as they are, confine their efforts to "good works" and to matters of faith. But historically, the Church has wielded great power in areas well beyond what we today think of as their purview: In the past, high-ranking church officials could (and did) both punish and reward people, granting property rights, distributing wealth (some of it confiscated from other citizens), or stripping people of their possessions for violating both church and secular law. In some cases, the Church could (and did) put people to death for what Church officials considered extreme violations of law. The separation of church and state on which many modern democracies are founded is a relatively new development.

**In the news**
**July, 1835**

The Charleston, SC post office is ransacked by a pro-slavery mob, which destroys sacks of abolitionist literature and anti-slavery mail sent to correspondents in the South. At the head of the mob is former South Carolina governor Robert Y. Hayne.

**...the venerable missions going rapidly to decay.** Without the priests running the day-to-day operations of the missions, and with only "broken down politicians and soldiers" in charge, the missions quickly fell into ruin.

northerly presidio is San Francisco; the next Monterey; the next Santa Barbara; including the mission of the same, St. Louis Obispo, and St. Buenaventura, which is the finest mission in the whole country, having very fertile soil and rich vineyards. The last, and most southerly, is San Diego, including the mission of the same, San Juan Campestrano, the Pueblo de los Angelos, the largest town in California, with the neighboring mission of San Gabriel. The priests in spiritual matters are subject to the Archbishop of Mexico, and in temporal matters to the governor-general, who is the great civil and military head of the country.

**The priests in spiritual matters are subject to the Archbishop of Mexico, and in temporal matters to the governor-general...** Here is an attempt at a type of separation of church and state: In religious matters, the priests answer to the archbishop; when secular ("temporal") issues arise, the priests must consult the governor-general.

The government of the country is an arbitrary democracy; having no common law, and no judiciary. Their only laws are made and unmade at the caprice of the legislature, and are as variable as the legislature itself. They pass through the form of sending representatives to the congress at Mexico, but as it takes several months to go and return, and there is very little communication between the capital and this distant province, a member usually stays there, as permanent member, knowing very well that there will be revolutions at home before he can write and receive an answer; if another member should be sent, he has only to challenge him, and decide the contested election in that way.

**The only object, of course, is the loaves and fishes...** From Matthew 14:17 ("And they say unto him, We have here but five loaves, and two fishes.") The Bible verse in which Jesus, having blessed five loaves of bread and two fish, miraculously uses them to feed a multitude of 5,000 men, "beside women and children." Dana is saying that the politicians are greedy men who are not looking to help their country or to see justice done, but who are instead out to line their own pockets. Not an uncommon accusation of politicians, then and now.

Revolutions are matters of constant occurrence in California. They are got up by men who are at the foot of the ladder and in desperate circumstances, just as a new political party is started by such men in our own country. The only object, of course, is the loaves and fishes; and instead of caucusing, paragraphing, libelling, feasting, promising, and lying, as with us, they take muskets and bayonets, and seizing upon the presidio and custom-house, divide the spoils, and declare a new dynasty. As for justice, they know no law but will and fear. A Yankee, who had been naturalized, and become a Catholic, and had married in the country, was sitting in his house at the Pueblo de los Angelos, with his wife and children, when a Spaniard, with whom he had had a difficulty, entered the house, and stabbed him to the heart before them all. The murderer was seized by some

**As for justice, they know no law but will and fear.** Dana is about to make the point that the laws in Mexico are muddled, unjust, and biased against outsiders and the poor. (But see the next note.)

Yankees who had settled there, and kept in confinement until a statement of the whole affair could be sent to the governor-general. He refused to do anything about it, and the countrymen of the murdered man, seeing no prospect of justice being administered, made known that if nothing was done, they should try the man themselves. It chanced that, at this time, there was a company of forty trappers and hunters from Kentucky, with their rifles, who had made their head-quarters at the Pueblo; and these, together with the Americans and Englishmen in the place, who were between twenty and thirty in number, took possession of the town, and waiting a reasonable time, proceeded to try the man according to the forms in their own country. A judge and jury were appointed, and he was tried, convicted, sentenced to be shot, and carried out before the town, with his eyes blindfolded. The names of all the men were then put into a hat and each one pledging himself to perform his duty, twelve names were drawn out, and the men took their stations with their rifles, and, firing at the word, laid him dead. He was decently buried, and the place was restored quietly to the proper authorities. A general, with titles enough for an hidalgo, was at San Gabriel, and issued a proclamation as long as the fore-top-bowline, threatening destruction to the rebels, but never stirred from his fort; for forty Kentucky hunters, with their rifles, were a match for a whole regiment of hungry, drawling, lazy half-breeds. This affair happened while we were at San Pedro, (the port of the Pueblo,) and we had all the particulars directly from those who were on the spot. A few months afterwards, another man, whom we had often seen in San Diego, murdered a man and his wife on the high road between the Pueblo and San Louis Rey, and the foreigners not feeling themselves called upon to act in this case, the parties being all natives, nothing was done about it; and I frequently afterwards saw the murderer in San Diego, where he was living with his wife and family.

When a crime has been committed by Indians, justice, or rather vengeance, is not so tardy. One Sunday afternoon, while I was at San Diego, an Indian was sitting on his horse, when another, with whom he had had

**...seeing no prospect of justice being administered, made known that if nothing was done, they should try the man themselves.** This is—by definition—vigilante justice: a group of people deciding amongst themselves that justice has not been served, and then taking matters into their own hands.

**...proceeded to try the man according to the forms in their own country.** Of course, part of the point here is that they're *not* in their own country. The man's actions are (or at least ought to be) subject to the laws of the country in which the crime was committed.

**...each one pledging himself to perform his duty...** Traditionally, one of the rifles would be loaded with a blank cartridge so that each member of the firing squad, should doubts assail him, can tell himself that he may not have had a hand in the execution. The members of the firing squad fire simultaneously so that neither the participants nor any onlookers can tell who fired the fatal shot.

**...titles enough for an hidalgo...** That is, a Spanish nobleman. Dana is being snide.

**...forty Kentucky hunters . . . were a match for a whole regiment of . . . lazy half-breeds.** Dana, who thinks little of the Californians, is saying (none too subtly) that the men from Kentucky are better fighters (and probably better men) than the Mexicans.

**...we had all the particulars directly from those who were on the spot.** Maybe so, but some critics contend that Dana's version of the story is garbled and that the real incident occurred in late March/early April when Gervasio Alipas and his lover, Maria del Rosario Villa, were shot by a "vigilance committee" after the pair murdered Maria's husband, Domingo Felix. (Which actually makes a much better story, anyway.)

some difficulty, came up to him, drew a long knife, and plunged it directly into the horse's heart. The Indian sprang from his falling horse, drew out the knife, and plunged it into the other Indian's breast, over his shoulder, and laid him dead. The poor fellow was seized at once, clapped into the calabozo, and kept there until an answer could be received from Monterey. A few weeks afterwards, I saw the poor wretch, sitting on the bare ground, in front of the calabozo, with his feet chained to a stake, and handcuffs about his wrists. I knew there was very little hope for him. Although the deed was done in hot blood, the horse on which he was sitting being his own, and a great favorite, yet he was an Indian, and that was enough. In about a week after I saw him, I heard that he had been shot. These few instances will serve to give one a notion of the distribution of justice in California.

In their domestic relations, these people are no better than in their public. The men are thriftless, proud, and extravagant, and very much given to gaming; and the women have but little education, and a good deal of beauty, and their morality, of course, is none of the best; yet the instances of infidelity are much less frequent than one would at first suppose. In fact, one vice is set over against another; and thus, something like a balance is obtained. The women have but little virtue, but then the jealousy of their husbands is extreme, and their revenge deadly and almost certain. A few inches of cold steel has been the punishment of many an unwary man, who has been guilty, perhaps, of nothing more than indiscretion of manner. The difficulties of the attempt are numerous, and the consequences of discovery fatal. With the unmarried women, too, great watchfulness is used. The main object of the parents is to marry their daughters well, and to this, the slightest slip would be fatal. The sharp eyes of a dueña, and the cold steel of a father or brother, are a protection which the characters of most of them—men and women—render by no means useless; for the very men who would lay down their lives to avenge the dishonor of their own family, would risk the same lives to complete the dishonor of another.

**...clapped into the calabozo...** Placed in jail. In Spanish, *calabozo* means dungeon. Since the 1830s, we have sometimes used the French-influenced word *calaboose* to mean the same thing.

**...yet he was an Indian, and that was enough.** Dana points out that in California "justice" (and one can sense the sarcasm here) generally depends on the social class of the criminal. (Some may argue that there might still be some truth to this.) An Indian, being of a lower class (in fact, barely human, according to some), is simply shot—the way one might put down a dog that bit a child. It is, after all, the easiest way out. (Unless you're the Indian in question.)

**...their morality, of course, is none of the best...** This is a touchy subject. At several points in the book, Dana discusses (and criticizes) the morality of others, including his fellow-sailors. However, he is largely silent about his own moral lapses. In this particular case, Dana is at the very least guilty of over-generalizing. Keep in mind that, even though he can be dismissive and condescending when speaking of other cultures, the idea of justice *matters* to Dana. This book, remember, was written as an outraged protest over what he saw as the injustices to which ordinary seamen were subjected.

**The sharp eyes of a dueña...** Also *duenna*. Used in this sense, a *dueña* is a chaperone. The more common word might be *doña*, since *dueña* can be taken to mean owner or landlady, which wouldn't fit at all.

**...the very men who would lay down their lives...** That is, the same men who would kill to protect the honor of a wife, daughter, or sister, often attempt to seduce someone else's wife, daughter, or sister. There is certainly some truth to this, but it's misleading to imply, as Dana does, that this is a feature only of Mexican life.

Of the poor Indians, very little care is taken. The priests, indeed, at the missions, are said to keep them very strictly, and some rules are usually made by the alcaldes to punish their misconduct; but it all amounts to but little. Indeed, to show the entire want of any sense of morality or domestic duty among them, I have frequently known an Indian to bring his wife, to whom he was lawfully married in the church, down to the beach, and carry her back again, dividing with her the money which she had got from the sailors. If any of the girls were discovered by the alcalde to be open evil-livers, they were whipped, and kept at work sweeping the square of the presidio, and carrying mud and bricks for the buildings; yet a few reáls would generally buy them off. Intemperance, too, is a common vice among the Indians. The Spaniards, on the contrary, are very abstemious, and I do not remember ever having seen a Spaniard intoxicated.

Such are the people who inhabit a country embracing four or five hundred miles of sea-coast, with several good harbors; with fine forests in the north; the waters filled with fish, and the plains covered with thousands of herds of cattle; blessed with a climate, than which there can be no better in the world; free from all manner of diseases, whether epidemic or endemic; and with a soil in which corn yields from seventy to eighty fold. In the hands of an enterprising people, what a country this might be! we are ready to say. Yet how long would a people remain so, in such a country? The Americans (as those from the United States are called) and Englishmen, who are fast filling up the principal towns, and getting the trade into their hands, are indeed more industrious and effective than the Spaniards; yet their children are brought up Spaniards, in every respect, and if the "California fever" (laziness) spares the first generation, it always attacks the second.

**I have frequently known an Indian to bring his wife...** Dana once again manages to denigrate an entire culture by over-generalizing, pointing out what he sees as the Indians' "want of any sense of morality." And, although silent on the details, one wonders exactly how Dana came to know this, and just what his own involvement might have been. Throughout the book, Dana is careful to avoid any mention of any dalliances he might have had with any of the native women. But he is, after all, a healthy 19-year-old male, far away from home, and in the company of both experienced sailors (as he says later, "rough & vulgar men") and willing women. In these circumstances, as several critics have mentioned, it's almost impossible to envision a young man such as Dana not establishing relationships with some of the women he meets. (And in fact, some years later, Dana confesses, "Not a man in my ship was more guilty in God's sight than myself.") Of course, by the time Dana sits down to write this book, he is courting (and will soon be engaged to—and then married to) the very conventional Sarah Watson. He would certainly wish to avoid mention of any such misbehaviors, which would have been viewed as scandalous in 19th-century Boston.

**...free from all manner of diseases...** Perhaps this is largely true of the Spanish and Mexicans, at least by this point. The Indians, however, were terribly vulnerable to diseases of European origin, such as smallpox. (In fact, there have been stories of settlers or soldiers purposely giving Indians smallpox-infected blankets. We do not know if that ever occurred, but we do know that during Pontiac's Rebellion (1763), for instance, doing so was at least discussed.) To Dana's point, to some extent much of the population of 19th-century California is disease-free simply because diseases breed and spread most rapidly in large cities, of which there are none in California.

# CHAPTER XXII

In the news
**July, 1835**

A Corsican named Giuseppe Fieschi attempts to assassinate Louis Philippe, the King of France, as the king and his sons ride in a parade. Fieschi constructs an "infernal machine," a device consisting of 24 (some accounts say 20) interconnected muskets on a single frame, all of which could fire simultaneously. Over a dozen people are killed and 40 others wounded. In fact, about the only people in the area who were *not* injured were the king and his sons.

## LIFE ON SHORE—THE ALERT

Saturday, July 18th. This day, sailed the Mexican hermaphrodite brig, Fazio, for San Blas and Mazatlan. This was the brig which was driven ashore at San Pedro in a south-easter, and had been lying at San Diego to repair and take in her cargo. The owner of her had had a good deal of difficulty with the government about the duties, etc., and her sailing had been delayed for several weeks; but everything having been arranged, she got under weigh with a light breeze, and was floating out of the harbor, when two horsemen came dashing down to the beach, at full speed, and tried to find a boat to put off after her; but there being none on the beach, they offered a handful of silver to any Kanaka who would swim off and take a letter on board. One of the Kanakas, a fine, active, well-made young fellow, instantly threw off everything but his duck trowsers, and putting the letter into his hat, swam off, after the vessel. Fortunately, the wind was very light and the vessel was going slowly, so that, although she was nearly a mile off when he started, he gained on her rapidly. He went through the water leaving a wake like a small steamboat. I certainly never saw such swimming before. They saw him coming from the deck, but did not heave-to, suspecting the nature of his errand; yet, the wind continuing light, he swam alongside and got on board, and delivered his letter. The captain read the letter, told the Kanaka there was no answer, and giving him a glass of brandy, left him to jump overboard and find the best of his way to the shore. The Kanaka swam in for the nearest point of land, and, in about an hour, made his appearance at the hide-house. He did not seem at all fatigued, had made three or four dollars, got a glass of brandy, and was in fine spirits. The brig kept on her course, and the government officers, who had come down to forbid her sailing, went back, each with something like a flea in his ear, having depended upon extorting a little more money from the owner.

**...although she was nearly a mile off when he started, he gained on her rapidly**. This is quite a feat. Swimming one mile in a pool would tax most of us. This young man did it in the ocean and in spite of any contrary currents or tides. The *Fazio* was a mile off when he started, but we must also add to that distance any further distance she might have sailed while he swam.

**...having depended upon extorting a little more money from the owner.** This sort of extortion (in the form of bribery or other "gifts") has long been common in many countries and cultures. (Including parts of contemporary Mexico, where it was possible fairly recently to pay a police officer to avoid a traffic citation and the attendant court appearance.)

It was now nearly three months since the Alert arrived

at Santa Barbara, and we began to expect her daily. About a half a mile behind the hide-house, was a high hill; and every afternoon, as soon as we had done our work, some one of us walked up to see if there were any sail in sight, coming down before the regular trades, which blow every afternoon. Each day, after the latter part of July, we went up the hill, and came back disappointed. I was anxious for her arrival, for I had been told by letter that the owners in Boston, at the request of my friends, had written to Captain T—— to take me on board the Alert, in case she returned to the United States before the Pilgrim; and I, of course, wished to know whether the order had been received, and what was the destination of the ship. One year more or less might be of small consequence to others, but it was everything to me. It was now just a year since we sailed from Boston, and at the shortest, no vessel could expect to get away under eight or nine months, which would make our absence two years in all. This would be pretty long, but would not be fatal. It would not necessarily be decisive of my future life. But one year more would settle the matter. I should be a sailor for life; and although I had made up my mind to it before I had my letters from home, and was, as I thought, quite satisfied; yet, as soon as an opportunity was held out to me of returning, and the prospect of another kind of life was opened to me, my anxiety to return, and, at least, to have the chance of deciding upon my course for myself, was beyond measure. Beside that, I wished to be "equal to either fortune," and to qualify myself for an officer's berth, and a hide-house was no place to learn seamanship in. I had become experienced in hide-curing, and everything went on smoothly, and I had many opportunities of becoming acquainted with the people, and much leisure for reading and studying navigation; yet practical seamanship could only be got on board ship; therefore, I determined to ask to be taken on board the ship when she arrived. By the first of August, we finished curing all our hides, stored them away, cleaned out our vats, (in which latter work we spent two days, up to our knees in mud and the sediments of six months' hide-curing, in a stench which would drive a donkey from his breakfast,) and got in readiness for the arrival of the

**...the owners in Boston, at the request of my friends...** Up to now, Dana has been pretty good about not pulling any strings to get special treatment. By this point, though, he is desperate to get home, so he seeks a place on *Alert*, which may return home sooner than *Pilgrim*. Dana feels that if he were to spend much more than two years onboard ship, he would end up "a sailor for life." If that is his lot, he notes, then he'd prefer to be an officer, and he knows that guarding and preparing hides at a hide-house is no way to gain the skills necessary for commanding a vessel. (For what it's worth, note that in his original manuscript, Dana had written "at the request of my father," rather than "at the request of my friends.")

**In the news**

**July, 1835**

Supreme Court Justice John Marshall, who had served as Chief Justice for some 34 years, dies in Philadelphia, PA, where he'd gone for medical treatment. Marshall, who had previously served as a state Representative from Virginia and as Secretary of State under President John Adams, was a powerful Chief Justice whose decisions helped shape the Supreme Court into the powerful branch of government we know today, co-equal with the executive and legislative branches. In fact, Marshall was Chief Justice when the Court handed down its opinion in the case of *Marbury v. Madison*–a decision in which the Court for the first time ruled an act of Congress to be unconstitutional and thus invalid.

ship, and had another leisure interval of three or four weeks; which I spent, as usual, in reading, writing, studying, making and mending my clothes, and getting my wardrobe in complete readiness, in case I should go on board the ship; and in fishing, ranging the woods with the dogs, and in occasional visits to the presidio and mission. A good deal of my time was spent in taking care of a little puppy, which I had selected from thirty-six, that were born within three days of one another, at our house. He was a fine, promising pup, with four white paws, and all the rest of his body of a dark brown. I built a little kennel for him, and kept him fastened there, away from the other dogs, feeding and disciplining him myself. In a few weeks, I got him in complete subjection, and he grew finely, was very much attached to me, and bid fair to be one of the leading dogs on the beach. I called him Bravo, and the only thing I regretted at the thought of leaving the beach, was parting with him.

**...the only thing I regretted...** This doesn't say much for the friendships he has struck up with the kanakas and the others. Dana modifies this stance later on, when it's time to leave the kanakas for good.

Day after day, we went up the hill, but no ship was to be seen, and we began to form all sorts of conjectures as to her whereabouts; and the theme of every evening's conversation at the different houses, and in our afternoon's paséo upon the beach, was the ship—where she could be—had she been to San Francisco?—how many hides she would bring, etc., etc.

**...where she could be–had she been to San Francisco?** Given the ubiquity of today's communicative technologies, it's difficult for us to appreciate just how completely out of touch these men were with their home port, their friends and loved ones, and the other ships with which they sailed. Although telegraphy existed in 1835, it was rudimentary; at the time, Samuel Morse had not yet invented the code bearing his name that would make the process efficient enough to be useful. Even 30 years later, when Lincoln is assassinated, it would take several days for the news to reach Europe.

Tuesday, August 25th. This morning, the officer in charge of our house went off beyond the point a fishing, in a small canoe, with two Kanakas; and we were sitting quietly in our room at the hide-house, when, just before noon, we heard a complete yell of "Sail ho!" breaking out from all parts of the beach, at once,—from the Kanakas' oven to the Rosa's house. In an instant, every one was out of his house; and there was a fine, tall ship, with royals and skysails set, bending over before the strong afternoon breeze, and coming rapidly round the point. Her yards were braced sharp up; every sail was set, and drew well; the Yankee ensign was flying from her mizen-peak; and having the tide in her favor, she came up like a race-horse. It was nearly six months since a new vessel had entered San Diego, and of

**...to the Rosa's house.** That is, to the hide-house being used by the crew of *La Rosa*.

**...a fine, tall ship...** Our very first glimpse of *Alert* is a favorable one. Dana wants us to realize from the start that this is a fine vessel, manned by a dedicated crew and led by a seasoned, professional captain.

course, every one was on the qui-vive. She certainly made a fine appearance. Her light sails were taken in, as she passed the low, sandy tongue of land, and clewing up her head sails, she rounded handsomely to, under her mizen topsail, and let go the anchor at about a cable's length from the shore. In a few minutes, the topsail yards were manned, and all three of the topsails furled at once. From the fore top-gallant yard, the men slid down the stay to furl the jib, and from the mizen top-gallant yard, by the stay, into the maintop, and thence to the yard; and the men on the topsail yards came down the lifts to the yard-arms of the courses. The sails were furled with great care, the bunts triced up by jiggers, and the jibs stowed in cloth. The royal yards were then struck, tackles got upon the yard-arms and the stay, the long-boat hoisted out, a large anchor carried astern, and the ship moored. Then the captain's gig was lowered away from the quarter, and a boat's crew of fine lads, between the ages of fourteen and eighteen, pulled the captain ashore. The gig was a light whale-boat, handsomely painted, and fitted up with cushions, etc., in the stern sheets. We immediately attacked the boat's crew, and got very thick with them in a few minutes. We had much to ask about Boston, their passage out, etc., and they were very curious to know about the life we were leading upon the beach. One of them offered to exchange with me; which was just what I wanted; and we had only to get the permission of the captain.

After dinner, the crew began discharging their hides, and, as we had nothing to do at the hide-houses, we were ordered aboard to help them. I had now my first opportunity of seeing the ship which I hoped was to be my home for the next year. She looked as well on board as she did from without. Her decks were wide and roomy, (there being no poop, or house on deck, which disfigures the after part of most of our vessels,) flush, fore and aft, and as white as snow, which the crew told us was from constant use of holystones. There was no foolish gilding and gingerbread work, to take the eye of landsmen and passengers, but everything was "ship-shape and Bristol fashion." There was no rust, no dirt, no rigging hanging slack, no fag ends of ropes and

**...clewing up her head sails...** Furling her sails as she enters the harbor. Dana continues describing the efficient, organized fashion in which the ship is brought to anchor.

### In the news
### August, 1835

The *Southern Literary Messenger* was a periodical published in Richmond, Virginia, from 1834 until June 1864. Edgar Allan Poe was hired as a staff writer and critic in August 1835, possibly based on a recommendation to founder Thomas White from John Pendleton Kennedy, a novelist and politician who would eventually serve as U.S. Secretary of the Navy. Just a month later, White fired Poe, allegedly for his drinking. Poe was rehired in October and made editor of the journal in December.

**One of them offered to exchange with me; which was just what I wanted...** This is what Dana is after: He has found an *Alert* crewmember who is willing to swap places with him, so that Dana can board (and perhaps return to Boston on) the *Alert*.

**...no poop, or house on deck...** A poop or poop-deck (from the Latin *puppis*, or stern) is a raised after-deck at the stern of a ship. Many vessels feature a deckhouse on the poop deck, in which the watch can be quartered or supplies kept.

**...foolish gilding and gingerbread work, to take the eye of landsmen...** Amongst sailors (then and now), a vessel's lines and equipment are greatly appreciated and often remarked upon. But a true sailor knows when he's looking at something that was added merely to impress the passengers; as when one adds superfluous fins or spoilers to an automobile, a true aficionado is not impressed by silly (and generally useless) frills and ornamentation.

"Irish pendants" aloft, and the yards were squared "to a t" by lifts and braces.

**...yet he was generally liked by the crew.** In other words, unlike the mate aboard *Pilgrim*, this man (his name is Richard Brown), is tough but fair, an experienced professional.

The mate was a fine, hearty, noisy fellow, with a voice like a lion, and always wide awake. He was "a man, every inch of him," as the sailors said; and though "a bit of a horse," and "a hard customer," yet he was generally liked by the crew. There was also a second and third mate, a carpenter, sailmaker, steward, cook, etc., and twelve, including boys, before the mast. She had, on board, seven thousand hides, which she had collected at the windward, and also horns and tallow. All these we began discharging, from both gangways at once, into the two boats, the second mate having charge of the launch, and the third mate of the pinnace. For several days, we were employed in this way, until all the hides were taken out, when the crew began taking in ballast, and we returned to our old work, hide-curing.

In the news
**July, 1835**

Roger B. Taney is appointed Chief Justice of the Supreme Court, although he will not be confirmed for several months. In 1857, Taney will author the infamous Dred Scott decision denying citizenship to blacks, and noting that they had, "for more than a century before been regarded as beings of an inferior order...altogether unfit to associate with the white race."

Saturday, Aug. 29th. Arrived, brig Catalina, from the windward.

**Arrived, brig Catalina, from the windward.** From 1832 to 1839, the *Catalina* is commanded by Joseph Snook and owned by Henry Virmond, a German merchant who owns businesses in Mexico. Snook, originally from a poverty-stricken family in England, eventually settles in California, acquiring a rancho of almost 9,000 acres north of San Francisco and stocking it with cattle.

Sunday, 30th. This was the first Sunday that the crew had been in San Diego, and of course they were all for going up to see the town. The Indians came down early, with horses to let for the day, and all the crew, who could obtain liberty, went off to the Presidio and mission, and did not return until night. I had seen enough of San Diego, and went on board and spent the day with some of the crew, whom I found quietly at work in the forecastle, mending and washing their clothes, and reading and writing. They told me that the ship stopped at Callao in the passage out, and there lay three weeks. She had a passage of little over eighty days from Boston to Callao, which is one of the shortest on record. There, they left the Brandywine frigate, and other smaller American ships of war, and the English frigate Blonde, and a French seventy-four. From Callao they came directly to California, and had visited every port on the coast, including San Francisco. The forecastle in which they lived was large, tolerably well lighted by bulls-eyes, and, being kept perfectly clean, had quite a comfortable appearance; at least, it was far better than

**...one of the shortest on record.** *Alert* is not only a well-built, well-maintained vessel, she's also fast; this is important, if one of your goals is to get home as quickly as possible.

**...the English frigate Blonde...** This is the same British warship that went to the islands in 1824, captained by Lord Byron, the poet's cousin.

**...a French seventy-four.** That is, a French warship mounting 74 guns (cannon).

the little, black, dirty hole in which I had lived so many months on board the Pilgrim. By the regulations of the ship, the forecastle was cleaned out every morning, and the crew, being very neat, kept it clean by some regulations of their own, such as having a large spitbox always under the steps and between the bits, and obliging every man to hang up his wet clothes, etc. In addition to this, it was holystoned every Saturday morning. In the after part of the ship was a handsome cabin, a dining-room, and a trade-room, fitted out with shelves and furnished with all sorts of goods. Between these and the forecastle was the "between-decks," as high as the gun deck of a frigate; being six feet and a half, under the beams. These between-decks were holystoned regularly, and kept in the most perfect order; the carpenter's bench and tools being in one part, the sailmaker's in another, and boatswain's locker, with the spare rigging, in a third. A part of the crew slept here, in hammocks swung fore and aft from the beams, and triced up every morning. The sides of the between-decks were clapboarded, the knees and stanchions of iron, and the latter made to unship. The crew said she was as tight as a drum, and a fine sea boat, her only fault being, that of most fast ships,—that she was wet, forward. When she was going, as she sometimes would, eight or nine knots on a wind, there would not be a dry spot forward of the gangway. The men told great stories of her sailing, and had great confidence in her as a "lucky ship." She was seven years old, and had always been in the Canton trade, and never had met with an accident of any consequence, and had never made a passage that was not shorter than the average. The third mate, a young man of about eighteen years of age, nephew of one of the owners, had been in the ship from a small boy, and "believed in the ship;" and the chief mate thought more of her than he would of a wife and family.

**...it was far better than the little, black, dirty hole in which I had lived so many months on board the Pilgrim.** Dana paints a picture in which *Alert* compares favorably to *Pilgrim* in just about every respect.

**...a large spitbox ...** This is exactly what it sounds like: a large box into which the sailors would spit. Perhaps a bit disgusting, but not as disgusting as having them spit all over the decking, which was the alternative.

**...the "between-decks," as high as the gun deck of a frigate...** On many vessels, the space between decks was cramped, but on the *Alert*, they were roomy and fitted out as fairly comfortable work areas. Six feet or more was plenty of clearance for the typically shorter men of that age, and quite roomy even today.

**...stanchions of iron, and the latter made to unship.** A stanchion is a vertical post or rod to which might be mounted lifelines or other gear. Those aboard *Alert* were made so as to be removable, making it easier to replace, repair, or work around them.

**...she was wet, forward.** Vessels of this size have displacement hulls: Rather than planing (riding up over the waves and skimming lightly across with a majority of the hull out of the water), a displacement hull plows through the waves, bouncing along as the bow strikes and drives through each wave. The faster the ship moves, the more the bow bounces and the harder it drives through the waves. The result is that the forward portion of such a vessel can become wet and uncomfortable.

The ship lay about a week longer in port, when, having discharged her cargo and taken in ballast, she prepared to get under weigh. I now made my application to the captain to go on board. He told me that I could go home in the ship when she sailed (which I knew before); and, finding that I wished to be on board while she was on

**...which I knew before...** Asking permission of Captain Thompson is something of a formality, thinks Dana, since Dana's friends (and father?) have already arranged this.

**...found myself once more afloat.** As far as Dana knows, he's (almost literally) "home free." He has transferred to the *Alert* and now plans to spend a few more weeks (or at most, months) on the West Coast loading hides aboard the ship, before departing for his hometown of Boston. (Dana had assumed—quite rightly—that *Pilgrim*, since she was being used to ferry hides to the hide-houses and thence to other ships, might spend many more months or even years on the coast, working the hide-houses and collecting hides for other, larger ships. This is one reason he is so anxious to transfer to the Alert.) However, Dana's plans are about to encounter an unforeseen hitch.

In the news

**August, 1835**

In what could have served as a cautionary tale from halfway around the world, the village that would soon become the Australian city of Melbourne is settled. At the time of its settlement, there were roughly 10,000 Aborigines in the area. Twenty years later, fewer than 2000 remained. The Aborigines in that region of Australia—like the Native Americans in California and elsewhere—were the victims of a largely (though not completely) unintentional genocide resulting mainly from disease and from a cultural clash of unimagined intensity.

the coast, said he had no objection, if I could find one of my own age to exchange with me, for the time. This, I easily accomplished, for they were glad to change the scene by a few months on shore, and, moreover, escape the winter and the south-easters; and I went on board the next day, with my chest and hammock, and found myself once more afloat.

## CHAPTER XXIII

## NEW SHIP AND SHIPMATES—MY WATCHMATE

Tuesday, Sept. 8th. This was my first day's duty on board the ship; and though a sailor's life is a sailor's life wherever it may be, yet I found everything very different here from the customs of the brig Pilgrim. After all hands were called, at day-break, three minutes and a half were allowed for every man to dress and come on deck, and if any were longer than that, they were sure to be overhauled by the mate, who was always on deck, and making himself heard all over the ship. The head-pump was then rigged, and the decks washed down by the second and third mates; the chief mate walking the quarter-deck and keeping a general supervision, but not deigning to touch a bucket or a brush. Inside and out, fore and aft, upper deck and between decks, steerage and forecastle, rail, bulwarks, and water-ways, were washed, scrubbed and scraped with brooms and canvas, and the decks were wet and sanded all over, and then holystoned. The holystone is a large, soft stone, smooth on the bottom, with long ropes attached to each end, by which the crew keep it sliding fore and aft, over the wet, sanded decks. Smaller hand-stones, which the sailors call "prayer-books," are used to scrub in among the crevices and narrow places, where the large holystone will not go. An hour or two, we were kept at this work, when the head-pump was manned, and all the sand washed off the decks and sides. Then came swabs and squilgees; and after the decks were dry, each one went to his particular morning job. There were five boats belonging to the ship,—launch, pinnace, jolly-boat, larboard quarter-boat, and gig,—each of which had a coxswain, who had charge of it, and was answerable for the order and cleanness of it. The rest of the cleaning was divided among the crew; one having the brass and composition work about the capstan; another the bell, which was of brass, and kept as bright as a gilt button; a third, the harness-cask; another, the man-rope stanchions; others, the steps of the forecastle and hatchways, which were hauled up and holystoned. Each of

**...I found everything very different here from the customs of the brig Pilgrim.** One of the differences is that on board the *Alert*, there is order and routine. One gets the impression that things on this ship are much more organized than on board *Pilgrim*.

**...but not deigning to touch a bucket or a brush.** The mate, as a senior officer, would not lower himself to do a mere seaman's work. And yet, this is as expected; the officer is a supervisor, not a laborer. If he's good (and this one is), then he's already done his stint as a common seaman.

**Then came swabs and squilgees...** That is, squeegees. This is a clean, organized, orderly ship.

**...the capstan...** A capstan is a sort of vertical windlass. That is, it's a pegged or geared barrel used for heavy hoisting, such as retrieving an anchor or lifting heavy gear up a mast.

**...the harness-cask...** A rimmed, covered cask used for storing salted meat.

these jobs must be finished before breakfast; and, in the meantime, the rest of the crew filled the scuttle-butt, and the cook scraped his kids (wooden tubs out of which the sailors eat) and polished the hoops, and placed them before the galley, to await inspection. When the decks were dry, the lord paramount made his appearance on the quarter-deck, and took a few turns, when eight bells were struck, and all hands went to breakfast. Half an hour was allowed for breakfast, when all hands were called again; the kids, pots, bread-bags, etc., stowed away; and, this morning, preparations were made for getting under weigh. We paid out on the chain by which we swung; hove in on the other; catted the anchor; and hove short on the first. This work was done in shorter time than was usual on board the brig; for though everything was more than twice as large and heavy, the cat-block being as much as a man could lift, and the chain as large as three of the Pilgrim's, yet there was a plenty of room to move about in, more discipline and system, more men, and more good will. Every one seemed ambitious to do his best: officers and men knew their duty, and all went well. As soon as she was hove short, the mate, on the forecastle, gave the order to loose the sails, and, in an instant, every one sprung into the rigging, up the shrouds, and out on the yards, scrambling by one another,—the first up the best fellow,—cast off the yard-arm gaskets and bunt gaskets, and one man remained on each yard, holding the bunt jigger with a turn round the tye, all ready to let go, while the rest laid down to man the sheets and halyards. The mate then hailed the yards—"All ready forward?"—"All ready the cross-jack yards?" etc., etc., and "Aye, aye, sir!" being returned from each, the word was given to let go; and in the twinkling of an eye, the ship, which had shown nothing but her bare yards, was covered with her loose canvas, from the royal-mast-heads to the decks. Every one then laid down, except one man in each top, to overhaul the rigging, and the topsails were hoisted and sheeted home; all three yards going to the mast-head at once, the larboard watch hoisting the fore, the starboard watch the main, and five light hands, (of whom I was one,) picked from the two watches, the

**...scraped his kids (wooden tubs out of which the sailors eat) and polished the hoops...** Although most editions of the book include a glossary as an appendix, this is one of the few times Dana defines a nautical term within the actual text. (Although he does provide a few footnoted definitions.) Hoops are metal bands that hold the shank of and anchor to the stock. In some types of sail configuration, hoops can also be wooden bands that slide up and down the mast as a sail is hoisted or lowered.

**...work was done in shorter time than was usual . . . for though everything was more than twice as large and heavy . . . there was a plenty of room to move about in, more discipline and system...** Dana again points out that *Alert* is better organized and manned by efficient, well-trained, and motivated sailors. The comparison to *Pilgrim*, though unstated, is obvious.

In the news

**September, 1835**

Recently established Oberlin College becomes the first U.S. college to admit African-American students. A few years later (1837), it will become the first to admit women. (Oberlin, the town and the college, has long been associated with progressive causes.)

**...five light hands...** Light hands are sailors who have been assigned light duty, sometimes due to illness or injury, but in Dana's case because he is still literally "learning the ropes" on board this new vessel.

**...the mizen.** The mizen is the lowest sail on the mizen (or mizzen) mast. The mizzenmast is the third, or aft-most mast on a three-masted, square-sailed vessel. (Or the after mast of a yawl or other two-masted vessel.)

mizen. The yards were then trimmed, the anchor weighed, the cat-block hooked on, the fall stretched out, manned by "all hands and the cook," and the anchor brought to the head with "cheerily men!" in full chorus. The ship being now under weigh, the light sails were set, one after another, and she was under full sail, before she had passed the sandy point. The fore royal, which fell to my lot, (being in the mate's watch,) was more than twice as large as that of the Pilgrim, and, though I could handle the brig's easily, I found my hands full, with this, especially as there were no jacks to the ship; everything being for neatness, and nothing left for Jack to hold on by, but his eyelids.

**...though I could handle the brig's easily, I found my hands full...** Even a small sail can be difficult to handle when the wind is blowing and the ship is pitching. In this case, although Dana had been able to handle this particular sail easily enough on board *Pilgrim*, he has difficulty doing it on *Alert* because the sail is much larger and because there are no convenient handholds. (The increased size matters greatly here, because only a few knots of wind striking a large sail can translate into hundreds—or even thousands—of pounds of pressure. Trying to manhandle a large sail single-handedly is a daunting and sometimes impossible task.)

As soon as we were beyond the point, and all sail out, the order was given, "Go below the watch!" and the crew said that, ever since they had been on the coast, they had had "watch and watch," while going from port to port; and, in fact, everything showed that, though strict discipline was kept, and the utmost was required of every man, in the way of his duty, yet, on the whole, there was very good usage on board. Each one knew that he must be a man, and show himself smart when at his duty, yet every one was satisfied with the usage; and a contented crew, agreeing with one another, and finding no fault, was a contrast indeed with the small, hard-used, dissatisfied, grumbling, desponding crew of the Pilgrim.

**... though strict discipline was kept, and the utmost was required of every man . . yet. . .there was very good usage on board.** Again Dana points out that *Alert* is manned by professionals who have been trained by a firm, fair leader of men. The contrast between the two vessels is obvious.

It being the turn of our watch to go below, the men went to work, mending their clothes, and doing other little things for themselves; and I, having got my wardrobe in complete order at San Diego, had nothing to do but to read. I accordingly overhauled the chests of the crew, but found nothing that suited me exactly, until one of the men said he had a book which "told all about a great highway-man," at the bottom of his chest, and producing it, I found, to my surprise and joy, that it was nothing else than Bulwer's Paul Clifford. This, I seized immediately, and going to my hammock, lay there, swinging and reading, until the watch was out. The between-decks were clear, the hatchways open, and a cool breeze blowing through them, the ship

**...overhauled the chests of the crew...** Aboard ship, to overhaul is to slacken a rope by pulling in the opposite direction. Here, Dana means that he looked through the men's belongings to locate some reading material.

**...Bulwer's Paul Clifford.** Edward Bulwer-Lytton's 1830 novel, *Paul Clifford*, was immensely popular, but the writer was subject to fits of "purple prose"—overly florid and extravagant writing. The first line in *Paul Clifford* is a good example and in fact the first seven words have become the punchline to many a literary joke: "It was a dark and stormy night; the rain fell in torrents—except at occasional intervals, when it was checked by a violent gust of wind which swept up the streets (for it is in London that our scene lies), rattling along the housetops, and fiercely agitating the scanty flame of the lamps that struggled against the darkness."

In the news
**September, 1835**

Only three months after their marriage, Jefferson Davis's wife, Sarah Knox Taylor, dies after having contracted malaria. Although only an army lieutenant when he met his young wife, Davis is the future president of the Confederacy, while Sarah was the daughter of future U.S. president Zachary Taylor.

**...three days on the passage...** The trip takes longer than expected, but Dana is glad of the delay, for it allows him time to enjoy his book.

**...this was a perfect feast to me.** Dana almost literally hungers for culture, for literature, for the sophisticated pleasures he has left behind in Boston. The discovery of such a book truly is a feast for his senses.

In the news
**September, 1835**

General José Figueroa dies. An able and respected administrator, soldier, and governor of Alta California, Figueroa is replaced by José Castro. Figueroa Street, which traverses much of Los Angeles, CA, is named for him.

**The sailmaker was the head man of the watch...** The sail maker is Rueben Herriot, a native New Yorker then living in Boston. An enormously experienced seaman, the men called him "Sails."

**...remarkable for drawing a long bow**. The longbow (a word that, not surprisingly, first appears in Joseph Ritson's 1790 collection of Robin Hood ballads; the ballads themselves go back to about the year 1500) is a tall bow with a correspondingly long pull. It takes great strength to draw and hold such a bow.

under easy way, and everything comfortable. I had just got well into the story, when eight bells were struck, and we were all ordered to dinner. After dinner came our watch on deck for four hours, and, at four o'clock, I went below again, turned into my hammock, and read until the dog watch. As no lights were allowed after eight o'clock, there was no reading in the night watch. Having light winds and calms, we were three days on the passage, and each watch below, during the daytime, I spent in the same manner, until I had finished my book. I shall never forget the enjoyment I derived from it. To come across anything with the slightest claims to literary merit, was so unusual, that this was a perfect feast to me. The brilliancy of the book, the succession of capital hits, lively and characteristic sketches, kept me in a constant state of pleasing sensations. It was far too good for a sailor. I could not expect such fine times to last long.

While on deck, the regular work of the ship went on. The sailmaker and carpenter worked between decks, and the crew had their work to do upon the rigging, drawing yarns, making spun-yarn, etc., as usual in merchantmen. The night watches were much more pleasant than on board the Pilgrim. There, there were so few in a watch, that, one being at the wheel, and another on the look-out, there was no one left to talk with; but here, we had seven in a watch, so that we had long yarns, in abundance. After two or three night watches, I became quite well acquainted with all the larboard watch. The sailmaker was the head man of the watch, and was generally considered the most experienced seaman on board. He was a thoroughbred old man-of-war's-man, had been to sea twenty-two years, in all kinds of vessels—men-of-war, privateers, slavers, and merchantmen;—everything except whalers, which a thorough sailor despises, and will always steer clear of, if he can. He had, of course, been in all parts of the world, and was remarkable for drawing a long bow. His yarns frequently stretched through a watch, and kept all hands awake. They were always amusing from their improbability, and, indeed, he never expected to be believed, but spun them merely for amusement; and as he had some humor and a good supply of man-of-war slang and sailor's salt phrases, he always madc fun. Next to him in age and experience, and, of course, in standing in the watch, was an Englishman, named Harris, of whom I shall have more to say hereafter. Then, came two or three Americans, who had been the common run of European and South American voyages, and one who had been in a "spouter," and, of course, had all the whaling stories to himself. Last of all, was a broad-backed, thick-headed boy from Cape Cod, who had been in mackerel schooners, and was making his first voyage in a square-rigged vessel. He was born in Hingham, and of course was called "Bucketmaker." The other watch was composed of about the same number. A tall, fine-looking Frenchman, with coal-black whiskers and curly hair, a first-rate seaman, and named John, (one name is enough for a sailor,) was the head man of the watch. Then came two Americans (one of whom had been a dissipated young man of property and family, and was reduced to duck trowsers and monthly wages,) a German, an English lad, named Ben, who belonged on the mizen topsail yard with me, and was a good sailor for his years, and two Boston boys just from the public schools. The carpenter sometimes mustered in the starboard watch, and was an old sea-dog, a Swede by birth, and accounted the best helmsman in the ship. This was our ship's company, beside cook and steward, who were blacks, three mates, and the captain.

The second day out, the wind drew ahead, and we had to beat up the coast; so that, in tacking ship, I could see the regulations of the vessel. Instead of going wherever was most convenient, and running from place to place, wherever work was to be done, each man had his station. A regular tacking and wearing bill was made out. The chief mate commanded on the forecastle, and had charge of the head sails and the forward part of the ship. Two of the best men in the ship—the sailmaker from our watch, and John, the Frenchman, from thc othcr, worked the forecastle. The third mate commanded in the waist, and, with the carpenter and one man, worked the main tack and bowlines; the cook, ex-officio, the fore sheet, and the steward the main. The second mate

**...an Englishman, named Harris...** Thomas Harris was an ordinary seaman. The official ship's records list his birthplace as Charleston, S.C., so either they or Dana must be in error.

**He was born in Hingham, and of course was called "Bucketmaker."** In 1815, the Wilders family opened a bucket factory in Hingham, MA. The factory was wildly successful, and the town became known as "Bucket Town." Even prior to that, though, the town was known for coopering and bucket-making; at one point, the Wilders' factory produced 1,000 wooden buckets per day.

**...a dissipated young man...** That is, one who has led a life dedicated to liquor, games of chance, and other self-indulgent pleasures.

In the news

**September, 1835**

Thousands of New Englanders head for Wisconsin when the U.S. government, aiming to encourage Wisconsin's bid to become a territory separate from Michigan, begins advertising prime Wisconsin land at $1.25 per acre. The plan works. On July 3, 1836, Wisconsin officially becomes a territory. In 1848, the eastern portion of the territory is admitted as the state of Wisconsin.

**...see the regulations of the vessel.** Dana means that the act of tacking provides him with an opportunity to see how the men behaved during the procedure. On a ship of this size, tacking (changing direction by bringing a vessel about and turning its bow across the wind) is a complex task, with many sails and spars needing to be shifted, lines changed, and rigging adjusted. Dana notes that the operation is carried out calmly and professionally, and that each man has a station and an area of responsibility, and that all of them seem to execute that responsibility quite well.

**...the weather side of the quarter-deck...** That is, on the windward side.

**"Helm's a lee'!"** Even on a small boat, coming about (that is, changing tacks) can be a tricky, sometimes dangerous procedure. Once the bow crosses the wind, the boom swings to the opposite side—often quickly and with great force. Someone who was not expecting the maneuver could be hurt (or even killed) if struck by the boom as it travels. For that reason, each step in the process is called out, so as to warn everyone in the area. In order to signal his intention, the helmsman first calls out "Ready about!" Then, when the helmsman is ready to turn the wheel (or push the tiller, if the vessel has no wheel), he calls out "Helm's alee!" to alert the crew.

In the news
**September, 1835**

A committee in San Felipe de Austin, Texas determines that because more peaceful measures have failed, "War [with Mexico] is our only resource. There is no other remedy but to defend our rights our country....." The delegates release a declaration of independence that states, "Whereas, General Antonio Lopez de Santa Anna, and other military chieftains, have, by force of arms, overthrown the federal institutions of Mexico...now the good people of Texas, availing themselves of their natural rights, [declare] . . . [t]hat they have taken up arms in defence of their rights and liberties, which were threatened by the encroachments of military despots, and in defence of the republican principles of the federal constitution of Mexico, of eighteen and twenty-four." (The 1824 constitution was much more liberal than the more centalized one recently adopted.)

had charge of the after yards, and let go the lee fore and main braces. I was stationed at the weather cross-jack braces; three other light hands at the lee; one boy at the spanker-sheet and guy; a man and a boy at the main topsail, top-gallant, and royal braces; and all the rest of the crew—men and boys—tallied on to the main brace. Every one here knew his station, must be there when all hands were called to put the ship about, and was answerable for every rope committed to him. Each man's rope must be let go and hauled in at the order, properly made fast, and neatly coiled away when the ship was about. As soon as all hands are at their stations, the captain, who stands on the weather side of the quarter-deck, makes a sign to the man at the wheel to put it down, and calls out "Helm's a lee'!" "Helm's a lee'!" answers the mate on the forecastle, and the head sheets are let go. "Raise tacks and sheets!" says the captain; "tacks and sheets!" is passed forward, and the fore tack and main sheet are let go. The next thing is to haul taut for a swing. The weather cross-jack braces and the lee main braces are each belayed together upon two pins, and ready to be let go; and the opposite braces hauled taut. "Main topsail haul!" shouts the captain; the braces are let go; and if he has taken his time well, the yards swing round like a top; but if he is too late, or too soon, it is like drawing teeth. The after yards are then braced up and belayed, the main sheet hauled aft, the spanker eased over to leeward, and the men from the braces stand by the head yards. "Let go and haul!" says the captain; the second mate lets go the weather fore braces, and the men haul in to leeward. The mate, on the forecastle, looks out for the head yards. "Well, the fore topsail yard!" "Top-gallant yard's well!" "Royal yard too much! Haul into windward! So! well that!" "Well all!" Then the starboard watch board the main tack, and the larboard watch lay forward and board the fore tack and haul down the jib sheet, clapping a tackle upon it, if it blows very fresh. The after yards are then trimmed, the captain generally looking out for them himself. "Well the cross-jack yard!" "Small pull the main top-gallant yard!" "Well that!" "Well the mizen top-gallant yard!" "Cross-jack yards all well!" "Well all aft!" "Haul taut to windward!" Everything being now trimmed and in order, each man coils up the rigging at his own station, and the order is given—"Go below the watch!"

During the last twenty-four hours of the passage, we beat off and on the land, making a tack about once in four hours, so that I had a sufficient opportunity to observe the working of the ship; and certainly, it took no more men to brace about this ship's lower yards, which were more than fifty feet square, than it did those of the Pilgrim, which were not much more than half the size; so much depends upon the manner in which the braces run, and the state of the blocks; and Captain Wilson, of the Ayacucho, who was afterwards a passenger with us, upon a trip to windward, said he had no doubt that our ship worked two men lighter than his brig.

Friday, Sept. 11th. This morning, at four o'clock, went below, San Pedro point being about two leagues ahead, and the ship going on under studding-sails. In about an hour we were waked up by the hauling of the chain about decks, and in a few minutes "All hands ahoy!" was called; and we were all at work, hauling in and making up the studding-sails, overhauling the chain forward, and getting the anchors ready. "The Pilgrim is there at anchor," said some one, as we were running about decks; and taking a moment's look over the rail, I saw my old friend, deeply laden, lying at anchor inside of the kelp. In coming to anchor, as well as in tacking, each one had his station and duty. The light sails were clewed up and furled, the courses hauled up and the jibs down; then came the topsails in the buntlines, and the anchor let go. As soon as she was well at anchor, all hands lay aloft to furl the topsails; and this, I soon found, was a great matter on board this ship; for every sailor knows that a vessel is judged of, a good deal, by the furl of her sails. The third mate, a sailmaker, and the larboard watch went upon the fore topsail yard; the second mate, carpenter, and the starboard watch upon the main; and myself and the English lad, and the two Boston boys, and the young Cape-Cod man, furled the mizen topsail. This sail belonged to us altogether, to

### In the news
### September, 1835

In what should not have been a particularly newsworthy event, a soldier named Orlando Reeves is killed by Seminole Indians in central Florida. Or maybe not. Apparently, regional histories of the incident differ, with some noting that settlers found the man's name carved into a tree and may have simply *assumed* that it marked his grave. And he might not have been a soldier, but a plantation owner whose name might not actually have been Reeves. In any event, the city of Orlando, FL owes its name to him, however muddled the story of its origin.

**...about two leagues ahead, and the ship going on under studding-sails.** They are about six miles out of San Pedro, with additional sails set outside of the ship's main sails in order to take advantage of the relatively calm weather. (The term studding-sail is usually pronounced stunsail. The term's origin is unknown, although it appears as early as the year 1550.)

**...my old friend, deeply laden, lying at anchor inside of the kelp.** The "old friend" is Dana's former vessel, *Pilgrim*. Live kelp grows only in fairly shallow water, so *Pilgrim* is relatively close to shore.

**...then came the topsails in the buntlines...** A buntline is a rope at the foot (or attached to a rope at the foot) of a sail and used to take in the sail.

**...by the furl of her sails.** There is still some truth to this. Often, one can fairly accurately judge a crew's skill by how neatly things aboard ship (including the sails themselves) are stowed.

**...and the bunt triced up...** That is, raised or hoisted with a line.

**With a voice like a young lion...** Dana often alludes to literature. This time he alludes to a biblical passage. See Psalms 104:21: "The young lions roar after their prey, and seek their meat from God." Irwin Shaw used the verse as the title of his 1948 novel, *The Young Lions*, about ordinary men during World War II attempting to come to grips with the carnage and confusion of war.

In the news
**September, 1835**

*The Penny Magazine* publishes a discourse on the history of smoking, calling it "repulsive to the natural taste." The magazine was aimed at working class readers and was an attempt to "diffuse useful knowledge" about everyday things. It did not cost a penny, but about 4 shillings, sixpence per year.

**...not so estimable a man, perhaps, but a far better mate...** After sailing for many months, Dana has come to an interesting conclusion: One need not be a good man to be a good sailor or even to be a good leader of men.

In the news
**September, 1835**

Darwin is at the Galapagos Islands, collecting samples. Some have said that it was Darwin's five weeks at The Galapagos that forever changed the world of science. While on the islands, Darwin collects samples of finches; back in London, he realizes that they are in fact different—*but closely related*—birds. The discovery leads him to formulate the principle of natural selection.

reef and to furl, and not a man was allowed to come upon our yard. The mate took us under his special care, frequently making us furl the sail over, three or four times, until we got the bunt up to a perfect cone, and the whole sail without a wrinkle. As soon as each sail was hauled up and the bunt made, the jigger was bent on to the slack of the buntlines, and the bunt triced up, on deck. The mate then took his place between the knight-heads to "twig" the fore, on the windlass to twig the main, and at the foot of the mainmast, for the mizen; and if anything was wrong,—too much bunt on one side, clews too taut or too slack, or any sail abaft the yard,—the whole must be dropped again. When all was right, the bunts were triced well up, the yard-arm gaskets passed, so as not to leave a wrinkle forward of the yard—short gaskets with turns close together.

From the moment of letting go the anchor, when the captain ceases his care of things, the chief mate is the great man. With a voice like a young lion, he was hallooing and bawling, in all directions, making everything fly, and, at the same time, doing everything well. He was quite a contrast to the worthy, quiet, unobtrusive mate of the Pilgrim; not so estimable a man, perhaps, but a far better mate of a vessel; and the entire change in Captain T——'s conduct, since he took command of the ship, was owing, no doubt, in a great measure, to this fact. If the chief officer wants force, discipline slackens, everything gets out of joint, the captain interferes continually; that makes a difficulty between them, which encourages the crew, and the whole ends in a three-sided quarrel. But Mr. Brown (the mate of the Alert) wanted no help from anybody; took everything into his own hands; and was more likely to encroach upon the authority of the master, than to need any spurring. Captain T—— gave his directions to the mate in private, and, except in coming to anchor, getting under weigh, tacking, reefing topsails, and other "all-hands-work," seldom appeared in person. This is the proper state of things, and while this lasts, and there is a good understanding aft, everything will go on well.

Having furled all the sails, the royal yards were next to

be sent down. The English lad and myself sent down the main, which was larger than the Pilgrim's main top-gallant yard; two more light hands, the fore; and one boy, the mizen. This order, we always kept while on the coast; sending them up and down every time we came in and went out of port. They were all tripped and lowered together, the main on the starboard side, and the fore and mizen, to port. No sooner was she all snug, than tackles were got up on the yards and stays, and the long-boat and pinnace hove out. The swinging booms were then guyed out, and the boats made fast by geswarps, and everything in harbor style. After breakfast, the hatches were taken off, and all got ready to receive hides from the Pilgrim. All day, boats were passing and repassing, until we had taken her hides from her, and left her in ballast trim. These hides made but little show in our hold, though they had loaded the Pilgrim down to the water's edge. This changing of the hides settled the question of the destination of the two vessels, which had been one of some speculation to us. We were to remain in the leeward ports, while the Pilgrim was to sail, the next morning, for San Francisco. After we had knocked off work, and cleared up decks for the night, my friend S—— came on board, and spent an hour with me in our berth between decks. The Pilgrim's crew envied me my place on board the ship, and seemed to think that I had got a little to windward of them; especially in the matter of going home first. S—— was determined to go home on the Alert, by begging or buying; if Captain T—— would not let him come on other terms, he would purchase an exchange with some one of the crew. The prospect of another year after the Alert should sail, was rather "too much of the monkey." About seven o'clock, the mate came down into the steerage, in fine trim for fun, roused the boys out of the berth, turned up the carpenter with his fiddle, sent the steward with lights to put in the between-decks, and set all hands to dancing. The between-decks were high enough to allow of jumping; and being clear, and white, from holystoning, made a fine dancing-hall. Some of the Pilgrim's crew were in the forecastle, and we all turned-to and had a regular sailor's shuffle, till eight bells. The Cape-Cod boy could dance the true

**The swinging booms were then guyed out, and the boats made fast by geswarps, and everything in harbor style.** The *Alert*'s crew has a system for everything; every man knows his job and has practiced at it long enough and often enough that it has become routine.

**...left her in ballast trim.** That is, the ships from which *Alert* acquires hides are left effectively empty, except for the ballast they carry for stability.

**These hides made but little show in our hold, though they had loaded the Pilgrim down to the water's edge.** The *Alert* is so much larger than *Pilgrim* that the hides she has taken on from the latter vessel have taken up very little space in her hold.

**...seemed to think that I had got a little to windward of them.** That is, they thought that Dana had taken advantage of his connections (which was certainly true) and that he thought himself better than they (which *may* have been true, at least to some extent).

**"too much of the monkey."** That is, more poor treatment than a sailor could (or should) bear. This odd phrase was common at the time, appearing in an 1829 issue of *The Literary Gazette*, for instance and also in an 1892 edition of short stories by Rolf Boldrewood—the pseudonym of Australian writer Thomas Alexander Browne. In a story entitled "In Bad Company," one character says, "I don't fancy free men like us shearers bein' under one man's thumb, and him lookin' out for himself all the time. It's too much of the monkey for me, and I'm not goin' to stand it after this season, no matter what comes of it."

In the news
**September, 1835**

The tuba (or "basstuba") is patented in Prussia by Wilhelm Friedrich Wieprecht and Carl Moritz, thus allowing thousands of future high school marching bands to do serious damage to hundreds of pop songs by attempting to play them in march tempo.

**...as he would a mackerel smack.** That is, as easily and casually as if *Pilgrim* were just a small, easily handled fishing boat.

**When Captain T— was in command of the Pilgrim, there was as much preparation and ceremony as there would be in getting a seventy-four under weigh. Captain Faucon was a sailor, every inch of him...** A seventy-four is a double-decked 74-gun warship—in other words, a large, complex vessel with a crew of several hundred men. Dana is saying that under Thompson, Pilgrim required as much preparation as the larger vessel would have required, but this was not the case under the much more experienced, better organized, and more respected Captain Faucon.

**The more, the merrier...** Not just a sailor's maxim, this saying goes all the way back to the 14th century. Even back then it was considered a proverb of long standing.

**...gloomy weeks we had spent in this dull place, in the brig...** Here Dana means the brig *Pilgrim*, not a military place of detention on board a ship. Although to Dana, working and living aboard *Pilgrim* may have felt the same as being in prison.

fisherman's jig, barefooted, knocking with his heels, and slapping the decks with his bare feet, in time with the music. This was a favorite amusement of the mate's, who always stood at the steerage door, looking on, and if the boys would not dance, he hazed them round with a rope's end, much to the amusement of the men.

The next morning, according to the orders of the agent, the Pilgrim set sail for the windward, to be gone three or four months. She got under weigh with very little fuss, and came so near us as to throw a letter on board, Captain Faucon standing at the tiller himself, and steering her as he would a mackerel smack. When Captain T—— was in command of the Pilgrim, there was as much preparation and ceremony as there would be in getting a seventy-four under weigh. Captain Faucon was a sailor, every inch of him; he knew what a ship was, and was as much at home in one, as a cobbler in his stall. I wanted no better proof of this than the opinion of the ship's crew, for they had been six months under his command, and knew what he was; and if sailors allow their captain to be a good seaman, you may be sure he is one, for that is a thing they are not always ready to say.

After the Pilgrim left us, we lay three weeks at San Pedro, from the 11th of September until the 2nd of October, engaged in the usual port duties of landing cargo, taking off hides, etc., etc. These duties were much easier, and went on much more agreeably, than on board the Pilgrim. "The more, the merrier," is the sailor's maxim; and a boat's crew of a dozen could take off all the hides brought down in a day, without much trouble, by division of labor; and on shore, as well as on board, a good will, and no discontent or grumbling, make everything go well. The officer, too, who usually went with us, the third mate, was a fine young fellow, and made no unnecessary trouble; so that we generally had quite a sociable time, and were glad to be relieved from the restraint of the ship. While here, I often thought of the miserable, gloomy weeks we had spent in this dull place, in the brig; discontent and hard usage on board, and four hands to do all the work on shore. Give me a big ship. There is more room, more hands, better outfit, better regulation, more life, and more company. Another thing was better arranged here: we had a regular gig's crew. A light whale-boat, handsomely painted, and fitted out with stern seats, yoke, tiller-ropes, etc., hung on the starboard quarter, and was used as the gig. The youngest lad in the ship, a Boston boy about thirteen years old, was coxswain of this boat, and had the entire charge of her, to keep her clean, and have her in readiness to go and come at any hour. Four light hands, of about the same size and age, of whom I was one, formed the crew. Each had his oar and seat numbered, and we were obliged to be in our places, have our oars scraped white, our tholepins in, and the fenders over the side. The bow-man had charge of the boat-hook and painter, and the coxswain of the rudder, yoke, and stern-sheets. Our duty was to carry the captain and agent about, and passengers off and on; which last was no trifling duty, as the people on shore have no boats, and every purchaser, from the boy who buys his pair of shoes, to the trader who buys his casks and bales, were to be taken off and on, in our boat. Some days, when people were coming and going fast, we were in the boat, pulling off and on, all day long, with hardly time for our meals; making, as we lay nearly three miles from shore, from forty to fifty miles' rowing in a day. Still, we thought it the best berth in the ship; for when the gig was employed, we had nothing to do with the cargo, except small bundles which the passengers carried with them, and no hides to carry, besides the opportunity of seeing everybody, making acquaintances, hearing the news, etc. Unless the captain or agent were in the boat, we had no officer with us, and often had fine times with the passengers, who were always willing to talk and joke with us. Frequently, too, we were obliged to wait several hours on shore; when we would haul the boat up on the beach, and leaving one to watch her, go up to the nearest house, or spend the time in strolling about the beach, picking up shells, or playing hop-scotch, and other games, on the hard sand. The rest of the crew never left the ship, except for bringing heavy goods and taking off hides; and though we were always in the water, the surf hardly leaving us a dry thread

**...used as the gig.** A gig is a light, narrow boat often used to ferry the captain, other officers, and important passengers to and from shore.

## In the news
## September, 1835

In Warren, OH, construction begins on the Pennsylvania and Ohio Canal. (Often called simply the P&O.) Using only picks and shovels, workers dig their way from New Castle, PA to Akron, OH, taking five years to finish the project. Used to ferry goods and passengers, the canal falls into disuse with the arrival of the railroads, and is abandoned in the 1870s. (In what should have been a clear sign of the canal's ultimate fate, at almost exactly the same time that work on the P&O begins, ground is broken for the construction of the Mad River and Lake Erie Railroad in Sandusky, OH—only 100 miles or so from Warren. This is the second railroad to be built in Ohio, the first being the Erie and Kalamazoo Railroad.)

**...the best berth in the ship...** Rowing that far that often is hard work, but there's also a lot of time to rest. Also, the gig's crew is excused from handling the heavy hides being stowed in the ship's hold.

**...playing hopscotch, and other games...** A *scotch* is a line or incision—originally in the flesh. Going back to the 15th century, the word is now obsolete, but it hangs on in terms such as the name for the popular children's game. (The game itself goes back at least to the 17th century, when it was called "scotch-hoppers.")

from morning till night, yet we were young, and the climate was good, and we thought it much better than the quiet, hum-drum drag and pull on board ship. We made the acquaintance of nearly half of California; for, besides carrying everybody in our boat,—men, women, and children,—all the messages, letters, and light packages went by us, and being known by our dress, we found a ready reception everywhere.

In the news
**September, 1835**

After the death (from tuberculosis) of his first wife, Ellen Louisa Tucker, Ralph Waldo Emerson marries Lydia Jackson, with whom he would have four children. The couple settles in Concord, MA, remaining there for the rest of their lives.

At San Pedro, we had none of this amusement, for, there being but one house in the place, we, of course, had but little company. All the variety that I had, was riding, once a week, to the nearest rancho, to order a bullock down for the ship.

**...a bullock down for the ship.** That is, for food. To sailors used to eating salted beef or pork and ship's biscuit, this ready supply of fresh meat must have seemed wonderful.

The brig Catalina came in from San Diego, and being bound up to windward, we both got under weigh at the same time, for a trial of speed up to Santa Barbara, a distance of about eighty miles. We hove up and got under sail about eleven o'clock at night, with a light land-breeze, which died away toward morning, leaving us becalmed only a few miles from our anchoring-place. The Catalina, being a small vessel, of less than half our size, put out sweeps and got a boat ahead, and pulled out to sea, during the night, so that she had the sea-breeze earlier and stronger than we did, and we had the mortification of seeing her standing up the coast, with a fine breeze, the sea all ruffled about her, while we were becalmed, in-shore. When the sea-breeze died away, she was nearly out of sight; and, toward the latter part of the afternoon, the regular north-west wind set in fresh, we braced sharp upon it, took a pull at every sheet, tack, and halyard, and stood after her, in fine style, our ship being very good upon a tautened bowline. We had nearly five hours of fine sailing, beating up to windward, by long stretches in and off shore, and evidently gaining upon the Catalina at every tack. When this breeze left us, we were so near as to count the painted ports on her side. Fortunately, the wind died away when we were on our inward tack, and she on her outward, so we were in-shore, and caught the land-breeze first, which came off upon our quarter, about the middle of the first watch. All hands were turned-up, and we set all sail, to the sky-

**...trial of speed...** A race. A race of 80 miles between two large sailing ships is quite a contest.

**...put out sweeps and got a boat ahead...** Sweeps were long, heavy oars carried aboard ship for use when the wind failed. Although *Alert* is too large to benefit from using sweeps, *Catalina* is small enough to use them to her advantage.

**...the regular north-west wind set in fresh...** In light winds, a smaller vessel generally has the advantage over a larger one. But when the wind freshens, the larger vessel can carry more sail and use that wind to its advantage. *Alert* has taken advantage of this fact for several hours and has caught up to *Catalina*.

sails and the royal studding-sails; and with these, we glided quietly through the water, leaving the Catalina, which could not spread so much canvas as we, gradually astern, and, by daylight, were off St. Buenaventura, and our antagonist nearly out of sight. The sea-breeze, however, favored her again, while we were becalmed under the headland, and laboring slowly along, she was abreast of us by noon. Thus we continued, ahead, astern, and abreast of one another, alternately; now, far out at sea, and again, close in under the shore. On the third morning, we came into the great bay of Santa Barbara, two hours behind the brig, and thus lost the bet; though, if the race had been to the point, we should have beaten her by five or six hours. This, however, settled the relative sailing of the vessels, for it was admitted that although she, being small and light, could gain upon us in very light winds, yet whenever there was breeze enough to set us agoing, we walked away from her like hauling in a line; and in beating to windward, which is the best trial of a vessel, we had much the advantage of her.

Sunday, Oct. 4th. This was the day of our arrival; and somehow or other, our captain always managed not only to sail, but to come into port, on a Sunday. The main reason for sailing on the Sabbath is not, as many people suppose, because Sunday is thought a lucky day, but because it is a leisure day. During the six days, the crew are employed upon the cargo and other ship's works, and the Sabbath, being their only day of rest, whatever additional work can be thrown into Sunday, is so much gain to the owners. This is the reason of our coasters, packets, etc, sailing on the Sabbath. They get six good days' work out of the crew, and then throw all the labor of sailing into the Sabbath. Thus it was with us, nearly all the time we were on the coast, and many of our Sabbaths were lost entirely to us. The Catholics on shore have no trading and make no journeys on Sunday, but the American has no national religion, and likes to show his independence of priestcraft by doing as he chooses on the Lord's day.

Santa Barbara looked very much as it did when I left it

**... off St. Buenaventura...** Now simply called Ventura, the mission here was founded in 1782. Named after a 13th-century saint, Ventura is now the dividing line between Los Angeles and Ventura counties.

**... if the race had been to the point...** That is, to Point Conception, to which *Alert* apparently beat *Catalina* by several hours. Point Conception is a high point or spit of land extending into the sea just southwest of Santa Barbara.

In the news

**September, 1835**

In Great Britain, bear baiting is outlawed. This "blood sport" pitted captured bears against specially trained dogs. The object was for the dogs to kill a bear that had been chained to a stake in a pit.

**They get six good days' work out of the crew, and then throw all the labor of sailing into the Sabbath.** Dana is complaining that once again the crew is denied its Sabbath, with no rest and no worship. (Remember that although he is now on the *Alert*, its current senior officer is Captain Thompson, and we know he rarely allows his crew any leisure time. Captain Faucon, meanwhile, is sailing *Pilgrim* up the coast to pick up more hides.)

**Day after day, the sun shone clear and bright...** October in San Diego is usually quite pleasant. It rains only rarely, and the temperatures are moderate. The average daily maximum temperature there in October is 74°F, while the daily minimum is usually in the 60s.

**...monkey-jackets...** Also called a mess jacket, at the time this was a thick jacket made of wool. These days the term refers to the everyday jacket worn by ships' officers.

## In the news
## October, 1835

Samuel Colt receives the British patent for his new revolver on October 22, 1835, the French one on November 16, and the American one on February 26, 1836, achieving a monopoly on revolver production until 1857. The patent laws being what they were at the time, Colt applied for the European patents first because if he had patented the gun first in the U.S., he would not have been allowed to file for European patents, meaning that European manufacturers could have begun developing weapons based on his designs.

**...Harris and myself had the deck to ourselves...** Harris is a seaman; the ship's papers list his hometown as Charleston, S.C., but Dana refers to him as an Englishman, so the papers are probably incorrect (as they often were, at the time). Dana is almost as impressed by Harris's accomplishments as he is by Bill Jackson's manly beauty, described earlier.

five months before: the long sand beach, with the heavy rollers, breaking upon it in a continual roar, and the little town, imbedded on the plain, girt by its amphitheatre of mountains. Day after day, the sun shone clear and bright upon the wide bay and the red roofs of the houses; everything being as still as death, the people really hardly seeming to earn their sun-light. Daylight actually seemed thrown away upon them. We had a few visitors, and collected about a hundred hides, and every night, at sundown, the gig was sent ashore, to wait for the captain, who spent his evenings in the town. We always took our monkey-jackets with us, and flint and steel, and made a fire on the beach with the driftwood and the bushes we pulled from the neighboring thickets, and lay down by it, on the sand. Sometimes we would stray up to the town, if the captain was likely to stay late, and pass the time at some of the houses, in which we were almost always well received by the inhabitants. Sometimes earlier and sometimes later, the captain came down; when, after a good drenching in the surf, we went aboard, changed our clothes, and turned in for the night—yet not for all the night, for there was the anchor watch to stand.

This leads me to speak of my watchmate for nine months—and, taking him all in all, the most remarkable man I have ever seen—Tom Harris. An hour, every night, while lying in port, Harris and myself had the deck to ourselves, and walking fore and aft, night after night, for months, I learned his whole character and history, and more about foreign nations, the habits of different people, and especially the secrets of sailors' lives and hardships, and also of practical seamanship, (in which he was abundantly capable of instructing me,) than I could ever have learned elsewhere. But the most remarkable thing about him, was the power of his mind. His memory was perfect; seeming to form a regular chain, reaching from his earliest childhood up to the time I knew him, without one link wanting. His power of calculation, too, was remarkable. I called myself pretty quick at figures, and had been through a course of mathematical studies; but, working by my head, I was unable to keep within sight of this man, who had never been beyond his arithmetic: so rapid was his calculation. He carried in his head not only a log-book of the whole voyage, in which everything was complete and accurate, and from which no one ever thought of appealing, but also an accurate registry of all the cargo; knowing, precisely, where each thing was, and how many hides we took in at every port.

One night, he made a rough calculation of the number of hides that could be stowed in the lower hold, between the fore and main masts, taking the depth of hold and breadth of beam, (for he always knew the dimension of every part of the ship, before he had been a month on board,) and the average area and thickness of a hide; he came surprisingly near the number, as it afterwards turned out. The mate frequently came to him to know the capacity of different parts of the vessel, so he could tell the sailmaker very nearly the amount of canvas he would want for each sail in the ship; for he knew the hoist of every mast, and spread of every sail, on the head and foot, in feet and inches. When we were at sea, he kept a running account, in his head, of the ship's way—the number of knots and the courses; and if the courses did not vary much during the twenty-four hours, by taking the whole progress, and allowing so many eighths southing or northing, to so many easting or westing; he would make up his reckoning just before the captain took the sun at noon, and often came wonderfully near the mark. Calculation of all kinds was his delight. He had, in his chest, several volumes giving accounts of inventions in mechanics, which he read with great pleasure, and made himself master of. I doubt if he ever forgot anything that he read. The only thing in the way of poetry that he ever read was Falconer's Shipwreck, which he was delighted with, and whole pages of which he could repeat. He knew the name of every sailor that had ever been his shipmate, and also, of every vessel, captain, and officer, and the principal dates of each voyage; and a sailor whom he afterwards fell in with, who had been in a ship with Harris nearly twelve years before, was very much surprised at having Harris tell him things about himself which he had entirely forgotten. His facts, whether dates

In the news
**October, 1835**

The battle of Gonzales: Colonel Domingo de Ugartechea, the commander of the Mexican garrison at San Antonio, sends soldiers to the town of Gonzales to recover a cannon that had previously been loaned to the town for protection. The townspeople refuse to return the gun, believing that Ugartechea's real intent is to ensure that any rebels in the town have been disarmed. After the Texans' refusal, Ugartechea sends troops to collect it. The Texans band together and, flying a flag designed by two women in the town, they attack the Mexican troops at dawn on October 2nd. The Mexicans retreat. This is the origin of the famous Texas flag bearing the star of Texas, a rudimentary drawing of a cannon, and the defiant legend, "Come and take it."

**... southing or northing...** Sailors have long used (and continue to use) dead reckoning (a term that derives from "deduced," rather than having anything to do with mortality) to estimate their position. Given a known starting point, the experienced seaman can keep track of a vessel's direction and speed and use those to determine, sometimes quite accurately, the vessel's position even days later. It's as much an art as a science, though, and many variables (drift, tides, leeway, etc.) must be taken into account. A southing or northing is a calculation of a distance south or north of a line or point of origin. Harris, though just a simple sailor, is quite accomplished at many facets of seamanship, including dead reckoning, a feat he seems to be able to accomplish without the aid of notes or a chart.

or events, no one thought of disputing; and his opinions, few of the sailors dared to oppose; for, right or wrong, he always had the best of the argument with them. His reasoning powers were remarkable. I have had harder work maintaining an argument with him in a watch, even when I knew myself to be right, and he was only doubting, than I ever had before; not from his obstinacy, but from his acuteness. Give him only a little knowledge of his subject, and, certainly among all the young men of my acquaintance and standing at college, there was not one whom I had not rather meet, than this man. I never answered a question from him, or advanced an opinion to him, without thinking more than once. With an iron memory, he seemed to have your whole past conversation at command, and if you said a thing now which ill agreed with something said months before, he was sure to have you on the hip. In fact, I always felt, when with him, that I was with no common man. I had a positive respect for his powers of mind, and felt often that if half the pains had been spent upon his education which are thrown away, yearly, in our colleges, he would have been a man of great weight in society. Like most self-taught men, he over-estimated the value of an education; and this, I often told him, though I profited by it myself; for he always treated me with respect, and often unnecessarily gave way to me, from an over-estimate of my knowledge. For the intellectual capacities of all the rest of the crew, captain and all, he had the most sovereign contempt. He was a far better sailor, and probably a better navigator, than the captain, and had more brains than all the after part of the ship put together. The sailors said, "Tom's got a head as long as the bowsprit," and if any one got into an argument with him, they would call out—"Ah, Jack! you'd better drop that, as you would a hot potato, for Tom will turn you inside out before you know it."

I recollect his posing me once on the subject of the Corn Laws. I was called to stand my watch, and, coming on deck, found him there before me; and we began, as usual, to walk fore and aft, in the waist. He talked about the Corn Laws; asked me my opinion about them, which I gave him; and my reasons; my small stock of

In the news
**October, 1835**

Benjamin Lundy, a Quaker abolitionist who sought to establish colonies of freed blacks around the world (including in Mexican Texas), publishes a pamphlet charging that the war in Texas is merely a disguised attempt to get Texas annexed to the U.S. as a slave state, thus geographically extending slavery.

In the news
**October, 1835**

In late October, the Utica Anti-Slavery Society holds its abolitionist convention at a Presbyterian church. The group had previously been denied permission to hold the gathering at Chancellor Square Academy Hall of Justice on the grounds that a public hall "should not be desecrated by such a radical meeting."

**...as long as the bowsprit...** A bowsprit is a long spar projecting from the bow of a ship. Used mainly as a place to mount tackle to receive rigging for a forward sail such as a jib (a triangular sail mounted forward of the foremast). Bowsprits are rarely seen on modern vessels.

**...the subject of the Corn Laws.** Repealed in 1846, the Corn Laws governed the import and export of grains in Great Britain. They functioned as trade barriers (in this case, taxes on imported corn and other grains), in an attempt to protect British producers of cereals. Harris turns out to be knowledgeable about this complex issue, surprising Dana.

which I set forth to the best advantage, supposing his knowledge on the subject must be less than mine, if, indeed, he had any at all. When I had got through, he took the liberty of differing from me, and, to my surprise, brought arguments and facts connected with the subject which were new to me, to which I was entirely unable to reply. I confessed that I knew almost nothing of the subject, and expressed my surprise at the extent of his information. He said that, a number of years before, while at a boarding-house in Liverpool, he had fallen in with a pamphlet on the subject, and, as it contained calculations, had read it very carefully, and had ever since wished to find some one who could add to his stock of knowledge on the question. Although it was many years since he had seen the book, and it was a subject with which he had no previous acquaintance, yet he had the chain of reasoning, founded upon principles of political economy, perfect in his memory; and his facts, so far as I could judge, were correct; at least, he stated them with great precision. The principles of the steam engine, too, he was very familiar with, having been several months on board of a steamboat, and made himself master of its secrets. He knew every lunar star in both hemispheres, and was a perfect master of his quadrant and sextant. Such was the man, who, at forty, was still a dog before the mast, at twelve dollars a month. The reason of this was to be found in his whole past life, as I had it, at different times, from himself.

He was an Englishman, by birth, a native of Ilfracomb, in Devonshire. His father was skipper of a small coaster, from Bristol, and dying, left him, when quite young, to the care of his mother, by whose exertions he received a common-school education, passing his winters at school and his summers in the coasting trade, until his seventeenth year, when he left home to go upon foreign voyages. Of his mother, he often spoke with the greatest respect, and said that she was a strong-minded woman, and had the best system of education he had ever known; a system which had made respectable men of his three brothers, and failed only in him, from his own indomitable obstinacy. One thing he often mentioned, in which he said his mother differed

In the news
**October, 1835**

A Boston crowd mobs journalist and prominent abolitionist William Lloyd Garrison and almost lynches him. He is eventually placed in jail for his own safety.

In the news
**October, 1835**

The United Tribes of New Zealand declare the country independent, but ask the U.K. for protection from the French. In response, Britain sends Royal Navy captain William Hobson to negotiate a treaty with the Maori. Hobson eventually (1840) declares British sovereignty over New Zealand.

**The principles of the steam engine...** The steam engine has been around, in one form or another, for thousands of years, although the first practical piston steam engine was not invented until 1690; steam turbines (still used in many applications, including some modern power plants) came some years later. By the late 1700s, steam engines were being employed to power machines in factories. Most sailors would be interested in advances in the area, because the technology was often applied (or at least an attempt was made to apply it) to powering ships. Eventually, steam power would put an end to the age of sail.

**...a perfect master of his quadrant and sextant.** Sophisticated tools for navigation, sextants and quadrants require careful measurements and precise mathematics in order to determine a vessel's position.

from all other mothers that he had ever seen disciplining their children; that was, that when he was out of humor and refused to eat, instead of putting his plate away, as most mothers would, and saying that his hunger would bring him to it, in time, she would stand over him and oblige him to eat it—every mouthful of it. It was no fault of hers that he was what I saw him; and so great was his sense of gratitude for her efforts, though unsuccessful, that he determined, at the close of the voyage, to embark for home with all the wages he should get, to spend with and for his mother, if perchance he should find her alive.

After leaving home, he had spent nearly twenty years, sailing upon all sorts of voyages, generally out of the ports of New York and Boston. Twenty years of vice! Every sin that a sailor knows, he had gone to the bottom of. Several times he had been hauled up in the hospitals, and as often, the great strength of his constitution had brought him out again in health. Several times, too, from his known capacity, he had been promoted to the office of chief mate, and as often, his conduct when in port, especially his drunkenness, which neither fear nor ambition could induce him to abandon, put him back into the forecastle. One night, when giving me an account of his life, and lamenting the years of manhood he had thrown away, he said that there, in the forecastle, at the foot of the steps—a chest of old clothes—was the result of twenty-two years of hard labor and exposure—worked like a horse, and treated like a dog. As he grew older, he began to feel the necessity of some provision for his later years, and came gradually to the conviction that rum had been his worst enemy. One night, in Havana, a young shipmate of his was brought aboard drunk, with a dangerous gash in his head, and his money and new clothes stripped from him. Harris had seen and been in hundreds of such scenes as these, but in his then state of mind, it fixed his determination, and he resolved never to taste another drop of strong drink, of any kind. He signed no pledge, and made no vow, but relied on his own strength of purpose. The first thing with him was a reason, and then a resolution, and the thing was done. The date of his resolution he knew,

**...he determined, at the close of the voyage, to embark for home with all the wages he should get...** As noted in a previous comment, Dana meets up with Harris after the voyage. At that time, he finds that Harris is in fact about to leave for England, carrying a tidy sum of money for his mother. They have a discussion that centers on the best form of currency to carry: gold, bills, etc. Dana advises Harris to visit with a banker, which he does. (We never find out the result of the conference, nor do we know if Harris made it back to his home in England—or whether his mother was still living when he did return.)

**Every sin that a sailor knows...** That's a fair number of sins.

### In the news
### October, 1835

On October 8th, H.M.S. *Beagle* anchors at James Island, in the Galapagos archipelago. Naturalist Charles Darwin wishes to explore the island, so he and ship's surgeon Benjamin Bynoe and their servants stay on James Island while the *Beagle* proceeds to Chatham for fresh water. The ship returns to pick up the explorers on the 13th of October, having been delayed by currents. About a week later, the ship, formerly a British man-of-war. but now on loan to various civilian expeditions, heads for Tahiti.

**...the conviction that rum had been his worst enemy.** Sadly, many a sailor (and accountant, police officer, attorney, etc.) has discovered the same thing. Harris seems to serve in the book as an object lesson, though: A brilliant man, laid low by drink and dissipation, he nonetheless recovers enough of his strength, skill, and diginity to function as a sailor and to save his money for a worthy cause—in this case, his (as far as Harris is concerned, saintly) mother.

of course, to the very hour. It was three years before I knew him, and during all that time, nothing stronger than cider or coffee had passed his lips. The sailors never thought of enticing Tom to take a glass, any more than they would of talking to the ship's compass. He was now a temperate man for life, and capable of filling any berth in a ship, and many a high station there is on shore which is held by a meaner man.

He understood the management of a ship upon scientific principles, and could give the reason for hauling every rope; and a long experience, added to careful observation at the time, and a perfect memory, gave him a knowledge of the expedients and resorts in times of hazard, which was remarkable, and for which I became much indebted to him, as he took the greatest pleasure in opening his stores of information to me, in return for what I was able to do for him. Stories of tyranny and hardship which had driven men to piracy;—of the incredible ignorance of masters and mates, and of horrid brutality to the sick, dead, and dying; as well as of the secret knavery and impositions practised upon seamen by connivance of the owners, landlords, and officers; all these he had, and I could not but believe them; for men who had known him for fifteen years had never taken him even in an exaggeration, and, as I have said, his statements were never disputed. I remember, among other things, his speaking of a captain whom I had known by report, who never handed a thing to a sailor, but put it on deck and kicked it to him; and of another, who was of the best connections in Boston, who absolutely murdered a lad from Boston that went out with him before the mast to Sumatra, by keeping him hard at work while ill of the coast fever, and obliging him to sleep in the close steerage. (The same captain has since died of the same fever on the same coast.)

In fact, taking together all that I learned from him of seamanship, of the history of sailors' lives, of practical wisdom, and of human nature under new circumstances,—a great history from which many are shut out,—I would not part with the hours I spent in the watch with that man for any given hours of my life passed in study and social intercourse.

**...a temperate man for life...** A non-drinker.

**...a meaner man.** That is, a lesser man.

**...the reason for hauling every rope...** Even a small sailboat can be somewhat complicated: The rigging, with dozens of ropes and stays and blocks, remains a mystery to most of us. On a ship of this size, there are literally hundreds of lines, ropes, blocks, cables, and the like. The fact that Harris knows them all—and why and how they should be used—is, as Dana notes, impressive.

**...the secret knavery and impositions practised upon seamen by connivance of the owners...** This becomes Dana's main reason for writing this book (and also *The Seaman's Friend*, which he publishes a few years later) and for becoming an attorney: He wishes to deliver these men from the horrors they routinely suffer at the hands of owners and officers, many (but certainly not all) of whom are bitter, malicious, spiteful men who make the lives of sailors miserable and who enjoy (and often revel in the exercise of) complete power over the men in their command.

**In the news**
**October, 1835**

The Texas Rangers, unofficially created by Stephen F. Austin in 1823, are formally constituted this month. Today, the Rangers are a law enforcement agency with statewide jurisdiction in Texas. Over the years, they have investigated crimes ranging from murder to political corruption, acted as riot police and as detectives, protected the governor of Texas, tracked down fugitives, and functioned as a paramilitary force at the service of both the Republic (1836–45) and the state of Texas.

# CHAPTER XXIV

## SAN DIEGO AGAIN—A DESCENT—HURRIED DEPARTURE—A NEW SHIPMATE

Sunday, Oct. 11th. Set sail this morning for the leeward; passed within sight of San Pedro, and, to our great joy, did not come to anchor, but kept directly on to San Diego, where we arrived and moored ship on.

Thursday, Oct. 15th. Found here the Italian ship La Rosa, from the windward, which reported the brig Pilgrim at San Francisco, all well. Everything was as quiet here as usual. We discharged our hides, horns, and tallow, and were ready to sail again on the following Sunday. I went ashore to my old quarters, and found the gang at the hide-house going on in the even tenor of their way, and spent an hour or two, after dark, at the oven, taking a whiff with my old Kanaka friends, who really seemed glad to see me again, and saluted me as the Aikane of the Kanakas. I was grieved to find that my poor dog Bravo was dead. He had sickened and died suddenly, the very day after I sailed in the Alert.

**...taking a whiff with my old Kanaka friends...** This could mean one of two things: Dana may have joined in the pipe-smoking enjoyed by his Kanaka friends. (An 1845 issue of Graham's Magazine includes an article in which the author describes a visitor to the Blackfeet tribe as "taking a whiff" when they share a pipe with him.) Or, and this is using "whiff" in a sense that was quite common in the 19th century, he may have joined them for some fishing: "Whiffing" was a term used to describe fishing with hand-lines. Given the hour and the context, though, the pipe-smoking scenario is the most likely one.

**...the Aikane of the Kanakas.** The good friend of the kanakas.

Sunday was again, as usual, our sailing day, and we got under weigh with a stiff breeze, which reminded us that it was the latter part of the autumn, and time to expect south-easters once more. We beat up against a strong head wind, under reefed top-sails, as far as San Juan, where we came to anchor nearly three miles from the shore, with slip-ropes on our cables, in the old south-easter style of last winter. On the passage up, we had an old sea captain on board, who had married and settled in California, and had not been on salt water for more than fifteen years. He was astonished at the changes and improvements that had been made in ships, and still more at the manner in which we carried sail; for he was really a little frightened; and said that while we had top-gallant sails on, he should have been under reefed top-sails. The working of the ship, and her progress to windward, seemed to delight him, for he said she went to windward as though she were kedging.

**Sunday was again, as usual, our sailing day...** While Captain Faucon might have given the men Sunday off, Captain Thompson is now in charge of *Alert*.

**...with slip-ropes on our cables...** The weather seems to be decidedly unpleasant. *Alert* has had a hard beat up to San Juan (that is, sailing more or less against the wind) with topsails reefed (shortened, so as not to expose much sail to the wind), followed by a careful anchorage using slip-ropes in case the weather worsened and the vessel needed to make a quick escape out to sea.

**...she went to windward as though she were kedging.** Kedging is pulling a vessel ahead by taking a small anchor and line forward of the vessel and then pulling the vessel up to the anchor. The operation is then repeated as necessary. The old captain is saying that *Alert* sails well (and smoothly) to windward.

Tuesday, Oct. 20th. Having got everything ready, we set the agent ashore, who went up to the mission to hasten down the hides for the next morning. This night we had the strictest orders to look out for south-easters; and the long, low clouds seemed rather threatening. But the night passed over without any trouble, and early the next morning, we hove out the long-boat and pinnace, lowered away the quarter-boats, and went ashore to bring off our hides. Here we were again, in this romantic spot; a perpendicular hill, twice the height of the ship's mast-head, with a single circuitous path to the top, and long sand beach at its base, with the swell of the whole Pacific breaking high upon it, and our hides ranged in piles on the overhanging summit. The captain sent me, who was the only one of the crew that had ever been there before, to the top, to count the hides and pitch them down. There I stood again, as six months before, throwing off the hides, and watching them, pitching and scaling, to the bottom, while the men, dwarfed by the distance, were walking to and fro on the beach, carrying the hides, as they picked them up, to the distant boats, upon the tops of their heads. Two or three boat-loads were sent off, until, at last, all were thrown down, and the boats nearly loaded again; when we were delayed by a dozen or twenty hides which had lodged in the recesses of the hill, and which we could not reach by any missiles, as the general line of the side was exactly perpendicular, and these places were caved in, and could not be seen or reached from the top. As hides are worth in Boston twelve and a half cents a pound, and the captain's commission was two per cent, he determined not to give them up; and sent on board for a pair of top-gallant studding-sail halyards, and requested some one of the crew to go to the top, and come down by the halyards. The older sailors said the boys, who were light and active, ought to go, while the boys thought that strength and experience were necessary. Seeing the dilemma, and feeling myself to be near the medium of these requisites, I offered my services, and went up, with one man to tend the rope, and prepared for the descent.

We found a stake fastened strongly into the ground, and

**...we hove out the long-boat and pinnace...** A pinnace is a ship's boat used mainly to carry equipment and communications back and forth between the ship and the shore.

In the news
**October, 1835**

In early October, a group of Texans attacks the presidio in Goliad. The Mexican garrison there quickly surrenders. A few months later, the first declaration of independence of the Republic of Texas is signed there. The following March, Santa Anna defeats the Texan troops at nearby Coleto, and orders the execution of all survivors. On March 27, 1836, in what would come to be called the Goliad Massacre (and in spite of pleas for clemency by the Mexican officer in charge at Goliad), those orders are carried out and about 340 men are killed. Along with "Remember the Alamo," "Remember Goliad" will become a rallying cry for the Texans in their fight for independence.

**...hides are worth in Boston twelve and a half cents a pound...** If a dry hide weighs, on average, 25 pounds, then each would sell for $5.20 or about $130 today. The captain's commission would net him about $2.60 or so per hide in today's currency. (Given that many thousands of hides are being shipped back to Boston, this is not an insubstantial sum of money; many captains became quite wealthy and either retired or went on to become ship owners themselves.) Note that hides today tend to weigh significantly more than 25 pounds, but that's because most cattle are larger these days, being much better-fed and better cared-for than those that ranged the sparse Mexican scrub of what is now Southern California.

apparently capable of holding my weight, to which we made one end of the halyards well fast, and taking the coil, threw it over the brink. The end, we saw, just reached to a landing-place, from which the descent to the beach was easy. Having nothing on but shirt, trowsers, and hat, the common sea-rig of warm weather, I had no stripping to do, and began my descent, by taking hold of the rope in each hand, and slipping down, sometimes with hands and feet round the rope, and sometimes breasting off with one hand and foot against the precipice, and holding on to the rope with the other. In this way I descended until I came to a place which shelved in, and in which the hides were lodged. Keeping hold of the rope with one hand, I scrambled in, and by the other hand and feet succeeded in dislodging all the hides, and continued on my way. Just below this place, the precipice projected again, and going over the projection, I could see nothing below me but the sea and the rocks upon which it broke, and a few gulls flying in mid-air. I got down in safety, pretty well covered with dirt; and for my pains was told, "What a d—d fool you were to risk your life for a half a dozen hides!"

**In this way I descended...** Dana has taken on a difficult and dangerous task. Suspended many feet in the air, he climbs partway down the rope, grabs a hide with one hand, and tosses it the rest of the way down the cliff.

**In the news**
**October, 1835**

James Maguire places an ad in the National Intelligencer, offering $50 to anyone who can give him the name of the person who broke into "the enclosure of the lock-up house" and "aided in the escape of" Jane Stewart, "aged 17 years and *a slave for life*." [Italics in the original.] Young female slaves were expecially valuable since, among other things, they were capable of giving birth to more slaves. The $50 reward would be roughly equivalent to well over $1,500 today.

While we were carrying the hides to the boat, I perceived, what I had been too busy to observe before, that heavy black clouds were rolling up from seaward, a strong swell heaving in, and every sign of a south-easter. The captain hurried everything. The hides were pitched into the boats; and, with some difficulty, and by wading nearly up to our armpits, we got the boats through the surf, and began pulling aboard. Our gig's crew towed the pinnace astern of the gig, and the launch was towed by six men in the jolly-boat. The ship was lying three miles off, pitching at her anchor, and the farther we pulled, the heavier grew the swell. Our boat stood nearly up and down several times; the pinnace parted her towline, and we expected every moment to see the launch swamped. We at length got alongside, our boats half full of water; and now came the greatest difficulty of all,—unloading the boats, in a heavy sea, which pitched them about so that it was almost impossible to stand in them; raising them sometimes even with the rail, and again dropping them below the bends. With

**Our boat stood nearly up and down...** That is, the boat rose almost vertically as it encountered large swells. If the seas became rough enough, the boat could "pitchpole," or turn completely stem-over-bow.

**...now came the greatest difficulty of all...** Another dangerous job for Dana and the crew: The boats are now full of water (meaning that the hides are now soaked and much heavier than before) and the boats are being tossed about by the rough seas.

great difficulty, we got all the hides aboard and stowed under hatches, the yard and stay tackles hooked on, and the launch and pinnace hoisted, checked, and griped. The quarter-boats were then hoisted up, and we began heaving in on the chain. Getting the anchor was no easy work in such a sea, but as we were not coming back to this port, the captain determined not to slip. The ship's head pitched into the sea, and the water rushed through the hawse-holes, and the chain surged so as almost to unship the barrel of the windlass. "Hove short, sir!" said the mate. "Aye, aye! Weather-bit your chain and loose the topsails! Make sail on her, men—with a will!" A few moments served to loose the topsails, which were furled with reefs, to sheet them home, and hoist them up. "Bear a hand!" was the order of the day; and every one saw the necessity of it, for the gale was already upon us. The ship broke out her own anchor, which we catted and fished, after a fashion, and stood off from the lee-shore against a heavy head sea, under reefed topsails, fore-topmast staysail and spanker. The fore course was given to her, which helped her a little; but as she hardly held her own against the sea which was settling her leeward—"Board the main tack!" shouted the captain; when the tack was carried forward and taken to the windlass, and all hands called to the handspikes. The great sail bellied out horizontally as though it would lift up the main stay; the blocks rattled and flew about; but the force of machinery was too much for her. "Heave ho! Heave and pawl! Yo, heave, hearty, ho!" and, in time with the song, by the force of twenty strong arms, the windlass came slowly round, pawl after pawl, and the weather clew of the sail was brought down to the waterways. The starboard watch hauled aft the sheet, and the ship tore through the water like a mad horse, quivering and shaking at every joint, and dashing from its head the foam, which flew off at every blow, yards and yards to leeward. A half hour of such sailing served our turn, when the clews of the sail were hauled up, the sail furled, and the ship, eased of her press, went more quietly on her way. Soon after, the foresail was reefed, and we mizen-top men were sent up to take another reef in the mizen topsail. This was the first time I had taken a weather earing, and I felt not a little proud to sit,

**...checked, and griped.** Gripes are ropes used to hold small boats against the davits in which they're mounted on (or hanging over) the deck.

**...the captain determined not to slip.** If the ship were returning to this spot, the crew could "slip" the anchor, leaving it where it was, knowing that they could pick it up later. Because they were not returning, Thompson opts not to leave it, given that anchors are very expensive and would be difficult to replace in California.

**"Hove short, sir!" said the mate.** If the scope (length) of the anchor line (or rode) is somewhat short, then violent swells will lift the vessel and tighten the line, which will either pull the anchor loose or cause the ship to be pulled up short at the crest of the swell; either outcome is undesirable and potentially dangerous.

**In the news**
**October, 1835**

Adlai Stevenson the elder is born in Kentucky. His family will relocate to Illinois. Leaving college, he returns to run the family sawmill after his father's death. A practicing lawyer, Stevenson will eventually become U.S. Vice President under Grover Cleveland and a Congressman representing Illinois. His son, Adlai Stevenson II, will become governor of Illinois, a U.N. ambassador, and a presidential candidate. *His* son, Adlai Stevenson III, will become a U.S. Senator, an Illinois State Representative, and a candidate for governor of Illinois. (Bucking the trend, Adlai Stevenson IV will become a journalist and businessman.)

**...served our turn...** That is, did the job, took care of the issue. The phrase goes back at least to Shakespeare. (In Richard II, King Richard says, "High be our thoughts: I know, my uncle York Hath power enough to serve our turn...")

**...I felt not a little proud to sit, astride of the weather yard-arm...** Dana is indeed proud of the sailor he's become. And he should be: In the space of a year or so, the soft-handed college student has become a hardened, knowledgeable veteran.

**...took the earings between us.** The earings are small ropes used to fasten the upper corners of a sail to a yard, or wooden spar that crosses the mast, and on which the sail is set.

**....the usual boating, hide-carrying, rolling of cargo up the steep hill...** Dana engages in a bit of humorously ironic understatement.

**...every thousand hides went toward completing the forty thousand which we were to collect before we could say good-by to California.** Dana and the crew are not happy about being bested by *La Rosa*, especially since it cost them 1000 hides—hides they would now have to stay longer in California to collect.

**He called himself George P. Marsh...** Marsh is a bit of a mystery. His story does not quite explain his education, which—as Dana points out about the man's English—was "far too good to have been learned in a smuggler." Many years later, Dana's son (also named Richard Henry Dana) received a letter from someone who knew Marsh, explaining that the man's name was actually George Walker Marsh, and that he was, "the eldest son of a retired English army officer and his wife, and was born in St. Malo, France...," thus Marsh's excellent French. Marsh eventually went to Chili on the *Ayacucho*, and there his trail vanishes.

astride of the weather yard-arm, pass the earing, and sing out "Haul out to leeward!" From this time until we got to Boston, the mate never suffered any one but our own gang to go upon the mizen topsail yard, either for reefing or furling, and the young English lad and myself generally took the earings between us.

Having cleared the point and got well out to sea, we squared away the yards, made more sail, and stood on, nearly before the wind, for San Pedro. It blew strong, with some rain, nearly all night, but fell calm toward morning, and the gale having gone over, we came-to,—

Thursday, Oct. 22d, at San Pedro, in the old south-easter berth, a league from shore, with a slip-rope on the cable, reefs in the topsails, and rope-yarns for gaskets. Here we lay ten days, with the usual boating, hide-carrying, rolling of cargo up the steep hill, walking barefooted over stones, and getting drenched in salt water.

The third day after our arrival, the Rosa came in from San Juan, where she went the day after the south-easter. Her crew said it was as smooth as a mill-pond, after the gale, and she took off nearly a thousand hides, which had been brought down for us, and which we lost in consequence of the south-easter. This mortified us; not only that an Italian ship should have got to windward of us in the trade, but because every thousand hides went toward completing the forty thousand which we were to collect before we could say good-by to California.

While lying here, we shipped one new hand, an Englishman, of about two or three and twenty, who was quite an acquisition, as he proved to be a good sailor, could sing tolerably, and, what was of more importance to me, had a good education, and a somewhat remarkable history. He called himself George P. Marsh; professed to have been at sea from a small boy, and to have served his time in the smuggling trade between Germany and the coasts of France and England. Thus he accounted for his knowledge of the French language, which he spoke and read as well as he did English; but his cutter education would not account for his English, which was far too good to have been learned in a smuggler; for he wrote an uncommonly handsome hand, spoke with great correctness, and frequently, when in private talk with me, quoted from books, and showed a knowledge of the customs of society, and particularly of the formalities of the various English courts of law, and of Parliament, which surprised me. Still, he would give no other account of himself than that he was educated in a smuggler. A man whom we afterwards fell in with, who had been a shipmate of George's a few years before, said that he heard at the boarding-house from which they shipped, that George had been at college, (probably a naval one, as he knew no Latin or Greek,) where he learned French and mathematics. He was by no means the man by nature that Harris was. Harris had made everything of his mind and character in spite of obstacles; while this man had evidently been born in a different rank, and educated early in life accordingly, but had been a vagabond, and done nothing for himself since. What had been given to him by others, was all that made him to differ from those about him; while Harris had made himself what he was. Neither had George the character, strength of mind, acuteness, or memory of Harris; yet there was about him the remains of a pretty good education, which enabled him to talk perhaps beyond his brains, and a high spirit and sense of honor, which years of a dog's life had not broken. After he had been a little while on board, we learned from him his remarkable history, for the last two years, which we afterwards heard confirmed in such a manner, as put the truth of it beyond a doubt.

He sailed from New York in the year 1833, if I mistake not, before the mast, in the brig Lascar, for Canton. She was sold in the East Indies, and he shipped at Manilla, in a small schooner, bound on a trading voyage among the Ladrone and Pelew Islands. On one of the latter islands, their schooner was wrecked on a reef, and they were attacked by the natives, and, after a desperate resistance, in which all their number except the captain, George, and a boy, were killed or drowned, they surrendered, and were carried bound, in a canoe, to a neighboring island. In about a month after this, an opportuni-

## In the news
**October, 1835**

The first newspaper in Texas with any real staying power, the *Telegraph and Texas Register*, begins publication at San Felipe de Austin. It will become the official paper of the short-lived Republic of Texas, eventually being printed in several cities, including Houston. The paper is published, with several interruptions and under various names, until February of 1877.

**...as he knew no Latin or Greek...** Naval colleges concentrated on teaching history, seamanship, and mathematics, while other colleges of the time required both Latin and Greek.

**...years of a dog's life...** That is, years spent "before the mast."

**...we afterwards heard confirmed...** Marsh tells a harrowing tale of adventure, complete with shipwreck and capture by natives. The story was indeed true, and was confirmed in most particulars by Dana's son's research some years later.

**...a trading voyage among the Ladrone and Pelew Islands.** These are two islands in the Western Pacific. The Pelew (or Palau) are part of the Carolines, located north of the Australian mainland and northwest of Papua, New Guinea, east of the Philippines. The Ladrone islands, east of the Philippine Sea, are now called the Marianas. (Guam, familiar to those who recall their WWII history, is at the southernmost tip of the chain.)

ty occurred by which one of their number might get away. I have forgotten the circumstances, but only one could go, and they yielded to the captain, upon his promising to send them aid if he escaped. He was successful in his attempt; got on board an American vessel, went back to Manilla, and thence to America, without making any effort for their rescue, or indeed, as George afterwards discovered, without even mentioning their case to any one in Manilla. The boy that was with George died, and he being alone, and there being no chance for his escape, the natives soon treated him with kindness, and even with attention. They painted him, tattooed his body, (for he would never consent to be marked in the face or hands,) gave him two or three wives; and, in fact, made quite a pet of him. In this way, he lived for thirteen months, in a fine climate, with a plenty to eat, half naked, and nothing to do. He soon, however, became tired, and went round the island, on different pretences, to look out for a sail. One day, he was out fishing in a small canoe with another man, when he saw a large sail to the windward, about a league and a half off, passing abreast of the island and standing westward. With some difficulty, he persuaded the islander to go off with him to the ship, promising to return with a good supply of rum and tobacco. These articles, which the islanders had got a taste of from American traders, were too strong a temptation for the fellow, and he consented. They paddled off in the track of the ship, and lay-to until she came down to them. George stepped on board the ship, nearly naked, painted from head to foot, and in no way distinguishable from his companion until he began to speak. Upon this, the people on board were not a little astonished; and, having learned his story, the captain had him washed and clothed, and sending away the poor astonished native with a knife or two and some tobacco and calico, took George with him on the voyage. This was the ship Cabot, of New York, Captain Low. She was bound to Manilla, from across the Pacific, and George did seaman's duty in her until her arrival in Manilla, when he left her, and shipped in a brig bound to the Sandwich Islands. From Oahu, he came, in the British brig Clementine, to Monterey, as second officer, where, hav-

In the news

**October, 1835**

The Texas War of Independence officially dates from this month. The war is an armed conflict that pits Mexico against (mainly U.S.) settlers in one portion of the Mexican state of Coahuila y Tejas. Officially, the war lasts from October 2, 1835 to April 21, 1836, after which time a Texas Republic is declared. (War at sea will actually continue for several years after the conclusion of the land war.) The war had its origins in the Siete Leyes (the "Seven Laws") of 1835, which allowed Mexican General Santa Anna to abolish the federal Constitution of 1824 (under the laws of which the Texans had originally settled in the area) and proclaimed a different (and much more rigorous and centralized) constitution in its place.

**...too strong a temptation for the fellow...** American traders seem to have made a habit of exposing indigenous populations to liquor, tobacco, and other vices, often to the great disadvantage of the natives.

**This was the ship Cabot, of New York, Captain Low.** The 339-ton *Cabot* was built in 1832 in Duxbury, MA.

**...to Monterey...** A few years later, Swiss businessman and storekeeper John (originally Johann) Sutter would be in Oregon Territory looking for a way to California. He would sign on as unpaid supercargo in *Clementine* and sail to Sitka and thence to what would eventually become San Francisco. About 10 years after arriving in San Francisco, Sutter and a partner discover gold when they set out to build a sawmill on Sutter's property. The discovery would kick off the California Gold Rush.

ing some difficulty with the captain, he left her, and coming down the coast, joined us at San Pedro. Nearly six months after this, among some papers we received by an arrival from Boston, we found a letter from Captain Low, of the Cabot, published immediately upon his arrival at New York, and giving all the particulars just as we had them from George. The letter was published for the information of the friends of George, and Captain Low added, that he left him at Manilia to go to Oahu, and he had heard nothing of him since.

George had an interesting journal of his adventures in the Pelew Islands, which he had written out at length, in a handsome hand, and in correct English.

**...left him at Manilia...** That is, at Manila, in the Phillipines. Many other editions include the correction.

**...in a handsome hand...** That is, with good penmanship. The word "hand" has been used to refer to the action (or product) of writing as far back as the 14th century, and even then one's handwriting could be regarded as a sign of authenticity or authorship. Thus, Steele & Addison, in a 1709 edition of *The Tattler* can say, "A Letter which he acknowledged to be his own Hand was read."

In the news
**October, 1835**

The Staedtler Company is established in Nuremberg, Germany. The company, which originally specialized in making what were erroneously called "lead pencils" (the "lead" is actually a form of graphite), still exists—and still makes pencils and other other writing instruments, including markers, pens, and accessories.

**Sunday, November 1st.** Note Dana's none-too-subtle dig at Captain Thompson's inclination to force his men to work on Sunday. Dana never misses a chance to point out Captain Thompson's failings, nor Captain Faucon's strengths.

**...low shear, sharp bows, and raking masts...** Rake refers to the degree to which a mast is swept forward or aft. (It can also refer to the amount of overhang present at the bow or stern.) In this context, shear (normally spelled sheer) is the upward curve of the ship's deck toward the bow and stern. A vessel with a great deal of sheer appears to curve up at bow and stern, with the lowest point in the center.

**...there was a war between the United States and France.** As is typical (and as is to be expected when accurate, timely communication is lacking), rumors are flying about a supposed war between the United States and France.

**...we were too salt to believe every yarn...** Dana and the crew are too experienced to be taken in. They're well aware that rumors usually prove to be untrue, or at least exaggerated.

# CHAPTER XXV

## RUMORS OF WAR—A SPOUTER—SLIPPING FOR A SOUTH-EASTER—A GALE

Sunday, November 1st. Sailed this day, (Sunday again,) for Santa Barbara, where we arrived on the 5th. Coming round St. Buenaventura, and nearing the anchorage, we saw two vessels in port, a large full-rigged, and a small hermaphrodite brig. The former, the crew said must be the Pilgrim; but I had been too long in the Pilgrim to be mistaken in her, and I was right in differing from them; for, upon nearer approach, her long, low shear, sharp bows, and raking masts, told quite another story. "Man-of-war brig," said some of them; "Baltimore clipper," said others; the Ayacucho, thought I; and soon the broad folds of the beautiful banner of St. George,—white field with blood-red border and cross,—were displayed from her peak. A few minutes put it beyond a doubt, and we were lying by the side of the Ayacucho, which had sailed from San Diego about nine months before, while we were lying there in the Pilgrim. She had since been to Valparaiso, Callao, and the Sandwich Islands, and had just come upon the coast. Her boat came on board, bringing Captain Wilson; and in half an hour the news was all over the ship that there was a war between the United States and France. Exaggerated accounts reached the forecastle. Battles had been fought, a large French fleet was in the Pacific, etc., etc.; and one of the boat's crew of the Ayacucho said that when they left Callao, a large French frigate and the American frigate Brandywine, which were lying there, were going outside to have a battle, and that the English frigate Blonde was to be umpire, and see fair play. Here was important news for us. Alone, on an unprotected coast, without an American man-of-war within some thousands of miles, and the prospect of a voyage home through the whole length of the Pacific and Atlantic oceans! A French prison seemed a much more probable place of destination than the good port of Boston. However, we were too salt to believe every yarn that comes into the forecastle, and waited to hear the truth of the matter from higher authority. By means of a supercargo's clerk, I got the account of the matter, which was, that the governments had had difficulty about the payment of a debt; that war had been threatened and prepared for, but not actually declared, although it was pretty generally anticipated. This was not quite so bad, yet was no small cause of anxiety. But we cared very little about the matter ourselves. "Happy go lucky" with Jack! We did not believe that a French prison would be much worse than "hide-droghing" on the coast of California; and no one who has not been on a long, dull voyage, shut up in one ship, can conceive of the effect of monotony upon one's thoughts and wishes. The prospect of a change is like a green spot in a desert, and the remotest probability of great events and exciting scenes gives a feeling of delight, and sets life in motion, so as to give a pleasure, which any one not in the same state would be entirely unable to account for. In fact, a more jovial night we had not passed in the forecastle for months. Every one seemed in unaccountably high spirits. An undefined anticipation of radical changes, of new scenes, and great doings, seemed to have possessed every one, and the common drudgery of the vessel appeared contemptible. Here was a new vein opened; a grand theme of conversation, and a topic for all sorts of discussions. National feeling was wrought up. Jokes were cracked upon the only Frenchman in the ship, and comparisons made between "old horse" and "soup meagre," etc., etc.

We remained in uncertainty as to this war for more than two months, when an arrival from the Sandwich Islands brought us the news of an amicable arrangement of the difficulties.

The other vessel which we found in port was the hermaphrodite brig Avon, from the Sandwich Islands. She was fitted up in handsome style; fired a gun and ran her ensign up and down at sunrise and sunset; had a band of four or five pieces of music on board, and appeared rather like a pleasure yacht than a trader; yet, in connection with the Loriotte, Clementine, Bolivar, Convoy, and other small vessels, belonging to sundry Americans at Oahu, she carried on a great trade—legal and illegal—in otter skins, silks, teas, specie, etc.

**...difficulty about the payment of a debt...** During the Napoleonic Wars (1803 to 1815), it had been determined that France owed the U.S. reparations due to damages to U.S. shipping. The "difficulty" mentioned here is the fact that France had failed to pay that debt, bringing the two nations close to war, until Great Britain stepped in to mediate the dispute.

In the news
**October, 1835**

Collecting plant samples along what would eventually be called The Oregon Trail, Harvard botany profesor Thomas Nuttall is about to catch a Philadelphia-bound ship that will carry him to the coast of California. Shortly after his arrival there, he will encounter Dana on the beach at San Diego. As unlikely as it sounds, the two will realize that they know one another from Harvard and will renew their acquaintance on the *Alert* as it sails back to Boston.

**...a more jovial night we had not passed in the forecastle for months.** The men are anticipating the possibility of being captured by a French warship, but they're not terribly worried about the possibility; after being cooped up on the ship for many months, most of them are actually looking forward to the change.

**..."old horse" and "soup meagre"...** Old horse is simply salt beef, but soup meagre has a more interesting story. A broth made mainly from vegetables and perhaps some fish, soup meagre (or soupe maigre, in French) was (and remains) popular as a meatless dish for those who are fasting. As you would expect, the French *maigre* translates to *meager*, *thin*, or *scant*.

In the news
**October, 1835**

Alcalde Francisco de Haro begins laying out what will eventually be the city of San Francisco, beginning with a street he calls La Calle de la Fundacion, or Foundation Street. The street runs from what is now the corner of Kearny and Pine toward what is now North Beach, and will eventually be renamed Grant Avenue.

The second day after our arrival, a full-rigged brig came round the point from the northward, sailed leisurely through the bay, and stood off again for the south-east, in the direction of the large island of Catalina. The next day the Avon got under weigh, and stood in the same direction, bound for San Pedro. This might do for marines and Californians, but we knew the ropes too well. The brig was never again seen on the coast, and the Avon arrived at San Pedro in about a week, with a full cargo of Canton and American goods.

This was one of the means of escaping the heavy duties the Mexicans lay upon all imports. A vessel comes on the coast, enters a moderate cargo at Monterey, which is the only custom-house, and commences trading. In a month or more, having sold a large part of her cargo, she stretches over to Catalina, or other of the large uninhabited islands which lie off the coast, in a trip from port to port, and supplies herself with choice goods from a vessel from Oahu, which has been lying off and on the islands, waiting for her. Two days after the sailing of the Avon, the Loriotte came in from the leeward, and without doubt had also a snatch at the brig's cargo.

**...Catalina, or other of the large uninhabited islands...** These days, of course Catalina is no longer uninhabited. Twenty-two miles long (and about 26 miles offshore, as the old song says), Santa Catalina is home to about 4,000 people, most of whom live in the island city of Avalon.

Tuesday, Nov. 10th. Going ashore, as usual, in the gig, just before sundown, to bring off the captain, we found, upon taking in the captain and pulling off again, that our ship, which lay the farthest out, had run up her ensign. This meant "Sail ho!" of course, but as we were within the point we could see nothing. "Give way, boys! Give way! Lay out on your oars, and long stroke!" said the captain; and stretching to the whole length of our arms, bending back again, so that our backs touched the thwarts, we sent her through the water like a rocket. A few minutes of such pulling opened the islands, one after another, in range of the point, and gave us a view of the Canal, where was a ship, under top-gallant sails, standing in, with a light breeze, for the anchorage. Putting the boat's head in the direction of the ship, the captain told us to lay out again; and we needed no spurring, for the prospect of boarding a new ship, perhaps from home, hearing the news and having something to tell of when we got back, was excitement

**This meant "Sail ho!" of course...** That is, it was a signal that crew remaining aboard *Pilgrim* had sighted a sail approaching the harbor.

**...our backs touched the thwarts...** Thwarts are the crosswise wooden seats on which the oarsmen sit.

**...the prospect of boarding a new ship, perhaps from home, hearing the news...** Once again, the men are eager to hear any news from home. That news wll likely be some weeks or months old, but no matter, since the crew has been away from Boston for well over a year now.

enough for us, and we gave way with a will. Captain Nye, of the Loriotte, who had been an old whaleman, was in the stern-sheets, and fell mightily into the spirit of it. "Bend your backs and break your oars!" said he. "Lay me on, Captain Bunker!" "There she flukes!" and other exclamations, peculiar to whalemen. In the meantime, it fell flat calm, and being within a couple of miles of the ship, we expected to board her in a few moments, when a sudden breeze sprung up, dead ahead for the ship, and she braced up and stood off toward the islands, sharp on the larboard tack, making good way through the water. This, of course, brought us up, and we had only to "ease larboard oars; pull round starboard!" and go aboard the Alert, with something very like a flea in the ear. There was a light land-breeze all night, and the ship did not come to anchor until the next morning. As soon as her anchor was down, we went aboard, and found her to be the whaleship, Wilmington and Liverpool Packet, of New Bedford, last from the "off-shore ground," with nineteen hundred barrels of oil. A "spouter" we knew her to be as soon as we saw her, by her cranes and boats, and by her stump top-gallant masts, and a certain slovenly look to the sails, rigging, spars and hull; and when we got on board, we found everything to correspond,—spouter fashion. She had a false deck, which was rough and oily, and cut up in every direction by the chimes of oil casks; her rigging was slack and turning white; no paint on the spars or blocks; clumsy seizings and straps without covers, and homeward-bound splices in every direction. Her crew, too, were not in much better order. Her captain was a slab-sided, shamble-legged Quaker, in a suit of brown, with a broad-brimmed hat, and sneaking about decks, like a sheep, with his head down; and the men looked more like fishermen and farmers than they did like sailors.

Though it was by no means cold weather, (we having on only our red shirts and duck trowsers,) they all had on woollen trowsers—not blue and shipshape—but of all colors—brown, drab, grey, aye, and green, with suspenders over their shoulders, and pockets to put their hands in. This, added to guernsey frocks, striped com-

**In the news**
**October, 1835**

Sally Jefferson becomes the first woman sentenced to prison in Illinois. Jefferson is described as "5 feet 4 inches high, black eyes and hair, fair complected [sic], about 24 years old. Her left hand and arm considerably seared by a burn when young. Sentenced for Arson to twelve months confinement in the penitentiary." Jefferson was pardoned and released six weeks after being admitted. It would be another five years before another woman is committed to the penitentiary in Illinois. As in most states at the time, female prisoners were incarcerated in the same prisons as were male offenders.

**...something very like a flea in the ear.** Having "a flea in one's ear" means to have received an unexpected or disappointing reply or a rebuke. The men were disappointed that the other vessel tacked away; now they must return to *Alert* without meeting the other crew and without receiving news from home. The saying goes all the way back to the early 15th century.

**...by her cranes and boats...** A whaling ship, of course, carries cranes and machinery meant to hoist whales up to deck level. The relatively large boats hanging on deck are used in the pursuit of whales.

**...shamble-legged...** That is, stumbling, shuffling, awkward.

**...the men looked more like fishermen and farmers than they did like sailors.** Dana, used to the rigorous discipline of the *Pilgrim* and the even more shipshape *Alert*, does not think much of this shabby vessel or its sloppy crew.

**This was a strange sight for a vessel coming to anchor...** Generally speaking, a vessel coming to anchor needs all hands on deck, quite literally: There are moorings to be located, anchor chain to be let out, lines to be worked, sails to be furled, a rudder to be controlled, and more. It would be very unusual to approach an anchorage with many of the crew seemingly unoccupied.

**There was only one "splicer" on board...** That is, only one true sailor, one who (literally) knows the ropes well enough to create or repair lines.

In the news
**November, 1835**

The Mexican government of Texas, having grown suspicious of the recent influx of Americans seeking land grants in the area, closes its land offices and stops issuing grants. In effect, the government had heretofore encouraged the American "colonization" of the area; this proves to be, from the government's perspective, unwise. The Mexican government has unknowingly populated the area with settlers eager to revolt against the Mexican government and either join the U.S. or establish a Texas republic. (Both of which events do in fact occur, of course.)

**...not very nice...** Not terribly concerned about.

forters about the neck, thick cowhide boots, woollen caps, and a strong, oily smell, and a decidedly green look, will complete the description. Eight or ten were on the fore-topsail yard, and as many more in the main, furling the topsails, while eight or ten were hanging about the forecastle, doing nothing. This was a strange sight for a vessel coming to anchor; so we went up to them, to see what was the matter. One of them, a stout, hearty-looking fellow, held out his leg and said he had the scurvy; another had cut his hand; and others had got nearly well, but said that there were plenty aloft to furl the sails, so they were sogering on the forecastle. There was only one "splicer" on board, a fine-looking old tar, who was in the bunt of the fore-topsail. He was probably the only sailor in the ship, before the mast. The mates, of course, and the boat-steerers, and also two or three of the crew, had been to sea before, but only whaling voyages; and the greater part of the crew were raw hands, just from the bush, as green as cabbages, and had not yet got the hay-seed out of their heads. The mizen topsail hung in the bunt-lines until everything was furled forward. Thus a crew of thirty men were half an hour in doing what would have been done in the Alert with eighteen hands to go aloft, in fifteen or twenty minutes.

We found they had been at sea six or eight months, and had no news to tell us; so we left them, and promised to get liberty to come on board in the evening, for some curiosities, etc. Accordingly, as soon as we were knocked off in the evening and had got supper, we obtained leave, took a boat, and went aboard and spent an hour or two. They gave us pieces of whalebone, and the teeth and other parts of curious sea animals, and we exchanged books with them—a practice very common among ships in foreign ports, by which you get rid of the books you have read and re-read, and a supply of new ones in their stead, and Jack is not very nice as to their comparative value.

Thursday, Nov. 12th. This day was quite cool in the early part, and there were black clouds about; but as it was often so in the morning, nothing was apprehended, and all the captains went ashore together, to spend the day. Towards noon, the clouds hung heavily over the mountains, coming half way down the hills that encircle the town of Santa Barbara, and a heavy swell rolled in from the south-east. The mate immediately ordered the gig's crew away, and at the same time, we saw boats pulling ashore from the other vessels. Here was a grand chance for a rowing match, and every one did his best. We passed the boats of the Ayacucho and Loriotte, but could gain nothing upon, and indeed, hardly hold our own with, the long, six-oared boat of the whale-ship. They reached the breakers before us; but here we had the advantage of them, for, not being used to the surf, they were obliged to wait to see us beach our boat, just as, in the same place, nearly a year before, we, in the Pilgrim, were glad to be taught by a boat's crew of Kanakas.

We had hardly got the boats beached, and their heads out, before our old friend, Bill Jackson, the handsome English sailor, who steered the Loriotte's boat, called out that the brig was adrift; and, sure enough, she was dragging her anchors, and drifting down into the bight of the bay. Without waiting for the captain, (for there was no one on board but the mate and steward,) he sprung into the boat, called the Kanakas together, and tried to put off. But the Kanakas, though capital water-dogs, were frightened by their vessel's being adrift, and by the emergency of the case, and seemed to lose their faculties. Twice, their boat filled, and came broadside upon the beach. Jackson swore at them for a parcel of savages, and promised to flog every one of them. This made the matter no better; when we came forward, told the Kanakas to take their seats in the boat, and, going two on each side, walked out with her till it was up to our shoulders, and gave them a shove, when, giving way with their oars, they got her safely into the long, regular swell. In the mean time, boats had put off from our ships and the whaler, and coming all on board the brig together, they let go the other anchor, paid out chain, braced the yards to the wind, and brought the vessel up.

In the news

**November, 1835**

Oddly enough, up to this point there has been no effective method of quickly making horseshoes. That changes when Henry Burden, of Troy, NY, patents a horseshoe manufacturing machine. Needless to say, the machine proves invaluable to the Union during the Civil War, some years later.

**...dragging her anchors, and drifting down into the bight of the bay.** A vessel can drag her anchor for any number of reasons, including unanticipated tides and currents or a gale or storm. The anchor may not have been set correctly in the first place, since anchoring is quite an art in itself, one that depends greatly on the vessel, the weather, and the composition of the ocean bottom. The *Loriotte* is in serious trouble here. If she were to drift onto the beach at the "bight" (bend) of the bay, it could be difficult to re-float her. And if she were driven onto rocks, the ship could be lost.

In a few minutes, the captains came hurrying down, on the run; and there was no time to be lost, for the gale promised to be a severe one, and the surf was breaking upon the beach, three deep, higher and higher every instant. The *Ayacucho*'s boat, pulled by four Kanakas, put off first, and as they had no rudder or steering oar, would probably never have got off, had we not waded out with them, as far as the surf would permit. The next that made the attempt was the whale-boat, for we, being the most experienced "beach-combers," needed no help, and staid till the last. Whalemen make the best boats' crews in the world for a long pull, but this landing was new to them, and notwithstanding the examples they had had, they slued round and were hove up—boat, oars, and men—altogether, high and dry upon the sand. The second time, they filled, and had to turn their boat over, and set her off again. We could be of no help to them, for they were so many as to be in one another's way, without the addition of our numbers. The third time, they got off, though not without shipping a sea which drenched them all, and half filled their boat, keeping them baling, until they reached their ship. We now got ready to go off, putting the boat's head out; English Ben and I, who were the largest, standing on each side of the bows, to keep her "head on" to the sea, two more shipping and manning the two after oars, and the captain taking the steering oar. Two or three Spaniards, who stood upon the beach looking at us, wrapped their cloaks about them, shook their heads, and muttered "Caramba!" They had no taste for such doings; in fact, the hydrophobia is a national malady, and shows itself in their persons as well as their actions.

Watching for a "smooth chance," we determined to show the other boats the way it should be done; and, as soon as ours floated, ran out with her, keeping her head on, with all our strength, and the help of the captain's oar, and the two after oarsmen giving way regularly and strongly, until our feet were off the ground, we tumbled into the bows, keeping perfectly still, from fear of hindering the others. For some time it was doubtful how it would go. The boat stood nearly up and down in the water, and the sea, rolling from under her, let her fall

In the news

**November, 1835**

Edward Everett becomes governor of Dana's home state of Massachusetts. In 1841, the esteemed orator and politician becomes the ambassador to the Court of St. James. Everett will go on to become president of Harvard University, Secretary of State, and a U.S. senator.

**Whalemen make the best boats' crews in the world for a long pull...** An interesting admission for Dana to make, given the disregard in which he holds the whalers. It makes sense, though, given that a whaleboat might have to row miles away from the ship in pursuit of a whale and then be prepared to row all the way back towing a dead whale.

**... the hydrophobia is a national malady...** Hydrophobia is a fear of water. (Often thought to be a symptom of rabies, although the real problem there is not a fear of water, but difficulty swallowing water—or anything else.) This is Dana being snide and casting more slurs on the Californians. He is saying that they don't bathe often enough. (*Caramba* itself is a Spanish oath, a euphemism for *carajo*, meaning *damn it*. When Bart Simpson says *Ay caramaba*! he's being a bit more vulgar than one might suppose.)

upon the water with a force which seemed almost to stave her bottom in. By quietly sliding two oars forward, along the thwarts, without impeding the rowers, we shipped two bow oars, and thus, by the help of four oars and the captain's strong arm, we got safely off, though we shipped several seas, which left us half full of water. We pulled alongside of the Loriotte, put her skipper on board, and found her making preparations for slipping, and then pulled aboard our own ship. Here Mr. Brown, always "on hand," had got everything ready, so that we had only to hook on the gig and hoist it up, when the order was given to loose the sails. While we were on the yards, we saw the Loriotte under weigh, and before our yards were mast-headed, the Ayacucho had spread her wings, and, with yards braced sharp up, was standing athwart our hawse. There is no prettier sight in the world than a full-rigged, clipper-built brig, sailing sharp on the wind. In a moment, our slip-rope was gone, the head-yards filled away, and we were off. Next came the whaler; and in a half an hour from the time when four vessels were lying quietly at anchor, without a rag out, or a sign of motion, the bay was deserted, and four white clouds were standing off to sea. Being sure of clearing the point, we stood off with our yards a little braced in, while the Ayacucho went off with a taut bowline, which brought her to windward of us. During all this day, and the greater part of the night, we had the usual south-easter entertainment, a gale of wind, variegated and finally topped off with a drenching rain of three or four hours. At daybreak, the clouds thinned off and rolled away, and the sun came up clear. The wind, instead of coming out from the northward, as is usual, blew steadily and freshly from the anchoring-ground. This was bad for us, for, being "flying light," with little more than ballast trim, we were in no condition for showing off on a taut bowline, and had depended upon a fair wind, with which, by the help of our light sails and studding-sails, we meant to have been the first at the anchoring-ground; but the Ayacucho was a good league to windward of us, and was standing in, in fine style. The whaler, however, was as far to leeward of us, and the Loriotte was nearly out of sight, among the islands, up the Canal. By hauling every brace and bow-

**...preparations for slipping...** That is, for slipping her anchor—letting go and leaving the anchor there to be retrieved after the storm.

**Mr. Brown, always "on hand," had got everything ready...** Richard Brown is the first mate, and a fine, experienced seaman. He has everything in hand and ready for the men's return.

<u>In the news</u>

**November, 1835**

Mark Twain is born—not in Hannibal, MO, as many suppose, but in Florida, MO, some 30 miles up the road. At the same time as Twain's birth, Halley's Comet makes its first appearance since about 1760. Twain is said to have commented that he came in with the comet and would leave with it—which is exactly what happened, Twain dying in April of 1910, just as the comet reappeared. According to Twain: "The Almighty has said, no doubt: 'Now here are these two unaccountable freaks; they came in together, they must go out together.'"

**...a full-rigged, clipper-built brig...** We know what a brig is, but the term *clipper* is quite vague. In general, it's a word that's applied to any sailing vessel built for speed. This tends to mean narrow-beamed, sharp-bowed ships that carry a good deal of sail, but that's about as specific as one can be.

**...the usual south-easter entertainment...** A bit of sarcastic understatement. There are better ways to be entertained than by being tossed about in a storm.

line, and clapping watch-tackles upon all the sheets and halyards, we managed to hold our own, and drop the leeward vessels a little in every tack. When we reached the anchoring-ground, the Ayacucho had got her anchor, furled her sails, squared her yards, and was lying as quietly as if nothing had happened for the last twenty-four hours.

We had our usual good luck in getting our anchor without letting go another, and were all snug, with our boats at the boom-ends, in half an hour. In about two hours more, the whaler came in, and made a clumsy piece of work in getting her anchor, being obliged to let go her best bower, and finally, to get out a kedge and a hawser. They were heave-ho-ing, stopping and unstopping, pawling, catting, and fishing, for three hours; and the sails hung from the yards all the afternoon, and were not furled until sundown. The Loriotte came in just after dark, and let go her anchor, making no attempt to pick up the other until the next day.

This affair led to a great dispute as to the sailing of our ship and the Ayacucho. Bets were made between the captains, and the crews took it up in their own way; but as she was bound to leeward and we to windward, and merchant captains cannot deviate, a trial never took place; and perhaps it was well for us that it did not, for the Ayacucho had been eight years in the Pacific, in every part of it—Valparaiso, Sandwich Islands, Canton, California, and all, and was called the fastest merchantman that traded in the Pacific, unless it was the brig John Gilpin, and perhaps the ship Ann McKim of Baltimore.

Saturday, Nov. 14th. This day we got under weigh, with the agent and several Spaniards of note, as passengers, bound up to Monterey. We went ashore in the gig to bring them off with their baggage, and found them waiting on the beach, and a little afraid about going off, as the surf was running very high. This was nuts to us; for we liked to have a Spaniard wet with salt water; and then the agent was very much disliked by the crew, one and all; and we hoped, as there was no officer in the

In the news
**November, 1835**

Andrew Carnegie, the future steel magnate and philanthropist, is born in Scotland. Carnegie, who began as a factory worker and a messenger boy, will revolutionize and greatly expand the steel industry. His company, Carnegie Steel, will eventually become the giant U.S. Steel. Carnegie founded the Carnegie Endowment for International Peace, the Carnegie Institution of Washington, Carnegie Mellon University, the Carnegie Museums of Pittsburgh, and many other philanthropic institutions, schools, and libraries.

**...getting our anchor without letting go another...** That is, because of their experience and skill, the crew was able to recover the slipped anchor without having to use another one to steady the vessel. The whaler's crew, in contrast, was unable to retrieve the slipped anchor, and ended up spending three hours (and using three smaller anchors) to get the ship settled. Note that the *Loriotte*, coming in at night, simply (and wisely) dropped a new anchor rather than attempting to recover the original one in the dark.

**...perhaps it was well for us that it did not...** Probably so. The *Ayacucho* was known for many years as the fastest vessel in the Pacific. The *Alert* would likely not have fared well in such a contest.

**...several Spaniards of note...** That is, important officials or wealthy Californian landowners. Dana and his colleagues do not think highly of these people, and are hoping for a chance to get them soaked.

boat, to have a chance to duck them; for we knew that they were such "marines" that they would not know whether it was our fault or not. Accordingly, we kept the boat so far from shore as to oblige them to wet their feet in getting into her; and then waited for a good high comber, and letting the head slue a little round, sent the whole force of the sea into the stern-sheets, drenching them from head to feet. The Spaniards sprang out of the boat, swore, and shook themselves and protested against trying it again; and it was with the greatest difficulty that the agent could prevail upon them to make another attempt. The next time we took care, and went off easily enough, and pulled aboard. The crew came to the side to hoist in their baggage, and we gave them the wink, and they heartily enjoyed the half-drowned looks of the company.

Everything being now ready, and the passengers aboard, we ran up the ensign and broad pennant, (for there was no man-of-war, and we were the largest vessel on the coast,) and the other vessels ran up their ensigns. Having hove short, cast off the gaskets, and made the bunt of each sail fast by the jigger, with a man on each yard; at the word, the whole canvas of the ship was loosed, and with the greatest rapidity possible, everything was sheeted home and hoisted up, the anchor tripped and catheaded, and the ship under headway. We were determined to show the "spouter" how things could be done in a smart ship, with a good crew, though not more than half their number. The royal yards were all crossed at once, and royals and skysails set, and, as we had the wind free, the booms were run out, and every one was aloft, active as cats, laying out on the yards and booms, reeving the studding-sail gear; and sail after sail the captain piled upon her, until she was covered with canvas, her sails looking like a great white cloud resting upon a black speck. Before we doubled the point, we were going at a dashing rate, and leaving the shipping far astern. We had a fine breeze to take us through the Canal, as they call this bay of forty miles long by ten wide. The breeze died away at night, and we were becalmed all day on Sunday, about half way between Santa Barbara and Point Conception. Sunday

**... they were such "marines"...** Especially coming from naval personnel, this was at the time an insult. Consider the saying, "Tell it to the marines." Some like to read this as meaning, "Just try and get away with telling that to the Marines, buddy!" implying that the Marines were too tough and too intelligent to be taken in. In fact, though, it meant exactly the opposite: "You'd best tell it to the Marines, because the Navy (or whomever) is too smart to be taken in. The Marines, on the other hand, are dumb enough to believe you."

**...we gave them the wink...** A sly gesture that may go back to the 15th century or before. It certainly goes back at least to Shakespeare, who has a character in Hamlet say of the mad Ophelia, "Her wincks, and nods, and gestures yeeld them, would make one thinke there might be thought."

**...the ensign and broad pennant...** A broad pennant is a swallow-tailed flag that flies from the masthead of an admiral's or commodore's vessel. Being the largest vessel in the bay, and in the absence of an actual high-ranking naval officer, *Alert* flies the pennant.

**...each sail fast by the jigger...** A jigger is a small block-and-tackle.

In the news
**November, 1835**

Texans skirmish with Mexican troops leading a pack train to San Antonio with reinforcements for the Mexican general who is holding the town under siege. Routing the troops and capturing the pack train, the Texans hope to find silver coin meant to pay the Mexican soldiers. However, when they open the packs, they find not silver but grass meant to feed the horses. Not surprisingly, the whole affair becomes known as "The Grass Fight."

**...where it begins to blow the first of January, and blows all the year round.** A bit of sailor's humor: That is to say, it's *always* windy off Point Conception.

In the news
**November, 1835**

Washington Irving writes *A Tour on The Prairies*, in which he describes his travels on what was then thought of as the "western frontier." Overall, he finds the native population (slowly being driven out of their native lands, of course) quite admirable and the white settlers significantly less so.

**...leaving her with as much sail as she could stagger under...** That is, with as much sail as she could safely handle, given the increasingly violent wind.

In the news
**November, 1835**

All through the month, Texian forces supporting either the Federalist constitution of 1824 or outright revolt against Texas (and then either an independent republic or annexation by the U.S.) gather outside San Antonio de Béxar. Centralist Mexican troops fortify the town, including a mission there called The Alamo.

**...off to the land of Nod...** That is, to sleep. An allusion to the biblical place-name: Nod is the land "east of Eden" to which Cain fled after murdering Abel. It may have become punningly associated with sleep because people often nod their heads when falling asleep. According to some sources, Jonathan Swift was (in a 1738 collection of tales) the first to make that connection—and therefore that little joke.

night we had a light, fair wind, which set us up again; and having a fine sea-breeze on the first part of Monday, we had the prospect of passing, without any trouble, Point Conception,—the Cape Horn of California, where it begins to blow the first of January, and blows all the year round. Toward the latter part of the afternoon, however, the regular northwest wind, as usual, set in, which brought in our studding-sails, and gave us the chance of beating round the Point, which we were now just abreast of, and which stretched off into the Pacific, high, rocky and barren, forming the central point of the coast for hundreds of miles north and south. A cap-full of wind will be a bag-full here, and before night our royals were furled, and the ship was laboring hard under her top-gallant sails. At eight bells our watch went below, leaving her with as much sail as she could stagger under, the water flying over the forecastle at every plunge. It was evidently blowing harder, but then there was not a cloud in the sky, and the sun had gone down bright.

We had been below but a short time, before we had the usual premonitions of a coming gale: seas washing over the whole forward part of the vessel, and her bows beating against them with a force and sound like the driving of piles. The watch, too, seemed very busy trampling about decks, and singing out at the ropes. A sailor can always tell, by the sound, what sail is coming in, and, in a short time, we heard the top-gallant sails come in, one after another, and then the flying jib. This seemed to ease her a good deal, and we were fast going off to the land of Nod, when—bang, bang, bang—on the scuttle, and "All hands, reef topsails, ahoy!" started us out of our berths; and, it not being very cold weather, we had nothing extra to put on, and were soon on deck. I shall never forget the fineness of the sight. It was a clear, and rather a chilly night; the stars were twinkling with an intense brightness, and as far as the eye could reach, there was not a cloud to be seen. The horizon met the sea in a defined line. A painter could not have painted so clear a sky. There was not a speck upon it. Yet it was blowing great guns from the north-west. When you can see a cloud to windward, you feel that there is a place for the wind to come from; but here it seemed to come from nowhere. No person could have told, from the heavens, by their eyesight alone, that it was not a still summer's night. One reef after another, we took in the topsails, and before we could get them hoisted up, we heard a sound like a short, quick rattling of thunder, and the jib was blown to atoms out of the bolt-rope. We got the topsails set, and the fragments of the jib stowed away, and the fore-topmast staysail set in its place, when the great mainsail gaped open, and the sail ripped from head to foot. "Lay up on that main-yard and furl the sail, before it blows to tatters!" shouted the captain; and in a moment, we were up, gathering the remains of it upon the yard. We got it wrapped, round the yard, and passed gaskets over it as snugly as possible, and were just on deck again, when, with another loud rent, which was heard throughout the ship, the fore-topsail, which had been double-reefed, split in two, athwartships, just below the reefband, from earing to earing. Here again it was down yard, haul out reef-tackles, and lay out upon the yard for reefing. By hauling the reef-tackles chock-a-block, we took the strain from the other earings, and passing the close-reef earing, and knotting the points carefully, we succeeded in setting the sail, close-reefed.

We had but just got the rigging coiled up, and were waiting to hear "go below the watch!" when the main royal worked loose from the gaskets, and blew directly out to leeward, flapping, and shaking the mast like a wand. Here was a job for somebody. The royal must come in or be cut adrift, or the mast would be snapped short off. All the light hands in the starboard watch were sent up, one after another, but they could do nothing with it. At length, John, the tall Frenchman, the head of the starboard watch, (and a better sailor never stepped upon a deck,) sprang aloft, and, by the help of his long arms and legs, succeeded, after a hard struggle,—the sail blowing over the yard-arm to leeward, and the skysail blowing directly over his head—in smothering it, and frapping it with long pieces of sinnet. He came very near being blown or shaken from the yard, several times, but he was a true sailor, every finger a fish-hook. Having made the sail snug, he prepared

**...the jib was blown to atoms...** That is, destroyed by the fierce wind. Because we associate the idea of atoms (and the adjective *atomic*) with bombs, reactors, and the like, this may sound jarringly anachronistic. But the idea that matter can be divided into smaller units and then those units further divided until at last one reaches the point beyond which no further division is possible is thousands of years old. Scientists thus referred to "atoms" long before they actually knew exactly what an atom was.

**...the fore-topsail, which had been double-reefed, split in two...** The violent wind is destroying one sail after another. That's probably better than the alternative, though, which would be to lose a mast. Sails can be repaired—and in fact, *Alert* has an expert sail maker on board: Rueben Herriot. (Masts can also be repaired, of course, but doing so would be very inv[illegible]

**In the news**
**November, 1835**

Henry Wadsworth Longfellow's wife, Mary Storer Potter, travels to Rotterdam with Longfellow as he prepares to take on a Harvard professorship, but Mary dies in Rotterdam after a miscarriage. Longfellow ("Paul Revere's Ride," *Song of Hiawatha*, *The Courtship of Miles Standish*, "The Village Blacksmith"), although already a writer of some note, had not yet established a reputation as a poet, publishing his first book of poems in 1839. Interestingly, in 1880 Longfellow will write a sonnet entitled "The Burial of The Poet." The poem is not about Longfellow himself, but about Richard Henry Dana's father, R.H. Dana, Sr.: "We laid him in the sleep that comes to all/And left him to his rest and his renown."

In the news
**November, 1835**

The Second Seminole War begins in Osceola, FL. Forced from their native lands, various Indian bands had settled in largely unoccupied (but Spanish-owned) Florida during the 1700s. When the U.S. annexed parts of Florida, a series of Indian wars began, of which this was perhaps the most devastating.

**It was a fine night for a gale...** Although it would be terrifying for us landlubbers (a derogatory term for landsmen, probably deriving from "land-lopers" and going back to the 17th century), experienced sailors do not fear such weather, assuming that their vessel is in good repair. As Dana says, it's "bracing" and makes for what a sailor might describe with deliberate understatement as "a spirited sail."

**...prepared to bend another staysail.** That is, prepared to attach or fasten new sails. A frapping is a lashing, in this case, one used to tighten the sail.

to send the yard down, which was a long and difficult job; for, frequently, he was obliged to stop and hold on with all his might, for several minutes, the ship pitching so as to make it impossible to do anything else at that height. The yard at length came down safe, and after it, the fore and mizen royal-yards were sent down. All hands were then sent aloft, and for an hour or two we were hard at work, making the booms well fast; unreeving the studding-sail and royal and skysail gear; getting rolling-ropes on the yards; setting up the weather breast-backstays; and making other preparations for a storm. It was a fine night for a gale; just cool and bracing enough for quick work, without being cold, and as bright as day. It was sport to have a gale in such weather as this. Yet it blew like a hurricane. The wind seemed to come with a spite, an edge to it, which threatened to scrape us off the yards. The mere force of the wind was greater than I had ever seen it before; but darkness, cold, and wet are the worst parts of a storm to a sailor.

Having got on deck again, we looked round to see what time of night it was, and whose watch. In a few minutes the man at the wheel struck four bells, and we found that the other watch was out, and our own half out. Accordingly, the starboard watch went below, and left the ship to us for a couple of hours, yet with orders to stand by for a call.

Hardly had they got below, before away went the foretopmast staysail, blown to ribbons. This was a small sail, which we could manage in the watch, so that we were not obliged to call up the other watch. We laid out upon the bowsprit, where we were under water half the time, and took in the fragments of the sail, and as she must have some head sail on her, prepared to bend another staysail. We got the new one out, into the nettings; seized on the tack, sheets, and halyards, and the hanks; manned the halyards, cut adrift the frapping lines, and hoisted away; but before it was half way up the stay, it was blown all to pieces. When we belayed the halyards, there was nothing left but the bolt-rope. Now large eyes began to show themselves in the foresail, and knowing that it must soon go, the mate ordered us upon the yard to furl it. Being unwilling to call up the watch who had been on deck all night, he roused out the carpenter, sailmaker, cook, steward, and other idlers, and, with their help, we manned the foreyard, and after nearly half an hour's struggle, mastered the sail, and got it well furled round the yard. The force of the wind had never been greater than at this moment. In going up the rigging, it seemed absolutely to pin us down to the shrouds; and on the yard, there was no such thing as turning a face to windward. Yet here was no driving sleet, and darkness, and wet, and cold, as off Cape Horn; and instead of a stiff oil-cloth suit, south-wester caps, and thick boots, we had on hats, round jackets, duck trowsers, light shoes, and everything light and easy. All these things make a great difference to a sailor. When we got on deck, the man at the wheel struck eight bells, (four o'clock in the morning,) and "All starbowlines, ahoy!" brought the other watch up. But there was no going below for us. The gale was now at its height, "blowing like scissors and thumb-screws;" the captain was on deck; the ship, which was light, rolling and pitching as though she would shake the long sticks out of her; and the sail gaping open and splitting, in every direction. The mizen topsail, which was a comparatively new sail, and close-reefed, split, from head to foot, in the bunt; the fore-topsail went, in one rent, from clew to earing, and was blowing to tatters; one of the chain bob-stays parted; the spritsail-yard sprung in the slings; the martingale had slued away off to leeward; and, owing to the long dry weather, the lee rigging hung in large bights, at every lurch. One of the main top-gallant shrouds had parted; and, to crown all, the galley had got adrift, and gone over to leeward, and the anchor on the lee bow had worked loose, and was thumping the side. Here was work enough for all hands for half a day. Our gang laid out on the mizen topsail yard, and after more than half an hour's hard work, furled the sail, though it bellied out over our heads, and again, by a slant of the wind, blew in under the yard, with a fearful jerk, and almost threw us off from the foot-ropes.

Double gaskets were passed round the yards, rolling tackles and other gear bowsed taut, and everything

## In the news
## November, 1835

The soon-to-be-proclaimed Republic of Texas develops a navy consisting of four schooners. The flagship is an 89-foot former United States Treasury cutter that the Texans rechristen *Independence*. The Texas Navy actually does see action, with *Independence* plying the coast between Galveston and Tampico (a distance of several hundred nautical miles), capturing several smaller craft, and generally making a nuisance of itself as far as Mexican General Santa Anna is concerned.

**All these things make a great difference to a sailor.** Because of the warm, dry weather, the men were at least able to wear comfortable clothing while they worked. Imagine trying to secure and replace these sails in cold, wet, snowy conditions, wearing stiff, heavy slickers and oilskins.

**...scissors and thumb-screws...** Among sailors, a phrase (now obsolete) that means, "something that's full of menace." One serialized 19th-century novel (*The Romance of a Wreck*) includes the sentence, "Mr Greenhew, with a glance full of scissors and thumbscrews, as the sailors say...."

**...the lee rigging hung in large bights, at every lurch.** The storm is battering the ship pretty severely.

**But this was too much after sail...** Even just a spanker and a close-reefed topsail are too much canvas for the violent conditions. The spanker was actually a fair-weather sail mounted on the mizzen-mast, although by the 1840s it became common to carry it in all weather.

**The brails were hauled up...** Brails are small ropes attached to the ends of sails and used to truss them prior to (or sometimes instead of) furling.

In the news

**November, 1835**

A new Chicago city ordinance requires citizens to A) have on hand as many buckets as there are stoves or fireplaces in their homes, and B) to convey those buckets to the scene of any fire. Later this month, the first official bucket brigade in the city is formed, the "Fire Guards Bucket Company," and a LaSalle Street location is selected for the first fire station, Engine Company No. 1. (Chicago's City Hall is currently located at that location, the fire station itself having long been demolished.)

**...and washing chock aft to the taffrail.** We tend to chafe (itself a nautical term) at Dana's repeated and seemingly endless store of sailor's lingo. And, as previously noted, many critics have advised landlubberly readers to simply skim (or skip altogether) those paragraphs that seem overburdened with nautical terminology. But we also need to remember that this book is the first to accurately and realistically describe the merchant sailor's life; the language used by Dana is the language of the sea, and the terminology is in fact important. While he is inordinately (and sometimes irritatingly) proud of his mastery of it, keep in mind that it is the true language of sailors—and that Dana, in mastering it and in becoming a skilled, toughened sailor, has in fact accomplished a great deal.

made as secure as could be. Coming down, we found the rest of the crew just coming down the fore rigging, having furled the tattered topsail, or, rather, swathed it round the yard, which looked like a broken limb, bandaged. There was no sail now on the ship but the spanker and the close-reefed main topsail, which still held good. But this was too much after sail; and order was given to furl the spanker. The brails were hauled up, and all the light hands in the starboard watch sent out on the gaff to pass the gaskets; but they could do nothing with it. The second mate swore at them for a parcel of "sogers," and sent up a couple of the best men; but they could do no better, and the gaff was lowered down. All hands were now employed in setting up the lee rigging, fishing the spritsail-yard, lashing the galley, and getting tackles upon the martingale, to bowse it to windward. Being in the larboard watch, my duty was forward, to assist in setting up the martingale. Three of us were out on the martingale guys and back-ropes for more than half an hour, carrying out, hooking and unhooking the tackles, several times buried in the seas, until the mate ordered us in, from fear of our being washed off. The anchors were then to be taken up on the rail, which kept all hands on the forecastle for an hour, though every now and then the seas broke over it, washing the rigging off to leeward, filling the lee scuppers breast high, and washing chock aft to the taffrail.

Having got everything secure again, we were promising ourselves some breakfast, for it was now nearly nine o'clock in the forenoon, when the main topsail showed evident signs of giving way. Some sail must be kept on the ship, and the captain ordered the fore and main spencer gaffs to be lowered down, and the two spencers (which were storm sails, bran new, small, and made of the strongest canvas) to be got up and bent; leaving the main topsail to blow away, with a blessing on it, if it would only last until we could set the spencers. These we bent on very carefully, with strong robands and seizings, and making tackles fast to the clews, bowsed them down to the water-ways. By this time the main topsail was among the things that have been, and we went aloft to stow away the remnant of the last sail of all those which were on the ship twenty-four hours before. The spencers were now the only whole sails on the ship, and, being strong and small, and near the deck, presenting but little surface to the wind above the rail, promised to hold out well. Hove-to under these, and eased by having no sail above the tops, the ship rose and fell, and drifted off to leeward like a line-of-battle ship.

It was now eleven o'clock, and the watch was sent below to get breakfast, and at eight bells (noon), as everything was snug, although the gale had not in the least abated, the watch was set, and the other watch and idlers sent below. For three days and three nights, the gale continued with unabated fury, and with singular regularity. There was no lulls, and very little variation in its fierceness. Our ship, being light, rolled so as almost to send the fore yard-arm under water, and drifted off bodily, to leeward. All this time there was not a cloud to be seen in the sky, day or night;—no, not so large as a man's hand. Every morning the sun rose cloudless from the sea, and set again at night, in the sea, in a flood of light. The stars, too, came out of the blue, one after another, night after night, unobscured, and twinkled as clear as on a still frosty night at home, until the day came upon them. All this time, the sea was rolling in immense surges, white with foam, as far as the eye could reach, on every side, for we were now leagues and leagues from shore.

The between-decks being empty, several of us slept there in hammocks, which are the best things in the world to sleep in during a storm; it not being true of them, as it is of another kind of bed, "when the wind blows, the cradle will rock;" for it is the ship that rocks, while they always hang vertically from the beams. During these seventy-two hours we had nothing to do, but to turn in and out, four hours on deck, and four below, eat, sleep, and keep watch. The watches were only varied by taking the helm in turn, and now and then, by one of the sails, which were furled, blowing out of the gaskets, and getting adrift, which sent us up on the yards; and by getting tackles on different parts of the rigging, which were slack. Once, the wheel-rope

**The spencers were now the only whole sails on the ship...** A spencer is a small, triangular sail mounted aft of the mainmast.

**In the news**
**November, 1835**

All through the months of October and November, Texan (or Texian) forces gather outside San Antonio de Béxar, the location of present-day San Antonio, TX. Centralist Mexican troops loyal to the new Mexican constitution fortify the town, but the Texans defeat the Mexican troops, seizing control of the town and of a former Spanish mission known as The Alamo. The Texians then establish a garrison at the mission.

**...not so large as a man's hand.** An allusion to the biblical passage in Kings: "And it came to pass at the seventh time, that he said, Behold, there ariseth a little cloud out of the sea, like a man's hand. And he said, Go up, say unto Ahab, Prepare thy chariot, and get thee down, that the rain stop thee not." This is doubly interesting, because we know that Herman Melville read and enjoyed both his Bible and *Two Years Before the Mast* and that he corresponded with Dana. Ahab was, of course, the name of the mad captain of the *Pequod* in Melville's *Moby Dick*.

**...it is the ship that rocks...** In effect, hammocks are gimbaled: Hanging from pillars and beams, they maintain their attitude, staying mostly still as the ship moves about them. Hammocks and other similar technologies are still used aboard many boats. Stoves on many yachts, for example, hang on gimbals so that the stove can remain horizontal even if its support tips; that way, the motion of the boat is less likely to toss pots and pans about. (Nonetheless, most such stoves also include a "fiddle rail"—a bar or stop meant to prevent cookware from sliding off the stovetop in rough weather.)

**...the wheel-rope parted...** That is, the rope connecting the wheel to the rudder. If the rope breaks, the rudder hangs uselessly; this is a dangerous position to be in, especially in bad weather, where it's important to keep the ship bow-on to the waves.

**Two spare courses...** Courses are sails set on the lower yards of a square-rigged vessel that can carry bonnets—extra strips of canvas sewn to the bottom of a sail to increase the sail's area. Eventually, the word was applied to any sails set to the lower yards, regardless of whether bonnets were in use.

In the news
**November, 1835**

Georgians marching to the aid of Texans receive from 17-year-old Johanna Troutman a flag that she had designed for the volunteers. In the center of the flag is a large star; on one side is the inscription, "Liberty or Death," and on the other is the Latin motto, "Ubi Libertas Habitat Ibi Patria Est." ("Where Liberty dwells, there is my country.") The flag, which will become one of several flags to fly over the Republic of Texas, is first raised on Texas soil at Velasco on Jan. 8, 1836. Johanna Troutman died on July 23, 1879; her portrait hangs in the state capitol.

**...no one of that ship's crew, I will venture to say, will ever desire again to unbend and bend five large sails...** The power of the wind as it strikes sails of any size at all is incredible—and these are large sails being handled in violent winds.

parted, which might have been fatal to us, had not the chief mate sprung instantly with a relieving tackle to windward, and kept the tiller up, till a new one could be rove. On the morning of the twentieth, at daybreak, the gale had evidently done its worst, and had somewhat abated; so much so, that all hands were called to bend new sails, although it was still blowing as hard as two common gales. One at a time, and with great difficulty and labor, the old sails were unbent and sent down by the bunt-lines, and three new topsails, made for the homeward passage round Cape Horn, and which had never been bent, were got up from the sailroom, and under the care of the sailmaker, were fitted for bending, and sent up by the halyards into the tops, and, with stops and frapping lines, were bent to the yards, close-reefed, sheeted home, and hoisted. These were done one at a time, and with the greatest care and difficulty. Two spare courses were then got up and bent in the same manner and furled, and a storm-jib, with the bonnet off, bent and furled to the boom. It was twelve o'clock before we got through; and five hours of more exhausting labor I never experienced; and no one of that ship's crew, I will venture to say, will ever desire again to unbend and bend five large sails, in the teeth of a tremendous north-wester. Towards night, a few clouds appeared in the horizon, and as the gale moderated, the usual appearance of driving clouds relieved the face of the sky. The fifth day after the commencement of the storm, we shook a reef out of each topsail, and set the reefed foresail, jib and spanker; but it was not until after eight days of reefed topsails that we had a whole sail on the ship; and then it was quite soon enough, for the captain was anxious to make up for leeway, the gale having blown us half the distance to the Sandwich Islands.

Inch by inch, as fast as the gale would permit, we made sail on the ship, for the wind still continued a-head, and we had many days' sailing to get back to the longitude we were in when the storm took us. For eight days more we beat to windward under a stiff top-gallant breeze, when the wind shifted and became variable. A light south-easter, to which we could carry a reefed topmast studding-sail, did wonders for our dead reckoning.

Friday, December 4th, after a passage of twenty days, we arrived at the mouth of the bay of San Francisco.

**...we arrived at the mouth of the bay of San Francisco.** This is as far north as Dana goes during this voyage. In 1835, San Francisco (which was of course still a part of Mexico at the time) is nothing like we think of it today. In fact, although the mission and presidio are called San Francisco (actually, Mission San Francisco de Asís), the city itself is not. That's because, during Dana's first visit, there really *is* no city. The first real dwelling in what was then called Yerba Buena was built only a few months prior to Dana's arrival.

In the news
**November, 1835**

In Courtland, AL, Dr. Jack Shackleford encourages the formation of a band of volunteers, the Red Rovers, to go to Texas and fight to help form the new republic. About 60 men volunteer, making the trip to Texas. A few months later, almost all of the men are executed at what came to be known as the Goliad Massacre. (See earlier note.)

In the news
**November, 1835**

The revised statutes of the Commonwealth of Massachusetts make it a crime to kidnap a person with intent to "cause such person to be sent out of this state against his will, or to be sold as a slave, or in any way held to service against his will." The new statute further requires that anyone who unlawfully seizes "any negro, mulatto, or other person of color, who shall have been unlawfully seized, taken, inveigled or kidnapped from this state, to any other state, place, or country, shall be punished by imprisonment in the state prison, not more than ten years...."

# CHAPTER XXVI

## SAN FRANCISCO—MONTEREY

**This large bay, which lies in latitude 37° 58', was discovered by Sir Francis Drake...** Dana's history and geography are a bit confused here. The bay was discovered (in 1769) by de Portola, not by Drake. The presidio to which he refers does not stand on the southeast side 30 miles inland, but on the south shore right at the mouth of the bay.

**...a newly begun settlement...called Yerba Buena...** Yerba Buena (which, perhaps somewhat ironically, means "good herb") will become the city of San Francisco, but it is currently sparsely populated, with only one permanent dwelling other than the mission and presidio.

**...Russian colors, from Asitka...** The 180-ton brig *Polifemia* is from what would someday be called Sitka, in what would eventually be called Alaska. In the 19th century, the Russians had settled in the area and established colonies and trading posts. In 1867, the United States would purchase Alaska for the sum of $7.2 million, or about .02 per acre.

**In the news**
**December, 1835**

The Mexican army surrenders San Antonio to Texan volunteers. Despite being told that the position is untenable, the volunteers choose to stay in town. They make their headquarters at an old mission named Misión San Antonio de Valero, but which had come to be called The Alamo. Almost all will die there in early March.

**...such a stupid and greasy-looking set, I certainly never saw before.** Once again, Dana thinks little of these representatives of a foreign culture.

**...Nova Zembla...** A Russian archipelago in the Arctic Ocean. Dana is saying that the Russian sailors wear their cold-weather gear at all times, even in warm weather.

Our place of destination had been Monterey, but as we were to the northward of it when the wind hauled ahead, we made a fair wind for San Francisco. This large bay, which lies in latitude 37° 58', was discovered by Sir Francis Drake, and by him represented to be (as indeed it is) a magnificent bay, containing several good harbors, great depth of water, and surrounded by a fertile and finely wooded country. About thirty miles from the mouth of the bay, and on the south-east side, is a high point, upon which the presidio is built. Behind this, is the harbor in which trading vessels anchor, and near it, the mission of San Francisco, and a newly begun settlement, mostly of Yankee Californians, called Yerba Buena, which promises well. Here, at anchor, and the only vessel, was a brig under Russian colors, from Asitka, in Russian America, which had come down to winter, and to take in a supply of tallow and grain, great quantities of which latter article are raised in the missions at the head of the bay. The second day after our arrival, we went on board the brig, it being Sunday, as a matter of curiosity; and there was enough there to gratify it. Though no larger than the Pilgrim, she had five or six officers, and a crew of between twenty and thirty; and such a stupid and greasy-looking set, I certainly never saw before. Although it was quite comfortable weather, and we had nothing on but straw hats, shirts, and duck trowsers, and were barefooted, they had, every man of them, double-soled boots, coming up to the knees, and well greased; thick woolen trowsers, frocks, waistcoats, pea-jackets, woolen caps, and everything in true Nova Zembla rig; and in the warmest days they made no change. The clothing of one of these men would weigh nearly as much as that of half our crew. They had brutish faces, looked like the antipodes of sailors, and apparently dealt in nothing but grease. They lived upon grease; eat it, drank it, slept in the midst of it, and their clothes were covered with it. To a Russian, grease is the greatest luxury. They looked with greedy eyes upon the tallow-bags as they were taken into the vessel, and, no doubt, would have eaten one up whole, had not the officer kept watch over it. The grease seemed actually coming through their pores, and out in their hair, and on their faces. It seems as if it were this saturation which makes them stand cold and rain so well. If they were to go into a warm climate, they would all die of the scurvy.

**...they would all die of the scurvy.** Scurvy, a disease caused by a vitamin C deficiency, is painful and debilitating and, left untreated, ultimately fatal. The cure is simple: Foods rich in vitamin C, such as limes or other fruits, will quickly bring about a cure. (This is why British sailors are called "limeys"—beginning in 1795, they were given a daily ration of limes or lime juice to combat scurvy.)

The vessel was no better than the crew. Everything was in the oldest and most inconvenient fashion possible; running trusses on the yards, and large hawser cables, coiled all over the decks, and served and parcelled in all directions. The topmasts, top-gallant masts and studding-sail booms were nearly black for want of scraping, and the decks would have turned the stomach of a man-of-war's-man. The galley was down in the forecastle; and there the crew lived, in the midst of the steam and grease of the cooking, in a place as hot as an oven, and as dirty as a pigsty. Five minutes in the forecastle was enough for us, and we were glad to get into the open air. We made some trade with them, buying Indian curiosities, of which they had a great number; such as bead-work, feathers of birds, fur moccasins, etc. I purchased a large robe, made of the skins of some animals, dried and sewed nicely together, and covered all over on the outside with thick downy feathers, taken from the breasts of various birds, and arranged with their different colors, so as to make a brilliant show.

**...served and parcelled in all directions.** That is, all was in disarray. This is a sloppy ship and a slovenly crew, at least in Dana's eyes.

In the news
**December, 1835**

The city of Chicago, a sleepy town founded only three years earlier, is growing rapidly. The *Chicago Democrat* reports this month that "[t]he population of Chicago, according to the last census is 3279. There are 44 stores (dry goods, hardware and groceries) 2 book stores, 4 druggists, 2 silversmiths and jewelers, 2 tin and copper manufactories, 2 printing offices, 2 breweries, 1 steam saw mill, 1 iron foundary, four storage and forwarding houses, 3 taverns, 1 lottery office, 1 bank, 5 churches, 7 schools, 22 lawyers, 14 physicians, a lyceum and a reading room. Nine brick buildings have been erected the past season, among which, are a tavern, three stories high, and a county clerk's office."

A few days after our arrival, the rainy season set in, and, for three weeks, it rained almost every hour, without cessation. This was bad for our trade, for the collecting of hides is managed differently in this port from what it is in any other on the coast. The mission of San Francisco near the anchorage, has no trade at all, but those of San José, Santa Clara, and others, situated on large creeks or rivers which run into the bay, and distant between fifteen and forty miles from the anchorage, do a greater business in hides than any in California. Large boats, manned by Indians, and capable of carrying nearly a thousand hides apiece, are attached to the missions, and sent down to the vessels with hides, to bring away goods in return. Some of the crews of the vessels are

**...a greater business in hides than any in California.** La Misión del Gloriosísimo Patriarca Señor San José, founded in 1797, was the 14th mission. It is in what is now Fremont, CA. The Mission Santa Clara de Asís, the 8th of the 21 California missions, was founded in 1777. It was rebuilt and relocated several times due to fire, floods, and earthquakes.

obliged to go and come in the boats, to look out for the hides and goods. These are favorite expeditions with the sailors, in fine weather; but now to be gone three or four days, in open boats, in constant rain, without any shelter, and with cold food, was hard service. Two of our men went up to Santa Clara in one of these boats, and were gone three days, during all which time they had a constant rain, and did not sleep a wink, but passed three long nights, walking fore and aft the boat, in the open air. When they got on board, they were completely exhausted, and took a watch below of twelve hours. All the hides, too, that came down in the boats, were soaked with water, and unfit to put below, so that we were obliged to trice them up to dry, in the intervals of sunshine or wind, upon all parts of the vessel. We got up tricing-lines from the jib-boom-end to each arm of the fore yard, and thence to the main and cross-jack yard-arms. Between the tops, too, and the mast-heads, from the fore to the main swifters, and thence to the mizen rigging, and in all directions athwartships, tricing-lines were run, and strung with hides. The head stays and guys, and the spritsail-yard, were lined, and, having still more, we got out the swinging booms, and strung them and the forward and after guys, with hides. The rail, fore and aft, the windlass, capstan, the sides of the ship, and every vacant place on deck, were covered with wet hides, on the least sign of an interval for drying. Our ship was nothing but a mass of hides, from the cat-harpins to the water's edge, and from the jib-boom-end to the taffrail.

**...trice them up...** A trice is a pulley or a windlass; the wet hides were stretched and tied in the open air to dry.

**...to the taffrail.** The taffrail is the aft-most rail at the stern of a ship. Oddly, the word began as "taferel," which meant a carved panel, so it should actually have nothing to do with rails. However, the -rel suffix sounded like rail, so through a process known as false etymology or folk etymology, it came to be applied to the thing for which it was mistaken.

In the news

**December, 1835**

In *Philosophical Transactions*, the journal of the Royal Society, Michael Faraday publishes a paper in which he points out, "...a very remarkable inductive action of electric currents, or of the different parts of the same current, and indicate an immediate connexion between such inductive action and the direct transmission of electricity through conducting bodies, or even that exhibited in the form of a spark." Giving due credit to a "Mr. Jenkin" for the idea, Faraday goes on to explain that if one wraps a wire around an electromagnet, "...a shock is felt each time the contact with the electromotor is broken, provided the ends of the wire be grasped one in each hand." Faraday has, with some readily acknowledged help, just invented the generator.

One cold, rainy evening, about eight o'clock, I received orders to get ready to start for San José at four the next morning, in one of these Indian boats, with four days' provisions. I got my oil-cloth clothes, south-wester, and thick boots all ready, and turned into my hammock early, determined to get some sleep in advance, as the boat was to be alongside before daybreak. I slept on till all hands were called in the morning; for, fortunately for me, the Indians, intentionally, or from mistaking their orders, had gone off alone in the night, and were far out of sight. Thus I escaped three or four days of very uncomfortable service.

Four of our men, a few days afterwards, went up in one of the quarter-boats to Santa Clara, to carry the agent, and remained out all night in a drenching rain, in the small boat, where there was not room for them to turn round; the agent having gone up to the mission and left the men to their fate, making no provision for their accommodation, and not even sending them anything to eat. After this, they had to pull thirty miles, and when they got on board, were so stiff that they could not come up the gangway ladder. This filled up the measure of the agent's unpopularity, and never after this could he get anything done by any of the crew; and many a delay and vexation, and many a good ducking in the surf, did he get to pay up old scores, or "square the yards with the bloody quill-driver."

**...agent having gone up to the mission and left the men to their fate...** The agent, you'll recall, is Alfred Robinson. His job is to acquire hides and supplies, and to make other financial arrangements on behalf of the owners back in Boston. Here he seems to be concentrating on business and ignoring the welfare of the men.

**...to pay up old scores...** That is, the men took every opportunity to get even with Robinson. A "quill driver" is a person whose job involves mainly writing, as opposed to "real" work. The depreciative term goes back to the late 1600s. ("Squaring the yards" means to brace the sails, making them even vertically and horizontally. Here the term is applied metaphorically to mean "making things right.")

Having collected nearly all the hides that were to be procured, we began our preparations for taking in a supply of wood and water, for both of which, San Francisco is the best place on the coast. A small island, situated about two leagues from the anchorage, called by us "Wood Island," and by the Spaniards "Isle de los Angelos," was covered with trees to the water's edge; and to this, two of our crew, who were Kennebec men, and could handle an axe like a plaything, were sent every morning to cut wood, with two boys to pile it up for them. In about a week, they had cut enough to last us a year, and the third mate, with myself and three others, were sent over in a large, schooner-rigged, open launch, which we had hired of the mission, to take in the wood, and bring it to the ship. We left the ship about noon, but, owing to a strong head wind, and a tide, which here runs four or five knots, did not get into the harbor, formed by two points of the island, where the boats lie, until sundown. No sooner had we come-to, than a strong south-easter, which had been threatening us all day, set in, with heavy rain and a chilly atmosphere. We were in rather a bad situation: an open boat, a heavy rain, and a long night; for in winter, in this latitude, it was dark nearly fifteen hours. Taking a small skiff which we had brought with us, we went ashore, but found no shelter, for everything was open to the rain, and collecting a little wood, which we found by

**...Isle de los Angelos...** Angel Island, located in San Francisco Bay, is now a state park, but it has seen use as a fort and a processing center for immigrants, among other things. In Dana's day, crews gathered firewood there. (The island has actually been logged several times in modern history.)

**...two of our crew, who were Kennebec men...** Kennebec County, in Maine, was at the time home to great forests and to the lumberjacks who worked those forests. The "Kennebec men" on board are evidently experienced lumbermen.

lifting up the leaves and brush, and a few mussels, we put aboard again, and made the best preparations in our power for passing the night. We unbent the mainsail, and formed an awning with it over the after part of the boat, made a bed of wet logs of wood, and, with our jackets on, lay down, about six o'clock, to sleep. Finding the rain running down upon us, and our jackets getting wet through, and the rough, knotty-logs, rather indifferent couches, we turned out; and taking an iron pan which we brought with us, we wiped it out dry, put some stones around it, cut the wet bark from some sticks, and striking a light, made a small fire in the pan. Keeping some sticks near, to dry, and covering the whole over with a roof of boards, we kept up a small fire, by which we cooked our mussels, and ate them, rather for an occupation than from hunger. Still, it was not ten o'clock, and the night was long before us, when one of the party produced an old pack of Spanish cards from his monkey-jacket pocket, which we hailed as a great windfall; and keeping a dim, flickering light by our fagots, we played game after game, till one or two o'clock, when, becoming really tired, we went to our logs again, one sitting up at a time, in turn, to keep watch over the fire. Toward morning, the rain ceased, and the air became sensibly colder, so that we found sleep impossible, and sat up, watching for daybreak. No sooner was it light than we went ashore, and began our preparations for loading our vessel. We were not mistaken in the coldness of the weather, for a white frost was on the ground, a thing we had never seen before in California, and one or two little puddles of fresh water were skimmed over with a thin coat of ice. In this state of the weather and before sunrise, in the grey of the morning, we had to wade off, nearly up to our hips in water, to load the skiff with the wood by armsfull. The third mate remained on board the launch, two more men staid in the skiff, to load and manage it, and all the water-work, as usual, fell upon the two youngest of us; and there we were, with frost on the ground, wading forward and back, from the beach to the boat, with armsfull of wood, barefooted, and our trowsers rolled up. When the skiff went off with her load, we could only keep our feet from freezing by racing up and down

In the news
**December, 1835**

Edgar Allan Poe composes—but never completes—*Politian*, the only play he'll ever write. The play, a fictionalized retelling of a Kentucky murder, is poorly received and, luckily for us, Poe turns to short stories as his preferred medium.

**...by which we cooked our mussels...** Some editions have "muscles." The (normally orange or yellow) flesh of cooked mussels is eaten boiled, smoked, roasted, or fried, and is popular around the world.

**...keeping a dim, flickering light by our fagots...** Fagots (or faggots) are branches or bundles of twigs—in this case, the wood Dana and his colleagues are using in their fire. Used in this sense, the word (originally from the French fagot) goes back to the 14th century.

In the news
**December, 1835**

The Missouri Compromise (1820) prohibited slavery north of the parallel located at 36°30' north, except in the state of Missouri itself. Thus, in December of 1835, we find a notice in the St. Louis County records of a slave named Daniel Banks who had escaped from his rightful owner in Kentucky. That owner, William Bagby, never shows up to claim his slave. After a required waiting period, the laws of Missouri now require the county sheriff to sell Banks to the highest bidder.

the beach on the hard sand, as fast as we could go. We were all day at this work, and towards sundown, having loaded the vessel as deep as she would bear, we hove up our anchor, and made sail, beating out the bay. No sooner had we got into the large bay, than we found a strong tide setting us out to seaward, a thick fog which prevented our seeing the ship, and a breeze too light to set us against the tide; for we were as deep as a sand-barge. By the utmost exertions, we saved ourselves from being carried out to sea, and were glad to reach the leewardmost point of the island, where we came-to, and prepared to pass another night, more uncomfortable than the first, for we were loaded up to the gunwale, and had only a choice among logs and sticks for a resting-place. The next morning, we made sail at slack water, with a fair wind, and got on board by eleven o'clock, when all hands were turned-to, to unload and stow away the wood, which took till night.

Having now taken in all our wood, the next morning a water-party was ordered off with all the casks. From this we escaped, having had a pretty good siege with the wooding. The water-party were gone three days, during which time they narrowly escaped being carried out to sea, and passed one day on an island, where one of them shot a deer, great numbers of which overrun the islands and hills of San Francisco Bay.

While not off, on these wood and water parties, or up the rivers to the missions, we had very easy times on board the ship. We were moored, stem and stern, within a cable's length of the shore, safe from south-easters, and with very little boating to do; and as it rained nearly all the time, awnings were put over the hatchways, and all hands sent down between decks, where we were at work, day after day, picking oakum, until we got enough to caulk the ship all over, and to last the whole voyage. Then we made a whole suit of gaskets for the voyage home, a pair of wheel-ropes from strips of green hide, great quantities of spun-yarn, and everything else that could be made between decks. It being now mid-winter and in high latitude, the nights were very long, so that we were not turned-to until seven in the morn-

**We were all day at this work...** This was a miserable day for the entire crew, but especially for Dana and the other young man. (Probably George Somerby, who was 15 years old when he shipped out.) It gets quite cold in San Francisco, and these men are working outdoors all day, often in the water and without shelter of any kind.

**...we were as deep as a sand-barge.** That is, their vessel was heavily loaded, and thus unwieldy and difficult to sail, even under the best of circumstances—which these were not, of course, given the tide and the fog.

**...we made sail at slack water...** That is, during that period of time when the tide is inactive, neither rising nor falling. As an interesting (and somewhat mysterious) side note, one source notes that during this period, regardless of whether the slack water occurs at high tide or low, birds in the area suddenly become silent.

**The water-party were gone three days...** One of Dana's frequent British usages: Many collective nouns that U.S. treats as singular (staff, party, group, etc.), are treated in British English as plural. A Brit would say, "The staff are at a meeting," while most U.S. speakers would say, "The staff is at a meeting." This is not an affectation on Dana's part: In the 1830s, the language simply hadn't diverged to the point it has now.

**...a deer, great numbers of which overrun the islands and hills of San Francisco Bay.** There are still deer in the hills around San Francisco, but imagine them in such numbers that they can be said to "overrun" the area.

**...picking oakum...** Tarred fibers used for caulking the seams of a wooden vessel. Oakum was gathered by picking loose fibers from old ropes or by unravelling them.

**...gaskets for the voyage home...** What a modern yachtsman would call a *tier*, a gasket was a rope or cord used to secure furled sails to a yard or other spar.

ing, and were obliged to knock off at five in the evening, when we got supper; which gave us nearly three hours before eight bells, at which time the watch was set.

As we had now been about a year on the coast, it was time to think of the voyage home; and knowing that the last two or three months of our stay would be very busy ones, and that we should never have so good an opportunity to work for ourselves as the present, we all employed our evenings in making clothes for the passage home, and more especially for Cape Horn. As soon as supper was over and the kids cleared away, and each one had taken his smoke, we seated ourselves on our chests round the lamp, which swung from a beam, and each one went to work in his own way, some making hats, others trowsers, others jackets, etc., etc.; and no one was idle. The boys who could not sew well enough to make their own clothes, laid up grass into sinnet for the men, who sewed for them in return. Several of us clubbed together and bought a large piece of twilled cotton, which we made into trowsers and jackets, and giving them several coats of linseed oil, laid them by for Cape Horn. I also sewed and covered a tarpaulin hat, thick and strong enough to sit down upon, and made myself a complete suit of flannel under-clothing, for bad weather. Those who had no south-wester caps, made them, and several of the crew made themselves tarpaulin jackets and trowsers, lined on the inside with flannel. Industry was the order of the day, and every one did something for himself; for we knew that as the season advanced, and we went further south, we should have no evenings to work in.

Friday, December 25th. This day was Christmas; and as it rained all day long, and there were no hides to take in, and nothing especial to do, the captain gave us a holiday, (the first we had had since leaving Boston,) and plum duff for dinner. The Russian brig, following the Old Style, had celebrated their Christmas eleven days before; when they had a grand blow-out and (as our men said) drank, in the forecastle, a barrel of gin, ate up a bag of tallow, and made a soup of the skin.

**...and more especially for Cape Horn.** The rough weather of the Cape demands that clothes be warm and in good repair.

**...laid up grass into sinnet for the men...** Sinnet is a flat, woven cord useful as chafing gear and (especially in later years) for decorative purposes.

**Those who had no south-wester caps, made them...** A sou'wester cap is the distinctive wide-brimmed hat common to Atlantic sailors and fishermen. The wide brim helps shed rain, keeping water away from the face and neck.

**...plum duff for dinner.** As noted earlier, plum duff is a pudding made of flour, raisins and other fruits and sweeteners. A duff was quite a treat for sailors hungry for sweets.

**...celebrated their Christmas eleven days before...** Dana is probably mistaken here, because the Russian Orthodox Church celebrates Christmas 11 days *after* Western churches, not before. One source comments that Dana may have mistaken the Russian celebration of the Feast of St. Nicholas for a Christmas celebration. Some other sources maintain that, because of this error, Dana's dates from this point on are off by 11 days. However, the dates appear to be correct at least from the point at which *Alert* sails for Boston in May of 1836.

Sunday, December 27th. We had now finished all our business at this port, and it being Sunday, we unmoored ship and got under weigh, firing a salute to the Russian brig, and another to the Presidio, which were both answered. The commandant of the Presidio, Don Gaudaloupe Villego, a young man, and the most popular, among the Americans and English, of any man in California, was on board when we got under weigh. He spoke English very well, and was suspected of being favorably inclined to foreigners.

We sailed down this magnificent bay with a light wind, the tide, which was running out, carrying us at the rate of four or five knots. It was a fine day; the first of entire sunshine we had had for more than a month. We passed directly under the high cliff on which the Presidio is built, and stood into the middle of the bay, from whence we could see small bays, making up into the interior, on every side; large and beautifully-wooded islands; and the mouths of several small rivers. If California ever becomes a prosperous country, this bay will be the centre of its prosperity. The abundance of wood and water, the extreme fertility of its shores, the excellence of its climate, which is as near to being perfect as any in the world, and its facilities for navigation, affording the best anchoring-grounds in the whole western coast of America, all fit it for a place of great importance; and, indeed, it has attracted much attention, for the settlement of "Yerba Buena," where we lay at anchor, made chiefly by Americans and English, and which bids fair to become the most important trading place on the coast, at this time began to supply traders, Russian ships, and whalers, with their stores of wheat and frijoles.

The tide leaving us, we came to anchor near the mouth of the bay, under a high and beautifully sloping hill, upon which herds of hundreds and hundreds of red deer, and the stag, with his high branching antlers, were bounding about, looking at us for a moment, and then starting off, affrighted at the noises which we made for the purpose of seeing the variety of their beautiful attitudes and motions.

**...Don Gaudaloupe Villego...** A more accurate rendition would be Guadalupe Vallejo. Vallejo was a rancher and military commander. The city of Vallejo, CA is named for him.

## In the news
## December, 1835

Mathematician and theologian Baden Powell publishes a paper discussing the science of light and "...the relation between the index of refraction and the length of period or wave for each definite ray...." Powell has 14 children, one of whom, Robert, founds the Scouting movement, giving rise to the Boy Scouts and Girl Scouts.

**If California ever becomes a prosperous country, this bay will be the centre of its prosperity.** Dana is perfectly correct. San Francisco—and its beautiful bay—do indeed become the center of a prosperous California, and for exactly the reasons he mentions.

**...the northerly point of the Bay of Monterey...** Point Año Nuevo is west of the current-day Silicon Valley cities of Los Gatos, Sunnyvale, and Cupertino.

**We spoke...the brig Diana...** Keep in mind that "spoke," in this context, means to have seen or encountered. *Diana* journeyed to and from the islands in search of sea otters, her principal item of trade.

In the news

**December, 1835**

In a Mexican prison in the port city of Tampico, James Cramp addresses to his family a declaration pledging that the roughly 130 men in his company were innocent of anti-government agitation and had no intention of "...participating or colleaguing with any persons or party, having for its object the revolutionizing or disturbing in any manner the tranquility of the country government of Mexico." While most of the expedition escapes, Camp and 30 other men are taken prisoner; all 31 are executed on 14 December. Camp's declaration claims that the men were tricked into fighting by José Antonio Mexia, a disaffected Mexican who was loyal to the 1824 Mexican Constitution.

At midnight, the tide having turned, we hove up our anchor and stood out of the bay, with a fine starry heaven above us,—the first we had seen for weeks and weeks. Before the light northerly winds, which blow here with the regularity of trades, we worked slowly along, and made Point Año Nuevo, the northerly point of the Bay of Monterey, on Monday afternoon. We spoke, going in, the brig Diana, of the Sandwich Islands, from the North-west Coast, last from Asitka. She was off the point at the same time with us, but did not get in to the anchoring-ground until an hour or two after us. It was ten o'clock on Tuesday morning when we came to anchor. The town looked just as it did when I saw it last, which was eleven months before, in the brig Pilgrim. The pretty lawn on which it stands, as green as sun and rain could make it; the pine wood on the south; the small river on the north side; the houses, with their white plastered sides and red-tiled roofs, dotted about on the green; the low, white presidio, with its soiled, tri-colored flag flying, and the discordant din of drums and trumpets for the noon parade; all brought up the scene we had witnessed here with so much pleasure nearly a year before, when coming from a long voyage, and our unprepossessing reception at Santa Barbara. It seemed almost like coming to a home.

## CHAPTER XXVII

### THE SUNDAY WASH-UP—ON SHORE—A SET-TO—A GRANDEE—"SAIL HO!"—A FANDANGO

The only other vessel in port was the Russian government bark, from Asitka, mounting eight guns, (four of which we found to be Quakers,) and having on board the ex-governor, who was going in her to Mazatlan, and thence overland to Vera Cruz. He offered to take letters, and deliver them to the American consul at Vera Cruz, whence they could be easily forwarded to the United States. We accordingly made up a packet of letters, almost every one writing, and dating them "January 1st, 1836." The governor was true to his promise, and they all reached Boston before the middle of March; the shortest communication ever yet made across the country.

The brig Pilgrim had been lying in Monterey through the latter part of November, according to orders, waiting for us. Day after day, Captain Faucon went up to the hill to look out for us, and at last, gave us up, thinking we must have gone down in the gale which we experienced off Point Conception, and which had blown with great fury over the whole coast, driving ashore several vessels in the snuggest ports. An English brig, which had put into San Francisco, lost both her anchors; the Rosa was driven upon a mud bank in San Diego; and the Pilgrim, with great difficulty, rode out the gale in Monterey, with three anchors a-head. She sailed early in December for San Diego and intermedios.

As we were to be here over Sunday, and Monterey was the best place to go ashore on the whole coast, and we had had no liberty-day for nearly three months, every one was for going ashore. On Sunday morning, as soon as the decks were washed, and we had got breakfast, those who had obtained liberty began to clean themselves, as it is called, to go ashore. A bucket of fresh water apiece, a cake of soap, a large coarse towel, and we went to work scrubbing one another, on the forecastle. Having gone through this, the next thing was to get

**...eight guns, (four of which we found to be Quakers,)...** That is, they were fake guns: wooden logs painted black and used to convince an enemy that a vessel was well-armed. The trick would be used fairly often during the Civil War, some 30 years later.

**...the ex-governor...** Ferdinand von Wrangel, once the governor of Russian America, had recently been relieved of his duties. He would now travel extensively, become minister of the Russian Navy, and eventually settle in Estonia. Von Wrangel was highly critical of the sale of Alaska to the United States.

**...Mazatlan, and . . . Vera Cruz.** Popular ports in Mexico.

**In the news**
**December, 1835**

Representatives of the Cherokee Nation sign the Treaty of New Echota, ceding all of the tribe's lands east of the Mississippi to the U.S. government. The treaty had been a long time coming. Although the tribe had by the 1830s developed its own written language and established a representative government, Georgia refused to recognize the tribe's autonomy and threatened to seize its lands. The Cherokees took their case to the U.S. Supreme Court and won, with Justice John Marshall ruling that the state of Georgia had no jurisdiction and no claim to the tribe's lands. Officials in Georgia simply ignored the decision, and President Jackson refused to enforce it. Many Cherokee resisted, noting that only a minority had approved the treaty. About 20,000 Cherokees were marched westward at gunpoint on what became known as The Trail of Tears. Nearly a quarter of the tribe died along the trail.

into the head,—one on each side—with a bucket apiece, and duck one another, by drawing up water and heaving over each other, while we were stripped to a pair of trowsers. Then came the rigging-up. The usual outfit of pumps, white stockings, loose white duck trowsers, blue jackets, clean checked shirts, black kerchiefs, hats well varnished, with a fathom of black ribbon over the left eye, a silk handkerchief flying from the outside jacket pocket, and four or five dollars tied up in the back of the neckerchief, and we were "all right." One of the quarter-boats pulled us ashore, and we steamed up to the town. I tried to find the church, in order to see the worship, but was told that there was no service, except a mass early in the morning; so we went about the town, visiting the Americans and English, and the natives whom we had known when we were here before. Toward noon we procured horses, and rode out to the Carmel mission, which is about a league from the town, where we got something in the way of a dinner—beef, eggs, frijoles, tortillas, and some middling wine—from the mayordomo, who, of course, refused to make any charge, as it was the Lord's gift, yet received our present, as a gratuity, with a low bow, a touch of the hat, and "Dios se lo pague!"

After this repast, we had a fine run, scouring the whole country on our fleet horses, and came into town soon after sundown. Here we found our companions who had refused to go to ride with us, thinking that a sailor has no more business with a horse than a fish has with a balloon. They were moored, stem and stern, in a grog-shop, making a great noise, with a crowd of Indians and hungry half-breeds about them, and with a fair prospect of being stripped and dirked, or left to pass the night in the calabozo. With a great deal of trouble, we managed to get them down to the boats, though not without many angry looks and interferences from the Spaniards, who had marked them out for their prey. The Diana's crew,—a set of worthless outcasts, who had been picked up at the islands from the refuse of whale-ships,—were all as drunk as beasts, and had a set-to, on the beach, with their captain, who was in no better state than themselves. They swore they would not go aboard,

**...the next thing was to get into the head...** To this day, a bathroom aboard a vessel is called a *head.* Originally the heads (plural to denote two areas, one on the weather side and one on the lee side) were simply grated (and thus easily cleaned) areas near the bow that the crew used as lavatories. Sailors always used the head on the lee side so that waste could fall clear into the ocean.

**...hats well varnished...** A helpful 1815 book lists several hundred "truly valuable receipts" (that is, recipes or formulae), including one explaining how to make "a black varnish for gentlemen's...hats." Varnish repelled water and also kept the hat stiff, enabling it to hold its shape.

In the news

**December, 1835**

José María Esparza and his family are advised to take refuge in the Alamo, since they are Tejanos, Mexican supporters of the Texans or Texians. This proves to be bad advice. Like most of the other defenders, Esparza is killed on March 6, 1836, when the Alamo is overrun. (His family survives, however.)

**...a sailor has no more business with a horse than a fish has with a balloon.** This is reminiscent of the sarcastic feminist slogan: "A woman needs a man like a fish needs a bicycle." (Sometimes rendered as "A woman without a man is like a fish without a bicycle.")

**...with a fair prospect of being stripped and dirked...** That is, robbed and possibly stabbed. (A dirk is a dagger or small sword.) This would not be the first time a drunken sailor was relieved of his wallet or purse.

and went back to the town, were stripped and beaten, and lodged in the calabozo, until the next day, when the captain bought them out. Our forecastle, as usual after a liberty-day, was a scene of tumult all night long, from the drunken ones. They had just got to sleep toward morning, when they were turned up with the rest, and kept at work all day in the water, carrying hides, their heads aching so that they could hardly stand. This is sailor's pleasure.

**This is sailor's pleasure.** Not really a pleasure, of course. But something with which a sailor learns to live if he intends to drink to excess the night before he's due back on duty.

In the news
**January, 1836**

In Illinois, a bill is introduced in the state legislature calling for the creation of a road from Peoria, through Pekin, and thence to the existing state road leading from Springfield to Peoria. The bill was introduced by Representative William Brown, but it was actually written by 27-year old Abraham Lincoln.

Nothing worthy of remark happened while we were here, except a little boxing-match on board our own ship, which gave us something to talk about. A broad-backed, big-headed Cape Cod boy, about sixteen years old, had been playing the bully, for the whole voyage, over a slender, delicate-looking boy, from one of the Boston schools, and over whom he had much the advantage, in strength, age, and experience in the ship's duty, for this was the first time the Boston boy had been on salt water. The latter, however, had "picked up his crumbs," was learning his duty, and getting strength and confidence daily; and began to assert his rights against his oppressor. Still, the other was his master, and, by his superior strength, always tackled with him and threw him down. One afternoon, before we were turned-to, these boys got into a violent squabble in the between-decks, when George (the Boston boy) said he would fight Nat, if he could have fair play. The chief mate heard the noise, dove down the hatchway, hauled them both up on deck, and told them to shake hands and have no more trouble for the voyage, or else they should fight till one gave in for beaten. Finding neither willing to make an offer for reconciliation, he called all hands up, (for the captain was ashore, and he could do as he chose aboard,) ranged the crew in the waist, marked a line on the deck, brought the two boys up to it, making them "toe the mark;" then made the bight of a rope fast to a belaying pin, and stretched it across the deck, bringing it just above their waists. "No striking below the rope!" And there they stood, one on each side of it, face to face, and went at it like two game-cocks. The Cape Cod boy, Nat, put in his double-fisters, starting the blood, and bringing the black and blue spots all over

**A broad-backed...Cape Cod boy...had been playing the bully...** The bully is most likely Nathaniel Prouty, listed in the records as an ordinary seaman hailing from Hingham. Although Dana says he's 16, the records indicate that he was 18 when he shipped; by this point, he's probably 19 years old. George is most likely George Somerby, who shipped out at age 15.

**...picked up his crumbs...** That is, he has grown. (Sometimes used to mean that one has grown fat or wealthy.) The word *crummy* was in the 19th century sometimes used to mean "grown fat" or "become rich."

**... made the bight of a rope fast to a belaying pin...** That is, looped the rope around a belaying pin, which is a short length of wood (or brass or iron) around which rigging is secured or belayed.

the face and arms of the other, whom we expected to see give in every moment: but the more he was hurt, the better he fought. Time after time he was knocked nearly down, but up he came again and faced the mark, as bold as a lion, again to take the heavy blows, which sounded so as to make one's heart turn with pity for him. At length he came up to the mark for the last time, his shirt torn from his body, his face covered with blood and bruises, and his eyes flashing fire, and swore he would stand there until one or the other was killed, and set-to like a young fury. "Hurrah in the bow!" said the men, cheering him on. "Well crowed!" "Never say die, while there's a shot in the locker!" Nat tried to close with him, knowing his advantage, but the mate stopped that, saying there should be fair play, and no fingering. Nat then came up to the mark, but looked white about the mouth, and his blows were not given with half the spirit of his first. He was evidently cowed. He had always been his master, and had nothing to gain, and everything to lose; while the other fought for honor and freedom, under a sense of wrong. It would not do. It was soon over. Nat gave in; not so much beaten, as cowed and mortified; and never afterwards tried to act the bully on board. We took George forward, washed him in the deck-tub, complimented his pluck, and from this time he became somebody on board, having fought himself into notice. Mr. Brown's plan had a good effect, for there was no more quarrelling among the boys for the rest of the voyage.

Wednesday, January 6th. Set sail from Monterey, with a number of Spaniards as passengers, and shaped our course for Santa Barbara. The Diana went out of the bay in company with us, but parted from us off Point Pinos, being bound to the Sandwich Islands. We had a smacking breeze for several hours, and went along at a great rate, until night, when it died away, as usual, and the land-breeze set in, which brought us upon a taut bowline. Among our passengers was a young man who was the best representation of a decayed gentleman I had ever seen. He reminded me much of some of the characters in Gil Blas. He was of the aristocracy of the country, his family being of pure Spanish blood, and

In the news
**January, 1836**

In Washington, DC, the House of Representatives considers a bill (H.R. 100) requesting an appropriation to be used to erect a "marine hospital" in the city of Baltimore. The bill passes, and the hospital—eventually known as the U.S. Public Health Hospital—is built.The facility is now part of Johns Hopkins.

In the news
**January, 1836**

Via an ad in a local paper, a Georgia sheriff offers for sale seized assets, including "...two negroes, to wit: Anderson, a boy about twelve years old, and also Priscilla, a girl about nine years old...." Later that month, the same newspaper carries an ad offering "For sale or to hire, a negro woman...accustomed to Cooking, Washing, and Ironing." The ad also notes that the (unnamed) woman "was previously considered a good field hand."

**... characters in Gil Blas.** A reference to a French novel, *Histoire de Gil Blas de Santillane*, by Alain-René Lesage. It depicts a hero who is something of a rogue and who lives by his wits. In this genre, called *picaresque*, we actually root for the rogue, partly because the society in which he lives is portrayed as corrupt, so it deserves to be taken advantage of, and in part because the rogue is himself a lovable—and essentially good-hearted—character.

once of great importance in Mexico. His father had been governor of the province, and having amassed a large property, settled at San Diego, where he built a large house with a court-yard in front, kept a great retinue of Indians, and set up for the grandee of that part of the country. His son was sent to Mexico, where he received the best education, and went into the first society of the capital. Misfortune, extravagance, and the want of funds, or any manner of getting interest on money, soon eat the estate up, and Don Juan Bandini returned from Mexico accomplished, poor, and proud, and without any office or occupation, to lead the life of most young men of the better families—dissolute and extravagant when the means are at hand; ambitious at heart, and impotent in act; often pinched for bread; keeping up an appearance of style, when their poverty is known to each half-naked Indian boy in the street, and they stand in dread of every small trader and shopkeeper in the place. He had a slight and elegant figure, moved gracefully, danced and waltzed beautifully, spoke the best of Castilian, with a pleasant and refined voice and accent, and had, throughout, the bearing of a man of high birth and figure. Yet here he was, with his passage given him, (as I afterwards learned,) for he had not the means of paying for it, and living upon the charity of our agent. He was polite to every one, spoke to the sailors, and gave four reáls—I dare say the last he had in his pocket—to the steward, who waited upon him. I could not but feel a pity for him, especially when I saw him by the side of his fellow-passenger and townsman, a fat, coarse, vulgar, pretending fellow of a Yankee trader, who had made money in San Diego, and was eating out the very vitals of the Bandinis, fattening upon their extravagance, grinding them in their poverty; having mortgages on their lands, forestalling their cattle, and already making an inroad upon their jewels, which were their last hope.

Don Juan had with him a retainer, who was as much like many of the characters in Gil Blas as his master. He called himself a private secretary, though there was no writing for him to do, and he lived in the steerage with the carpenter and sailmaker. He was certainly a charac-

**...ambitious at heart, and impotent in act...** An interesting phrase. We all know those who aspire to greatness, but who never actually work to achieve it; they have grand plans that, because they lack either means or commitment, will never be achieved. Near the end of his life, Dana comes to feel that he himself turned out to be "impotent in act." That is, he had expected greatness from himself—largely in the form of a political career leading to honorable (and honored) statesmanship. That never happened, and Dana lived his later years worried that the only thing he'd done of any import was to write this book. (To some degree, that may indeed be the case. But the book was a classic: It helped launch a genre—*Moby Dick* would certainly not have existed without it—and it helped vast numbers of merchant seamen whose treatment was improved by Dana's work.)

**Don Juan Bandini...** Juan Bandini was, technically, the inspector of customs at San Diego, so although his circumstances are greatly reduced, it's not as if he were a vagrant.

**...a Yankee trader...** These are harsh words indeed. The man's name is Henry Fitch. A later (1840-1842) visitor to San Diego also met Fitch and noted that he was indeed both fat and a trader, but also called him honest and kind-hearted. The later visitor commented that perhaps Dana didn't like Fitch because Dana, he said, "entered Fitch's house intoxicated and was kicked out!"

**In the news**

**January, 1836**

Back in Boston, Samuel T. Armstrong, a Whig bookseller-turned-politician, becomes mayor of the city. Armstrong had previously been the governor of Massachusetts, having taken over when then-governor John Davis resigned to take his recently won senate seat.

ter; could read and write extremely well; spoke good Spanish; had been all over Spanish America, and lived in every possible situation, and served in every conceivable capacity, though generally in that of confidential servant to some man of figure. I cultivated this man's acquaintance, and during the five weeks that he was with us,—for he remained on board until we arrived at San Diego,—I gained a greater knowledge of the state of political parties in Mexico, and the habits and affairs of the different classes of society, than I could have learned from almost any one else. He took great pains in correcting my Spanish, and supplying me with colloquial phrases, and common terms and exclamations in speaking. He lent me a file of late newspapers from the city of Mexico, which were full of triumphal receptions of Santa Ana, who had just returned from Tampico after a victory, and with the preparations for his expedition against the Texans. "Viva Santa Ana!" was the by-word everywhere, and it had even reached California, though there were still many here, among whom was Don Juan Bandini, who were opposed to his government, and intriguing to bring in Bustamente. Santa Ana, they said, was for breaking down the missions; or, as they termed it—"Santa Ana no quiere religion." Yet I had no doubt that the office of administrador of San Diego would reconcile Don Juan to any dynasty, and any state of the church. In these papers, too, I found scraps of American and English news; but which were so unconnected, and I was so ignorant of everything preceding them for eighteen months past, that they only awakened a curiosity which they could not satisfy. One article spoke of Taney as Justicia Mayor de los Estados Unidos, (what had become of Marshall? was he dead, or banished?) and another made known, by news received from Vera Cruz, that "El Vizconde Melbourne" had returned to the office of "primer ministro," in place of Sir Roberto Peel. (Sir Robert Peel had been minister, then? and where were Earl Grey and the Duke of Wellington?) Here were the outlines of a grand parliamentary overturn, the filling up of which I could imagine at my leisure.

In the news
**January, 1836**

Betsy Ross (Elizabeth Griscom), the seamstress widely (but perhaps incorrectly) credited with designing and sewing the first American flag, dies in Philadelphia. Ross was the 8th of 17 children born to devout Quakers Samuel and Rebecca Griscom. In 1773, Betsy married John Ross, the son of an Episcopalian church official; the interdenominational marriage caused a permanent break with Ross's family. Legend (occasionally disputed or possibly overstated) has it that, after John died in an explosion at an ammunition depot, Betsy met with George Washington, George Ross (no relation), and Robert Morris, to discuss the design and sewing of the first flag.

**...still many here, among whom was Don Juan Bandini, who were opposed to his government, and intriguing to bring in Bustamente.** When Santa Anna fails to prevent the Texas revolution (see "In the news" sidebars), Bustamente does in fact become president of Mexico. It was true that "Santa Ana no quiere religion" ("Santa Ana does not want religion"), at least in the sense that the general wanted to completely secularize the missions, but implying that Santa Anna was simply against religion in general is probably overstating things.

**One article spoke of Taney as Justicia Mayor de los Estados Unidos...** Yes, Justice Marshall had in fact died (see the sidebars), and Taney had become Chief Justice of the U.S. Supreme Court.

The second morning after leaving Monterey, we were off Point Conception. It was a bright, sunny day, and the wind, though strong, was fair; and everything was in striking contrast with our experience in the same place two months before, when we were drifting off from a northwester under a fore and main spencer. "Sail ho!" cried a man who was rigging out a top-gallant studding-sail boom.—"Where away?"—"Weather beam, sir!" and in a few minutes a full-rigged brig was seen standing out from under Point Conception. The studding-sail halyards were let go, and the yards boom-ended, the after yards braced aback, and we waited her coming down. She rounded to, backed her main top-sail, and showed her decks full of men, four guns on a side, hammock nettings, and everything man-of-war fashion, except that there was no boatswain's whistle, and no uniforms on the quarter-deck. A short, square-built man, in a rough grey jacket, with a speaking-trumpet in hand, stood in the weather hammock nettings. "Ship ahoy!"—"Hallo!"—"What ship is that, pray?"—"Alert."—"Where are you from, pray?" etc., etc. She proved to be the brig Convoy, from the Sandwich Islands, engaged in otter hunting, among the islands which lie along the coast. Her armament was from her being an illegal trader. The otter are very numerous among these islands, and being of great value, the government require a heavy sum for a license to hunt them, and lay a high duty upon every one shot or carried out of the country. This vessel had no license, and paid no duty, besides being engaged in smuggling goods on board other vessels trading on the coast, and belonging to the same owners in Oahu. Our captain told him to look out for the Mexicans, but he said they had not an armed vessel of his size in the whole Pacific. This was without doubt the same vessel that showed herself off Santa Barbara a few months before. These vessels frequently remain on the coast for years, without making port, except at the islands for wood and water, and an occasional visit to Oahu for a new outfit.

Sunday, January 10th. Arrived at Santa Barbara, and on the following Wednesday, slipped our cable and

### In the news
### January, 1836

James Gillespie Birney, a former slave-owner who has become a virulent abolitionist, starts an anti-slavery newspaper in Ohio, the *Cincinnati Weekly and Abolitionist*. The paper aims anti-slavery propaganda at Kentucky slave-owners across the Ohio River. This angers Cincinnati businessmen hoping to do business with the Kentuckians. The result, a few months later, is a riot that is quelled only when the governor declares martial law.

**"Where away?"–"Weather beam, sir!"** That is, "Where is the ship you spotted?" And the answer: "Off to the side of your vessel facing the wind."

**...everything man-of-war fashion, except that there was...no uniforms on the quarter-deck.** The *Convoy* is rigged and manned as a warship, even sporting eight cannon. This turns out to be because the vessel engages in illegal trade, having no licenses and skipping out on the duties owed at her various ports of call.

**...he said they had not an armed vessel of his size in the whole Pacific.** The captain (whose name is Alpheus B. Thompson) is very likely correct. *Convoy* was a well-armed 137-ton brig with a crew of 13. She had little to fear from the Mexican navy.

**...slipped our cable and went to sea, on account of a south-easter.** We're once more reminded that, during a storm, a ship is generally safer at sea rather than anchored near shore, where she could be driven upon the rocks. In this case, *Alert* slips her cable, leaving the cable and anchor or other ground tackle where it is, since she plans to return.

**...G— De N— y C—, youngest daughter of Don Antonio N—...** The agent plans to marry Donna Maria de la Guerra y Noriega. Dana is a bit confused here, because Donna is actually not the youngest daughter of Jose de la Guerra y Noriega. Instead, it appears that the agent, Alfred Robinson, married the third sister, Anita (also called Anna—or Ana—Maria). (The fourth sister was named María Antonia, not Donna.) Don Antonio was definitely a grandee—in Spanish, a nobleman. By the time of the marriage, Guerra y Noriega has retired from the army and from political office, and owns some 1/2 million acres of land in what are now Santa Barbara, Sacramento, Ventura, and other counties in modern-day California.

**In the news**
**January, 1836**

A Vermont newspaper carries an ad from Pangborn & Brinsmaid for "elegant otter caps" made of the skins that were widely traded on the California coast (a trade mentioned several times by Dana) and then brought back to New England. (The mercantile partnership will survive in Burlington, VT until 1843, when the company will become simply Brinsmaid's.)

**Twenty-three guns followed...** Most of us have heard of a 21-gun salute, the so-called Royal Salute, normally reserved for the most important recipients. (Presidents, for example, are so saluted.) Dana may simply have miscounted, or perhaps there was at the time some other significance attached to a salute of 23 guns. (The salute is always an odd number, though. The tradition of cannon salute evolved because firing a cannon out to sea for no reason disarmed the vessel—or at least that gun—and was thus a gesture of trust and respect.)

went to sea, on account of a south-easter. Returned to our anchorage the next day. We were the only vessel in the port. The Pilgrim had passed through the Canal and hove-to off the town, nearly six weeks before, on her passage down from Monterey, and was now at the leeward. She heard here of our safe arrival at San Francisco.

Great preparations were making on shore for the marriage of our agent, who was to marry Donna Anneta De G—— De N—— y C——, youngest daughter of Don Antonio N——, the grandee of the place, and the head of the first family in California. Our steward was ashore three days, making pastry and cake, and some of the best of our stores were sent off with him. On the day appointed for the wedding, we took the captain ashore in the gig, and had orders to come for him at night, with leave to go up to the house and see the fandango. Returning on board, we found preparations making for a salute. Our guns were loaded and run out, men appointed to each, cartridges served out, matches lighted, and all the flags ready to be run up. I took my place at the starboard after gun, and we all waited for the signal from on shore. At ten o'clock the bride went up with her sister to the confessional, dressed in deep black. Nearly an hour intervened, when the great doors of the mission church opened, the bells rang out a loud, discordant peal, the private signal for us was run up by the captain ashore, the bride, dressed in complete white, came out of the church with the bridegroom, followed by a long procession. Just as she stepped from the church door, a small white cloud issued from the bows of our ship, which was full in sight, the loud report echoed among the surrounding hills and over the bay, and instantly the ship was dressed in flags and pennants from stem to stern. Twenty-three guns followed in regular succession, with an interval of fifteen seconds between each when the cloud cleared away, and the ship lay dressed in her colors, all day. At sun-down, another salute of the same number of guns was fired, and all the flags run down. This we thought was pretty well—a gun every fifteen seconds—for a merchantman with only four guns and a dozen or twenty men.

After supper, the gig's crew were called, and we rowed ashore, dressed in our uniform, beached the boat, and went up to the fandango. The bride's father's house was the principal one in the place, with a large court in front, upon which a tent was built, capable of containing several hundred people. As we drew near, we heard the accustomed sound of violins and guitars, and saw a great motion of the people within. Going in, we found nearly all the people of the town—men, women, and children—collected and crowded together, leaving barely room for the dancers; for on these occasions no invitations are given, but every one is expected to come, though there is always a private entertainment within the house for particular friends. The old women sat down in rows, clapping their hands to the music, and applauding the young ones. The music was lively, and among the tunes, we recognized several of our popular airs, which we, without doubt, have taken from the Spanish. In the dancing, I was much disappointed. The women stood upright, with their hands down by their sides, their eyes fixed upon the ground before them, and slided about without any perceptible means of motion; for their feet were invisible, the hem of their dresses forming a perfect circle about them, reaching to the ground. They looked as grave as though they were going through some religious ceremony, their faces as little excited as their limbs; and on the whole, instead of the spirited, fascinating Spanish dances which I had expected, I found the Californian fandango, on the part of the women at least, a lifeless affair. The men did better. They danced with grace and spirit, moving in circles round their nearly stationary partners, and showing their figures to great advantage.

A great deal was said about our friend Don Juan Bandini, and when he did appear, which was toward the close of the evening, he certainly gave us the most graceful dancing that I had ever seen. He was dressed in white pantaloons neatly made, a short jacket of dark silk, gaily figured, white stockings and thin morocco slippers upon his very small feet. His slight and graceful figure was well calculated for dancing, and he moved about with the grace and daintiness of a young fawn.

**...went up to the fandango.** Originally the fandango was an erotic courtship dance, but in English the term eventually came to signify any dance or large party.

**In the news**

**January, 1836**

Captain James Barron brings to a U.S. House committee a proposal for a ship that is in essence a giant, floating battering ram. The committee notes that the idea came from an incident more than a decade before when a whaling ship, the *Essex*, "was struck multiple times by a whale." Barron claims that, "The proof of the effects made by a whale on the ship *Essex*...are conclusive that no construction of a ship now known, could resist the shock by a vessel like the ram." The House rejects the prow ship authorization bill, so Barron writes directly (and futilely) to President Andrew Jackson, saying that he was convinced he had "long been excluded from any participation in the concerns of the affairs of the Navy, and cannot but consider that [I have] been subject to an unnatural and cruel degree of persecution." He noted that his appeal was to "the heart of a hero" (i.e., Jackson) who would "know but how to appreciate the feelings of an officer." (Note that the tale of the whale attacking the *Essex* is said to have inspired Herman Melville's writing of *Moby Dick*.)

**...appeared to be rather repressing a strong tendency to motion.** Don Bandini is one of those men who can move about seemingly without effort, and the dance is one that benefits from that illusion.

**...a very few of the "gente de razón"...** As noted earlier, the term refers to Hispanic (as opposed to Native American) people, and means "people of reason." The implication is that people other than Hispanics were not capable of reason, that is, they were somehow less than human.

**... the sister of the bride...** Actually, there is no sister named Donna. The four daughters were, in order of birth, Teresa, Augustias, Anita (also known as Anna Maria), and María Antonia. (In 1847, Augustias will marry Dr. Santiago Ord, a U.S. citizen living in Washington, D.C. and visiting California. After marrying Augustias, Dr. Ord and his wife lived in Monterey, where he practiced medicine. Tragically, Anna Maria died just a year after the marriage.) Dana's occasional errors are understandable: Keep in mind that the Spanish naming conventions were somewhat confusing, nicknames and endearments abounded, and that Dana is working years later and largely without notes.

**... to me, offensive figures...** Offensive because, to the "civilized" Dana, they were unacceptably erotic.

In the news
**January, 1836**

In one of the nation's first domestic abuse trials, a jury in Muncy, PA, takes less than one hour to convict John Earls of poisoning his wife, Catharine, by placing arsenic in her hot chocolate. Earls, who had been having an affair with one Maria Moritz, had previously attempted to murder his wife by placing arsenic in an apple. Earls is hanged in May of 1836.

An occasional touch of the toe to the ground, seemed all that was necessary to give him a long interval of motion in the air. At the same time he was not fantastic or flourishing, but appeared to be rather repressing a strong tendency to motion. He was loudly applauded, and danced frequently toward the close of the evening. After the supper, the waltzing began, which was confined to a very few of the "gente de razón," and was considered a high accomplishment, and a mark of aristocracy. Here, too, Don Juan figured greatly, waltzing with the sister of the bride, (Donna Angustia, a handsome woman and a general favorite,) in a variety of beautiful, but, to me, offensive figures, which lasted as much as half an hour, no one else taking the floor. They were repeatedly and loudly applauded, the old men and women jumping out of their seats in admiration, and the young people waving their hats and handkerchiefs. Indeed among people of the character of these Mexicans, the waltz seemed to me to have found its right place. The great amusement of the evening,—which I suppose was owing to its being carnival—was the breaking of eggs filled with cologne, or other essences, upon the heads of the company. One end of the egg is broken and the inside taken out, then it is partly filled with cologne, and the whole sealed up. The women bring a great number of these secretly about them, and the amusement is to break one upon the head of a gentleman when his back is turned. He is bound in gallantry to find out the lady and return the compliment, though it must not be done if the person sees you. A tall, stately Don, with immense grey whiskers, and a look of great importance, was standing before me, when I felt a light hand on my shoulder, and turning round, saw Donna Angustia, (whom we all knew, as she had been up to Monterey, and down again, in the Alert,) with her finger upon her lip, motioning me gently aside. I stepped back a little, when she went up behind the Don, and with one hand knocked off his huge sombrero, and at the same instant, with the other, broke the egg upon his head, and springing behind me, was out of sight in a moment. The Don turned slowly round, the cologne, running down his face, and over his clothes, and a loud laugh breaking out from every quarter. He looked round in vain, for some time, until the direction of so many laughing eyes showed him the fair offender. She was his niece, and a great favorite with him, so old Don Domingo had to join in the laugh. A great many such tricks were played, and many a war of sharp manoeuvering was carried on between couples of the younger people, and at every successful exploit a general laugh was raised.

Another singular custom I was for some time at a loss about. A pretty young girl was dancing, named, after what would appear to us the sacrilegious custom of the country—Espiritu Santo, when a young man went behind her and placed his hat directly upon her head, letting it fall down over her eyes, and sprang back among the crowd. She danced for some time with the hat on, when she threw it off, which called forth a general shout; and the young man was obliged to go out upon the floor and pick it up. Some of the ladies, upon whose heads hats had been placed, threw them off at once, and a few kept them on throughout the dance, and took them off at the end, and held them out in their hands, when the owner stepped out, bowed, and took it from them. I soon began to suspect the meaning of the thing, and was afterward told that it was a compliment, and an offer to become the lady's gallant for the rest of the evening, and to wait upon her home. If the hat was thrown off, the offer was refused, and the gentleman was obliged to pick up his hat amid a general laugh. Much amusement was caused sometimes by gentlemen putting hats on the ladies' heads, without permitting them to see whom it was done by. This obliged them to throw them off, or keep them on at a venture, and when they came to discover the owner, the laugh was often turned upon them. The captain sent for us about ten o'clock, and we went aboard in high spirits, having enjoyed the new scene much, and were of great importance among the crew, from having so much to tell, and from the prospect of going every night until it was over; for these fandangos generally last three days. The next day, two of us were sent up to the town, and took care to come back by way of Capitan Noriego's and take a look into the booth. The musicians were still there,

**...sharp manoeuvering was carried on between couples of the younger people...** In a conservative (some would say sexually repressed) society in which it would be unheard of for young men and women to be left alone together, this game (and similar ones at like gatherings) serves the purpose of allowing young people to flirt harmlessly and to meet and get to know members of the opposite sex.

**...Espiritu Santo...** The Holy Ghost or The Holy Spirit. The dance constitutes a sanctioned (and safely chaperoned) form of flirting in which the young woman is able to let the man know if she's open to his advances.

In the news
**January, 1836**

Radical abolitionist John Brown settles in Ohio. He becomes a "stationmaster" in the Underground Railroad, and his hatred of slavery—and of slave-owners—leads him to speak out against the institution. Brown eventually leads a violent anti-slavery revolt, culminating in a failed attack on the federal arsenal at Harper's Ferry, VA. Found guilty of murder and treason, Brown is hanged in December of 1859.

**...these fandangos generally last three days.** They did indeed last for three days—and nights. One earlier writer described the fandango as consisting "principally in drinking brandy and wine, intermixed with [what seemed to him] indecent and scandalous motions and gestures...." The party sometimes became boisterous, and quarrels were not uncommon.

**...took care to come back by way of Capitan Noriego's...** Dana made sure to drop by the scene of the party on his way back.

In the news
**January, 1836**

Queen Emma, of the recently unified Hawaiian islands, is born. Emma Kalanikaumakaamano Kaleleonālani Naʻea Rooke was the consort of King Kamehameha IV. Emma was a respected leader and a close friend of Britain's Queen Victoria. After her husband's death, Emma ran for chief monarch against King David Kalākaua, but lost.

**...we thought they had had enough of Yankee grace.** Meaning of course, that the yankees—including the agent, Robinson—were anything but graceful, especially when compared to the elegant Spaniards.

**...getting into a high-go...** A high-go is a frolic or a bout of merriment. Although common in 19th century usage, the word is now obsolete. Perhaps the word "spree" comes close to the same meaning. Note that a "high go" (as defined in an 1851 book about college customs) seems always to involve drinking. Imagine that

In the news
**January, 1836**

Botanist Miles Joseph Berkeley coins the term "mycology" to describe the study of fungi. Because if you're going to study fungus . . . well, you have to call it *something*. (Note that this is *not* the Berkeley after whom the city of Berkeley, CA was named. That honor goes to Anglo-Irish philosopher George Berkeley.)

upon their platform, scraping and twanging away, and a few people, apparently of the lower classes, were dancing. The dancing is kept up, at intervals, throughout the day, but the crowd, the spirit, and the élite, come in at night. The next night, which was the last, we went ashore in the same manner, until we got almost tired of the monotonous twang of the instruments, the drawling sounds which the women kept up, as an accompaniment, and the slapping of the hands in time with the music, in place of castanets. We found ourselves as great objects of attention as any persons or anything at the place. Our sailor dresses—and we took great pains to have them neat and shipshape—were much admired, and we were invited, from every quarter, to give them an American sailor's dance; but after the ridiculous figure some of our countrymen cut, in dancing after the Spaniards, we thought it best to leave it to their imaginations. Our agent, with a tight, black, swallow-tailed coat, just imported from Boston, a high stiff cravat, looking as if he had been pinned and skewered, with only his feet and hands left free, took the floor just after Bandini; and we thought they had had enough of Yankee grace.

The last night they kept it up in great style, and were getting into a high-go, when the captain called us off to go aboard, for, it being south-easter season, he was afraid to remain on shore long; and it was well he did not, for that very night, we slipped our cables, as a crowner to our fun ashore, and stood off before a south-easter, which lasted twelve hours, and returned to our anchorage the next day.

## CHAPTER XXVIII

## AN OLD FRIEND—A VICTIM—CALIFORNIA RANGERS—NEWS FROM HOME—LAST LOOKS

Monday, Feb. 1st. After having been in port twenty-one days, we sailed for San Pedro, where we arrived on the following day, having gone "all fluking," with the weather clew of the mainsail hauled up, the yards braced in a little, and the lower studding-sails just drawing; the wind hardly shifting a point during the passage. Here we found the Ayacucho and the Pilgrim, which last we had not seen since the 11th of September,—nearly five months; and I really felt something like an affection for the old brig which had been my first home, and in which I had spent nearly a year, and got the first rough and tumble of a sea life. She, too, was associated, in my mind with Boston, the wharf from which we sailed, anchorage in the stream, leave-taking, and all such matters, which were now to me like small links connecting me with another world, which I had once been in, and which, please God, I might yet see again. I went on board the first night, after supper; found the old cook in the galley, playing upon the fife which I had given him, as a parting present; had a hearty shake of the hand from him; and dove down into the forecastle, where were my old ship-mates, the same as ever, glad to see me; for they had nearly given us up as lost, especially when they did not find us in Santa Barbara. They had been at San Diego last, had been lying at San Pedro nearly a month, and had received three thousand hides from the pueblo. These were taken from her the next day, which filled us up, and we both got under weigh on the 4th, she bound up to San Francisco again, and we to San Diego, where we arrived on the 6th.

We were always glad to see San Diego; it being the depot, and a snug little place, and seeming quite like home, especially to me, who had spent a summer there. There was no vessel in port, the Rosa having sailed for Valparaiso and Cadiz, and the Catalina for Callao, nearly a month before. We discharged our hides, and in four

**...having gone "all fluking," with the weather clew of the mainsail hauled up...** That is, running free before the wind. Dana notes that the wind barely shifted during the passage, so the vessel, once rigging and sails were set, could remain on course with very little work on the part of the crew.

**In the news**
**January, 1836**

Ohio teacher William Holmes McGuffey signs a contract with publishers Truman and Smith for the creation of four readers to be used in elementary grades. The result is the *McGuffey's Readers*, a series of books (not all of them actually written by William McGuffey, of course) that between 1836 and 1960 sold some 120 million copies or more.

**...and which, please God, I might yet see again.** Dana repeatedly reminds us that he wishes to return to his more sophisticated roots, and that this stint as a sailor is meant to be temporary. He truly does fear that he might never see his old life again, either due to mischance during the voyage or else due simply to the fact that he had spent so long at sea that he was now fit for nothing else.

**...the Catalina for Callao...** Dana is most likely referring to the port city in Peru, located just west of Lima.

days were ready to sail again for the windward; and, to our great joy—for the last time! Over thirty thousand hides had been already collected, cured, and stowed away in the house, which, together with what we should collect, and the Pilgrim would bring down from San Francisco, would make out her cargo. The thought that we were actually going up for the last time, and that the next time we went round San Diego point it would be "homeward bound," brought things so near a close, that we felt as though we were just there, though it must still be the greater part of a year before we could see Boston.

**...hides had been already collected, cured, and stowed away in the house...** The *Alert*'s cargo is ultimately to consist of some 40,000 valuable hides. If each hide weighed 25 pounds (a conservative estimate), then the ship would head for home carrying about 1 million pounds of cargo.

In the news
**February, 1835**

The Texas rebellion is heating up. William Barret Travis, commander of The Alamo, writes a letter in which he vows never to retreat from or surrender to the Mexican army. (A contemporary copy of that letter, made for distribution at the time, was recently sold for almost $300,000. The original remains in the archives of the Texas State Library in Austin.)

I spent one evening, as had been my custom, at the oven with the Sandwich Islanders; but it was far from being the usual noisy, laughing time. It has been said, that the greatest curse to each of the South Sea islands, was the first man who discovered it; and every one who knows anything of the history of our commerce in those parts, knows how much truth there is in this; and that the white men, with their vices, have brought in diseases before unknown to the islanders, and which are now sweeping off the native population of the Sandwich Islands, at the rate of one fortieth of the entire population annually. They seem to be a doomed people. The curse of a people calling themselves Christian, seems to follow them everywhere; and even here, in this obscure place, lay two young islanders, whom I had left strong, active young men, in the vigor of health, wasting away under a disease, which they would never have known but for their intercourse with Christianized Mexico and people from Christian America. One of them was not so ill; and was moving about, smoking his pipe, and talking, and trying to keep up his spirits; but the other, who was my friend, and Aikane—Hope, was the most dreadful object I had ever seen in my life: his eyes sunken and dead, his cheeks fallen in against his teeth, his hands looking like claws; a dreadful cough, which seemed to rack his whole shattered system, a hollow whispering voice, and an entire inability to move himself. There he lay, upon a mat, on the ground, which was the only floor of the oven, with no medicine, no comforts, and no one to care for, or help him, but a few

**...the greatest curse to each of the South Sea islands, was the first man who discovered it...** Not surprisingly, by this Dana means the first *white* or *European* man. The islands themselves had been inhabited by Polynesians who traveled there in canoes between AD 300 and AD 800. Tahitians may have come somewhat later to what became known during Dana's time as "the Sandwich Islands." Dana's "first man" may have been Captain James Cook, who came upon the islands in 1778 while seeking a "Northwest Passage" between Alaska and Asia. (Some sources note that Spanish explorers may have beaten Cook to the islands.)

**They seem to be a doomed people.** In a way, Dana is quite literally correct here. When Cook arrived, the population of the islands stood at somewhere between 300,000 and 400,000. Over the next century, the native population dropped as much as 90%, due mainly to the impact of foreign diseases to which the natives had no resistance.

Kanakas, who were willing enough, but could do nothing. The sight of him made me sick, and faint. Poor fellow! During the four months that I lived upon the beach, we were continually together, both in work, and in our excursions in the woods, and upon the water. I really felt a strong affection for him, and preferred him to any of my own countrymen there; and I believe there was nothing which he would not have done for me. When I came into the oven he looked at me, held out his hand, and said, in a low voice, but with a delightful smile, "Aloha, Aikane! Aloha nui!" I comforted him as well as I could, and promised to ask the captain to help him from the medicine-chest, and told him I had no doubt the captain would do what he could for him, as he had worked in our employ for several years, both on shore and aboard our vessels on the coast. I went aboard and turned into my hammock, but I could not sleep.

**The sight of him made me sick, and faint.** Dana had come to love the kanakas with whom he had worked and lived. The sight of his friend simply waiting to die for lack of medicine is almost more than he can bear.

**"Aloha, Aikane! Aloha nui!"** "Hello, Friend! Hello, good [literally, *large*] friend."

**I comforted him as well as I could...** In later editions of the book, Dana comments here about "the wickedness of the beach, which was habitual...and not to be escaped from." This may indicate that the man's condition was due either to a venereal disease or to drink, or to a combination of the two.

Thinking, from my education, that I must have some knowledge of medicine, the Kanakas had insisted upon my examining him carefully; and it was not a sight to be forgotten. One of our crew, an old man-of-war's man, of twenty years' standing, who had seen sin and suffering in every shape, and whom I afterwards took to see Hope, said it was dreadfully worse than anything he had ever seen, or even dreamed of. He was horror-struck, as his countenance showed; yet he had been among the worst cases in our naval hospitals. I could not get the thought of the poor fellow out of my head all night; his horrible suffering, and his apparently inevitable, horrible end.

## In the news
### February, 1836

The Mexican army, under General Antonio López de Santa Anna, besieges the defenders of San Antonio, who occupy the Alamo (the name of which came from the cottonwood grove in which the chapel was based). The defenders, said to have numbered fewer than 200 men, hold their positions for 13 days until they are attacked by the 3,000 Mexican troops that surrounded them. Some 183 men are killed, while Santa Anna is said to have spared the handful of women and children that were there. William B. Travis's slave, Joe, also survived.

The next day I told the captain of Hope's state, and asked him if he would be so kind as to go and see him.

"What? a d——d Kanaka?"

"Yes, sir," said I; "but he has worked four years for our vessels, and has been in the employ of our owners, both on shore and aboard."

"Oh! he be d——d!" said the captain, and walked off.

**"Oh! he be d——d!" said the captain...** Here Dana is being discreet, abbreviating *damn* and *damned*, as befits a gentleman of his standing and of that time.

**This same man died afterwards of a fever on the deadly coast of Sumatra; and God grant he had better care taken of him in his sufferings, than he ever gave to any one else!** Recall that at this point, the captain of the *Alert* is Francis Thompson, a man who has many times proven that he cares little for his men. He cares even less for a "damned kanaka." Thompson does indeed die of a fever in Sumatra only a short time later (1837).

**...although a driving fellow, and a taught hand in a watch, he had good feelings...** Brown is a tough, gruff man, but unlike the captain, he is kindhearted enough to find medicine for Hope, who was, after all, employed by the *Alert*.

**... any chance was worth running.** Hope is so very ill that there is really nothing to be lost by trying the medicines, some of which were quite harsh. Calomel is a cathartic, a strong purgative used to stimulate evacuation of the bowels.

### In the news
### February, 1836

The theory of glacier movement (often called *glacial motion*) is given a boost when botanist Karl Schimper, studying mosses in Bavaria, begins to wonder about the origin of the boulders on which the moss is growing. He ultimately concludes that the boulders must have come from higher up in the Alps and had been transferred by the movement of glacial ice.

This same man died afterwards of a fever on the deadly coast of Sumatra; and God grant he had better care taken of him in his sufferings, than he ever gave to any one else! Finding nothing was to be got from the captain, I consulted an old shipmate, who had much experience in these matters, and got from him a recipe, which he always kept by him. With this I went to the mate, and told him the case. Mr. Brown had been entrusted with the general care of the medicine-chest, and although a driving fellow, and a taut hand in a watch, he had good feelings, and was always inclined to be kind to the sick. He said that Hope was not strictly one of the crew, but as he was in our employ when taken sick, he should have the medicines; and he got them and gave them to me, with leave to go ashore at night. Nothing could exceed the delight of the Kanakas, when I came bringing the medicines. All their terms of affection and gratitude were spent upon me, and in a sense wasted, (for I could not understand half of them,) yet they made all known by their manner. Poor Hope was so much revived at the bare thought of anything's being done for him, that he was already stronger and better. I knew he must die as he was, and he could but die under the medicines, and any chance was worth running. An oven, exposed to every wind and change of weather, is no place to take calomel; but nothing else would do, and strong remedies must be used, or he was gone. The applications, internal and external, were powerful, and I gave him strict directions to keep warm and sheltered, telling him it was his only chance for life. Twice, after this, I visited him, having only time to run up, while waiting in the boat. He promised to take his medicines regularly until we returned, and insisted upon it that he was doing better.

We got under weigh on the 10th, bound up to San Pedro, and had three days of calm and head winds, making but little progress. On the fourth, we took a stiff south-easter, which obliged us to reef our topsails. While on the yard, we saw a sail on the weather bow, and in about half an hour, passed the Ayacucho, under double-reefed topsails, beating down to San Diego.

Arrived at San Pedro on the fourth day, and came-to in the old place, a league from shore, with no other vessel in port, and the prospect of three weeks, or more, of dull life, rolling goods up a slippery hill, carrying hides on our heads over sharp stones, and, perhaps, slipping for a south-easter.

There was but one man in the only house here, and him I shall always remember as a good specimen of a California ranger. He had been a tailor in Philadelphia, and getting intemperate and in debt, he joined a trapping party and went to the Columbia river, and thence down to Monterey, where he spent everything, left his party, and came to the Pueblo de los Angelos, to work at his trade. Here he went dead to leeward among the pulperias, gambling rooms, etc., and came down to San Pedro, to be moral by being out of temptation. He had been in the house several weeks, working hard at his trade, upon orders which he had brought with him, and talked much of his resolution, and opened his heart to us about his past life. After we had been here some time, he started off one morning, in fine spirits, well dressed, to carry the clothes which he had been making to the pueblo, and saying he would bring back his money and some fresh orders the next day. The next day came, and a week passed, and nearly a fortnight, when, one day, going ashore, we saw a tall man, who looked like our friend the tailor, getting out of the back of an Indian's cart, which had just come down from the pueblo. He stood for the house, but we bore up after him; when finding that we were overhauling him, he hove-to and spoke us. Such a sight I never saw before. Barefooted, with an old pair of trowsers tied round his waist by a piece of green hide, a soiled cotton shirt, and a torn Indian hat; "cleaned out," to the last reál, and completely "used up." He confessed the whole matter; acknowledged that he was on his back; and now he had a prospect of a fit of the horrors for a week, and of being worse than useless for months. This is a specimen of the life of half of the Americans and English who are adrift over the whole of California. One of the same stamp was Russell, who was master of the hide-house at San Diego, while I was there, and afterwards turned

**...the prospect of three weeks, or more, of dull life, rolling goods up a slippery hill...** Dana has little to look forward to here, other than a great deal of hard work. He is buoyed, though, by the thought that this will be the last time he engages in this sort of backbreaking labor, since the *Alert* should be heading back to Boston soon.

**...a good specimen of a California ranger.** Briefly there existed a statewide law enforcement agency called the California Rangers (organized in 1853 and disbanded later that year), but that is of course not what Dana means here. Since the 16th century, a ranger has been a rake or a wanderer. That is, someone of little means who is up to no good and who has no permanent home. The man is essentially what we might call a bum.

**Here he went dead to leeward among the pulperias....** That is, he gave in to the temptations of the bars and gambling halls, as a ship might be blown by the wind.

In the news
**February, 1836**

Samuel Colt patents the first revolver. (But see previous note about Colt's European patents for the same device. Colt had already patented the revolver in Europe, reserving the U.S. patent until last, since doing so carried certain legal advantages.)

**...now he had a prospect of a fit of the horrors for a week...** Dana is probably referring to delirium tremens (the so-called DTs), a delirium brought on by excessive use of (and then withdrawal from) alcohol. Delusions and trembling are the hallmarks of the disease. Symptoms normally last from seven to 10 days.

**...the half-bloods upon the beach...** That is, he spent his money on liquor and prostitutes and was left with nothing.

**...sent him off "between two days,"...** In other words, overnight, or in the middle of the night.

**"Capitán de la playa," "Maéstro de la casa,"...** That is, the captain of the beach, the master of the house. Russell has indeed fallen far, having gone from rich dandy to tattered fugitive.

In the news
**February, 1836**

State Representative Abraham Lincoln addresses a crowd in Petersburg, IL, promoting the Beardstown and Sangamon Canal, and delivering a plea for subscriptions. Two weeks later, Lincoln himself buys stock in the canal. The plan is abandoned when estimated costs exceed $800,000.

**...commenced Ranchéro...** Working as a ranch hand but, like many ranch hands in those days, gambling and fallen into thievery.

**...saying he was going to paseár with our captain a little.** Spanish for "take a walk." From the Spanish verb, *pasar—to walk* or *pass.*

away for his misconduct. He spent his own money and nearly all the stores among the half-bloods upon the beach, and being turned away, went up to the Presidio, where he lived the life of a desperate "loafer," until some rascally deed sent him off "between two days," with men on horseback, dogs, and Indians in full cry after him, among the hills. One night, he burst into our room at the hide-house, breathless, pale as a ghost, covered with mud, and torn by thorns and briers, nearly naked, and begged for a crust of bread, saying he had neither eaten nor slept for three days. Here was the great Mr. Russell, who a month before was "Don Tomàs," "Capitán de la playa," "Maéstro de la casa," etc., etc., begging food and shelter of Kanakas and sailors. He staid with us till he gave himself up, and was dragged off to the calabozo.

Another, and a more amusing specimen, was one whom we saw at San Francisco. He had been a lad on board the ship California, in one of her first voyages, and ran away and commenced Ranchéro, gambling, stealing horses, etc. He worked along up to San Francisco, and was living on a rancho near there, while we were in port. One morning, when we went ashore in the boat, we found him at the landing-place, dressed in California style,—a wide hat, faded velveteen trowsers, and a blanket cloak thrown over his shoulders—and wishing to go off in the boat, saying he was going to paseár with our captain a little. We had many doubts of the reception he would meet with; but he seemed to think himself company for any one. We took him aboard, landed him at the gangway, and went about our work, keeping an eye upon the quarter-deck, where the captain was walking. The lad went up to him with the most complete assurance, and raising his hat, wished him a good afternoon. Captain T—— turned round, looked at him from head to foot, and saying coolly, "Hallo! who the h—- are you?" kept on his walk. This was a rebuff not to be mistaken, and the joke passed about among the crew by winks and signs, at different parts of the ship. Finding himself disappointed at headquarters, he edged along forward to the mate, who was overseeing some work on the forecastle, and tried to begin a yarn; but it would not do. The mate had seen the reception he had met with aft, and would have no cast-off company. The second mate was aloft, and the third mate and myself were painting the quarter-boat, which hung by the davits, so he betook himself to us; but we looked at one another, and the officer was too busy to say a word. From us, he went to one and another of the crew, but the joke had got before him, and he found everybody busy and silent. Looking over the rail a few moments afterward, we saw him at the galley-door talking to the cook. This was a great comedown, from the highest seat in the synagogue to a seat in the galley with the black cook. At night, too, when supper was called, he stood in the waist for some time, hoping to be asked down with the officers, but they went below, one after another, and left him. His next chance was with the carpenter and sail-maker, and he lounged round the after hatchway until the last had gone down. We had now had fun enough out of him, and taking pity on him, offered him a pot of tea, and a cut at the kid, with the rest, in the forecastle. He was hungry, and it was growing dark, and he began to see that there was no use in playing the caballero any longer, and came down into the forecastle, put into the "grub" in sailor's style, threw off all his airs, and enjoyed the joke as much as any one; for a man must take a joke among sailors. He gave us the whole account of his adventures in the country,—roguery and all—and was very entertaining. He was a smart, unprincipled fellow, was at the bottom of most of the rascally doings of the country, and gave us a great deal of interesting information in the ways of the world we were in.

Saturday, Feb. 13th. Were called up at midnight to slip for a violent north-easter, for this rascally hole of San Pedro is unsafe in every wind but a south-wester, which is seldom known to blow more than once in a half century. We went off with a flowing sheet, and hove-to under the lee of Catalina island, where we lay three days, and then returned to our anchorage.

Tuesday, Feb. 23d. This afternoon, a signal was made from the shore, and we went off in the gig, and found the agent's clerk, who had been up to the pueblo, waiting at the landing-place, with a package under his arm, covered with brown papers and tied carefully with

### In the news
### February, 1836

The Virginia Assembly passes an act forming the Kanawha Slave Insurance Company in Charleston, VA for the purpose of compensating slaveholders of runaway slaves. Somewhat ironically, Charleston is now in West Virginia: During the Civil War, the western part of the state actually seceded from Virginia, entering the U.S. as a free state in June of 1863. This is the only instance of a U.S. state being formed by secession from a Confederate state. (The state of Nevada was formed in 1861 by secession from Utah, but Utah was at the time a territory, not a state. Nevada itself did not become a state until 1864.)

**He was a smart, unprincipled fellow...** Which makes sense, after all: One must be smart (if unprincipled) in order to make a living as a rogue. The man is dissolute, but he's far from stupid. (Dana may also be using "smart" in its 19th-century sense of one who is affected in dress or manners.)

**Has the old bundle of bones got him at last?** That is, Death. The crewman is asking if the (universally disliked) agent, Robinson, has died.

**Our hearts were all up in our mouths...** After months with little news or communication, the crew is excited by the possibility of word from home.

> In the news
> **February, 1836**
>
> In Boston, Mrs. John Farrar publishes *The Young Lady's Friend*, a book that explains how a young woman is expected to behave in 19th-century America. Much of the book's advice boils down to reminders that a young woman should modestly "cover her body." The book also discusses how to treat "the help," and how to arrange a dinner party. The chapter on "Behaviour To Gentlemen" notes that religion is "the only cure for a wounded heart."

**...you angel of darkness...** The cook is black, so this—while probably intended in a kindly fashion—was nonetheless a racist jibe. Now named Joy Street, Belknap Street is (or was) a real street in Boston, running north between the Common (Beacon Street) and Cambridge. It was an African-American enclave even then, the home of the African Meeting House (the oldest African Meeting house in America, and now open to the public) and of Rebecca Lee Crumpler, considered the first black woman in the country to receive a medical degree.

**An overstrained sense of manliness...** Dana is describing what we might call a sense of *machismo*: an exaggerated masculinity that pretends to be completely absent of weakness or even of sensitivity—although possibly without the fierce readiness to defend against any (real or imagined) slights to one's honor.

twine. No sooner had we shoved off than he told us there was good news from Santa Barbara. "What's that?" said one of the crew; "has the bloody agent slipped off the hooks? Has the old bundle of bones got him at last?"—"No; better than that. The California has arrived." Letters, papers, news, and, perhaps,—friends, on board! Our hearts were all up in our mouths, and we pulled away like good fellows; for the precious packet could not be opened except by the captain. As we pulled under the stern, the clerk held up the package, and called out to the mate, who was leaning over the taffrail, that the California had arrived.

"Hurrah!" said the mate, so as to be heard fore and aft; "California come, and news from Boston!"

Instantly there was a confusion on board which no one could account for who has not been in the same situation. All discipline seemed for a moment relaxed.

"What's that, Mr. Brown?" said the cook, putting his head out of the galley—"California come?"

"Aye, aye! you angel of darkness, and there's a letter for you from Bullknop 'treet, number two-two-five—green door and brass knocker!"

The packet was sent down into the cabin, and every one waited to hear of the result. As nothing came up, the officers began to feel that they were acting rather a child's part, and turned the crew to again and the same strict discipline was restored, which prohibits speech between man and man, while at work on deck; so that, when the steward came forward with letters for the crew, each man took his letters, carried them below to his chest, and came up again immediately; and not a letter was read until we had cleared up decks for the night.

An overstrained sense of manliness is the characteristic of seafaring men, or, rather, of life on board ship. This often gives an appearance of want of feeling, and even of cruelty. From this, if a man comes within an ace of breaking his neck and escapes, it is made a joke of; and no notice must be taken of a bruise or cut; and any expression of pity, or any show of attention, would look sisterly, and unbecoming a man who has to face the rough and tumble of such a life. From this, too, the sick are neglected at sea, and whatever sailors may be ashore, a sick man finds little sympathy or attention, forward or aft. A man, too, can have nothing peculiar or sacred on board ship; for all the nicer feelings they take pride in disregarding, both in themselves and others. A thin-skinned man could not live an hour on ship-board. One would be torn raw unless he had the hide of an ox. A moment of natural feeling for home and friends, and then the frigid routine of sea-life returned. Jokes were made upon those who showed any interest in the expected news, and everything near and dear was made common stock for rude jokes and unfeeling coarseness, to which no exception could be taken by any one.

**Jokes were made upon those who showed any interest in the expected news...** An obvious longing for home or for news of loved ones could (and almost certainly *would*) be interpreted amongst this rough-and-tumble group as a form of weakness.

Supper, too, must be eaten before the letters were read; and when, at last, they were brought out, they all got round any one who had a letter, and expected to have it read aloud, and have it all in common. If any one went by himself to read, it was—"Fair play, there; and no skulking!" I took mine and went into the sailmaker's berth, where I could read it without interruption. It was dated August, just a year from the time I had sailed from home; and every one was well, and no great change had taken place. Thus, for one year, my mind was set at ease, yet it was already six months from the date of the letter, and what another year would bring to pass, who could tell? Every one away from home thinks that some great thing must have happened, while to those at home there seems to be a continued monotony and lack of incident.

**In the news**
**February, 1836**

The U.S. Treasury Department issues a report noting that the country now possesses a surplus of funds in the amount of $30 million. Arguments follow regarding the distribution of those funds. Henry Clay and Daniel Webster favor distributing the money among the states. President Andrew Jackson and other strict federalists favor the U.S. government keeping the money. In the end, Congress passes an act (June 23, 1836) distributing all but $5 million, "...with the several States, in proportion to their respective representation in the Senate and the House of Representatives."

As much as my feelings were taken up by my own intelligence from home, I could not but be amused by a scene in the steerage. The carpenter had been married just before leaving Boston, and during the voyage had talked much about his wife, and had to bear and forbear, as every man, known to be married, must, aboard ship; yet the certainty of hearing from his wife by the first ship, seemed to keep up his spirits. The California came, the packet was brought on board; no one was in higher spirits than he; but when the letters came forward, there was none for him. The captain looked again, but there was no mistake. Poor "Chips," could eat no supper. He was completely down in the mouth. "Sails" (the sailmaker) tried to comfort him, and told him he was a bloody fool to give up his grub for any woman's daughter, and reminded him that he had told him a dozen times that he'd never see or hear from his wife again.

"Ah!" said "Chips," "you don't know what it is to have a wife, and"—

"Don't I?" said Sails; and then came, for the hundredth time, the story of his coming ashore at New York, from the Constellation frigate, after a cruise of four years round the Horn,—being paid off with over five hundred dollars,—marrying, and taking a couple of rooms in a four-story house,—furnishing the rooms, (with a particular account of the furniture, including a dozen flag-bottomed chairs, which he always dilated upon, whenever the subject of furniture was alluded to,)—going off to sea again, leaving his wife half-pay, like a fool,—coming home and finding her "off, like Bob's horse, with nobody to pay the reckoning;" furniture gone,—flag-bottomed chairs and all;—and with it, his "long togs," the half-pay, his beaver hat, white linen shirts, and everything else. His wife he never saw, or heard of, from that day to this, and never wished to. Then followed a sweeping assertion, not much to the credit of the sex, if true, though he has Pope to back him. "Come, Chips, cheer up like a man, and take some hot grub! Don't be made a fool of by anything in petticoats! As for your wife, you'll never see her again; she was 'up keeleg and off' before you were outside of Cape Cod. You hove your money away like a fool; but every man must learn once, just as I did; so you'd better square the yards with her, and make the best of it."

This was the best consolation "Sails" had to offer, but it

**Poor "Chips," could eat no supper.** Aboard ship, every carpenter (provided he has proven his skill) is known as *Chips*—just as every sailmaker is known as *Sails*.

**He was completely down in the mouth.** That is, sad. One who has the corners of one's mouth turned down as a sign of dejection or unhappiness. An interesting phrase that goes back at least to the 17th century.

**...tried to comfort him...** Calling someone a fool is a harsh way to comfort him, but then these men are a bit rough around the edges.

**... like Bob's horse...** In the British slang of a few years later, the phrase "Bob's your uncle" was used to mean "And there you go. Settled. Done. No problem. You've achieved your goal." That phrase probably derives from A. J. Balfour's promotion to Chief Secretary for Ireland by his uncle (Robert) Lord Salisbury in 1887. Even before that, though, there was a tendency for Brits to use the name Bob as meaning "everyman." (*High Bradford*, a 1912 novel by Mary Rogers Bangs, describes someone as "...off with the girl like Bob's horse and nobody to pay the reckoning.") However, the pedigree of "...off, like Bob's horse" is murky. It may or may not be British in origin; it may simply be a nautical saying encountered by Dana and used here as a form of dialect-based "local color."

**...he has Pope to back him.** This may be a reference to part of Alexander Pope's *Moral Essays*, which is based on the very 19th-century idea that women—being morally inferior to men—lack character. What he said was, "Most Women have no Characters at all." This was, oddly enough, meant as a compliment. Pope was addressing this specific epistle to a woman whom he believes actually *does* have character, and he was pointing out that she was in this way different from other women.

did not seem to be just the thing the carpenter wanted; for, during several days, he was very much dejected, and bore with difficulty the jokes of the sailors, and with still more difficulty their attempts at advice and consolation, of most of which the sailmaker's was a good specimen.

Thursday, Feb. 25th. Set sail for Santa Barbara, where we arrived on Sunday, the 28th. We just missed of seeing the California, for she had sailed three days before, bound to Monterey, to enter her cargo and procure her license, and thence to San Francisco, etc. Captain Arthur left files of Boston papers for Captain T——, which, after they had been read and talked over in the cabin, I procured from my friend the third mate. One file was of all the Boston Transcripts for the month of August, 1835, and the rest were about a dozen Daily Advertisers and Couriers, of different dates. After all, there is nothing in a strange land like a newspaper from home. Even a letter, in many respects, is nothing, in comparison with it. It carries you back to the spot, better than anything else. It is almost equal to clairvoyance. The names of the streets, with the things advertised, are almost as good as seeing the signs; and while reading "Boy lost!" one can almost hear the bell and well-known voice of "Old Wilson," crying the boy as "strayed, stolen, or mislaid!" Then there was the Commencement at Cambridge, and the full account of the exercises at the graduating of my own class. A list of all those familiar names, (beginning as usual with Abbot, and ending with W., ) which, as I read them over, one by one, brought up their faces and characters as I had known them in the various scenes of college life. Then I imagined them upon the stage, speaking their orations, dissertations, colloquies, etc., with the gestures and tones of each, and tried to fancy the manner in which each would handle his subject, *****, handsome, showy, and superficial; *****, with his strong head, clear brain, cool self-possession; *****, modest, sensitive, and underrated; *****, the mouthpiece of the debating clubs, noisy, vaporous, and democratic; and so following. Then I could see them receiving their A. Bs. from the dignified, feudal-looking

In the news

**February, 1836**

King William IV of England gives a speech to parliament in which he reiterates his 1834 proclamation that proceeds from "captures and seizures" made by the Royal Navy during wartime shall be distributed amongst the officers and men on board the vessels taking part in the conflict. (Except that the proclamation also noted that flag officers not actually on board during the fight "shall have one sixteenth part of the whole net proceeds....") This sharing of spoils was perfectly acceptable—in fact, expected—at the time. After all, it was one way that Britain replenished her treasury and was not viewed as a conflict of interest nor as underhanded. Today we would consider such a policy to be akin to encouraging piracy.

**...well-known voice of "Old Wilson," crying the boy as "strayed, stolen, or mislaid!"** Jimmy Wilson was at the time a town crier in Boston, and well-known for his powerful voice. Wilson dies in 1841, but not before founding The Bell In Hand Tavern, today claimed to be the oldest operating tavern in the U.S. These days the tavern is said, during the day, to be a relaxed place where tourists and local business people can get a decent meal and a beer or two. At night, though, things apparently get a little raucous, with multiple bars on separate floors, DJs, and lines of young people waiting to get in.

**...the Commencement at Cambridge...** Not Cambridge University, which is in the U.K. (And which is more correctly called the University of Cambridge.) Dana is referring to Harvard University, located in Cambridge, MA.

**...with his "auctoritate mihi commis-sâ,"...** Latin for "by the authority entrusted in me."

**In the news**
**February, 1836**

Early in the month, Alamo commander J.C. Neill leaves the mission in order to respond to a family illness. He appoints William Travis commander. Travis, who opts to share command with Col. Jim Bowie, sends out letters pleading for men and supplies. Soon afterward, General Santa Anna enters San Antonio and The Alamo comes under artillery fire from Mexican troops.

**In the news**
**February, 1836**

Charles Dickens publishes *Sketches by Boz*. Much of this collection of 56 short stories and essays (the full title of which is *Sketches by "Boz," Illustrative of Every-day Life and Every-day People*) had previously been published in magazines and journals, but this is the first publication of the entire collection in book form.

**..."Time for us to go!" was raised for the first time...** A popular song often sung by sailors preparing to return home. (Discussed more fully in a subsequent note.)

**...the young Englishman, George Marsh...** This is the (somewhat mysterious) Englishman who seems to have signed on as an American and who went by the name George P. Marsh, and whose real name was apparently George Walker Marsh. (See previous note.)

President, with his "auctoritate mihi commissâ," and walking off the stage with their diplomas in their hands; while upon the very same day, their classmate was walking up and down California beach with a hide upon his head.

Every watch below, for a week, I pored over these papers, until I was sure there could be nothing in them that had escaped my attention, and was ashamed to keep them any longer.

Saturday, March 5th. This was an important day in our almanac, for it was on this day that we were first assured that our voyage was really drawing to a close. The captain gave orders to have the ship ready for getting under weigh; and observed that there was a good breeze to take us down to San Pedro. Then we were not going up to windward. Thus much was certain, and was soon known, fore and aft; and when we went in the gig to take him off, he shook hands with the people on the beach, and said that he never expected to see Santa Barbara again. This settled the matter, and sent a thrill of pleasure through the heart of every one in the boat. We pulled off with a will, saying to ourselves (I can speak for myself at least)—"Good-by, Santa Barbara!—This is the last pull here—No more duckings in your breakers, and slipping from your cursed south-easters!" The news was soon known aboard, and put life into everything when we were getting under weigh. Each one was taking his last look at the mission, the town, the breakers on the beach, and swearing that no money would make him ship to see them again; and when all hands tallied on to the cat-fall, the chorus of "Time for us to go!" was raised for the first time, and joined in, with full swing, by everybody. One would have thought we were on our voyage home, so near did it seem to us, though there were yet three months for us on the coast.

We left here the young Englishman, George Marsh, of whom I have before spoken, who was wrecked upon the Pelew Islands. He left us to take the berth of second mate on board the Ayacucho, which was lying in port. He was well qualified for this, and his education would enable him to rise to any situation on board ship. I felt really sorry to part from him. There was something about him which excited my curiosity; for I could not, for a moment, doubt that he was well born, and, in early life, well bred. There was the latent gentleman about him, and the sense of honor, and no little of the pride, of a young man of good family. The situation was offered him only a few hours before we sailed; and though he must give up returning to America, yet I have no doubt that the change from a dog's berth to an officer's, was too agreeable to his feelings to be declined. We pulled him on board the Ayacucho, and when he left the boat he gave each of its crew a piece of money, except myself, and shook hands with me, nodding his head, as much as to say,—"We understand one another," and sprang on board. Had I known, an hour sooner, that he was to leave us, I would have made an effort to get from him the true history of his early life. He knew that I had no faith in the story which he told the crew, and perhaps, in the moment of parting from me, probably forever, he would have given me the true account. Whether I shall ever meet him again, or whether his manuscript narrative of his adventures in the Pelew Islands, which would be creditable to him and interesting to the world, will ever see the light, I cannot tell. His is one of those cases which are more numerous than those suppose, who have never lived anywhere but in their own homes, and never walked but in one line from their cradles to their graves. We must come down from our heights, and leave our straight paths, for the byways and low places of life, if we would learn truths by strong contrasts; and in hovels, in forecastles, and among our own outcasts in foreign lands, see what has been wrought upon our fellow-creatures by accident, hardship, or vice.

Two days brought us to San Pedro, and two days more (to our no small joy) gave us our last view of that place, which was universally called the hell of California, and seemed designed, in every way, for the wear and tear of sailors. Not even the last view could bring out one feeling of regret. No thanks, thought I, as we left the sandy shores in the distance, for the hours I have walked over

<u>In the news</u>
**March, 1836**

After a 13-day siege (beginning on Feb. 23), Texans under Col. William B. Travis are overwhelmed by the Mexican army at the Battle of the Alamo in San Antonio. Santa Anna's predawn assault catches the weary Texans by surprise, and 138 defenders are killed, most remaining at their posts until their final moments. "Remember the Alamo" will become the Texans' battle cry as they fight for independence from Mexico.

**...I would have made an effort to get from him the true history of his early life.** We never do get to find out what happens to Marsh. When Dana returns to the coast many years later and looks up some old acquaintances, all trace of Marsh has been lost.

<u>In the news</u>
**March, 1836**

In Springfield, IL, a young Abraham Lincoln places an ad in the *Sangamo Journal* seeking return of his lost horse. Lincoln notes, "Any person who will take up said horse, and leave information at the Journal office, or with the subscriber at New-salem, shall be liberally paid for their trouble."

**...the hell of California...** The residents of present-day San Pedro might disagree, of course. But for Dana, San Pedro meant nothing but a bad harbor, backbreaking work, and long, lonely nights spent guarding a pile of damp, smelly hides.

your stones, barefooted, with hides on my head;—for the burdens I have carried up your steep, muddy hill; for the duckings in your surf; and for the long days and longer nights passed on your desolate hill, watching piles of hides, hearing the sharp bark of your eternal coati, and the dismal hooting of your owls.

**...the chain of my servitude.** By this point, Dana really does feel as if he's been committed to some sort of involuntary servitude. (In spite of the fact that he volunteered.) This is now somewhat offset by the fact that he's preparing to leave: Each time he has to suffer, he can now tell himself, "This is the last time I'll have to do this."

**"Forsan et haec olim," thought I...** Dana purposely doesn't complete the Latin phrase, which is properly rendered, "Forsan et haec olim, meminisse iuvabit" and which means, "Perhaps someday it will be pleasant to remember even this." The quotation comes from Virgil's *The Aeneid*, and the well-read Dana expects his reader to be able to complete the quotation.

In the news
**March, 1836**

Miles Goodyear, a teenaged orphan originally from Hamden, CT, is hired by the Whitman missionary party traveling what would soon be known as the Oregon Trail. Hired as a servant and herder, Goodyear leaves the company at Wyeth's Fort (i.e., Ft. Hall, in eastern Oregon), intending to become a trapper. Goodyear later builds Fort Buenaventura in what will eventually become Ogden, Utah.

**...taking sailor's pleasure...** That is, enjoying some well-earned (and rare) private time.

As I bade good-by to each successive place, I felt as though one link after another were struck from the chain of my servitude. Having kept close in shore, for the land-breeze, we passed the mission of San Juan Campestráno the same night, and saw distinctly, by the bright moonlight, the hill which I had gone down by a pair of halyards in search of a few paltry hides. "Forsan et haec olim," thought I, and took my last look of that place too. And on the next morning we were under the high point of San Diego. The flood tide took us swiftly in, and we came-to, opposite our hide-house, and prepared to get everything in trim for a long stay. This was our last port. Here we were to discharge everything from the ship, clean her out, smoke her, take in our hides, wood, water, etc., and set sail for Boston. While all this was doing, we were to lie still in one place, and the port was a safe one, and there was no fear of south-easters. Accordingly, having picked out a good berth, in the stream, with a good smooth beach opposite, for a landing-place and within two cables' length of our hide-house, we moored ship, unbent all the sails, sent down the top-gallant yards and all the studding-sail booms, and housed the top-gallant masts. The boats were then hove out, and all the sails, spare spars, the stores, the rigging not rove, and, in fact, everything which was not in daily use, sent ashore, and stowed away in the house. Then went all our hides and horns, and we left hardly anything in the ship but her ballast, and this we made preparation to heave out, the next day. At night, after we had knocked off, and were sitting round in the forecastle, smoking and talking and taking sailor's pleasure, we congratulated ourselves upon being in that situation in which we had wished ourselves every time we had come into San Diego. "If we were only here for the last time," we had often said, "with our top-gallant masts housed and our sails unbent!"—and now we had our wish. Six weeks, or two months, of the hardest work we had yet seen, was before us, and then—"Good-by to California!"

**...and then—"Good-by to California!"** Dana knows that he can look forward to several more weeks of hard work, but that then they will board ship and head for home. His feeling is that one can stand almost any unpleasantness if one knows that it will soon end.

In the news
**March, 1836**

A few weeks after the fall of The Alamo, General José Urrea marches into Texas from Matamoros, Mexico. His troops easily surround the roughly 300 men in the Texan (or Texian) army near Goliad. After a two-day battle, Urrea's now-reinforced troops are able to bring cannon to bear on the Texans. When the Texans surrender, they are taken back to their fort (Fort Defiance) in Goliad and held prisoner. Although Urrea writes to Santa Anna requesting clemency for the Texans, Santa Anna orders Colonel Jose Nicolas de la Portilla to execute the men. All 300 are marched out of the fort and shot point-blank by the side of the road. (Survivors are clubbed and knifed.) The Goliad Massacre will become another rallying cry for the Texans in their (ultimately successful) fight for independence.

In the news

**March, 1836**

Texas officially proclaims its independence from Mexico. Next month, just east of present-day Houston, Gen. Sam Houston's troops defeat the Mexican Army and capture General Santa Anna, lending credence to Texas's declaration as a sovereign republic, no longer part of Mexico, but not (yet) part of the United States.

**...more than a week of labor...** Ballast, usually in the form of rocks or sand, helped to stabilize the ship. In fact, without a great deal of weight stored low in the vessel, the ship might easily capsize in a storm. At this point, with the ship about to be filled with hides, little additional ballast is needed. Loading tons of rock into small boats and then rowing to shore and unloading that rock would indeed have been laborious, so the *Alert*'s crew (and apparently every other crew) hedges a bit. The remark about "inferior foreign nations" is telling, though: The Americans think little of the laws, customs, or people of some other nations.

**...a good day for smoking ship...** As noted earlier, this procedure is used before heading for home (or whenever else it's deemed necessary) as a way of ridding the ship of insects and rodents.

**...brimstone, and other matters...** A few years later, it would be common to "smoke ship" by using a boiling pot of what was at the time called quicksilver. This method was so efficient that 30 minutes with the hatches closed and seams caulked was deemed sufficient to rid a ship of rats, cockroaches, and other unwelcome visitors. Of course, what they called quicksilver, we know as the poisonous element mercury. These days, most countries regulate exposure to mercury and class it as an occupational hazard.

# CHAPTER XXIX

## LOADING FOR HOME—A SURPRISE—LAST OF AN OLD FRIEND—THE LAST HIDE—A HARD CASE—UP ANCHOR, FOR HOME!—HOMEWARD BOUND

We turned-in early, knowing that we might expect an early call; and sure enough, before the stars had quite faded, "All hands ahoy!" and we were turned-to, heaving out ballast. A regulation of the port forbids any ballast to be thrown overboard; accordingly, our long-boat was lined inside with rough boards and brought alongside the gangway, but where one tub-full went into the boat, twenty went overboard. This is done by every vessel, for the ballast can make but little difference in the channel, and it saves more than a week of labor, which would be spent in loading the boats, rowing them to the point, and unloading them. When any people from the Presidio were on board, the boat was hauled up and ballast thrown in; but when the coast was clear, she was dropped astern again, and the ballast fell overboard. This is one of those petty frauds which every vessel practises in ports of inferior foreign nations, and which are lost sight of, among the countless deeds of greater weight which are hardly less common. Fortunately a sailor, not being a free agent in work aboard ship, is not accountable; yet the fact of being constantly employed, without thought, in such things, begets an indifference to the rights of others.

Friday, and a part of Saturday, we were engaged in this work, until we had thrown out all but what we wanted under our cargo on the passage home; when, as the next day was Sunday, and a good day for smoking ship, we cleared everything out of the cabin and forecastle, made a slow fire of charcoal, birch bark, brimstone, and other matters, on the ballast in the bottom of the hold, calked up the hatches and every open seam, and pasted over the cracks of the windows, and the slides of the scuttles, and companionway. Wherever smoke was seen coming out, we calked and pasted, and, so far as we could, made the ship smoke tight. The captain and officers slept under the awning which was spread over the quarter-deck; and we stowed ourselves away under an old studding-sail, which we drew over one side of the forecastle. The next day, from fear that something might happen, orders were given for no one to leave the ship, and, as the decks were lumbered up with everything, we could not wash them down, so we had nothing to do, all day long. Unfortunately, our books were where we could not get at them, and we were turning about for something to do, when one man recollected a book he had left in the galley. He went after it, and it proved to be Woodstock. This was a great windfall, and as all could not read it at once, I, being the scholar of the company, was appointed reader. I got a knot of six or eight about me, and no one could have had a more attentive audience. Some laughed at the "scholars," and went over the other side of the forecastle, to work, and spin their yarns; but I carried the day, and had the cream of the crew for my hearers. Many of the reflections, and the political parts, I omitted, but all the narrative they were delighted with; especially the descriptions of the Puritans, and the sermons and harangues of the Round-head soldiers. The gallantry of Charles, Dr. Radcliffe's plots, the knavery of "trusty Tompkins,"—in fact, every part seemed to chain their attention. Many things which, while I was reading, I had a misgiving about, thinking them above their capacity, I was surprised to find them enter into completely.

I read nearly all day, until sundown; when, as soon as supper was over, as I had nearly finished, they got a light from the galley; and by skipping what was less interesting, I carried them through to the marriage of Everard, and the restoration of Charles the Second, before eight o'clock.

The next morning, we took the battens from the hatches, and opened the ship. A few stifled rats were found; and what bugs, cockroaches, fleas, and other vermin, there might have been on board, must have unrove their life-lines before the hatches were opened. The ship being now ready, we covered the bottom of the hold over, fore and aft, with dried brush for dunnage, and

**... it proved to be Woodstock.** This was Sir Walter Scott's enormously successful 1826 historical novel, *Woodstock: Or the Cavalier.*

In the news
**March, 1836**

Much of what we know about early attempts to travel the Oregon Trail comes from the journals of Narcissa Whitman, wife of missionary Marcus Whitman. The two led a small group of missionary Presbyterians from New York to Oregon in 1836 and, at the request of her mother, Narcissa kept a diary of the journey. The party established a mission near present-day Walla Walla. A measles outbreak some 10 years later killed many local Indians, and some of the survivors blamed tthe outbreak on Dr. Whitman. The Indians attacked, and the Whitmans were killed.

**...I was surprised to find them enter into completely.** The novel is a dense fictionalized treatment of complex palace intrigues surrounding Charles II's escape from London in 1652 and his return in 1660. Dana is surprised that the men are interested in and can follow the narrative.

**...dried brush for dunnage...** Dunnage is any inexpensive material that is used to protect more expensive cargo. In this case, it will protect the hides from the rough wood and from any seepage of the hold.

having levelled everything away, we were ready to take in our cargo. All the hides that had been collected since the California left the coast, (a little more than two years,) amounting to about forty thousand, were cured, dried, and stowed away in the house, waiting for our good ship to take them to Boston.

**Now began the operation of taking in our cargo...** Most of the 40,000 hides collected are not yet on the vessel, but have been treated onshore and stored in the hide-house. Loading 40,000 hides (roughly 1 million pounds) onto the ship will take several weeks of very hard work.

Now began the operation of taking in our cargo, which kept us hard at work, from the grey of the morning till star-light, for six weeks, with the exception of Sundays, and of just time to swallow our meals. To carry the work on quicker, a division of labor was made. Two men threw the hides down from the piles in the house, two more picked them up and put them on a long horizontal pole, raised a few feet from the ground, where they were beaten, by two more, with flails, somewhat like those used in threshing wheat. When beaten, they were taken from this pole by two more, and placed upon a platform of boards; and ten or a dozen men, with their trowsers rolled up, were constantly going, back and forth, from the platform to the boat, which was kept off where she would just float, with the hides upon their heads. The throwing the hides upon the pole was the most difficult work, and required a sleight of hand which was only to be got by long practice. As I was known for a hide-curer, this post was assigned to me, and I continued at it for six or eight days, tossing, in that time, from eight to ten thousand hides, until my wrists became so lame that I gave in; and was transferred to the gang that was employed in filling the boats, where I remained for the rest of the time. As we were obliged to carry the hides on our heads from fear of their getting wet, we each had a piece of sheepskin sewed into the inside of our hats, with the wool next to our heads, and thus were able to bear the weight, day after day, which would otherwise have soon worn off our hair, and borne hard upon our skulls. Upon the whole, ours was the best berth; for though the water was nipping cold, early in the morning and late at night, and being so continually wet was rather an exposure, yet we got rid of the constant dust and dirt from the beating of the hides, and being all of us young and hearty, did not mind the exposure. The older men of the

**In the news**
**March, 1836**

Traveling from England to Fort Vancouver (located on the southern bank of the Columbia River, northeast of present-day Portland, OR), William Copendale and his wife arrive on the British ship *Columbia*. Copendale was to oversee agriculture at Ft. Vancouver while his wife had been assigned to run the dairy. The commander of the fort, Dr. John McLoughlin, was apparently angry at the outside interference in fort operations and the criticisms that implied, so he delayed assigning quarters to the couple.

**...I continued at it for six or eight days...** If Dana's estimate is correct, and assuming that the men worked 12 hours per day, then he was "tossing" about 104 hides per hour, or one every 90 seconds or so. This seems reasonable and not terribly strenuous, until one realizes that he would have to keep that up for hours on end, with few breaks, and that he would have to do so day after day, covered in dust and dirt all the while.

crew, whom it would have been dangerous to have kept in the water, remained on board with the mate, to stow the hides away, as fast as they were brought off by the boats.

We continued at work in this manner until the lower hold was filled to within four feet of the beams, when all hands were called aboard to commence steeving. As this is a peculiar operation, it will require a minute description.

Before stowing the hides, as I have said, the ballast is levelled off, just above the keelson, and then loose dunnage placed upon it, on which the hides rest. The greatest care is used in stowing, to make the ship hold as many hides as possible. It is no mean art, and a man skilled in it is an important character in California. Many a dispute have I heard raging high between professed "beach-combers," as to whether the hides should be stowed "shingling," or "back-to-back, and flipper-to-flipper;" upon which point there was an entire and bitter division of sentiment among the savans. We adopted each method at different periods of the stowing, and parties ran high in the forecastle, some siding with "old Bill" in favor of the former, and others scouting him, and relying upon "English Bob" of the Ayacucho, who had been eight years in California, and was willing to risk his life and limb for the latter method. At length a compromise was effected, and a middle course, of shifting the ends and backs at every lay, was adopted, which worked well, and which, though they held it inferior to their own, each party granted was better than that of the other.

Having filled the ship up, in this way, to within four feet of her beams, the process of steeving commenced, by which an hundred hides are got into a place where one could not be forced by hand, and which presses the hides to the utmost, sometimes starting the beams of the ship, resembling in its effects the jack-screws which are used in stowing cotton. Each morning we went ashore, and beat and brought off as many hides as we could steeve in the course of the day, and, after breakfast,

**...all hands were called aboard to commence steeving.** As noted earlier, steeving is the stowing of cargo by compressing it so that more cargo will fit into the allotted space. (The term derives from French, Spanish, Portuguese, and Italian words meaning to crowd or pack tightly.) The men argue here about the most efficient steeving method, and eventually arrive at a compromise in which they alternate the direction of each hide.

**...division of sentiment among the savans.** Dana refers somewhat sarcastically to the men as *savants*, that is, learned persons or scholars.

**In the news**
**March, 1836**

Charles Dickens publishes the first of *The Pickwick Papers*. Dickens' first novel, *The Posthumous Papers of the Pickwick Club*, actually grew out of a contract Dickens had signed to contribute to a monthly publication containing installments of the novel. Soon after he agreed to take on the task, the other contributor (contracted mainly to provide illustrations) committed suicide, and Dickens found himself writing the entire thing (and seeking other illustrators). The book, in which a group of club members (memorable characters, all) travel England seeking curiosities and report back on their findings, was a sensation—perhaps the first such sensation, in fact.

**...resembling in its effects the jack-screws which are used in stowing cotton.** Not surprising, since the word *steeve* was originally used in reference to compressing and stowing bales of cotton.

In the news
**March, 1836**

An unincorporated region along the Brazos River becomes known as "Washington-on-the Brazos" or "the birthplace of Texas" when it hosts both the Convention of 1836 and then the signing of the Texas Declaration of Independence (although drafters of the latter document were forced to flee the area temporarily in the face of the advancing Mexican army).

**...when these tackles were nippered...** A nipper is a short length of rope used to bind something.

**...an hundred or an hundred and fifty were often driven in by this complication of purchases.** All of this boils down to the use of various forms of pulleys, ropes, and other machines aimed at increasing the mechanical advantage that could be brought to bear in order to squeeze the pile of hides such that more hides could be inserted into the pile.

In the news
**March, 1836**

Jefferson Franklin Long is born a slave near Knoxville, GA. Self-educated, he becomes a successful merchant in Macon, GA. In November of 1870, Long becomes the first black man elected to Congress from the state of Georgia.

went down into the hold, where we remained at work until night. The whole length of the hold, from stem to stern, was floored off level, and we began with raising a pile in the after part, hard against the bulkhead of the run, and filling it up to the beams, crowding in as many as we could by hand and pushing in with oars; when a large "book" was made of from twenty-five to fifty hides, doubled at the backs, and put into one another, like the leaves of a book. An opening was then made between two hides in the pile, and the back of the outside hide of the book inserted. Two long, heavy spars, called steeves, made of the strongest wood, and sharpened off like a wedge at one end, were placed with their wedge ends into the inside of the hide which was the centre of the book, and to the other end of each, straps were fitted, into which large tackles were hooked, composed each of two huge purchase blocks, one hooked to the strap on the end of the steeve, and the other into a dog, fastened into one of the beams, as far aft as it could be got. When this was arranged, and the ways greased upon which the book was to slide, the falls of the tackles were stretched forward, and all hands tallied on, and bowsed away until the book was well entered; when these tackles were nippered, straps and toggles clapped upon the falls, and two more luff tackles hooked on, with dogs, in the same manner; and thus, by luff upon luff, the power was multiplied, until into a pile in which one hide more could not be crowded by hand, an hundred or an hundred and fifty were often driven in by this complication of purchases. When the last luff was hooked on, all hands were called to the rope—cook, steward, and all—and ranging ourselves at the falls, one behind the other, sitting down on the hides, with our heads just even with the beams, we set taut upon the tackles, and striking up a song, and all lying back at the chorus, we bowsed the tackles home, and drove the large books chock in out of sight.

The sailor's songs for capstans and falls are of a peculiar kind, having a chorus at the end of each line. The burden is usually sung, by one alone, and, at the chorus, all hands join in,—and the louder the noise, the better. With us, the chorus seemed almost to raise the decks of the ship, and might be heard at a great distance, ashore. A song is as necessary to sailors as the drum and fife to a soldier. They can't pull in time, or pull with a will, without it. Many a time, when a thing goes heavy, with one fellow yo-ho-ing, a lively song, like "Heave, to the girls!" "Nancy oh!" "Jack Cross-tree," etc., has put life and strength into every arm. We often found a great difference in the effect of the different songs in driving in the hides. Two or three songs would be tried, one after the other; with no effect;—not an inch could be got upon the tackles—when a new song, struck up, seemed to hit the humor of the moment, and drove the tackles "two blocks" at once. "Heave round hearty!" "Captain gone ashore!" and the like, might do for common pulls, but in an emergency, when we wanted a heavy, "raise-the-dead" pull, which should start the beams of the ship, there was nothing like "Time for us to go!" "Round the corner," or "Hurrah! hurrah! my hearty bullies!"

This was the most lively part of our work. A little boating and beach work in the morning; then twenty or thirty men down in a close hold, where we were obliged to sit down and slide about, passing hides, and rowsing about the great steeves, tackles, and dogs, singing out at the falls, and seeing the ship filling up every day. The work was as hard as it could well be. There was not a moment's cessation from Monday morning till Saturday night, when we were generally beaten out, and glad to have a full night's rest, a wash and shift of clothes, and a quiet Sunday. During all this time,—which would have startled Dr. Graham—we lived upon almost nothing but fresh beef; fried beefsteaks, three times a day,—morning, noon, and night. At morning and night we had a quart of tea to each man; and an allowance of about a pound of hard bread a day; but our chief article of food was the beef. A mess, consisting of six men, had a large wooden kid piled up with beefsteaks, cut thick, and fried in fat, with the grease poured over them. Round this we sat, attacking it with our jack-knives and teeth, and with the appetite of young lions, and sent back an empty kid to the galley. This was done three times a day. How many pounds each man ate in a day, I will not attempt to compute. A whole bullock (we ate liver

**A song is as necessary to sailors as the drum and fife to a soldier.** Sailors' songs are sometimes called "sea shanties"—usually spelled "shanties," not "chanties," although the term probably derives from "chant." (Which in turn may have come to us from the French *chanter*, meaning to sing.) The shanty is a work song whose rhythm helps sailors perform a repetitive task. A sailor known as the "shantyman" leads the song, and the other crewmembers join in on the choruses. Singing truly did help the work move along, and a good shantyman was much respected.

In the news
**March, 1836**

An anonymous 1836 etiquette manual (*The Laws of Etiquette, or, Short Rules and Reflections for Conduct in Society*) lists instructions for managing social interactions, reminding people to bow to one another and to doff their hats—even to "an individual of the lowest rank, or without any rank at all" if he removes his hat first. The book also notes that "If you have remarkably fine teeth, you may smile affectionately upon the bowee, without speaking," and cautions that, "It is a mark of high breeding not to speak to a lady in the street, until you perceive that she has noticed you by an inclination of the head."

**...which would have startled Dr. Graham...** Sylvester Graham was a minister who advocated what at the time was thought to be radical dietary reform, including the use of bread made without chemical additives. Graham thought that bad diet led to sexual excesses, which in turn caused disease. We have Dr. Graham to thank for the graham cracker. (Which, being sweet, is actually more of a cookie than a cracker.)

and all) lasted us but four days. Such devouring of flesh, I will venture to say, was seldom known before. What one man ate in a day, over a hearty man's allowance, would make a Russian's heart leap into his mouth. Indeed, during all the time we were upon the coast, our principal food was fresh beef, and every man had perfect health; but this was a time of especial devouring; and what we should have done without meat, I cannot tell. Once or twice, when our bullocks failed and we were obliged to make a meal upon dry bread and water, it seemed like feeding upon shavings. Light and dry, feeling unsatisfied, and, at the same time, full, we were glad to see four quarters of a bullock, just killed, swinging from the fore-top. Whatever theories may be started by sedentary men, certainly no men could have gone through more hard work and exposure for sixteen months in more perfect health, and without ailings and failings, than our ship's crew, let them have lived upon Hygeia's own baking and dressing.

**...would make a Russian's heart leap into his mouth.** We've already encountered Dana's thoughts on Russians. He characterizes them as lazy, dirty gluttons who eat grease.

**...let them have lived upon Hygeia's own baking and dressing.** In Greek mythology, Hygeia was the goddess of health. It is from her that we get the word hygiene.

Friday, April 15th. Arrived, brig Pilgrim, from the windward. It was a sad sight for her crew to see us getting ready to go off the coast, while they, who had been longer on the coast than the Alert, were condemned to another year's hard service. I spent an evening on board, and found them making the best of the matter, and determined to rough it out as they might; but my friend S—— was determined to go home in the ship, if money or interest could bring it to pass. After considerable negotiating and working, he succeeded in persuading my English friend, Tom Harris,—my companion in the anchor watch—for thirty dollars, some clothes, and an intimation from Captain Faucon that he should want a second mate before the voyage was up, to take his place in the brig as soon as she was ready to go up to windward.

In the news
**April, 1836**

At the Battle of San Jacinto, General Sam Houston leads the Texians into battle against Santa Anna. The fight lasts only 15 minutes or so, during which time more than 600 Mexican soldiers are killed and over 700 captured. Santa Anna is captured and forced to sign a peace treaty that forces the Mexican army to leave the region and requires that Santa Anna encourage Mexico City to recognize Texas as a sovereign nation. The victory essentially ensures that Texas will become an independent republic.

The first opportunity I could get to speak to Captain Faucon, I asked him to step up to the oven and look at Hope, whom he knew well, having had him on board his vessel. He went to see him, but said that he had so little medicine, and expected to be so long on the coast, that he could do nothing for him, but that Captain

**He went to see him...** Unlike Captain Thompson, Faucon is at least willing to visit with Hope and, since he can do little for him, arranges for the captain of the *California* to help.

Arthur would take care of him when he came down in the California, which would be in a week or more. I had been to see Hope the first night after we got into San Diego this last time, and had frequently since spent the early part of a night in the oven. I hardly expected, when I left him to go to windward, to find him alive upon my return. He was certainly as low as he could well be when I left him, and what would be the effect of the medicines that I gave him, I hardly then dared to conjecture. Yet I knew that he must die without them. I was not a little rejoiced, therefore, and relieved, upon our return, to see him decidedly better. The medicines were strong, and took hold and gave a check to the disorder which was destroying him; and, more than that, they had begun the work of exterminating it. I shall never forget the gratitude that he expressed. All the Kanakas attributed his escape solely to my knowledge, and would not be persuaded that I had not all the secrets of the physical system open to me and under my control. My medicines, however, were gone, and no more could be got from the ship, so that his life was left to hang upon the arrival of the California.

Sunday, April 24th. We had now been nearly seven weeks in San Diego, and had taken in the greater part of our cargo, and were looking out, every day, for the arrival of the California, which had our agent on board; when, this afternoon, some Kanakas, who had been over the hill for rabbits and to fight rattlesnakes, came running down the path, singing out, "Kail ho!" with all their might. Mr. H., our third mate, was ashore, and asking them particularly about the size of the sail, etc., and learning that it was "Moku—Nui Moku," hailed our ship, and said that the California was on the other side of the point. Instantly, all hands were turned up, the bow guns run out and loaded, the ensign and broad pennant set, the yards squared by lifts and braces, and everything got ready to make a good appearance. The instant she showed her nose round the point, we began our salute. She came in under top-gallant sails, clewed up and furled her sails in good order, and came-to, within good swinging distance of us. It being Sunday, and nothing to do, all hands were on the forecastle, crit-

## In the news
## April, 1836

Charles Darwin is in Mauritius, Australia and seems surprised to find the inhabitants civilized and literate: "30th April 1836 - Mauritius - I spent the greater part of the next day in walking about the town & visiting different people. The town is of considerable size, & is said to contain 20,000 inhabitants; the streets are very clean & regular. Although the island has been so many years under the English government, the general character of the place is quite French. Englishmen speak to their servants in French, & the shops are all French; indeed I should think that Calais or Boulogne was much more Anglefied. There is a very pretty little theatre, in which operas are excellently performed, & are much preferred by the inhabitants to common plays. We were also surprised at seeing large booksellers shops with well stored shelves."

**"Kail ho!"** That is, "Sail ho!"

**...the bow guns run out and loaded...** As noted earlier, the cannon salute is a mark of respect. *Alert* wishes to welcome *California*, and also to make a good impression.

**...wall-sided and kettle-bottomed...** That is, the ship has a flat hull. A hull could theoretically range from perfectly round to perfectly flat, although they tend to fall in between those extremes. The flatter a vessel's hull, the more stable she tends to be. However, there's a trade-off to be considered: Although a flatter hull will roll less, when such a vessel is forced to roll, the action can be violent, and could even lead to the ship capsizing in conditions in which a rounder hull would simply roll back to the vertical after having been forced over.

icising the new-comer. She was a good, substantial ship, not quite so long as the Alert, and wall-sided and kettle-bottomed, after the latest fashion of south-shore cotton and sugar wagons; strong, too, and tight, and a good average sailor, but with no pretensions to beauty, and nothing in the style of a "crack ship." Upon the whole, we were perfectly satisfied that the Alert might hold up her head with a ship twice as smart as she.

At night, some of us got a boat and went on board, and found a large, roomy forecastle, (for she was squarer forward than the Alert,) and a crew of a dozen or fifteen men and boys, sitting around on their chests, smoking and talking, and ready to give a welcome to any of our ship's company. It was just seven months since they left Boston, which seemed but yesterday to us. Accordingly, we had much to ask, for though we had seen the newspapers that she brought, yet these were the very men who had been in Boston and seen everything with their own eyes. One of the green-hands was a Boston boy, from one of the public schools, and, of course, knew many things which we wished to ask about, and on inquiring the names of our two Boston boys, found that they had been schoolmates of his. Our men had hundreds of questions to ask about Ann street, the boarding-houses, the ships in port, the rate of wages, and other matters.

**...a Boston boy, from one of the public schools...** These days, a public school in the U.S. is one supported by tax dollars and run by a local government, such as a city or county. In the 1830s (and still today, in the U.K.), a public school was (somewhat confusingly) what we would call a private school: one funded by private endowments and tuition and run as a private enterprise.

**...questions to ask about Ann street...** Ann Street was a very rough waterfront area of Boston, known for raucous pubs, drunken brawls, gambling halls, and houses of prostitution. As such, it was always a good source of interesting (and titillating) news. It was renamed North Street in 1852.

Among her crew were two English man-of-war's-men, so that, of course, we soon had music. They sang in the true sailor's style, and the rest of the crew, which was a remarkably musical one, joined in the choruses. They had many of the latest sailor songs, which had not yet got about among our merchantmen, and which they were very choice of. They began soon after we came on board, and kept it up until after two bells, when the second mate came forward and called "the Alerts away!" Battle-songs, drinking-songs, boat-songs, love-songs, and everything else, they seemed to have a complete assortment of, and I was glad to find that "All in the Downs," "Poor Tom Bowline," "The Bay of Biscay," "List, ye Landsmen!" and all those classical songs of the sea, still held their places. In addition to these, they

**...all those classical songs of the sea, still held their places.** Those four were popular songs written by John Gay (1685-1732), Charles Dibdin (1745-1814), Andrew Cherry (1762-1812), and George A. Stephens (1710-1780).

had picked up at the theatres and other places a few songs of a little more genteel cast, which they were very proud of; and I shall never forget hearing an old salt, who had broken his voice by hard drinking on shore, and bellowing from the mast-head in a hundred north-westers, with all manner of ungovernable trills and quavers in the high notes, breaking into a rough falsetto—and in the low ones, growling along like the dying away of the boatswain's "all hands ahoy!" down the hatchway, singing, "Oh, no, we never mention him."

"Perhaps, like me, he struggles with
Each feeling of regret;
But if he's loved as I have loved,
He never can forget!"

The last line, being the conclusion, he roared out at the top of his voice, breaking each word up into half a dozen syllables. This was very popular, and Jack was called upon every night to give them his "sentimental song." No one called for it more loudly than I, for the complete absurdity of the execution, and the sailors' perfect satisfaction in it, were ludicrous beyond measure.

The next day, the California commenced unloading her cargo; and her boats' crews, in coming and going, sang their boat-songs, keeping time with their oars. This they did all day long for several days, until their hides were all discharged, when a gang of them were sent on board the Alert, to help us steeve our hides. This was a windfall for us, for they had a set of new songs for the capstan and fall, and ours had got nearly worn out by six weeks' constant use. I have no doubt that this timely reinforcement of songs hastened our work several days.

Our cargo was now nearly all taken in; and my old friend, the Pilgrim, having completed her discharge, unmoored, to set sail the next morning on another long trip to windward. I was just thinking of her hard lot, and congratulating myself upon my escape from her, when I received a summons into the cabin. I went aft, and there

**Perhaps, like me, he struggles with Each feeling of regret...** Some sources say that this song, written by popular poet and songwriter Thomas Haynes Bayly (1797-1839), is actually called, "Oh, No, We Never Mention Her." In fact, it originated as "...Him," but was often sung, depending on the singer and the situation, as "...Her." The lyrics are a bit saccharine for today's tastes:

*For oh! there are so many things recall the past to me, The breeze upon the sunny hills, the billows of the sea, The rosy tint that decks the sky before the sun is set; Ay every leaf I look upon forbids me to forget.*

In the news
**April, 1836**

The *Far West* newspaper, published in Liberty, MO, rails in a brief editorial about the fact that easterners are importing wheat from abroad. "It will not be astonishing," sniffs the editor, "if we soon import our bacon, beef, cabbages and potatoes."

In the news
**April, 1836**

The town of Lowell, MA officially becomes a city, a notable achievement given that only Boston and Salem before it had been granted city governments. At the time, Lowell's population stood at just over 17,000. That population would double over the next 15 years, making Lowell the second-largest city in the state.

found, seated round the cabin table, my own captain, Captain Faucon of the Pilgrim, and Mr. R——, the agent. Captain T—— turned to me and asked abruptly—

**"D—, do you want to go home in the ship?"** "D—" is Dana, of course. The two captains and the agent have decided, out of the blue, as far as Dana can tell, that Dana must now get someone from Alert to switch over to Pilgrim. This is an unexpected (and cruel) development. Dana had assumed that this had all been worked out; in fact, he had been assured as much. Now it seems as if his plan was in danger of coming undone.

"D——, do you want to go home in the ship?"

"Certainly, sir," said I; "I expect to go home in the ship."

"Then," said he, "you must get some one to go in your place on board the Pilgrim."

**...completely "taken aback" by this...** It's interesting to note that the phrase "taken aback" is in fact of nautical origin. We use it to mean surprised or startled by some sudden turn of events. Originally, though, "taken aback" was used to describe sails that had been blown back until they lay flattened against a mast.

I was so completely "taken aback" by this sudden intimation, that for a moment I could make no reply. I knew that it would be hopeless to attempt to prevail upon any of the ship's crew to take twelve months more upon the California in the brig. I knew, too, that Captain T—— had received orders to bring me home in the Alert, and he had told me, when I was at the hide-house, that I was to go home in her; and even if this had not been so, it was cruel to give me no notice of the step they were going to take, until a few hours before the brig would sail. As soon as I had got my wits about me, I put on a bold front, and told him plainly that I had a letter in my chest informing me that he had been written to, by the owners in Boston, to bring me home in the ship, and moreover, that he had told me that I was to go in the ship.

**...more than my lord paramount had been used to.** Dana is being sarcastic here. Paramount means of the highest authority or importance. In feudal law, a lord paramount was one who did not hold his fiefdom by the authority or pleasure of some other lord, but who was instead beholden to no superior.

To have this told him, and to be opposed in such a manner, was more than my lord paramount had been used to.

He turned fiercely upon me, and tried to look me down, and face me out of my statement; but finding that that wouldn't do, and that I was entering upon my defence in such a way as would show to the other two that he was in the wrong,—he changed his ground, and pointed to the shipping papers of the Pilgrim, from which my name had never been erased, and said that there was my name,—that I belonged to her,—that he had an absolute discretionary power,—and, in short, that I must be on board the Pilgrim by the next morning with my chest and hammock, or have some one ready to go in my place, and that he would not hear another word from me. No court or star chamber could proceed more summarily with a poor devil, than this trio was about to do with me; condemning me to a punishment worse than a Botany Bay exile, and to a fate which would alter the whole current of my future life; for two years more in California would have made me a sailor for the rest of my days. I felt all this, and saw the necessity of being determined. I repeated what I had said, and insisted upon my right to return in the ship.

I "raised my arm, and tauld my crack,
Before them a'."

But it would have all availed me nothing, had I been "some poor body," before this absolute, domineering tribunal. But they saw that I would not go, unless "vi et armis," and they knew that I had friends and interest enough at home to make them suffer for any injustice they might do me. It was probably this that turned the matter; for the captain changed his tone entirely, and asked me if, in case any one went in my place, I would give him the same sum that S—— gave Harris to exchange with him. I told him that if any one was sent on board the brig, I should pity him, and be willing to help him to that, or almost any amount; but would not speak of it as an exchange.

"Very well," said he. "Go forward about your business, and send English Ben here to me!"

I went forward with a light heart, but feeling as angry, and as much contempt as I could well contain between my teeth. English Ben was sent aft, and in a few moments came forward, looking as though he had received his sentence to be hung. The captain had told him to get his things ready to go on board the brig the next morning; and that I would give him thirty dollars and a suit of clothes. The hands had "knocked off" for dinner, and were standing about the forecastle, when

**No court or star chamber...** The Star Chamber was a powerful 17th century English court of law designed to ensure that even prominent people—those who were so powerful that an ordinary court might never convict them of a crime—were in fact held accountable and were forced to answer to the law. Star Chamber sessions were held in secret and there were no witnesses and no right of appeal. It was therefore ripe with opportunity for misuse, and in fact it eventually became a political weapon, a symbol of the very abuse of power it was originally set up to combat.

**...raised my arm...** Not quite a word-for-word quote of Robert Burns' poem, "The Author's Earnest Cry and Prayer." The 1786 poem—written in Scottish dialect—was directed at the Scottish representatives in the British House of Commons. The full line is:

*In gath'rin votes you were na slack; Now stand as tightly by your tack: Ne'er claw your lug, an' fidge your back, An' hum an' haw; But raise your arm, an' tell your crack Before them a'.*

**...and they knew that I had friends...** Latin for "by force of arms." Here Dana is not above pulling strings, reminding the officers that he (or his father, at least) has powerful friends in Boston. This seems to do the trick, and the captains back down, agreeing instead that Dana should pay if someone does agree to board *Pilgrim*.

In the news
**April, 1836**

Grove Pomeroy is awarded the first tavern (or "pub") license in Marshall County, IN. For $10 per year, Pomeroy is allowed to operate a tavern in the two-story log building on the south-west corner of Michigan and La Porte streets. Currently there are about a dozen bars to serve the 13,000 residents of the county.

Ben came forward and told his story. I could see plainly that it made a great excitement, and that, unless I explained the matter to them, the feeling would be turned against me. Ben was a poor English boy, a stranger in Boston, and without friends or money; and being an active, willing lad, and a good sailor for his years, was a general favorite. "Oh, yes!" said the crew, "the captain has let you off, because you are a gentleman's son, and have got friends, and know the owners; and taken Ben, because he is poor, and has got nobody to say a word for him!" I knew that this was too true to be answered, but I excused myself from any blame, and told them that I had a right to go home, at all events. This pacified them a little, but Jack had got a notion that a poor lad was to be imposed upon, and did not distinguish very clearly; and though I knew that I was in no fault, and, in fact, had barely escaped the grossest injustice, yet I felt that my berth was getting to be a disagreeable one. The notion that I was not "one of them," which, by a participation in all their labor and hardships, and having no favor shown me, had been laid asleep, was beginning to revive. But far stronger than any feeling for myself, was the pity I felt for the poor lad. He had depended upon going home in the ship; and from Boston, was going immediately to Liverpool, to see his friends. Beside this, having begun the voyage with very few clothes, he had taken up the greater part of his wages in the slop-chest, and it was every day a losing concern to him; and, like all the rest of the crew, he had a hearty hatred of California, and the prospect of eighteen months or two years more of hide-droghing seemed completely to break down his spirit. I had determined not to go myself, happen what would, and I knew that the captain would not dare to attempt to force me. I knew, too, that the two captains had agreed together to get some one, and that unless I could prevail upon somebody to go voluntarily, there would be no help for Ben. From this consideration, though I had said that I would have nothing to do with an exchange, I did my best to get some one to go voluntarily. I offered to give an order upon the owners in Boston for six months' wages, and also all the clothes, books, and other matters, which I should not want upon the voyage

**...unless I explained the matter to them, the feeling would be turned against me.** This whole thing is not Dana's fault, nor was the exchange his idea. He doesn't want the men to think that he sacrificed Ben and that the captain is letting him (Dana) off because of his connections. Nonetheless, that's at least partly true (as Dana himself admits), and we have only Dana's word for the rest. We already know that Dana, writing some years later, is not above shading the truth a bit, if doing so is to his advantage.

**The notion that I was not "one of them,"...** This has been a recurring theme all along. Dana—who in fact is most definitely not one of them—wishes nonetheless to be considered "one of the boys" and often fears that he may not be accepted as such.

**But far stronger than any feeling for myself, was the pity I felt for the poor lad.** Dana means well here, but this is a bit self-serving. The pity he feels is most certainly not "far stronger than any feeling" he might have for himself; if it were, he would have gone back to the captain and turned down the deal.

### In the news
### April, 1836

In the middle of a full-blown pro-slavery riot in Cincinnati, OH, previously mentioned abolitionist editor James G. Birney maintains that the (mostly non-violent) abolitionists have done nothing to deserve the physical threats they have received: "What are the abolitionists doing? Have they levied a military force? Laid up magazines of arms? They talk and they print, to persuade their fellow countrymen to do justice and to show mercy to the poor."

home. When this offer was published in the ship, and the case of poor Ben was set forth in strong colors, several, who would not have dreamed of going themselves, were busy in talking it up to others, who, they thought, might be tempted to accept it; and, at length, one fellow, a harum-scarum lad, whom we called Harry Bluff, and who did not care what country or ship he was in, if he had clothes enough and money enough—partly from pity for Ben, and partly from the thought he should have "cruising money" for the rest of his stay,—came forward, and offered to go and "sling his hammock in the bloody hooker." Lest his purpose should cool, I signed an order for the sum upon the owners in Boston, gave him all the clothes I could spare, and sent him aft to the captain, to let him know what had been done. The skipper accepted the exchange, and was, doubtless, glad to have it pass off so easily. At the same time he cashed the order, which was endorsed to him,[1] and the next morning, the lad went aboard the brig, apparently in good spirits, having shaken hands with each of us and wished us a pleasant passage home, jingling the money in his pockets, and calling out, "Never say die, while there's a shot in the locker." The same boat carried off Harris, my old watchmate, who had previously made an exchange with my friend S——.

I was sorry to part with Harris. Nearly two hundred hours (as we had calculated it) had we walked the ship's deck together, at anchor watch, when all hands were below, and talked over and over every subject which came within the ken of either of us. He gave me a strong gripe with his hand; and I told him, if he came to Boston again, not to fail to find me out, and let me see an old watchmate. The same boat brought on board S——, my friend, who had begun the voyage with me from Boston, and, like me, was going back to his family and to the society which we had been born and brought up in. We congratulated one another upon finding what we had long talked over and wished for, thus brought about; and none on board the ship were more glad than ourselves to see the old brig standing round the point, under full sail. As she passed abreast of us, we all collected in the waist, and gave her three loud, hearty

**...one fellow, a harum-scarum lad...came forward...** This is getting a bit complicated. Now Dana is working up a plan to find a replacement for his replacement. "Harum-scarum" means reckless and wild. Harry Bluff is a 16 year-old who signed on as Henry R. May.

**..."sling his hammock in the bloody hooker."** Dana points out in his notes that this is a common sailor's expression for signing on to a ship. In this context, "hooker" is a slightly contemptuous term for an older, somewhat battered vessel.

In the news

**April, 1836**

Peter Studebaker is born in northeast Ohio to John and Rebecca. John is a blacksmith and mechanic who finds work repairing stagecoaches and who then starts a company that manufactures wagons, eventually supplying wagons to the Union army. By 1857, Peter has opened the first Studebaker "dealership," in Goshen, IN. The company will prosper, with sales exceeding $1 million by 1877. Peter dies in 1897, but the company carries on, designing and manufacturing an electric car (1902) and then building gasoline-powered vehicles. Studebaker becomes one of the world's largest automobile manufacturers, manufacturing popular models such as the Lark and the Avanti. The company is eventually purchased by Packard, and the last Studebaker is produced in 1966.

**I told him, if he came to Boston again, not to fail to find me out, and let me see an old watchmate.** In fact, although Tom Harris never made it to Boston, Dana does meet up with him when, 24 years later, Dana returns to the California coast.

cheers, waving our hats in the air. Her crew sprang into the rigging and chains, answered us with three as loud, to which we, after the nautical custom, gave one in return. I took my last look of their familiar faces as they got over the rail, and saw the old black cook put his head out of the galley, and wave his cap over his head. The crew flew aloft to loose the top-gallant sails and royals; the two captains waved their hands to one another; and, in ten minutes, we saw the last inch of her white canvas, as she rounded the point.

Relieved as I was to see her well off, (and I felt like one who had just sprung from an iron trap which was closing upon him) I had yet a feeling of regret at taking the last look at the old craft in which I had spent a year, and the first year, of my sailor's life—which had been my first home in the new world into which I had entered—and with which I had associated so many things,—my first leaving home, my first crossing the equator, Cape Horn, Juan Fernandez, death at sea, and other things, serious and common. Yet, with all this, and the feeling I had for my old shipmates, condemned to another term of California life, the thought that we were done with it, and that one week more would see us on our way to Boston, was a cure for everything.

Friday, May 6th, completed the taking of our cargo, and was a memorable day in our calendar. The time when we were to take in our last hide, we had looked forward to, for sixteen months, as the first bright spot. When the last hide was stowed away, and the hatches calked down, the tarpaulins battened on to them, the long-boat hoisted in and secured, and the decks swept down for the night,—the chief mate sprang upon the top of the long-boat, called all hands into the waist, and giving us a signal by swinging his cap over his head,—we gave three long, loud cheers, which came from the bottom of our hearts, and made the hills and valleys ring again. In a moment, we heard three, in answer, from the California's crew, who had seen us taking in our long-boat, and—"the cry they heard—its meaning knew."

The last week, we had been occupied in taking in a sup-

**In the news**
**May, 1836**

Illinois' Fort Armstrong is abandoned May 4, 1836. Erected on Rock Island after the War of 1812, the small (300 square feet) fort was actively garrisoned through 1832. It was meant to dissuade French and English Canadians from encroaching on U.S. territory as much as it was meant as protection against Indian attack. The fort was abandoned after a cholera epidemic struck, killing almost 200 people on the island.

**...the thought that we were done with it, and that one week more would see us on our way to Boston, was a cure for everything.** For Dana, this is something of a bittersweet moment. He's glad to be quit of *Pilgrim* and happy to be about to head home. But, as he looks back at his year aboard his earlier berth, he realizes that however uncomfortable the vessel and however brutal its captain, it was home—and it was the place he "learned the ropes," and where he became a sailor. In a way, he will miss it.

**..."the cry they heard–its meaning knew."** The ever-literary Dana is quoting from Sir Walter Scott's epic 1808 poem, *Marmion*. (Two famous lines from the poem are often mistakenly thought to be from either Shakespeare or the Bible: "Oh, what a tangled web we weave/When first we practise to deceive!")

ply of wood and water for the passage home, and bringing on board the spare spars, sails, etc. I was sent off with a party of Indians to fill the water-casks, at a spring, about three miles from the shipping, and near the town, and was absent three days, living at the town, and spending the daytime in filling the casks and transporting them on ox-carts to the landing-place, whence they were taken on board by the crew with boats. This being all done with, we gave one day to bending our sails; and at night, every sail, from the courses to the skysails, was bent, and every studding-sail ready for setting.

**...living at the town...** The town, you will recall, is San Diego, at this point a small Mexican pueblo (village) the outskirts of which are still occasionally attacked by local Indians who live in the surrounding mountains.

Before our sailing, an unsuccessful attempt was made by one of the crew of the California to effect an exchange with one of our number. It was a lad, between fifteen and sixteen years of age, who went by the name of the "reefer," having been a midshipman in an East India Company's ship. His singular character and story had excited our interest ever since the ship came into the port. He was a delicate, slender little fellow, with a beautiful pearly complexion, regular features, forehead as white as marble, black haired, curling beautifully, rounded, tapering, delicate fingers, small feet, soft voice, gentle manners, and, in fact, every sign of having been well born and bred. At the same time there was something in his expression which showed a slight deficiency of intellect. How great the deficiency was, or what it resulted from; whether he was born so; whether it was the result of disease or accident; or whether, as some said, it was brought on by his distress of mind, during the voyage, I cannot say. From his own account of himself, and from many circumstances which were known in connection with his story, he must have been the son of a man of wealth. His mother was an Italian woman. He was probably a natural son, for in scarcely any other way could the incidents of his early life be accounted for. He said that his parents did not live together, and he seemed to have been ill treated by his father. Though he had been delicately brought up, and indulged in every way, (and he had then with him trinkets which had been given him at home,) yet his education had been sadly neglected; and when only twelve

**...who went by the name of the "reefer,"...** A reefer is someone who reefs sails; at the time, it was slang for a midshipman: a noncommissioned officer.

In the news

**May, 1836**

After the Republic of Texas is established, David G. Burnet, President of the Republic of Texas, and His Excellency General Antonio Lopez de Santa Anna, General of the Mexican Army sign the Treaty of Velasco. The treaty formalizes the end of hostilities and calls for the evacuation of Mexican troops from Texan territory and the release of both Texian and Mexican POWs.

**He was probably a natural son...** That is, an "illegitimate" child—one born to parents who are not married to one another. The question of a child's legitimacy was once of great legal importance, since only a legitimate child could inherit, but U.S. courts have since struck down such restrictions.

**...the ship Rialto, Captain Holmes, for Boston.** The *Rialto* is a 459-ton vessel built in 1834.

**...sailor's boarding-house, in Ann street...** From previous notes, we know that Ann Street is an unsavory place full of brothels, gambling halls, and the sorts of people who frequent them. It's not a place for a young boy on his own.

**...and advised him to ship.** Misleading would-be sailors (or, in extreme cases, simply drugging or beating men on the street and dragging them aboard ship) has been going on for a long time. The term most widely used to describe the practice, impressment, originally referred to a state-sponsored "draft" of citizens recruited to serve in the Navy or merchant marine. It eventually came to encompass even instances in which (often drunken) men were simply forced aboard a ship and awoke out at sea with no way of returning until the end of the voyage. What's interesting here—and it stands as proof of the writer's altruistic intent—is the fact that Dana would speak of it (and of practices related to it) so openly. But Dana, enraged as he was by the treatment of sailors, did not shy away from such issues, in this or later writings.

**...shipping-master, who had been in search of him, popped upon him...** The shipping-master is the official who supervises the signup and discharge of sailors. He is most likely paid a commission on the men who show up for duty, so it would be worth his time to go out and find men and boys who had signed up and were now having second thoughts.

years old, he was sent as midshipman in the Company's service. His own story was, that he afterwards ran away from home, upon a difficulty which he had with his father, and went to Liverpool, whence he sailed in the ship Rialto, Captain Holmes, for Boston. Captain Holmes endeavored to get him a passage back, but there being no vessel to sail for some time, the boy left him, and went to board at a common sailor's boarding-house, in Ann street, where he supported himself for a few weeks by selling some of his valuables. At length, according to his own account, being desirous of returning home, he went to a shipping-office, where the shipping articles of the California were open. Upon asking where the ship was going, he was told by the shipping-master that she was bound to California. Not knowing where that was, he told him that he wanted to go to Europe, and asked if California was in Europe. The shipping-master answered him in a way which the boy did not understand, and advised him to ship. The boy signed the articles, received his advance, laid out a little of it in clothes, and spent the rest, and was ready to go on board, when, upon the morning of sailing, he heard that the ship was bound upon the North-west Coast, on a two or three years' voyage, and was not going to Europe. Frightened at this prospect, he slipped away when the crew was going aboard, wandered up into another part of the town, and spent all the forenoon in straying about the common, and the neighboring streets.

Having no money, and all his clothes and other things being in the chest, on board, and being a stranger, he became tired and hungry, and ventured down toward the shipping, to see if the vessel had sailed. He was just turning the corner of a street, when the shipping-master, who had been in search of him, popped upon him, seized him, and carried him on board. He cried and struggled, and said he did not wish to go in the ship, but the topsails were at the mast-head, the fasts just ready to be cast off, and everything in the hurry and confusion of departure, so that he was hardly noticed; and the few who did inquire about the matter were told that it was merely a boy who had spent his advance and tried to run away. Had the owners of the vessel known anything of the matter, they would have interfered at once; but they either knew nothing of it, or heard, like the rest, that it was only an unruly boy who was sick of his bargain. As soon as the boy found himself actually at sea, and upon a voyage of two or three years in length, his spirits failed him; he refused to work, and became so miserable, that Captain Arthur took him into the cabin, where he assisted the steward, and occasionally pulled and hauled about decks. He was in this capacity when we saw him; and though it was much better for him than the life in the forecastle, and the hard work, watching, and exposure, which his delicate frame could not have borne, yet, to be joined with a black fellow in waiting upon a man whom he probably looked upon as but little, in point of education and manners, above one of his father's servants, was almost too much for his spirit to bear. Had he entered upon his situation of his own free will, he could have endured it; but to have been deceived, and, in addition to that, forced into it, was intolerable. He made every effort to go home in our ship, but his captain refused to part with him except in the way of exchange, and that he could not effect. If this account of the whole matter, which we had from the boy, and which was confirmed by all the crew, be correct, I cannot understand why Captain Arthur should have refused to let him go, especially being a captain who had the name, not only with that crew, but with all whom he had ever commanded, of an unusually kind-hearted man.

The truth is, the unlimited power which merchant captains have, upon long voyages on strange coasts, takes away a sense of responsibility, and too often, even in men otherwise well-disposed, substitutes a disregard for the rights and feelings of others. The lad was sent on shore to join the gang at the hide-house; from whence, I was afterwards rejoiced to hear, he effected his escape, and went down to Callao in a small Spanish schooner; and from Callao, he probably returned to England.

Soon after the arrival of the California, I spoke to Captain Arthur about Hope; and as he had known him on the voyage before, and was very fond of him, he

**In the news**
**May, 1836**

Edgar Allan Poe marries his first cousin, Virginia Clemm. Poe, 26 years of age, had already married the girl (she was only 13 years old) in a private ceremony the previous September. Marriage between first cousins was (and remains) legal in many states, including Maryland, where the marriage took place. The marriage certificate lists Virginia's age as 21, but that was strictly for appearances. Some have suggested that the marriage was never consummated, but friends of the family insisted that the marriage was "normal" in every respect.

**In the news**
**May, 1836**

One way to deal with the continuing contentious debate about slavery was simply to outlaw the argument. In effect, that's what the U.S. House of Representatives did when it passed what amounted to a "gag rule." President Martin Van Buren helped pass a watered-down version of the law. Southerners accused him of lukewarm support for their interests, while northerners pilloried him for supporting the measure at all.

**The truth is...** This is a recurring theme with Dana, reminiscent of Lord Acton's dictum (formulated some 50 years after Dana's voyage) that "Power tends to corrupt, and absolute power corrupts absolutely." Dana argues that even good men, when possessed of "unlimited power," become insensitive to the needs of others and in fact are sometimes devoid of simple, common decency.

**...he immediately went to see him...** In spite of his unwillingness to free "Reefer," Captain Arthur is a kind man, as we see here.

**...this was the only thing connected with leaving California which was in any way unpleasant.** Dana has come to love these men, and to appreciate their kindness, their generosity, and their good spirits. Dana too is a good and kind man, but one who is, after all, a product of his times. (To him, anyone who is not white, European, and male, might be considered "simple.")

In the news
**May, 1836**

Virginia's *Staunton Spectator* publishes an article calling into question the results of the siege at the Alamo and the massacre at Goliad, and claiming that Col. David Crockett, "although covered with wounds...is slowly recovering." The article is, of course, in error. After a 13-day siege, Crockett and about 200 other men, among them James "Jim" Bowie and William B. Travis, perished during the predawn attack by General Santa Anna's Mexican army.

**...and the hatches calked down.** Later editions of the book included Dana's comment that the ship also "carried a small quantity of gold dust," brought to the ship by Mexicans or Indians. The first meaningful gold strikes in California would occur near what is now San Fernando, CA, in 1841. Strikes further north in 1848 would ignite the firestorm of entrepreneurial avarice and expansion known as the California Gold Rush.

immediately went to see him, gave him proper medicines, and, under such care, he began rapidly to recover. The Saturday night before our sailing, I spent an hour in the oven, and took leave of my Kanaka friends; and, really, this was the only thing connected with leaving California which was in any way unpleasant. I felt an interest and affection for many of these simple, true-hearted men, such as I never felt before but for a near relation. Hope shook me by the hand, said he should soon be well again, and ready to work for me when I came upon the coast, next voyage, as officer of the ship; and told me not to forget, when I became captain, how to be kind to the sick. Old "Mr. Bingham" and "King Mannini" went down to the boat with me, shook me heartily by the hand, wished us a good voyage, and went back to the oven, chanting one of their deep monotonous songs, the burden of which I gathered to be about us and our voyage.

Sunday, May 8th. This promised to be our last day in California.

Our forty thousand hides, thirty thousand horns, besides several barrels of otter and beaver skins, were all stowed below, and the hatches calked down. All our spare spars were taken on board and lashed; our water-casks secured; and our live stock, consisting of four bullocks, a dozen sheep, a dozen or more pigs, and three or four dozen of poultry, were all stowed away in their different quarters: the bullocks in the long-boat, the sheep in a pen on the fore-hatch, and the pigs in a sty under the bows of the long-boat, and the poultry in their proper coop; and the jolly-boat was full of hay for the sheep and bullocks. Our unusually large cargo, together with the stores for a five months' voyage, brought the ship channels down into the water. In addition to this, she had been steeved so thoroughly, and was so bound by the compression of her cargo, forced into her by so powerful machinery, that she was like a man in a straight-jacket, and would be but a dull sailer, until she had worked herself loose.

The California had finished discharging her cargo, and

was to get under weigh at the same time with us. Having washed down decks and got our breakfast, the two vessels lay side by side, in complete readiness for sea, our ensigns hanging from the peaks, and our tall spars reflected from the glassy surface of the river, which, since sunrise, had been unbroken by a ripple. At length, a few whiffs came across the water, and, by eleven o'clock, the regular north-west wind set steadily in. There was no need of calling all hands, for we had all been hanging about the forecastle the whole forenoon, and were ready for a start upon the first sign of a breeze.

All eyes were aft upon the captain, who was walking the deck, with, every now and then, a look to windward. He made a sign to the mate, who came forward, took his station, deliberately between the knight-heads, cast a glance aloft, and called out, "All hands, lay aloft and loose the sails!" We were half in the rigging before the order came, and never since we left Boston were the gaskets off the yards, and the rigging overhauled, in a shorter time. "All ready forward, sir!"—"All ready the main!"—"Cross-jack yards all ready, sir!"—"Lay down, all hands but one on each yard!" The yard-arm and bunt gaskets were cast off; and each sail hung by the jigger, with one man standing by the tie to let it go. At the same moment that we sprang aloft, a dozen hands sprang into the rigging of the California, and in an instant were all over her yards; and her sails, too, were ready to be dropped at the word. In the mean time our bow gun had been loaded and run out, and its discharge was to be the signal for dropping sails. A cloud of smoke came out of our bows; the echoes of the gun rattled our farewell among the hills of California; and the two ships were covered, from head to foot, with their white canvas. For a few minutes, all was uproar and apparent confusion: men flying about like monkeys in the rigging; ropes and blocks flying; orders given and answered, and the confused noises of men singing out at the ropes. The top-sails came to the mast-heads with "Cheerily, men!" and, in a few minutes, every sail was set; for the wind was light. The head sails were backed, the windlass came round "slip-slap" to the cry of the

**In the news**
**May, 1836**

John King begins printing *The Dubuque Visitor* in Dubuque, believed to be the first newspaper to be printed in Iowa. (At the time, Dubuque was part of the Michigan Territory.) Originally from Ohio, King settled in Dubuque in 1834 and returned to Cincinnati to purchase a press and find a typesetter. The first issue is dated May 11, 1836. King was the publisher only briefly, as the paper would change hands several times over the next few years.

**...ready for a start upon the first sign of a breeze.** The men are, after all, more than ready to head home.

**...between the knight-heads...** The knightheads are two large supporting timbers rising from the ship's keel to the bowsprit. (They are sometimes called bollard timbers.) The mate is attempting to look calm, deliberate, and nonchalant, even though he is probably just as excited as the men to be heading home.

**A cloud of smoke came out of our bows...** This must have been a beautiful and stirring sight: both vessels firing their cannons, hoisting their profusion of sails, and setting out to sea together.

**...to the tune of "Time for us to go," with a loud chorus.** This was a popular seafaring ballad, and was obviously an appropriate way to start the voyage home. A sample verse is as follows:

*With sails let fall and sheeted home and clear of the ground were we. We passed the bank, stood round the Light, and sailed away to sea. The wind was fair. the coast was clear. The brig was noways slow, For she was built in Baltimore, and 'twas time for us to go.*

A version of the song became popular with slavers.

**...being low in the water...** The *Alert* is so weighed down by her heavy cargo that she's sitting very low in the water; as a result, the ship gets stuck on a sand bar.

**...observed the redheaded second mate, most mal-a-propos.** That is, most inappropriately.

sailors;—"Hove short, sir," said the mate;—"Up with him!"—"Aye, aye, sir."—A few hearty and long heaves, and the anchor showed its head. "Hook cat!"—The fall was stretched along the decks; all hands laid hold;—"Hurrah, for the last time," said the mate; and the anchor came to the cat-head to the tune of "Time for us to go," with a loud chorus. Everything was done quick, as though it were for the last time. The head yards were filled away, and our ship began to move through the water on her homeward-bound course.

The California had got under weigh at the same moment; and we sailed down the narrow bay abreast and were just off the mouth, and finding ourselves gradually shooting ahead of her, were on the point of giving her three parting cheers, when, suddenly, we found ourselves stopped short, and the California ranging fast ahead of us. A bar stretches across the mouth of the harbor, with water enough to float common vessels, but, being low in the water, and having kept well to leeward, as we were bound to the southward, we had stuck fast, while the California, being light, had floated over.

We kept all sail on, in the hope of forcing over, but failing in this, we hove aback, and lay waiting for the tide, which was on the flood, to take us back into the channel. This was somewhat of a damper to us, and the captain looked not a little mortified and vexed. "This is the same place where the Rosa got ashore," observed the redheaded second mate, most mal-a-propos. A malediction on the Rosa, and him too, was all the answer he got, and he slunk off to leeward. In a few minutes, the force of the wind and the rising of the tide backed us into the stream, and we were on our way to our old anchoring-place, the tide setting swiftly up, and the ship barely manageable, in the light breeze. We came-to, in our old berth, opposite the hide-house, whose inmates were not a little surprised to see us return. We felt as though we were tied to California; and some of the crew swore that they never should get clear of the bloody coast.

In about half an hour, which was near high water, the

order was given to man the windlass, and again the anchor was catted; but not a word was said about the last time. The California had come back on finding that we had returned, and was hove-to, waiting for us, off the point. This time we passed the bar safely, and were soon up with the California, who filled away, and kept us company.

She seemed desirous of a trial of speed, and our captain accepted the challenge, although we were loaded down to the bolts of our chain plates, as deep as a sand-barge, and bound so taut with our cargo that we were no more fit for a race than a man in fetters;—while our antagonist was in her best trim. Being clear of the point, the breeze became stiff, and the royal masts bent under our sails, but we would not take them in until we saw three boys spring aloft into the rigging of the California; when they were all furled at once, but with orders to stay aloft at the top-gallant mastheads, and loose them again at the word. It was my duty to furl the fore royal; and while standing by to loose it again, I had a fine view of the scene. From where I stood, the two vessels seemed nothing but spars and sails, while their narrow decks, far below, slanting over by the force of the wind aloft, appeared hardly capable of supporting the great fabrics raised upon them. The California was to windward of us, and had every advantage; yet, while the breeze was stiff, we held our own. As soon as it began to slacken, she ranged a little ahead, and the order was given to loose the royals. In an instant the gaskets were off and the bunt dropped. "Sheet home the fore royal!—Weather sheet's home!"—"Hoist away, sir!" is bawled from aloft. "Overhaul your clew-lines!" shouts the mate. "Aye, aye, sir, all clear!"—"taut leech! belay! Well the lee brace; haul taut to windward"—and the royals are set. These brought us up again; but the wind continuing light, the California set hers, and it was soon evident that she was walking away from us. Our captain then hailed, and said that he should keep off to his course; adding—"She isn't the Alert now. If I had her in your trim, she would have been out of sight by this time." This was good-naturedly answered from the California, and she braced sharp up, and stood close

**In the news**
**May, 1836**

The Champlain and St. Lawrence Railway takes delivery of Canada's first locomotive, the "Iron Kitten." (Which for some reason is quickly renamed "Dorchester.") The engine, built in England by Robert Stephenson, was a wood-burner with a top speed of about 31 mph.

upon the wind up the coast; while we squared away our yards, and stood before the wind to the south-south-west. The California's crew manned her weather rigging, waved their hats in the air, and gave up three hearty cheers, which we answered as heartily, and the customary single cheer came back to us from over the water. She stood on her way, doomed to eighteen months' or two years' hard service upon that hated coast, while we were making our way to our home, to which every hour and every mile was bringing us nearer.

In the news
**May, 1836**

In the face of a continuing influx of settlers clamoring for Indian lands, a band of Creek Indians attacks the town of Roanoke, GA, killing several residents and burning their homes. After the residents retreat, the Indians burn the town to the ground. The Creeks were angered, of course, by being driven from their lands and also by the fact that the U.S. government was not interested in abiding by the 1832 Treaty of Cusseta, which had stipulated that Alabama Creeks would be given a parcel of 320 acres if they decided to stay in that state.

As soon as we parted company with the California, all hands were sent aloft to set the studding-sails. Booms were rigged out, tacks and halyards rove, sail after sail packed upon her, until every available inch of canvas was spread, that we might not lose a breath of the fair wind. We could now see how much she was cramped and deadened by her cargo; for with a good breeze on her quarter, and every stitch of canvas spread, we could not get more than six knots out of her. She had no more life in her than if she were water-logged. The log was hove several times; but she was doing her best. We had hardly patience with her, but the older sailors said—"Stand by! you'll see her work herself loose in a week or two, and then she'll walk up to Cape Horn like a race-horse."

When all sail had been set, and the decks cleared up, the California was a speck in the horizon, and the coast lay like a low cloud along the north-east. At sunset they were both out of sight, and we were once more upon the ocean where sky and water meet.

**When the crew were paid off in Boston...** To Dana's credit, he is willing to attempt to coerce the owners to pay Harry Bluff six months' wages. And to the owners' credit, they do so. Note that this is a footnote that refers back to early in the chapter. Dana occasionally adds these as explanatory measures.

[1] When the crew were paid off in Boston, the owners answered the order, but generously refused to deduct the amount from the pay-roll, saying that the exchange was made under compulsion. They also allowed S—— his exchange money.

## Chapter XXX

### Beginning the Long Return Voyage–A Scare

At eight o'clock all hands were called aft, and the watches set for the voyage. Some changes were made; but I was glad to find myself still in the larboard watch. Our crew was somewhat diminished; for a man and a boy had gone in the Pilgrim; another was second mate of the Ayacucho; and a third, the oldest man of the crew, had broken down under the hard work and constant exposure on the coast, and, having had a stroke of the palsy, was left behind at the hide-house under the charge of Captain Arthur. The poor fellow wished very much to come home in the ship; and he ought to have been brought home in her. But a live dog is better than a dead lion, and a sick sailor belongs to nobody's mess; so he was sent ashore with the rest of the lumber, which was only in the way. By these diminutions, we were short-handed for a voyage round Cape Horn in the dead of winter. Besides S— and myself, there were only five in the forecastle; who, together with four boys in the steerage, the sailmaker, carpenter, etc., composed the whole crew. In addition to this, we were only three or four days out, when the sailmaker, who was the oldest and best seaman on board, was taken with the palsy, and was useless for the rest of the voyage. The constant wading in the water, in all weathers, to take off hides, together with the other labors, is too much for old men, and for any who have not good constitutions. Beside these two men of ours, the second officer of the California and the carpenter of the Pilgrim broke down under the work, and the latter died at Santa Barbara. The young man, too, who came out with us from Boston in the Pilgrim, had to be taken from his berth before the mast and made clerk, on account of a fit of rheumatism which attacked him soon after he came upon the coast. By the loss of the sailmaker, our watch was reduced to five, of whom two were boys, who never steered but in fine weather, so that the other two and myself had to stand at the wheel four hours apiece out of every twenty-four; and the other watch had only four helmsmen. "Never mind–we're homeward bound!"

**...the oldest man of the crew, had broken down under the hard work...** The man is Harry Bennett. The records list him as having stated his age as 31 when he signed on, which, in that day and age and in that company, was fairly old. Captain Faucon later said that Bennett was at least 40. Dana says elsewhere that Bennett came home on the *Pilgrim*, and that Dana helped him get into the hospital for treatment. Bennett was last seen selling cakes and ale from a stall he had set up in the marketplace in Boston.

**...a live dog is better than a dead lion...** From the Bible, Ecclesiastes 9:4: "For to him that is joined to all the living there is hope: for a living dog is better than a dead lion."

**...the sailmaker, who was the oldest and best seaman on board, was taken with the palsy...** "Sails," as he was called, was Rueben Herriot, born in New York and living in Boston. (He's the oldest on board, now that Bennett has left.) Ship's records have his age as 26, which must be wrong, since Faucon says elsewhere that Herriot had been at sea at least 22 years. Palsy is a condition in which one loses the ability to move a part of one's body or is afflicted with uncontrollable tremors. There are various forms (and causes) of palsy: Bell's palsy, for instance, is a partial (and often temporary) facial paralysis caused by inflammation of facial nerves; cerebral palsy is caused by lesions in the brain. We don't know what sort of palsy has afflicted the two men, but the term was widely (and often incorrectly) used during the 19th century to describe a variety of ailments.

**...on account of a fit of rheumatism...** In those days, any painful disorder of the joints was characterized as rheumatism.

was the answer to everything; and we should not have minded this, were it not for the thought that we should be off Cape Horn in the very dead of winter. It was now the first part of May; and two months would bring us off the cape in July, which is the worst month in the year there; when the sun rises at nine and sets at three, giving eighteen hours night, and there is snow and rain, gales and high seas, in abundance.

The prospect of meeting this in a ship half manned, and loaded so deep that every heavy sea must wash her fore and aft, was by no means pleasant. The Alert, in her passage out, doubled the Cape in the month of February, which is midsummer; and we came round in the Pilgrim in the latter part of October, which we thought was bad enough. There was only one of our crew who had been off there in the winter, and that was in a whaleship, much lighter and higher than our ship; yet he said they had man-killing weather for twenty days without intermission, and their decks were swept twice, and they were all glad enough to see the last of it. The Brandywine frigate, also, in her passage round, had sixty days off the Cape, and lost several boats by the heavy sea. All this was for our comfort; yet pass it we must; and all hands agreed to make the best of it.

During our watches below we overhauled our clothes, and made and mended everything for bad weather. Each of us had made for himself a suit of oil-cloth or tarpaulin, and these we got out, and gave thorough coatings of oil or tar, and hung upon the stays to dry.

Our stout boots, too, we covered over with a thick mixture of melted grease and tar, and hung out to dry. Thus we took advantage of the warm sun and fine weather of the Pacific to prepare for its other face. In the forenoon watches below, our forecastle looked like the workshop of what a sailor is,–a Jack at all trades. Thick stockings and drawers were darned and patched; mittens dragged from the bottom of the chest and mended; comforters made for the neck and ears; old flannel shirts cut up to line monkey jackets; south-westers lined with flannel, and a pot of paint smuggled forward to give them a coat

**"Never mind–we're homeward bound!" was the answer to everything...** After all, Dana seems to be saying, one can stand anything if one knows that the suffering will be short-lived.

**The prospect of meeting this in a ship half manned, and loaded so deep...** The weather off Cape Horn, especially at this time of year, is horrendous. It's not uncommon for ships to fail in their attempt to round the cape, and then have to stand off for weeks waiting for better weather. It is a miserable and very dangerous undertaking and even more dangerous in an undermanned, overloaded ship.

**....their decks were swept twice...** That is, the seas were so large and so violent that waves swept across the deck from bow to stern, taking with them anything that wasn't secured. (This can include even lifeboats and workboats, such as those lost by the frigate *Brandywine*.)

### In the news
### May, 1836

In Russia, construction begins on the Tsarskoye Selo Railway, the first public railway line in the Russian Empire. The project is finished in October of 1837, at which point a train consisting of eight cars is hauled by a steam locomotive between Saint Petersburg and Tsarskoye Selo, the birthplace of writer Alexandr Pushkin. Czar Nicholas I and his family participate in several of the test runs, helping to prove to awestruck citizens that railway travel was safe.

**...we took advantage of the warm sun and fine weather of the Pacific to prepare for its other face.** A bitter and sometimes deadly irony: The Pacific, as befits its name, is a calm, peaceful ocean—except for when it's not.

on the outside; and everything turned to hand; so that, although two years had left us but a scanty wardrobe, yet the economy and invention which necessity teaches a sailor, soon put each of us in pretty good trim for bad weather, even before we had seen the last of the fine. Even the cobbler's art was not out of place. Several old shoes were very decently repaired, and with waxed ends, an awl, and the top of an old boot, I made me quite a respectable sheath for my knife.

There was one difficulty, however, which nothing that we could do would remedy; and that was the leaking of the forecastle, which made it very uncomfortable in bad weather, and rendered half of the berths tenantless. The tightest ships, in a long voyage, from the constant strain which is upon the bowsprit, will leak, more or less, round the heel of the bowsprit, and the bitts, which come down into the forecastle; but, in addition to this, we had an unaccountable leak on the starboard bow, near the cat-head, which drove us from the forward berths on that side, and, indeed, when she was on the starboard tack, from all the forward berths. One of the after berths, too, leaked in very bad weather; so that in a ship which was in other respects as tight as a bottle, and brought her cargo to Boston perfectly dry, we had, after every effort made to prevent it, in the way of caulking and leading, a forecastle with only three dry berths for seven of us. However, as there is never but one watch below at a time, by 'turning in and out,' we did pretty well. And there being, in our watch, but three of us who lived forward, we generally had a dry berth apiece in bad weather.(1)

———- 1. On removing the cat-head, after the ship arrived at Boston, it was found that there were two holes under it which had been bored for the purpose of driving tree-nails, and which, accidentally, had not been plugged up when the cat-head was placed over them. This was sufficient to account for the leak, and for our not having been able to discover and stop it. ———-

All this, however, was but anticipation. We were still in fine weather in the North Pacific, running down the

**...I made me quite a respectable sheath for my knife.** One of the things of which Dana is understandably proud is the level of self-sufficiency he's attained since shipping out. In those days especially, sailors on an extended voyage had to learn to sew, mend, and fix their gear and garments. There were no malls in California at the time, no place to purchase new boots or jackets as the old ones wore out during the two-year trip.

**The tightest ships, in a long voyage, from the constant strain which is upon the bowsprit, will leak...** Wooden vessels leak. Even today, owners of wooden boats know that a boat that has been out of the water will leak quite a bit when "splashed"—placed back into a lake or ocean, at least until the wood swells and tightens up the seams. But even after the seams swell, a certain amount of leakage is normal for a wooden boat, if a bit disconcerting for its landlubberly passengers. The leak Dana describes, though, sounds bad enough to be uncomfortable at best and dangerous at worst. (In his notes, Dana describes the problem, discovered and resolved after *Alert* made it back to Boston.)

north-east trades, which we took on the second day after leaving San Diego.

**...thirteen hundred miles in seven days.** At about 185 miles per day (or a bit over 7 miles in an hour), this is roughly in keeping with Dana's earlier estimate that *Alert* was making about 7 knots. Keep in mind that the ship sails 24 hours per day; there is no handy rest stop to pull into and sleep. (Although vessels will sometimes "heave to," especially in a storm. This involves setting the helm and sails such that they need no attention and the ship makes little or no headway. The crew can thus stay below and rest, safe from the storm.)

Sunday, May 15th, one week out, we were in latitude 14° 56' N., long. 116° 14' W., having gone, by reckoning, over thirteen hundred miles in seven days. In fact, ever since leaving San Diego, we had had a fair wind, and as much as we wanted of it. For seven days, our lower and topmast studding-sails were set all the time, and our royals and top-gallant studding-sails, whenever she could stagger under them. Indeed, the captain had shown, from the moment we got to sea, that he was to have no boy's play, but that the ship had got to carry all she could, and that he was going to make up, by "cracking on" to her, what she wanted in lightness. In this way, we frequently made three degrees of latitude, besides something in longitude, in the course of twenty-four hours.–Our days were spent in the usual ship's work. The rigging which had become slack from being long in port was to be set up; breast backstays got up; studding-sail booms rigged upon the main yard; and the royal studding-sails got ready for the light trades; ring-tail set; and new rigging fitted and sails got ready for Cape Horn. For, with a ship's gear, as well as a sailor's wardrobe, fine weather must be improved to get ready for the bad to come. Our forenoon watch below, as I have said, was given to our own work, and our night watches were spent in the usual manner:–a trick at the wheel, a look-out on the forecastle, a nap on a coil of rigging under the lee of the rail; a yarn round the windlass-end; or, as was generally my way, a solitary walk fore and aft, in the weather waist, between the windlass-end and the main tack. Every wave that she threw aside brought us nearer home, and every day's observation at noon showed a progress which, if it continued, would in less than five months, take us into Boston Bay. This is the pleasure of life at sea, –fine weather, day after day, without interruption,–fair wind, and a plenty of it,–and homeward bound. Every one was in good humor; things went right; and all was done with a will. At the dog watch, all hands came on deck, and stood round the weather side of the forecastle, or sat upon the windlass, and sung sea songs, and those ballads of pirates and

**...he was going to make up, by "cracking on" to her...** This is a very old nautical expression that means to carry as much sail as possible in order to increase a vessel's speed.

**In the news**

**May, 1836**

The *New York Times* weighs in on the ongoing war in Texas, with an editorial that, although noting that "our neutrality must be preserved, if possible," also lays the groundwork for a possible American invasion of Mexico. The paper comments that there is reason to believe that "the accounts of the butcheries of Santa Anna are correct" and notes that "there is good ground for the opinion that [Santa Anna] has invaded our territory." Public sentiment in support of the Texians was high in the U.S., with many favoring outright annexation of Texas, by force if necessary.

**This is the pleasure of life at sea, – fine weather, day after day, without interruption,–fair wind, and a plenty of it,–and homeward bound.** For Dana, and for most sailors, this would indeed be a good description of how pleasant the life of a sailor can be.

highwaymen, which sailors delight in. Home, too, and what we should do when we got there, and when and how we should arrive, was no infrequent topic. Every night, after the kids and pots were put away, and we had lighted our pipes and cigars at the galley, and gathered about the windlass, the first question was,–

"Well, Tom, what was the latitude to-day?"

"Why fourteen, north, and she has been going seven knots ever since."

"Well, this will bring us up to the line in five days."

"Yes, but these trades won't last twenty-four hours longer," says an old salt, pointing with the sharp of his hand to leeward, –"I know that by the look of the clouds."

Then came all manner of calculations and conjectures as to the continuance of the wind, the weather under the line, the south-east trades, etc., and rough guesses as to the time the ship would be up with the Horn; and some, more venturous, gave her so many days to Boston light, and offered to bet that she would not exceed it.

"You'd better wait till you get round Cape Horn," says an old croaker.

"Yes," says another, "you may see Boston, but you've got to 'smell hell' before that good day."

Rumors also of what had been said in the cabin, as usual, found their way forward. The steward had heard the captain say something about the straits of Magellan, and the man at the wheel fancied he had heard him tell the "passenger" that, if he found the wind ahead and the weather very bad off the Cape, he should stick her off for New Holland, and come home round the Cape of Good Hope.

This passenger–the first and only one we had had, except to go from port to port, on the coast, was no one

## In the news
## May, 1836

The *Daily Commercial Bulletin* reports the death of Dr. Warren Noel, killed in an accident of the sort not uncommon at the time. As the paper has it: "On Monday last, as the steamboat Science was preparing to leave Evansville, Ia., one of her boilers burst with a terrible explosion, throwing about a dozen persons overboard. ... Seven persons were scalded, some of them dangerously...." One reason that accidents such as this are common is that the captains and passengers enjoyed racing other vessels up and down the rivers and lakes. That often meant stoking the boilers beyond the point of safety.

**...you've got to 'smell hell'...** That is, come so close to death that you can smell hell from where you stand.

**...he should stick her off for New Holland...** Dutch explorer Abel Tasman (whose name we now recall in "Tasmania") gave this name to the country (and continent) of Australia in 1644. The Cape of Good Hope is on the Atlantic coast of South Africa; Cape Horn, for which *Alert* is headed, is off of South America. The former route would be longer, but possibly safer than the latter.

**...Professor N—, of Cambridge.** Thomas Nuttall was a professor at Harvard, and curator of the university's botanical gardens. Nuttall had, as noted earlier, taken a leave of absence from Harvard in 1832 to traverse the U.S. via what would eventually be known as the Oregon Trail, examining the flora and collecting samples. He then went to the Sandwich Islands (i.e., Hawaii), then back to California, and has now boarded *Alert* to sail back home to Boston. In an incredible coincidence, it turns out that Dana knows the ship's only passenger.

In the news

**May, 1836**

On May 8th, 1836, Dr. John Emerson arrives at Fort Snelling (the future site of St. Paul, MN), in what was then the Wisconsin Territory. Accompanying him is his servant, a black man named Dred Scott. Scott will eventually (1857) sue for his freedom (and that of his family) on the grounds that he had resided (with Emerson) in states and territories where slavery was illegal. The U.S. Supreme Court, in a decision that would echo through the ages, ruled against Scott, not because he was in the wrong, but because he was of African ancestry and thus could not claim citizenship; since only citizens can sue, Scott had no legal basis from which to pursue his argument, said the Court.

**...I should not have been more surprised to have seen...** Dana is referring to the steeple of the Old South Meeting House, a church originally located at the corner of Washington and Milk Streets. Legend has it that the church was used as a base from which the Boston Tea Party was organized. The church was damaged by fire in 1872, and a new building, still in use today, was built at Copley Square.

else than a gentleman whom I had known in my better days; and the last person I should have expected to have seen on the coast of California–Professor N—, of Cambridge. I had left him quietly seated in the chair of Botany and Ornithology, in Harvard University; and the next I saw of him, was strolling about San Diego beach, in a sailor's pea-jacket, with a wide straw hat, and bare-footed, with his trowsers roiled up to his knees, picking up stones and shells. He had travelled overland to the North-west Coast, and come down in a small vessel to Monterey. There he learned that there was a ship at the leeward, about to sail for Boston; and, taking passage in the Pilgrim, which was then at Monterey, he came slowly down, visiting the intermediate ports, and examining the trees, plants, earths, birds, etc., and joined us at San Diego shortly before we sailed. The second mate of the Pilgrim told me that they had an old gentleman on board who knew me, and came from the college that I had been in.

He could not recollect his name, but said he was a "sort of an oldish man," with white hair, and spent all his time in the bush, and along the beach, picking up flowers and shells, and such truck, and had a dozen boxes and barrels, full of them. I thought over everybody who would be likely to be there, but could fix upon no one; when, the next day, just as we were about to shove off from the beach, he came down to the boat, in the rig I have described, with his shoes in his hand, and his pockets full of specimens. I knew him at once, though I should not have been more surprised to have seen the Old South steeple shoot up from the hide-house. He probably had no less difficulty in recognizing me. As we left home about the same time, we had nothing to tell one another; and, owing to our different situations on board, I saw but little of him on the passage home. Sometimes, when I was at the wheel of a calm night, and the steering required no attention, and the officer of the watch was forward, he would come aft and hold a short yarn with me; but this was against the rules of the ship, as is, in fact, all intercourse between passengers and the crew. I was often amused to see the sailors puzzled to know what to make of him, and to hear their conjectures about him and his business. They were as much puzzled as our old sailmaker was with the captain's instruments in the cabin.

He said there were three:–the chro-nometer, the chre-nometer, and the the-nometer. (Chronometer, barometer, and thermometer.) The Pilgrim's crew christened Mr. N. "Old Curious," from his zeal for curiosities, and some of them said that he was crazy, and that his friends let him go about and amuse himself in this way. Why else a rich man (sailors call every man rich who does not work with his hands, and wears a long coat and cravat) should leave a Christian country, and come to such a place as California, to pick up shells and stones, they could not understand. One of them, however, an old salt, who had seen something more of the world ashore, set all to rights, as he thought,–"Oh, 'vast there!–You don't know anything about them craft. I've seen them colleges, and know the ropes. They keep all such things for cur'osities, and study 'em, and have men a' purpose to go and get 'em. This old chap knows what he's about. He a'n't the child you take him for. He'll carry all these things to the college, and if they are better than any that they have had before, he'll be head of the college. Then, by-and-by, somebody else will go after some more, and if they beat him, he'll have to go again, or else give up his berth. That's the way they do it. This old covey knows the ropes. He has worked a traverse over 'em, and come 'way out here, where nobody's ever been afore, and where they'll never think of coming." This explanation satisfied Jack; and as it raised Mr. N.'s credit for capacity, and was near enough to the truth for common purposes, I did not disturb it.

With the exception of Mr. N., we had no one on board but the regular ship's company, and the live stock. Upon this, we had made a considerable inroad. We killed one of the bullocks every four days, so that they did not last us up to the line. We, or, rather, they, then began upon the sheep and the poultry, for these never come into Jack's mess.(1) The pigs were left

———— 1. The customs as to the allowance of "grub"

**...sailors call every man rich who does not work with his hands, and wears a long coat and cravat...** Nuttall is not looked down upon so much as he's looked at warily; the men aren't quite sure what to make of him, although they figure he must be wealthy. (And he probably is, compared to most of them.) A cravat is an early (though sometimes still worn) form of necktie. The word comes from the French "cravate," which is itself a mispronunciation of "Hirvat," or "Croat," the country in which this form of necktie originated.

**This old covey...** The worldy sailor (who's not far wrong, actually, in his assessment of academic politics and pecking order) is using "covey" in its sense of "an associate."

**This explanation satisfied Jack...** That is, made sense to the sailors.

**...for these never come into Jack's mess.** The sailors and the officers they serve are of two distinct classes, and there is very little mingling. The cabin (the officers' mess) gets the best food and eats with utensils and with real plates. For the most part, the sailors get what's left, and some food they never taste at all. When they do eat, the sailors use their sheath knives and eat out of a "kid," a small wooden tub used for holding food. Generally, sailors before the mast did not use plates and forks, let alone the china or pewter that was often used in the officers' mess.

are very nearly the same in all American merchantmen. Whenever a pig is killed, the sailors have one mess from it. The rest goes to the cabin. The smaller live stock, poultry, etc., they never taste.

And, indeed, they do not complain of this, for it would take a great deal to supply them with a good meal, and without the accompaniments, (which could hardly be furnished to them,) it would not be much better than salt beef. But even as to the salt beef, they are scarcely dealt fairly with; for whenever a barrel is opened, before any of the beef is put into the harness-cask, the steward comes up, and picks it all over, and takes out the best pieces, (those that have any fat in them) for the cabin.

This was done in both the vessels I was in, and the men said that it was usual in other vessels. Indeed, it is made no secret, but some of the crew are usually called to help in assorting and putting away the pieces. By this arrangement the hard, dry pieces, which the sailors call "old horse," come to their share.

There is a singular piece of rhyme, traditional among sailors, which they say over such pieces of beef. I do not know that it ever appeared in print before. When seated round the kid, if a particularly bad piece is found, one of them takes it up, and addressing it, repeats these lines: "Old horse! old horse! what brought you here?"

–"From Sacarap to Portland pier I've carted stone this many a year: Till, killed by blows and sore abuse, They salted me down for sailors' use.

The sailors they do me despise: They turn me over and damn my eyes; Cut off my meat, and pick my bones, And pitch the rest to Davy Jones."

There is a story current among seamen, that a beef-dealer was convicted, at Boston, of having sold old horse for ship's stores, instead of beef, and had been sentenced to be confined in jail, until he should eat the whole of it; and that he is now lying in Boston jail. I

In the news
**May, 1836**

Up and down the coast from Virginia to New Jersey, mariners had been pleading for a breakwater that might provide a safe harbor. In 1828, the government allocates funds to begin building such a breakwater near Lewes, DE. The breakwater was to be huge, 2,586 feet long, and some 835,000 tons of stone would be required. Work proceeded slowly. The May 5th, 1836 edition of the *American Daily Advertiser* carries a letter to the editor noting that the recent loss of the schooner *Amanda* and her entire crew was entirely preventable—if only the breakwater had been completed. The writer, Henry F. Rodney, says that, far from offering safety, the partially completed breakwater, "...is in fact the most dangerous trap to vessels coming into this harbor and this crew was lost by reason of it."

**This was done in both the vessels I was in...** This is one of the more extensive notes the author included in the book. Dana normally explicates, when he bothers doing so, within the text itself and only rarely adds a separate footnote. This fairly longwinded explanation is unusual, but it does reflect Dana's strong feelings about the mistreatment of the sailors, which extends to the bad food they're forced to eat while the officers dine on better-tasting, more nutritious fare.

have heard this story often, on board other vessels beside those of our own nation. It is very generally believed, and is always highly commended, as a fair instance of retaliatory justice. ————

for the latter part of the voyage, for they are sailors, and can stand all weathers. We had an old sow on board, the mother of a numerous progeny, who had been twice round the Cape of Good Hope, and once round Cape Horn. The last time going round, was very nearly her death. We heard her squealing and moaning one dark night, after it had been snowing and hailing for several hours, and getting into the sty, we found her nearly frozen to death. We got some straw, an old sail, and other things, and wrapped her up in a corner of the sty, where she staid until we got into fine weather again.

Wednesday, May 18th. Lat. 9° 54' N., long. 113° 17' W. The north-east trades had now left us, and we had the usual variable winds, which prevail near the line, together with some rain. So long as we were in these latitudes, we had but little rest in our watch on deck at night, for, as the winds were light and variable, and we could not lose a breath, we were all the watch bracing the yards, and taking in and making sail, and "humbugging" with our flying kites. A little puff of wind on the larboard quarter, and then –"larboard fore braces!" and studding-booms were rigged out, studding-sails set alow and aloft, the yards trimmed, and jibs and spanker in; when it would come as calm as a duck-pond, and the man at the wheel stand with the palm of his hand up, feeling for the wind. "Keep her off a little!" "All aback forward, sir!" cries a man from the forecastle. Down go the braces again; in come the studding-sails, all in a mess, which half an hour won't set right; yards braced sharp up; and she's on the starboard tack, close hauled.

The studding-sails must now be cleared away, and set up in the tops, and on the booms. By the time this is done, and you are looking out for a soft plank for a nap,–"Lay aft here, and square in the head yards!" and the studding-sails are all set again on the starboard side. So it goes until it is eight bells,–call the watch,–heave

**...for they are sailors...** The "they" in this sentence refers to the pigs on board, this being a continuation of the main text after being interrupted by the long footnote. The pigs are hardy and can withstand the rigors of a sea voyage. They are spared (for a time) not due to any sentiment on the part of the crew, but simply because the other livestock would have to be eaten first regardless, since those animals would have died early in the voyage anyway.

**... the winds were light and variable...** Because the winds were light and often changed direction, the crew was kept busy working the sails, tacking, and in general doing everything they could to take advantage of what little wind there was. It's when the winds are strong and steady that sailors can relax.

## In the news
## May, 1836

James Gordon Bennett, editor (and writer and ad salesman and publisher) of the popular *New York Herald*, takes his usual morning walk around Wall Street. He encounters James Watson Webb, editor of the rival *Morning Courier and New-York Enquirer*. A fight ensues (fights, and sometimes duels, between rival editors were not all that uncommon at the time), and Webb pushes Bennett down a flight of stone stairs, follows him to the bottom of the stairway, and beats him senseless with a cane. The beating was never officially explained, but it could have had something to do with the fact that Bennett had poked fun (in print) at Webb's obesity and called him "a defaulter" who was guilty of "disgraceful conduct." Bennett, whose paper was covering the sensational trial of a murdered prostitute at the time, had also offered to send Webb a piece of the dead prostitute's bed as a memento.

the log,–relieve the wheel, and go below the larboard watch.

Sunday, May 22d. Lat. 5° 14' N., long. 166° 45' W. We were now a fortnight out, and within five degrees of the line, to which two days of good breeze would take us; but we had, for the most part, what sailors call "an Irishman's hurricane,–right up and down."

This day it rained nearly all day, and being Sunday, and nothing to do, we stopped up the scuppers and filled the decks with rain water, and bringing all our clothes on deck, had a grand wash, fore and aft. When this was through, we stripped to our drawers, and taking pieces of soap and strips of canvas for towels, we turned-to and soaped, washed, and scrubbed one another down, to get off, as we said, the California dust; for the common wash in salt water, which is all Jack can get, being on an allowance of fresh, had little efficacy, and was more for taste than utility. The captain was below all the afternoon, and we had something nearer to a Saturnalia than anything we had yet seen; for the mate came into the scuppers, with a couple of boys to scrub him, and got into a battle with them in heaving water. By unplugging the holes, we let the soap-suds off the decks, and in a short time had a new supply of rain water, in which we had a grand rinsing. It was surprising to see how much soap and fresh water did for the complexions of many of us; how much of what we supposed to be tan and sea-blacking, we got rid of. The next day, the sun rising clear, the ship was covered, fore and aft, with clothes of all sorts, hanging out to dry.

As we approached the line, the wind became more easterly, and the weather clearer, and in twenty days from San Diego,–

Saturday, May 28th, at about three P. M., with a fine breeze from the east-south-east, we crossed the equator. In twenty-four hours after crossing the line, which was very unusual, we took the regular south-east trades. These winds come a little from the eastward of south-east, and, with us, they blew directly from the east-

**Sunday, May 22d. Lat. 5° 14' N., long. 166° 45' W.** Due to a combination of errors, this lat/long is probably incorrect. The manuscript has it as 106° 45' W, which is probably close to correct. Some critics, having looked closely at preceding and subsequent readings, argue that it should read 116° 45' W. The difference between 166° and 116° is meaningful, amounting to almost 3,000 nautical miles.

**...nothing to do...** This is quite a difference from Captain Thompson's *Pilgrim*, on which the sailors were forced to work most Sundays.

In the news
**May, 1836**

Antislavery editor Reverend Elijah Lovejoy moves from St. Louis to Alton, IL, in the hopes of escaping the virulent attacks, numerous incidents of vandalism, and vicious threats that had ensued ever since he began campaigning against slavery. Illinois is a "free" state, which might lead one to assume that pro-slavery sentiment was rare, but as soon as he and his press arrive in Illinois, a group of men smash the press and throw the pieces in the Mississippi River. Local citizens contribute funds toward a new press, but only on the condition that Lovejoy agree not to print antislavery articles. Lovejoy agrees, but later finds that his conscience will not allow him to stay silent. Not surprisingly, the citizens become disenchanted, and two more of his presses are destroyed. Eventually an angry mob (protected, some said, by the pro-slavery Illinois Attorney General) set fire to Lovejoy's building and shoot him five times when he runs out. Lovejoy crawls back inside, but dies near his press.

south-east, which was fortunate for us, for our course was south-by-west, and we could thus go one point free. The yards were braced so that every sail drew, from the spanker to the flying-jib; and the upper yards being squared in a little, the fore and main top-gallant studding-sails were set, and just drew handsomely. For twelve days this breeze blew steadily, not varying a point, and just so fresh that we could carry our royals; and, during the whole time, we hardly started a brace. Such progress did we make, that at the end of seven days from the time we took the breeze, on Sunday, June 5th, we were in lat. 19° 29' S., and long. 118° 01' W., having made twelve hundred miles in seven days, very nearly upon a taught bowline. Our good ship was getting to be herself again, had increased her rate of sailing more than one-third since leaving San Diego. The crew ceased complaining of her, and the officers hove the log every two hours with evident satisfaction. This was glorious sailing. A steady breeze; the light trade-wind clouds over our heads; the incomparable temperature of the Pacific, –neither hot nor cold; a clear sun every day, and clear moon and stars each night; and new constellations rising in the south, and the familiar ones sinking in the north, as we went on our course, –"stemming nightly toward the pole." Already we had sunk the north star and the Great Bear in the northern horizon, and all hands looked out sharp to the southward for the Magellan Clouds, which, each succeeding night, we expected to make. "The next time we see the north star," said one, "we shall be standing to the northward, the other side of the Horn." This was true enough, and no doubt it would be a welcome sight; for sailors say that in coming home from round Cape Horn, and the Cape of Good Hope, the north star is the first land you make.

These trades were the same that, in the passage out in the Pilgrim, lasted nearly all the way from Juan Fernandez to the line; blowing steadily on our starboard quarter for three weeks, without our starting a brace, or even brailing down the skysails. Though we had now the same wind, and were in the same latitude with the Pilgrim on her passage out, yet we were nearly twelve hundred miles to the westward of her course; for the

**...we could thus go one point free.** The steady breeze is blowing within one point (about 11 degrees) of the direction they wish to travel. Thus, little tacking or adjusting of sails is required. (There are 32 points on a 360 degree compass. 360/32 = 11.25.)

**...having made twelve hundred miles in seven days...** One or the other of Dana's figures is wrong. Either his previous comment about having made "over thirteen hundred miles in seven days" or this more recent estimate is in error, since they amount to a similar rate of speed; yet, Dana says the ship had "increased her rate of sailing more than one-third." Those figures do not support a meaningful increase in speed. (Unless Dana is measuring purely "speed over ground" and discounting leeway—sideways slippage caused by tides, currents, and wind acting on the side of the vessel. If that were the case, the ship could be moving at a faster rate but not gaining as much headway as before. However, leeway caused by wind is certainly not likely, since Dana notes that they're sailing only one point off the wind.)

**..."stemming nightly toward the pole."** Dana is making another literary allusion. To stem is to move forward against some sort of obstacle: wind, current, etc. See Milton's *Paradise Lost*: "Through the wide Ethiopian, to the Cape Ply, stemming nightly toward the Pole. So seem'd Far off the flying fiend."

**...or even brailing down the skysails.** To brail is to temporarily take sails in (or for that matter, to haul anything in) using a brail, which is a small rope. As noted earlier, a skysail is a sail that flies above the royal.

captain, depending upon the strong south-west winds which prevail in high southern latitudes during the winter months, took the full advantage of the trades, and stood well to the westward, so far that we passed within about two hundred miles of Ducie's Island.

**...we passed within about two hundred miles of Ducie's Island.** Properly called Ducie Island, this is an uninhabited atoll that's part of the Pitcairn Islands. (Pitcairn Island itself—about 290 miles from Ducie Island—is famous for being the home of descendents of the HMS *Bounty* mutineers.)

It was this weather and sailing that brought to my mind a little incident that occurred on board the Pilgrim, while we were in the same latitude. We were going along at a great rate, dead before the wind, with studding-sails out on both sides, alow and aloft, on a dark night, just after midnight, and everything was as still as the grave, except the washing of the water by the vessel's side; for, being before the wind, with a smooth sea, the little brig, covered with canvas, was doing great business, with very little noise. The other watch was below, and all our watch, except myself and the man at the wheel, were asleep under the lee of the boat. The second mate, who came out before the mast, and was always very thick with me, had been holding a yarn with me, and just gone aft to his place on the quarter-deck, and I had resumed my usual walk to and from the windlass-end, when, suddenly, we heard a loud scream coming from ahead, apparently directly from under the bows. The darkness, and complete stillness of the night, and the solitude of the ocean, gave to the sound a dreadful and almost supernatural effect. I stood perfectly still, and my heart beat quick.

**...when, suddenly, we heard a loud scream coming from ahead...** This is an odd interlude. Dana's description is eerie and perhaps gothic—surrounded as it is by gloom and mystery. But the explanation is anticlimactic and ordinary: a sailor is having a nightmare, which some readers have found disappointing. It turns out to be nothing special, really, so why bring it up? What the story does do, however, is serve to point out some of the risks and dangers one encounters out on the open ocean: a shipwreck or a rundown whaleboat, for example. (Recall that whaleboats were often rowed—or towed by a whale—many miles from their ship; it was not at all uncommon for a whaleboat to make its way back to its ship long after dark with only a dim lantern to light its way and to ward off other vessels. To this day, a sailor's greatest fear—especially a lone sailor—is being overrun by a larger ship that does not see the smaller vessel in the dark. That sort of accident happens all too frequently, even though modern maritime law supposedly requires a 24-hour lookout on all ships.)

The sound woke up the rest of the watch, who stood looking at one another. "What, in the name of God, is that?" said the second mate, coming slowly forward. The first thought I had was, that it might be a boat, with the crew of some wrecked vessel, or perhaps the boat of some whaleship, out over night, and we had run them down in the darkness. Another scream, but less loud than the first. This started us, and we ran forward, and looked over the bows, and over the sides, to leeward, but nothing was to be seen or heard. What was to be done. Call the captain, and heave the ship aback? Just at this moment, in crossing the forecastle, one of the men saw a light below, and looking down the scuttle, saw the watch all out of their berths, and afoul of one poor

In the news
**May, 1836**

Lest we forget just how early in the country's history Dana's journey took place, consider that in May of this year, the state treasurer of Pennsylvania sends to each county treasurer a list of Revolutionary War veterans and widows who are due to receive their yearly pensions.

fellow, dragging him out of his berth, and shaking him, to wake him out of a nightmare.

They had been waked out of their sleep, and as much alarmed at the scream as we were, and were hesitating whether to come on deck, when the second sound, coming directly from one of the berths, revealed the cause of the alarm. The fellow got a good shaking for the trouble he had given. We made a joke of the matter and we could well laugh, for our minds were not a little relieved by its ridiculous termination.

We were now close upon the southern tropical line, and, with so fine a breeze, were daily leaving the sun behind us, and drawing nearer to Cape Horn, for which it behoved us to make every preparation. Our rigging was all examined and overhauled, and mended, or replaced with new, where it was necessary: new and strong bob-stays fitted in the place of the chain ones, which were worn out; the spritsail yard and martingale guys and back-ropes set well taught; bran new fore and main braces rove; top-gallant sheets, and wheel-ropes, made of green hide, laid up in the form of rope, were stretched and fitted; and new top-sail clewlines, etc., rove; new fore-topmast back-stays fitted; and other preparations made, in good season, that the ropes might have time to stretch and become limber before we got into cold weather.

Sunday, June 12th. Lat. 26° 04' S., 116° 31' W. We had now lost the regular trades, and had the winds variable, principally from the westward, and kept on, in a southerly course, sailing very nearly upon a meridian, and at the end of the week,

Sunday, June 19th, were in lat. 34° 15' S., and long. 116° 38' W.

-------

Editor's Note: In some editions, Dana's explanatory notes for the chapter are appended as follows:

**In the news**

**May, 1836**

In Illinois, work begins on a canal connecting the Chicago River with the Illinois River at La Salle. Completed in 1848, the final cost ran over $700 million, about 10 times what consultants had estimated back in 1824, when the idea was first proposed. With no active railroads in the area, the canal for the first time allows boat traffic to pass from the Great Lakes to the Mississippi River and the Gulf of Mexico, helping to establish the city as a major hub for the transportation of people and goods. With demand reduced due to the growth of railroads and the presence of alternative canals, the Illinois and Michigan Canal ceases operations in 1933.

**...for which it behoved us to make every preparation.** This is the crew's last chance to get ready for rounding the Cape. Once they enter the zone around Cape Horn, they will be much too busy—and the weather will likely be too bad—to take time to repair rigging, replace sails, and adjust, repair, or replace stays and fittings.

**In the news**

**May, 1836**

The Auburn and Rochester Railroad is chartered, with the goal of connecting Auburn, Rochester, Geneva, and Canandaigua, NY. The new railroad would come close to putting New York's Erie Canal out of business, since it provided a faster and cheaper way to transport goods. (Ironically, most of the materials used to build the railroad were brought to the site via the canal.)

## In the news
## May, 1836

All through May, the U.S. Congress debates various ways to restore funds that had been bequeathed to the government (and which had been invested in flawed bonds that soon defaulted) by British scientist James Smithson. Smithson had originally left the money to the U.S. government for the establishment of an institution devoted to the "increase & diffusion of Knowledge among men." The result, once Congress restores the squandered funds (amounting to about $11 million in today's dollars), is the establishment of the Smithsonian Institute, a now-famous research-oriented museum complex with headquarters in Washington, D.C. With a yearly budget today somewhere in the neighborhood of $800 million, the institution maintains sites in various cities, publishes two magazines, and maintains its own police force. The fact that The Smithsonian exhibits or stores some 136 million items has led some to call it "our nation's attic."

[1] On removing the cat-head, after the ship arrived at Boston, it was found that there were two holes under it which had been bored for the purpose of driving tree-nails, and which, accidentally, had not been plugged up when the cat-head was placed over them. This was sufficient to account for the leak, and for our not having been able to discover and stop it.

[2] The customs as to the allowance of "grub" are very nearly the same in all American merchantmen. Whenever a pig is killed, the sailors have one mess from it. The rest goes to the cabin. The smaller live stock, poultry, etc., they never taste.

And, indeed, they do not complain of this, for it would take a great deal to supply them with a good meal, and without the accompaniments, (which could hardly be furnished to them,) it would not be much better than salt beef. But even as to the salt beef, they are scarcely dealt fairly with; for whenever a barrel is opened, before any of the beef is put into the harness-cask, the steward comes up, and picks it all over, and takes out the best pieces, (those that have any fat in them) for the cabin.

This was done in both the vessels I was in, and the men said that it was usual in other vessels. Indeed, it is made no secret, but some of the crew are usually called to help in assorting and putting away the pieces. By this arrangement the hard, dry pieces, which the sailors call "old horse," come to their share.

There is a singular piece of rhyme, traditional among sailors, which they say over such pieces of beef. I do not know that it ever appeared in print before. When seated round the kid, if a particularly bad piece is found, one of them takes it up, and addressing it, repeats these lines: "Old horse! old horse! what brought you here?"

[...]

There is a story current among seamen, that a beef-dealer was convicted, at Boston, of having sold old horse for ship's stores, instead of beef, and had been sentenced to be confined in jail, until he should eat the whole of it; and that he is now lying in Boston jail. I have heard this story often, on board other vessels beside those of our own nation. It is very generally believed, and is always highly commended, as a fair instance of retaliatory justice.

## Chapter XXXI

### Bad Prospects–First Touch of Cape Horn–Icebergs–Temperance Ships–Lying-Up–Ice–Difficulty On Board–Change of Course–Straits of Magellan

There now began to be a decided change in the appearance of things. The days became shorter and shorter; the sun running lower in its course each day, and giving less and less heat; and the nights so cold as to prevent our sleeping on deck; the Magellan Clouds in sight, of a clear night; the skies looking cold and angry; and, at times, a long, heavy, ugly sea, setting in from the southwards told us what we were coming to. Still, however, we had a fine, strong breeze, and kept on our way, under as much sail as our ship would bear. Toward the middle of the week, the wind hauled to the southward, which brought us upon a taught bowline, made the ship meet, nearly head on, the heavy swell which rolled from that direction; and there was something not at all encouraging in the manner in which she met it. Being so deep and heavy, she wanted the buoyancy which should have carried her over the seas, and she dropped heavily into them, the water washing over the decks; and every now and then, when an unusually large sea met her fairly upon the bows, she struck it with a sound as dead and heavy as that with which a sledge-hammer falls upon the pile, and took the whole of it in upon the forecastle, and rising, carried it aft in the scuppers, washing the rigging off the pins, and carrying along with it everything which was loose on deck. She had been acting in this way all of our forenoon watch below; as we could tell by the washing of the water over our heads, and the heavy breaking of the seas against her bows, (with a sound as though she were striking against a rock,) only the thickness of the plank from our heads, as we lay in our berths, which are directly against the bows. At eight bells, the watch was called, and we came on deck, one hand going aft to take the wheel, and another going to the galley to get the grub for dinner. I stood on the forecastle, looking at the seas, which were rolling high, as far as the eye could reach, their tops white with foam, and the body of them

**The days became shorter and shorter...** With the days becoming shorter and the nights colder, the crew knows they're coming within range of the Cape, even though they're able—for now—to continue with a full complement of sails.

**...the Magellan Clouds...** Visible from the southern hemisphere, the Magellanic Clouds are galaxies that orbit our own. The "clouds" (they're not clouds at all, of course) have been known for thousands of years, but they were not named after Magellan until many years subsequent to Magellan's death.

**...which brought us upon a taught bowline...** That is, *Alert* is sailing as close to the wind as she can. (Which, on a square-sailed ship, is not terribly close, especially compared to today's nimble vessels, such as sloops, cutters, and yawls, all of which can sail quite close to the wind—though of course not directly into it.)

**...took the whole of it in upon the forecastle...** Overloaded as she is, *Alert* is not handling the rising seas very well.

**...another going to the galley to get the grub for dinner.** "Grub" is an interesting word. Used as a rough-hewn slang synonym for "food," it goes back at least to the mid-17th century. It does not appear to have been nautical in origin, and in fact was common among cowboys, ranchers, and farmers of the era.

**...their tops white with foam...** The weather and the sea are worsening. Whitecaps are universally viewed as a sign of rough water—the only thing more alarming would be if the wind were strong enough to whip the foam off the wavetops.

**...she would not rise over.** Dana is rightfully proud of the sea-sense he's gained over the past 18 months or so. He's seen enough of these (and he's knowledgeable enough about his ship's behavior) to know that *Alert* will not rise over the oncoming wave.

**...new-reaped...** Freshly shaven.

**In the scuppers lay the galley...** Scuppers are channels with drain holes that run alongside the bulwarks (raised sides of the ship meant to keep gear and people from washing overboard). The channels and drain holes are there to help drain off water such as left by the wave the ship has encountered.

In the news
**June, 1836**

In what might have been viewed as a warning (had there been anyone around to be warned), on June 10th, 1836, an earthquake strikes the San Francisco Bay area. Since there are few people in the town (and in fact, at that point there's very little that constitutes a town), not much notice is taken until 32 years later, when another earthquake strikes, this time centered in Hayward, CA and causing heavy damage: The town of Hayward is pretty much destroyed, and several buildings are toppled in San Francisco, San Jose, and elsewhere. On hand to witness the 1868 quake is 33-year-old Mark Twain, who is living across the bay from Hayward at the time. He will describe the quake in 1872's *Roughing It*.

of a deep indigo blue, reflecting the bright rays of the sun. Our ship rose slowly over a few of the largest of them, until one immense fellow came rolling on, threatening to cover her, and which I was sailor enough to know, by "the feeling of her" under my feet, she would not rise over. I sprang upon the knight-heads, and seizing hold of the fore-stay with my hands, drew myself upon it. My feet were just off the stanchion, when she struck fairly into the middle of the sea, and it washed her fore and aft, burying her in the water. As soon as she rose out of it, I looked aft, and everything forward of the main-mast, except the long-boat, which was griped and double-lashed down to the ring-bolts, was swept off clear. The galley, the pig-sty, the hen-coop, and a large sheep-pen which had been built upon the forehatch, were all gone, in the twinkling of an eye–leaving the deck as clean as a chin new-reaped–and not a stick left, to show where they had stood. In the scuppers lay the galley, bottom up, and a few boards floating about, the wreck of the sheep-pen,–and half a dozen miserable sheep floating among them, wet through, and not a little frightened at the sudden change that had come upon them. As soon as the sea had washed by, all hands sprung out of the forecastle to see what had become of the ship and in a few moments the cook and old Bill crawled out from under the galley, where they had been lying in the water, nearly smothered, with the galley over them. Fortunately, it rested against the bulwarks, or it would have broken some of their bones. When the water ran off, we picked the sheep up, and put them in the long-boat, got the galley back in its place, and set things a little to rights; but, had not our ship had uncommonly high bulwarks and rail, everything must have been washed overboard, not excepting Old Bill and the cook.

Bill had been standing at the galley-door, with the kid of beef in his hand for the forecastle mess, when, away he went, kid, beef, and all. He held on to the kid till the last, like a good fellow, but the beef was gone, and when the water had run off, we saw it lying high and dry, like a rock at low tide–nothing could hurt that. We took the loss of our beef very easily, consoling ourselves with the recollection that the cabin had more to lose than we; and chuckled not a little at seeing the remains of the chicken-pie and pan-cakes floating in the scuppers. "This will never do!" was what some said, and every one felt. Here we were, not yet within a thousand miles of the latitude of Cape Horn, and our decks swept by a sea not one half so high as we must expect to find there. Some blamed the captain for loading his ship so deep, when he knew what he must expect; while others said that the wind was always southwest, off the Cape, in the winter; and that, running before it, we should not mind the seas so much. When we got down into the forecastle, Old Bill, who was somewhat of a croaker,–having met with a great many accidents at sea–said that if that was the way she was going to act, we might as well make our wills, and balance the books at once, and put on a clean shirt. "'Vast there, you bloody old owl! You're always hanging out blue lights! You're frightened by the ducking you got in the scuppers, and can't take a joke! What's the use in being always on the look-out for Davy Jones?" "Stand by!" says another, "and we'll get an afternoon watch below, by this scrape;" but in this they were disappointed, for at two bells, all hands were called and set to work, getting lashings upon everything on deck; and the captain talked of sending down the long top-gallant masts; but, as the sea went down toward night, and the wind hauled abeam, we left them standing, and set the studding-sails.

The next day, all hands were turned-to upon unbending the old sails, and getting up the new ones; for a ship, unlike people on shore, puts on her best suit in bad weather. The old sails were sent down, and three new topsails, and new fore and main courses, jib, and fore-topmast staysail, which were made on the coast, and never had been used, were bent, with a complete set of new earings, robands and reef-points; and reef-tackles were rove to the courses, and spilling-lines to the top-sails. These, with new braces and clew-lines, fore and aft, gave us a good suit of running rigging.

The wind continued westerly, and the weather and sea less rough since the day on which we shipped the heavy

**...the cabin had more to lose...** That is, the men had lost only some tough beef, while "the cabin" (that is, the officers and passenger, pampered as they are) is losing fancy foodstuffs such as chicken pot pie and cakes.

In the news
**June, 1836**

In New York, the murder trial of Richard Robinson begins. With his client accused of bludgeoning prostitute Helen Jewett, Robinson's lawyer produces a witness who provides an alibi for Robinson. The case has everything: sex, murder, betrayal, and mystery, so the "penny press" (see the previous sidebars about James Gordon Bennett and the *New York Herald*) of the time has a field day. In the end, Robinson is acquitted, partly because many of the prosecution's witnesses are prostitutes whose credibility is therefore suspect.

**...who was somewhat of a croaker...** A croaker was someone who always looks on the dark side of things and foresees evil and gloom. (Of course, if Old Bill has been around for many years and has seen "a great many accidents at sea," then perhaps he's right to be despondent.) "Davy Jones" is an evil spirit of the sea, akin to a sea-going version of the Devil.

**...a ship, unlike people on shore, puts on her best suit in bad weather.** A witty and apt turn of phrase, and possibly Dana's own, rather than a popular aphorism of the time. When aboard ship, and especially when bad weather is expected, it is always best to have the newest sails, the best rope, the best-made rigging deployed. The pressure that a storm brings to bear on a boat is extreme, and any weakness—any at all—will surely result in a ripped sail or a parted line, which in bad weather could prove disasterous. Here the men are preparing for the Cape by making sure that all of the gear is in good repair.

sea, and we were making great progress under studding-sails, with our light sails all set, keeping a little to the eastward of south; for the captain, depending upon westerly winds off the Cape, had kept so far to the westward, that though we were within about five hundred miles of the latitude of Cape Horn, we were nearly seventeen hundred miles to the westward of it. Through the rest of the week, we continued on with a fair wind, gradually, as we got more to the southward, keeping a more easterly course, and bringing the wind on our larboard quarter, until–

**...had kept so far to the westward...** The *Alert*, heading for Cape Horn, is at nearly the correct latitude: The Cape's latitude is 55°58'S, while *Alert* is currently at 47°50'S. Dana is correct; the difference is about 570 miles. However, *Alert*'s longitude is 113°49'W, while the Cape's longitude is about 067°16'W. The difference is about 2000 miles, so Dana's calculation is correct here, also. *Alert* is fairly close in terms of latitude, but quite a bit west of where she needs to be.

Sunday, June 26th, when, having a fine, clear day, the captain got a lunar observation, as well as his meridian altitude, which made us in lat. 47° 50' S., long. 113° 49' W.; Cape Horn bearing, according to my calculation, E. S. E. 1/2 E., and distant eighteen hundred miles.

**...captain got a lunar observation...** The captain can average the two different readings and come up with a fairly accurate estimate of both latitude (position north or south of a point) and longitude (position east or west of a point). Keep in mind that accurate and complete charts were rare, and of course electronics such as GPS and LORAN were 150 years or more in the future. About all the captain had to help him cross the vast expanse of featureless ocean were a sextant, some rough charts, a clock, and his skill at dead reckoning. (A term described in an earlier note.)

Monday, June 27th. During the first part of this day, the wind continued fair, and, as we were going before it, it did not feel very cold, so that we kept at work on deck, in our common clothes and round jackets. Our watch had an afternoon watch below, for the first time since leaving San Diego, and having inquired of the third mate what the latitude was at noon, and made our usual guesses as to the time she would need, to be up with the Horn, we turned-in, for a nap. We were sleeping away "at the rates of knots," when three knocks on the scuttle, and "All hands ahoy!" started us from our berths. What could be the matter? It did not appear to be blowing hard, and looking up through the scuttle, we could see that it was a clear day, overhead; yet the watch were taking in sail.

**...our common clothes and round jackets.** A round jacket is a short, tailless coat of the sort worn by a naval cadet.

**We were sleeping away "at the rates of knots,"...** If someone is said to be doing something "at a rate of knots," he is doing it well or quickly.

In the news
**June, 1836**

As we can see from ads in small-town newspapers of the time, home sales often included not merely a house and outbuildings, but also a specific pew at the local church. (One ad includes the note: "Also, a good Horse.")

We thought there must be a sail in sight, and that we were about to heave-to and speak her; and were just congratulating ourselves upon it–for we had seen neither sail nor land since we had left port–when we heard the mate's voice on deck, (he turned-in "all standing," and was always on deck the moment he was called,) singing out to the men who were taking in the studding-sails, and asking where his watch were. We did not wait for a second call, but tumbled up the ladder; and there,

**...he turned-in "all standing,"...** That is, he went to bed fully clothed, having removed no more than his boots, if that.

on the starboard bow, was a bank of mist, covering sea and sky, and driving directly for us. I had seen the same before, in my passage round in the Pilgrim, and knew what it meant, and that there was no time to be lost. We had nothing on but thin clothes, yet there was not a moment to spare, and at it we went.

The boys of the other watch were in the tops, taking in the top-gallant studding-sails, and the lower and top-mast studding-sails were coming down by the run. It was nothing but "haul down and clew up," until we got all the studding-sails in, and the royals, flying-jib, and mizen top-gallant sail furled, and the ship kept off a little, to take the squall. The fore and main top-gallant sails were still on her, for the "old man" did not mean to be frightened in broad daylight, and was determined to carry sail till the last minute.

**...determined to carry sail till the last minute.** The storm is approaching, but the captain will wait until the last minute to reef or furl the sails.

We all stood waiting for its coming, when the first blast showed us that it was not be trifled with. Rain, sleet, snow, and wind, enough to take our breath from us, and make the toughest turn his back to windward! The ship lay nearly over on her beam-ends; the spars and rigging snapped and cracked; and her top-gallant masts bent like whip-sticks. "Clew up the fore and main top-gallant sails!" shouted the captain, and all hands sprang to the clewlines. The decks were standing nearly at an angle of forty-five degrees, and the ship going like a mad steed through the water, the whole forward part of her in a smother of foam. The halyards were let go and the yard clewed down, and the sheets started, and in a few minutes the sails smothered and kept in by clewlines and buntlines. –"Furl 'em, sir?" asked the mate.–"Let go the topsail halyards, fore and aft!" shouted the captain, in answer, at the top of his voice. Down came the topsail yards, the reef-tackles were manned and hauled out, and we climbed up to windward, and sprang into the weather rigging. The violence of the wind, and the hail and sleet, driving nearly horizontally across the ocean, seemed actually to pin us down to the rigging. It was hard work making head against them. One after another, we got out upon the yards. And here we had work to do; for our new sails, which had hardly been

**...nearly over on her beam-ends...** It makes landlubbers nervous when a sailing vessel heels sharply; neophytes always fear that the boat will simply keep heeling until she's capsized. But heeling is exactly what a sailboat is supposed to do. In fact, a modern well-built, well-balanced keeled sailboat can heel 45 degrees or more, until it's literally lying flat, with masts almost horizontal; barring any other problems, it will return to the vertical if left to its own devices. A large square-sailed vessel such as the *Alert* is not quite that nimble, nor that forgiving, but it can heel almost as far and still recover.

**In the news**
**June, 1836**

French physicist and mathematician André-Marie Ampère dies in Marseille, France at age 61. Ampère, a foreign member of the Royal Swedish Academy of Science, was known for his researches into electromagnetism. His name was given to Ampère's Law, which is used to determine the strength of a magnetic field produced by a given current. In a nod to Ampère, electric current is today measured in amperes (or "amps")—the amount of charge that flows through a given surface per second.

bent long enough to get the starch out of them, were as stiff as boards, and the new earings and reef-points, stiffened with the sleet, knotted like pieces of iron wire. Having only our round jackets and straw hats on, we were soon wet through, and it was every moment growing colder. Our hands were soon stiffened and numbed, which, added to the stiffness of everything else, kept us a good while on the yard. After we had got the sail hauled upon the yard, we had to wait a long time for the weather earing to be passed; but there was no fault to be found, for French John was at the earing, and a better sailor never laid out on a yard; so we leaned over the yard, and beat our hands upon the sail to keep them from freezing. At length the word came–"Haul out to leeward,"–and we seized the reef-points and hauled the band taught for the lee earing. "Taught band–Knot away," and we got the first reef fast, and were just going to lay down, when–"Two reefs–two reefs!" shouted the mate, and we had a second reef to take, in the same way. When this was fast, we laid down on deck, manned the halyards to leeward, nearly up to our knees in water, set the topsail, and then laid aloft on the main topsail yard, and reefed that sail in the same manner; for, as I have before stated, we were a good deal reduced in numbers, and, to make it worse, the carpenter, only two days before, cut his leg with an axe, so that he could not go aloft. This weakened us so that we could not well manage more than one topsail at a time, in such weather as this, and, of course, our labor was doubled. From the main topsail yard, we went upon the main yard, and took a reef in the mainsail. No sooner had we got on deck, than–"Lay aloft there, mizen-topmen, and close-reef the mizen topsail!" This called me; and being nearest to the rigging, I got first aloft, and out to the weather earing. English Ben was on the yard just after me, and took the lee earing, and the rest of our gang were soon on the yard, and began to fist the sail, when the mate considerately sent up the cook and steward, to help us. I could now account for the long time it took to pass the other earings, for, to do my best, with a strong hand to help me at the dog's ear, I could not get it passed until I heard them beginning to complain in the bunt. One reef after another we took in, until the sail

**...there was no fault to be found...** That is, all was well. French John is someone on whom the men can rely to do his job. Oddly, although French John (or "John, the Frenchman") is mentioned several times in the book, we have no idea who he is. His name does not appear on the crew lists; in fact, the name "John" does not appear in the lists at all. There was, however, a seaman named Cotton Pratt on the list, whom no one on board, when contacted later by Dana, seems to recall. Thus, it may be that Pratt left during the voyage and French John took his place, and no one ever updated the crew list.

**..."Two reefs–two reefs!" shouted the mate...** As noted earlier, taking in a reef is a way of shortening or reducing sail. Each sail contains "reef points," short lengths of rope set into the sail at various points. The sail is slacked off, furled up to the appropriate line of reef points, and then tied off. The result is less sail exposed, which is what one wants when the wind gets too strong. In this case, the crew reefed once and were then told to reef again, so the wind must be getting quite violent. (But not yet strong enough to warrant taking the sail down altogether.)

was close-reefed, when we went down and hoisted away at the halyards. In the mean time, the jib had been furled and the staysail set, and the ship, under her reduced sail, had got more upright and was under management; but the two top-gallant sails were still hanging in the buntlines, and slatting and jerking as though they would take the masts out of her. We gave a look aloft, and knew that our work was not done yet; and, sure enough, no sooner did the mate see that we were on deck, than–"Lay aloft there, four of you, and furl the top-gallant sails!" This called me again, and two of us went aloft, up the fore rigging, and two more up the main, upon the top-gallant yards.

The shrouds were now iced over, the sleet having formed a crust or cake round all the standing rigging, and on the weather side of the masts and yards. When we got upon the yard, my hands were so numb that I could not have cast off the knot of the gasket to have saved my life. We both lay over the yard for a few seconds, beating our hands upon the sail, until we started the blood into our fingers' ends, and at the next moment our hands were in a burning heat. My companion on the yard was a lad, who came out in the ship a weak, puny boy, from one of the Boston schools,– "no larger than a spritsail sheet knot," nor "heavier than a paper of lampblack," and "not strong enough to haul a shad off a gridiron," but who was now "as long as a spare topmast, strong enough to knock down an ox, and hearty enough to eat him." We fisted the sail together, and after six or eight minutes of hard hauling and pulling and beating down the sail, which was as stiff as sheet iron, we managed to get it furled; and snugly furled it must be, for we knew the mate well enough to be certain that if it got adrift again, we should be called up from our watch below, at any hour of the night, to furl it.

I had been on the look-out for a moment to jump below and clap on a thick jacket and south-wester; but when we got on deck we found that eight bells had been struck, and the other watch gone below, so that there were two hours of dog watch for us, and a plenty of

**...until the sail was close-reefed...** That is, until very little sail was left exposed. Given the increasing violence of the storm, the captain is reducing sail on all of the masts, and has put the jib away altogether. (The jib is a sail, normally triangular, forward of the main mast.)

**In the news**
**June, 1836**

Around the country, "Thomsonian medicine" is all the rage. Named after Samuel Thomson, a self-taught herbalist who developed a method based on plant-mediated removal of toxins from the body, Thomsonian medicine came into conflict with traditional practitioners, but appealed greatly to rural dwellers. Thomson eventually writes a book, *New Guide to Health; or Botanic Family Physician*, and sells to individual families the right to use his system of medicine, including his herbs and formulas.

**...no larger than a spritsail sheet knot...** Dana is playing with language here, enjoying the picturesque sailors' lingo. He repeats several popular nautical figurative speech idioms used to show how frail and fragile the boy was when he came on board, and compares him to the hale and hearty young man he has become: "...strong enough to knock down an ox, and hearty enough to eat him."

**...two hours of dog watch...** As mentioned in an earlier note, the dog watches are the two watches of two hours each that are used to produce an uneven number of watches, so that the crews do not keep the same watches every day. One source notes that these are called the First Watch and the Last Watch, but never the First Watch and the Second Watch, although no one knows why. Nor is there any agreement as to why they came to be called "dog watches" in the first place.

work to do. It had now set in for a steady gale from the south-west; but we were not yet far enough to the southward to make a fair wind of it, for we must give Terra del Fuego a wide berth. The decks were covered with snow, and there was a constant driving of sleet. In fact, Cape Horn had set in with good earnest. In the midst of all this, and before it became dark, we had all the studding-sails to make up and stow away, and then to lay aloft and rig in all the booms, fore and aft, and coil away the tacks, sheets, and halyards. This was pretty tough work for four or five hands, in the face of a gale which almost took us off the yards, and with ropes so stiff with ice that it was almost impossible to bend them. I was nearly half an hour out on the end of the fore yard, trying to coil away and stop down the topmast studding-sail tack and lower halyards. It was after dark when we got through, and we were not a little pleased to hear four bells struck, which sent us below for two hours, and gave us each a pot of hot tea with our cold beef and bread, and, what was better yet, a suit of thick, dry clothing, fitted for the weather, in place of our thin clothes, which were wet through and now frozen stiff.

This sudden turn, for which we were so little prepared, was as unacceptable to me as to any of the rest; for I had been troubled for several days with a slight toothache, and this cold weather, and wetting and freezing, were not the best things in the world for it.

I soon found that it was getting strong hold, and running over all parts of my face; and before the watch was out I went aft to the mate, who had charge of the medicine-chest, to get something for it.

But the chest showed like the end of a long voyage, for there was nothing that would answer but a few drops of laudanum, which must be saved for any emergency; so I had only to bear the pain as well as I could.

When we went on deck at eight bells, it had stopped snowing, and there were a few stars out, but the clouds were still black, and it was blowing a steady gale. Just

In the news
**June, 1836**

The dangers of steamboat travel (with some likelihood of horrific boiler explosions) have already been mentioned (see previous sidebar). In a sign of the times, a June issue of the *Burlington Free Press* carries an ad for a "Valuable Salve," specifically noting that it "...would be found very useful on board Steam Boats or vessels of any kind, where accidents may happen; especially such as scalds or burns...."

**...I had been troubled for several days with a slight tooth-ache...** Not a big deal for us; if we get a toothache, we head to the drugstore for some over-the-counter pain meds or oral "gels." If it doesn't go away, then we head to the dentist. But this is 1836, and Dana is on a ship in the middle of the ocean, thousands of miles from anywhere. At that time and place, a toothache—or any major illness or injury—was a serious problem. In those days (and occasionally still), people *died* from the infections that accompany (or cause) the typical toothache.

**...a few drops of laudanum...** Laudanum was a popular (and very addictive) pain medicine that was widely used (and widely abused) in the 19th century. It is essentially a tincture made up of alcohol and opium. In this case, the mate has decreed that the laudanum must be saved for serious emergencies such as broken limbs (fairly common aboard ship) or even amputations (not as common, but certainly not unheard of).

before midnight, I went aloft and sent down the mizen royal yard, and had the good luck to do it to the satisfaction of the mate, who said it was done "out of hand and ship-shape." The next four hours below were but little relief to me, for I lay awake in my berth, the whole time, from the pain in my face, and heard every bell strike, and, at four o'clock, turned out with the watch, feeling little spirit for the hard duties of the day. Bad weather and hard work at sea can be borne up against very well, if one only has spirit and health; but there is nothing brings a man down, at such a time, like bodily pain and want of sleep.

There was, however, too much to do to allow time to think; for the gale of yesterday, and the heavy seas we met with a few days before, while we had yet ten degrees more southing to make, had convinced the captain that we had something before us which was not to be trifled with, and orders were given to send down the long top-gallant masts. The top-gallant and royal yards were accordingly struck, the flying jib-boom rigged in, and the top-gallant masts sent down on deck, and all lashed together by the side of the long-boat.

The rigging was then sent down and coiled away below, and everything was made snug aloft. There was not a sailor in the ship who was not rejoiced to see these sticks come down; for, so long as the yards were aloft, on the least sign of a lull, the top-gallant sails were loosed, and then we had to furl them again in a snow-squall, and shin up and down single ropes caked with ice, and send royal yards down in the teeth of a gale coming right from the south pole. It was an interesting sight, too, to see our noble ship, dismantled of all her top-hamper of long tapering masts and yards, and boom pointed with spear-head, which ornamented her in port; and all that canvas, which a few days before had covered her like a cloud, from the truck to the water's edge, spreading far out beyond her hull on either side, now gone; and she, stripped, like a wrestler for the fight. It corresponded, too, with the desolate character of her situation;–alone, as she was, battling with storms, wind, and ice, at this extremity of the globe, and in almost

**...it was done "out of hand and ship-shape."** That is, quickly and to the mate's satisfaction.

**...we had yet ten degrees more southing to make...** The *Alert* was still too far north; unless they headed about 10 degrees south, she would miss the Cape.

**...convinced the captain that we had something before us which was not to be trifled with...** The ship has now entered the region near Cape Horn, and can expect continued bad weather. It's time to stow any sails and gear that will not be needed during the passage. Anything *not* carefully stowed away will probably be damaged or even washed overboard.

In the news
**June, 1836**

Andrew Jackson's proposed bill on "incendiary publications" fails in the Senate. Although a law aimed at banning "incendiary publications intended to instigate the slaves to insurrection" could be considered pro-slavery, several prominent pro-slavery states'-rights legislators, including John C. Calhoun, argue against the bill for two reasons: First, any law that gives more power to the federal government is going to be looked at suspiciously by legislators who feel that states must control their own destiny. Secondly, while the bill is certainly a form of anti-slavery censorship, if it's allowed, what's to prevent the government from censoring *pro-slavery* materials down the road?

**...shook a reef out of the fore-topsail...** This is the *opposite* of reefing: The crew now exposes a bit more sail, in order to take advantage of a stiff (but no longer dangerous) breeze, with the hope of making good time to the Cape.

**...a man as well as a sailor...** The mate, gruff though he is, is a fair and kindhearted man. By rights, Dana should be resting in his bunk or hammock, but he's trying not to shirk his duty.

In the news
**July, 1836**

The exact date is unknown, but the unfortunately named plumber and inventor Thomas Crapper was probably born this month. (He was baptized in September of 1836.) Crapper was a sanitary engineer operating in London. Contrary to myth, he did not invent the flush toilet, although he did popularize and improve upon it. In a perhaps odd coincidence, the word "crap" (meaning "excrement") did not derive from Crapper's name; rather, it is comes from Middle English, having originally been combined from two even older Dutch and Old French words. Thus, the word predates Mr. Crapper by a long while.

In the news
**July, 1836**

Construction begins on the Illinois and Michigan Canal, only three years after the city of Chicago is incorporated. The 96-mile-long canal allows boat traffic to proceed from the Great Lakes on into the Mississippi and the Gulf of Mexico, and helps establish Chicago as a major transportation hub.

constant night.

Friday, July 1st. We were now nearly up to the latitude of Cape Horn, and having over forty degrees of easting to make, we squared away the yards before a strong westerly gale, shook a reef out of the fore-topsail, and stood on our way, east-by-south, with the prospect of being up with the Cape in a week or ten days. As for myself, I had had no sleep for forty-eight hours; and the want of rest, together with constant wet and cold, had increased the swelling, so that my face was nearly as large as two, and I found it impossible to get my mouth open wide enough to eat. In this state, the steward applied to the captain for some rice to boil for me, but he only got a–"No! d–- you! Tell him to eat salt junk and hard bread, like the rest of them." For this, of course, I was much obliged to him, and in truth it was just what I expected. However, I did not starve, for the mate, who was a man as well as a sailor, and had always been a good friend to me, smuggled a pan of rice into the galley, and told the cook to boil it for me, and not let the "old man" see it. Had it been fine weather, or in port, I should have gone below and lain by until my face got well; but in such weather as this, and short-handed as we were, it was not for me to desert my post; so I kept on deck, and stood my watch and did my duty as well as I could.

Saturday, July 2nd. This day the sun rose fair, but it ran too low in the heavens to give any heat, or thaw out our sails and rigging; yet the sight of it was pleasant; and we had a steady "reef topsail breeze" from the westward. The atmosphere, which had previously been clear and cold, for the last few hours grew damp, and had a disagreeable, wet chilliness in it; and the man who came from the wheel said he heard the captain tell "the passenger" that the thermometer had fallen several degrees since morning, which he could not account for in any other way than by supposing that there must be ice near us; though such a thing had never been heard of in this latitude, at this season of the year. At twelve o'clock we went below, and had just got through dinner, when the cook put his head down the scuttle and told us to come on deck and see the finest sight that we had ever seen. "Where away, cook?" asked the first man who was up. "On the larboard bow." And there lay, floating in the ocean, several miles off, an immense, irregular mass, its top and points covered with snow, and its center of a deep indigo color.

This was an iceberg, and of the largest size, as one of our men said who had been in the Northern ocean. As far as the eye could reach, the sea in every direction was of a deep blue color, the waves running high and fresh, and sparkling in the light, and in the midst lay this immense mountain-island, its cavities and valleys thrown into deep shade, and its points and pinnacles glittering in the sun.

All hands were soon on deck, looking at it, and admiring in various ways its beauty and grandeur. But no description can give any idea of the strangeness, splendor, and, really, the sublimity, of the sight.

Its great size;–for it must have been from two to three miles in circumference, and several hundred feet in height;–its slow motion, as its base rose and sank in the water, and its high points nodded against the clouds; the dashing of the waves upon it, which, breaking high with foam, lined its base with a white crust; and the thundering sound of the cracking of the mass, and the breaking and tumbling down of huge pieces; together with its nearness and approach, which added a slight element of fear,–all combined to give to it the character of true sublimity. The main body of the mass was, as I have said, of an indigo color, its base crusted with frozen foam; and as it grew thin and transparent toward the edges and top, its color shaded off from a deep blue to the whiteness of snow.

It seemed to be drifting slowly toward the north, so that we kept away and avoided it. It was in sight all the afternoon; and when we got to leeward of it, the wind died away, so that we lay-to quite near it for a greater part of the night. Unfortunately, there was no moon, but it was a clear night, and we could plainly mark the long,

**"Where away, cook?" asked the first man...** In a later edition, Dana changed this to, "Where away, Doctor?" and added a note that cooks on board were universally addressed by that term. He is correct, and we can find the term used in that fashion as far back as 1821, although no one is quite sure why it came to be used that way. It's possible that it's an ironically humorous application of an honorific normally applied to learned professors and physicians applied instead to a lowly ship's cook. (And yet, the ship's cook *was* an important person, one who was treated with a certain amount of deference: He did control the food, after all, and he also controlled the stove that the men used to warm themselves and to dry clothes. And at least on board most vessels, the cook had the ear of the captain.)

**...sparkling in the light, and in the midst lay this immense mountain-island, its cavities and valleys thrown into deep shade...** This book is largely a sober undertaking with serious political and social ramifications: It's a book that helped define an entire genre of literature and one that had an impact on the well-being of countless generations of sailors. It's not poetry. Yet, every once in a while, we're reminded that Dana really has a talent for writing. These vivid descriptions of the iceberg serve as examples of that talent.

**It seemed to be drifting slowly toward the north...** These days, icebergs longer than 10 nautical miles are named and tracked, being both of scientific interest and possible hazards to navigation. (Not surprisingly, the system for measuring and tracking icebergs came about as a direct result of the 1912 sinking of the *Titanic*, which struck an iceberg in April of that year. The huge ship sank in less than three hours, and over 1,500 people were killed.)

regular heaving of the stupendous mass, as its edges moved slowly against the stars. Several times in our watch loud cracks were heard, which sounded as though they must have run through the whole length of the ice-berg, and several pieces fell down with a thundering crash, plunging heavily into the sea. Toward morning, a strong breeze sprang up, and we filled away, and left it astern, and at daylight it was out of sight. The next day, which was

Sunday, July 3d, the breeze continued strong, the air exceedingly chilly, and the thermometer low. In the course of the day we saw several icebergs, of different sizes, but none so near as the one which we saw the day before. Some of them, as well as we could judge, at the distance at which we were, must have been as large as that, if not larger. At noon we were in latitude 55° 12' south, and supposed longitude 89° 5' west. Toward night the wind hauled to the southward, and headed us off our course a little, and blew a tremendous gale; but this we did not mind, as there was no rain nor snow, and we were already under close sail.

Monday, July 4th. This was "independence day" in Boston. What firing of guns, and ringing of bells, and rejoicings of all sorts, in every part of our country! The ladies (who have not gone down to Nahant, for a breath of cool air, and sight of the ocean) walking the streets with parasols over their heads, and the dandies in their white pantaloons and silk stockings! What quantities of ice-cream have been eaten, and what quantities of ice brought into the city from a distance, and sold out by the lump and the pound! The smallest of the islands which we saw today would have made the fortune of poor Jack, if he had had it in Boston; and I dare say he would have had no objection to being there with it. This, to be sure, was no place to keep the fourth of July. To keep ourselves warm, and the ship out of the ice, was as much as we could do. Yet no one forgot the day; and many were the wishes, and conjectures, and comparisons, both serious and ludicrous, which were made among all hands. The sun shone bright as long as it was up, only that a scud of black clouds was ever and anon

In the news

**July, 1836**

Delegates from Kentucky, Georgia, and the Carolinas meet in Knoxville, TN to discuss possible railway projects—and also ways to get the government to help pay for them. Given the country's immense rate of expansion, the need for railroads, canals, and roads was quickly becoming dire.

**The ladies (who have not gone down to Nahant...** The East Coast gets very hot and sticky during the summer, of course, and in 1835 there were no air conditioners. Those who could afford to leave the hot, crowded cities for cooler towns on the ocean or in the mountains often did so. In the case of Boston, one popular seaside destination was Nahant, in northeastern Massachusetts.

**The smallest of the islands which we saw today...** Along with there being no air conditioners in 19th-century Boston, there were also no refrigerators. (The first electric refrigerators were introduced in 1915, and became common in the late 1930s.) There were, however, iceboxes. An icebox is an insulated appliance (usually made of wood and often quite a handsome piece of furniture) into the top of which was inserted a large block of ice and perhaps some insulation. Air chilled by the ice flowed down into a compartment in which food was kept. Naturally, this required the delivery to homes and businesses of large blocks of ice, originally in the iceman's wagon, and then later in a truck. Icemen were paid for their labor, of course, and owners of large ice companies could make a good living. This is what Dana means when he says that "the smallest of the islands" they were viewing "would have made the fortune of poor Jack." The tons of ice in the icebergs in the area would have been worth a great deal of money back in hot, sticky Boston.

driving across it. At noon we were in lat. 54° 27' S., and long. 85° 5' W., having made a good deal of easting, but having lost in our latitude by the heading of the wind. Between daylight and dark–that is, between nine o'clock and three–we saw thirty-four ice islands, of various sizes; some no bigger than the hull of our vessel, and others apparently nearly as large as the one that we first saw; though, as we went on, the islands became smaller and more numerous; and, at sundown of this day, a man at the mast-head saw large fields of floating ice called "field-ice" at the south-east. This kind of ice is much more dangerous than the large islands, for those can be seen at a distance, and kept away from; but the field-ice, floating in great quantities, and covering the ocean for miles and miles, in pieces of every size- -large, flat, and broken cakes, with here and there an island rising twenty and thirty feet, and as large as the ship's hull;– this, it is very difficult to sheer clear of. A constant look-out was necessary; for any of these pieces, coming with the heave of the sea, were large enough to have knocked a hole in the ship, and that would have been the end of us; for no boat (even if we could have got one out) could have lived in such a sea; and no man could have lived in a boat in such weather. To make our condition still worse, the wind came out due east, just after sundown, and it blew a gale dead ahead, with hail and sleet, and a thick fog, so that we could not see half the length of the ship. Our chief reliance, the prevailing westerly gales, was thus cut off; and here we were, nearly seven hundred miles to the westward of the Cape, with a gale dead from the eastward, and the weather so thick that we could not see the ice with which we were surrounded, until it was directly under our bows.

At four, P. M. (it was then quite dark) all hands were called, and sent aloft in a violent squall of hail and rain, to take in sail. We had now all got on our "Cape Horn rig"–thick boots, south-westers coming down over our neck and ears, thick trowsers and jackets, and some with oil-cloth suits over all. Mittens, too, we wore on deck, but it would not do to go aloft with them on, for it was impossible to work with them, and, being wet

**In the news**

**July, 1836**

British law has gone through some draconian periods, and modern sensibilities might be surprised at the severity of punishments for relatively minor crimes. Case in point: In July of this year in London, 19-year-old Henry Williams is tried for burglary. Williams is found guilty of breaking into the dwelling of one Arabella Mann and stealing a wide variety of silverware, including thimbles, a "scent-box," and a "pencil-case." The unfortunate young man is sentenced to death. On the same day, 20-year-old George Willoughby is tried for the theft of a handkerchief; he is found guilty and sentenced to be transported (that is, sent to the penal colony in Australia) for seven years.

**...and that would have been the end of us...** Just another reminder of how precarious life was (and still is, often enough) for sailors in hostile climates. The average life expectancy for a person lacking specialized protective gear in water below 40 degrees Fahrenheit is less than one hour.

**...weather so thick that we could not see...** Fog is universally disliked by sailors and yachtsmen. A good sailor can prepare for and overcome many challenges—but not if he can't *see* the challenges. There's very little that's good about fog, other than the fact that it usually occurs in calm water. In this case, the *Alert* is traversing a sea of cake ice, but the crew cannot see the ice until it's almost too late. This makes for dangerous, nerve-wracking sailing.

In the news
**July, 1836**

Although General Winfield Scott (known as "Old Fuss and Feathers" for his love of fancy uniforms and his meticulous attention to detail) declares that the Creek War in Alabama and Georgia is over, his announcement proves premature. While Seminole Chief Neamathla and hundreds of his warriors are marched to Montgomery, AL in chains, the war continues; in Florida, for example, the militia battles the Creeks all through the summer and into late October.

**...while Jack...can have nothing to wet his lips or warm his stomach.** Once again, Dana is at pains to point out the inequities of the system: The captain can always retire to his cozy, private cabin for rest and refreshment, and can also order coffee or tea whenever he likes. In the meantime, the common sailors (i.e., "Jack") have nothing, even though they're exposed to the elements all night.

**This was a "temperance ship," and, like too many such ships, the temperance was all in the forecastle.** A "temperance ship" is one in which alcohol is used moderately, if at all. Dana is saying that the rule often applies only to the crew, not to the officers, and certainly not to the captain. He points out that it was common to issue to sailors a ration of rum (usually in the form of a weak rum-water solution called grog), and that if that should not be allowed, it should be disallowed for all (officers included) and that it should be replaced by some other comfort, such as hot chocolate or coffee.

and stiff, they might let a man slip overboard, for all the hold he could get upon a rope; so, we were obliged to work with bare hands, which, as well as our faces, were often cut with the hail-stones, which fell thick and large. Our ship was now all cased with ice,–hull, spars, and standing rigging;–and the running rigging so stiff that we could hardly bend it so as to belay it, or, still worse, take a knot with it; and the sails nearly as stiff as sheet iron. One at a time, (for it was a long piece of work and required many hands,) we furled the courses, mizen topsail, and fore-topmast staysail, and close-reefed the fore and main topsails, and hove the ship to under the fore, with the main hauled up by the clewlines and buntlines, and ready to be sheeted home, if we found it necessary to make sail to get to windward of an ice island. A regular look-out was then set, and kept by each watch in turn, until the morning. It was a tedious and anxious night. It blew hard the whole time, and there was an almost constant driving of either rain, hail, or snow. In addition to this, it was "as thick as muck," and the ice was all about us. The captain was on deck nearly the whole night, and kept the cook in the galley, with a roaring fire, to make coffee for him, which he took every few hours, and once or twice gave a little to his officers; but not a drop of anything was there for the crew. The captain, who sleeps all the daytime, and comes and goes at night as he chooses, can have his brandy and water in the cabin, and his hot coffee at the galley; while Jack, who has to stand through everything, and work in wet and cold, can have nothing to wet his lips or warm his stomach.

This was a "temperance ship," and, like too many such ships, the temperance was all in the forecastle. The sailor, who only takes his one glass as it is dealt out to him, is in danger of being drunk; while the captain, who has all under his hand, and can drink as much as he chooses, and upon whose self-possession and cool judgment the lives of all depend, may be trusted with any amount, to drink at his will. Sailors will never be convinced that rum is a dangerous thing, by taking it away from them, and giving it to the officers; nor that, that temperance is their friend, which takes from them what they have always had, and gives them nothing in the place of it. By seeing it allowed to their officers, they will not be convinced that it is taken from them for their good; and by receiving nothing in its place, they will not believe that it is done in kindness. On the contrary, many of them look upon the change as a new instrument of tyranny. Not that they prefer rum. I never knew a sailor, in my life, who would not prefer a pot of hot coffee or chocolate, in a cold night, to all the rum afloat. They all say that rum only warms them for a time; yet, if they can get nothing better, they will miss what they have lost. The momentary warmth and glow from drinking it; the break and change which is made in a long, dreary watch by the mere calling all hands aft and serving of it out; and the simply having some event to look forward to, and to talk about; give it an importance and a use which no one can appreciate who has not stood his watch before the mast. On my passage round Cape Horn before, the vessel that I was in was not under temperance articles, and grog was served out every middle and morning watch, and after every reefing of topsails; and though I had never drank rum before, and never intend to again, I took my allowance then at the capstan, as the rest did, merely for the momentary warmth it gave the system, and the change in our feelings and aspect of our duties on the watch. At the same time, as I have stated, there was not a man on board who would not have pitched the rum to the dogs, (I have heard them say so, a dozen times) for a pot of coffee or chocolate; or even for our common beverage– "water bewitched, and tea begrudged," as it was.(1)

——— 1. The proportions of the ingredients of the tea that was made for us (and ours, as I have before stated, was a favorable specimen of American merchantmen) were, a pint of tea, and a pint and a half of molasses, to about three gallons of water.

These are all boiled down together in the "coppers," and before serving it out, the mess is stirred up with a stick, so as to give each man his fair share of sweetening and tea-leaves. The tea for the cabin is, of course, made in the usual way, in a tea-pot, and drank with sugar. ———

**...simply having some event to look forward to...** At work or school, we've all found ourselves looking forward to a cup of coffee or a soft drink, not so much because we were tired or thirsty, but mostly for the break it provided, and for the opportunity to visit with friends. Dana is pointing out that it's not the lack of grog that's the problem (many of the sailors would actually have preferred hot chocolate or coffee, he says), it's the fact that the "temperance articles" do away with the *occasion*, in addition to the drink itself.

## In the news
## July, 1836

A retired judge named James Doty, having purchased over 1,000 acres of land (much of it swampland) in the Wisconsin Territory, plats a city he names Madison, and encourages the territorial legislature to declare the (currently imaginary) city of Madison as the territory's capital. The legislature promptly accedes to Doty's wishes (he stands to make a great deal of money, after all), and Wisconsin—which is not yet a state—now has as its capital a city that does not yet exist. (The first cornerstone for the Wisconsin capitol building will not be laid until 1837, and the legislature won't meet there for the first time until 1838. Wisconsin will not become a state until 1848.)

**The tea for the cabin is, of course, made in the usual way...** Once again, Dana takes the opportunity to point out the inequity: The officers get real tea, with sugar, and made full-strength in a teapot. The sailors get a weak, watered-down concoction sweetened with molasses.

—

**The temperance reform is the best thing that ever was undertaken for the sailor...** Dana is actually quite in favor of the temperance movement, having seen what intemperate use of alcohol can do to a man. He's also a fairly religious man, and an aversion to strong drink fits that aspect of his personality, also. But he thinks that the removal of grog from the list of supplies was more of a cost-cutting measure than anything else, even if the owners like to pretend that it has a moral basis. If not, he says, then why not substitute some other drink that might help warm a sailor when he turns in after his watch?

**I do not wish these remarks...to be applied to the owners of our ship...** Dana is careful here to note that he is criticizing the system in general, and not the owners and officers of his ship in particular. As we have seen, Dana thinks highly of the *Alert*'s owners and officers.

The temperance reform is the best thing that ever was undertaken for the sailor; but when the grog is taken from him, he ought to have something in its place. As it is now, in most vessels, it is a mere saving to the owners; and this accounts for the sudden increase of temperance ships, which surprised even the best friends of the cause. If every merchant, when he struck grog from the list of the expenses of his ship, had been obliged to substitute as much coffee, or chocolate, as would give each man a pot-full when he came off the topsail yard, on a stormy night;–I fear Jack might have gone to ruin on the old road.(2) But this is not doubling

———- (2) I do not wish these remarks, so far as they relate to the saving of expense in the outfit, to be applied to the owners of our ship, for she was supplied with an abundance of stores, of the best kind that are given to seamen;, though the dispensing of them is necessarily left to the captain, Indeed, so high was the reputation of "the employ" among men and officers, for the character and outfit of their vessels, and for their liberality in conducting their voyages, that when it was known that they had a ship fitting out for a long voyage, and that hands were to be shipped at a certain time,–a half hour before the time, as one of the crew told me, numbers of sailors were steering down the wharf, hopping over the barrels, like flocks of sheep. ———-

Cape Horn. Eight hours of the night, our watch was on deck, and during the whole of that time we kept a bright look-out: one man on each bow, another in the bunt of the fore yard, the third mate on the scuttle, one on each quarter, and a man always standing by the wheel. The chief mate was everywhere, and commanded the ship when the captain was below.

When a large piece of ice was seen in our way, or drifting near us, the word was passed along, and the ship's head turned one way and another; and sometimes the yards squared or braced up. There was little else to do than to look out; and we had the sharpest eyes in the ship on the forecastle. The only variety was the monotonous voice of the look-out forward–"Another island!"–"Ice ahead!"– "Ice on the lee bow!"–"Hard up the helm!"–"Keep her off a little!"–"Stead-y!"

In the meantime, the wet and cold had brought my face into such a state that I could neither eat nor sleep; and though I stood it out all night, yet, when it became light, I was in such a state, that all hands told me I must go below, and lie-by for a day or two, or I should be laid up for a long time, and perhaps have the lock-jaw.

When the watch was changed I went into the steerage, and took off my hat and comforter, and showed my face to the mate, who told me to go below at once, and stay in my berth until the swelling went down, and gave the cook orders to make a poultice for me, and said he would speak to the captain.

I went below and turned-in, covering myself over with blankets and jackets, and lay in my berth nearly twenty-four hours, half asleep and half awake, stupid, from the dull pain. I heard the watch called, and the men going up and down, and sometimes a noise on deck, and a cry of "ice," but I gave little attention to anything. At the end of twenty-four hours the pain went down, and I had a long sleep, which brought me back to my proper state; yet my face was so swollen and tender, that I was obliged to keep to my berth for two or three days longer. During the two days I had been below, the weather was much the same that it had been, head winds, and snow and rain; or, if the wind came fair, too foggy, and the ice too thick, to run. At the end of the third day the ice was very thick; a complete fog-bank covered the ship. It blew a tremendous gale from the eastward, with sleet and snow, and there was every promise of a dangerous and fatiguing night. At dark, the captain called all hands aft, and told them that not a man was to leave the deck that night; that the ship was in the greatest danger; any cake of ice might knock a hole in her, or she might run on an island and go to pieces. No one could tell whether she would be a ship the next morning. The look-outs were then set, and

**...or I should be laid up for a long time, and perhaps have the lock-jaw.** Lockjaw is a condition in which the mouth is clamped shut by muscle spasms. It is a symptom of tetanus, which itself is caused by various forms of wound contamination. The mate is correct, in a sense: If Dana's infection is not cured, he could get tetanus, which is ultimately fatal. It's more likely, though, that the wound would become gangrenous, and tissue could begin to die. In that case, absent surgery and medicines, Dana would almost certainly die. Either way, Dana needs to get treatment and also some sleep, since a well-rested body can fight infections much more effectively.

**...make a poultice for me...** A poultice is a soft mass of medicines or herbs that is spread on a soft cloth, which is then placed over a wound.

**In the news**
**July, 1836**

Back in Boston, the editor of *Parley's Magazine* pens an essay aimed at children in which he decries the evils of...*sugar*. The ingestion of sugar will, according to the editor, lead children "...to become intemperate or gluttonous, or both." He notes further that, "...intemperate and gluttonous people are very likely to become, in the end, bestial and filthy. They often stoop to the most shameful deeds, and lose their good name." He ends by warning the children to simply avoid the confectioners' shops because, "We should not go, if we can help it, where temptation exists." Who knew sugar was so evil?

**...she might run on an island...** The captain is referring here not to a land mass, but to an iceberg.

every man was put in his station. When I heard what was the state of things, I began to put on my clothes to stand it out with the rest of them, when the mate came below, and looking at my face, ordered me back to my berth, saying that if we went down, we should all go down together, but if I went on deck I might lay myself up for life. This was the first word I had heard from aft; for the captain had done nothing, nor inquired how I was, since I went below.

**This was the first word I had heard from aft...** Dana was brought up in a gentle (and genteel) culture in which people cared (or at least pretended to care) about one another. He's a little annoyed that he's not been visited by the captain and that, as far as he knows, the captain has not inquired after his health.

In obedience to the mate's orders, I went back to my berth; but a more miserable night I never wish to spend. I never felt the curse of sickness so keenly in my life. If I could only have been on deck with the rest, where something was to be done, and seen, and heard; where there were fellow-beings for companions in duty and danger–but to be cooped up alone in a black hole, in equal danger, but without the power to do, was the hardest trial. Several times, in the course of the night, I got up, determined to go on deck; but the silence which showed that there was nothing doing, and the knowledge that I might make myself seriously ill, for nothing, kept me back. It was not easy to sleep, lying, as I did, with my head directly against the bows, which might be dashed in by an island of ice, brought down by the very next sea that struck her. This was the only time I had been ill since I left Boston, and it was the worst time it could have happened. I felt almost willing to bear the plagues of Egypt for the rest of the voyage, if I could but be well and strong for that one night. Yet it was a dreadful night for those on deck.

**...a more miserable night I never wish to spend.** At least in retrospect (remember that he is writing this some years after the voyage), Dana recalls feeling so miserable that he might have fared better if he were on deck helping out, where at least he could have had company and the distraction of doing something useful.

**...willing to bear the plagues of Egypt...** Dana alludes to the book of Exodus, in which Pharaoh's Egypt is struck by 10 plagues, including swarms of frogs, gnats, and locusts; the changing of Egypt's rivers and streams to blood; an epidemic of boils; and the death of every firstborn in the country (even firstborn animals). This is a form of *hyperbole*—an exaggeration of just how much Dana would have been willing to endure if only he could have been able to help out during the storm that night.

A watch of eighteen hours, with wet, and cold, and constant anxiety, nearly wore them out; and when they came below at nine o'clock for breakfast, they almost dropped asleep on their chests, and some of them were so stiff that they could with difficulty sit down. Not a drop of anything had been given them during the whole time, (though the captain, as on the night that I was on deck, had his coffee every four hours,) except that the mate stole a potful of coffee for two men to drink behind the galley, while he kept a look-out for the captain. Every man had his station, and was not allowed to

**In the news**
**July, 1836**

Britain's King William IV issues Letters Patent declaring the establishment of the province of South Australia. Unlike the rest of the continent, South Australia is to be free of "the convict taint"—that is, no convicts are to be transported there. Today's inhabitants are still acutely aware of this difference, although historians are divided about what the lasting effect—if any—might have been on the culture.

leave it; and nothing happened to break the monotony of the night, except once setting the main topsails to run clear of a large island to leeward, which they were drifting fast upon. Some of the boys got so sleepy and stupefied, that they actually fell asleep at their posts; and the young third mate, whose station was the exposed one of standing on the fore scuttle, was so stiff, when he was relieved, that he could not bend his knees to get down. By a constant look-out, and a quick shifting of the helm, as the islands and pieces came in sight, the ship went clear of everything but a few small pieces, though daylight showed the ocean covered for miles. At daybreak it fell a dead calm, and with the sun, the fog cleared a little, and a breeze sprung up from the westward, which soon grew into a gale. We had now a fair wind, daylight, and comparatively clear weather; yet, to the surprise of every one, the ship continued hove-to. Why does not he run? What is the captain about? was asked by every one; and from questions, it soon grew into complaints and murmurings. When the daylight was so short, it was too bad to lose it, and a fair wind, too, which every one had been praying for. As hour followed hour, and the captain showed no sign of making sail, the crew became impatient, and there was a good deal of talking and consultation together, on the forecastle. They had been beaten out with the exposure and hardship, and impatient to get out of it, and this unaccountable delay was more than they could bear in quietness, in their excited and restless state. Some said that the captain was frightened,–completely cowed, by the dangers and difficulties that surrounded us, and was afraid to make sail; while others said that in his anxiety and suspense he had made a free use of brandy and opium, and was unfit for his duty. The carpenter, who was an intelligent man, and a thorough seaman, and had great influence with the crew, came down into the forecastle, and tried to induce the crew to go aft and ask the captain why he did not run, or request him, in the name of all hands, to make sail. This appeared to be a very reasonable request, and the crew agreed that if he did not make sail before noon, they would go aft. Noon came, and no sail was made. A consultation was held again, and it was proposed to take the ship from the

**Why does not he run?** In spite of the improved weather and a fresh breeze, the captain keeps the ship "hove to"—that is, with sails and rudder set such that the ship sits almost motionless. Heaving to is common during a storm, since it affords some rest for the crew, but now that both the storm and the calm have passed, the vessel would normally be gotten underway.

In the news
**July, 1836**

If you think that it's difficult to get a straight answer from a politician today, keep in mind that not much has changed over the years. In early July a debate occurs in Britain's House of Lords in which Sir Robert Peel poses to Viscount Palmerston a seemingly simple question relating to Britain's then-current relationship with Spain. After a bit of sparring, Lord Mahon chimes in: "[I wish] to put one very plain question to the noble Lord. Was Great Britain at peace or at war? That was a very plain question, and he thought it must be a very tortuous policy not to give a plain answer to it." Palmerston then speaks for several minutes, ending with, "Lord John Hay had represented that such a force was necessary, in order to secure his anchorage, and...for the protection of his Majesty's ships, an undertaking he had not been able to complete with the men under his command. An officer and a certain number of sappers and miners had therefore been directed to proceed to Spain...in order to assist him...." The session adjourned with the members still unsure whether the country was at war. (Officially, it was not.)

**...it was proposed to take the ship from the captain and give the command of her to the mate...** This is a very serious course of action to be considering. It is essentially a form of mutiny in which a captain is declared "unfit for duty," and command is given to another officer. It's entirely legal—in some cases, even obligatory. But it would be a very rash and dangerous move; if the officers and crew were unable to prove that the captain deserved to lose his command, the crew could be jailed or, if in time of war, even executed.

captain and give the command of her to the mate, who had been heard to say that, if he could have his way, the ship would have been half the distance to the Cape before night,–ice or no ice. And so irritated and impatient had the crew become, that even this proposition, which was open mutiny, punishable with state prison, was entertained, and the carpenter went to his berth, leaving it tacitly understood that something serious would be done, if things remained as they were many hours longer. When the carpenter left, we talked it all over, and I gave my advice strongly against it. Another of the men, too, who had known something of the kind attempted in another ship by a crew who were dissatisfied with their captain, and which was followed with serious consequences, was opposed to it. S—-, who soon came down, joined us, and we determined to have nothing to do with it. By these means, they were soon induced to give it up, for the present, though they said they would not lie where they were much longer without knowing the reason.

**The carpenter...had sounded the mate as to whether he would take command of the ship...** This, of course, is the problem with conspiracies: Rarely can the conspirators rely on one another not to say too much to the wrong person. In this case, the carpenter asks the mate if he would entertain the idea of taking control of the ship. The mate, whom one assumes is aghast at the suggestion that he seize command from the captain whom he has vowed to serve faithfully, goes directly to the captain to inform him of the plot.

**...he received the crew in a manner quiet, and even almost kind.** The captain is wise enough not to overreact. He even treats the carpenter, who has emerged as the chief instigator of the conspiracy, with a certain amount of restraint. He warns the man that he's treading on thin ice (and one assumes that he was pretty imperious and threatening when he did so), but keep in mind that the captain would have been well within his rights to have the man flogged.

The affair remained in this state until four o'clock, when an order came forward for all hands to come aft upon the quarter-deck. In about ten minutes they came forward again, and the whole affair had been blown. The carpenter, very prematurely, and without any authority from the crew, had sounded the mate as to whether he would take command of the ship, and intimated an intention to displace the captain; and the mate, as in duty bound, had told the whole to the captain, who immediately sent for all hands aft. Instead of violent measures, or, at least, an outbreak of quarter-deck bravado, threats, and abuse, which they had every reason to expect, a sense of common danger and common suffering seemed to have tamed his spirit, and begotten something like a humane fellow-feeling; for he received the crew in a manner quiet, and even almost kind. He told them what he had heard, and said that he did not believe that they would try to do any such thing as was intimated; that they had always been goodmen,–obedient, and knew their duty, and he had no fault to find with them; and asked them what they had to complain of–said that no one could say that he was slow to carry sail, (which was true enough;) and that, as soon as he thought it was safe and proper, he should make sail. He added a few words about their duty in their present situation, and sent them forward, saying that he should take no further notice of the matter; but, at the same time, told the carpenter to recollect whose power he was in, and that if he heard another word from him he would have cause to remember him to the day of his death.

This language of the captain had a very good effect upon the crew, and they returned quietly to their duty.

For two days more the wind blew from the southward and eastward; or in the short intervals when it was fair, the ice was too thick to run; yet the weather was not so dreadfully bad, and the crew had watch and watch. I still remained in my berth, fast recovering, yet still not well enough to go safely on deck. And I should have been perfectly useless; for, from having eaten nothing for nearly a week, except a little rice, which I forced into my mouth the last day or two, I was as weak as an infant. To be sick in a forecastle is miserable indeed. It is the worst part of a dog's life; especially in bad weather. The forecastle, shut up tight to keep out the water and cold air;–the watch either on deck, or asleep in their berths;–no one to speak to;–the pale light of the single lamp, swinging to and fro from the beam, so dim that one can scarcely see, much less read by it;–the water dropping from the beams and carlines, and running down the sides; and the forecastle so wet, and dark, and cheerless, and so lumbered up with chests and wet clothes, that sitting up is worse than lying in the berth! These are some of the evils. Fortunately, I needed no help from any one, and no medicine; and if I had needed help, I don't know where I should have found it. Sailors are willing enough; but it is true, as is often said–No one ships for nurse on board a vessel. Our merchant ships are always under-manned, and if one man is lost by sickness, they cannot spare another to take care of him. A sailor is always presumed to be well, and if he's sick, he's a poor dog. One has to stand his wheel, and another his lookout, and the sooner he gets on deck again, the better.

In the news
**July, 1836**

John Ross, a chief of the Cherokee Nation, pens a 6,000-word letter to the U.S. government in which he explains why his people cannot accept the Treaty of Echota, in spite of the fact that several Cherokees professing to represent the tribe have already signed it, thus acceding to the state of Georgia's demands that the tribe turn over its lands and relocate to the Indian Territory (originally, present-day Arkansas and Oklahoma) by 1838. The "removal" culminates in the Trail of Tears, a forced march during which 4,000 of the 15,000 Native American marchers die. Among the dead is John Ross's wife, Quatie.

**The forecastle, shut up tight to keep out the water and cold air...** Another example of Dana's powerfully descriptive prose: This is as good a picture of the misery of life in a 19th-century forecastle as we're likely to see. Keep in mind that, because previous nautically themed books were mostly romanticized versions of life "in the cabin," this is essentially the *first* such picture the public has seen.

**A sailor is always presumed to be well...** As with any other intense and dangerous occupation undertaken while undermanned, if one team member cannot perform, others must take up the slack. This does not endear the "slacker" (for that's what he is considered) to the rest of the crew; after all, it makes their lives even more exhausting and more dangerous.

In the news
**July, 1836**

Mary Wollstonecraft Shelley, who at age 19 had written *Frankenstein*, agrees to edit her father's papers and issue them as a memoir, largely to help support her now-widowed mother, early feminist writer Mary Wollstonecraft. The younger Mary had previously edited an edition of her husband's papers (he was famed poet Percy Bysshe Shelley) and now hoped to do the same with her philosopher/writer father's papers. In the end, Mary drops the project, worried that her father's radical views would upset the public—including her father-in-law, Sir Timothy Shelley.

Accordingly, as soon as I could possibly go back to my duty, I put on my thick clothes and boots and southwester, and made my appearance on deck. Though I had been but a few days below, yet everything looked strangely enough. The ship was cased in ice,–decks, sides, masts, yards, and rigging. Two close-reefed topsails were all the sail she had on, and every sail and rope was frozen so stiff in its place, that it seemed as though it would be impossible to start anything. Reduced, too, to her top-masts, she had altogether a most forlorn and crippled appearance. The sun had come up brightly; the snow was swept off the decks, and ashes thrown upon them, so that we could walk, for they had been as slippery as glass.

It was, of course, too cold to carry on any ship's work, and we had only to walk the deck and keep ourselves warm. The wind was still ahead, and the whole ocean, to the eastward, covered with islands and field-ice. At four bells the order was given to square away the yards; and the man who came from the helm said that the captain had kept her off to N. N. E. What could this mean? Some said that he was going to put into Valparaiso, and winter, and others that he was going to run out of the ice and cross the Pacific, and go home round the Cape of Good Hope. Soon, however, it leaked out, and we found that we were running for the straits of Magellan. The news soon spread through the ship, and all tongues were at work, talking about it. No one on board had been through the straits, but I had in my chest an account of the passage of the ship A. J. Donelson, of New York, through those straits, a few years before.

The account was given by the captain, and the representation was as favorable as possible. It was soon read by every one on board, and various opinions pronounced. The determination of our captain had at least this good effect; it gave every one something to think and talk about, made a break in our life, and diverted our minds from the monotonous dreariness of the prospect before us. Having made a fair wind of it, we were going off at a good rate, and leaving the thickest of the ice behind

**...Valparaiso...** A large seaport in Chile.

**...running for the straits of Magellan.** The Strait (or Straits) of Magellan is a navigable route across the tip of South America, just north of Tierra del Fuego. Prior to the opening of the Panama Canal (1914), this was a typical route between the Atlantic and Pacific oceans, although a rough and dangerous passage.

**...I had in my chest an account of the passage of the ship A. J. Donelson...** The *A.J. Donaldson*, under Captain Cunningham, had traversed the Straits in April of 1833, and his letter to the vessel's owner, Silas E. Burrows, had been extracted in *The Knickerbocker* magazine that September and elsewhere. Cunningham notes that the passage, which was smooth and fast, "saved twelve days" transit. (In noting his experience trading with natives in the area, Cunningham calls them "the most miserable beings I ever saw.")

us. This, at least, was something.

Having been long enough below to get my hands well warmed and softened, the first handling of the ropes was rather tough; but a few days hardened them, and as soon as I got my mouth open wide enough to take in a piece of salt beef and hard bread, I was all right again.

Sunday, July 10th. Lat. 54° 10', long. 79° 07'. This was our position at noon. The sun was out bright; the ice was all left behind, and things had quite a cheering appearance. We brought our wet pea-jackets and trowsers on deck, and hung them up in the rigging, that the breeze and the few hours of sun might dry them a little; and, by the permission of the cook, the galley was nearly filled with stockings and mittens, hung round to be dried. Boots, too, were brought up; and having got a little tar and slush from below, we gave them a thick coat. After dinner, all hands were turned-to, to get the anchors over the bows, bend on the chains, etc. The fish-tackle was got up, fish-davit rigged out, and after two or three hours of hard and cold work, both the anchors were ready for instant use, a couple of kedges got up, a hawser coiled away upon the fore-hatch, and the deep-sea-lead-line overhauled and got ready. Our spirits returned with having something to do; and when the tackle was manned to bowse the anchor home, notwithstanding the desolation of the scene, we struck up "Cheerily ho!" in full chorus. This pleased the mate, who rubbed his hands and cried out–"That's right, my boys; never say die! That sounds like the old crew!" and the captain came up, on hearing the song, and said to the passenger, within hearing of the man at the wheel,–"That sounds like a lively crew. They'll have their song so long as there're enough left for a chorus!"

This preparation of the cable and anchors was for the passage of the straits; for, being very crooked, and with a variety of currents, it is necessary to come frequently to anchor. This was not, by any means, a pleasant prospect, for, of all the work that a sailor is called upon to do in cold weather, there is none so bad as working the ground-tackle. The heavy chain cables to be hauled

**In the news**
**July, 1836**

President Andrew Jackson issues an executive order known as the "specie circular," which forbids the government's Land Office to accept anything but gold and silver as payment for land. The order is an attempt to reduce the likelihood of speculation, but it also creates a credit crunch and eventually a full-scale panic.

**...tar and slush from below...** Recall that slush is fat skimmed from pots and barrels and used to protect masts and spars. (The extra often being sold to coastal residents, from whence we get the phrase "slush fund.")

**...the deep-sea-lead-line...** A lead line is a weighted and marked line used to measure depth. It is heaved overboard ahead of the ship such that by the time the vessel reaches it, the line is more or less vertical, hanging directly beneath the hull. A coastal lead line was used to measure depths of up to about 20 fathoms (120 feet); a deep-sea lead line could measure depths of up to 100 fathoms (600 feet).

**In the news**
**July, 1836**

Indiana is growing rapidly, thanks partly to an influx in immigrants. The state's Receiver of Public Moneys notes that he expects his office to take in the then-enormous sum of $1.5 million from the sale of government land. The government is selling prime land ("to which the Indian title had been extinguished," as one source notes dryly) for 1/4 down, another 1/4 due after two years, another after three years, and the final 1/4 due at the close of the fourth year.

and pulled about the decks with bare hands; wet hawsers, slip-ropes, and buoy-ropes to be hauled aboard, dripping in water, which is running up your sleeves, and freezing; clearing hawse under the bows; getting under weigh and coming-to, at all hours of the night and day, and a constant look-out for rocks and sands and turns of tides;–these are some of the disagreeables of such a navigation to a common sailor. Fair or foul, he wants to have nothing to do with the ground-tackle between port and port. One of our hands, too, had unluckily fallen upon a half of an old newspaper which contained an account of the passage, through the straits, of a Boston brig, called, I think, the Peruvian, in which she lost every cable and anchor she had, got aground twice, and arrived at Valparaiso in distress. This was set off against the account of the A. J. Donelson, and led us to look forward with less confidence to the passage, especially as no one on board had ever been through, and the captain had no very perfect charts. However, we were spared any further experience on the point; for the next day, when we must have been near the Cape of Pillars, which is the south-west point of the mouth of the straits, a gale set in from the eastward, with a heavy fog, so that we could not see half of the ship's length ahead. This, of course, put an end to the project, for the present; for a thick fog and a gale blowing dead ahead are not the most favorable circumstances for the passage of difficult and dangerous straits. This weather, too, seemed likely to last for some time, and we could not think of beating about the mouth of the straits for a week or two, waiting for a favorable opportunity; so we braced up on the larboard tack, put the ship's head due south, and struck her off for Cape Horn again.

**...of all the work...there is none so bad as working the ground-tackle.** As Dana notes, it's very difficult (and often dangerous) to haul heavy wet ropes and slippery chains in freezing weather. This is true at any time, but never more than during a difficult passage that will require many tacks and anchorages to account for the twists and turns of the Straits.

**...a Boston brig, called, I think, the Peruvian...** There seems to be no record of a Boston brig called *Peruvian*, although there are British and Irish brigs of that name. There was, however, a Boston brig called *Peru*, owned by the brothers Charles and Andrew Cunningham (later the firm of Dabney & Cunningham).

**...we must have been near the Cape of Pillars...** Cape Pilar (or Cape Pillar) is at Desolación (Desolation) Island, off the coast of southern Chile.

**...and struck her off for Cape Horn again.** Thus end's the *Alert*'s first bid to transit the passage. Given the bad weather, the captain wisely opts to hold off until conditions improve. Remember that the vessel is seriously overloaded: The men would be nervous about a passage under any circumstances, let alone in a ship that's this sluggish and sitting this low in the water.

In the news
**July, 1836**

Ibrahim Pasha, commander of Egyptian forces and the eldest son of Egypt's Muhammad Ali, informs members of the press that rather than pay for new stones to erect dams on the Nile, he will instead deconstruct "one of the smaller pyramids at Ghiza, and make use of the materials." Luckily for history and for the future of Egyptian tourism, the plan never comes to fruition.

## Chapter XXXII

### Ice Again–A Beautiful Afternoon–Cape Horn–"Land Ho!"–Heading For Home

In our first attempt to double the Cape, when we came up to the latitude of it, we were nearly seventeen hundred miles to the westward, but, in running for the straits of Magellan, we stood so far to the eastward, that we made our second attempt at a distance of not more than four or five hundred miles; and we had great hopes, by this means, to run clear of the ice; thinking that the easterly gales, which had prevailed for a long time, would have driven it to the westward. With the wind about two points free, the yards braced in a little, and two close-reefed topsails and a reefed foresail on the ship, we made great way toward the southward and, almost every watch, when we came on deck, the air seemed to grow colder, and the sea to run higher. Still, we saw no ice, and had great hopes of going clear of it altogether, when, one afternoon, about three o'clock, while we were taking a siesta during our watch below, "All hands!" was called in a loud and fearful voice. "Tumble up here, men!–tumble up!–don't stop for your clothes– before we're upon it!" We sprang out of our berths and hurried upon deck.

The loud, sharp voice of the captain was heard giving orders, as though for life or death, and we ran aft to the braces, not waiting to look ahead, for not a moment was to be lost. The helm was hard up, the after yards shaking, and the ship in the act of wearing.

Slowly, with stiff ropes and iced rigging, we swung the yards round, everything coming hard, and with a creaking and rending sound, like pulling up a plank which had been frozen into the ice. The ship wore round fairly, the yards were steadied, and we stood off on the other tack, leaving behind us, directly under our larboard quarter, a large ice island, peering out of the mist, and reaching high above our tops, while astern; and on either side of the island, large tracts of field-ice were dimly seen, heaving and rolling in the sea. We were

**In our first attempt to double the Cape...** This nautical usage of the word "double" to mean "pass around to the other side" goes back to the 16th century. In a pre-Shakespearean telling of the story of Henry VIII (by Edward Hall, in 1548), we find "If you wil bring your shippe into the bay of Hardines, you must double ye poynt of Gentilnes." It's a perfectly viable metaphor in that sense, of course, since one of its meanings is to fold over or bend—which is exactly what happens to the vessel's course as she rounds a cape or point.

**In the news**
**July, 1836**

In mid-July, the governor of Kentucky calls for volunteers to go to Camp Sabine to help guard the state's southwestern frontier from the potential ravages of the Texas Revolution. Some 1,000 men respond, and officers are appointed. However, hostilities in the area now having wound down somewhat after the Battle of San Jacinto, the men receive discharge orders before they can begin the trek to the camp.

**...giving orders, as though for life or death...** Which, of course, was exactly the case. A large floe or iceberg could easily punch a hole in the ship's wooden hull, sinking the ship. Once in the icy water, the men would perish within minutes. (Or even seconds, given that almost none of them knew how to swim.)

**...the Southern ocean.** That is, the South Polar Ocean—the Antarctic Ocean, the exact boundaries of which are unclear and sometimes disputed.

**"Ice on the lee bow!"** Rather than referring to the starboard (right) bow or port (left) bow (if facing forward from the stern), the "lee bow" would be the side of the bow opposite that from which the wind is coming.

**...and we lay hove-to...** A sensible idea. A vessel that heaves to has sails and rudder set so as to minimize headway—ideally, the vessel would sit perfectly still, aside from being wave-tossed. (In reality, the ship will drift some, but that's OK so long as you're far enough away from land so that you can't accidentally drift onto shore or rocks.) A ship that's hove-to needs no tending; except for the men on watch, the crew can rest, relatively safe and warm belowdecks.

In the news
**July, 1836**

Aboard the *Beagle*, Charles Darwin arrives at St. Helena island, where he stays for about two weeks, setting sail for Ascension Island on the 14th of the month. At Ascension Island, he climbs Green Hill, a volcano almost 3,000 feet tall. During his visit to what he perceives as an arid, mostly-empty "cinder" of an island with little useful vegetation, Darwin conceives a plan to "terra-form" the island: With the help of his friend, British explorer and botanist Joseph Hooker, he wishes to introduce thousands of trees to the barren landscape to transform the island into a paradise. Years later, thousands of trees are indeed imported and planted on the island; by the 1870s, enough trees had been planted at Green Mountain to create a tropical cloud forest.

now safe, and standing to the northward; but, in a few minutes more, had it not been for the sharp look-out of the watch, we should have been fairly upon the ice, and left our ship's old bones adrift in the Southern ocean. After standing to the northward a few hours, we wore ship, and the wind having hauled, we stood to the southward and eastward. All night long, a bright look-out was kept from every part of the deck; and whenever ice was seen on the one bow or the other, the helm was shifted and the yards braced, and by quick working of the ship she was kept clear. The accustomed cry of "Ice ahead!"–"Ice on the lee bow!"–"Another island!" in the same tones, and with the same orders following them, seemed to bring us directly back to our old position of the week before.

During our watch on deck, which was from twelve to four, the wind came out ahead, with a pelting storm of hail and sleet, and we lay hove-to, under a close-reefed main topsail, the whole watch. During the next watch it fell calm, with a drenching rain, until daybreak, when the wind came out to the westward, and the weather cleared up, and showed us the whole ocean, in the course which we should have steered, had it not been for the head wind and calm, completely blocked up with ice. Here then our progress was stopped, and we wore ship, and once more stood to the northward and eastward; not for the straits of Magellan, but to make another attempt to double the Cape, still farther to the eastward; for the captain was determined to get round if perseverance could do it; and the third time, he said, never failed.

With a fair wind we soon ran clear of the field-ice, and by noon had only the stray islands floating far and near upon the ocean.

The sun was out bright, the sea of a deep blue, fringed with the white foam of the waves which ran high before a strong south-wester; our solitary ship tore on through the water, as though glad to be out of her confinement; and the ice islands lay scattered upon the ocean here and there, of various sizes and shapes, reflecting the bright rays of the sun, and drifting slowly northward before the gale. It was a contrast to much that we had lately seen, and a spectacle not only of beauty, but of life; for it required but little fancy to imagine these islands to be animate masses which had broken loose from the "thrilling regions of thick-ribbed ice," and were working their way, by wind and current, some alone, and some in fleets, to milder climes. No pencil has ever yet given anything like the true effect of an iceberg. In a picture, they are huge, uncouth masses, stuck in the sea, while their chief beauty and grandeur,–their slow, stately motion; the whirling of the snow about their summits, and the fearful groaning and cracking of their parts,–the picture cannot give. This is the large iceberg; while the small and distant islands, floating on the smooth sea, in the light of a clear day, look like little floating fairy isles of sapphire.

From a north-east course we gradually hauled to the eastward, and after sailing about two hundred miles, which brought us as near to the western coast of Terra del Fuego as was safe, and having lost sight of the ice altogether,–for the third time we put the ship's head to the southward, to try the passage of the Cape. The weather continued clear and cold, with a strong gale from the westward, and we were fast getting up with the latitude of the Cape, with a prospect of soon being round. One fine afternoon, a man who had gone into the fore-top to shift the rolling tackles, sung out, at the top of his voice, and with evident glee,–"Sail ho!" Neither land nor sail had we seen since leaving San Diego; and any one who has traversed the length of a whole ocean alone, can imagine what an excitement such an announcement produced on board. "Sail ho!" shouted the cook, jumping out of his galley; "Sail ho!" shouted a man, throwing back the slide of the scuttle, to the watch below, who were soon out of their berths and on deck; and "Sail ho!" shouted the captain down the companion-way to the passenger in the cabin. Besides the pleasure of seeing a ship and human beings in so desolate a place, it was important for us to speak a vessel, to learn whether there was ice to the eastward, and to ascertain the longitude; for we had no chronometer, and

**...the "thrilling regions of thick-ribbed ice," and were working their way...** This is an allusion to Act III of Shakespeare's *Measure for Measure*:

*To bathe in fiery floods, or to reside*
*In thrilling regions of thick-ribbed ice;*

Dana's penchant for literary allusion is to be expected from one who has studied the classics and who loves books, language, and literature. His allusions would seem obscure to most of the crew, but they would be readily recognized by educated men of his era. In this case, the allusion is quite appropriate, as the soliloquy has to do with the nature of death—and at this point, the specter of death surrounds the crew: One mistake and they are all doomed.

**... little floating fairy isles of sapphire.** Every so often we are reminded that Dana can sound decidedly poetic when he wishes.

**...we gradually hauled to the eastward...** Began sailing due east or nearly so, after having spent time on a northeasterly course.

**...which brought us as near to the western coast of Terra del Fuego as was safe...** Safe for two reasons: First, approaching an unfamiliar coast that offers little in the way of safe harbors would have been unwise; a ship could easily end up on the rocks. Second, an enduring legend had it that Terra del Fuego was the home of cannibal bands of natives. (This was apparently never true, and yet the rumors persist. In 1836, they were not merely vague rumors, but instead were widely accepted as fact.)

**...drifting about so long that we had nearly lost our reckoning...** Dead (i.e., deduced) reckoning relies on accurately tracking a vessel's course and speed over time. If *Alert* has no clock (chronometer), then this would be difficult, especially if she's been drifting. With a fuzzy idea of her latitude and (lacking lunar observations) longitude, *Alert* would be glad indeed to "speak" (encounter, communicate with) another vessel.

**"Land in your eye!" said the mate...** Not true land, of course, but ice. Imagine the disappointment of the captain and crew at finding that the first "sails" sighted since leaving San Diego were in fact not sails at all.

In the news

**July, 1836**

Composer and pianist Frédéric Chopin travels to Marienbad, in what is now the Czech Republic, following Maria Wodzinski, whom he had met earlier in Paris. Chopin had previously known her brothers in Poland. While in Marienbad, the two become engaged, and a huge party travels to Dresden for several weeks of merrymaking. Maria, however, is quite young (17 years old), and Chopin is dealing with health issues, which leads to the postponement of the marriage. In the end, the marriage never does take place.

**...as though the genius of the place had been roused at finding that we had nearly slipped through his fingers...** An interesting bit of personification and, apart from occasional references to Davy Jones, one of few such instances in the book.

had been drifting about so long that we had nearly lost our reckoning, and opportunities for lunar observations are not frequent or sure in such a place as Cape Horn. For these various reasons, the excitement in our little community was running high, and conjectures were made, and everything thought of for which the captain would hail, when the man aloft sung out–"Another sail, large on the weather bow!"

This was a little odd, but so much the better, and did not shake our faith in their being sails. At length the man in the top hailed, and said he believed it was land, after all. "Land in your eye!" said the mate, who was looking through a telescope; "they are ice islands, if I can see a hole through a ladder;" and a few moments showed the mate to be right and all our expectations fled; and instead of what we most wished to see, we had what we most dreaded, and what we hoped we had seen the last of. We soon, however, left these astern, having passed within about two miles of them; and at sundown the horizon was clear in all directions.

Having a fine wind, we were soon up with and passed the latitude of the Cape, and having stood far enough to the southward to give it a wide berth, we began to stand to the eastward, with a good prospect of being round and steering to the northward on the other side, in a very few days.

But ill luck seemed to have lighted upon us. Not four hours had we been standing on in this course, before it fell dead calm; and in half an hour it clouded up; a few straggling blasts, with spits of snow and sleet, came from the eastward; and in an hour more, we lay hove-to under a close-reefed main topsail, drifting bodily off to leeward before the fiercest storm that we had yet felt, blowing dead ahead, from the eastward. It seemed as though the genius of the place had been roused at finding that we had nearly slipped through his fingers, and had come down upon us with tenfold fury. The sailors said that every blast, as it shook the shrouds, and whistled through the rigging, said to the old ship, "No, you don't!"–"No, you don't!"

For eight days we lay drifting about in this manner. Sometimes,– generally towards noon,–it fell calm; once or twice a round copper ball showed itself for a few moments in the place where the sun ought to have been; and a puff or two came from the westward, giving some hope that a fair wind had come at last. During the first two days, we made sail for these puffs, shaking the reefs out of the topsails and boarding the tacks of the courses; but finding that it only made work for us when the gale set in again, it was soon given up, and we lay-to under our close-reefs.

We had less snow and hail than when we were farther to the westward, but we had an abundance of what is worse to a sailor in cold weather–drenching rain. Snow is blinding, and very bad when coming upon a coast, but, for genuine discomfort, give me rain with freezing weather. A snow-storm is exciting, and it does not wet through the clothes (which is important to a sailor); but a constant rain there is no escaping from. It wets to the skin, and makes all protection vain. We had long ago run through all our dry clothes, and as sailors have no other way of drying them than by the sun, we had nothing to do but to put on those which were the least wet.

At the end of each watch, when we came below, we took off our clothes and wrung them out; two taking hold of a pair of trowsers,–one at each end,–and jackets in the same way. Stockings, mittens, and all, were wrung out also and then hung up to drain and chafe dry against the bulk-heads. Then, feeling of all our clothes, we picked out those which were the least wet, and put them on, so as to be ready for a call, and turned-in, covered ourselves up with blankets, and slept until three knocks on the scuttle and the dismal sound of "All starbowlines ahoy! Eight bells, there below! Do you hear the news?" drawled out from on deck, and the sulky answer of "Aye, aye!" from below, sent us up again.

On deck, all was as dark as a pocket, and either a dead calm, with the rain pouring steadily down, or, more generally, a violent gale dead ahead, with rain pelting horizontally, and occasional variations of hail and

**...some hope that a fair wind had come at last.** This (again) brings to mind Coleridge's "Rime of the Ancient Mariner" and its depiction of a ship caught in a seemingly endless calm:

*Day after day, day after day,*
*We stuck, nor breath nor motion;*
*As idle as a painted ship*
*Upon a painted ocean.*
*Water, water, every where,*
*And all the boards did shrink;*
*Water, water, every where,*
*Nor any drop to drink.*

Note that the line about the boards shrinking has to do with the fact that wet boards swell a ship's seams shut, reducing leaks; boards drying in the sun shrink, allowing water (none of it fit to drink, as the poem says) to leak into the vessel.

**...sailors have no other way of drying them than by the sun...** We tend to forget that the crew had no way to dry their clothes, other than to hang them near the stove—which would have quickly become inconvenient to the cook and to all who needed access to (or past) the stove.

**In the news**
**July, 1836**

The U.S. Patent Office updates its method of registering patents, beginning use of a numbered system that replaces the old method, which referred to inventions by name and date. The recipient of Patent #1 (July 13) issued under the new system is one John Ruggles, a lawyer, politician, and inventor from New England, who patents an enhanced-traction type of train wheel.

sleet;–decks afloat with water swashing from side to side, and constantly wet feet; for boots could not be wrung out like drawers, and no composition could stand the constant soaking. In fact, wet and cold feet are inevitable in such weather, and are not the least of those little items which go to make up the grand total of the discomforts of a winter passage round the Cape. Few words were spoken between the watches as they shifted, the wheel was relieved, the mate took his place on the quarter-deck, the look-outs in the bows; and each man had his narrow space to walk fore and aft in, or, rather, to swing himself forward and back in, from one belaying pin to another,– for the decks were too slippery with ice and water to allow of much walking. To make a walk, which is absolutely necessary to pass away the time, one of us hit upon the expedient of sanding the deck; and afterwards, whenever the rain was not so violent as to wash it off, the weatherside of the quarter-deck and a part of the waist and forecastle were sprinkled with the sand which we had on board for holystoning; and thus we made a good promenade, where we walked fore and aft, two and two, hour after hour, in our long, dull, and comfortless watches. The bells seemed to be an hour or two apart, instead of half an hour, and an age to elapse before the welcome sound of eight bells. The sole object was to make the time pass on. Any change was sought for, which would break the monotony of the time; and even the two hours' trick at the wheel, which came round to each of us, in turn, once in every other watch, was looked upon as a relief. Even the never-failing resource of long yarns, which eke out many a watch, seemed to have failed us now; for we had been so long together that we had heard each other's stories told over and over again, till we had them by heart; each one knew the whole history of each of the others, and we were fairly and literally talked out. Singing and joking, we were in no humor for, and, in fact, any sound of mirth or laughter would have struck strangely upon our ears, and would not have been tolerated, any more than whistling, or a wind instrument. The last resort, that of speculating upon the future, seemed now to fail us, for our discouraging situation, and the danger we were really in, (as we expected every

**...the discomforts of a winter passage round the Cape.** It's easy to forget that, although it is July, it is winter in the Southern Hemisphere, as the seasons are reversed. (However, the legend about water circling the drain in the opposite direction in the Southern Hemisphere is just that: a legend, and patently untrue. The direction in which water spins as it enters or exits a toilet or sink depends entirely on the manner and direction in which it is introduced into or pulled from the toilet or sink.)

In the news
**July, 1836**

Sam Houston arrives in San Augustine this month for treatment of injuries received during the battle of San Jacinto. Houston is eventually elected first (and later, third) president of the new Republic of Texas. His first term runs from October of 1836 to December of 1838, while his second runs from December of 1841 to December of 1844. (Texas is annexed by the United States in 1846, ending the succession of Texas presidents.)

**...would not have been tolerated, any more than whistling...** Sailors are a superstitious lot, and one of their superstitions concerns whistling: Whistling on deck is forbidden, lest one "whistle up a storm." (Other actions thought to bring bad luck included angering the ship's cat, having a priest [or a woman or flowers] on board, a shark following a ship, and losing a mop or bucket overboard.)

day to find ourselves drifted back among the ice) "clapped a stopper" upon all that. From saying–"when we get home"–we began insensibly to alter it to–"if we get home"–and at last the subject was dropped by a tacit consent.

In this state of things, a new light was struck out, and a new field opened, by a change in the watch. One of our watch was laid up for two or three days by a bad hand, (for in cold weather the least cut or bruise ripens into a sore,) and his place was supplied by the carpenter. This was a windfall, and there was quite a contest, who should have the carpenter to walk with him. As "Chips" was a man of some little education, and he and I had had a good deal of intercourse with each other, he fell in with me in my walk. He was a Fin, but spoke English very well, and gave me long accounts of his country;–the customs, the trade, the towns, what little he knew of the government, (I found he was no friend of Russia), his voyages, his first arrival in America, his marriage and courtship;–he had married a countrywoman of his, a dress-maker, whom he met with in Boston. I had very little to tell him of my quiet, sedentary life at home; and, in spite of our best efforts, which had protracted these yarns through five or six watches, we fairly talked one another out, and I turned him over to another man in the watch, and put myself upon my own resources.

I commenced a deliberate system of time-killing, which united some profit with a cheering up of the heavy hours. As soon as I came on deck, and took my place and regular walk, I began with repeating over to myself a string of matters which I had in my memory, in regular order. First, the multiplication table and the tables of weights and measures; then the states of the union, with their capitals; the counties of England, with their shire towns; the kings of England in their order; and a large part of the peerage, which I committed from an almanac that we had on board; and then the Kanaka numerals. This carried me through my facts, and, being repeated deliberately, with long intervals, often eked out the two first bells. Then came the ten commandments; the thirty-ninth chapter of Job, and a few other passages from

**...in cold weather the least cut or bruise ripens into a sore...** There may be some small bit of truth to this. Some studies, for instance, have shown that certain viruses (such as the ones that cause cold sores) can be reactivated by cold weather. Too, if an unrested sailor has been working in cold, wet weather for an extended time, his immune system may well be weakened, reducing the body's ability to heal. That's about the extent of it, though. By and large, cold weather has little effect on cuts and bruises.

**...my quiet, sedentary life at home...** This is, in fact, exactly how Dana views his life—at least, up until he went to sea: quiet, sedentary, and largely without excitement or purpose. But then, that's how most young people feel until they get out into the world.

In the news

**July, 1836**

Charles Dickens is staying at Furnival's Inn in London, while he writes *The Pickwick Papers*. The inn, like several other Inns of Chancery, was originally built to serve as offices for solicitors. Over time the inns became associations. By the 19th century, they were no longer used as such, and instead had become temporary accommodations for well-heeled travelers and visitors. By the early 20th century, the inns had disappeared altogether.

**...the counties of England...** While most of us could recite the multiplication tables and the states and capitals of the union, few of us know the counties and shires of England, the peerage (the British system of hereditary titles of nobility), and Hawaiian numerals.

**...Cowper's Castaway...the solemn measure and gloomy character of which...made it well suited to a lonely watch at sea.** "The Castaway" is a gloomy 1799 poem by William Cowper, an English pre-Romantic poet.

**"Ille et nefasto" from Horace, and Goethe's Erl King.** The first is an ode from Horace, the Roman poet who lived from 56 BC to 8 BC. The Erlking is a malevolent spirit that haunts forests. In Goethe's poem, *Der Erlkönig*, the spirit preys on children.

In the news
**July, 1836**

The U.S. having wrested control of the area from the British during the War of 1812, Wisconsin becomes a territory. Many of the Native Americans in the area had already been removed from the area, partly as a result of the Winnebago and Black Hawk wars. Wisconsin will become a state in 1848 and will soon become a center of abolitionist sentiment.

In the news
**July, 1836**

Abraham Lincoln, a Whig candidate for the state senate, spends much of the month traveling the state and participating in debates with the likes of John C. Calhoun and Jacob M. Early. (Ultimately, Lincoln is elected to the state assembly in November.)

**...no nectar and ambrosia were sweeter to the lazy immortals...** Ambrosia is the food of the Greek gods, while nectar is the drink of the gods, although the two are reversed in some of the myths.

Scripture. The next in the order, that I never varied from, came Cowper's Castaway, which was a great favorite with me; the solemn measure and gloomy character of which, as well as the incident that it was founded upon, made it well suited to a lonely watch at sea. Then his lines to Mary, his address to the jackdaw, and a short extract from Table Talk; (I abounded in Cowper, for I happened to have a volume of his poems in my chest;) "Ille et nefasto" from Horace, and Goethe's Erl King. After I had got through these, I allowed myself a more general range among everything that I could remember, both in prose and verse. In this way, with an occasional break by relieving the wheel, heaving the log, and going to the scuttle-butt for a drink of water, the longest watch was passed away; and I was so regular in my silent recitations, that if there was no interruption by ship's duty, I could tell very nearly the number of bells by my progress.

Our watches below were no more varied than the watch on deck.

All washing, sewing, and reading was given up; and we did nothing but eat, sleep, and stand our watch, leading what might be called a Cape Horn life. The forecastle was too uncomfortable to sit up in; and whenever we were below, we were in our berths. To prevent the rain, and the sea-water which broke over the bows, from washing down, we were obliged to keep the scuttle closed, so that the forecastle was nearly air-tight. In this little, wet, leaky hole, we were all quartered, in an atmosphere so bad that our lamp, which swung in the middle from the beams, sometimes actually burned blue, with a large circle of foul air about it. Still I was never in better health than after three weeks of this life. I gained a great deal of flesh, and we all ate like horses. At every watch, when we came below, before turning-in, the bread barge and beef kid were overhauled. Each man drank his quart of hot tea night and morning; and glad enough we were to get it, for no nectar and ambrosia were sweeter to the lazy immortals, than was a pot of hot tea, a hard biscuit, and a slice of cold salt beef, to us after a watch on deck. To be sure, we were mere animals and had this life lasted a year instead of a month we should have been little better than the ropes in the ship. Not a razor, nor a brush, nor a drop of water, except the rain and the spray, had come near us all the time; for we were on an allowance of fresh water; and who would strip and wash himself in salt water on deck, in the snow and ice, with the thermometer at zero?

**Not a razor...nor a drop of water...had come near us all the time.** One can imagine what this must have smelled like, with dirty, smelly men and moldering, wet clothing filling the dank, airless forecastle.

In the news
**July, 1836**

The ailing Stephen F. Austin, the "father of Texas," writes: "The prosperity of Texas has been the object of my labors, the idol of my existence—it has assumed the character of a religion, for the guidance of my thoughts and actions, for fifteen years." In five months, Austin will die and be buried in the state cemetery in the Texas city that bears his name.

After about eight days of constant easterly gales, the wind hauled occasionally a little to the southward, and blew hard, which, as we were well to the southward, allowed us to brace in a little and stand on, under all the sail we could carry. These turns lasted but a short while, and sooner or later it set again from the old quarter; yet each time we made something, and were gradually edging along to the eastward. One night, after one of these shifts of the wind, and when all hands had been up a great part of the time, our watch was left on deck, with the mainsail hanging in the buntlines, ready to be set if necessary. It came on to blow worse and worse, with hail and snow beating like so many furies upon the ship, it being as dark and thick as night could make it. The mainsail was blowing and slatting with a noise like thunder, when the captain came on deck, and ordered it to be furled. The mate was about to call all hands, when the captain stopped him, and said that the men would be beaten out if they were called up so often; that as our watch must stay on deck, it might as well be doing that as anything else.

**...beating like so many furies...** In Roman mythology, the Furies were female goddesses of vengeance. (This is where we get the word "furious" and its variants.)

In the news
**July, 1836**

In a sign of things to come, the first English-language newspaper in Hawaii begins publication. The paper was called the *Sandwich Island Gazette and Journal of Commerce*, and it lasted about three years. Hawaii will become a U.S. state in 1959.

Accordingly, we went upon the yard; and never shall I forget that piece of work. Our watch had been so reduced by sickness, and by some having been left in California, that, with one man at the wheel, we had only the third mate and three beside myself, to go aloft; so that at most, we could only attempt to furl one yard-arm at a time. We manned the weather yard-arm, and set to work to make a furl of it. Our lower masts being short, and our yards very square, the sail had a head of nearly fifty feet, and a short leach, made still shorter by the deep reef which was in it, which brought the clew away out on the quarters of the yard, and made a bunt nearly

**...a head of nearly fifty feet...** In this context, the head is the top part of a four-sided sail, while the leech (note the spelling) is the sail's vertical edge. If the sail is 50 feet across and the wind is blowing, it is exerting a tremendous amount of pressure on the sail, which will make it very difficult to handle, especially undermanned as they are. Doubly difficult when it's freezing and both the sail and the men's hands are stiff.

**We had to fist the sail...** That is, furl it.

In the news
**July, 1836**

Seeking ways to improve the performance of steam-powered paddle-wheel-driven craft, Swedish native John Ericsson patents a screw propeller that consists of a helix or spiral of several turns. Today's boat "props" are only vaguely similar to these early screw propellers, although it's obvious that later designs are informed by and built on the same fundamental principles.

as square as the mizen royal-yard. Beside this difficulty, the yard over which we lay was cased with ice, the gaskets and rope of the foot and leach of the sail as stiff and hard as a piece of suction-hose, and the sail itself about as pliable as though it had been made of sheets of sheathing copper. It blew a perfect hurricane, with alternate blasts of snow, hail, and rain. We had to fist the sail with bare hands. No one could trust himself to mittens, for if he slipped, he was a gone man. All the boats were hoisted in on deck, and there was nothing to be lowered for him. We had need of every finger God had given us. Several times we got the sail upon the yard, but it blew away again before we could secure it. It required men to lie over the yard to pass each turn of the gaskets, and when they were passed, it was almost impossible to knot them so that they would hold. Frequently we were obliged to leave off altogether and take to beating our hands upon the sail, to keep them from freezing.

After some time,–which seemed forever,–we got the weather side stowed after a fashion, and went over to leeward for another trial.

**...the yard was a-cock-bill...** That is, at an angle with the deck.

This was still worse, for the body of the sail had been blown over to leeward, and as the yard was a-cock-bill by the lying over of the vessel, we had to light it all up to windward. When the yard-arms were furled, the bunt was all adrift again, which made more work for us. We got all secure at last, but we had been nearly an hour and a half upon the yard, and it seemed an age. It just struck five bells when we went up, and eight were struck soon after we came down. This may seem slow work, but considering the state of everything, and that we had only five men to a sail with just half as many square yards of canvas in it as the mainsail of the Independence, sixty-gun ship, which musters seven hundred men at her quarters, it is not wonderful that we were no quicker about it. We were glad enough to get on deck, and still more, to go below. The oldest sailor in the watch said, as he went down,–"I shall never forget that main yard;–it beats all my going a fishing. Fun is fun, but furling one yard-arm of a course, at a time,

**...a sail with just half as many square yards of canvas in it as...the Independence, sixty-gun ship...** The *Independence*, built after (and as a response to) the War of 1812, would sail the world for almost 100 years. She actually carried 74 guns, not 60, but Dana's point was nonetheless valid: She carried twice as much canvas as *Alert*, but then she boasted a crew of 700 to handle her sails and gear.

off Cape Horn, is no better than man-killing."

**...no better than man-killing.** In later editions, Dana replaced this with "no better than bloody murder."

During the greater part of the next two days, the wind was pretty steady from the southward. We had evidently made great progress, and had good hope of being soon up with the Cape, if we were not there already. We could put but little confidence in our reckoning, as there had been no opportunities for an observation, and we had drifted too much to allow of our dead reckoning being anywhere near the mark. If it would clear off enough to give a chance for an observation, or if we could make land, we should know where we were; and upon these, and the chances of falling in with a sail from the eastward, we depended almost entirely.

**...we had drifted too much to allow of our dead reckoning being anywhere near the mark.** Since the weather had been so bad and given that he had been unable to confirm his longitude, the captain has only the vaguest idea of his position.

Friday, July 22d. This day we had a steady gale from the southward, and stood on under close sail, with the yards eased a little by the weather braces, the clouds lifting a little, and showing signs of breaking away. In the afternoon, I was below with Mr. H—-, the third mate, and two others, filling the bread locker in the steerage from the casks, when a bright gleam of sunshine broke out and shone down the companion-way and through the skylight, lighting up everything below, and sending a warm glow through the heart of every one. It was a sight we had not seen for weeks,–an omen, a god-send. Even the roughest and hardest face acknowledged its influence. Just at that moment we heard a loud shout from all parts of the deck, and the mate called out down the companion-way to the captain, who was sitting in the cabin. What he said, we could not distinguish, but the captain kicked over his chair, and was on deck at one jump. We could not tell what it was; and, anxious as we were to know, the discipline of the ship would not allow of our leaving our places. Yet, as we were not called, we knew there was no danger. We hurried to get through with our job, when, seeing the steward's black face peering out of the pantry, Mr. H—- hailed him, to know what was the matter. "Lan' o, to be sure, sir! No you hear 'em sing out, 'Lan' o?' De cap'em say 'im Cape Horn!"

**...I was below with Mr. H—-, the third mate...** The third mate is James Hatch, shipped at 19 years of age, and hailing from Springfield, MA.

In the news
**July, 1836**

Canada's first railway opens. Called the Champlain and Saint Lawrence Railroad, it connects Montreal and Lake Champlain. It actually carries little freight, instead serving largely as a sort of "portage" over the most difficult parts of the journey from Montreal to New York. The locomotive used is the previously mentioned "Kitten."

**...anxious as we were to know, the discipline of the ship would not allow of our leaving our places.** This is a good example of one of the differences between the *Alert* and the *Pilgrim*. Even though the men are tempted to leave their places to find out what was going on, they did not (and would not) do so. The *Alert* is a "taut" ship, crewed by well-trained, disciplined men.

This gave us a new start, and we were soon through our

work, and on deck; and there lay the land, fair upon the larboard beam, and slowly edging away upon the quarter. All hands were busy looking at it–the captain and mates from the quarter-deck, the cook from his galley, and the sailors from the forecastle; and even Mr. N., the passenger, who had kept in his shell for nearly a month, and hardly been seen by anybody, and who we had almost forgotten was on board, came out like a butterfly, and was hopping round as bright as a bird.

**...Mr. N., the passenger, who had kept in his shell for nearly a month...** Dana likens his old professor, Nuttall, to a bleary-eyed turtle—and then immediately compares him instead to a butterfly and then a bird.

The land was the island of Staten Land, and, just to the eastward of Cape Horn; and a more desolate-looking spot I never wish to set eyes upon;–bare, broken, and girt with rocks and ice, with here and there, between the rocks and broken hillocks, a little stunted vegetation of shrubs. It was a place well suited to stand at the junction of the two oceans, beyond the reach of human cultivation, and encounter the blasts and snows of a perpetual winter. Yet, dismal as it was, it was a pleasant sight to us; not only as being the first land we had seen, but because it told us that we had passed the Cape,–were in the Atlantic,–and that, with twenty-four hours of this breeze, might bid defiance to the Southern Ocean. It told us, too, our latitude and longitude better than any observation; and the captain now knew where we were, as well as if we were off the end of Long wharf.

**...the island of Staten Land...** According to an 1817 guidebook, the Argentinian island east of Tierra del Fuego is a largely barren collection of craggy rocks and mountains, but vessels often stopped there to fish and to collect water and wood. Its modern name is Isla de los Estados.

**...as well as if we were off the end of Long wharf.** When Dana was writing, Long Wharf was the main wharf of the port of Boston. It was built in the mid-1700s, and served as a busy pier for loading and unloading for well over 150 years. In a shortened and much-modified form, the Wharf still exists, though it no longer plays an important part in nautical commerce. Instead, it is now occupied by hotels and restaurants, while serving as a landing point for cruise boats and ferries.

In the general joy, Mr. N. said he should like to go ashore upon the island and examine a spot which probably no human being had ever set foot upon; but the captain intimated that he would see the island–specimens and all,–in–another place, before he would get out a boat or delay the ship one moment for him.

**...he would see the island–specimens and all,–in–another place...** That is, he would see the entire island in hell before he would waste time just so Professor Nuttall can wander about collecting (what would have appeared to the captain to be) useless samples of the island's flora.

We left the land gradually astern; and at sundown had the Atlantic Ocean clear before us.

**...at sundown had the Atlantic Ocean clear before us.** This is a key turning point. The *Alert* is back in the Atlantic ocean proper and headed for Boston.

## Chapter XXXIII

### Cracking On–Progress Homeward–A Pleasant Sunday–A Fine Sight–By-Play

It is usual, in voyages round the Cape from the Pacific, to keep to the eastward of the Falkland Islands; but as it had now set in a strong, steady, and clear south-wester, with every prospect of its lasting, and we had had enough of high latitudes, the captain determined to stand immediately to the northward, running inside the Falkland Islands. Accordingly, when the wheel was relieved at eight o'clock, the order was given to keep her due north, and all hands were turned up to square away the yards and make sail. In a moment, the news ran through the ship that the captain was keeping her off, with her nose straight for Boston, and Cape Horn over her taffrail. It was a moment of enthusiasm. Every one was on the alert, and even the two sick men turned out to lend a hand at the halyards. The wind was now due south-west, and blowing a gale to which a vessel close hauled could have shown no more than a single close-reefed sail; but as we were going before it, we could carry on.

**...running inside the Falkland Islands.** The captain decides to take advantage of the fair winds and stays inside the Falkland Islands (instead of running east of them) in order to save time and shorten the return trip. The Falklands (or the Malvinas) consist of a chain of hundreds of islands, home to a large fishing and tourist industry. The islands have been claimed by multiple countries, most famously by Argentina and Great Britain; that claim has led to several diplomatic clashes and armed skirmishes, and occasionally to outright war.

**...a gale to which a vessel close hauled could have shown no more than a single close-reefed sail...** If the ship were sailing close-hauled—that is, more or less into the wind—it would have been a very rough go, and sail would have had to have been reduced. However, because the wind is mainly behind *Alert* and pushing her the direction she wishes to go, she can carry more sail.

Accordingly, hands were sent aloft, and a reef shaken out of the top-sails, and the reefed foresail set. When we came to masthead the topsail yards, with all hands at the halyards, we struck up "Cheerily, men," with a chorus which might have been heard half-way to Staten Land. Under her increased sail, the ship drove on through the water. Yet she could bear it well; and the captain sang out from the quarter-deck–"Another reef out of that fore-topsail, and give it to her!" Two hands sprang aloft; the frozen reef-points and earings were cast adrift, the halyards manned, and the sail gave out her increased canvas to the gale. All hands were kept on deck to watch the effect of the change. It was as much as she could well carry, and with a heavy sea astern, it took two men at the wheel to steer her. She flung the foam from her bows; the spray breaking aft as far as the gangway. She was going at a prodigious rate.

**In the news**
**July, 1836**

Andrew Stevenson becomes U.S. ambassador to Great Britain. However, Britain's King William IV dies 11 months later, and Stevenson is issued new credentials addressed to the new monarch. She is William's 18-year-old niece, the newly crowned Queen Victoria. Victoria will rule Britain for the next 64 years.

Still, everything held. Preventer braces were reeved and hauled taught; tackles got upon the backstays; and each thing done to keep all snug and strong. The captain walked the deck at a rapid stride, looked aloft at the sails, and then to windward; the mate stood in the gangway, rubbing his hands, and talking aloud to the ship–"Hurrah, old bucket! the Boston girls have got hold of the tow-rope!" and the like; and we were on the forecastle, looking to see how the spars stood it, and guessing the rate at which she was going,–when the captain called out–"Mr. Brown, get up the topmast studding-sail! What she can't carry she may drag!" The mate looked a moment; but he would let no one be before him in daring.

**Preventer braces were reeved...** A preventer is simply a line, chain, or other device that is used to back up stays and rigging in severe weather.

**...the Boston girls have got hold of the tow-rope!"** A common saying among sailors of the time. Obviously, the idea is that the women of Boston are so eager for the return of their men that they are pulling the ship toward home. Sailors then and now have always thought highly of themselves and of their appeal to members of the opposite sex.

**What she can't carry she may drag!** If a vessel is carrying too much sail for the weather, the spars and masts supporting some of those sails may snap. At that point, she is no longer carrying sail, but dragging both it and the broken spars.

He sprang forward–"Hurrah, men! rig out the topmast studding-sail boom! Lay aloft, and I'll send the rigging up to you!"–We sprang aloft into the top; lowered a girt-line down, by which we hauled up the rigging; rove the tacks and halyards; ran out the boom and lashed it fast, and sent down the lower halyards, as a preventer. It was a clear starlight night, cold and blowing; but everybody worked with a will. Some, indeed, looked as though they thought the "old man" was mad, but no one said a word. We had had a new topmast studding-sail made with a reef in it,–a thing hardly ever heard of, and which the sailors had ridiculed a good deal, saying that when it was time to reef a studding-sail, it was time to take it in. But we found a use for it now; for, there being a reef in the topsail, the studding-sail could not be set without one in it also. To be sure, a studding-sail with reefed topsails was rather a new thing; yet there was some reason in it, for if we carried that away, we should lose only a sail and a boom; but a whole topsail might have carried away the mast and all.

**...when it was time to reef a studding-sail, it was time to take it in.** Recall that a studding sail (pronounced *stunsail*) is an additional sail set forward of the mast. Normally used in good weather, one would typically not set one in bad, since sail is generally *reduced* in bad weather.

While we were aloft, the sail had been got out, bent to the yard, reefed, and ready for hoisting. Waiting for a good opportunity, the halyards were manned and the yard hoisted fairly up to the block; but when the mate came to shake the catspaw out of the downhaul, and we began to boom-end the sail, it shook the ship to her centre. The boom buckled up and bent like a whip-stick,

**...the mate came to shake the catspaw out of the downhaul...** A catspaw is a type of hitch made by twisting two sides in a bight so as to form a strengthened loop that can be hooked and lifted by a block-and-tackle. In this case, the mate loosens the catspaw, freeing the boom, which then swings freely; although under great strain, the boom does not break.

and we looked every moment to see something go; but, being of the short, tough upland spruce, it bent like whalebone, and nothing could break it. The carpenter said it was the best stick he had ever seen. The strength of all hands soon brought the tack to the boom-end, and the sheet was trimmed down, and the preventer and the weather brace hauled taught to take off the strain. Every rope-yarn seemed stretched to the utmost, and every thread of canvas; and with this sail added to her, the ship sprang through the water like a thing possessed. The sail being nearly all forward, it lifted her out of the water, and she seemed actually to jump from sea to sea. From the time her keel was laid, she had never been so driven; and had it been life or death with every one of us, she could not have borne another stitch of canvas.

Finding that she would bear the sail, the hands were sent below, and our watch remained on deck. Two men at the wheel had as much as they could do to keep her within three points of her course, for she steered as wild as a young colt. The mate walked the deck, looking at the sails, and then over the side to see the foam fly by her, slapping his hands upon his thighs and talking to the ship–"Hurrah, you jade, you've got the scent!–you know where you're going!" And when she leaped over the seas, and almost out of the water, and trembled to her very keel, the spars and masts snapping and creaking,– "There she goes!–There she goes,–handsomely!–as long as she cracks she holds!"–while we stood with the rigging laid down fair for letting go, and ready to take in sail and clear away, if anything went. At four bells we hove the log, and she was going eleven knots fairly; and had it not been for the sea from aft which sent the ship home, and threw her continually off her course, the log would have shown her to have been going much faster. I went to the wheel with a young fellow from the Kennebec, who was a good helmsman; and for two hours we had our hands full. A few minutes showed us that our monkey-jackets must come off; and, cold as it was, we stood in our shirt-sleeves, in a perspiration; and were glad enough to have it eight bells, and the wheel relieved. We turned-in and slept as well as we could, though the sea made a constant roar under her

**...the ship sprang through the water like a thing possessed.** In spite of the fierce wind, *Alert* is carrying just about all the sail she can manage, a feat possible only because the wind is almost directly behind her.

**Hurrah, you jade...** This (now obscure) bit of idiom worked on a couple of levels back in the 19th century. "Jade" was a common name for a horse, especially an old, worn out nag—generally used as a playful and loving endearment. *Alert* is certainly running like a horse headed down the straightaway for the finish line—in this case, Boston. But the term was also playfully applied to women of the time, in much the same was as "hussy" or "minx," to mean a seductive flirt or a tease. That characterization *also* fits when applied to the ship.

**...as long as she cracks she holds!** An old saying meaning that as long as the masts and spars are making noises that indicate that they're being stressed, they've not yet given way. The same phrase was also uttered by children skating on ice that was threatening to break, but which had not yet done so.

**...had it not been for the sea from aft which sent the ship home...** Much as when flying an airplane with a tailwind, getting an accurate measure of speed from a vessel sailing with a current is complicated. In the aircraft, you're not simply moving at, say, the indicated airspeed; you're moving at that rate *plus* the speed of the tailwind. The same applies to a ship's speed in a current; the log will not indicate a true speed over the ocean bottom, because the log itself is floating within the current that's pushing you.

bows, and washed over the forecastle like a small cataract.

**...water poured over the spritsail yard...** The spritsail was a smallish sail set forward of the main mast and beneath the bowsprit. The forerunner of today's triangular jibs and staysails, the spritsail was used mainly to balance the vessel as much as to speed it along. Because the spritsail is set so far forward and so low, the spar ("yard") on which it was mounted was often underwater in violent weather.

**...enough to last a Dutchman a week...** That is, with plenty to spare. The phrase derives from the fact that the Dutch, with a reputation as tremendous traders, were held to be frugal in the extreme.

**...just in time to save her from broaching to...** The safest way to meet violent waves is at an oblique angle, "quartering the wave" as nearly as possible. Failing that, you can try to meet the wave head on; that could result in a great deal of pitching, but that's normally not dangerous unless it becomes excessive enough to result in "pitchpoling"—flipping the vessel end over end as she careens down the face of the wave. The one thing you do *not* want to do is broach: end up facing broadside to the oncoming wave. A large wave that is broached could easily result in the vessel capsizing. This is what the mate and the crewmember (just barely) managed to avoid.

At four o'clock, we were called again. The same sail was still on the vessel, and the gale, if there was any change, had increased a little. No attempt was made to take the studding-sail in; and, indeed, it was too late now. If we had started anything toward taking it in, either tack or halyards, it would have blown to pieces, and carried something away with it. The only way now was to let everything stand, and if the gale went down, well and good; if not, something must go–the weakest stick or rope first–and then we could get it in. For more than an hour she was driven on at such a rate that she seemed actually to crowd the sea into a heap before her; and the water poured over the spritsail yard as it would over a dam. Toward daybreak the gale abated a little, and she was just beginning to go more easily along, relieved of the pressure, when Mr. Brown, determined to give her no respite, and depending upon the wind's subsiding as the sun rose, told us to get along the lower studding-sail. This was an immense sail, and held wind enough to last a Dutchman a week,–hove-to. It was soon ready, the boom topped up, preventer guys rove, and the idlers called up to man the halyards; yet such was still the force of the gale, that we were nearly an hour setting the sail; carried away the outhaul in doing it, and came very near snapping off the swinging boom. No sooner was it set than the ship tore on again like one that was mad, and began to steer as wild as a hawk. The men at the wheel were puffing and blowing at their work, and the helm was going hard up and hard down, constantly. Add to this, the gale did not lessen as the day came on, but the sun rose in clouds. A sudden lurch threw the man from the weather wheel across the deck and against the side. The mate sprang to the wheel, and the man, regaining his feet, seized the spokes, and they hove the wheel up just in time to save her from broaching to; though nearly half the studding-sail went under water; and as she came to, the boom stood up at an angle of forty five degrees. She had evidently more on her than she could bear; yet it was in vain to try to take it in–the clewline was not strong enough; and they were thinking of cutting away, when another wide yaw and a come-to, snapped the guys, and the swinging boom came in, with a crash, against the lower rigging. The outhaul block gave way, and the topmast studding-sail boom bent in a manner which I never before supposed a stick could bend. I had my eye on it when the guys parted, and it made one spring and buckled up so as to form nearly a half circle, and sprang out again to its shape.

**...buckled up so as to form nearly a half circle, and sprang out again...** This is a very strong and very flexible piece of wood. Any sailor or yachtsman knows that as soon as you sail (or, these days, motor) away from your home mooring, the sea begins acting upon your boat, and not in a good way. Under the stresses of a long voyage, weaknesses in sails, lines, rigging, spars, and the like *will* show up—and always at the most inopportune time. The *Alert* has been under stress for many months; the men have done a good job of staying on top of things, but this ferocious weather is beginning to tell on the ship.

The clewline gave way at the first pull; the cleat to which the halyards were belayed was wrenched off, and the sail blew round the spritsail yards and head guys, which gave us a bad job to get it in.

A half hour served to clear all away, and she was suffered to drive on with her topmast studding-sail set, it being as much as she could stagger under.

During all this day and the next night, we went on under the same sail, the gale blowing with undiminished force; two men at the wheel all the time; watch and watch, and nothing to do but to steer and look out for the ship, and be blown along;–until the noon of the next day–

Sunday, July 24th, when we were in latitude 50° 27' S., longitude 62° 13' W., having made four degrees of latitude in the last twenty-four hours. Being now to northward of the Falkland Islands, the ship was kept off, north-east, for the equator; and with her head for the equator, and Cape Horn over her taffrail, she went gloriously on; every heave of the sea leaving the Cape astern, and every hour bringing us nearer to home, and to warm weather. Many a time, when blocked up in the ice, with everything dismal and discouraging about us, had we said,–if we were only fairly round, and standing north on the other side, we should ask for no more:–and now we had it all, with a clear sea, and as much wind as a sailor could pray for. If the best part of the voyage is the last part, surely we had all now that we could wish. Every one was in the highest spirits, and the ship seemed as glad as any of us at getting out of her confinement. At each change of the watch, those coming on

**...when blocked up in the ice, with everything dismal and discouraging about us, had we said,–if we were only fairly round, and standing north on the other side, we should ask for no more...** Even after a grueling few days, and still many days from home, the men take solace in the fact that they are in fact on the way home, and getting closer by the minute.

deck asked those going below–"How does she go along?" and got for answer, the rate, and the customary addition–"Aye! and the Boston girls have had hold of the tow-rope all the watch, and can't haul half the slack in!" Each day the sun rose higher in the horizon, and the nights grew shorter; and at coming on deck each morning, there was a sensible change in the temperature. The ice, too, began to melt from off the rigging and spars, and, except a little which remained in the tops and round the hounds of the lower masts, was soon gone. As we left the gale behind us, the reefs were shaken out of the topsails, and sail made as fast as she could bear it; and every time all hands were sent to the halyards, a song was called for, and we hoisted away with a will.

**Each day the sun rose higher in the horizon, and the nights grew shorter...** At higher latitudes during the summer, days are in fact longer than at lower latitudes. At the equator, day and night should each (theoretically) last for exactly 12 hours. (But they don't, exactly, because atmospheric refraction can add a few minutes to each daylight period.)

**...and we hoisted away with a will.** This has always been a good crew, better trained and more disciplined than the crew of *Pilgrim*. But now that they're nearing home, they're even happier than usual, quite willing to work very hard, because they know that when they do, they're helping the ship get back to Boston even sooner.

Sail after sail was added, as we drew into fine weather; and in one week after leaving Cape Horn, the long topgallant masts were got up, topgallant and royal yards crossed, and the ship restored to her fair proportions.

The Southern Cross we saw no more after the first night; the Magellan Clouds settled lower and lower in the horizon; and so great was our change of latitude each succeeding night, that we sank some constellation in the south, and raised another in the northern horizon.

**The Southern Cross we saw no more...** Also called Crux (Latin for "cross"), this constellation is clearly visible in the southern hemisphere most of the time, and only rarely seen in the Northern Hemisphere.

Sunday, July 31st. At noon we were in lat. 36° 41' S., long. 38° 08' W.; having traversed the distance of two thousand miles, allowing for changes of course, in nine days. A thousand miles in four days and a half!–This is equal to steam.

**This is equal to steam.** If four days equal 108 hours, *Alert* has been averaging about 9.25 mph, or about 8 knots, which is indeed an impressive rate. For that time, 8 knots really was about equal to the speed of a steam-powered vessel. (In 1849, the steamer *Pacific* set an eastbound transatlantic record with an average speed of 13.03 knots. On the other hand, a few years after *that*, in 1854, the *Pacific* sank without a trace, with the loss of all 200 passengers and crew.)

Soon after eight o'clock, the appearance of the ship gave evidence that this was the first Sunday we had yet had in fine weather. As the sun came up clear, with the promise of a fair, warm day, and, as usual on Sunday, there was no work going on, all hands turned-to upon clearing out the forecastle. The wet and soiled clothes which had accumulated there during the past month, were brought up on deck; the chests moved; brooms, buckets of water, swabs, scrubbing-brushes, and scrapers carried down, and applied, until the forecastle floor

**...as usual on Sunday, there was no work going on...** Dana points out again one of the differences between the two vessels on which he served: On board *Alert*, the men do not work on Sunday. (One can almost hear Dana mutter, "As it should be!") Instead, the crew takes advantage of the first decent weather they've had in many weeks to clean out their quarters and wash their clothes. Imagine the smell of tattered, damp clothing that had lain wadded up wet for week after week in the dark corners of the forecastle.

was as white as chalk, and everything neat and in order. The bedding from the berths was then spread on deck, and dried, and aired; the deck-tub filled with water; and a grand washing begun of all the clothes which were brought up. Shirts, frocks, drawers, trowsers, jackets, stockings, of every shape and color, wet and dirty–many of them mouldy from having been lying a long time wet in a foul corner–these were all washed and scrubbed out, and finally towed overboard for half an hour; and then made fast in the rigging to dry. Wet boots and shoes were spread out to dry in sunny places on deck; and the whole ship looked like a back yard on a washing day. After we had done with our clothes, we began upon our own persons. A little fresh water, which we had saved from our allowance, was put in buckets, and with soap and towels, we had what sailors call a fresh-water wash. The same bucket, to be sure, had to go through several hands, and was spoken for by one after another, but as we rinsed off in salt water, pure from the ocean, and the fresh was used only to start the accumulated grime and blackness of five weeks, it was held of little consequence.

In the news

**July, 1836**

Although the so-called Toledo War (a tempestuous boundary dispute involving the territories of Michigan and Ohio; see earlier sidebar) will delay the entry of the state of Michigan into the union until 1837, the United States District Court for the District of Michigan is established on July 1 of this year. It includes a single judgeship.

**...we had what sailors call a fresh-water wash.** Although this is accounted as quite a big deal by the men, note that it's not as if they're taking real showers or baths. They've got a little fresh water (quickly dirtied, since it's shared by the men), some soap, and some buckets of seawater. Nonetheless, it must be quite an improvement, and the men would have enjoyed it greatly.

We soaped down and scrubbed one another with towels and pieces of canvas, stripping to it; and then, getting into the head, threw buckets of water upon each other. After this, came shaving, and combing, and brushing; and when, having spent the first part of the day in this way, we sat down on the forecastle, in the afternoon, with clean duck trowsers, and shirts on, washed, shaved, and combed, and looking a dozen shades lighter for it, reading, sewing, and talking at our ease, with a clear sky and warm sun over our heads, a steady breeze over the larboard quarter, studding-sails out alow and aloft, and all the flying kites aboard;–we felt that we had got back into the pleasantest part of a sailor's life. At sundown the clothes were all taken down from the rigging–clean and dry–and stowed neatly away in our chests; and our southwesters, thick boots, guernsey frocks, and other accompaniments of bad weather, put out of the way, we hoped, for the rest of the voyage, as we expected to come upon the coast early in the autumn.

**... and all the flying kites aboard...** Not what we think of when we see the word "kite." A kite is a sail added above the vessel's main square sails. One is said to be "flying kites" when one sets such sails to help catch a light breeze.

**...a ship never has all her sail upon her, except when she has a light, steady breeze...** It is certainly true that a ship leaving or coming into port flying a profusion of white, billowing sails is a beautiful sight and often said to be "under full sail." But, as Dana points out, that's almost never true. A ship would only be under full sail under the conditions he notes. (The "regularity" of the wind is worth noting: It doesn't pay to set all of those dozens of sails, only to have the winds die or shift such that the crew has to go through the effort of dousing, reefing, furling, or otherwise dealing with the sails every time the wind changes.)

**Such a sight, very few, even some who have been at sea a great deal, have ever beheld...** Ironic, but true. From the deck of a ship, you don't see the majestic spread of the sails or the towering masts looming above a seemingly small hull. From the sailor's point of view, a sailing ship is a confusing welter of ropes and lines, with masts and spars sticking out every which way. From that perspective, it's difficult to appreciate the beauty of the vessel, although Dana manages to come close, having climbed up and lain out upon a boom suspended high above the deck.

**So quiet, too, was the sea, and so steady the breeze, that if these sails had been sculptured marble, they could not have been more motionless.** Another piece of poetic writing from Dana. This book was a huge success in its day, and the quality of Dana's writing—whether describing the life of a simple sailor in straightforward, blunt language, or waxing poetic, as he does here—is why. This was not only an important book, it was a masterpiece of honest, informative expository writing.

Notwithstanding all that has been said about the beauty of a ship under full sail, there are very few who have ever seen a ship, literally, under all her sail. A ship coming in or going out of port, with her ordinary sails, and perhaps two of three studding-sails, is commonly said to be under full sail; but a ship never has all her sail upon her, except when she has a light, steady breeze, very nearly, but not quite, dead aft, and so regular that it can be trusted, and is likely to last for some time. Then, with all her sails, light and heavy, and studding-sails, on each side, alow and aloft, she is the most glorious moving object in the world. Such a sight, very few, even some who have been at sea a great deal, have ever beheld; for from the deck of your own vessel you cannot see her, as you would a separate object.

One night, while we were in these tropics, I went out to the end of the flying-jib-boom, upon some duty, and, having finished it, turned round, and lay over the boom for a long time, admiring the beauty of the sight before me. Being so far out from the deck, I could look at the ship, as at a separate vessel;–and there rose up from the water, supported only by the small black hull, a pyramid of canvas, spreading out far beyond the hull, and towering up almost, as it seemed in the indistinct night air, to the clouds. The sea was as still as an inland lake; the light trade-wind was gently and steadily breathing from astern; the dark blue sky was studded with the tropical stars; there was no sound but the rippling of the water under the stem; and the sails were spread out, wide and high;–the two lower studding-sails stretching, on each side, far beyond the deck; the topmast studding-sails, like wings to the topsails; the top-gallant studding-sails spreading fearlessly out above them; still higher, the two royal studding-sails, looking like two kites flying from the same string; and, highest of all, the little skysail, the apex of the pyramid, seeming actually to touch the stars, and to be out of reach of human hand. So quiet, too, was the sea, and so steady the breeze, that if these sails had been sculptured marble, they could not have been more motionless. Not a ripple upon the surface of the canvas; not even a quivering of the extreme edges of the sail–so perfectly were they distended by the breeze. I was so lost in the sight, that I forgot the presence of the man who came out with me, until he said, (for he, too, rough old man-of-war's-man as he was, had been gazing at the show,) half to himself, still looking at the marble sails–"How quietly they do their work!"

The fine weather brought work with it; as the ship was to be put in order for coming into port. This may give a landsman some notion of what is done on board ship.–All the first part of a passage is spent in getting a ship ready for sea, and the last part in getting her ready for port. She is, as sailors say, like a lady's watch, always out of repair. The new, strong sails, which we had up off Cape Horn, were to be sent down, and the old set, which were still serviceable in fine weather, to be bent in their place; all the rigging to be set up, fore and aft; the masts stayed; the standing rigging to be tarred down; lower and topmast rigging rattled down, fore and aft; the ship scraped, inside and out, and painted; decks varnished; new and neat knots, seizings and coverings to be fitted; and every part put in order, to look well to the owner's eye, on coming into Boston. This, of course, was a long matter; and all hands were kept on deck at work for the whole of each day, during the rest of the voyage. Sailors call this hard usage; but the ship must be in crack order, and "we're homeward bound" was the answer to everything.

We went on for several days, employed in this way, nothing remarkable occurring; and, at the latter part of the week, fell in with the south-east trades, blowing about east-south-east, which brought them nearly two points abaft our beam. These blew strong and steady, so that we hardly started a rope, until we were beyond their latitude. The first day of "all hands," one of those little incidents occurred, which are nothing in themselves, but are great matters in the eyes of a ship's company, as they serve to break the monotony of a voyage, and afford conversation to the crew for days afterwards. These small matters, too, are often interesting, as they show the customs and state of feeling on shipboard.

**...like a lady's watch, always out of repair.** Or, as rendered in Nathaniel Ames' *A Mariner's Sketches*, "A ship is like a lady's watch, always out of repair." The saying was widespread enough that it showed up in a British Parliamentary budget debate about fortifications and breakwaters, with a member noting that "They were, indeed, like a lady's watch, always out of repair and always requiring expenditure." All of which is (or was) true, of course. Ladies' watches of the time, being small and delicate (as ladies themselves were presumed at the time to be), were in constant need of adjustment. The larger men's pocket-watches were (as indeed the men themselves were presumed at the time to be) stronger, more robust, and more substantial.

**In the news**
**July, 1836**

The Barnstable, MA newspaper advertises that the effects of "the late widow Bradford" will be sold at auction, including "one or two COWS [perhaps one of the cows was ill and might not survive 'til the auction?], a variety of household furniture, such as Chairs, Tables. Beds, and Bedding." Also to be sold were "one good Crock, Iron Ware, Glass, &c. &c." Barnstable is less than 100 miles from Dana's residence in Boston, although the cross-country journey could take days at that time.

**...we hardly started a rope...** That is, the men had very little to do, because the winds were so steady.

**...is never infringed upon by a wise master...** This has parallels in the armed services and even in the world of work. A smart newly commissioned Army officer (known somewhat contemptuously as a "shavetail"), for example, trusts his experienced noncommissioned officers (NCOs) to run things until the newly minted lieutenant has learned the ropes and proved his mettle. At work, a wise manager sets policy but avoids "micromanaging"; instead, he or she lets subordinates figure out how to implement the strategies and tactics the manager wishes to see in place.

**...when the captain came forward, and also began to give orders.** The captain should know better than this. Having two bosses is having one too many, and their orders are sure to be seen as confusing and contradictory.

In the news

**July, 1836**

In a speech in Boston, David Henshaw (eventually U.S. Secretary of the Navy, but at the time an official of the Port of Boston), rails against the then-current system of appointing state judges for life, pointing out that "adjoining States of Rhode Island and Vermont, and in some other States, Judges hold their office for limited terms, and are elected to their places by the representatives of the people." Henshaw partly gets his wish: Massachusetts state judges are now nominated by the governor and voted on by the state legislature. However, they are still appointed for life—or at least until the mandatory retirement age of 70.

**I didn't come through the cabin windows!** That is, he (Mr. Brown, the mate) had worked his way up through the ranks and had proved himself as a seaman. Passengers are said to have "come through the cabin windows."

In merchant vessels, the captain gives his orders as to the ship's work, to the mate, in a general way, and leaves the execution of them, with the particular ordering, to him. This has become so fixed a custom, that it is like a law, and is never infringed upon by a wise master, unless his mate is no seaman; in which case, the captain must often oversee things for himself. This, however, could not be said of our chief mate; and he was very jealous of any encroachment upon the borders of his authority.

On Monday morning, the captain told him to stay the fore-topmast plumb. He accordingly came forward, turned all hands to, with tackles on the stays and backstays, coming up with the seizings, hauling here, belaying there, and full of business, standing between the knightheads to sight the mast,–when the captain came forward, and also began to give orders. This made confusion, and the mate, finding that he was all aback, left his place and went aft, saying to the captain–

"If you come forward, sir, I'll go aft. One is enough on the forecastle."

This produced a reply, and another fierce answer; and the words flew, fists were doubled up, and things looked threateningly.

"I'm master of this ship."

"Yes, sir, and I'm mate of her, and know my place! My place is forward, and yours is aft!"

"My place is where I choose! I command the whole ship; and you are mate only so long as I choose!"

"Say the word, Capt. T., and I'm done! I can do a man's work aboard! I didn't come through the cabin windows! If I'm not mate, I can be man," etc., etc.

This was all fun for us, who stood by, winking at each other, and enjoying the contest between the higher powers. The captain took the mate aft; and they had a long talk, which ended in the mate's returning to his duty.

The captain had broken through a custom, which is a part of the common-law of a ship, and without reason; for he knew that his mate was a sailor, and needed no help from him; and the mate was excusable for being angry. Yet he was wrong, and the captain right. Whatever the captain does is right, ipso facto, and any opposition to it is wrong, on board ship; and every officer and man knows this when he signs the ship's articles.

It is a part of the contract. Yet there has grown up in merchant vessels a series of customs, which have become a well understood system, and have almost the force of prescriptive law. To be sure, all power is in the captain, and the officers hold their authority only during his will; and the men are liable to be called upon for any service; yet, by breaking in upon these usages, many difficulties have occurred on board ship, and even come into courts of justice, which are perfectly unintelligible to any one not acquainted with the universal nature and force of these customs. Many a provocation has been offered, and a system of petty oppression pursued towards men, the force and meaning of which would appear as nothing to strangers, and doubtless do appear so to many "'long-shore" juries and judges.

The next little diversion, was a battle on the forecastle one afternoon, between the mate and the steward. They had been on bad terms the whole voyage; and had threatened a rupture several times. This afternoon, the mate asked him for a tumbler of water, and he refused to get it for him, saying that he waited upon nobody but the captain: and here he had the custom on his side. But in answering, he left off "the handle to the mate's name." This enraged the mate, who called him a "black soger;" and at it they went, clenching, striking, and rolling over and over; while we stood by, looking on, and enjoying the fun. The darky tried to butt him, but the mate got him down, and held him, the steward singing out, "Let me go, Mr. Brown, or there'll be blood spilt!" In the midst of this, the captain came on deck, separated them, took the steward aft, and gave him half a dozen with a rope's end.

**Yet he was wrong, and the captain right. Whatever the captain does is right, ipso facto...** One of Dana's reasons for writing this book: On board a vessel, the captain is king. He literally cannot be wrong—even when he's wrong. Like the Pope, he is held to be infallible. On a ship, the captain's word is quite literally law. Obviously, this can lead to abuses of power. One of the things that Dana wished to achieve by writing *Two Years Before the Mast* was to curb captains' power, or at least to ensure that it was less likely to be abused. (*Ipso facto* is Latin for *by the fact itself.*)

**...to many "'long-shore" juries and judges.** Note the apostrophe used to indicate a shortened word. An "along-shore" judge or jury would be one on the shore and thus far from the sea and unfamiliar with its customs. (What we call "longshoremen" these days, men who load and unload cargo along the shore or at a wharf, were originally called "'longshoremen," with the apostrophe used at the time to indicate the shortened word.)

**...a battle on the forecastle one afternoon, between the mate and the steward.** The steward is James Luyck, a 27-year-old black man from Boston. The steward is not normally the cook, but he is in overall charge of provisions and dining arrangements.

**...he left off "the handle to the mate's name."** That is, he failed to call Mr. Brown "mister."

**...that was enough to earn him his flogging...** This is a good example of the captain's absolute power. A fistfight or shoving match is one thing, but when the steward threatens to spill blood, he is saying in essence that he intends to kill the mate. Threatening murder (at least that's the way the captain interprets it) earns him a flogging, and the captain, by law and by custom, is perfectly within his rights to flog a sailor. This is exactly the sort of thing that Dana wishes to publicize. (Note, though, that he does not argue *against* a captain's right to flog his men; Dana feels that captains need absolute power in order to keep things running smoothly onboard ship, but he hopes to put in place mechanisms designed to minimize the likelihood that a captain will abuse that power.)

The steward tried to justify himself; but he had been heard to talk of spilling blood, and that was enough to earn him his flogging; and the captain did not choose to inquire any further.

## Chapter XXXIV

### Narrow Escapes–The Equator–Tropical Squalls–A Thunder Storm

The same day, I met with one of those narrow escapes, which are so often happening in a sailor's life. I had been aloft nearly all the afternoon, at work, standing for as much as an hour on the fore top-gallant yard, which was hoisted up, and hung only by the tie; when, having got through my work, I balled up my yarns, took my serving-board in my hand, laid hold deliberately of the top-gallant rigging, took one foot from the yard, and was just lifting the other, when the tie parted, and down the yard fell. I was safe, by my hold upon the rigging, but it made my heart beat quick. Had the tie parted one instant sooner, or had I stood an instant longer on the yard, I should inevitably have been thrown violently from the height of ninety or a hundred feet, overboard; or, what is worse, upon the deck. However, "a miss is as good as a mile;" a saying which sailors very often have occasion to use. An escape is always a joke on board ship. A man would be ridiculed who should make a serious matter of it. A sailor knows too well that his life hangs upon a thread, to wish to be always reminded of it; so, if a man has an escape, he keeps it to himself, or makes a joke of it. I have often known a man's life to be saved by an instant of time, or by the merest chance,–the swinging of a rope,–and no notice taken of it. One of our boys, when off Cape Horn, reefing top-sails of a dark night, and when there were no boats to be lowered away, and where, if a man fell overboard he must be left behind,–lost his hold of the reef-point, slipped from the foot-rope, and would have been in the water in a moment, when the man who was next to him on the yard caught him by the collar of his jacket, and hauled him up upon the yard, with–"Hold on, another time, you young monkey, and be d—d to you!"–and that was all that was heard about it.

Sunday, August 7th. Lat. 25° 59' S., long. 27° 0' W. Spoke the English bark Mary-Catherine, from Bahia, bound to Calcutta. This was the first sail we had fallen

**...took my serving-board in my hand...** A tool used, along with (or instead of) a serving mallet, to wind a "serving" around a rope. (A serving is a length of twine or thread used to finish off the ends of a rope to keep it from unravelling.)

**...or, what is worse, upon the deck.** We don't know if Dana could swim; typically, sailors of that era did *not* know how to swim, but Dana may have learned (at Harvard or elsewhere) before shipping out. Even if he couldn't swim, in decent weather there's a chance that someone could have pulled him from the water if he could at least have managed to surface and float for a few moments. Still, it would have been a tremendous risk. Falling from that height and hitting the deck, though, is another story: He would surely have died. (Which certainly would have been ironic, given that the day on which this incident occurs happens to be Dana's birthday.)

**...a miss is as good as a mile...** In other words, to fail at something is to fail at it, regardless of how close one might have come to succeeding. (Of course, in this case, "failure" is a good thing, since Dana refers to his "failure" to fall.) There are many variants of this (including "an inch in a miss is as good as an ell," an English ell being a measure of length roughly equal to 45 inches), going back to at least the mid-16th century. (As Sir Walter Scott said of one hapless writer, "He was very near being a poet—but a miss is as good as a mile, and he always fell short of the mark.")

**A man would be ridiculed who should make a serious matter of it.** There's a macho thing going on here that one still encounters aboard ship, in the trenches, or wherever men and women work in peril. Frightening though the incident may be, real "troupers" are expected to make light of it. At most, a wry joke may be made about one's close encounter, but few would admit to actually being frightened.

**...studding-sails out alow and aloft...** The vessel was rigged to take advantage of the breeze as best she could, but was not performing well. This may be the same bark that went aground in New Zealand in 1847, but with no loss of life reported.

**...going six on an easy bowline.** Sailing "on a bowline" means sailing close-hauled, i.e., close to the wind. *Alert*, sailing more or less into the wind, is sailing faster than the *Mary-Catherine*, even though the latter has studding sails set, implying that she'd been sailing with the wind directly behind her. (See previous note.)

**...a large corvette-built ship...** At the time, a corvette was a fast, maneuverable, three-masted, flush-deck warship. (From which vessel the Chevrolet sports car gets its name.)

**...banner of St. George...** One of several flags of England—and also of several other states, countries, and muncipalities. (See previous note.) St. George is the patron saint of England.

In the news
**August, 1836**

General Sam Houston is nominated for the presidency of the Republic of Texas. Given his victory at the Battle of San Jacinto, Houston's popularity is immense, and his election is almost a foregone conclusion. Houston had already served as Governor of Tennessee and as a general of the Texas Army. When Texas becomes part of the Union, Houston becomes governor of the state, but he resigns the governorship when the Civil War begins, due to his opposition to Texas joining the confederacy.

**Friday, August 12th.** This coming Sunday will mark the point at which Dana will have been gone two years from Boston.

in with, and the first time we had seen a human form or heard the human voice, except of our own number, for nearly a hundred days. The very yo-ho-ing of the sailors at the ropes sounded sociably upon the ear. She was an old, damaged-looking craft, with a high poop and top-gallant forecastle, and sawed off square, stem and stern, like a true English "tea-wagon," and with a run like a sugar-box. She had studding-sails out alow and aloft, with a light but steady breeze, and her captain said he could not get more than four knots out of her and thought he should have a long passage. We were going six on an easy bowline.

The next day, about three P. M., passed a large corvette-built ship, close upon the wind, with royals and skysails set fore and aft, under English colors. She was standing south-by-east, probably bound round Cape Horn. She had men in her tops, and black mast-heads; heavily sparred, with sails cut to a t, and other marks of a man-of-war. She sailed well, and presented a fine appearance; the proud, aristocratic-looking banner of St. George, the cross in a blood-red field, waving from the mizen. We probably were as fine a sight, with our studding-sails spread far out beyond the ship on either side, and rising in a pyramid to royal studding-sails and skysails, burying the hull in canvas, and looking like what the whale-men on the Banks, under their stump top-gallant masts, call "a Cape Horn-er under a cloud of sail."

Friday, August 12th. At daylight made the island of Trinidad, situated in lat. 20° 28' S., long. 29° 08' W. At twelve M., it bore N. W. 1/2 N., distant twenty-seven miles. It was a beautiful day, the sea hardly ruffled by the light trades, and the island looking like a small blue mound rising from a field of glass.

Such a fair and peaceful-looking spot is said to have been, for a long time, the resort of a band of pirates, who ravaged the tropical seas.

Thursday, August 18th. At three P. M., made the island of Fernando Naronha, lying in lat. 3° 55' S., long. 32° 35' W.; and between twelve o'clock Friday night and one o'clock Saturday morning, crossed the equator, for the fourth time since leaving Boston, in long. 35° W.; having been twenty-seven days from Staten Land–a distance, by the courses we had made, of more than four thousand miles.

We were now to the northward of the line, and every day added to our latitude. The Magellan Clouds, the last sign of South latitude, were sunk in the horizon, and the north star, the Great Bear, and the familiar signs of northern latitudes, were rising in the heavens.

**...the familiar signs of northern latitudes...** Perhaps more familiar to most 19th century citizens than to many of us today. These days, the constellations are usually a matter of curiosity and, perhaps, scientific interest. Back then, the constellations were used to help navigate during long trips on both land and sea. In any case, "light pollution" has made the identification of constellations much more difficult now, unless they're being viewed from a vantage point far from a city.

Next to seeing land, there is no sight which makes one realize more that he is drawing near home, than to see the same heavens, under which he was born, shining at night over his head. The weather was extremely hot, with the usual tropical alternations of a scorching sun and squalls of rain; yet not a word was said in complaint of the heat, for we all remembered that only three or four weeks before we would have given nearly our all to have been where we now were. We had plenty of water, too, which we caught by spreading an awning, with shot thrown in to make hollows. These rain squalls came up in the manner usual between the tropics.–A clear sky; burning, vertical sun; work going lazily on, and men about decks with nothing but duck trowsers, checked shirts, and straw hats; the ship moving as lazily through the water; the man at the helm resting against the wheel, with his hat drawn over his eyes; the captain below, taking an afternoon nap; the passenger leaning over the taffrail, watching a dolphin following slowly in our wake; the sailmaker mending an old topsail on the lee side of the quarter-deck; the carpenter working at his bench, in the waist; the boys making sinnet; the spun-yarn winch whizzing round and round, and the men walking slowly fore and aft with their yarns.–A cloud rises to windward, looking a little black; the sky-sails are brailed down; the captain puts his head out of the companion-way, looks at the cloud, comes up, and begins to walk the deck.–The cloud spreads and comes on;–the tub of yarns, the sail, and other matters, are thrown below, and the sky-light and booby-hatch put on, and the slide drawn over the forecastle.–"Stand by

<u>In the news</u>

**August, 1836**

Alabama judge Eli S. Shorter publishes in a Georgia newspaper a spirited defense of himself and a passionate denouncement of a previous article by Col. John B. Hogan, who was at the time Superintendent of [Indian] Removals. Hogan, charged with ensuring the tribes' (preferably peaceful) emigration to the newly created Indian Territories, had the temerity to suggest that the current war (i.e., the Seminole War) was caused, at least in part, by wrongs committed by the U.S. government (and its citizens) upon the Indians, who acted in large part merely to secure their rights and recover their lands.

**...the sailmaker mending an old topsail...** This is quite a peaceful, idyllic description of life on board *Alert*, especially compared to some weeks ago, when the men were fighting sleet, snow, ice, and howling winds.

**...the sky-light and booby-hatch put on...** A booby hatch is a one-piece raised hatch covering placed over an existing opening (companionway).

the royal halyards;"–the man at the wheel keeps a good weather helm, so as not to be taken aback. The squall strikes her. If it is light, the royal yards are clewed down, and the ship keeps on her way; but if the squall takes strong hold, the royals are clewed up, fore and aft; light hands lay aloft and furl them; top-gallant yards clewed down, flying-jib hauled down, and the ship kept off before it,–the man at the helm laying out his strength to heave the wheel up to windward. At the same time a drenching rain, which soaks one through in an instant. Yet no one puts on a jacket or cap; for if it is only warm, a sailor does not mind a ducking; and the sun will soon be out again. As soon as the force of the squall has passed, though to a common eye the ship would seem to be in the midst of it,–"Keep her up to her course, again!"–"Keep her up, sir," (answer);–"Hoist away the top-gallant yards!"–"Run up the flying jib!"–"Lay aloft, you boys, and loose the royals!"–and all sail is on her again before she is fairly out of the squall; and she is going on in her course. The sun comes out once more, hotter than ever, dries up the decks and the sailors' clothes; the hatches are taken off; the sail got up and spread on the quarter-deck; spun-yarn winch set a whirling again; rigging coiled up; captain goes below; and every sign of an interruption is removed.

**...the man at the wheel keeps a good weather helm...** That is, holds the wheel to leeward (the side opposite the wind) in order to stay on a steady course.

**"Keep her up to her course, again!"–"Keep her up, sir..."** As Dana points out in a later edition, it is customary on large vessels for a sailor to repeat an order that has been given to him in order to assure the officer that the order has been understood. A ship can be a noisy, confusing place, and this rule helps minimize mistakes caused by miscommunications.

These scenes, with occasional dead calms, lasting for hours, and sometimes for days, are fair specimens of the Atlantic tropics. The nights were fine; and as we had all hands all day, the watch were allowed to sleep on deck at night, except the man at the wheel, and one look-out on the forecastle. This was not so much expressly allowed, as winked at. We could do it if we did not ask leave. If the look-out was caught napping, the whole watch was kept awake.

**...not so much expressly allowed, as winked at.** Winked at in the merchant marine, perhaps, but not in the navies of either Britain or the United States. In 2007, a Royal Navy officer received a court martial and a reprimand for falling asleep on watch. (Punishment can be severe for sleeping on watch during time of war. According to the Uniform Code of Military Justice, "Any sentinel or look-out who is found drunk or sleeping upon his post, or leaves it before he is regularly relieved, shall be punished, if the offense is committed in time of war, by death or such other punishment as a court-martial may direct, but if the offense is committed at any other time, by such punishment other than death as a court-martial may direct.") In fact, a recent study noted that 73% of merchant mariners admitted to falling asleep on watch.

We made the most of this permission, and stowed ourselves away upon the rigging, under the weather rail, on the spars, under the windlass, and in all the snug corners; and frequently slept out the watch, unless we had a wheel or a look-out. And we were glad enough to get this rest; for under the "all hands" system, out of every other thirty-six hours, we had only four below; and even an hour's sleep was a gain not to be neglected. One would have thought so, to have seen our watch, some nights, sleeping through a heavy rain. And often have we come on deck, and finding a dead calm and a light, steady rain, and determined not to lose our sleep, have laid a coil of rigging down so as to keep us out of the water which was washing about decks, and stowed ourselves away upon it, covering a jacket over us, and slept as soundly as a Dutchman between two feather beds.

**...a Dutchman between two feather beds.** A common saying of the time, and especially popular amongst sailors. A number of "Dutchman" sayings were prevalent at the time, most of them based on the perception of the Dutch people as bad-tempered and miserly. (Keep in mind that the Dutch—long a world power—fought multiple wars with the British during the 17th century; no doubt some of the rancor generated by those conflicts still lingered.) From that, we get such phrases as "a Dutch auction," "Dutch reckoning," "Dutch courage," etc.

For a week or ten days after crossing the line, we had the usual variety of calms, squalls, head winds, and fair winds;–at one time braced sharp upon the wind, with a taught bowline, and in an hour after, slipping quietly along, with a light breeze over the taffrail, and studding-sails out on both sides;–until we fell in with the north-east trade-winds; which we did on the afternoon of

Sunday, August 28th, in lat. 12° N. The trade-wind clouds had been in sight for a day or two previously, and we expected to take them every hour. The light southerly breeze, which had been blowing languidly during the first part of the day, died away toward noon, and in its place came puffs from the north-east, which caused us to take our studding-sails in and brace up; and in a couple of hours more, we were bowling gloriously along, dashing the spray far ahead and to leeward, with the cool, steady north-east trades, freshening up the sea, and giving us as much as we could carry our royals to. These winds blew strong and steady, keeping us generally upon a bowline, as our course was about north-north-west; and sometimes, as they veered a little to the eastward, giving us a chance at a main top-gallant studding-sail; and sending us well to the northward, until–

### In the news
### August, 1836

A Vermont newspaper prints a perfectly straight-faced news item reporting that a Massachusetts man has discovered the secret of "perpetual motion," and has built a machine demonstrating the principle. The newspaper notes that "in our candid opinion, the power of one man...would be sufficient to propel the largest ship across the Atlantic...." The inventor is reported to be "on his way to Washington to secure his patent." The patent does not show up in a search of patents of that era, but it was (and is) perfectly possible to apply for a patent for a perpetual motion machine. Of course, whether the patent will ever be granted is another issue.

Sunday, Sept. 4th, when they left us, in lat. 22° N., long. 51° W., directly under the tropic of Cancer.

For several days we lay "humbugging about" in the Horse latitudes, with all sorts of winds and weather, and occasionally, as we were in the latitude of the West Indies–a thunder storm. It was hurricane month, too,

**...we lay "humbugging about" in the Horse latitudes...** The horse latitudes are (two) high-pressure regions characterized by very light winds; ships were often becalmed there for days on end. The origin of the term "horse latitudes" is disputed. Some have conjectured that they were so-called because desperate sailors would throw horses and other livestock overboard in order to lighten the load. This is unlikely, since one would have to be carrying a great many animals for their absence to make any difference in how (or whether) the ship sails.

**...it was as black as Erebus...** Depending on how you interpret Greek mythology, Erebus was either Hades (i.e., Hell), a passage to Hades, or the god of darkness himself.

In the news

**September, 1836**

Poet/journalist Walt Whitman has been working as a printer in New York, but the great downtown fire (see earlier sidebars) leaves him unemployed. He quickly secures a position as a schoolteacher on Long Island. (Whitman becomes a vocal abolitionist, eventually editing and publishing a "free-soil" newspaper in Brooklyn. Publication of the first issue results in the paper's office being burned to the ground.) In addition to *Leaves of Grass*—the work for which he is perhaps best remembered—Whitman will also write "When Lilacs Last in the Dooryard Bloom'd" and "O Captain! My Captain!" both of which deal with the assassination of Abraham Lincoln.

**...there, directly over where we had been standing, upon the main top-gallant-mast-head, was a ball of light...** Sailors are a suspicious lot, and many believed in portents of both good and evil. The *corpus sancti* (holy body) is also called St. Elmo's Fire. It generally appears during or just after a thunderstorm, and presents as glowing balls or streams of blue light that seem to "dance" about a ship's masts and spars. (A few years before this, Charles Darwin, anchored on the Rio Plata River aboard the *Beagle*, describes a similar experience: "At this present minute we are at anchor in the mouth of the river: & such a strange scene as it is.— Every thing is in flames,—the sky with lightning,—the water with luminous particles, & even the very masts are pointed with a blue flame.")

and we were just in the track of the tremendous hurricane of 1830, which swept the North Atlantic, destroying almost everything before it. The first night after the tradewinds left us, while we were in the latitude of the island of Cuba, we had a specimen of a true tropical thunder storm. A light breeze had been blowing directly from aft during the first part of the night which gradually died away, and before midnight it was dead calm, and a heavy black cloud had shrouded the whole sky. When our watch came on deck at twelve o'clock, it was as black as Erebus; the studding-sails were all taken in, and the royals furled; not a breath was stirring; the sails hung heavy and motionless from the yards; and the perfect stillness, and the darkness, which was almost palpable, were truly appalling. Not a word was spoken, but every one stood as though waiting for something to happen. In a few minutes the mate came forward; and in a low tone, which was almost a whisper, told us to haul down the jib. The fore and mizen top-gallant sails were taken in, in the same silent manner; and we lay motionless upon the water, with an uneasy expectation, which, from the long suspense, became actually painful. We could hear the captain walking the deck, but it was too dark to see anything more than one's hand before the face. Soon the mate came forward again, and gave an order, in a low tone, to clew up the main top-gallant sail; and so infectious was the awe and silence, that the clewlines and buntlines were hauled up without any of the customary singing out at the ropes. An English lad and myself went up to furl it; and we had just got the bunt up, when the mate called out to us, something, we did not hear what,–but supposing it to be an order to bear-a-hand, we hurried, and made all fast, and came down, feeling our way among the rigging. When we got down we found all hands looking aloft, and there, directly over where we had been standing, upon the main top-gallant-mast-head, was a ball of light, which the sailors name a corposant (corpus sancti), and which the mate had called out to us to look at. They were all watching it carefully, for sailors have a notion that if the corposant rises in the rigging, it is a sign of fair weather, but if it comes lower down, there will be a storm. Unfortunately, as an omen, it came down, and showed itself on the top-gallant yard-arm. We were off the yard in good season, for it is held a fatal sign to have the pale light of the corposant thrown upon one's face. As it was, the English lad did not feel comfortably at having had it so near him, and directly over his head. In a few minutes it disappeared, and showed itself again on the fore top-gallant yard; and after playing about for some time, disappeared again; when the man on the forecastle pointed to it upon the flying-jib-boom-end. But our attention was drawn from watching this, by the falling of some drops of rain and by a perceptible increase of the darkness, which seemed suddenly to add a new shade of blackness to the night. In a few minutes, low, grumbling thunder was heard, and some random flashes of lightning came from the south-west. Every sail was taken in but the topsails, still, no squall appeared to be coming. A few puffs lifted the topsails, but they fell again to the mast, and all was as still as ever. A moment more, and a terrific flash and peal broke simultaneously upon us, and a cloud appeared to open directly over our heads and let down the water in one body, like a falling ocean. We stood motionless, and almost stupefied; yet nothing had been struck. Peal after peal rattled over our heads, with a sound which seemed actually to stop the breath in the body, and the "speedy gleams" kept the whole ocean in a glare of light. The violent fall of rain lasted but a few minutes, and was succeeded by occasional drops and showers; but the lightning continued incessant for several hours, breaking the midnight darkness with irregular and blinding flashes. During all which time there was not a breath stirring, and we lay motionless, like a mark to be shot at, probably the only object on the surface of the ocean for miles and miles. We stood hour after hour, until our watch was out, and we were relieved, at four o'clock. During all this time, hardly a word was spoken; no bells were struck, and the wheel was silently relieved. The rain fell at intervals in heavy showers, and we stood drenched through and blinded by the flashes, which broke the Egyptian darkness with a brightness which seemed almost malignant; while the thunder rolled in peals, the concussion of which appeared to shake the very ocean.

In the news
**September, 1836**

The USS *Porpoise*, a 224-ton hermaphrodite brig (see previous notes) is on her maiden voyage, with orders to conduct surveys along the southern coast. *Porpoise* will spend much of her career doing exploratory surveys and seeking illegal slavers. (Slavery was still legal in the U.S., but beginning with the passage of the 1817 "Act Prohibiting Importation of Slaves," *importing* slaves was not.) After participating in the Mexican-American War, she is assigned to explore and chart Pacific islands. Departing China in September of 1854, *Porpoise* leaves the other vessels in the flotilla, and is never seen again.

**...flashes, which broke the Egyptian darkness...** Possibly a reference to a color of ceramics known as "Egyptian black," after a style and color of pottery said to have originated in Egypt, but made popular by English potters in the early 18th century, or to the fact that Egypt itself is located in what was then often called "darkest Africa."

**...A ship is not often injured by lightning...** It is true that a mast towering above a ship provides a partial "cone of protection," but Dana is deluding himself here—as he admits in the very next sentence, when he comments on the men's (understandable) fear that the "very next flash may tear the ship in two, or set her on fire." There have been many reports of ships burned to the waterline by fires that were started by a lightning strike.

**...a man is no sailor if he cannot sleep when he turns-in...** Perhaps a bit more macho posturing: A "real man" doesn't fear these things, and can unconcernedly roll over and go to sleep as if he were safe at home on a feather bed. Then again, sailors (and soldiers, and firefighters, etc.) really do learn to fall asleep almost anywhere and at any opportunity; after all, they never know when they'll next get the chance.

A ship is not often injured by lightning, for the electricity is separated by the great number of points she presents, and the quantity of iron which she has scattered in various parts. The electric fluid ran over our anchors, top-sail sheets and ties; yet no harm was done to us. We went below at four o'clock, leaving things in the same state. It is not easy to sleep, when the very next flash may tear the ship in two, or set her on fire; or where the deathlike calm may be broken by the blast of a hurricane, taking the masts out of the ship. But a man is no sailor if he cannot sleep when he turns-in, and turn out when he's called. And when, at seven bells, the customary "All the larboard watch, ahoy?" brought us on deck, it was a fine, clear, sunny morning, the ship going leisurely along, with a good breeze and all sail set.

## Chapter XXXV

### A Double-Reef-Top-Sail Breeze–Scurvy–A Friend in Need–Preparing For Port–The Gulf Stream

From the latitude of the West Indies, until we got inside the Bermudas, where we took the westerly and south-westerly winds, which blow steadily off the coast of the United States early in the autumn, we had every variety of weather, and two or three moderate gales, or, as sailors call them, double-reef-topsail breezes, which came on in the usual manner, and of which one is a specimen of all.–A fine afternoon; all hands at work, some in the rigging, and others on deck; a stiff breeze, and ship close upon the wind, and skysails brailed down.–Latter part of the afternoon, breeze increases, ship lies over to it, and clouds look windy. Spray begins to fly over the forecastle, and wets the yarns the boys are knotting;–ball them up and put them below.–Mate knocks off work and clears up decks earlier than usual, and orders a man who has been employed aloft to send the royal halyards over to windward, as he comes down. Breast backstays hauled taught, and tackle got upon the martingale back-rope.–One of the boys furls the mizen royal.–Cook thinks there is going to be "nasty work," and has supper ready early.–Mate gives orders to get supper by the watch, instead of all hands, as usual.–While eating supper, hear the watch on deck taking in the royals.–Coming on deck, find it is blowing harder, and an ugly head sea is running.–Instead of having all hands on the forecastle in the dog watch, smoking, singing, and telling yarns, one watch goes below and turns-in, saying that it's going to be an ugly night, and two hours' sleep is not to be lost.

Clouds look black and wild; wind rising, and ship working hard against a heavy sea, which breaks over the forecastle, and washes aft through the scuppers. Still, no more sail is taken in, for the captain is a driver, and, like all drivers, very partial to his top-gallant sails. A top-gallant sail, too, makes the difference between a breeze and a gale. When a top-gallant sail is on a ship,

**A fine afternoon; all hands at work, some in the rigging, and others on deck...** This is an interesting stylistic shift for Dana. Suddenly, 35 chapters into a 36-chapter book, he adopts a fast-paced, telegraphic style, almost as if he's hoping to hurry the reader along, here near the end of the journey, attempting to make the reader feel the crew's headlong rush to finally get home.

**Cook thinks there is going to be "nasty work," and has supper ready early.** Anticipating bad weather, the cook sensibly prepares supper early, both so that the men can have eaten before having to deal with the bad weather, and also because it's much easier (and safer) to cook when the seas are calm.

**... and two hours' sleep...** Another example of a point made earlier: Sailors learn to sleep when and where they can. The watch hopes to get in a couple hours' sleep before the weather turns ugly.

**...the captain is a driver, and, like all drivers, very partial to his top-gallant sails.** The captain is not at all afraid to push his ship, especially as he nears home. The topgallant is near the top of the mast; carrying canvas there adds much sail area, but can make for a rougher sail.

it is only a breeze, though I have seen ours set over a reefed topsail, when half the bowsprit was under water, and it was up to a man's knees in the scuppers. At eight bells, nothing is said about reefing the topsails, and the watch go below, with orders to "stand by for a call." We turn-in, growling at the "old man" for not reefing the topsails when the watch was changed, but putting it off so as to call all hands, and break up a whole watch below. Turn-in "all standing," and keep ourselves awake, saying there is no use in going asleep to be waked up again.–Wind whistles on deck, and ship works hard, groaning and creaking, and pitching into a heavy head sea, which strikes against the bows, with a noise like knocking upon a rock.–The dim lamp in the forecastle swings to and fro, and things "fetch away" and go over to leeward.–"Doesn't that booby of a second mate ever mean to take in his top-gallant sails?– He'll have the sticks out of her soon," says old Bill, who was always growling, and, like most old sailors, did not like to see a ship abused.–By-and-by an order is given–"Aye, aye, sir!" from the forecastle;–rigging is heaved down on deck;–the noise of a sail is heard fluttering aloft, and the short, quick cry which sailors make when hauling upon clewlines.–"Here comes his fore-top-gallant sail in!"–We are wide awake, and know all that's going on as well as if we were on deck.–A well-known voice is heard from the mast-head singing out the officer of the watch to haul taught the weather brace.–"Hallo! There's S—– aloft to furl the sail!"–Next thing, rigging is heaved down directly over our heads, and a long-drawn cry and a rattling of hanks announce that the flying-jib has come in.–The second mate holds on to the main top-gallant sail until a heavy sea is shipped, and washes over the forecastle as though the whole ocean had come aboard; when a noise further aft shows that that sail, too, is taking in. After this, the ship is more easy for a time; two bells are struck, and we try to get a little sleep. By-and-by, bang, bang, bang, on the scuttle–"All ha-a-ands, a ho-o-y!"–We spring out of our berths, clap on a monkey-jacket and southwester, and tumble up the ladder.–Mate up before us, and on the forecastle, singing out like a roaring bull; the captain singing out on the quarter-deck, and the second mate

**...growling at the "old man"...** The customary name for the captain of a ship, regardless of his actual age.

**...Wind whistles on deck, and ship works hard...** Dana slips back into the breathlessly present-tense, telegraphic style used earlier.

**He'll have the sticks out of her soon," says old Bill...** That is, if he doesn't take in the topgallant sails, the fierce wind may destroy the mast. (Keep in mind that at this point, "old Bill" is about 30 years of age.)

**There's S—– aloft to furl the sail!** Later editions have this as, "There's Ben aloft...."

**...a rattling of hanks...** A hank is a small ring or metal loop used to bend (tie) a sail to a stay (cable or line used to support a mast).

In the news

**September, 1836**

With the help of testimonials from local hoteliers and innkeepers, businessmen around the country are busily marketing a new "patent washing machine" that promises to wash clothes "cheaper, and with less wear, than when washed by hand, and in one quarter of the time." Wright's patent washing machine, exhibited at the American Institute the previous fall, is a hand-operated table with built-in wringers and high sides that form a tub-on-legs that holds several quarts of soapy water.

**The ship is lying over half upon her beam-ends; lee scuppers under water, and forecastle all in a smother of foam.** Another poetic description, this time of a frightening scene: *Alert* is keeled far over on her side, with the sea rushing over the deck.

yelling, like a hyena, in the waist. The ship is lying over half upon her beam-ends; lee scuppers under water, and forecastle all in a smother of foam.–Rigging all let go, and washing about decks; topsail yards down upon the caps, and sails flapping and beating against the masts; and starboard watch hauling out the reef-tackles of the main topsail. Our watch haul out the fore, and lay aloft and put two reefs into it, and reef the foresail, and race with the starboard watch, to see which will mast-head its topsail first. All hands tally-on to the main tack, and while some are furling the jib, and hoisting the staysail, we mizen-topmen double-reef the mizen topsail and hoist it up. All being made fast –"Go below, the watch!" and we turn-in to sleep out the rest of the time, which is perhaps an hour and a half. During all the middle, and for the first part of the morning watch, it blows as hard as ever, but toward daybreak it moderates considerably, and we shake a reef out of each topsail, and set the top-gallant sails over them and when the watch come up, at seven bells, for breakfast, shake the other reefs out, turn all hands to upon the halyards, get the watch-tackle upon the top-gallant sheets and halyards, set the flying-jib, and crack on to her again.

Our captain had been married only a few weeks before he left Boston; and, after an absence of over two years, it may be supposed he was not slow in carrying sail. The mate, too, was not to be beaten by anybody; and the second mate, though he was afraid to press sail, was afraid as death of the captain, and being between two fears, sometimes carried on longer than any of them. We snapped off three flying-jib booms in twenty-four hours, as fast as they could be fitted and rigged out; sprung the spritsail yard; and made nothing of studding-sail booms. Beside the natural desire to get home, we had another reason for urging the ship on. The scurvy had begun to show itself on board. One man had it so badly as to be disabled and off duty, and the English lad, Ben, was in a dreadful state, and was daily growing worse. His legs swelled and pained him so that he could not walk; his flesh lost its elasticity, so that if it was pressed in, it would not return to its shape; and his gums swelled until he could not open his mouth. His

In the news

**September, 1836**

Nathaniel Hawthorne, eventually to become the author of *The Scarlet Letter*, *The House of Seven Gables*, and other works, accepts a position at the Boston Custom House, having earlier resigned his position as editor of *The American Magazine of Useful and Entertaining Knowledge* in Salem, MA. An obscure clerk living in poverty, Hawthorne begins writing the short stories that will bring him fame and fortune, including "Young Goodman Brown" and others.

**We snapped off three flying-jib booms in twenty-four hours...** This is why ships of that time carried as part of their crew trained carpenters and sailmakers. In general, crews aboard blue-water (i.e., open ocean, long distance) sailing vessels had to be close to 100% self-sufficient.

**His legs swelled and pained him so that he could not walk.** Ben has scurvy, a potentially fatal disease caused by a vitamin C deficiency. Early symptoms include weakness and lethargy, but the disease quickly leads to swollen joints, loss of teeth, and hemorrhaging. Although the exact cause was unknown during Dana's time, scurvy had been known for centuries, and by Dana's time, most were aware that consumption of citrus fruits, berries, potatoes, and other fresh fruits and vegetables could quickly effect a cure.

breath, too, became very offensive; he lost all strength and spirit; could eat nothing; grew worse every day; and, in fact, unless something was done for him, would be a dead man in a week, at the rate at which he was sinking. The medicines were all, or nearly all, gone; and if we had had a chest-full, they would have been of no use; for nothing but fresh provisions and terra firma has any effect upon the scurvy. This disease is not so common now as formerly; and is attributed generally to salt provisions, want of cleanliness, the free use of grease and fat (which is the reason of its prevalence among whalemen,) and, last of all, to laziness. It never could have been from the latter cause on board our ship; nor from the second, for we were a very cleanly crew, kept our forecastle in neat order, and were more particular about washing and changing clothes than many better-dressed people on shore. It was probably from having none but salt provisions, and possibly from our having run very rapidly into hot weather, after having been so long in the extremest cold.

**...nothing but fresh provisions and terra firma has any effect upon the scurvy.** This was more or less true at the time. Even citrus juice became ineffective against scurvy after a period of months, losing its potency in storage. (As part of its battle against scurvy, the Royal Navy had been issuing rations of lime juice to sailors since the late 18th century, thus the nickname of "limey" for a British sailor. These days, of course, we're able to preserve fruits and vegetables for longer periods of time, and we've also managed to synthesize vitamin C itself. Few first-world doctors see even one case of scurvy during their careers, although it is not unknown in third-world countries.)

Depending upon the westerly winds, which prevail off the coast in the autumn, the captain stood well to the westward, to run inside of the Bermudas, and in the hope of falling in with some vessel bound to the West Indies or the Southern States. The scurvy had spread no farther among the crew, but there was danger that it might; and these cases were bad ones.

Sunday, Sept. 11th. Lat. 30° 04' N., long. 63° 23' W.; the Bermudas bearing north-north-west, distant one hundred and fifty miles. The next morning, about ten o'clock, "Sail ho!" was cried on deck; and all hands turned up to see the stranger. As she drew nearer, she proved to be an ordinary-looking hermaphrodite brig, standing south-south-east; and probably bound out, from the Northern States, to the West Indies; and was just the thing we wished to see. She hove-to for us, seeing that we wished to speak her; and we ran down to her; boom-ended our studding-sails; backed our main topsail, and hailed her–"Brig, ahoy!"–"Hallo!"–"Where are you from, pray?"–"From New York, bound to Curaçoa."–"Have you any fresh provisions to spare?"–

**"Sail ho!" was cried on deck...** This is truly a serendipitous encounter. The *Solon* was "bound out," that is, on her outward-bound leg—she was thus still likely to have provisions to spare.

"Aye, aye! plenty of them!" We lowered away the quarter-boat, instantly; and the captain and four hands sprang in, and were soon dancing over the water, and alongside the brig. In about half an hour, they returned with half a boat-load of potatoes and onions, and each vessel filled away, and kept on her course. She proved to be the brig Solon, of Plymouth, from the Connecticut river, and last from New York, bound to the Spanish Main, with a cargo of fresh provisions, mules, tin bake-pans, and other notions. The onions were genuine and fresh; and the mate of the brig told the men in the boat, as he passed the bunches over the side, that the girls had strung them on purpose for us the day he sailed. We had supposed, on board, that a new president had been chosen, the last winter, and, just as we filled away, the captain hailed and asked who was president of the United States. They answered, Andrew Jackson; but thinking that the old General could not have been elected for a third time, we hailed again, and they answered–Jack Downing; and left us to correct the mistake at our leisure.

It was just dinner-time when we filled away; and the steward, taking a few bunches of onions for the cabin, gave the rest to us, with a bottle of vinegar. We carried them forward, stowed them away in the forecastle, refusing to have them cooked, and ate them raw, with our beef and bread. And a glorious treat they were. The freshness and crispness of the raw onion, with the earthy taste, give it a great relish to one who has been a long time on salt provisions.

We were perfectly ravenous after them. It was like a scent of blood to a hound. We ate them at every meal, by the dozen; and filled our pockets with them, to eat in our watch on deck; and the bunches, rising in the form of a cone, from the largest at the bottom, to the smallest, no larger than a strawberry, at the top, soon disappeared.

The chief use, however, of the fresh provisions, was for the men with the scurvy. One of them was able to eat, and he soon brought himself to, by gnawing upon raw

**... the brig Solon, of Plymouth...** *Solon* is most likely under the command of Captain Charles Hammond; at least, Hammond is the captain listed when the vessel is sold a few years later.

**...bound to the Spanish Main...** That is, to the Caribbean Sea and Gulf of Mexico—Spanish possessions in America. By the 1830s, the term was dying out, except as a historical (and somewhat romanticized) reference, since Spain no longer possessed most of these lands. By the 18th century, the term was being used to refer more often to the seas in the area than to the land.

**...they answered–Jack Downing...** Jack Downing is a character created by humorist Seba Smith and used by that writer as the butt of various forms of political satire. Thus, the *Solon*'s crew is simply tossing a mild insult at the crew, for not believing that Jackson was president. However, the statement itself is confusing, because the election of 1836 did not take place until December, and the winner (over William Henry Harrison) was Martin Van Buren. Technically, Jackson remained president until March of 1837, when Van Buren took office.

**We ate them at every meal, by the dozen; and filled our pockets with them...** One can only imagine the state of the forecastle, filled with unwashed, onion-eating men.

**The chief use, however, of the fresh provisions, was for the men with the scurvy.** Whatever the effect on the men's breath, the onions (and potatoes) rapidly restored the scurvy-ridden men to health. Raw onions, as it turns out, are an excellent source of vitamin C.

potatoes; but the other, by this time, was hardly able to open his mouth; and the cook took the potatoes raw, pounded them in a mortar, and gave him the juice to drink. This he swallowed, by the tea-spoonful at a time, and rinsed it about his gums and throat. The strong earthy taste and smell of this extract of the raw potato at first produced a shuddering through his whole frame, and after drinking it, an acute pain, which ran through all parts of his body; but knowing, by this, that it was taking strong hold, he persevered, drinking a spoonful every hour or so, and holding it a long time in his mouth; until, by the effect of this drink, and of his own restored hope, (for he had nearly given up, in despair) he became so well as to be able to move about, and open his mouth enough to eat the raw potatoes and onions pounded into a soft pulp. This course soon restored his appetite and strength; and in ten days after we spoke the Solon, so rapid was his recovery, that, from lying helpless and almost hopeless in his berth, he was at the mast-head, furling a royal.

**...in ten days after we spoke the Solon...he was at the mast-head, furling a royal.** Ben recovers very quickly, as is typical of normally healthy men suffering from scurvy, so long as the disease can be arrested before it causes permanent harm.

With a fine south-west wind, we passed inside of the Bermudas; and notwithstanding the old couplet, which was quoted again and again by those who thought we should have one more touch of a storm before our voyage was up,–

**...notwithstanding the old couplet...** The couplet is a well-known one, used partly as a poetic warning and also as the sort of mnemonic device that sailors (many of them unable to read) used to help them learn and remember the lore and legend of the sea. (Others include: "Red sky at morning, sailor take warning; red sky at night, sailor's delight," "Quick rise after low Foretells a stronger blow," and "If clouds appear as if scratched by a hen, Get ready to reef your topsails then.")

"If the Bermudas let you pass, You must beware of Hatteras–"

we were to the northward of Hatteras, with good weather, and beginning to count, not the days, but the hours, to the time when we should be at anchor in Boston harbor.

Our ship was in fine order, all hands having been hard at work upon her from daylight to dark, every day but Sunday, from the time we got into warm weather on this side the Cape.

It is a common notion with landsmen that a ship is in her finest condition when she leaves port to enter upon her voyage; and that she comes home, after a long

**In the news**
**September, 1836**

According to a New England newspaper account of the time, a quick sailing voyage from Crocker's Wharf in Barnstable, MA to Boston takes about four days: A schooner is scheduled to leave Barnstable on Wednesdays ("wind and weather permitting," says the paper) and arrive at Boston's Central Wharf on Saturdays. By car today, this is a "journey" of some 90 minutes, at most.

absence,

"With over-weathered ribs and ragged sails; Lean, rent and beggared by the strumpet wind."

But so far from that, unless a ship meets with some accident, or comes upon the coast in the dead of winter, when work cannot be done upon the rigging, she is in her finest order at the end of the voyage. When she sails from port, her rigging is generally slack; the masts need staying; the decks and sides are black and dirty from taking in cargo; riggers' seizings and overhand knots in place of nice seamanlike work; and everything, to a sailor's eye, adrift.

But on the passage home, the fine weather between the tropics is spent in putting the ship into the neatest order. No merchant vessel looks better than an Indiaman, or a Cape Horn-er, after a long voyage; and many captains and mates will stake their reputation for seamanship upon the appearance of their ship when she hauls into the dock. All our standing rigging, fore and aft, was set up and tarred; the masts stayed; the lower and top-mast rigging rattled down, (or up, as the fashion now is;) and so careful were our officers to keep the rattlins taught and straight, that we were obliged to go aloft upon the ropes and shearpoles with which the rigging was swifted in; and these were used as jury rattlins until we got close upon the coast. After this, the ship was scraped, inside and out, decks, masts, booms and all; a stage being rigged outside, upon which we scraped her down to the water-line; pounding the rust off the chains, bolts and fastenings. Then, taking two days of calm under the line, we painted her on the outside, giving her open ports in her streak, and finishing off the nice work upon the stern, where sat Neptune in his car, holding his trident, drawn by sea-horses; and re-touched the gilding and coloring of the cornucopia which ornamented her billet-head. The inside was then painted, from the sky-sail truck to the waterways–the yards black; mast-heads and tops, white; monkey-rail, black, white, and yellow; bulwarks, green; plank-shear, white; waterways, lead color, etc., etc. The anchors and ring-bolts, and other

**"With over-weathered ribs and ragged sails; Lean, rent and beggared by the strumpet wind."** This quote from Shakespeare's *The Merchant of Venice* is an interesting example of Dana's erudition, gained from a classical education; its scholarly tone contrasts nicely with the more homely (but no less important) seaman's lore quoted above. As Dana points out, Shakespeare—not much of a sailor himself, apparently—is wrong about the typical vessel's appearance as it returns to port. When weather allows, it is a point of pride for a ship to sail into harbor looking shipshape: sails clean and mended, gear stowed neatly, hull scraped and painted, and the sailors themselves neatly dressed.

In the news
**September, 1836**

Newspapers are filled with articles and editorials relating to "the Nullifiers," members of a southern political party (the Nullifier Party, headed by John C. Calhoun) that held that states had the right to nullify federal laws within their borders.

**...finishing off the nice work upon the stern...** That is, the fine painted and gilded carvings that decorate the stern of the vessel.

**The inside was then painted...** This is a serious attempt to clean up the ship, including painting every panel and fitting. (One is tempted to characterize this as "dressing ship," but that term is reserved for the celebratory flying of an array of flags from mast and stays.)

iron work, were blackened with coal-tar; and the steward kept at work, polishing the brass of the wheel, bell, capstan, etc. The cabin, too, was scraped, varnished, and painted; and the forecastle scraped and scrubbed; there being no need of paint and varnish for Jack's quarters. The decks were then scraped and varnished, and everything useless thrown overboard; among which the empty tar barrels were set on fire and thrown overboard, on a dark night, and left blazing astern, lighting up the ocean for miles. Add to all this labor, the neat work upon the rigging;–the knots, flemish-eyes, splices, seizings, coverings, pointings, and graftings, which show a ship in crack order. The last preparation, and which looked still more like coming into port, was getting the anchors over the bows, bending the cables, rowsing the hawsers up from between decks, and overhauling the deep-sea-lead-line.

**...there being no need of paint and varnish for Jack's quarters.** Dana cannot resist pointing out that the common sailors' quarters need no repainting, because they were never painted in the first place. And, given that the whole point of the book was to publicize inequities in the treatment of the men, one would expect nothing less of Dana.

Thursday, September 15th. This morning the temperature and peculiar appearance of the water, the quantities of gulf-weed floating about, and a bank of clouds lying directly before us, showed that we were on the border of the Gulf Stream. This remarkable current, running north-east, nearly across the ocean, is almost constantly shrouded in clouds, and is the region of storms and heavy seas. Vessels often run from a clear sky and light wind, with all sail, at once into a heavy sea and cloudy sky, with double-reefed topsails. A sailor told me that on a passage from Gibraltar to Boston, his vessel neared the Gulf Stream with a light breeze, clear sky, and studding-sails out, alow and aloft; while, before it, was a long line of heavy, black clouds, lying like a bank upon the water, and a vessel coming out of it, under double-reefed topsails, and with royal yards sent down. As they drew near, they began to take in sail after sail, until they were reduced to the same condition; and, after twelve or fourteen hours of rolling and pitching in a heavy sea, before a smart gale, they ran out of the bank on the other side, and were in fine weather again, and under their royals and skysails. As we drew into it, the sky became cloudy, the sea high, and everything had the appearance of the going off, or the coming on, of a storm. It was blowing no more than a stiff breeze; yet the wind, being north-east, which is directly against the course of the current, made an ugly, chopping sea, which heaved and

**...we were on the border of the Gulf Stream.** This is a warm, fast-moving current with a width of about 60 miles.

In the news

**September, 1836**

In Britain, legislators are slowly removing less serious crimes from the list of those punishable by death. This year, the last men to be hanged for arson and robbery are put to death.

**...the wind, being...directly against the course of the current, made an ugly, chopping sea...** Sailors call this a "confused" or "lumpy" sea: Often created when current and wind run in opposite directions, it is characterized by choppy seas with swells and waves coming from multiple (and sometimes opposite) directions.

pitched the vessel about, so that we were obliged to send down the royal yards, and to take in our light sails. At noon, the thermometer, which had been repeatedly lowered into the water, showed the temperature to be seventy; which was considerably above that of the air,–as is always the case in the centre of the Stream. A lad who had been at work at the royal mast-head, came down upon the deck, and took a turn round the long-boat; and looking very pale, said he was so sick that he could stay aloft no longer, but was ashamed to acknowledge it to the officer. He went up again, but soon gave out and came down, and leaned over the rail, "as sick as a lady passenger."

He had been to sea several years, and had, he said, never been sick before. He was made so by the irregular, pitching motion of the vessel, increased by the height to which he had been above the hull, which is like the fulcrum of the lever. An old sailor, who was at work on the top-gallant yard, said he felt disagreeably all the time, and was glad, when his job was done, to get down into the top, or upon the deck. Another hand was sent to the royal mast-head, who staid nearly an hour, but gave up. The work must be done, and the mate sent me. I did very well for some time, but began at length to feel very unpleasantly, though I had never been sick since the first two days from Boston, and had been in all sorts of weather and situations. Still, I kept my place, and did not come down, until I had got through my work, which was more than two hours. The ship certainly never acted so badly before. She was pitched and jerked about in all manner of ways; the sails seeming to have no steadying power over her. The tapering points of the masts made various curves and angles against the sky overhead, and sometimes, in one sweep of an instant, described an arc of more than forty-five degrees, bringing up with a sudden jerk which made it necessary to hold on with both hands, and then sweeping off, in another long, irregular curve. I was not positively sick, and came down with a look of indifference, yet was not unwilling to get upon the comparative terra firma of the deck. A few hours more carried us through, and when we saw the sun go down, upon our larboard beam, in the direction of the continent of North America, we had left the bank of dark, stormy clouds astern, in the twilight.

**...leaned over the rail, "as sick as a lady passenger."** Dana quotes this phrase as if it were a popular saying of the day, but references to it are few and far between. We know, of course, that it is a reference to the supposed "frailty" of women in general, and is used as a gentle insult to the (literally) green hand who gave up his post. As it happens, a pitching movement is more likely than any other to lead quickly to severe motion sickness. (Studies of passengers in airliners note that most can handle up-and-down and side-to-side movements relatively well. A few sharp pitching movements, however, can debilitate even the hardiest of flyers.)

In the news
**September, 1836**

According to the *London Gazette*, the King of England (William IV) appoints "John Austin, Esq. to be His Majesty's Commissioner of Enquiry into the affairs of the Island of Malta." Austin, who will eventually gain a measure of fame as a legal philosopher, had recently resigned his position as lecturer at the University of London. (He was a poor lecturer, and attendance was spotty in his courses.) Malta, in the meantime, proved an important geopolitical asset for the British empire, eventually achieving independence in 1964.

**...the tapering points of the masts made various curves and angles against the sky overhead, and sometimes, in one sweep of an instant, described an arc of more than forty-five degrees...** This description makes standing watch abovedecks sound a bit like riding a 400-ton bull—for hours on end. No wonder the men were getting sick.

## Chapter XXXVI

## Soundings–Sights From Home–Boston Harbor–Leaving the Ship

Friday, Sept. 16th. Lat. 38° N., long. 69° 00' W. A fine south-west wind; every hour carrying us nearer in toward land. All hands on deck at the dog watch, and nothing talked about, but our getting in; where we should make the land; whether we should arrive before Sunday; going to church; how Boston would look; friends; wages paid;–and the like. Every one was in the best of spirits; and, the voyage being nearly at an end, the strictness of discipline was relaxed; for it was not necessary to order in a cross tone, what every one was ready to do with a will.

**...on George's Bank before to-morrow noon...** Dividing the Atlantic Ocean from the Gulf of Maine, Georges Bank (some editions have it, incorrectly, as George's Banks) is a 150-mile raised area—a submerged plateau—of the sea floor about 200 miles southeast of Boston. Long a lucrative and productive fishing area, fishing on the Bank is now restricted. After complex rulings related to international fishing rights, during the 1970s and 1980s the bank became an object of contention, with U.S. and Canadian fishermen arguing over disputed areas.

The little differences and quarrels which a long voyage breeds on board a ship, were forgotten, and every one was friendly; and two men, who had been on the eve of a battle half the voyage, were laying out a plan together for a cruise on shore. When the mate came forward, he talked to the men, and said we should be on George's Bank before to-morrow noon; and joked with the boys, promising to go and see them, and to take them down to Marblehead in a coach.

Saturday, 17th. The wind was light all day, which kept us back somewhat; but a fine breeze springing up at nightfall, we were running fast in toward the land. At six o'clock we expected to have the ship hove-to for soundings, as a thick fog, coming up showed we were near them; but no order was given, and we kept on our way. Eight o'clock came, and the watch went below, and, for the whole of the first hour, the ship was tearing on, with studding-sails out, alow and aloft, and the night as dark as a pocket. At two bells the captain came on deck, and said a word to the mate, when the studding sails were hauled into the tops, or boom-ended, the after yards backed, the deep-sea-lead carried forward, and everything got ready for sounding. A man on the sprit-sail yard with the lead, another on the cathead with a handful of the line coiled up, another in the fore chains,

**...everything got ready for sounding.** As described in an earlier note, a lead line was used for sounding—that is, determining the current depth of the water. The weighted line is cast out ahead of the vessel so that at the point the vessel passes over it, the line is nearly perpendicular. The sailor taking the sounding can tell the current depth by the marks on the line.

another in the waist, and another in the main chains, each with a quantity of the line coiled away in his hand. "All ready there, forward?"–"Aye, aye, sir!"–"He-e-e-ave!"–"Watch! ho! watch!" sings out the man on the spritsail yard, and the heavy lead drops into the water. "Watch! ho! watch!" bawls the man on the cat-head, as the last fake of the coil drops from his hand, and "Watch! ho! watch!" is shouted by each one as the line falls from his hold; until it comes to the mate, who tends the lead, and has the line in coils on the quarter-deck. Eighty fathoms, and no bottom! A depth as great as the height of St. Peter's! The line is snatched in a block upon the swifter, and three or four men haul it in and coil it away. The after yards are braced full, the studding-sails hauled out again, and in a few minutes more the ship had her whole way upon her. At four bells, backed again, hove the lead, and–soundings! at sixty fathoms! Hurrah for Yankee land! Hand over hand, we hauled the lead in, and the captain, taking it to the light, found black mud on the bottom.

**...the last fake of the coil...** A winding of a coil of rope or line. A properly faked line will run out clear, without one fake fouling a subsequent one as line is paid out. The term goes back to the early 17th century, but its origin is obscure.

**A depth as great as the height of St. Peter's!** St. Peter's cathedral in Rome is said to be one of the largest churches in the Christian world. (In Dana's day, it was the largest.) More correctly called St. Peter's Basilica, the church stands on the site where Peter is said to have been buried, and it rises to a height of some 400 feet or more.

**...the captain, taking it to the light, found black mud on the bottom.** The captain and crew now know they are nearing Boston. They are in 60 fathoms (360 feet) of water, and the bottom is black mud. Experienced coastal navigators know not only the landforms but also the depth and composition of the bottom as they near these landforms. (For one thing, understanding the composition of the bottom makes it easier to ensure an effective anchoring.) Below, Dana notes that the composition of the bottom tells mariners where they are as surely as if they could see the land itself.

Studding-sails taken in; after yards filled, and ship kept on under easy sail all night; the wind dying away.

The soundings on the American coast are so regular that a navigator knows as well where he has made land, by the soundings, as he would by seeing the land. Black mud is the soundings of Block Island. As you go toward Nantucket, it changes to a dark sand; then, sand and white shells; and on George's Banks, white sand; and so on. Being off Block Island, our course was due east, to Nantucket Shoals, and the South Channel; but the wind died away and left us becalmed in a thick fog, in which we lay the whole of Sunday. At noon of

**...becalmed in a thick fog...** In fact, fog is *usually* accompanied by calm.

Sunday, 18th, Block Island bore, by calculation, N. W. 1/4 W. fifteen miles; but the fog was so thick all day that we could see nothing.

Having got through the ship's duty, and washed and shaved, we went below, and had a fine time overhauling our chests, laying aside the clothes we meant to go ashore in and throwing overboard all that were worn out and good for nothing. Away went the woollen caps in which we had carried hides upon our heads, for sixteen months, on the coast of California; the duck frocks, for tarring down rigging; and the worn-out and darned mittens and patched woollen trowsers which had stood the tug of Cape Horn.

**...ate the last "duff"...** Duff, something of a treat aboard ship, is a flour pudding, often flavored with raisins, figs, or molasses, when they're available.

**...and not stop till I'm out of the sight of salt water!** Reminiscent of Ulysses (Odysseus) who, having finally returned from the sea, is resolved never again to have anything to do with the ocean. He decides to carry an oar and walk the country until he finally arrives at a land so far removed from the sea that people gaze at the oar in bewilderment, wondering what it is.

In the news
**September, 1836**

Charles Darwin has recently left Pernambuco, in northeastern Brazil. While there, he describes a prominent reef near the harbor, and hypothesizes about its formation, noting that the reef is not a true coral reef, for no corals were involved in its creation. Instead, he notes that it was "formed by the successive growth of several kinds of organic bodies, chiefly serpulae, balani, corallinae, but no true corals. It is a process strictly analogous to the formation of peat, & like that substance, its effects are to preserve from degradations the matter on which it rests." The reef still exists, forming a "safe but rather shallow harbour."

**...and ship for navigator of a Hingham packet!** The men are joking with one another, one promising never again to touch liquor (a claim loudly derided by his doubting fellows) and another pointing out that the first sailor's sobriety is about as likely as him, a mere sailor, buying a quadrant (a navigational instrument) and serving as an officer. As mentioned earlier, Hingham is a coastal Massachusetts town. A packet is a fast ship used to deliver mail, packages ("packets"), and passengers.

We hove them overboard with a good will; for there is nothing like being quit of the very last appendages and remnants of our evil fortune. We got our chests all ready for going ashore, ate the last "duff" we expected to have on board the ship Alert; and talked as confidently about matters on shore as though our anchor were on the bottom.

"Who'll go to church with me a week from to-day?"

"I will," says Jack; who said aye to everything.

"Go away, salt water!" says Tom. "As soon as I get both legs ashore, I'm going to shoe my heels, and button my ears behind me, and start off into the bush, a straight course, and not stop till I'm out of the sight of salt water!"

"Oh! belay that! Spin that yarn where nobody knows your filling! If you get once moored, stem and stern, in old B—'s grog-shop, with a coal fire ahead and the bar under your lee, you won't see daylight for three weeks!"

"No!" says Tom, "I'm going to knock off grog, and go and board at the Home, and see if they won't ship me for a deacon!"

"And I," says Bill, "am going to buy a quadrant and ship for navigator of a Hingham packet!"

These and the like jokes served to pass the time while we were lying waiting for a breeze to clear up the fog and send us on our way.

Toward night a moderate breeze sprang up; the fog

however continuing as thick as before; and we kept on to the eastward. About the middle of the first watch, a man on the forecastle sang out, in a tone which showed that there was not a moment to be lost,–"Hard up the helm!" and a great ship loomed up out of the fog, coming directly down upon us. She luffed at the same moment, and we just passed one another; our spanker boom grazing over her quarter. The officer of the deck had only time to hail, and she answered, as she went into the fog again, something about Bristol–probably, a whaleman from Bristol, Rhode Island, bound out. The fog continued through the night, with a very light breeze, before which we ran to the eastward, literally feeling our way along. The lead was heaved every two hours, and the gradual change from black mud to sand, showed that we were approaching Nantucket South Shoals. On Monday morning, the increased depth and deep blue color of the water, and the mixture of shells and white sand which we brought up, upon sounding, showed that we were in the channel, and nearing George's; accordingly, the ship's head was put directly to the northward, and we stood on, with perfect confidence in the soundings, though we had not taken an observation for two days, nor seen land; and the difference of an eighth of a mile out of the way might put us ashore. Throughout the day a provokingly light wind prevailed, and at eight o'clock, a small fishing schooner, which we passed, told us we were nearly abreast of Chatham lights.

Just before midnight, a light land-breeze sprang up, which carried us well along; and at four o'clock, thinking ourselves to the northward of Race Point, we hauled upon the wind and stood into the bay, west-north-west, for Boston light, and commenced firing guns for a pilot. Our watch went below at four o'clock, but could not sleep, for the watch on deck were banging away at the guns every few minutes. And, indeed, we cared very little about it, for we were in Boston Bay; and if fortune favored us, we could all "sleep in" the next night, with nobody to call the watch every four hours.

We turned out, of our own will, at daybreak, to get a

**...we just passed one another...** Even today, with radar, GPS, AIS (Automatic Identification System, a system that labels vessel traffic on a display and notes the vessels' speed and heading, even when the vessels cannot be seen), and other such technology, sailing in fog remains treacherous. Here, the *Alert* narrowly averts a disaster—one that would have been tragically ironic, occurring so near the end of the voyage.

**...though we had not taken an observation for two days, nor seen land...** Because they know the depth and makeup of the bottom, the captain and crew know exactly where they are, even absent lunar or solar observations and without having glimpsed land.

**...we were nearly abreast of Chatham lights.** The Chatham Light is a lighthouse near Cape Cod. From this point on, Dana notes the approach to each lighthouse (Race Point Light, Boston Light, etc.), as well as other landmarks that indicate *Alert*'s proximity to Boston.

**In the news**
**September, 1836**

Across the United States, the fall of the Alamo is the topic on everyone's lips and in their hearts. Homage is paid in the form of treacly prose and heartfelt but saccharine poetry, such as this from the *Carolina Watchman*: "Here falls the patriot–there the tyrant dies...Brave Crockett falls and helpless freedom weeps ...A deafening shout—the Alamo is no more; The fallen fortress forms a funeral pyre..."

sight of land.

**...a stirring sight for us, who had been months on the ocean without seeing anything but two solitary sails...** Boston harbor, then and now a very busy place, seems positively alive with vessels, large and small. The way Dana describes his first glimpse of the harbor, one can almost visualize the bustling waters of the bay.

In the grey of the morning, one or two small fishing smacks peered out of the mist; and when the broad day broke upon us, there lay the low sand-hills of Cape Cod, over our larboard quarter, and before us, the wide waters of Massachusetts Bay, with here and there a sail gliding over its smooth surface. As we drew in toward the mouth of the harbor, as toward a focus, the vessels began to multiply until the bay seemed actually alive with sails gliding about in every direction; some on the wind, and others before it, as they were bound to or from the emporium of trade and centre of the bay. It was a stirring sight for us, who had been months on the ocean without seeing anything but two solitary sails; and over two years without seeing more than the three or four traders on an almost desolate coast. There were the little coasters, bound to and from the various towns along the south shore, down in the bight of the bay, and to the eastward; here and there a square-rigged vessel standing out to seaward; and, far in the distance, beyond Cape Ann, was the smoke of a steamer, stretching along in a narrow, black cloud upon the water. Every sight was full of beauty and interest. We were coming back to our homes; and the signs of civilization, and prosperity, and happiness, from which we had been so long banished, were multiplying about us. The high land of Cape Ann and the rocks and shore of Cohasset were full in sight, the lighthouses, standing like sentries in white before the harbors, and even the smoke from the chimney on the plains of Hingham was seen rising slowly in the morning air. One of our boys was the son of a bucket-maker; and his face lighted up as he saw the tops of the well-known hills which surround his native place. About ten o'clock a little boat came bobbing over the water, and put a pilot on board, and sheered off in pursuit of other vessels bound in.

**...a little boat came bobbing over the water, and put a pilot on board...** Then and now, ships the size of *Alert* are rarely brought into port by their captains alone. Instead, a pilot, assigned by the harbormaster and possessing specialized knowledge of the area, boards the ship and guides it in.

**...sharks in Ann street learned that there was a rich prize for them down in the bay...** Recall that Ann Street was an unsavory neighborhood full of gamblers, prostitutes, and other questionable characters.

Being now within the scope of the telegraph stations, our signals were run up at the fore, and in half an hour afterwards, the owner on 'change, or in his counting-room, knew that his ship was below; and the landlords, runners, and sharks in Ann street learned that there was a rich prize for them down in the bay: a ship from round the Horn, with a crew to be paid off with two years' wages.

The wind continuing very light, all hands were sent aloft to strip off the chafing gear; and battens, parcellings, roundings, hoops, mats, and leathers, came flying from aloft, and left the rigging neat and clean, stripped of all its sea bandaging. The last touch was put to the vessel by painting the skysail poles; and I was sent up to the fore, with a bucket of white paint and a brush, and touched her off, from the truck to the eyes of the royal rigging. At noon, we lay becalmed off the lower light-house; and it being about slack water, we made little progress. A firing was heard in the direction of Hingham, and the pilot said there was a review there.

**... the pilot said there was a review there.** A ceremonial inspection of local military forces, often accompanied by a parade and carnival-like atmosphere.

The Hingham boy got wind of this, and said if the ship had been twelve hours sooner, he should have been down among the soldiers, and in the booths, and having a grand time. As it was, we had little prospect of getting in before night. About two o'clock a breeze sprang up ahead, from the westward, and we began beating up against it. A full-rigged brig was beating in at the same time, and we passed one another, in our tacks, sometimes one and sometimes the other, working to windward, as the wind and tide favored or opposed. It was my trick at the wheel from two till four; and I stood my last helm, making between nine hundred and a thousand hours which I had spent at the helms of our two vessels. The tide beginning to set against us, we made slow work; and the afternoon was nearly spent, before we got abreast of the inner light. In the meantime, several vessels were coming down, outward bound; among which, a fine, large ship, with yards squared, fair wind and fair tide, passed us like a race-horse, the men running out upon her yards to rig out the studding-sail booms. Toward sundown the wind came off in flaws, sometimes blowing very stiff, so that the pilot took in the royals, and then it died away; when, in order to get us in before the tide became too strong, the royals were set again. As this kept us running up and down the rigging all the time, one hand was sent aloft at each mast-head,

**...between nine hundred and a thousand hours which I had spent at the helms of our two vessels.** From his beginnings as a soft college boy prone to sea-sickness, Dana has become a skilled and knowledgeable sailor, and a much stronger, more robust young man.

**...the wind came off in flaws...** A flaw is a sudden gust or burst of wind. After having sailed thousands of miles, *Alert* is having trouble making those last few miles, due mainly to undependable winds.

**...between Rainsford Island and the Castle.** Castle Island was at the time a sea fort located near Boston Harbor. It is now a recreational area. In the 1830s, Rainsford Island served as a quarantine hospital.

**...fortifications on George's Island...** Georges Island (no apostrophe), is an island in Boston Harbor. At the time of Dana's voyage, it was fortified with gun emplacements meant to protect Boston. (It would eventually become home to Fort Warren, which itself would in the 1860s become a Civil War prison.)

**...weather-bowing the tide...** Turning the bow to the side from which the wind is coming. If the wind and current don't cooperate, the vessel can lose ground by "weather-bowing."

**...our long voyage ended...** It has been 135 days since *Alert* left San Diego, but Dana has been away from Boston for a little over two years.

**...the well-known tone of the Old South.** A reference to the well-known (and previously mentioned) Old South Church in Boston.

**...the junior partner of the firm to which our ship belonged, jumped on board.** This is Samuel Hooper, a clerk working for the ship's owners. He and Dana were acquaintances in Boston. (Not the same Samuel Hooper who ships out on *Pilgrim* at age 12.)

to stand-by to loose and furl the sails, at the moment of the order. I took my place at the fore, and loosed and furled the royal five times between Rainsford Island and the Castle. At one tack we ran so near to Rainsford Island, that, looking down from the royal yard, the island, with its hospital buildings, nice gravelled walks, and green plats, seemed to lie directly under our yard-arms. So close is the channel to some of these islands, that we ran the end of our flying-jib-boom over one of the out-works of the fortifications on George's Island; and had an opportunity of seeing the advantages of that point as a fortified place; for, in working up the channel, we presented a fair stem and stern, for raking, from the batteries, three or four times. One gun might have knocked us to pieces.

We had all set our hearts upon getting up to town before night and going ashore, but the tide beginning to run strong against us, and the wind, what there was of it, being ahead, we made but little by weather-bowing the tide, and the pilot gave orders to cock-bill the anchor and overhaul the chain. Making two long stretches, which brought us into the roads, under the lee of the castle, he clewed up the topsails, and let go the anchor; and for the first time since leaving San Diego,–one hundred and thirty-five days–our anchor was upon bottom. In half an hour more, we were lying snugly, with all sails furled, safe in Boston harbor; our long voyage ended; the well-known scene about us; the dome of the State House fading in the western sky; the lights of the city starting into sight, as the darkness came on; and at nine o'clock the clangor of the bells, ringing their accustomed peals; among which the Boston boys tried to distinguish the well-known tone of the Old South.

We had just done furling the sails, when a beautiful little pleasure-boat luffed up into the wind, under our quarter, and the junior partner of the firm to which our ship belonged, jumped on board. I saw him from the mizen topsail yard, and knew him well.

He shook the captain by the hand, and went down into the cabin, and in a few moments came up and inquired of the mate for me.

The last time I had seen him, I was in the uniform of an undergraduate of Harvard College, and now, to his astonishment, there came down from aloft a "rough alley" looking fellow, with duck trowsers and red shirt, long hair, and face burnt as black as an Indian's. He shook me by the hand, congratulated me upon my return and my appearance of health and strength, and said my friends were all well. I thanked him for telling me what I should not have dared to ask; and if–

**...a "rough alley" looking fellow...** A tough, a thug.

"the first bringer of unwelcome news Hath but a losing office; and his tongue Sounds ever after like a sullen bell–"

**...the first bringer of unwelcome news Hath but a losing office...** Another quote from Shakespeare, this time from *Henry IV, Pt. II.* Dana is relieved to discover that his friends and family are well.

certainly I shall ever remember this man and his words with pleasure.

The captain went up to town in the boat with Mr. H—-, and left us to pass another night on board ship, and to come up with the morning's tide under command of the pilot.

So much did we feel ourselves to be already at home, in anticipation, that our plain supper of hard bread and salt beef was barely touched; and many on board, to whom this was the first voyage, could scarcely sleep. As for myself, by one of those anomalous changes of feeling of which we are all the subjects, I found that I was in a state of indifference, for which I could by no means account. A year before, while carrying hides on the coast, the assurance that in a twelvemonth we should see Boston, made me half wild; but now that I was actually there, and in sight of home, the emotions which I had so long anticipated feeling, I did not find, and in their place was a state of very nearly entire apathy. Something of the same experience was related to me by a sailor whose first voyage was one of five years upon the North-west Coast. He had left home, a lad, and after several years of very hard and trying experience, found himself homeward bound; and such was the excitement of his feelings that, during the whole passage, he could

**...I found that I was in a state of indifference...** Many editors and critics have remarked on Dana's odd reaction to finally making it back to Boston: He does not feel elated, nor relieved, nor overjoyed. He feels. . .*apathetic.* But, as he himself points out, that feeling isn't unheard of after such a voyage. Perhaps after a voyage during which one is sorely tested—and during which one feels one's self to have become a man—everything else becomes superfluous; surely the humdrum life of a college student headed for a career in law will be nowhere near as exciting as the two-year period Dana has just spent traveling the world and becoming both a seasoned sailor and a man.

talk and think of nothing else but his arrival, and how and when he should jump from the vessel and take his way directly home. Yet when the vessel was made fast to the wharf and the crew dismissed, he seemed suddenly to lose all feeling about the matter. He told me that he went below and changed his dress; took some water from the scuttle-butt and washed himself leisurely; overhauled his chest, and put his clothes all in order; took his pipe from its place, filled it, and sitting down upon his chest, smoked it slowly for the last time. Here he looked round upon the forecastle in which he had spent so many years, and being alone and his shipmates scattered, he began to feel actually unhappy. Home became almost a dream; and it was not until his brother (who had heard of the ship's arrival) came down into the forecastle and told him of things at home, and who were waiting there to see him, that he could realize where he was, and feel interest enough to put him in motion toward that place for which he had longed, and of which he had dreamed, for years. There is probably so much of excitement in prolonged expectation, that the quiet realizing of it produces a momentary stagnation of feeling as well as of effort. It was a good deal so with me. The activity of preparation, the rapid progress of the ship, the first making land, the coming up the harbor, and old scenes breaking upon the view, produced a mental as well as bodily activity, from which the change to a perfect stillness, when both expectation and the necessity of labor failed, left a calmness, almost of indifference, from which I must be roused by some new excitement. And the next morning, when all hands were called, and we were busily at work, clearing the decks, and getting everything in readiness for going up to the wharves,–loading the guns for a salute, loosing the sails, and manning the windlass–mind and body seemed to wake together.

**There is probably so much of excitement in prolonged expectation, that the quiet realizing of it produces a momentary stagnation of feeling as well as of effort.** That is, having looked forward for so long (and so heartily) to an event, the actual event often strikes us as anticlimactic.

**...when all hands were called, and we were busily at work, clearing the decks...mind and body seemed to wake together.** Notice that the only thing that dispels Dana's apathetic lethargy is the opportunity to act once more as a sailor: manning the windlass, getting everything ready, loading the guns, etc.

About ten o'clock, a sea-breeze sprang up, and the pilot gave orders to get the ship under weigh. All hands manned the windlass, and the long-drawn "Yo, heave, ho!" which we had last heard dying away among the desolate hills of San Diego, soon brought the anchor to the bows; and, with a fair wind and tide, a bright sunny morning, royals and sky-sails set, ensign, streamer, signals, and pennant, flying, and with our guns firing, we came swiftly and handsomely up to the city. Off the end of the wharf, we rounded-to and let go our anchor; and no sooner was it on the bottom, than the decks were filled with people: custom-house officers; Topliff's agent, to inquire for news; others, inquiring for friends on board, or left upon the coast; dealers in grease, besieging the galley to make a bargain with the cook for his slush; "loafers" in general; and last and chief, boarding-house runners, to secure their men.

**...we came swiftly and handsomely up to the city.** This is a contradictory sentence, unless we parse it in a non-nautical sense. Dana notes that *Alert* came "swiftly" but also "handsomely"—handsomely, in the nautical sense means "slowly and carefully." So, Dana must be using the term in its more common non-nautical sense of "good-looking" or "beautiful."

**...besieging the galley to make a bargain with the cook for his slush...** Recall that the cook sells his slush (fats and oils skimmed from the cookpot and elsewhere and used to weatherproof and oil spars and masts) and pockets the money—a practice that gave rise to the term "slush fund." Here, he has a chance to sell his slush to dealers in Boston.

Nothing can exceed the obliging disposition of these runners, and the interest they take in a sailor returned from a long voyage with a plenty of money. Two or three of them, at different times, took me by the hand; remembered me perfectly; were quite sure I had boarded with them before I sailed; were delighted to see me back; gave me their cards; had a hand-cart waiting on the wharf, on purpose to take my things up: would lend me a hand to get my chest ashore; bring a bottle of grog on board if we did not haul in immediately,–and the like. In fact, we could hardly get clear of them, to go aloft and furl the sails. Sail after sail, for the hundredth time, in fair weather and in foul, we furled now for the last time together, and came down and took the warp ashore, manned the capstan, and with a chorus which waked up half the North End, and rang among the buildings in the dock, we hauled her in to the wharf. Here, too, the landlords and runners were active and ready, taking a bar to the capstan, lending a hand at the ropes, laughing and talking and telling the news. The city bells were just ringing one when the last turn was made fast, and the crew dismissed; and in five minutes more, not a soul was left on board the good ship Alert, but the old ship-keeper, who had come down from the counting-house to take charge of her.

**...were delighted to see me back...** These are people whom in reality Dana does not know, and has never met; they're out to "make a buck" off the newly returned sailor. The crew has (or will soon have) two years' wages in their' pockets, making them likely targets for every con man, bar-keeper, prostitute, and gambler in Boston.

**...taking a bar to the capstan...** That is, willing to insert a bar into the capstan to help turn it. A capstan, used for heavy lifting, is a rotating vertical cylinder around which lines can be wrapped and which the men turn using bars inserted into the barrel-like cylinder.

## Concluding Chapter

I trust that they who have followed me to the end of my narrative, will not refuse to carry their attention a little farther, to the concluding remarks which I here present to them.

**...in it I design to offer those views of what may be done for seamen...** Dana's book has been called "the greatest sea-book that was ever written," and it may be exactly that, for three reasons. First, it is eminently readable, or so it must have seemed to the 19th-century reader. Although filled with what may seem to us unfamiliar cadences and laborious syntax, it really was for its time a shining example of honest, unadorned, forthright (occasionally even blunt) writing. Second, the book was conceived essentially as a protest: Its purpose, and Dana made no bones about it, was to inform and perhaps enrage the public, who until now knew little about the often brutal daily lives of men "before the mast." He succeeded. The book was immensely popular, and led to reforms of exactly the type that Dana had envisioned. Finally, Dana launched a new genre of much more realistic, occasionally even gritty, sea stories of the type popularized in later years by such writers as Melville. As many have noted, without *Two Years Before the Mast*, there would have been no *Moby Dick*.

This chapter is written after the lapse of a considerable time since the end of my voyage, and after a return to my former pursuits; and in it I design to offer those views of what may be done for seamen, and of what is already doing, which I have deduced from my experiences, and from the attention which I have since gladly given to the subject.

The romantic interest which many take in the sea, and in those who live upon it, may be of use in exciting their attention to this subject, though I cannot but feel sure that all who have followed me in my narrative must be convinced that the sailor has no romance in his every-day life to sustain him, but that it is very much the same plain, matter-of-fact drudgery and hardship, which would be experienced on shore. If I have not produced this conviction, I have failed in persuading others of what my own experience has most fully impressed upon myself.

There is a witchery in the sea, its songs and stories, and in the mere sight of a ship, and the sailor's dress, especially to a young mind, which has done more to man navies, and fill merchantmen, than all the press-gangs of Europe. I have known a young man with such a passion for the sea, that the very creaking of a block stirred up his imagination so that he could hardly keep his feet on dry ground; and many are the boys, in every seaport, who are drawn away, as by an almost irresistible attraction, from their work and schools, and hang about the decks and yards of vessels, with a fondness which, it is plain, will have its way. No sooner, however, has the young sailor begun his new life in earnest, than all this fine drapery falls off, and he learns that it is but work and hardship, after all. This is the true light in which a sailor's life is to be viewed; and if in our books, and

**...he learns that it is but work and hardship, after all.** Young men and boys are fed, says Dana, romanticized notions of what it means to go to sea—perhaps not unlike what a later generation of young boys would believe of running away to join the circus. And in both cases, the boys' romantic notions are quickly dispelled: Circuses and sailing ships both are mainly "work and hardship" and occasional brutality.

anniversary speeches, we would leave out much that is said about "blue water," "blue jackets," "open hearts," "seeing God's hand on the deep," and so forth, and take this up like any other practical subject, I am quite sure we should do full as much for those we wish to benefit. The question is, what can be done for sailors, as they are,–men to be fed, and clothed, and lodged, for whom laws must be made and executed, and who are to be instructed in useful knowledge, and, above all, to be brought under religious influence and restraint? It is upon these topics that I wish to make a few observations.

**The question is, what can be done for sailors...** This is in fact *the* question that drives Dana. What can be done to make them better people and to make their lives better?

In the first place, I have no fancies about equality on board ship, It is a thing out of the question, and certainly, in the present state of mankind, not to be desired. I never knew a sailor who found fault with the orders and ranks of the service; and if I expected to pass the rest of my life before the mast, I would not wish to have the power of the captain diminished an iota. It is absolutely necessary that there should be one head and one voice, to control everything, and be responsible for everything. There are emergencies which require the instant exercise of extreme power. These emergencies do not allow of consultation; and they who would be the captain's constituted advisers might be the very men over whom he would be called upon to exert his authority. It has been found necessary to vest in every government, even the most democratic, some extraordinary, and, at first sight, alarming powers; trusting in public opinion, and subsequent accountability to modify the exercise of them. These are provided to meet exigencies, which all hope may never occur, but which yet by possibility may occur, and if they should, and there were no power to meet them instantly, there would be an end put to the government at once. So it is with the authority of the shipmaster. It will not answer to say that he shall never do this and that thing, because it does not seem always necessary and advisable that it should be done. He has great cares and responsibilities; is answerable for everything; and is subject to emergencies which perhaps no other man exercising authority among civilized people is subject to. Let him, then, have powers commensurate

**It is a thing out of the question, and certainly, in the present state of mankind, not to be desired.** In reading Dana's passionate defense of (and arguments for better treatment of) the common sailor, it's easy to forget that Dana was not a radical liberal—he was in many ways a product of his times, and he felt strongly that "the orders and ranks of the service" were necessities for keeping discipline on board. He even defended the right of captains to flog sailors when necessary—and he was confident that floggings *were* in fact sometimes necessary.

**He has great cares and responsibilities; is answerable for everything...** Dana's argument here is that a captain has great responsibility, and is therefore entitled (or even *required*) to wield great power ("at first sight, alarming powers") as a way of dealing with those responsibilities in an effective manner.

**...only let him be held strictly responsible for the exercise of them.** What Dana does wish to see are ways to hold officers responsible for the appropriate use of those "alarming" powers.

with his utmost possible need; only let him be held strictly responsible for the exercise of them. Any other course would be injustice, as well as bad policy.

**He is liable at common law for murder, assault and battery, and other offences...** As this book is being prepared for publication, Dana has recently been admitted to the bar. He is a practicing attorney, as well as an experienced sailor. He therefore understands better than most the laws as they apply to the officers and men of the merchant marine.

In the treatment of those under his authority, the captain is amenable to the common law, like any other person. He is liable at common law for murder, assault and battery, and other offences; and in addition to this, there is a special statute of the United States which makes a captain or other officer liable to imprisonment for a term not exceeding five years, and to a fine not exceeding a thousand dollars, for inflicting any cruel punishment upon, withholding food from, or in any other way maltreating a seaman. This is the state of the law on the subject; while the relation in which the parties stand, and the peculiar necessities, excuses, and provocations arising from that relation, are merely circumstances to be considered in each case. As to the restraints upon the master's exercise of power, the laws themselves seem, on the whole, to be sufficient. I do not see that we are in need, at present, of more legislation on the subject. The difficulty lies rather in the administration of the laws; and this is certainly a matter that deserves great consideration, and one of no little embarrassment.

**I do not see that we are in need, at present, of more legislation on the subject**. Dana does not argue that new laws are required to protect the men, only that the existing laws be administered more consistently and fairly.

**Many lives and a great amount of property are constantly in their hands, for which they are strictly responsible.** Essentially a restatement of Dana's earlier position that positions of great responsibility require great power.

In the first place, the courts have said that public policy requires the power of the master and officers should be sustained. Many lives and a great amount of property are constantly in their hands, for which they are strictly responsible. To preserve these, and to deal justly by the captain, and not lay upon him a really fearful responsibility, and then tie up his hands, it is essential that discipline should be supported. In the second place, there is always great allowance to be made for false swearing and exaggeration by seamen, and for combinations among them against their officers; and it is to be remembered that the latter have often no one to testify on their side. These are weighty and true statements, and should not be lost sight of by the friends of seamen. On the other hand, sailors make many complaints, some of which are well founded.

**...for combinations among them against their officers...** Dana points out that the men greatly outnumber the officers. It would be easy for the men to get together and make up stories about their treatment.

On the subject of testimony, seamen labor under a difficulty full as great as that of the captain. It is a well-known fact, that they are usually much better treated when there are passengers on board.

The presence of passengers is a restraint upon the captain, not only from his regard to their feelings and to the estimation in which they may hold him, but because he knows they will be influential witnesses against him if he is brought to trial. Though officers may sometimes be inclined to show themselves off before passengers, by freaks of office and authority, yet cruelty they would hardly dare to be guilty of. It is on long and distant voyages, where there is no restraint upon the captain, and none but the crew to testify against him, that sailors need most the protection of the law. On such voyages as these, there are many cases of outrageous cruelty on record, enough to make one heartsick, and almost disgusted with the sight of man; and many, many more, which have never come to light, and never will be known, until the sea shall give up its dead. Many of these have led to mutiny and piracy,–stripe for stripe, and blood for blood. If on voyages of this description the testimony of seamen is not to be received in favor of one another, or too great a deduction is made on account of their being seamen, their case is without remedy; and the captain, knowing this, will be strengthened in that disposition to tyrannize which the possession of absolute power, without the restraints of friends and public opinion, is too apt to engender.

It is to be considered, also, that the sailor comes into court under very different circumstances from the master. He is thrown among landlords, and sharks of all descriptions; is often led to drink freely; and comes upon the stand unaided, and under a certain cloud of suspicion as to his character and veracity. The captain, on the other hand, is backed by the owners and insurers, and has an air of greater respectability; though, after all, he may have but a little better education than the sailor, and sometimes, (especially among those engaged in certain voyages that I could mention) a very hackneyed conscience.

**...they are usually much better treated when there are passengers on board.** Though Dana cites no sources for this claim, it does ring true: Few captains would willfully mistreat their men in front of a paying passenger who might report back to the owners or be called as a witness in the event of a civil or criminal suit.

**...and many, many more, which have never come to light...** In an 1886 debate in the House of Commons, British legislators (members of the Royal Commission on Loss of Life at Sea) discussed the fact that it was common for a captain, having killed a crewmember, to record that the man "died of heart disease or that sort of complaint, when it is not really the case." A 1915 U.S. statute, sometimes described as "the Magna Carta of sailor' rights," was aimed at protecting crew members from abuse by officers—it did so by holding the ships' *owners* responsible for monetary damages. While the law allowed sailors charged with certain offenses to be held in irons or fed reduced rations, it explicitly disallowed flogging. Both Dana's book and Jack London's *The Sea-Wolf* were cited as influences by the sponsor of the law, Senator Robert LaFollette.

**...sometimes, (especially among those engaged in certain voyages that I could mention) a very hackneyed conscience**. An interesting turn of phrase and a powerful, if understated, allusion. We use the term "hackneyed" to mean *trite* or *commonplace*, but its original meaning had to do with something that was hired or kept for hire. (Hence the term *hack*, meaning a taxicab.) Here, it takes on something of both meanings. Dana's allusion is to the slave trade—something about which he harbored passionately abolitionist feelings—and to captains who, because they were interested only in money, took part in that trade in spite of the fact that the import of slaves had been illegal since 1817. He's saying, in effect, that these men *have* no conscience, that they've been bought off.

**The effect of a sailor's testimony in deciding a case must depend altogether upon the reputation of the class to which he belongs...** Dana is well aware that a well-educated, sophisticated, and relatively wealthy man such as himself would be treated more equitably in a court of law than would an uneducated, unwashed, barely literate sailor—notwithstanding that the illiterate sailor might be in the right. To his credit, he argues that this is patently unfair and results in the inconsistent application of the law.

These are the considerations most commonly brought up on the subject of seamen's evidence; and I think it cannot but be obvious to every one that here, positive legislation would be of no manner of use. There can be no rule of law regulating the weight to be given to seamen's evidence. It must rest in the mind of the judge and jury; and no enactment or positive rule of court could vary the result a hair, in any one case. The effect of a sailor's testimony in deciding a case must depend altogether upon the reputation of the class to which he belongs, and upon the impression he himself produces in court by his deportment, and by those infallible marks of character which always tell upon a jury.

**...we must be satisfied to labor in the less easy and less exciting task of gradual improvement, and abide the issue of things working slowly together for good.** Again, for all of his liberal leanings, Dana does not advocate a revolutionary approach to the problem. He believes that change can come from within, from working within the system, and that it must come slowly in order to avoid destabilizing the entire industry. (This is not unlike conservative civil rights activists who preached that change would have to come slowly, that blacks could not—and should not—demand instant integration, that society would be better-served if change proceeded slowly.) This argument, Dana says, extends even to the more mundane aspects of the treatment of the crew, such as those relating to food, sleep, and lodging.

In fine, after all the well-meant and specious projects that have been brought forward, we seem driven back to the belief, that the best means of securing a fair administration of the laws made for the protection of seamen, and certainly the only means which can create any important change for the better, is the gradual one of raising the intellectual and religious character of the sailor, so that as an individual and as one of a class, he may, in the first instance, command the respect of his officers, and if any difficulty should happen, may upon the stand carry that weight which an intelligent and respectable man of the lower class almost always does with a jury. I know there are many men who, when a few cases of great hardship occur, and it is evident that there is an evil somewhere, think that some arrangement must be made, some law passed, or some society got up, to set all right at once. On this subject there can be no call for any such movement; on the contrary, I fully believe that any public and strong action would do harm, and that we must be satisfied to labor in the less easy and less exciting task of gradual improvement, and abide the issue of things working slowly together for good.

Equally injudicious would be any interference with the economy of the ship. The lodging, food, hours of sleep, etc., are all matters which, though capable of many changes for the better, must yet be left to regulate themselves. And I am confident that there will be, and that there is now a gradual improvement in all such particulars. The forecastles of most of our ships are small, black, and wet holes, which few landsmen would believe held a crew of ten or twelve men on a voyage of months or years; and often, indeed in most cases, the provisions are not good enough to make a meal anything more than a necessary part of a day's duty;(1)

———- 1. I am not sure that I have stated, in the course of my narrative, the manner in which sailors eat, on board ship. There are neither tables, knives, forks, nor plates, in a forecastle; but the kid (a wooden tub, with iron hoops) is placed on the floor and the crew sit round it, and each man cuts for himself with the common jack-knife or sheath-knife, that he carries about him. They drink their tea out of tin pots, holding little less than a quart each.

These particulars are not looked upon as hardships, and, indeed, may be considered matters of choice. Sailors, in our merchantmen, furnish their own eating utensils, as they do many of the instruments which they use in the ship's work, such as knives, palms and needles, marline-spikes, rubbers, etc. And considering their mode of life in other respects, the little time they would have for laying and clearing away a table with its apparatus, and the room it would take up in a forecastle, as well as the simple character of their meals, consisting generally of only one piece of meat,–it is certainly a convenient method, and, as the kid and pans are usually kept perfectly clean, a neat and simple one. I had supposed these things to be generally known, until I heard, a few months ago, a lawyer of repute, who has had a good deal to do with marine cases, ask a sailor upon the stand whether the crew had "got up from table" when a certain thing happened. ———-

and on the score of sleep, I fully believe that the lives of merchant seamen are shortened by the want of it. I do not refer to those occasions when it is necessarily broken in upon; but, for months, during fine weather, in many merchantmen, all hands are kept, throughout the day, and, then, there are eight hours on deck for one

**They drink their tea out of tin pots...** Keep in mind that the tea served on most vessels is a watered-down concoction consisting of about one pint of actual tea and some molasses to about three gallons of water.

**...simple character of their meals...it is certainly a convenient method...** Dana points out that given the limited space and the demands on their time, it's probably best that mealtime preparations and cleanup be kept quick and simple. He finds it funny that a supposedly knowledgeable attorney would ask about the men getting "up from table"—as if these men ever ate at a proper table.

**...on the score of sleep, I fully believe that the lives of merchant seamen are shortened by the want of it.** A perennial complaint of sailors, soldiers, pilots, firefighters, and the like. Not only are they allotted little time for sleep, but what sleep they do get is often interrupted by emergencies to which they are obligated to respond. Sleep deprivation definitely does have long- and short-term effects, and it may not be overstating the issue to claim that it shortens one's life. In the first place, fatigued people make mistakes, and mistakes on board a ship (or in an airplane, at a fire, etc.) can kill you. Secondly, research indicates that people suffering from long-term sleep deprivation are apparently more prone to heart trouble, stroke, and other medical issues that could certainly be said to shorten one's life.

watch each night. Thus it is usually the case that at the end of a voyage, where there has been the finest weather, and no disaster, the crew have a wearied and worn-out appearance. They never sleep longer than four hours at a time, and are seldom called without being really in need of more rest. There is no one thing that a sailor thinks more of as a luxury of life on shore, than a whole night's sleep. Still, all these things must be left to be gradually modified by circumstances.

**...all these things must be left to be gradually modified by circumstances.** Dana repeats his admonition to take things slowly when advocating for change.

Whenever hard cases occur, they should be made known, and masters and owners should be held answerable, and will, no doubt, in time, be influenced in their arrangements and discipline by the increased consideration in which sailors are held by the public.

It is perfectly proper that the men should live in a different part of the vessel from the officers; and if the forecastle is made large and comfortable, there is no reason why the crew should not live there as well as in any other part. In fact, sailors prefer the forecastle. It is their accustomed place, and in it they are out of the sight and hearing of their officers.

**It is perfectly proper that the men should live in a different part of the vessel from the officers...** There is definitely something to the idea that the men would probably prefer not to live with the officers; after all, would an employee want to spend all of his time in close quarters with his boss? Probably not. It would be difficult to be yourself, to relax. It would certainly be impossible to discuss the officers themselves—something that was (then and now) surely a popular topic in the forecastle. On the other hand, one cannot escape the faint echoes of paternalistic apologists insisting that slavery is the proper state for "simple darkies," and that offering "separate but equal" accomodations is really a kindness to them. Is it possible that Dana, in spite of his own experiences before the mast, is condescending toward the men with whom he'd recently—but always temporarily—spent many months?

As to their food and sleep, there are laws, with heavy penalties, requiring a certain amount of stores to be on board, and safely stowed; and, for depriving the crew unnecessarily of food or sleep, the captain is liable at common law, as well as under the statute before referred to. Farther than this, it would not be safe to go.

The captain must be the judge when it is necessary to keep his crew from their sleep; and sometimes a retrenching, not of the necessaries, but of some of the little niceties of their meals, as, for instance, duff on Sunday, may be a mode of punishment, though I think generally an injudicious one.

**...generally an injudicious one.** Duff (previously defined) on Sundays is a perk for the men, a treat to which they can look forward all week. Dana is implying that rather than punish the men for bad behavior by taking away one of their (few) pleasures, perhaps it might be better instead to reward them for good behavior.

I could not do justice to this subject without noticing one part of the discipline of a ship, which has been very much discussed of late, and has brought out strong expressions of indignation from many,–I mean the infliction of corporal punishment. Those who have followed me in my narrative will remember that I was witness to an act of great cruelty inflicted upon my own shipmates; and indeed I can sincerely say that the simple mention of the word flogging, brings up in me feelings which I can hardly control. Yet, when the proposition is made to abolish it entirely and at once; to prohibit the captain from ever, under any circumstances, inflicting corporal punishment; I am obliged to pause, and, I must say, to doubt exceedingly the expediency of making any positive enactment which shall have that effect. If the design of those who are writing on this subject is merely to draw public attention to it, and to discourage the practice of flogging, and bring it into disrepute, it is well; and, indeed, whatever may be the end they have in view, the mere agitation of the question will have that effect, and, so far, must do good. Yet I should not wish to take the command of a ship to-morrow, running my chance of a crew, as most masters must, and know, and have my crew know, that I could not, under any circumstances, inflict even moderate chastisement. I should trust that I might never have to resort to it; and, indeed, I scarcely know what risk I would not run, and to what inconvenience I would not subject myself, rather than do so. Yet not to have the power of holding it up in terrorem, and indeed of protecting myself, and all under my charge, by it, if some extreme case should arise, would be a situation I should not wish to be placed in myself, or to take the responsibility of placing another in.

**...I am obliged to pause...** Dana is a kind man. He can barely even *consider* the topic of flogging without feeling abased and disgusted. But he nonetheless refrains from suggesting that it be entirely and universally abolished.

**...I should not wish to take the command of a ship to-morrow...** As repugnant as the idea is, Dana wishes to reserve a captain's right to flogging as a last-ditch punishment, something that the captain and the men know can be ordered if deemed necessary. It is, if nothing else, a deterrent—one that Dana hopes that most captains hope will never be necessary.

**...the power of holding it up in terrorem...** Latin for *as a warning*.

Indeed, the difficulties into which masters and officers are liable to be thrown, are not sufficiently considered by many whose sympathies are easily excited by stories, frequent enough, and true enough of outrageous abuse of this power. It is to be remembered that more than three-fourths of the seamen in our merchant vessels are foreigners. They are from all parts of the world. A great many from the north of Europe, beside Frenchmen, Spaniards, Portuguese, Italians, men from all parts of the Mediterranean, together with Lascars, Negroes, and, perhaps worst of all, the off-casts of British men-of-war, and men from our own country who have gone to sea because they could not be permitted to live on land.

**...because they could not be permitted to live on land.** In an interesting turn of phrase, later editions have, "...who have gone to sea because they have made the land too hot to hold them." The sentiment and logic are the same, though: Merchant crews are often rough-hewn castoffs, reformed (or possibly not at all reformed) criminals, and the like. They can be a rough bunch to deal with, and the captain needs all of the tools at his disposal—including the right to resort to corporal punishment in extreme situations. Note, though, that Dana singles out "foreigners" (and "Negroes") as the most problematic.

As things now are, many masters are obliged to sail without knowing anything of their crews, until they get out at sea. There may be pirates or mutineers among them; and one bad man will often infect all the rest; and it is almost certain that some of them will be ignorant foreigners, hardly understanding a word of our language, accustomed all their lives to no influence but force, and perhaps nearly as familiar with the use of the knife as with that of the marline-spike. No prudent master, however peaceably inclined, would go to sea without his pistols and handcuffs. Even with such a crew as I have supposed, kindness and moderation would be the best policy, and the duty of every conscientious man; and the administering of corporal punishment might be dangerous, and of doubtful use. But the question is not, what a captain ought generally to do, but whether it shall be put out of the power of every captain, under any circumstances, to make use of, even moderate, chastisement. As the law now stands, a parent may correct moderately his child, and the master his apprentice; and the case of the shipmaster has been placed upon the same principle. The statutes, and the common law as expounded in the decisions of courts, and in the books of commentators, are express and unanimous to this point, that the captain may inflict moderate corporal chastisement, for a reasonable cause. If the punishment is excessive, or the cause not sufficient to justify it, he is answerable; and the jury are to determine, by their verdict in each case, whether, under all the circumstances, the punishment was moderate, and for a justifiable cause.

**Even with such a crew as I have supposed, kindness and moderation would be the best policy...** Dana's point here is that such tools (flogging, handcuffs, pistols, etc.) must be available, but that the wise and temperate captain should rarely (perhaps never) have need of them; the mere fact that they exist and could legally be brought to bear should serve to militate against their use.

**...the case of the shipmaster has been placed upon the same principle.** Dana's interpretation of the law is that captains, like teachers and masters, act much like (and in place of) parents. They should endeavor to act reasonably, but they are empowered to act as severely as necessitated by circumstances. If the captain (or parent, etc.) acts more severely than the occasion warrants, he is answerable to the courts.

This seems to me to be as good a position as the whole subject can be left in. I mean to say, that no positive enactment, going beyond this, is needed, or would be a benefit either to masters or men, in the present state of things. This again would seem to be a case which should be left to the gradual working of its own cure. As seamen improve, punishment will become less necessary; and as the character of officers is raised, they will be less ready to inflict it; and, still more, the infliction of it upon intelligent and respectable men, will be

**This again would seem to be a case which should be left to the gradual working of its own cure.** Not surprisingly, Dana returns to his theme that the law as it stands is more than adequate to safeguard the rights of both officers and men, if it were interpreted correctedly and consistently; any desired change should come slowly and from within the existing system.

an enormity which will not be tolerated by public opinion, and by juries, who are the pulse of the body politic. No one can have a greater abhorrence of the infliction of such punishment than I have, and a stronger conviction that severity is bad policy with a crew; yet I would ask every reasonable man whether he had not better trust to the practice becoming unnecessary and disreputable; to the measure of moderate chastisement and a justifiable cause being better understood, and thus, the act becoming dangerous, and in course of time to be regarded as an unheard-of barbarity–than to take the responsibility of prohibiting it, at once, in all cases, and in what ever degree, by positive enactment?

There is, however, one point connected with the administration of justice to seamen, to which I wish seriously to call the attention of those interested in their behalf, and, if possible, also of some of those concerned in that administration. This is, the practice which prevails of making strong appeals to the jury in mitigation of damages, or to the judge, after a verdict has been rendered against a captain or officer, for a lenient sentence, on the grounds of their previous good character, and of their being poor, and having friends and families depending upon them for support. These appeals have been allowed a weight which is almost incredible, and which, I think, works a greater hardship upon seamen than any one other thing in the laws, or the execution of them. Notwithstanding every advantage the captain has over the seaman in point of evidence, friends, money, and able counsel, it becomes apparent that he must fail in his defence. An appeal is then made to the jury, if it is a civil action, or to the judge for a mitigated sentence, if it is a criminal prosecution, on the two grounds I have mentioned. The same form is usually gone through in every case. In the first place, as to the previous good character of the party. Witnesses are brought from the town in which he resides, to testify to his good character, and to his unexceptionable conduct when on shore. They say that he is a good father, or husband, or son, or neighbor, and that they never saw in him any signs of a cruel or tyrannical disposition. I have even known evidence admitted to show the character he bore when a

**...the practice which prevails of making strong appeals...for a lenient sentence, on the grounds of their previous good character...** One thing that Dana feels must change quickly is the tendency of captains found guilty to seek leniency on the grounds of their good name, their poverty, or the fact that their families depend on them for continued sustenance. Historically, this sort of appeal has been effective, and this angers Dana: After all, compared to the sailors, the captain has the advantages of evidence, friends, money, etc.

**...if it is a civil action, or to the judge for a mitigated sentence, if it is a criminal prosecution...** A civil action is a lawsuit brought to recover damages alleged to have been caused by the action of the defendant. The idea is that a court (or jury) can determine how much damage has been suffered (if any) and what those damages are worth (if anything). That's different than a criminal prosecution, which results when the defendant is accused of having broken a law—in which case the burden (at least, in the United States) is on the prosecution to prove the defendent's guilt "beyond a reasonable doubt." It is possible (perhaps even likely) that a criminal defendant will also be the subject of a civil suit brought by those (or those representing) person(s) alleged to have been harmed by the defendant's actions. It is even possible for a defendent to be found not guilty in a criminal trial and then be found liable for damages in a related civil suit. (That's what happened when, in a Los Angeles criminal trial, former football star O.J. Simpson was found not guilty of murdering his wfe and a friend. A year later, and in spite of the previous acquittal, a jury hearing the civil suit brought by the families of the victims found Simpson liable for damages totalling over $45 million.)

boy at school. The owners of the vessel, and other merchants, and perhaps the president of the insurance company, are then introduced; and they testify to his correct deportment, express their confidence in his honesty, and say that they have never seen anything in his conduct to justify a suspicion of his being capable of cruelty or tyranny. This evidence is then put together, and great stress is laid upon the extreme respectability of those who give it. They are the companions and neighbors of the captain, it is said,–men who know him in his business and domestic relations, and who knew him in his early youth. They are also men of the highest standing in the community, and who, as the captain's employers, must be supposed to know his character. This testimony is then contrasted with that of some half dozen obscure sailors, who, the counsel will not forget to add, are exasperated against the captain because he has found it necessary to punish them moderately, and who have combined against him, and if they have not fabricated a story entirely, have at least so exaggerated it, that little confidence can be placed in it.

**This testimony is then contrasted with that of some half dozen obscure sailors...** Dana points out that the deck is stacked here (and perhaps always) against the poor, the uneducated, the lower classes—into which categories most sailors fall. They have few neighbors to speak for them, and no banker or powerful businessman is going to come to their aid.

The next thing to be done is to show to the court and jury that the captain is a poor man, and has a wife and family, or other friends, depending upon him for support; that if he is fined, it will only be taking bread from the mouths of the innocent and helpless, and laying a burden upon them which their whole lives will not be able to work off; and that if he is imprisoned, the confinement, to be sure, he will have to bear, but the distress consequent upon the cutting him off from his labor and means of earning his wages, will fall upon a poor wife and helpless children, or upon an infirm parent. These two topics, well put, and urged home earnestly, seldom fail of their effect.

**...the captain is a poor man, and has a wife and family, or other friends, depending upon him for support...** The final claim by many officers, says Dana, is that they are supporting a family and that to punish the officer would be to punish the (surely guiltless) wife and children. (Although it varies widely by region and by type of vessel, the typical captain these days makes a comfortable living wage, of course, but is unlikely to become wealthy. Keep in mind, too, that a ship's captain must have years of experience and training, and works under arduous and sometimes dangerous conditions.)

In deprecation of this mode of proceeding, and in behalf of men who I believe are every day wronged by it, I would urge a few considerations which seem to me to be conclusive.

First, as to the evidence of the good character the captain sustains on shore. It is to be remembered that masters of vessels have usually been brought up in a forecastle; and upon all men, and especially upon those taken from lower situations, the conferring of absolute power is too apt to work a great change. There are many captains whom I know to be cruel and tyrannical men at sea, who yet, among their friends, and in their families, have never lost the reputation they bore in childhood. In fact, the sea-captain is seldom at home, and when he is, his stay is short, and during the continuance of it he is surrounded by friends who treat him with kindness and consideration, and he has everything to please, and at the same time to restrain him. He would be a brute indeed, if, after an absence of months or years, during his short stay, so short that the novelty and excitement of it has hardly time to wear off, and the attentions he receives as a visitor and stranger hardly time to slacken,–if, under such circumstances, a townsman or neighbor would be justified in testifying against his correct and peaceable deportment. With the owners of the vessel, also, to which he is attached, and among merchants and insurers generally, he is a very different man from what he may be at sea, when his own master, and the master of everybody and everything about him. He knows that upon such men, and their good opinion of him, he depends for his bread. So far from their testimony being of any value in determining what his conduct would be at sea, one would expect that the master who would abuse and impose upon a man under his power, would be the most compliant and deferential to his employers at home.

**...masters of vessels have usually been brought up in a forecastle; and...the conferring of absolute power is too apt to work a great change.** Captains who once lived in the forecastle, says Dana, are just as likely as anyone else to fall victim to the undesirable effects of the sudden acquisition of power, as noted by Lord Action: "Power tends to corrupt, and absolute power corrupts absolutely." Dana also comments that one cannot base one's judgment of a captain on his behavior at home, because he is in fact so rarely at home that we don't (and cannot) know much about how he behaves when not at sea.

**He knows that upon such men, and their good opinion of him, he depends for his bread.** We must discount the testimony of the owners, says Dana, because they are, after all, his bosses. Naturally he will behave himself when in their presence.

As to the appeal made in the captain's behalf on the ground of his being poor and having persons depending upon his labor for support, the main and fatal objection to it is, that it will cover every case of the kind, and exempt nearly the whole body of masters and officers from the punishment the law has provided for them. There are very few, if any masters or other officers of merchantmen in our country, who are not poor men, and having either parents, wives, children, or other relatives, depending mainly or wholly upon their exertions for support in life. Few others follow the sea for subsistence. Now if this appeal is to have weight with courts

**...the main and fatal objection to it is, that it will cover every case of the kind...** This portion of the argument is weak, says Dana, because it applies to everyone: We *all* have parents or spouses or children who depend on us. We're all poor—or at least, not as well off as we would like to be. Almost all ships' officers, being of a certain age and having achieved a certain standing in society, have wives and children or aging parents who depend on them, and homes they could stand to lose if punished too severely. If this argument were to be given any weight, it would mean that no one—certainly no officer—could ever be punished for anything.

in diminishing the penalty the law would otherwise inflict, is not the whole class under a privilege which will, in a degree, protect it in wrong-doing? It is not a thing that happens now and then. It is the invariable appeal, the last resort, of counsel, when everything else has failed. I have known cases of the most flagrant nature, where after every effort has been made for the captain, and yet a verdict rendered against him, and all other hope failed, this appeal has been urged, and with such success that the punishment has been reduced to something little more than nominal, the court not seeming to consider that it might be made in almost every such case that could come before them. It is a little singular, too, that it seems to be confined to cases of shipmasters and officers. No one ever heard of a sentence, for an offence committed on shore, being reduced by the court on the ground of the prisoner's poverty, and the relation in which he may stand to third persons. On the contrary, it had been thought that the certainty that disgrace and suffering will be brought upon others as well as himself, is one of the chief restraints upon the criminally disposed. Besides, this course works a peculiar hardship in the case of the sailor. For if poverty is the point in question, the sailor is the poorer of the two; and if there is a man on earth who depends upon whole limbs and an unbroken spirit for support, it is the sailor. He, too, has friends to whom his hard earnings may be a relief, and whose hearts will bleed at any cruelty or indignity practised upon him. Yet I never knew this side of the case to be once adverted to in these arguments addressed to the leniency of the court, which are now so much in vogue; and certainly they are never allowed a moment's consideration when a sailor is on trial for revolt, or for an injury done to an officer.
Notwithstanding the many difficulties which lie in a seaman's way in a court of justice, presuming that they will be modified in time, there would be little to complain of, were it not for these two appeals.

It is no cause of complaint that the testimony of seamen against their officers is viewed with suspicion, and that great allowance is made for combinations and exaggeration. On the contrary, it is the judge's duty to charge the

**It is the invariable appeal, the last resort, of counsel...** By now we see that Dana is a logician. He is able to break an argument down to its component parts and then deal with those parts, pointing out the flaws in each piece of an argument. He is an attorney, after all, and well-suited to be one.

**No one ever heard of a sentence, for an offence committed on shore, being reduced by the court on the ground of the prisoner's poverty...** Dana points out that since an accused ashore cannot receive a reduced sentence by virtue of his poverty or because of positive testimony from character witnesses, why should a ship's officer be allowed to do so? Dana is being disingenuous here. Surely the testimony of powerful community figures is often effective in swaying a jury—otherwise, why would such testimony be offered in the first place? In addition, first-time offenders are quite often given the benefit of the doubt and either paroled or given reduced (or even deferred) sentences. This was not nearly as true in Dana's day as it is now, but to say that "no one ever heard" of such a thing is inaccurate.

**...there would be little to complain of, were it not...** In later editions, Dana inserts at this point a recounting of two specific cases in which captains were accused of excess cruelty, found guilty, and then given sentences so lenient that it "...made the conviction hardly worth proving."

**It is no cause of complaint...** Dana returns to the point that complaints by seamen are (and *should* be) viewed with a certain amount of suspicion. He reiterates his earlier point that the sailors can, after all, band together (in "combinations") to cast aspersions upon an officer who was either completely innocent or who was simply acting in a manner appropriate to the circumstances. Nonetheless, Dana points out, there are cases in which the sailors' testimony is the only existing evidence against the officer, and it would be unfair to discount that.

jury on these points strongly. But there is reason for objection, when, after a strict cross-examination of witnesses, after the arguments of counsel, and the judge's charge, a verdict is found against the master, that the court should allow the practice of hearing appeals to its lenity, supported solely by evidence of the captain's good conduct when on shore, (especially where the case is one in which no evidence but that of sailors could have been brought against the accused), and then, on this ground, and on the invariable claims of the wife and family, be induced to cut down essentially the penalty imposed by a statute made expressly for masters and officers of merchantmen, and for no one else.

There are many particulars connected with the manning of vessels, the provisions given to crews, and the treatment of them while at sea, upon which there might be a good deal said; but as I have, for the most part, remarked upon them as they came up in the course of my narrative, I will offer nothing further now, except on the single point of the manner of shipping men. This, it is well known, is usually left entirely to the shipping-masters, and is a cause of a great deal of difficulty, which might be remedied by the captain, or owner, if he has any knowledge of seamen, attending to it personally. One of the members of the firm to which our ship belonged, Mr. S—-, had been himself a master of a vessel, and generally selected the crew from a number sent down to him from the shipping-office. In this way he almost always had healthy, serviceable, and respectable men; for any one who has seen much of sailors can tell pretty well at first sight, by a man's dress, countenance, and deportment, what he would be on board ship. This same gentleman was also in the habit of seeing the crew together, and speaking to them previously to their sailing. On the day before our ship sailed, while the crew were getting their chests and clothes on board, he went down into the forecastle and spoke to them about the voyage, the clothing they would need, the provision he had made for them, and saw that they had a lamp and a few other conveniences. If owners or masters would more generally take the same pains, they would often save their crews a good deal of inconvenience, beside

**...Mr. S—-, had been himself a master of a vessel, and generally selected the crew from a number sent down to him from the shipping-office.** Dana refers to Mr. (William) Sturgis, one of the owners, pointing out that Sturgis, having once been a captain, knows how to select a respectable (and respectful) crew. Intelligent crew selection, says Dana, does much to avoid future trouble on board ship. Keep in mind earlier references to men "shanghaied" into service, taken against their will and forced (or tricked) into compulsory service. Gathering a crew in that fashion (and it was not an uncommon approach in those days) is almost sure to result in serious conflict once at sea. Dana argues instead for the sort of kind, intelligent, informed approach utilized by Sturgis.

creating a sense of satisfaction and gratitude, which makes a voyage begin under good auspices, and goes far toward keeping up a better state of feeling throughout its continuance.

It only remains for me now to speak of the associated public efforts which have been making of late years for the good of seamen: a far more agreeable task than that of finding fault, even where fault there is. The exertions of the general association, called the American Seamen's Friend Society, and of the other smaller societies throughout the Union, have been a true blessing to the seaman; and bid fair, in course of time, to change the whole nature of the circumstances in which he is placed, and give him a new name, as well as a new character. These associations have taken hold in the right way, and aimed both at making the sailor's life more comfortable and creditable, and at giving him spiritual instruction. Connected with these efforts, the spread of temperance among seamen, by means of societies, called, in their own nautical language, Windward-Anchor Societies, and the distribution of books; the establishment of Sailors' Homes, where they can be comfortably and cheaply boarded, live quietly and decently, and be in the way of religious services, reading and conversation; also the institution of Savings Banks for Seamen; the distribution of tracts and Bibles;–are all means which are silently doing a great work for this class of men. These societies make the religious instruction of seamen their prominent object. If this is gained, there is no fear but that all other things necessary will be added unto them. A sailor never becomes interested in religion, without immediately learning to read, if he did not know how before; and regular habits, forehandedness (if I may use the word) in worldly affairs, and hours reclaimed from indolence and vice, which follow in the wake of the converted man, make it sure that he will instruct himself in the knowledge necessary and suitable to his calling. The religious change is the great object. If this is secured, there is no fear but that knowledge of things of the world will come in fast enough. With the sailor, as with all other men in fact, the cultivation of the intellect, and

**...the American Seamen's Friend Society...** The American Seamen's Friend Society was formed in the late 1820s, with the goal of improving the lives of seamen by providing reading rooms, libraries, and religious instruction. The Society eventually opened boarding houses for sailors, some of which included chapels, recreational facilities, and even concert halls, in addition to living facilities. The Society officially ceased to exist in 1986, though its influence had waned years before.

**...temperance among seamen...** Dana equates "decency" with religion and with temperance: that is, with abstinence from liquor. (Indeed, he has seen—and described for us—the results of habitual drunkenness.) And note an interesting inclusion: he advocates the establishment of savings banks for seamen. He has seen what happens to a sailor's hard-earned pay when he jumps off the gangway and into the teeming streets of a large port city. One result is that many sailors reach old age as paupers: They have no one to care for them and no money to care for (or even house) themselves. It would be best if they learned to put part of their money in (or better still, have it deposited directly to) a bank, where the money could stay safe and earn interest, and where the bank itself can serve as a resource for the sailor's (or his family's) later years.

**...immediately learning to read...** There are, says Dana, many benefits to religion: It encourages one to learn to read, to plan for the future (i.e., what Dana calls "forehandedness"), and to acquire other important knowledge and skills. On the other hand says Dana, when religion is neglected—even if the sailor does learn to plan and to read—he is likely to be led down the path to sin, becoming nothing more, in that case, than "an intelligent and powerful" sinner, rather than an ignorant one.

the spread of what is commonly called useful knowledge, while religious instruction is neglected, is little else than changing an ignorant sinner into an intelligent and powerful one. That sailor upon whom, of all others, the preaching of the Cross is least likely to have effect, is the one whose understanding has been cultivated, while his heart has been left to its own devices. I fully believe that those efforts which have their end in the intellectual cultivation of the sailor; in giving him scientific knowledge; putting it in his power to read everything, without securing, first of all, a right heart which shall guide him in judgment; in giving him political information, and interesting him in newspapers;–an end in the furtherance of which he is exhibited at ladies' fairs and public meetings, and complimented for his gallantry and generosity,–are all doing a harm which the labors of many faithful men cannot undo.

The establishment of Bethels in most of our own seaports, and in many foreign ports frequented by our vessels, where the gospel is regularly preached and the opening of "Sailors' Homes," which I have before mentioned, where there are usually religious services and other good influences, are doing a vast deal in this cause. But it is to be remembered that the sailor's home is on the deep. Nearly all his life must be spent on board ship; and to secure a religious influence there, should be the great object. The distribution of Bibles and tracts into cabins and forecastles, will do much toward this. There is nothing which will gain a sailor's attention sooner, and interest him more deeply, than a tract, especially one which contains a story. It is difficult to engage their attention in mere essays and arguments, but the simplest and shortest story, in which home is spoken of, kind friends, a praying mother or sister, a sudden death, and the like, often touches the heart of the roughest and most abandoned. The Bible is to the sailor a sacred book. It may lie in the bottom of his chest, voyage after voyage; but he never treats it with positive disrespect. I never knew but one sailor who doubted its being the inspired word of God; and he was one who had received an uncommonly good education, except that he had been brought up without any

**The establishment of Bethels in most of our own seaports...** Originally the name of a small village located not far from Jerusalem, a Bethel (original meaning: "house of God") in this context was a seaman's chapel, the first one of which was built in New Bedford, MA in 1832. Today, the Bedford Bethel is nondenominational, and serves as both a chapel and as host to weddings and memorial services. (The names of area sailors and fishermen lost at sea are inscribed on the walls of the building, which is said to have been the inspiration for the "fire and brimstone" church scene in Melville's *Moby Dick*.)

**... especially one which contains a story.** Sailors of the time certainly did enjoy a good story, whether it was reading one, telling one, or hearing one. And really, not much has changed: We all enjoy a good story. What Dana is saying is that the men's love of stories can be put to good use, as a way of encouraging religious instruction.

**The most abandoned man of our crew...** That is, the most irreligious.

early religious influence. The most abandoned man of our crew, one Sunday morning, asked one of the boys to lend him his Bible. The boy said he would, but was afraid he would make sport of it. "No!" said the man, "I don't make sport of God Almighty." This is a feeling general among sailors, and is a good foundation for religious influence.

**There are occurrences at sea which he may turn to great account...** What educators might today call "teachable moments." A death at sea, for example, would surely turn men's thoughts to God and to the hereafter, says Dana. A wise captain would take advantage of such occurrences as opportunities for further religious instruction and exploration.

A still greater gain is made whenever, by means of a captain who is interested in the eternal welfare of those under his command, there can be secured the performance of regular religious exercises, and the exertion, on the side of religion, of that mighty influence which a captain possesses for good, or for evil. There are occurrences at sea which he may turn to great account,–a sudden death, the apprehension of danger, or the escape from it, and the like; and all the calls for gratitude and faith. Besides, this state of thing alters the whole current of feeling between the crew and their commander. His authority assumes more of the parental character; and kinder feelings exist. Godwin, though an infidel, in one of his novels, describing the relation in which a tutor stood to his pupil, says that the conviction the tutor was under, that he and his ward were both alike awaiting a state of eternal happiness or misery, and that they must appear together before the same judgment-seat, operated so upon his naturally morose disposition, as to produce a feeling of kindness and tenderness toward his ward, which nothing else could have caused. Such must be the effect upon the relation of master and common seaman.

**Godwin, though an infidel...**William Godwin was a radical English writer, and a proponent of anarchism, a political theory that proposed the abolition of governments. (We've encountered Godwin's family before. His wife was pioneering feminist Mary Wollstonecraft. Their daughter, Mary Shelley, was the author of *Frankenstein*.) The novel to which Dana refers is *Mandeville*, written in 1817. Dana suggests now that the relationship between a master (captain) and crew member should be much like that of benevolent tutor and pupil.

There are now many vessels sailing under such auspices, in which great good is done. Yet I never happened to fall in with one of them. I did not hear a prayer made, a chapter read in public, nor see anything approaching to a religious service, for two years and a quarter. There were, in the course of the voyage, many incidents which made, for the time, serious impressions upon our minds, and which might have been turned to our good; but there being no one to use the opportunity, and no services, the regular return of which might have kept something of the feeling alive in us, the advantage of them was lost, to some, perhaps, forever.

**I did not hear a prayer made, a chapter read in public, nor see anything approaching to a religious service...** Dana's point is valid, though his experience is limited. He served for only two years on only two vessels, both commanded much of the time by (the brutal and irreligious) Captain Francis Thompson.

The good which a single religious captain may do can hardly be calculated. In the first place, as I have said, a kinder state of feeling exists on board the ship. There is no profanity allowed; and the men are not called by any opprobrious names, which is a great thing with sailors. The Sabbath is observed. This gives the men a day of rest, even if they pass it in no other way. Such a captain, too, will not allow a sailor on board his ship to remain unable to read his Bible and the books given to him; and will usually instruct those who need it, in writing, arithmetic, and navigation; since he has a good deal of time on his hands, which he can easily employ in such a manner. He will also have regular religious services; and, in fact, by the power of his example, and, where it can judiciously be done, by the exercise of his authority, will give a character to the ship and all on board. In foreign ports, a ship is known by her captain; for, there being no general rules in the merchant service, each master may adopt a plan of his own. It is to be remembered, too, that there are, in most ships, boys of a tender age, whose characters for life are forming, as well as old men, whose lives must be drawing toward a close. The greater part of sailors die at sea; and when they find their end approaching, if it does not, as is often the case, come without warning, they cannot, as on shore, send for a clergyman, or some religious friend, to speak to them of that hope in a Saviour, which they have neglected, if not despised, through life; but if the little hull does not contain such an one within its compass, they must be left without human aid in their great extremity. When such commanders and such ships, as I have just described, shall become more numerous, the hope of the friends of seamen will be greatly strengthened; and it is encouraging to remember that the efforts among common sailors will soon raise up such a class; for those of them who are brought under these influences will inevitably be the ones to succeed to the places of trust and authority. If there is on earth an instance where a little leaven may leaven the whole lump, it is that of the religious shipmaster.

It is to the progress of this work among seamen that we must look with the greatest confidence for the remedy-

**The good which a single religious captain may do can hardly be calculated.** Dana goes on to catalogue all of the good things that occur when men serve on a ship under a religious captain. But he must be relying on hearsay, since as he just mentioned, he's never actually been on board such a vessel.

**...by the power of his example...will give a character to the ship...** It's certainly true that a ship (or an office, or a department, or a battallion, etc.) tend to take on something of the character of its commanding officer.

**...there are, in most ships, boys of a tender age, whose characters for life are forming...** As shown by the rosters of the men (and boys) aboard *Alert* and *Pilgrim*. Not including the captain, *Pilgrim* sets sail with a crew of 14, the average age of whom is not quite 23, even accounting for "oldsters" such as Thomas Curtis (the cook, 40 years of age) and John Holtz (the carpenter, 37 years of age) on the roster. (If we discount those two, the average age aboard *Pilgrim* drops to barely 20 years of age.) The *Alert*, meanwhile, shipped with a crew of 20, not counting the captain. The average age on that vessel was 25, counting the few older crewmembers. (Again discounting the older crewmembers, the average age aboard *Alert* drops to 23.) Both vessels set sail with crew as young as 15 and 16. (Samuel Hooper, who sailed on *Pilgrim* and then transferred to *Alert*, was only 12 years old when *Pilgrim* departed Boston.) (Note that this is not the same Samuel Hooper who serves as clerk for the owners back in Boston.)

**...a little leaven may leaven the whole lump...** The metaphor here is a culinary one in which a very small bit of a leavening agent (e.g., yeast) in an about-to-be-baked loaf of bread causes the entire loaf to rise. Dana is pointing out that one person, when that person is the master of a ship, can have an outsized impact on the entire crew.

ing of those numerous minor evils and abuses that we so often hear of. It will raise the character of sailors, both as individuals and as a class. It will give weight to their testimony in courts of justice, secure better usage to them on board ship, and add comforts to their lives on shore and at sea. There are some laws that can be passed to remove temptation from their way and to help them in their progress; and some changes in the jurisdiction of the lower courts, to prevent delays, may, and probably will, be made. But, generally speaking, more especially in things which concern the discipline of ships, we had better labor in this great work, and view with caution the proposal of new laws and arbitrary regulations, remembering that most of those concerned in the making of them must necessarily be little qualified to judge of their operation.

Without any formal dedication of my narrative to that body of men, of whose common life it is intended to be a picture, I have yet borne them constantly in mind during its preparation. I cannot but trust that those of them, into whose hands it may chance to fall, will find in it that which shall render any professions of sympathy and good wishes on my part unnecessary. And I will take the liberty, on parting with my reader, who has gone down with us to the ocean, and "laid his hand upon its mane," to commend to his kind wishes, and to the benefit of his efforts, that class of men with whom, for a time, my lot was cast. I wish the rather to do this, since I feel that whatever attention this book may gain, and whatever favor it may find, I shall owe almost entirely to that interest in the sea, and those who follow it, which is so easily excited in us all.

**...the proposal of new laws...** Dana points out that new laws are not necessary to safeguard the interests of seamen; what is needed are mechanisms to ensure that existing laws are followed consistently and fairly. In any case, he says, those who are charged with making such laws are neither sailors nor officers; they know little of the sea and are therefore not really qualified to judge how one should behave aboard a ship.

**...and "laid his hand upon its mane..."** Dana leaves us with a final literary allusion, this one an adaptation of a line from Byron's *Childe Harold's Pilgrimage*. The full quote is actually:

*And I have loved thee, Ocean! and my joy*
*Of youthful sports was on thy breast to be*
*Borne like thy bubbles, onward: from a boy*
*I wantoned with thy breakers - they to me*
*Were a delight; and if the freshening sea*
*Made them a terror - 'twas a pleasing fear,*
*For I was as it were a child of thee,*
*And trusted to thy billows far and near,*
*And laid my hand upon thy mane - as I do here.*

This is an apostrophe to the ocean: an address to what is in this case an inanimate—but profoundly powerful and much loved—object. The poet expresses both his affection and his respect for the sea.

**...so easily excited in us all...** Most of us do love the sea, and that love has been the topic of many a poem, book, or philosphical treatise. And, as many have noted, we are tied to the sea; when we go back to it, we are returning from whence we came. Dana, like most of us, loves the sea, and he knows that the men with whom he has sailed also love it. Because of this, Dana feels himself part of a community, one of which he is proud to be a member. He has, after all, earned that membership through hard work; long, miserable hours; and shared danger. It is the purpose of this book to ensure that the members of the seafaring community who occupy the lowest rung of the nautical hierarchy—common sailors—are treated fairly.

## Acknowledgments

For this release of Dana's classic book, we used the text of the original edition. Dana's powerful (and occasionally beautiful) prose speaks for itself on every page; my goal was simply to comment on his words—and perhaps in doing so, to illuminate his work and make it more accessible to modern readers.

That attempt at clarification required much reading and discussion, a good deal of research, and a comparison of many editions of the book. Dozens of editors before me have provided astoundingly erudite commentary on Dana and his work, including Anne Spencer, John Seelye, John Haskell Kemble, and the inimitable (and somewhat intimidating) Thomas Philbrick. I borrowed unashamedly from them all, and I hereby acknowledge my considerable debt to their pioneering work.

I'm proud enough of the result of my efforts here, but there is no doubt in my mind that others could have done as good a job or better; I was simply lucky enough to have had the opportunity to try my hand at working with one of my favorite books, written by one of my favorite authors. I'll take this occasion to apologize for the inadequacy of the attempt.

The research was aided by speaking with many people and by reading hundreds of publications. While any errors are ultimately mine alone, I would like to acknowledge the gracious support of the following:

- The American Leather Chemists Association for facts and figures about hides and hide preparation
- Josh Benton, Lone Star Cattle Co., for information about hides and the hide trade
- Dr. Stephen Buhler, Aaron Douglas Professor of English, University of Nebraska-Lincoln, for help with seemingly endless (and occasionally futile) language-related queries
- Michael D. Harlick, USCG Ret., for still more nautical information
- Mike Jackson, M/V Lady Mick, Seattle, WA, boating instructor, for astute nautical advice and suggestions
- Dr. David Schneider, M.D., for information about scurvy and other medical topics that arose in Dana's narrative
- Patricia Wood, liveaboard (and author of *Lottery*), S/V Orion, Ko 'Olina, HI, for answering the occasional (and proverbial) "dumb question" about sailing

Finally, I'd like to dedicate this book to my wife, Lesley. Thank you for your love and support, and thanks especially for your understanding during those many months I was only rarely able to help around the house and yard because I was in the basement, buried under a pile of books.